Employment Law

New Challenges in the Business Environment

THIRD EDITION

John Jude Moran, J.D., M.B.A.

Professor of Business and Employment Law
Wagner College

PEARSON

Prentice Hall

Upper Saddle River, New Jersey 07458

Library of Congress Cataloging-in-Publication Data

Moran, John Jude.
  Employment law: new challenges in the business environment/John Jude Moran.
    --3rd ed. p. cm.
  Includes bibliographical references and indexes.
  ISBN 0-13-147735-8 (alk. paper)
  1. Labor laws and legislation—United States. I. Title.

KF3455.M67 2004
344.7301-dc22

2004050705

Senior Managing Editor (Editorial): Alana Bradley
VP/Editor-in-Chief: Jeff Shelstad
Assistant Editor: Sam Goffinet
Senior Editorial Assistant: Jane Avery
Media Project Manager: Caroline Kasterine
Executive Marketing Manager: Beth Toland
Marketing Assistant: Melissa Owens
Managing Editor (Production): John Roberts
Production Editor: Renata Butera
Production Supervisor: Charles Morris
Manufacturing Buyer: Michelle Klein
Design Director: Maria Lange
Art Director: Pat Smythe
Cover Design: JMG Graphics
Director, Image Resource Center: Melinda Reo
Manager, Rights and Permissions: Zina Arabia
Manager: Visual Research: Beth Brenzel
Manager, Cover Visual Research & Permissions: Karen Sanatar
Manager, Print Production: Christy Mahon
Composition: Integra Software Services
Full-Service Project Management: BookMasters, Inc.
Printer/Binder: Von Hoffmann
Typeface: Palatino

Credits and acknowledgments borrowed from other sources and reproduced, with permission, in this textbook appear on appropriate page within the text.

Pearson Education LTD.
Pearson Education Singapore, Pte. Ltd
Pearson Education, Canada, Ltd
Pearson Education–Japan

Pearson Education Australia PTY, Limited
Pearson Education North Asia Ltd
Pearson Educación de Mexico, S. A. de C. V.
Pearson Education Malaysia, Pte. Ltd

10 9 8 7 6 5 4 3 2
ISBN 0-13-147735-8

Employment Law

To my mother and father

CONTENTS

PART III: EMPLOYMENT REGULATION   397

PREFACE

Employment law is an area that is constantly changing. Decisions are being rendered that redefine the parameters of selection, discrimination, privacy, and termination. Sexual harassment has become one of the most litigated areas of employment law. The number of cases involving disability discrimination is growing rapidly. Sexual orientation may soon be considered a suspect classification under gender discrimination. Family leave may soon be given with pay. At-will employment may soon be displaced by the Model Termination in Employment Act's termination for cause contracts in lieu of an employee's right to sue. Arbitration will be the method for dispute resolution. The right of privacy advocates will continue to do battle with the proponents of drug and polygraph testing. As companies continue to find ways to improve the bottom line, diminishing employee theft of goods, services, and time will be a likely target. Surveillance will increase through the implementation of subtle methods. A trend has developed eliminating affirmative action in certain jurisdictions.

Employment issues used to be handled by personnel departments with a director as the head. Now, a human resources division is often in place with countless more workers and a vice president as its leader. At the other end of the spectrum, NAFTA and GATT has made inroads against unions, labor laws, OSHA, workers' compensation, unemployment insurance, pension and health benefits, minimum and hourly wage laws, child labor laws, and the number of high-paying skilled and office positions through the deployment of jobs to Mexico and overseas, where these laws are not in effect. The global business environment will entice companies to seek out the most efficient labor force per dollar of wages and the least expensive manufacturing plants and office space. American workers will have to work longer, harder, and more efficiently while continuously learning skills to keep them competitive.

Employment issues are now high profile. The study of employment law is important because of the impact it will have on businesses, management, and employees. The focus of *Employment Law: New Challenges in the Business Environment* is on discrimination and employment regulation. As with my first book, *Practical Business Law*, I have written this book presenting principles of law in a step-building approach and illustrating those principles with stimulating employment perspectives (there are more than 100 employment perspectives in this book).

Seventy-five cases from the year 2000 to present have been added to this edition. Each case is followed by case questions and commentary. Human resource advice and a chapter checklist appear at the beginning of each chapter with a hypothetical scenario illustrating employment law problems confronted by a small business. Employee lessons, human resource dilemmas, case problems, review questions, and a Web site assignment close out each chapter.

Employment Law: New Challenges in the Business Environment is a simple approach to employment law, with a foundation of legal principles explained in the layperson's language. The principles, once learned, can be applied to understand the judges' opinions in the cases presented.

The ultimate task in learning is to apply the principles of law to factual situations. This can be accomplished through having the students resolve the issues in dispute. In each chapter, cases are included that focus on the important principles of law to be learned. These cases are extracted from actual cases to enhance class discussions while providing the student with a pragmatic view of the reasoning behind court decisions. This makes the book timely. It also provides the student with a text he or she can truly understand and appreciate. At the same time, the text affords the professor the opportunity to discuss the principles more fully by introducing his or her own examples and instances of practical experience.

A hypothetical scenario involving a small business, its owners, and their attorney continues through the text. In each chapter, the owners are confronted with a legal challenge involving their employees. With the legal guidance of their attorney, they attempt to resolve the conflict.

Chapter checklists are incorporated into each chapter to highlight the important principles students should glean from the text.

Employee lessons located toward the culmination of each chapter speak to the issues that employers and employees should concern themselves with to minimize potential litigation.

One hundred percent of the cases, which are incorporated into the end of the chapter review questions, are from no earlier than 1995.

Part I sets forth the parameters of the relationship between employer and employee and independent contractor. The distinction between an employer and independent contractor is identified. The rights and duties of the parties are spelled out in an employment contract along with the resulting liability should a breach occur.

The procedure for selecting and testing employees is also discussed. A considerable problem for employers is employee theft. Balancing the privacy interests of employees with the employer's desire to utilize testing, investigations, inspections, and surveillance is discussed. Finally, the issues of at-will employment, termination for cause, wrongful discharge, and arbitration are explained.

Part II presents the Civil Rights Act, affirmative action, and the various forms of discrimination found in employment. Hot issues include sexual harassment, racial discrimination, disability discrimination, and sexual orientation.

Part III addresses government regulation of the workplace with regard to unions, collective bargaining, minimum and maximum wage hours, safety, health, compensation for injuries, and pension and health benefits.

Web site addresses are cited at the end of each chapter for student reference. The Web sites are current as of May 2004.

This book was written because of the timeliness and importance of employment law and its interaction with the business curriculum. It is important that students understand the impact that employment law has on both management and employees.

I wish to express gratitude to my parents, Rita and John, for their love and support.

I appreciate the fine words written by Richard Guarasci, President of Wagner College, in the Foreword. President Guarasci developed the Wagner Plan, a program designed around learning communities to involve students in experiential learning. This plan has gained national recognition and placed Wagner College among the finest small liberal arts colleges with professional programs in the northeast.

I am indebted to Anthony Ginetto for his thought-provoking and insightful commentary. Mr. Ginetto is a highly regarded legal scholar in the field of employment law. He received his J.D. degree from St. John's University Law School and his L.L.M. degree from New York University Law School.

I appreciate the tireless efforts of the following individuals from Prentice Hall: Alana Bradley, Managing Editor; Jane Avery, Senior Editorial Assistant; John Roberts, Managing Editor of Production; Renata Butera, Production Editor; Beth Toland, Executive Marketing Manager; and Jeff Shelstad, Editor-in-Chief. Rebecca Roby copyedited with aplomb and Jennifer Welsch of BookMasters, Inc. did an exemplary job regarding the layout and composition, for which I am grateful.

I wish to thank the following people for their review of the manuscript: Joanne S. Bochis, Montclair State University; Gerald A. Loy, Broome Community College; Anne W. Schacherl, Madison Area Technical College; and Mary-Kathryn Zachery, State University of West Georgia.

J. J. Moran, J.D., M.B.A.

FOREWORD

The development of critical thinking is one of the greatest lessons that a student can learn during his or her college studies. This occurs in a myriad of ways. In Professor Moran's text, he has set forth several scenarios and dilemmas that will confront human resource specialists and employment law attorneys. Students are asked to critically analyze the factual situations and arrive at possible solutions.

In the business world, managers are confronted with personnel issues involving privacy, discrimination, harassment, termination, and labor on a daily basis. Professor Moran has explained what human resource managers and those who practice employment and labor law need to know. He has done so in a simplified approach using a combination of real-life cases and hypothetical examples to illustrate the application of the principles of law to factual situations.

Students will appreciate the value of this textbook not only in the classroom, but in their careers as well. Many students will experience employment law issues both as employees and later in their careers as managers. Having a text which can provide guidance on these complicated and often controversial topics, is worth its weight in gold.

We at Wagner College are proud of Professor Moran for his work in the classroom and for his written contributions in the fields of employment and business law.

Richard Guarasci, Ph.D.

President

Wagner College

FOREWORD FROM SECOND EDITION

When I was asked to write the foreword for Professor Moran's textbook *Employment Law: New Challenges in the Business Environment*, second edition my first thought was what can I possibly say about this comprehensive and informative text that has not already been said? Well, as a practitioner who has specialized in the area of employment law for 25 years, in both federal service and private industry, I have found that this text has not only been an informative tool for my use as an adjunct professor, but it has also served as an invaluable resource to me in researching legal issues in this very complex area.

Employment law has been subject to numerous substantial changes in the past 10 years—notably the erosion of the "at-will employment" concept, development of new affirmative defenses in sexual harassment cases, the extension of the hostile work environment doctrine from sexual harassment to race and age discrimination cases; and Supreme Court recognition that sexual orientation discrimination may be prohibited under Title VII. In addition to changes in traditional labor law, the text also covers succinctly new areas of employment law previously not encountered: privacy, drug and polygraph testing, and new OSHA ergonomic rules, first issued and then withdrawn by joint congressional resolution.

Today in corporate America, companies are paying particular attention to diversity issues in the workplace. In this regard, employment lawyers and human resource professionals must keep current with new laws and decisions in order to ensure compliance with them and achieve a diverse workforce. With so many demands, one may be overwhelmed by the accumulation of so much to learn and know. Professor Moran's text deals with all of these areas in a manner that has helped me keep abreast of new developments while keeping significant past developments fresh.

I highly recommend Professor Moran's text for attorneys, human resource professionals, and those who, although not specialists in the area, wish to become more informed about an area of law that has an impact on us all. I am certain that students will find this text to be informative and written in a style that will easily facilitate their understanding of a very complex area of law. Many may even be encouraged to further pursue their studies in this increasingly dynamic and important facet of the business world.

Anthony C. Ginetto, J.D., L.L.M.
Associate General Counsel
Employment Law Division
MetLife Insurance Co.

FOREWORD FROM FIRST EDITION

It is a privilege to write the foreword to this new textbook *Employment Law: New Challenges in the Business Environment.*

Professor John Jude Moran, a well noted authority in the employment field, has written a book which brings this fast-changing area of law up-to-date in a most lucid and perceptive manner.

Not so many years ago, Employment Law was one of the backwaters of the legal system. This is no longer true. The number of cases involving labor law has grown probably more rapidly than any other area of law in the last decade.

Sexual orientation appears to becoming a suspect classification under gender discrimination. This book deals with this challenging area in details and with great understanding. Even more significant to those of us trained in the common law tradition, is the rapid changes occurring with "at-will employment," which is being changed beyond recognition from what we previously knew to be its parameters. Those of us who are keenly interested in privacy are being faced with the constant barrage of the demand by the government and employers for drug and polygraph testing. All of these subjects are dealt with in this book and dealt with well.

An entire new division in management has grown up in corporate America and that is the human resources division. Indeed, "human resources" is no longer merely a personnel department, but a major concern for most of corporate America. There are so many changes which have occurred in this area that one would almost have to write a book every month to keep the reader informed of the latest developments in labor law. NAFTA, GATT, OSHA worker's compensation, unemployment insurance, health benefits, pension benefits, and so many more topics are dealt with by Professor Moran in an understandable and comprehensive manner.

What Professor Moran has accomplished is nothing short of a minor miracle. He has taken an extremely difficult subject matter and made it understandable to all of us who are not labor law specialists. This is a book which I know you will not only enjoy reading and from which you will learn, but also a book which will serve as a valuable resource tool in your future undertakings in this field.

There is no question that Professor Moran deserves high praise from all of us in the legal field as well as corporate America for what he has accomplished

E. Donald Shapiro
The Joseph Solomon Distinguished
Professor of Law and Supernumerary Fellow
of St. Cross College at Oxford University

ABOUT THE AUTHOR

John Jude Moran was born in Bay Ridge, Brooklyn, New York. After graduating from Xaverian High School at the age of 16, John received his Bachelor's Degree in Business Administration from St. John's University's Notre Dame College in 2 years at the age of 18. John then attended New York Law School, from which he received his Doctor of Law Degree at the age of 21. John's first teaching experience was at the City University of New York, which he began while still in law school. John also taught part-time at St. John's University MBA program. After becoming a member of the New York Bar, John worked for a law firm and then a corporation in Manhattan.

In 1982, John moved to Cameron Lake in Staten Island. At that time, John began writing his first book, *Practical Business Law*. This book was published in 1985. It is now in its third edition and has been used in almost 100 colleges in the United States and six foreign countries. John returned to St. John's University to pursue an MBA in finance, which he received at the age of 30.

After teaching at St. Peter's College for 1 year, John became a member of Wagner College's faculty in 1985. He has served as chairman of the Department of Business Administration and is currently a Professor of Business and Employment Law. In 1995, the first edition of *Employment Law: New Challenges in the Business Environment* was published. John resides in Grasmere, Staten Island, with his dog, Cuddles and his cats, Sweetheart and Chubby.

Employment Law

Chapter

1

Employment Relationship

Employment Scenario

Tom Long and Mark Short form a business called "The Long and the Short of It" and abbreviated it, "L&S."

L&S is a men's clothing store dedicated to large, tall, and short men. These are sizes not generally catered to by department stores and other men's clothing stores. Tom and Mark met while working at a well-known men's clothing store. Their idea for L&S stemmed from their experience of being unable to fulfill requests for clothing from customers who were very large, tall, or short. Niche marketing had intrigued both of them. They wanted to open their own clothing store and thought it was far better to specialize rather than attempt to be all things to all people.

For the first 8 months of the business, Tom and Mark handle the ordering, selling, measuring, and tailoring. Through an effective advertising campaign emphasizing the name of the company and its owners, many customers are attracted to the store. Sales are brisk. Tom and Mark begin to feel overwhelmed by the amount of work. Currently, store hours are Monday through Friday 10 A.M. to 6 P.M. and Saturday 12 noon to 6 P.M. The tailoring and paperwork are done after hours.

Tom and Mark make an appointment with Susan North, an employment law specialist. They retain her services and ask her to advise them as employment issues arise with the growth of the business.

Employment Scenario

Long and Short tell Susan that they are considering expanding store hours and advertising. They wish to concentrate their efforts on management and growth. There are several workers they wish to hire, but they are uncertain whether or not these workers would be designated as employees or independent contractors. Susan asks Long and Short to describe the nature of each position, the hours worked, and the control they exercise over each worker. Jack Walker, Grant

Worthington, and Phil Costello are first-rate salespeople who have extensive experience in selling men's clothing. They would each work 40 hours per week and be paid a base salary plus commission. The salesmen would be prohibited from working elsewhere. They would be required to wear suits, and their work schedules would be set by L&S. Paid vacation and sick leave would be given as well. Jack, Grant, and Phil would have no discretion in deciding whether to attend a customer's needs, and they would have no authority to hire assistants.

Nancy Cooke is being employed as an administrative assistant. Her duties will include bookkeeping, ordering, and typing, as well as telephone reception. She will work from 10 A.M. to 6 P.M. Monday through Friday. Martha Winslow, a seamstress by trade, is being hired to perform the necessary alterations on the clothing. She would be available for appointments on Tuesdays and Thursdays from 6 P.M. to 8 P.M. and on Saturday afternoons from 2 P.M. to 4 P.M. Martha would set her own hours in addition to these, depending on the workload. Martha has set a fee schedule covering the various types of alterations performed on a per item basis.

(*The next paragraph is a continuation of the scenario*)

Stephanie Russo is a Web page design specialist with a degree in graphic arts. She is being trained to create a Web page for The Long and the Short of It. After that, she will act as a consultant for purposes of Web advertising. Lucy Johnson is being hired to clean the store after hours. She will set her own schedule, and she estimates working 1 to 2 hours per night. Stephanie is being paid on a one-time fee basis for the Web design work and then will be retained on an hourly basis as a consultant. Lucy is being paid a flat fee per night, regardless of the length of time it takes for her to clean the store. Which of these people are employees and which are independent contractors?

Employment Scenario

L&S approaches Susan with a concern over whether it can restrict its salespeople from leaving to work for a competitor. Susan explains that a noncompete agreement would have to be drafted designating the duration and geographical restriction. The latter is usually limited to the area from where L&S draws its customers. Each salesperson would have to sign the noncompete agreement. The enforceability of this agreement hinges upon whether L&S could show harm to its business. Susan adds that courts do not look with favor upon noncompete agreements absent the showing of actual loss of profits to the business, because the employee would be precluded from working in his or her profession. Enforcement of such an agreement mandates relocation or a career change. L&S states that it is the salespeople who develop a rapport with the customers. L&S worries that the salespeople, upon leaving, could influence customers to follow them to another store. Should L&S require a noncompete agreement?

Chapter Checklist

➤ *Define employment relationship.*

➤ *Distinguish between an employee and an independent contractor.*

➤ *Understand the duties of the employer and the worker.*

➤ *Appreciate the types of authority given to the worker.*

➤ *Know the parameters of a "covenant not to compete" and when it is enforceable.*

➤ *Discern when an employee's actions occurred within the scope of employment.*

➤ *Identify situations that could lead to potential liability involving contract disputes and the torts of assault, battery, defamation, and invasion of privacy.*

INTRODUCTION

The employment relationship is a contractual one between an employer and a worker. The worker may be either an employee or an independent contractor. Distinguishing between the two is very important. It has an effect on compensation, benefits, harassment, family leave, workers' compensation, unemployment insurance, and discrimination.

In an employment relationship, authority is conveyed by an employer to an employee. Deciding what kinds of authority and how much authority to grant are important issues for employers to resolve. Inherent in every employment relationship is the employee's duties of loyalty and good faith and the employer's duties to compensate and maintain a safe working environment. Violations of these duties give rise to contractual and tort liability. A contract is a legally enforceable agreement. A tort is a private civil wrong. Tort liability encompasses assault and battery, defamation, invasion of privacy, and negligence. The key to an employer's responsibility is whether the tort was committed within the scope of employment—in other words, "on the job." Employers may attempt to employ restrictive covenants, also known as "covenants not to compete." These covenants are used to protect the employer's business against theft of trade secrets, stealing clients, and competing against the former employer. Courts generally do not like to restrict people from working, but the courts will enforce these covenants where they are voluntarily signed and designed to protect the business from unfair competition.

HUMAN RESOURCE ADVICE

- Develop an understanding of the implementation of the Economic Realities test as it relates to the distinction between employees and independent contractors.
- Discern what kind of authority employees should have and how much authority should be given to them.
- Reprimand employees if they exceed the authority given to them.
- Indoctrinate employees concerning the loyalty owed to the employer and their need to always act in the best interests of the company.
- Implore employees to act in good faith, give their best effort, and carry out their jobs in a responsible manner.
- Compensate employees fairly and be concerned about their workplace safety to enhance employee morale.
- Understand when employees' actions occur within the scope of employment.
- Appreciate the torts of defamation, invasion of privacy, and interference with business relations when speaking to others about employees.
- Remember that contracts are binding and lawsuits are filed for breaches of contracts.
- Minimize tort liability by emphasizing to employees that they should never assault, defame, harass, inflict emotional distress, or interfere in the business relations of others.

The word *employment* may be defined as the rendering of personal service by one person on behalf of another in return for compensation. The person requesting the service is the *employer*. The person performing the service may be either the *employee* or an *independent contractor*. Employment law has its roots in the law of agency.

Agency is a contractual relationship, involving an agent and a principal, in which the agent is given the authority to represent the principal in dealings with third parties. The most common example is an employer–employee relationship wherein an *agent* (employee) is given the power by a *principal* (employer) to act on his or her behalf. An agent may be an employee or an independent contractor. A principal is a person who employs an agent to act on his or her behalf. A principal (employer) has full control over his or her employee. The employee must complete the work assigned by following the instructions of the employer.

INDEPENDENT CONTRACTOR

An *independent contractor* is an individual hired by an employer to perform a specific task. The employer has no control over the methods used by the independent contractor. The following are among those who act independently of an employer: electricians, carpenters, plumbers, television repairpersons, and automobile mechanics. Independent contractors also include professional agents such as lawyers, physicians, accountants, securities brokers, insurance brokers, real estate brokers, and investment advisors. Independent contractors may also employ others in their field who will be bound to them as employees.

At times there is conflict over whether a worker is an employee or an independent contractor. This arises with workers who are salespeople, delivery and car service drivers, home workers, and others who work for tips or commissions. Employers prefer the independent contractor status because there is no paid vacation, sick time, personal leave, or any life, health, and unemployment insurance involved. In addition, pension benefits do not have to be paid; there are no workers' compensation suits; taxes do not have to be withheld; there are no minimum wages, maximum hours, or overtime; and there is minimal or no tort liability for the actions of the independent contractor. Employers initially designate a worker as an employee or an independent contractor. The Internal Revenue Service weighs in on this as well concerning tax matters. How then is the distinction made? Courts often employ an economic realities test, which encompasses an employer's control over the worker's behavior. First, factors indicating behavioral control include instructing, training, setting work hours, and designating dress codes, as well as where, when, and how the work is to be done, and restricting the worker from being employed by others. Second, financial control is determined by the following: The worker does not have a significant investment in the business; the worker cannot perform services for the public; the worker has no unrealized personal profit or loss; the worker does not pay business expenses or provide tools; the worker is compensated for a job on an hourly basis; and the worker files reports as required by the employer. Third, the type of relationship is indicative of employment status. Factors include the following: the relationship is continuous; the worker plays an essential part in the business; the worker has no power to employ others without the employer's authorization; the worker is liable if the job is done poorly or is not completed; and the worker may be terminated at will, not solely for breach of contract.

Affirmative responses to these criteria would indicate that the worker is an employee. Negative responses signify that the worker is an independent contractor. Often, indicators are split between employee and independent contractor. Some courts have used a balanced approach, in which the criteria supporting employee status will be counted or weighed against the criteria supporting independent contractor status to determine the employment relationship.

The issue in this case is whether the delivery drivers are to be considered employees or independent contractors.

Alexis M. Herman, Secretary of Labor v. Express Sixty-Minutes Delivery Service
161 F.3d 299 (5th Cir. 1998)

Parker, Circuit Judge.

Appellant, the Secretary of Labor, brought this FLSA action seeking to enjoin appellee Express 60-Minutes Delivery Service, Inc. from violating the minimum wage, overtime compensation, and record keeping provisions of the Act. After a six-day bench trial, the district court concluded that no violation of the FLSA occurred because the courier delivery drivers were independent contractors.

FACTUAL BACKGROUND
Drivers

Express operates a courier delivery service in Dallas and Tarrant Counties, Texas. Express contracts with various businesses, including law firms, hospitals, and laboratories, to deliver packages on a 24-hour basis in and around the Dallas-Fort Worth metropolitan area. Over 50% of the packages delivered by Express contain medical blood or tissue samples. Express averages around 525 deliveries each day. To make these deliveries, Express relies on about fifty drivers on its payroll at any given time. The drivers are recruited by Express through newspaper advertisements and word of mouth.

Customers of Express choose among various delivery options under which Express agrees to complete its deliveries within either one, two, or four hours of when an order is placed. Express uses a computer-dispatch system wherein orders are taken by customer service personnel over the telephone, entered into the computer, and transferred to dispatchers who assign the deliveries. The dispatchers communicate with the drivers by pager, two-way closed-channel radio, and telephone. While different factors guide their decisions, the dispatchers generally offer a delivery to the last on-duty driver to have received an offer who is closest to the pick-up point. Express bills its customers based upon several factors including the size of the package, the priority of its delivery, and the distance between the pick-up and delivery points.

Potential drivers are required to attend an orientation session at which they must sign an Independent Contractor Agreement providing that they will make deliveries for Express using their own vehicles in exchange for receiving a commission for each delivery equal to a percentage of the customer's cost. Under the agreement, drivers also pay the costs of their gasoline, vehicle maintenance, and insurance. Most drive a vehicle that they also use personally.

The Independent Contractor Agreement also provides that drivers will furnish their own uniforms, radios and pagers, as well as the biohazard bags and dry ice required for transporting medical samples. These items are supplied to the drivers by Express, which leases some of the items to the drivers and deducts the cost from their first few paychecks. Drivers supply their own dollies and MAPSCOs, and, if needed, their own tarps and cords for covering and securing items.

The drivers can and do negotiate for increased commissions, but most drivers do not negotiate their commissions. The drivers have no input into how Express's business is conducted, the amount charged its customers, or the allocation or frequency of deliveries.

The drivers may use only those radios supplied by the company, because the radios operate on a private channel that Express licenses from the Federal Communication Commission. Most drivers wear a uniform consisting of a blue shirt and khaki pants. One shoulder of the shirt has a patch with an Express logo and the other shoulder sports an Independent Contractor patch. Uniforms are not required, but preferred.

Pursuant to their contracts, drivers agree to make themselves available to work on-call for Express's 24-hour delivery service. A majority of the drivers who testified stated either that they were required to work on-call or that they had no input into when their on-call time was scheduled. Express posts the on-call schedules at its offices and informs drivers that if unable to work, they are responsible for finding a replacement.

Drivers work for Express for varying lengths of time, with the majority working for relatively short periods. Several drivers testified that they had worked for other courier companies in the Dallas-Fort Worth area either prior to or after working for Express. Only one driver testified that he worked for another courier company while working for Express. The Independent Contractor Agreement does not contain a covenant-not-to-compete.

No prior experience is necessary to become a courier driver, but couriers need to be able to drive, read maps, and be courteous to customers. By using their judgment as to the best routes available and their knowledge about area traffic patterns, drivers may earn more money because they can make their deliveries faster and be available to make more deliveries.

Under the terms of the contract, the drivers have the right to accept or reject individual offers of delivery jobs, and have no obligation to accept any specified number of jobs during any given period. Drivers confirmed that they could decline offers without being subjected to retaliation.

In addition to the drivers that Express considers independent contractors, the company employs four drivers it considers employees. The employee-drivers run errands for Express and make routine deliveries when the office is busy. They attend the same initial orientation session as the other drivers. Unlike the contract drivers, the employee-drivers (1) report for work at a specified time; (2) are paid by the hour; (3) work a set number of hours that are determined by Express; (4) are required to wear a uniform; (5) are provided with a company vehicle and all of the necessary tools of the trade; (6) are reimbursed for expenses; (7) are not allowed to turn down deliveries; and (8) are under the control and supervision of Express.

ANALYSIS
Drivers

To determine employee status under the FLSA, we focus on whether the alleged employee, as a matter of economic reality, is economically dependent upon the business to which he or she renders his or her services. In other words, our task is to determine whether the individual is, as a matter of economic reality, in business for himself or herself.

To aid us in this task, we consider five factors: the degree of control exercised by the alleged employer; the extent of the relative investments of the worker and alleged employer; the degree to which the worker's opportunity for profit and loss is determined by the alleged employer; the skill and initiative required in performing the job; and the permanency of the relationship.

No single factor is determinative. We review the district court's findings as to these five factors for clear error, but we review the district court's ultimate determination of employee status de novo.

1. *Degree of control exercised by the alleged employer* The district court found that Express had minimal control over its drivers. We agree. The drivers set their own hours and days of work and can reject deliveries without retaliation. It is preferred that drivers wear a uniform and become notaries, but it is not required of all contract drivers. The drivers can work for other courier delivery systems, and the Independent Contractor Agreement does not contain a covenant-not-to-compete. Although the drivers are required to attend an orientation session and required to be on-call, these facts do not outweigh the other facts indicating a lack of control and independent contractor status. This result is even clearer when one contrasts Express's employee-drivers who, unlike contract drivers, report for work at a specified time; are paid by the hour; work a set number of hours that are determined by Express; are required to wear a uniform; are not allowed to turn down deliveries; and are under the control and supervision of Express.

The degree-of-control factor points toward independent contractor status. Such a finding by the district court is not clearly erroneous.

2. *Relative investment of worker and alleged employer* The district court found that the investment on the part of the drivers was significant. The district court first pointed out that Express does not provide drivers with any equipment—drivers were required to purchase or lease all the necessary tools of the trade including a vehicle, automobile insurance, dolly, MAPSCO, tarp, two-way radio, pager, and a medical delivery bag. The drivers also were responsible for all fuel, maintenance, and depreciation of their vehicles.

The Secretary counters that most drivers use their automobiles for personal and recreational purposes as well as for business, so that the capital risk on the part of the drivers is not substantial. Further, the Secretary argues that the relative investment of Express far exceeds that of the drivers, explaining that Express operates offices in two locations, uses a sophisticated computer system, purchases the equipment that it leases to its drivers, pays to license a closed-channel radio frequency from the Federal Communications Commission, and pays the salaries of twenty-five office employees. While the Secretary did not discuss in her brief the dollar amount of investment of Express, an independent review of the record reveals the following:
   a. monthly lease on Fort Worth office = $1500–$1900
   b. Monthly lease on Dallas office = several hundred dollars
   c. 60–65 radios at $600 a piece
   d. Air time for radio = $17 per month for each radio
   e. Biweekly payroll = approximately $19,000
   f. four vehicles = approximately $14,000 each
   g. fax machine = $250
   h. computer system = $25,000

The relative investment by Express is indeed significant. Although the driver's investment of a vehicle is no small matter, that investment is somewhat diluted when one considers that most drivers also use the vehicle for personal purposes.

The district court also concluded that, although no direct testimony was presented on this point, the aggregate investment of all the contract drivers is substantially more than that of Express. However, we find no support for the application of an aggregation principle with respect to the relative investment factor.

The relative investment factor weighs in favor of the Secretary and toward employee status.

3. *Degree to which employee's opportunity for profit and loss is determined by the alleged employer* The district court found that the drivers are compensated on a commission basis. According to the district court a driver's profit or loss is determined largely on his or her skill, initiative, ability to cut costs, and understanding of the courier business. The district court observed that the drivers who made the most money appeared to be the most experienced and most concerned with efficiency, while the less successful drivers tended to be inexperienced and less concerned with efficiency.

Although the Secretary maintains that Express controls customer volume and the amount charged to customers, we cannot say that the district court clearly erred in finding that the drivers' opportunity for profit and loss was determined by the drivers to a greater degree than Express. This is especially true because the drivers had the ability to choose how much they wanted to work and the experienced drivers knew which jobs were most profitable.

This factor points toward independent contractor status. The district court did not clearly err.

4. *Skill and initiative required* The district court found that once a job is offered to the driver, the driver is not told which route to take—the driver must rely on his own judgment, knowledge of traffic patterns and road conditions in the Dallas-Fort Worth metroplex,

ability to read a MAPSCO, and ability to anticipate the need for an alternate route. According to the district court, experienced drivers possess specialized skills beyond that of merely driving an automobile and more experienced drivers tended to make more money than less experienced drivers.

The Secretary argues that the contract drivers are more like wage earners than independent entrepreneurs seeking a return on their risky capital investment. The Secretary is correct. The district court did not discuss initiative during its evaluation of this factor. We agree with the Secretary that the skill and initiative factor points toward employee status. The district court clearly erred in finding to the contrary.

5. *Permanency of the relationship* The Secretary conceded at oral argument that the district court correctly determined the permanency issue. We agree. The majority of drivers work for Express for a short period of time. Drivers are able to work for other courier delivery companies, and the Independent Contractor Agreement does not contain a covenant-not-to-compete. The permanency factor points toward independent contractor status.

6. *Other factors* Both sides encourage the court to look to other factors in addition to the preceding five factors. The Secretary emphasizes that the work performed by the drivers is an integral and indispensable part of Express' business. Express argues that the contract provided that the drivers were independent contractors and the drivers' uniforms indicate same.

The determination of employee status is very fact intensive, and as with most employee-status cases, there are facts pointing in both directions. In this case, three of the five traditional factors point toward independent contractor status. We conclude that the district court did not err in finding that the drivers were independent contractors. We are confident in this result not only because the various factors weigh in favor of independent contractor status, but also because of Supreme Court precedent with respect to this issue.

The conclusion of the district court that the drivers were independent contractors is affirmed.

Judgment for Express.

Case Commentary

This case illustrates that a worker can exhibit traits of both an employee and an independent contractor. Here, the Fifth Circuit employed a five-prong test. The conclusion reached was that three criteria pointed to independent contractor status, while two criteria pointed to employee status. Thus, the workers for Express were independent contractors. It is not necessary that all factors point one way or the other. ∎

CASE QUESTIONS

1. Do you agree with the court's assessment of the criteria?
2. Is a simple 3-to-2 majority sufficient to make a decision here?
3. Why do some businesses prefer the independent contractor designation for their employees?

Employment is a contractual relationship wherein the employee or independent contractor is given authority to act on behalf of the employer. All the requirements of contract law are applicable to the creation of employment.

In the case that follows, Trayon Redd's claim of disability discrimination depends on whether she is considered to be an employee or an independent contractor.

Redd v. Summers, Secretary of the Treasury
232 F.3d 933 (D.C. Cir. 2000)

Williams, Circuit Judge.

The Treasury Department's Bureau of Engraving and Printing retained Aspen Personnel Services, Inc., to provide tour services at the Bureau. In July 1995 Aspen hired Trayon Redd as a tour guide. In March 1996 Aspen removed Redd from her job at the Bureau. When Redd complained to Aspen about her dismissal, Aspen rehired Redd and attempted to reinstate her at the Bureau. The Bureau refused. Redd, who is 5'7" tall and weighs about

348 pounds, perceived the Bureau's behavior in these affairs as a response to her weight. (So far as appears, Redd's weight did not change between her hiring in 1995 and her dismissal in 1996.) She has brought claims against the Bureau under §§ 501 and 504 of the Rehabilitation Act of 1973 (RHA). Redd brought claims against the Bureau claiming that it was her employer.

Under the contract between Aspen and the Bureau, Aspen was responsible for training all tour guides, paying guides' wages and providing benefits, including annual leave. Aspen and the Bureau each had a representative to handle their relationship—in the Bureau's case a liaison officer, the Contracting Officer's Technical Representative, and in Aspen's an on-site supervisor for its workers, the Lead Tour Guide. The Technical Representative and her supervisor at the Bureau had the right to reject any tour guide, but Aspen did all the hiring and firing. The Bureau appointed Antoinette Banks as Technical Representative, and Aspen appointed Henrietta Walls as the Lead Tour Guide.

Redd's complaint against the Bureau stems from five episodes involving Banks and Redd between June 1995 and March 1996. First, Redd alleges that on the occasion of her hiring Banks told Redd and her mother that the tour guide job required a lot of walking in the sun, drinking water and limiting one's consumption of milk. Redd regards these remarks as obesity-based aspersions on her ability to guide tours. Second, Redd finds another obesity-based aspersion in Banks's remark to Redd's mother, in December 1995, that with all the walking the tour work required Redd would surely lose some weight.

Third, Redd says that on March 12, 1996, Banks and Walls said that Redd's tour "spiel" was deficient and temporarily suspended her from guiding tours. In the next few days Walls and Banks tested the guides on their spiels and criticized Redd for her pronunciation; on March 20, Banks accompanied Redd on a tour and evaluated her performance. Redd evidently sees the scrutiny as derived from Banks's perception of her obesity.

Fourth, Redd alleges that in a phone conversation on March 21, 1996, Redd's mother asked Banks if the latter's concerns with Redd's performance were related to Banks's comments in June 1995 (referring to walking in the sun, and drinking water but not much milk, which Redd perceived as relating to obesity). In the phone call Redd's mother told Banks that "full-figured" women are not unable to perform the job of a tour guide. Redd alleges that later that day, after a conversation with Banks, Walls told Redd that her evaluation was sub-standard and that she would be terminated. Redd's view is that Banks's opposition was behind the termination, and was driven by obesity concerns and/or a desire to retaliate for Redd's mother's "full-figured" remarks.

Finally, Redd wrote to Aspen on April 12, 1996, complaining at length about what she saw as her mistreatment by Aspen and the Bureau. Aspen rehired her on June 3, 1996, but the Bureau refused to allow her reinstatement as a Bureau guide. Redd alleges that Banks's superior, Teresa Brooks, who had the authority to reject Redd, made her decision solely on the advice of Banks. Again, Redd infers that Banks's alleged advice was obesity motivated and retaliatory (both for the mother's remarks about "full-figured" women and for the protests in the April 12 letter).

Aspen suggested that Redd fill out applications for jobs on other Aspen contracts, but she didn't do so and was terminated by Aspen in July 1996.

She argues—and Treasury accepts—that we should apply the test stated in *Spirides v. Reinhardt*, a case considering whether the plaintiff was an employee or an independent contractor.

This court has never invoked *Spirides* to resolve an issue of joint employment. For a joint employment test, a fairly standard formulation is whether "one employer[,] while contracting in good faith with an otherwise independent company, has retained for itself sufficient control of the terms and conditions of employment of the employees who are employed by the other employer."

In this context it is telling that Banks did not get involved in Redd's initial training, the work that produced the finished product—the performances themselves. Banks's interventions, well into Redd's tenure, amount to little more than an inspection of the quality of Aspen's services.

None of the other interactions between Banks and Redd amounts to controlling the "means and manner" of Redd's routine. Banks's comments to Redd and Redd's mother in June and December 1995, evidently understood by Redd as relating to her weight, and Banks's conversation with Redd's mother in March 1996, are not assertions of control over Redd. At most they bear on the question of discrimination—not control.

Spirides's eleven "additional" factors do not alter our conclusion:

(1) the kind of occupation, with reference to whether the work usually is done under the direction of a supervisor or is done by a specialist without supervision; (2) the skill required in the particular occupation; (3) whether the "employer" or the individual in question furnishes the equipment used and the place of work; (4) the length of time during which the individual has worked; (5) the method of payment, whether by time or by the job; (6) the manner in which the work relationship is terminated; *i.e.*, by one or both parties, with or without notice and explanation; (7) whether annual leave is afforded; (8) whether the work is an integral part of the business of the "employer"; (9) whether the worker accumulates

retirement benefits; (10) whether the "employer" pays social security taxes; and (11) the intention of the parties.

Rather than simply plow through the eleven factors, we think it more useful to collect them in groups of items that seem to perform similar functions in getting to a sound result. We find four such groups. The first we see as comprised of a single factor: (11) the intent of the parties, primarily as reflected in the contract between the "contractor" and its "client" (here the Bureau). As the *Spirides* court noted, of course, the intent of the parties alone cannot "waive protections granted to an individual under . . . any act of Congress." Thus, intent to make the individual an employee of the client is more likely to prove the relationship than the opposite intent is to disprove it. Here the contract explicitly states that the contractor's personnel "shall not at any time during the contract period be employees of the U.S. Government.

The second group of factors can be seen as addressing whether contracting out work is justifiable as a prudent business decision: (1) whether supervision of the contractor by the client is required; (2) whether the contractor's work does not require special skills; and (8) whether the work performed by the contractor is an integral part of the client's business. An affirmative answer to these questions may call into question the business bona fides of the decision to hire an independent contractor, possibly suggesting a purpose to circumvent rights afforded to employees.

Here, Redd's work required supervision, but Aspen provided it via the Lead Tour Guide, Walls. While Banks, the Bureau's Technical Representative, evaluated Redd twice, Aspen was responsible for all training. Banks appears not to have supervised Redd before March 12, 1996, and even after that date, Walls accompanied Banks on all occasions but two: a brief encounter on March 14, 1996, and the evaluation tour of March 20, 1996. As Walls and Banks were equals—liaisons under the terms of the contract—Walls was by no means Banks's messenger. Finally, the Bureau is a printer of currency and stamps; tours are part of its public relations, not an integral part of its business. There is nothing to suggest that the Bureau's decision to contract out tours was a sham.

If hiring independent contractors cannot be dismissed as an implausible business decision, it is sensible to turn to a third group of factors, which seem to renew the question of the client's control over the work (which, we recall, is in a sense the ultimate determinant): (3) whether the client furnishes the equipment used and place of work; and (6) the manner in which the work relationship was terminated. Here the inquiry is whether the business is exercising a degree of control that seems excessive in comparison to a reasonable client-contractor relationship in the same circumstances.

The evidence on these matters does little to prove Redd an employee of the Bureau. Of course the Bureau provided office space and the tour guides worked at the Bureau, but in context this proves little. That a landscaper's employees worked at the site of a landscaping job would hardly support an inference that they were the client's employees; the nature of the work compels the site. It is true that the Bureau also provided tour guides with office supplies, two-way radios and uniforms. But the Bureau presumably would want continuity in uniforms regardless of who held the tour guide contract, while Aspen's interest was contract dependent. The office supplies and radios seem de minimis.

As to Redd's termination, while the contract gives the Bureau the right to reject any guide, under the contract the decision to terminate the guide's employment with Aspen is solely within Aspen's power. To pursue the landscape example: the client's command to remove a specific worker (say, on grounds of rudeness or just personal incompatibility) would hardly render the worker an employee of the client. Here, in fact, the link of the Bureau to Redd's termination with Aspen was especially tenuous: Aspen asked her to file another employment application in July 1996 and Redd did not.

The final group of factors appears to ask whether the relationship shares attributes commonly found in arrangements with independent contractors or with employees: (4) the duration of the engagement; (5) the method of payment; (7) whether annual leave is afforded; (9) whether the worker accumulates retirement benefits; and (10) whether the client pays social security taxes. Employment relationships tend to be longer or at any rate more likely of indefinite length, to afford annual leave and retirement payments, and to assign payment of social security taxes to the employer. Payment by time period suggests employment; payment by product suggests an independent contractor relation. Here, of course, the *Spirides* factors' misfit with the issue is most acute: Redd indisputably *was* the employee of Aspen. It paid Redd's wages, provided for her vacation time, and paid the social security taxes due. Her employment appears to have been at will. Nothing here suggests Redd was the Bureau's employee.

We conclude that an application of the *Spirides* test, however ill-suited to an analysis of whether an employee of a[n] independent contractor is also an employee of the contractor's client, suggests that Redd is not an employee of the Bureau.

We therefore affirm the district court's grant of summary judgment for Treasury.

Case Commentary

The D.C. Circuit concluded that Redd was not an employee. Her disability discrimination suit against the Treasury was dismissed. ■

CASE QUESTIONS

1. Do you agree with the court's decision?
2. What reason motivated Redd to sue the Treasury?

3. Do you believe Redd has a viable lawsuit against Aspen Personnel Services?

ELEMENTS OF AN EMPLOYMENT CONTRACT

An *employment contract* is a legally enforceable agreement. For an agreement to be legally enforceable, the following elements must be present: a mutual agreement, executed in proper form, voluntarily made by two or more capable parties wherein each party promises to perform or not to perform a specific legal act for valuable consideration. Each element in this definition must be satisfied by each party for the contract to be valid. The validity of the contract is what gives it legal effect. The elements of an employment contract are:

- Lawful purpose
- Agreement
- Legal capacity
- Promise to perform
- Consideration
- Executed in proper form

Employment contracts are personal service contracts. Personal service contracts are contracts in which one person promises to perform a service for an employer in return for the employer's promise to provide compensation for the services rendered. Personal service contracts include employment contracts, in which an individual is employed on a salary basis, as well as contracts with professionals or independent contractors, in which performance is on an hourly or per case basis.

Assignments of employment contracts are permissible under certain circumstances.

An employment contract may be created expressly, through a writing or a verbal conversation, or impliedly, through the actions of the parties. Generally employment contracts are not required to be in writing because they are indefinite in nature.

Actual Authority

The scope of an employee's authority is usually determined by the employer. Actual authority is the express authority conveyed by the employer to the employee, which also includes the implied authority to do whatever is reasonably necessary to complete the task. This implied authority also gives the employee power to act in an emergency. Implied authority is authority that the employee actually has. It comes with the job.

Employment Perspective

Charlie Moore is a garage mechanic at the Seagate Service Station. His actual authority is limited to servicing automobiles. He has no authority to enter into contracts with customers for his services and has no authority to decide on which cars he will work on. One day while the gas attendant is out to lunch, a customer pulls up to the gas pump. Does Charlie Moore have the authority to service the customer? Yes! Inherent in the authority delegated to Charlie is the implied authority to perform those routine tasks necessary for the continuation of the business when the other mechanics or gas attendants are out to lunch or otherwise occupied. Is Charlie an employee or an independent contractor? If Charlie works exclusively for Seagate, he would be an employee. For example, if a boy threw a brick through the office window and it had to be repaired before closing, Charlie would have the authority to board up the window or have a glazier replace the glass—assuming that the service station manager could not be notified—because Charlie would be acting in an emergency.

Apparent Authority

Apparent authority is the authority the employee professes to have that induces a reasonable person to believe in the employee. The reliance on apparent authority must be justifiable. With apparent authority, the employee appears to have the authority to act, but he or she actually does not.

Employment Perspective

In the previous example, suppose Charlie is alone at the service station, finishing a tune-up on a Monte Carlo, when Arthur Moriarity drives up in his Rolls-Royce. Charlie had previously been assigned by his manager to perform a brake job on this Rolls 6 months ago. Moriarity recognizes Charlie and tells him that there is a rumbling sound in the engine. Charlie inspects the engine and tells Arthur Moriarity that the valves are worn and need to be reseated. Moriarity agrees to leave the car overnight. The next morning, Charlie has completed the valve job, but the engine's rumbling has become worse. When Moriarity calls for the Rolls-Royce, he threatens to sue the service station for negligence in its attempted repair of his car. Can the service station raise the defense that Charlie Moore acted without authority. No! Although Charlie did not possess the actual authority to bind the Seagate Service Station to a contract, he appeared to have the authority in entering into the contract of repair. Arthur Moriarity was justified because a reasonable person would believe a garage mechanic would possess the authority to decide whether a car could be repaired at the service station for which he or she worked. How could Seagate prevent Charlie from agreeing to service cars on Seagate's behalf? Seagate could post conspicuous notices instructing customers to speak only with the manager, and it could warn Charlie that if he takes it upon himself to accept a car for service, he will be severely reprimanded or terminated.

DUTIES OF EMPLOYEES AND INDEPENDENT CONTRACTORS

Duty of Loyalty

The relationship between employers and employees or independent contractors is a fiduciary one, based on trust and confidence. Inherent in this relationship is the employee's or independent contractor's duty of loyalty. An employee has a duty to inform, to obey instructions, and to protect confidential information. An employee or independent contractor has a duty to disclose all pertinent information he or she learns of that will affect the employer, the employer's business, or the task at hand. An employee or independent contractor must not take advantage of the employer's prospective business opportunities or enter into contracts on behalf of the employer for personal aggrandizement without the employer's knowledge. An employee, and in some cases an independent contractor (lawyer, investment banker, sports-team scout), may not work for two employers who have competing interests.

Employment Perspective

Peter Stapelton works as a salesclerk and mechanic at South Shore Auto Parts and Repair Shop. One day, Stapelton is approached by Malcolm Ripkin, owner of Ripkin's Limousine Service, who informs him that he would like South Shore to maintain his fleet of 17 limousines. Stapelton takes Ripkin's card, but instead of passing it along to the owners of South Shore, he decides to negotiate with Ripkin on his own behalf. Stapelton reasons that if he can get the contract for the maintenance of the 17 limousines, it would enable him to establish his own auto repair station. Stapelton enters into a personal service contract with Ripkin and then contracts with South Shore to purchase all the supplies he needs at wholesale prices. Six months later, South Shore learns of Stapelton's disloyalty. What recourse does the company have? South Shore may sue Stapelton for breach of contract because he violated his duty of loyalty in failing to disclose Ripkin's offer and in taking advantage of South Shore's business opportunity. Stapelton also contracted on behalf of South Shore for his own benefit without telling the company of what he was doing. Stapelton will be liable to South Shore for consequential damages—that is, the loss of profits South Shore sustained because of Stapelton's unauthorized contracts made on behalf of South Shore with himself at wholesale prices. South Shore will be able to recover the difference between the wholesale price and the retail price, and may also fire Stapelton for his disloyal actions.

Duty to Act in Good Faith

An employee or independent contractor has an obligation to perform all duties in good faith. He or she must carry out the task assigned by using reasonable skill and care. The employee or independent contractor has a further duty to follow the employer's instructions and not to exceed the authority delegated to him or her.

Employment Perspective

Steve Torrino worked in a Burgerville Restaurant for 3 years. During his employment, he felt that the manager was continually mistreating him by using abusive language, assigning him hours that purposely conflicted with his class studies, and making him perform janitorial services that were not included in his job description. When an opening arose at a nearby House of Burgers on a late shift, Torrino accepted the position, but he retained his regular job with Burgerville. During the manager's absence one busy Saturday afternoon, Torrino neglected his routine duties and took charge of the cash register. He proceeded to give away three jumbo burgers free with every purchase of a small soda. He informed the customers that it was an anniversary celebration. Torrino's intent was to repay the Burgerville manager for his unkindness by causing him to lose profits. What recourse does the Burgerville manager have against Torrino? Torrino violated his duty of loyalty to Burgerville by working for a competing employer, House of Burgers, and by purposely causing Burgerville to lose profits. Torrino refused to obey instructions to perform his delegated duties. He exceeded his authority through the authorization of a free offer. If Torrino was displeased with his job, he should have left to find another position rather than allowing his resentment to build up for 3 years. In all respects, Torrino violated his duty to act in good faith.

Duty to Account

An employee or independent contractor has a duty to account for all compensations received, including kickbacks. Upon the employer's request, an employee or independent contractor must make a full disclosure, known as an *accounting*, of all receipts and expenditures. The employee or independent contractor must not commingle funds but rather must keep the employer's funds in an account separate from his or her own. Furthermore, an employee or independent contractor must not use the employer's funds for his or her own purposes.

Employment Perspective

Ted Murphy is a securities broker at a branch office of Pearlman & Associates, located in Silver City, New Mexico. All of Murphy's clients signed an agreement appointing him as their agent to buy and sell securities. Murphy would often borrow from individual accounts in order to further his own investment opportunities. He did this without telling either the client or the company; later, he would repay the amount borrowed. Because Silver City is not a large city, many clients make deposits in cash. Murphy would stamp the deposit slip but then deposit the cash in his own account, expecting to repay the money at a later date. Finally, Murphy has a streak of bad luck and is unable to repay the money before the monthly statements are sent out. The clients sue Pearlman & Associates and Ted Murphy for conversion of the funds in their accounts. What recourse does Pearlman & Associates have against Murphy? The company may sue Murphy for breach of contract and for reimbursement of any of the clients' losses. Murphy breached his duty of loyalty, his duty to act in good faith, and his duty to disclose fully all deposits he received. He commingled clients' funds with his own for the purpose of furthering his own investment schemes.

EMPLOYER'S DUTIES

Duty to Compensate

An employer has the duty to compensate the employee or independent contractor for the work performed. An employee or independent contractor will be entitled to the amount agreed upon in the contract; otherwise, he or she will be entitled to the reasonable value of the services rendered. Sales representatives are usually paid according to a commission-based pay structure, which incorporates a minimum level of compensation against which the sales representatives are entitled to draw. An employer must also reimburse an employee for the expenses incurred by the employee during the course of conducting the employer's business. For tax purposes, an employer has a duty to keep a record of the compensation earned by an employee and the reimbursements made for expenditures. Employers are required to withhold payroll taxes from employees' paychecks. This is not so with fees paid to independent contractors.

Duty to Maintain Safe Working Conditions

The maintenance of safe working conditions is another obligation placed on the employer. Any tools or equipment furnished to the employee must be in proper working order; otherwise, the employer may be liable for the harm resulting to an employee under the Occupational Safety and Health Administration (OSHA).

If an employee is injured during the scope of employment, then the employee will be covered under workers' compensation. The scope of employment means the worker is on the job.

NONCOMPETE AGREEMENTS

A *noncompete agreement* is a contract wherein the employer provides employment or a severance package (in the case where the noncompete agreement is entered into upon termination) in return for the employee's promise not to work for a competitor or open a competing business within the geographic area in which the employer transacts business for a reasonable length of time. A noncompete agreement may be a separate document or it may be a clause or covenant contained in an employment contract. The latter is often identified as noncompete clauses, restrictive covenants, or covenants not to compete. Enforcement of these deprives the employee of being able to work in his or her area of expertise. Courts will restrict the employee only when the employer has established harm to its business. The limitations set forth in the contract must be reasonable. The courts will not enforce restrictions upon employees that are unduly harsh and permit employers to derive more protection than that necessary to guard their secrets or to protect their business interests.

In most states, noncompete agreements are enforceable within the confines set forth here. Some states place restrictions on them. In California, noncompete agreements are restricted to the sale of a business and cannot be used in employment.

Employment Perspective

David Williams bought a liquor store on the South Side of Chicago. He hired Brian Jackson to manage the store for him. A provision in the contract prohibited Brian from opening a liquor store within the city limits for the rest of his natural life. After learning the trade, Brian quit and opened his own place in the downtown section of Chicago known as The Loop. Can David enforce the provision? No! The provision is too broad in its geographic area and much too unreasonable in its time restraints.

NONDISCLOSURE AGREEMENTS

An employee's sale or use of trade secrets, confidential information, and/or a work in progress that has commercial value or will result in harm to the employer may be restricted through a nondisclosure agreement. Courts will enjoin an employee where the employer is protecting its legitimate business interests. The Uniform Trade Secrets Act provides guidelines for employers in those states that have ratified it.

Noncompete and nondisclosure agreements are often used in high-tech, product development, sales, and financial services where employees have proprietary information or access to customer lists. Under the inevitable disclosure doctrine, employees may be restricted even where they have not signed a noncompete and/or a nondisclosure document under the theory that it is inevitable that the employees will use the information gleaned from their employer to benefit themselves or a competitor. This doctrine is predominantly applicable to intellectual property.

SAMPLE NONCOMPETE AND NONDISCLOSURE AGREEMENTS

Employee agrees that during a 1-year period following the termination of employment with X Corp., employee agrees to refrain from the following:

1. Conduct business that would place employee in competition with X Corp.
2. Work for an employer who is in competition with X Corp.
3. Entice coworkers and/or customers to cease their relationship with X Corp.
4. Disclose to a competitor of X Corp. any confidential information belonging or pertaining to X Corp.

The issue in the case that follows is whether the noncompete clause should be enforceable.

Paglia v. Franco
206 F. Supp. 2d 597 (S.D.N.Y. 2002)

McMahon, J.

On June 22, 2000, this Court, after a bench trial on a consolidated motion for a preliminary and permanent injunction, imposed an injunction precluding Defendant Dr. Michael Franco from practicing medicine at Greenwich Hospital, to which he had repaired following his departure from practice with Plaintiff corporation, for a period of three years.

The injunction was entered to enforce a clause in plaintiff's employment agreement that prevented him, for three years after his termination from GPS, from practicing medicine within a 15-mile radius of Mamaroneck and Port Chester, New York, excepting only Stamford, Connecticut. The prohibition, I found, was directed especially at Greenwich, Connecticut, where GPS hoped to expand its patient base and hospital affiliation. Concluding that the covenant was reasonable in time, place and scope, and that defendant had deliberately procured his own discharge in the hope of evading the

covenant, I enjoined Dr. Franco from engaging in any sort of patient care—including teaching involving patient care—at Greenwich Hospital for a period to conclude on May 1 of next year.

Now defendant moves for vacatur of the final judgment. He contends that GPS, while still an active and registered professional corporation, has in fact gone out of business and no longer practices medicine, and that its principals have become shareholders and employees of a still larger medical group, the Westchester Medical Group. Noting (correctly) that the benefits under his restrictive covenant are not assignable without his consent, Franco points out that he did not agree to the assignment of GPS's contract rights to Westchester Medical Group. He argues that the judgment should be vacated because plaintiff no longer has any interest in preventing him from practicing medicine in Greenwich.

Plaintiff retorts that, while GPS has sold its assets, and its employees (including Drs. Gismondi, Paglia and Sherling) have become employees of Westchester Medical Group, the corporation's "protectable interest" in preventing plaintiff from practicing medicine in Greenwich has not diminished since the injunction was entered. The corporation still exists. While it is not currently engaged in the practice of medicine, Drs. Gismondi, Paglia and Sherling have the right to return to the status quo if things don't work out with WMG. Plaintiff further notes that the benefits of Franco's restrictive covenant inure by the contract's terms to GPS's "successors" as well as to consensual assigns, and contends that WMG is the "revocable successor" (whatever that means) of GPS.

Defendant replies that the law recognizes no such thing as a "revocable successor" to a corporation, especially to a corporation that has not dissolved and remains in active status under the law of the State of New York. It notes that WMG did not purport to acquire all the assets of GPS and expressly declined to assume the liabilities and obligations of GPS.

After reviewing the documents, there is no way I can describe WMG as a "successor" to GPS within the law's understanding of that term. WMG neither became invested with GPS's rights nor assumed its liabilities. Rather, it bought GPS's assets (or at least those of it that were for sale, such as furnishings and equipment), subleased its premises, and employed its physicians and its other personnel. GPS did not merge into WMG—plaintiff proffers no evidence to suggest that it is not still an active corporation, while defendant has established that GPS is still registered with the Secretary of State. Thus, WMG does not fit within the definition of the legal term "successor," and cannot claim any benefit from Dr. Franco's restrictive covenant by virtue of his employment agreement with GPS. Since there is no other way that WMG could have become invested with GPS's right to restrict Franco's employment (except by consensual assignment, which did not occur), WMG is not entitled to the benefits of the injunction entered by this Court.

The question then becomes whether GPS has any continuing interest in barring Dr. Franco from practicing medicine in Greenwich. Given the extreme disfavor in which the law holds restrictive covenants, and the strict construction that must be given to such covenants, it would be inequitable for the injunction to continue in force if GPS as an entity no longer has any interest in where Franco works. I conclude that GPS has no such interest.

As part of GPS's arrangement with WMG, Drs. Gismondi, Paglia, Sherling and the physicians associated with them all signed employment contracts obligating them to work exclusively for WMG—to be precise, requiring that each of them "devote his entire time, attention and

energies to the business of [WMG] during its regular office hours and at any other time during the week as may from time to time be requested by [WMG] . . . and shall not, during the term of this agreement without the consent of the Board of Directors of [WMG], either directly or indirectly engage in the practice of medicine except on behalf of [WMG]." Thus, GPS is no longer in the practice of medicine, and has no present interest in restricting Dr. Franco's employment. It has not had any such interest since last May. The fact that a corporate shell remains in existence is irrelevant, because that corporate shell cannot engage in the practice of medicine as long as its principals are contractually bound to devote their full efforts to WMG's practice.

Plaintiff argues that, if things do not go well between the principals of the now dormant GPS and WMG, the old practice can be reconstituted (minus those of its employees who have signed restrictive covenants as a condition of their employment by WMG). However, that inchoate (not to mention unlikely) possibility does not alter the analysis. Restrictive covenants are disfavored at law, and so their terms must be construed strictly. The only party entitled to benefit from the Court's injunction is GPS, and the reason GPS is entitled to that injunction is so that it can further its interest in practicing medicine in and near Greenwich. But GPS is not practicing medicine at all, let alone in or near Greenwich, and the record does not contain the slightest indication that GPS intends to resume the active practice of medicine any time soon. At present, the only party benefiting from Dr. Franco's situation is WMG, the employer of Drs. Gismondi, Paglia and Sherling. But WMG has no right to this benefit absent Dr. Franco's consent—which defendant has no intention of providing.

The conclusion that GPS has no present interest in restricting Dr. Franco's employment is inescapable. The physicians who are affiliated with GPS chose to practice medicine under corporate form and they must live with the consequences of their choice. "Combining" rather than merging with WMG may be the way that GPS found to "expand" its practice into Connecticut, but that combination came with a cost—the cost of losing the benefit of the restrictive covenant barring Dr. Franco from practicing at Greenwich Hospital. Indeed, had this Court been confronted with the facts now before it two years ago, no injunction would have issued.

I do, however, vacate the injunction enforcing the restrictive covenant against Dr. Franco, and I direct that the injunction dissolve immediately.

Case Commentary

The southern District of New York vacated its injunction against Dr. Franco because his former employer no longer engages in business in the area in which Dr. Franco is now located. ■

CASE QUESTIONS

1. Do you agree with the court's decision?
2. Was the noncompete clause against Dr. Franco properly drafted?
3. Do noncompete clauses serve a legitimate purpose?

In the following case, the issue is whether a noncompete agreement is assignable.

Managed Health Care Associates, Inc. v. Ronald Kethan and First Choice Cooperative

2000 FED App. 0143P (6th Cir.)

Gilman, Circuit Judge.

Managed Health Care Associates, Inc. and MHCA Acquisition, Inc., d/b/aMHA/MedEcon (collectively MHA), commenced an action in state court against Ronald Kethan (Kethan) and East Texas Regional Cooperative, d/b/a First Choice Cooperative (First Choice). MHA sought a preliminary injunction to prevent Kethan from violating the noncompetition clause that he had signed when employed by MedEcon Services, Inc. (MedEcon).

BACKGROUND

On December 27, 1991, Kethan signed an employment agreement with MedEcon, a group purchasing organization (GPO) for hospitals with its principal place of business in Kentucky. GPOs contract for the purchase of a vast array of products for use by member healthcare facilities. They also enter into agreements directly with suppliers to allow member facilities to purchase the products at reduced prices, thereby providing a substantial savings of both time and money for their members. GPOs also engage in bulk purchasing in order to provide their members even greater discounts.

From 1992 through 1996, Kethan worked as a salesman and an agreement administrator for MedEcon. Kethan's job responsibilities included meeting with various representatives from hospitals and encouraging them to use the products covered by MedEcon's agreements. He contacted numerous representatives in Texas and Oklahoma on MedEcon's behalf.

During this period, Kethan had the opportunity to develop strong business relationships with MedEcon's customers, including First Choice. Kethan eventually became the agreement administrator for the First Choice account.

In June of 1998, MHA, which is also a GPO, began negotiations with MedEcon for the acquisition of MedEcon's assets. On September 9, 1998, most of MedEcon's assets were purchased by MHA. Included in those assets was Kethan's employment agreement. Neither MedEcon nor MHA obtained Kethan's written consent to the assignment. Following the transaction, Kethan continued to be an at-will employee, performing the same job, receiving the same salary and benefits, and reporting to the same supervisor. Twenty days after the sale of MedEcon's assets to MHA, Kethan gave thirty-days' notice of his resignation. Two days after Kethan tendered his resignation notice, First Choice ceased using MHA/MedEcon for group purchasing services. When the thirty days had passed from Kethan's resignation notice, he commenced employment with First Choice. Shortly thereafter, MHA brought suit seeking to enforce Kethan's noncompetition agreement with MedEcon.

The noncompetition clause provides as follows:

"Employee, during the term of this agreement and for a period of two (2) years after the termination thereof, will not do, directly or indirectly, for himself or herself or as an agent of, or on behalf of, or in conjunction with, any person, trust, firm, partnership, corporation, or business organization other than the Company ("Other Firm"), nor will he or she, directly or indirectly, cause or permit any Other Firm in which he or she has a proprietary or financial interest, or of which he or she is a director, officer, employee, shareholder, partner, or representative, to do any of the following:

a. solicit or cause any past, present or future (up to the time of the termination of employment) customers (or members) of the Company or of any of the existing or future subsidiaries or affiliates of the Company ("Subsidiaries or Affiliates") to transfer all or part of their business from the Company or the Subsidiaries or Affiliates or render competitive services to any such customers (or members).
b. induce or attempt to influence any existing or future employee of the Company or any of the Subsidiaries or Affiliates to leave such employment; and
c. engage in any of the kinds of business activities in which the Company or any of the Subsidiaries or Affiliates have been or is now engaged within the States of Texas, Kansas, Nebraska, Oklahoma, Colorado, Idaho, Arizona, Wyoming, and Missouri.

In addition to the noncompetition clause, the agreement contained a provision requiring that any modifications be in writing and signed by both parties. The agreement also provided that any disputes were to be governed by Kentucky law. No clause in the contract, however, directly addressed the issue of whether Kethan's contract could be assigned. The district court concluded that the assignment of Kethan's contract was a modification. Because any modification had to be in writing, and there was no such writing, the district court held that Kethan was no longer bound by the noncompetition clause. The district court also held that noncompetition clauses are not assignable under Kentucky law.

ANALYSIS

[A]ssignments and modifications are completely different concepts, and that assignability is not impacted by "boilerplate" modification provisions. Based on this reasoning, we conclude that the terms of Kethan's employment were not modified by the assignment of his contract and the substitution of MHA for MedEcon. Following the assignment, Kethan's contractual rights and duties as an employee did not change. The only thing that changed was the entity now entitled to enforce the terms and conditions that Kethan had previously agreed to when he entered into his employment agreement. Accordingly, we hold that the district court erred when it concluded that the assignment

of Kethan's employment contract modified the terms of his agreement. A noncompetition clause is assignable in Kentucky

Under Kentucky law, it has long been recognized "that a contract is generally assignable, unless forbidden by public policy or the contract itself, or its provisions are such as to show that one of the parties reposes a personal confidence in the other, which he would have unwilling to repose in any other person." Kentucky courts have also acknowledged that noncompetition clauses play a critical role in business and are favored as long as they are reasonable in geographic scope and duration.

"The policy of this state is to enforce noncompetition clauses unless very serious inequities would result." The policy behind enforcing noncompetition clauses is to protect businesses against employees resigning and taking valued clients with them. In this case, while working for MedEcon, Kethan had access to MedEcon's customer lists. He eventually became First Choice's primary advisor. Because of that, Kethan developed a special business relationship with First Choice.

Shortly after First Choice decided to end its business relationship with MHA/MedEcon, Kethan ceased working for MHA and commenced working for First Choice. The reason that Kethan was able to develop his unique business relationship with First Choice, and later go to work for it, was because MedEcon employed him and placed him in charge of the First Choice account. He is thus precisely the type of employee for whom noncompetition clauses were designed.

Here, Kethan was an at will employee who was free to resign at any time. Consequently, the noncompetition clause does not require any affirmative action on the part of Kethan, and is thus assignable.

Judgment for Managed Health Care Associates.

Case Commentary

The Sixth Circuit ruled that noncompetition clauses are assignable. Here MHA acquired MedEcon, who had entered into a noncompete agreement with Kethan for the purpose of protecting its business from the loss of the customers he was dealing with should he go elsewhere, which he did. MHA, as assignee to the noncompete agreement, has the right to enforce it against Kethan. ■

CASE QUESTIONS

1. Why should noncompetition clauses be assignable?
2. Are noncompetition clauses ethical? After all, noncompetition clauses prevent workers from seeking employment in the trade or profession they know or do best.

3. Would MHA have suffered harm had the noncompetition clause not been enforced?

Injunction

An *injunction* is an equitable remedy that prevents a party breaching a contract from rendering the same performance elsewhere. An injunction is personal in nature and negative in effect in that it precludes a person from performing certain acts. However, because the breaching party cannot be compelled to perform a certain act, an injunction can prohibit the party from performing the same act elsewhere. An injunction acts as a restraint against the party breaching an employment contract. An injunction is the appropriate remedy to enforce a noncompete clause.

Employment Perspective

Wild Bill Cary is under a 5-year contract with the Texas Tornadoes to play quarterback for them for $100,000 per year. After leading his team to successive central division titles, he is offered a 4-year contract from the Hawaii Hurricanes for $500,000 per year. There are still 3 years remaining on Wild Bill's contract with Texas, but he decides to accept Hawaii's offer. Can Texas prevent Wild Bill from quarterbacking for Hawaii? Yes! An injunction can be granted, but Texas cannot legally force Wild Bill to quarterback for them through specific performance. Wild Bill is bound to Texas for the 3 years remaining on his contract unless they renegotiate his contract or trade him. The terms of Wild Bill's original contract were designed to protect him from being cut from the team while ensuring him a substantial yearly salary. After the contract expires, Wild Bill will have free-agent status.

Contractual Conditions

A condition occurs when the parties' contractual duties are contingent upon the occurrence of a future event. Parties must expressly agree when making the contract if they are conditioning their obligations on the occurrence of a particular event.

Sales quotas in car dealerships, insurance, brokerage, and so on, are conditions that must be continuously satisfied for the worker to retain his or her job.

Tort Liability

An employer is liable for any tort committed by his or her employee if the tort is committed within the scope of employment—that is, if it is related to the business at hand. A *tort* is a private civil wrong as opposed to a *crime*, which is a wrong committed against the public. However, an employer is not liable for the torts of an independent contractor even if the torts are committed during the scope of employment because the employer has no control over the work of an independent contractor.

The issue in the following case is whether the employee was acting within the scope of employment when he negligently injured the plaintiff.

Clamor v. United States
240 F.3d 1215 (9th Cir. 2001)

Hawkins, Judge.

Erlinda Clamor appeals the district court's dismissal of her tort claim, which arose from a car accident on the Pearl Harbor Naval Base with James Karagiorgis, a civilian employee. The district court concluded that Karagiorgis had been acting within the scope of his employment as a federal employee at the time of the accident, and that therefore the case was governed by the Federal Tort Claims Act ("FTCA"). The district court dismissed the case because Clamor had failed to exhaust her administrative remedies under the FTCA. Because we conclude that Karagiorgis was not acting within the scope of his employment at the time of the accident, we reverse and remand for further proceedings.

FACTS AND PROCEDURAL HISTORY

James Karagiorgis is a civilian employee of the United States Navy who is ordinarily assigned to the Naval Sea System Command ("NAVSEA") in Washington, D.C. For a few weeks in 1996, Karagiorgis was temporarily assigned to perform an "engineering reliability backfit" on the USS Los Angeles, which was moored at the Pearl Harbor Naval Base in Hawaii. Because no government quarters were available on the base, Karagiorgis arranged commercial lodging through a government travel agent and procured a rental car for use while in Hawaii. The cost of both the car and hotel were reimbursed by the Navy.

On January 24, 1996, James Karagiorgis finished his day's work on the USS Los Angeles, left the ship and began driving toward the exit of the base, which was some distance from the ship where he had been working. While still just inside the base, he rear-ended a car that was stopped in traffic, injuring Clamor.

After first exhausting her no-fault benefits as required by Hawaii state law, Clamor filed a complaint against Karagiorgis in Hawaii state court. The United States Attorney for the District of Hawaii certified that Karagiorgis was acting within the scope of his employment at the time of the accident, removed the case to federal court, and substituted the United States as defendant pursuant to 28 U.S.C. § 2679(d). The United States then moved to dismiss the case for lack of subject matter jurisdiction because Clamor had not exhausted her administrative remedies as required by the FTCA. 28 U.S.C. § 2675(a). The district court concluded that Karagiorgis had been acting within the scope of his employment and that therefore the certification, removal and substitution had been proper. The district court granted the United States' motion to dismiss.

DISCUSSION

Karagiorgis was temporarily assigned to perform a special engineering project on the U.S.S. Los Angeles. At the time of the accident, however, Karagiorgis was off duty and was leaving the base to drive to his temporary home. This is not conduct "of the kind he was employed to perform," and was not "actuated by a purpose to serve the master." Hawaii courts have specifically rejected the notion that any action by an employee on temporary assignment can give rise to respondeat superior liability:

> We do not believe that the respondeat superior doctrine is so pliant that where an employee is hired in one locality and relocated to another by his employer for an indefinite period of time, any act of the employee before, during or after his working hours is one within the scope of his employment as long as he works for the employer in the latter locality.

If Karagiorgis had been on call around the clock or working until "his head hit the pillow," we might reach a different result. Karagiorgis, however, was not working the entire time he was in Hawaii, and was, in fact, off duty when the accident occurred. He was not engaged in any errand for his employer, but was leaving work and free to do whatever he wished. The fact that the United States reimbursed the cost of his rental car is more indicative of the inconvenience of working on an island in the middle of the Pacific Ocean (which makes it difficult for a temporary employee to bring his own car to work) than an indication that the employer considered all actions taken while driving that car to be within the scope of employment. The United States derived no benefit from Karagiorgis' activities once he stopped working on the U.S.S. Los Angeles and left for the day, any more than it does when any other employee departs for the evening (test is whether conduct was related to employment or if enterprise derived benefit from the activity). Accordingly, Karagiorgis was not acting within the scope of his employment under Hawaii law.

Because we hold that the scope of employment certification was erroneous, Karagiorgis must be substituted back as a defendant; therefore, the FTCA does not govern this case and it was error for the district court to dismiss the action.

REVERSED AND REMANDED for further proceedings consistent with this opinion.

Judgment for the United States.

Tallman, Circuit Judge, Dissenting:

Erlinda Clamor was injured on a military base in a minor car accident caused by another government employee. Her state court lawsuit was removed to federal district court by the United States. The district court dismissed the case because Mrs. Clamor failed to exhaust her FTCA remedies before bringing suit. I would affirm. I am unable to join the Court's opinion because it ignores the overwhelming evidence and case law supporting the U.S. Attorney's certification that the government employee was within the scope of his employment at the time of the accident.

The district court determined that Karagiorgis was within the scope of his federal employment under Hawaii law. First, in driving from his temporary duty station to his temporary lodging (arranged by his employer), Karagiorgis was engaged in the type of conduct he was employed to perform on orders of the Department of Defense. His orders authorized his use of a rental car to permit him to travel in and around his temporary duty area, which included the Pearl Harbor Naval Base and the Honolulu hotel where he was staying. This was no vacation or personal frolic. Karagiorgis's orders authorized reimbursement for his Government travel, including the cost of the Government rental car under federal contract with Alamo Rent A Car. He was also reimbursed for his subsistence lodging expenses incurred during his month-long assignment at Pearl Harbor.

Second, Karagiorgis's conduct was substantially within authorized time and space limits. Karagiorgis was still on the naval base at the time of the accident and just minutes earlier he was performing his assigned tasks aboard the USS Los Angeles. He was driving his authorized rental car in the authorized duty area in order to return directly to his authorized lodging.

Third, use of the rental car was necessary to serve the needs of the Government. There was no lodging available for Karagiorgis on the naval base. The Government was in need of his technical expertise in nuclear submarine work. To obtain his assistance, it was necessary to temporarily house Karagiorgis (while on this remote assignment 6,000 miles from his normal duty station) by arranging lodging at a nearby hotel and by providing him a car with which to commute. This arrangement was related directly to Karagiorgis's federal employment and it benefitted the Government because it allowed him to work on the submarine even though there was no room for him to stay on the Pearl Harbor base.

The opinion of the Court fails to recognize that Karagiorgis was within the scope of his Government employment at the time of the car accident. It overlooks the fact that the accident occurred on a naval base and was therefore within the special maritime and territorial jurisdiction of the United States. Clamor failed to establish by a preponderance of the evidence that the scope of employment certification was improper under Hawaii law. I would affirm the dismissal of Clamor's tort claim for lack of subject matter jurisdiction because she failed to first exhaust her administrative remedies.

I respectfully dissent.

Case Commentary
The Ninth Circuit decided that Karagiorgis was not acting within the scope of his employment. Therefore, the United States, as employer, could not be held liable for his negligence. ∎

CASE QUESTIONS

1. Do you agree with the decision in this case?
2. Should the government be liable because the accident occurred on the base?

3. Is Karagiorgis personally liable?

Employment Perspective
Luis Manulto is a construction worker who was hired by Valenti Construction Company. Currently, Luis is working on the 44th floor of an office building in downtown Houston. Manulto has his toolbox at his feet, but when someone calls him abruptly, he accidentally knocks it off the beam. The toolbox falls onto a pedestrian walkway that was covered by a heavy plastic grating. Linda Anderson, who was walking through the passageway at the time, is severely injured. Is Manulto an employee or an independent contractor? Manulto is an employee because he works exclusively for Valenti and is under Valenti's direct control. Who is liable for Linda's injuries? Linda may sue both Luis Manulto (employee) and Valenti Construction Company (employer). Manulto acted negligently in knocking over the toolbox. Valenti Construction Company is liable for Manulto's negligence because it occurred during his scope of employment; the accident was related directly to the business at hand.

Suppose that at lunchtime, Manulto stops at a bar across the street to drown his sorrows and that a patron comments, "I saw the whole episode, and it was a real stupid thing you did." Manulto, angered by the patron's comments, punches him in the face, causing the patron to suffer a fractured nose and a concussion. Is the principal liable for Manulto's acts? No! Valenti Construction Company is not liable for Manulto's tort of assault and battery because it did not occur within the scope of employment—the tort was not related to the business at hand. Manulto will be solely liable.

The issue in the next case is whether an employee could be held personally liable for a negligent act committed within the scope of employment.

Warren v. Cooper Tire & Rubber Company

2002 U.S. Dist. Lexis 22843 (N.D. MI)

Davidson, Chief Judge.

The Plaintiff Harvis Elton Warren worked at the Defendant Cooper Tire & Rubber Company's Tupelo, Mississippi, warehouse as an independent contractor. In April of 2000, Mr. Warren was severely injured when a column of stacked tires and tire pallets fell on him while he was working at the warehouse.

In the case at bar, the Plaintiffs allege that the individual Defendant Carmickel was negligent in connection with the circumstances surrounding the Plaintiff Harvis Elton Warren's injuries.

Under Mississippi law, an agent for a disclosed principal can be held personally liable for his own tortious acts committed within the scope of his employment, and a tort claim can be maintained against that agent. The agent is subject to personal liability when he "directly participates in or authorizes the commission of a tort." [T]he Plaintiffs have alleged that Carmickel, as the agent for Cooper Tire who was in charge of the warehouse where Mr. Warren was injured, directly participated in the commission of at least one tort, negligence, while within the scope of his employment.

A PREMISES OWNER'S OR MANAGER'S POTENTIAL LIABILITY TO INDEPENDENT CONTRACTORS

While Mississippi law makes it burdensome for independent contractors or business invitees to successfully sue premises owners (or those in charge of the premises) for negligence for injuries sustained while working on the premises, the court finds that such relief is not necessarily foreclosed in this case.

While premises owners or managers have no duty to protect independent contractors against risks "arising from or intimately connected with defects of the premises, or of machinery or appliances located thereon, which the contractor has undertaken to repair," the Defendants have made no effort to establish that this "intimately connected" exception to liability is applicable here; and, based on the record before it, the court cannot hold as a matter of law that the exception applies. Accordingly, at this stage of the proceedings and based on the evidence presently before the court, the Plaintiffs' negligence claim against Carmickel survives this potential ground for dismissal.

A corollary to the "intimately connected" exception to liability states that a premises owner or manager is not liable when the independent contractor assumes "the right and fact of control" of the premises and the nature and details of the work. No evidence currently before the court suggests that Mr. Warren had "the right and fact of control" of the warehouse where he was working, although he did control the nature and details of his work. Accordingly, this exception to liability potentially does not apply.

Finally, an owner or manager is not liable for injuries suffered by an independent contractor "resulting from dangers which the contractor, as an expert, has known, or as to which he and his employees 'assumed the risk.'" This "knowledge of danger" exception to liability applies to dangerous conditions of which the contractor has actual or constructive knowledge. The Defendants have not asserted this exception as a bar to recovery by the Plaintiffs, and the court finds that the exception may not apply because there is no evidence presently before the court indicating that Mr. Warren knew or should have known of the dangerous condition that purportedly caused his injuries. Accordingly, the court finds that the Defendants have failed to establish that there is no possibility that the Plaintiffs will be able to state a claim for negligence against the individual Defendant David Carmickel based on this exception to potential liability.

Conclusion

In sum, upon careful review of the parties' submissions, and after construing all state law ambiguities in favor of the Plaintiffs, the court finds that the scenario set forth in the Plaintiffs' pleadings, if true, could possibly result in liability being imposed on David Carmickel for his alleged tortious acts. The Plaintiffs have sufficiently set forth specific allegations, including that Carmickel was aware of the danger posed at the warehouse and took no action to address the danger, demonstrating that Carmickel may have been negligent.

Judgment for Warren.

Case Commentary

The Northern District Court of Mississippi held that an employee may be held to be personally liable for the commission of a negligent act within the scope of his employment. ■

CASE QUESTIONS

1. Are you in agreement with the decision of the court?
2. Why is the plaintiff concerned with suing a coworker when Cooper Tire & Rubber Company represents the deep pocket?
3. Are employees always personally liable for their negligent acts that occur during the scope of employment?

An employer is also liable for the fraud or misrepresentations committed by an employee where the principal has placed the employee in a position that leads people to believe that the agent has the apparent authority to make certain actual representations.

Employment Perspective

Keith Stewart, a representative of Super Duper Vacuum Company, calls on Thelma Williams at her house. Although at first Thelma is reluctant to make a purchase, Stewart convinces her when he makes the false representation that this household vacuum cleaner will also clean basements and garages, with the separate purchase of certain attachments. He does this intentionally to get the sale. Thelma purchases the vacuum cleaner as well as the attachments. When her husband comes home, she gives him a demonstration in the living room, where the vacuum cleaner works perfectly. Then using the attachments, Thelma's husband attempts to clean the garage floor. The machine breaks down. Thelma and her husband sue Super Duper Vacuum Company and Keith Stewart for fraud. Super Duper never instructed Stewart to make false statements of fact and never advertised its vacuum cleaner for anything more than household use. Who will be responsible for the fraud? If Keith is an employee working exclusively for Super Duper, then both Super Duper and Keith Stewart will be liable. Super Duper is liable for its employee's fraudulent representations because it placed Stewart in a position where people would reasonably believe that he had the authority to make such a statement. Super Duper may seek indemnification from Stewart because of his breach of duty of loyalty. Stewart breached the duty by exceeding his authority through the making of statements that were false and unauthorized.

Employment Perspective

One day while strolling through Richmond Hill Mall, Bill Cominsky decides to browse around Peter's Jewelry Store. He spots what appears to be a gold necklace on sale for $49. He figures this would be perfect for his fiancee's upcoming birthday. Bill goes in and asks the clerk, Marjorie Travers, whether the necklace is made of gold. She excuses herself and goes into a back room where she questions Bernard Peters, the store owner. He replies that the necklace is 14K gold, knowing this to be false. Marjorie conveys the message to Bill, ignorant of its falsehood. Bill, relying on the statement, makes the purchase. On his fiancee's birthday, they discover that the necklace is not 14K gold. What recourse is available to Bill Cominsky? Bill may sue Marjorie Travers, the employee, for misrepresentation and Bernard Peters, the employer, for fraud. Marjorie Travers made a material misrepresentation of fact that Bill justifiably relied on to his detriment. She made this statement innocently, without an intent to defraud. Bernard Peters is guilty of fraud because his misrepresentation was intentional.

EMPLOYEE LESSONS

1. Know whether your employment status is that of an employee or independent contractor.
2. Understand the rights and responsibilities of both.
3. Learn what authority you have been given.
4. Acknowledge the limits of your authority by not exceeding them.
5. Recognize that you are to be loyal to your employer and act in the best interests of your employer.
6. Undertake your tasks in good faith by giving your best efforts.
7. Appreciate the concept of "scope of employment" and make certain to act within it.
8. Refrain from assaulting, defaming, invading the privacy of others, interfering with the business relations of others, harassing or inflicting emotional distress on customers, management, or coworkers.
9. Remember that contracts are binding and lawsuits result from breaches of contracts.
10. Discern the effects of limiting one's employment opportunities by signing a covenant "not to compete."

SUMMARY

The key to a successful business is the existence of a positive relationship between employers and employees. Employers are confronted with issues concerning employees' authority, duties, compensation, and liability. Employers must be concerned with elucidating in a clear and concise manner the employees' authority and duties. Employers must fairly compensate their workers. Employers should limit their liability by adequately educating and training their employees with regard to specific torts and breaches of contracts. Adapting the concept of "scope of employment" (which means whether the action or complaint occurred on the job) to the business will clearly define an employer's liability for torts and breaches of contracts.

A good understanding of the appropriate time to employ a covenant "not to compete" in an employment contract is essential. Finally, the distinction between employees and independent contractors has been defined. Courts employ an Economic Realities test to determine the extent of control the employer has over the behavior and compensation of workers and whether the relationship is permanent.

REVIEW QUESTIONS

1. Define *agency, principal, agent, employment, employer, employee,* and *independent contractor.*
2. What is the difference between express and implied actual authority? Give an example of each.
3. What is apparent authority? Give an example.
4. Define the employee's duty of loyalty, duty to act in good faith, and duty to account, and give an example of a breach of each duty.
5. Explain the employer's duty to compensate and the employer's duty to maintain safe working conditions.
6. What is the main difference between an employee and an independent contractor?
7. Why does employment create a fiduciary relationship?
8. When will a restrictive covenant be enforced?
9. When is an employer contractually liable?
10. Explain the types of torts for which an employer may be liable.

CASE PROBLEMS

1. Shell Oil Company fired petitioner Charles T. Robinson, Sr., in 1991. Shortly thereafter, petitioner filed a charge with the EEOC, alleging that respondent had discharged him because of his race. While that charge was pending, petitioner applied for a job with another company. That company contacted respondent, as petitioner's former employer, for an employment reference. Petitioner claims that respondent gave him a negative reference in retaliation for his having filed the EEOC charge.

    The District Court's determined that former employees may not bring suit under section; 704(a) for retaliation occurring after termination of their employment. The issue in this case is whether the term *employees* includes former employees.

    The Fourth Circuit affirmed. What result? *Robinson v. Shell Oil Company*, 519 U.S. 337 (1997)

2. David Jones, a Rogers city policeman, worked for appellee during his off-duty hours as a loss-prevention officer. On March 25, 1996, he supposedly observed appellant stealing a pack of cigarettes. Appellant was apprehended and arrested and charged with shoplifting. It was later determined that the cigarettes did not come from appellee's store, and the shoplifting charge was nolle prossed. As a result of the incident, appellant filed suit in federal court against David Jones, the City of Rogers, and the city's police chief. In the same action, he sued appellee for battery, assault, false imprisonment, defamation, malicious prosecution, and negligence. What result? *Guidry v. Harp's Food Stores, Inc.*, 987 S.W.2d 755 (Ark. 1999)

3. This case arises from a physical altercation that took place in northern Virginia between Eduardo Burkhart, plaintiff–appellee, and Archie Smith, a Washington Metropolitan Area Transit Authority (WMATA) bus operator. On May 5, 1994, Burkhart and a friend, Basram Salman, both of whom are deaf, boarded a Metrobus in Arlington, Virginia. Burkhart and Salman each placed a 30 token in the fare box. The correct fare for those with disabilities is 50. As the bus pulled away from the curb, Smith called both Burkhart and Salman back to pay the correct fare.

    However, because they are deaf, neither Salman nor Burkhart understood Smith's request. A series of blows was exchanged between Smith and Burkhart. In any event, Smith then grabbed Burkhart's finger. Burkhart responded by kicking Smith in the groin, causing him to release his hold of Burkhart's finger. Burkhart asserted claims against Smith, and against WMATA vicariously, for assault, battery, gross negligence, and infliction of emotional distress. In addition, Burkhart alleged that WMATA negligently hired, trained, and supervised its bus operators and, as a result, caused the assault and battery at issue. WMATA admitted that Smith was acting within the scope of his employment with WMATA when the events at issue occurred. What result? *Burkhart v. Washington Metropolitan Area Transit Authority*, 112 F.3d 1207 (D.C. Cir. 1997).

HUMAN RESOURCE DILEMMAS

1. Pharmmedix employs 13 salespeople to market its wonder drug "Rejuvenate," which has been designed to reverse the aging process. Each salesperson has been designated to cover a 50-mile radius. The number of hours worked, the number of physicians visited, the enticements such as gifts, dinners, and so on, offered to

physicians who prescribe Rejuvenate are all within the discretion of the salespeople. A generous commission based wage is given, but each salesperson is responsible for his or her transportation. Pharmmedix regards its sales staff as independent contractors. The sales staff bring a lawsuit claiming they are employees entitled to all of the required benefits. Pharmmedix is seeking advice.

2. Upon graduation from Moran University with her MBA, Carol Lewis was offered a position with the firm of Harry the Headhunter, specializing in the placement of MBA graduates with advertising and public relations firms. When Carol accepted the position, she was asked to sign a noncompete agreement restricting her from working for a competitor or opening her own placement service for a period of 1 year. Excited about the position and not thinking of the future ramifications, Carol signed the agreement. Seven years later, Carol and an acquaintance from another headhunter decide to follow their entrepreneurial urges and open their own placement business in the same area in which her employer does business. During her exit interview from Harry the Headhunter, Carol is reminded of the noncompete agreement she signed. She seeks counsel. What course of action do you recommend?

3. Todd Peterson is a lineman for Bright Light Electric Utility in the North Central States Region. While driving from a repair site on Route 17, Todd comes upon Melinda Porter, who is stranded with her broken-down Hyundai. Todd approaches Melinda and offers to phone for assistance. Melinda asks Todd to drop her off at her parents' home, which is 3 miles down the road. Todd tells Melinda it is against company policy to take a passenger. Upon Melinda's pleading that nothing will happen and if it did she would never sue, Todd relents. After driving a short distance, a car attempting to pass Todd on the 2-lane highway, sideswipes the Bright Light vehicle to avoid oncoming traffic. Melinda is seriously injured. She files suit against Bright Light. Bright Light seeks legal advice. What course of action do you recommend with respect to Melinda's lawsuit and Todd's employment?

4. After working for 9 months in the receiving department of Soho Express, Bruce Miller was terminated by his boss, Jack Chandler. Miller, distraught and perplexed, attempts to question Chandler, but is rebuffed. After 4 days of harboring anger and resentment, Miller returns, gun in hand, to Soho Express and shoots Chandler and his secretary, Becky Finch. Soho is seeking a consultation to discern whether Soho Express is liable to Chandler and/or Finch for their injuries.

5. Under pressure to meet his annual car sales quota, Roy Gifford tells prospective customers that Mighty Motors will throw in at no additional cost antilock breaks and durable paint sealer, a combined $1,400 value. Roy has no intention of including these features because he believes the customers will never know. Roy is able to realize the sale of nine vehicles due to his slick promotion. Samantha Martin and Christine Evers, two of the nine purchasers, discover the fraud after Samantha's teal blue vehicle is badly scratched and Christina's burgundy vehicle skids when its brakes lock. They both confront Mighty Motors, which disclaims knowledge of the fraud. Mighty Motors seeks legal advice. How should we proceed?

WEB SITE ASSIGNMENT

Research: The IRS has claimed that Pharmmedix was in violation of the Internal Revenue Code for failing to withhold taxes from sales reps whom Pharmmedix treated as independent contractors, but who the IRS believe are employees. Research the criteria the IRS employs to decide whether sales reps are employees or independent contractors and apply it to Pharmmedix. Utilizing the following Web sites, advise Pharmmedix as to how to decide in the future which workers are employees and which are independent contractors.

www.bizjournals.com/albany/stories/1999/08/16/smallb5.html? = printable
www.findlaw.com
www.gov.on.ca/lab/es/ese.htm
pf.inc.com/articles/2001/03/22361.html
editorial.careers.msn.com/articles/noncompete
jobsearchtech.about.com/library/weekly/aa042202.htm
www.nolo.com/lawcenter
zdnet.com/2102–1103_2–274247.html?tag = printthis
lawsmart.lawinfo.com

Chapter

Selection

Employment Scenario

During an office visit with Susan North, Esq., Tom Long and Mark Short ask Susan her opinion regarding some problems they have encountered during the interview process. Susan listens as Tom and Mark recall their experiences. Tom mentioned that he asked Martha if she had small children. He thought that was a legitimate concern given the evening hours needed for coverage. Mark wondered about which country Lucy Jimenez was from and asked her about it. Tom remembered that both he and Mark refused to hire Bruce Wood because of his effeminate mannerisms. They thought that he was gay. Mark added that Mildred Peterson was refused employment as a sales representative because she was a woman. They told her that this was a men's clothing store. Tom and Mark were seeking affirmation for their business conduct. What advice should be given?

Employment Scenario

Roger Thorpe, an African-American candidate, was refused employment after revealing during an interview with L&S that he had a prior conviction for the sale of cocaine 14 years ago. Tom and Mark discussed this situation with Susan after the fact. Susan asked Tom and Mark how they came to know of the prior drug conviction. They responded that during the interview they required every candidate to reveal all prior criminal convictions. Was this an appropriate request?

Employment Scenario

The Long and Short of It (L&S) approach Susan with a plan to hire relatives, friends, and individuals referred by those employed at L&S. Tom and Mark's explanation is that they are comfortable with the composition of their current staff, and they would prefer hiring similar people. How should Susan reply?

Chapter Checklist

➤ Understand that the selection process must be nondiscriminatory.

➤ Identify when an employer's recruitment process may be discriminatory.

➤ Distinguish between job-related questions and questions that are discriminatory.

➤ Understand the importance of undertaking a job analysis that will define the qualifications necessary for the job.

➤ Appreciate why record keeping is important.

➤ Discern when the EEOC may investigate for discrimination.

➤ Know why job-related criteria should be established before employees are evaluated for a promotion.

➤ Understand why only criminal convictions related to a particular job should be checked.

➤ Appreciate the employer's liability for a negligent hire.

INTRODUCTION

The purpose of this chapter is to give instruction on the proper methods for selecting employees for employment, training, and promotion. Recruiting a broad range of candidates is key. Nepotism and promoting from within are acceptable as long as they do not compromise this end. Accurate record keeping is essential for evidence in Equal Employment Opportunity Commission (EEOC) investigations and lawsuits. Screening candidates for job-related criminal convictions to preclude negligent hiring is an important task.

Human Resource Advice

- Address the concerns of those candidates who have been refused employment expeditiously and with great care.
- Establish criteria for promotions that are necessary for those positions.
- Draft policies for nepotism and promoting from within that will not hamper the attainment of a diverse workforce.
- Evaluate which criminal convictions are related to an available job before you ask candidates about their criminal records.
- Guard against negligent hiring by screening candidates thoroughly.
- Attempt to achieve a work environment that is free from discrimination.
- Query candidates about the qualifications that are related to the job.
- Train interviewers to refrain from asking those questions that may be discriminatory.
- Recruit from as wide a variety of sources as possible to assure a diverse pool of candidates.
- Maintain accurate records.

Discrimination in Selection

The purpose of recruitment and selection is to obtain the best possible workers for a business. Discrimination is permissible with respect to selecting candidates based on interpersonal relations, communication skills, training, and education. It is not permissible with respect to suspect classifications such as race, religion, gender, age, disability, and national origin. Because employees are valuable assets to a business, employers must be able to choose those employees who will perform the best work for the business. Education, training, communication skills, and interpersonal relations are key qualities that employees must possess to help a business be more successful.

The easiest way to discriminate against individuals is to do so in the recruitment and selection process. Employers may use a myriad of methods to evaluate an individual and his or her particular traits. Testing, interviews, writing samples, demonstrations, and role-playing are a few examples. If these methods are job-related, then the employer has every right to use them. What an employer may not do is discourage potential candidates who belong to a particular suspect classification as defined by Title VII of the Civil Rights Act, the Age Discrimination in Employment Act, and the Americans with Disabilities Act.

Employment Perspective

Speedy Delivery Service (SDS) delivers packages to residential and business customers. All the delivery personnel are men, and SDS would like to keep it that way. Sandra Musial applied for a position. SDS discouraged her by showing her extremely bulky and heavy parcels. Sandra was told she would have to carry these packages up two, sometimes three, flights of stairs. Sandra withdrew her application. Later, she learned that other female applicants were told the same story but males were not. Sandra filed a claim with the EEOC. Will she win? Yes! The selection process is tainted. Males are encouraged; females are not. They must be treated the same. Suppose SDS advertised the position only in a men's fitness magazine. Would this be discriminatory? Yes! It would be designed to attract only male applicants. If the job entailed only minor lifting, but in its advertisements, SDS stated that heavy lifting was required in order to discourage female applicants, would this be discriminatory? Yes! SDS would be misrepresenting the requirements for the position.

Employers may also not seek prospective applicants from pools that do not contain certain groups, such as recruiting from predominantly white male schools.

Employment Perspective

SDS is at it again. This time the company is recruiting candidates exclusively from Prestige College, a predominantly white male school. Is this practice discriminatory? Yes! SDS's purpose is to exclude women and minorities from its hiring process.

Selection Process

The selection process must be free of discrimination. Great care must be taken to ensure that statements, overtures, and advertisements are not suspect. References to age must not be made because age is not a qualitative criterion to be used in the selection process. In an advertisement of a job description, the use of terms such as *high school student*, *college student*, *recent college graduate*, *boy*, *girl*, and *only those under 40 need apply* are all examples of possible violations of the Age Discrimination in Employment Act.

ADVERTISING AND RECRUITING

Employers are barred from indicating in any advertisement for employment that they prefer an applicant of a particular race, religion, gender, or national origin. An exception to this condition exists if it can be shown that a bona fide occupational qualification requires a person of a particular religion, gender, or national origin. There is no exception for race and color.

Employment Perspective

Lilly's Lingerie Shop places an advertisement in a local paper for a position admitting women to its dressing-room area. The ad states that only females need apply. Is this advertisement in violation of Title VII? Most likely! Lilly's must establish that it is a business necessity that only a woman should work in this position where the attendant is in close proximity to an area where female customers are undressing. However, if the attendant is visibly outside the dressing-room area where other employees and customers are, then no invasion of privacy exists to warrant a same sex attendant.

Recruiting at colleges, graduate schools, and professional schools has long been a practice followed by many companies. This is a process in which a large pool of people seeking professional and office work are located and, for the most part, are unemployed. This practice may not in and of itself be discriminatory unless done exclusively. A company or professional firm that recruits only students at graduation is discriminating against people already in the labor force and possibly those without the mandated degree. Recruiting candidates solely from colleges for a position where a degree is not a justifiable necessity is discriminatory.

Employment Perspective

Rhodes, Lucas, and Reed is a prestigious accounting firm that recruits its entry-level candidates solely from college. The firm advertises, "entry-level positions available for this year's graduates only." Amanda Stewart graduated from college 20 years ago and is currently a homemaker looking to return to work. She applies for the entry-level position with Rhodes, Lucas, and Reed. Amanda is rejected. She claims age discrimination. The firm argues that students right out of college can be trained and indoctrinated more easily. Amanda argues that her age and her experience would not hamper that process in the least. Who wins? Amanda has a good chance of winning because of the exclusivity of the firm's policy with regard to hiring only college students.

Employment Perspective

Safe T Alarm Systems advertises a position available for alarm-system planning and installation. Scott Feeney, age 50, applies for the position but is rejected because he does not possess a college diploma. Scott argues an alarm-system installer does not need a college education. Safe T recounts that college graduates have better interpersonal skills for dealing with people and possess sound reasoning skills for planning the layout of the alarm system. Who will be victorious? Scott! Although Safe T may incorporate reasoning ability and interpersonal skills in its job qualifications, its argument will most likely fail because a college diploma is not a justifiable business necessity for this kind of position. This requirement discriminates against older workers who do not possess a college degree. Many individuals can and do perform this job adequately without possessing the college degree. Although college graduates may be more qualified on average, it does not mean there are no qualified candidates among the remainder. To exclude this entire group because they do not possess a characteristic not crucial to the job is arbitrary and capricious.

Employment Perspective

Simon, Matthews, and Stevens, a Park Avenue law firm, consistently recruit new associates from three predominantly white male schools exclusively. Their firm is comprised of 17 attorneys, all of whom are protestant white males. They will not visit any other law schools. Simon, Matthews, and Stevens conduct on-site interviews and, if interested, invite the select few for a visit to its office. Is the procedure discriminatory? Definitely! The firm is dismissing other qualified applicants without a justifiable reason. Simon, Matthews, and Stevens may be looking to perpetuate the old-boy network by persisting in the maintenance of its policy of exclusivity.

Questioning

Questioning an applicant about his or her religion, national origin, race, and age is discriminatory. Inquiries regarding marital status, the number of children, or the prospects of having children are also suspect. An employer may not require an applicant to state whether he or she has a disability or to submit information concerning the disability. This would be an unfair employment practice. However, the employer may require the applicant to undergo a physical or mental examination to determine whether the person has the ability to perform the job. The examination must relate only to the essential job-related functions and must not be a fishing expedition. It must be required of all applicants, not just those with a perceived disability.

The Americans with Disabilities Act (ADA), along with most state civil rights acts, prohibits discriminating against an individual in the selection process because of a disability. A disability is defined as a physical or mental condition that results in a substantial handicap. The employer may be required to reasonably accommodate disabled individuals to enable them to perform the jobs that but for their handicap they would be qualified to do.

Employment Perspective

Mary Thomas applied for a position as a computer programmer with Computer Wizard. She was given a computer language exam. Her references and educational background were checked, and she was required to undergo a physical examination. Mary's qualifications were superb except for the physical examination, which disclosed that she had had a breast removed 4 years ago because of cancer. Mary was not hired. She filed a claim with the EEOC, alleging disability discrimination. Computer Wizard claimed it did not want to hire someone with a history of cancer. Such a person might incur huge medical expenses in the future, and the company's medical insurance premiums might skyrocket. Is this a valid reason for not hiring her? No! Her breast removal is not related to an essential job-related function. Had she been missing fingers or an arm that related to her typing skills, that disability might be a consideration. However, even then a reasonable accommodation may be made or possibly the person may type as fast with one hand as someone with two hands. In that case, the disability would have no effect.

Uniform Guidelines on Employee Selection Procedures

Uniform guidelines on employee selection procedures were enacted in 1978 to provide counsel in the proper methodology used in the selection process to avoid infringement of Title VII, Equal Employment Opportunity Act (Affirmative Action), and the Equal Pay Act. Although not applying directly to the Age Discrimination in Employment Act and the Americans with Disabilities Act, other guidelines are available for consultation in these areas.

The main thrust of the uniform guidelines is to recognize and encourage the discontinuance of selection procedures that have a disparate impact on minorities and women. Disparate impact may be defined as having an adverse or detrimental effect on a particular group. Men are also covered in situations where gender is a determining factor in the selection process. Minority groups include blacks, Hispanics, Asians, and American Indians.

To eliminate a disparate impact, records must be kept of the number of each minority group and gender that apply and the number of each group selected. If the percentage of minorities selected is at least 80 percent of the percentage of whites selected, there is no adverse effect. If the 80 percent rule is not met, then a detriment in employment selection exists against the particular group of minority or women applicants.

Employment Perspective

ABC Mutual Fund places an advertisement for customer service representatives. One hundred positions are available. Three hundred applicants are received: 100 women and 200 men, including 150 whites, 50 blacks, 50 Asians, and 50 Hispanics. The selections made are 20 women and 80 men, including 75 whites, 5 blacks, 20 Asians, and no Hispanics. Does the selection procedure have an adverse effect on minorities and women? Yes! A disparate impact exists against blacks, Hispanics, and women. The percentage of whites chosen out of those whites who applied was 50 percent. That means all minority group selection rates must be within 80 percent of the 50 percent white rate. Minority group selection rates must be at least 40 percent. The selection rate of Asians met the test: 50 applicants of whom 20 were chosen—that is, 40 percent. The black selection rate was 10 percent, and the Hispanic selection rate was 0 percent. Both of these fall far short of the required rate and are evidence of discrimination, according to the Uniform Guidelines on Employee Selection Procedures. The selection rate of women was 20 percent: 20 out of 100. The selection rate of men was 40 percent: 80 out of 200. The women's percentage was only one-half, or 50 percent, of the men's percentage. This result does not meet the 80 percent rule and is evidence of discrimination.

Selection Procedure

The term *selection procedure* encompasses the use of aptitude testing, physical evaluations, educational credentials, employment experience, training programs, probationary terms, résumés, interviews, and application forms to evaluate prospective candidates. These guidelines apply to employers, employment agencies, testing organizations, and labor unions.

Employment Perspective

E.J. Roberts receives about 50 unsolicited résumés each month for positions with his marketing research firm. He dumps most of these in the garbage. Every once in awhile he leafs through a few while he is having a cup of herbal tea. If something catches his eye, he notifies his secretary to contact the person for an interview. Is E.J.'s procedure in contradiction with the Uniform Guidelines on Employee Selection Procedures? Yes! There is no objective standard of judgment employed in E.J.'s procedure. It is arbitrary and capricious.

The employer's right to investigate the employee's background including past criminal records is based on the employer's showing of a justifiable business necessity.

The issue in the following case deals with whether an applicant for a teaching position should be denied a teaching license because of a prior drug sale conviction.

The Matter of Arrocha v. Board of Education of the City of New York
93 N.Y.2d 361 (1999)

Levine, Judge.

In 1996, petitioner applied for a Pedagogical Certificate from the Board of Education of the City of New York licensing him to teach high school Spanish in the New York City public school system. In his application, petitioner disclosed that he had been convicted in 1987, at age 36, of criminal sale of a controlled substance (a B felony) for selling a $10 bag of cocaine to an undercover officer, and subsequently served the minimum of a two-to-six year prison term. As evidence of rehabilitation, petitioner submitted to the Board a certificate of relief from disabilities, designed to remove any automatic bar to employment or licensure. He also provided five current letters of recommendation, attesting to his teaching ability and professional skills, as well as evidence of his educational achievements during and since incarceration.

The Board nevertheless denied petitioner's application, stating that his conviction "is serious in nature" and that the granting of employment "would pose a risk to the safety and welfare of the student population and Board of Education employees." Petitioner thereafter challenged the Board's determination in this article 78 proceeding, arguing that the Board's reliance on the nine-year-old conviction was arbitrary and capricious and in violation of article 23-A of the New York Correction Law, which prohibits discrimination against ex-offenders. Supreme Court agreed and ordered the Board to grant petitioner the teaching license. The Appellate Division affirmed over a two-Justice dissent. The Board appealed to this Court as of right, and we now reverse. The Board's decision denying petitioner the privilege of a teaching license is the type of administrative action that, at common law, was subject to challenge through a writ of mandamus to review and thus cannot be disturbed unless it is arbitrary and capricious. In such situations, "the courts cannot interfere unless there is no rational basis for the exercise of discretion" by the administrative agency."It is well settled that a court may not substitute its judgment for that of the board or body it reviews unless the decision under review is arbitrary and unreasonable and constitutes an abuse of discretion."

Mindful of these restraints on the judicial power of review here, we turn to petitioner's claims that the Board acted unlawfully, and thus arbitrarily, when it denied him a high school teaching license on the basis of his previous conviction. Article 23-A of the Correction Law provides that "no application for any license or employment shall be denied by reason of the applicant's having been previously convicted of one or more criminal offenses." The statute, however, recognizes exceptions either where there is "a direct relationship between the previous criminal offense and the specific license or employment sought," or where granting the license or employment would "involve an unreasonable risk to property or to the safety or welfare of specific individuals or the general public." Here, the Board denied petitioner's license under the second exception, stating in its letter to petitioner denying the license that, in light of his prior conviction, his employment in the City's high schools would "pose a risk to the safety and welfare of the student population and Board of Education employees." Such a finding of unreasonable risk "depends upon a subjective analysis of a variety of considerations relating to the nature of the license or employment sought and the prior misconduct." Thus, Correction Law § 753 sets forth a series of eight factors to be considered by the Board in determining whether it would pose an unreasonable risk to issue a license. Specifically, the Board must consider:

a. "The public policy of this state, as expressed in this act, to encourage the licensure and employment of persons previously convicted of one or more criminal offenses.

b. The specific duties and responsibilities necessarily related to the license or employment sought.

c. The bearing, if any, the criminal offense or offenses for which the person was previously convicted will have

on his fitness or ability to perform one or more such duties or responsibilities.

d. The time which has elapsed since the occurrence of the criminal offense or offenses.

e. The age of the person at the time of occurrence of the criminal offense or offenses.

f. The seriousness of the offense or offenses.

g. Any information produced by the person, or produced on his behalf, in regard to his rehabilitation and good conduct.

h. The legitimate interest of the public agency or private employer in protecting property, and the safety and welfare of specific individuals or the general public."

The statute also creates a presumption of rehabilitation where, as here, the applicant has obtained a certificate of relief from disabilities. Nonetheless, the certificate does not establish a prima facie entitlement to the license or employment, but only establishes, if not rebutted, that the applicant has been rehabilitated—just one of the eight factors that the Board must consider in determining whether an exception applies.

On the record before Supreme Court, there is evidence that the Board considered all eight of the factors set forth in section 753 in reaching its conclusion. Significantly, the Board considered those positive factors on which petitioner heavily relies, namely that the conviction was nine years old[d], the positive references submitted on petitioner's behalf, evidence of rehabilitation]), his educational achievements and the presumption that he is rehabilitated [g].

The Board, however, balanced these considerations against the other five factors delineated by the statute. In particular, the Board averred that it considered the fact that high school teachers must serve as role models to students at an impressionable age and are held to a high ethical standard and that petitioner's conviction might impact his ability to serve as such a role model [c]). The affidavit submitted by the Board noted that petitioner was a mature adult when he committed the crime [e]), and that the offense was a serious felony conviction [f]. Finally, the Board considered the fact that criminal sale of a controlled substance is one of the six specifically enumerated crimes that the Board has deemed to be of special concern with respect to carrying out its duty to protect the welfare of New York City school children[h]).

Nevertheless, the courts below annulled the Board's determination because the Board failed to submit any evidence to rebut the presumption of rehabilitation and because the Board unduly relied on the prior drug sale conviction in the face of the evidence of petitioner's more recent academic and professional accomplishments. As previously discussed, the presumption of rehabilitation does not preclude the Board from considering any of the other seven factors, unrelated to rehabilitation, including prior convictions in the context of the license or employment being sought.

Thus, the Board was not obligated to rebut the presumption of rehabilitation and was entirely justified in considering the nature and seriousness of this particular crime, a B felony cocaine sale committed by petitioner at the mature age of 36, of overriding significance when issuing a high school teaching license.

Moreover, all that the record establishes here is that, in denying petitioner a high school teaching license, the Board gave greater weight to the statutory factors adversely affected by the fact and circumstances of his conviction than to the statutory factors favorably affected by his subsequent accomplishments and the presumption of rehabilitation. This did not afford a basis for the lower courts to conclude that factors favorable to petitioner were not considered, and there is nothing additional in the record that would support that conclusion. Thus, there is no justification for overturning the Board's determination without engaging in essentially a reweighing of the factors, which is beyond the power of judicial review.

Accordingly, the order of the Appellate Division should be reversed, without costs, and the petition dismissed. Judgment for the Board of Education

Case Commentary

The Board of Education applied an eight-prong test to determine whether the prior drug sale conviction posed a threat to the safety of the students and employees of the school system. In doing so, the Board gave greater weight to a drug sale conviction than to the applicant's subsequent rehabilitation and accomplishments. The New York Court of Appeals stated there is no justification for overturning the Board of Education's decision. ∎

CASE QUESTIONS

1. Do you believe Arrocha was entitled to the license?
2. Should the Board of Education be entitled to assign different weights to the licensing criteria?
3. Should the Court have the right to review the weight assigned to each criterion?

Investigation and Record Keeping

Private employers of 100 or more employees must file annual reports with the EEOC.

To properly conduct an investigation, the EEOC has the right to evidence, which has a bearing on the alleged unlawful employment practice. This would include the right of access to documentation, as well as to the coworkers, superiors, and subordinates of the employee alleging a Title VII violation for the purpose of questioning them.

Employers are obligated to keep records relating to their methods of selection, compensation, promotion, training, and termination of employees. Test scores and the chronological order of applications for hiring, training, and promotion must be part of the record keeping.

These records must be made available to the EEOC to enable them to determine whether unlawful employment practices have been committed. An employer may seek an exemption from the EEOC if it can prove the burden of record keeping presents undue hardship. A notification of excerpts of Title VII is required to be posted by each employer in a conspicuous setting to apprise current employees as well as applicants of the existence of Title VII.

Record keeping can be burdensome, especially for small firms that do not have a human resources department. In addition to keeping records denoting the number of persons who applied and the number of persons who were selected in each job category for each suspect classification, similar record keeping must be kept for promotions and terminations as well.

Samples

Where the number of applicants and those selected are so numerous that maintaining records on every individual would be too burdensome, the Uniform Guidelines on Employee Selection Procedures permit the company to select samples and maintain records on them. The sample must be adequate in size and representative of the various groups. If it is not, then the sample may be challenged, and an inference of discrimination may be drawn. If the sample is viable but results in a disparate impact, the company is bound by it. The company may not dispute the authenticity of its own sample.

The Bottom Line

The Uniform Guidelines on Employee Selection Procedures adopts the bottom-line approach where a myriad of selection procedures are utilized. If one criterion is tainted, the selection process will not be found to be discriminatory where other criteria have offset it and the final results do not violate the 80 percent rule.

Employment Perspective

Thompson Meat Packing Plant employs three criteria in its employee selection process: a weight-lifting test, a dexterity test, and an application form. Hispanics, Asians, and women who apply have difficulty with the weight-lifting test because of their small stature. Their overall selection rate satisfies the 80 percent rule. Regardless, these groups claim that a greater number of them would have been selected but for this test and that weight lifting is not a job necessity. Will they win? No! Because a significant number of women, Asians, and Hispanics are being selected, the bottom line is not discriminatory. The weight-lifting component does not have to be justified as a business necessity.

DISCRIMINATION IN PROMOTIONS

The reason that certain groups are promoted less frequently is due in part to discrimination and in part to social factors. Promotions often entail more responsibility, longer hours, travel requirements, attendance at social affairs, decision-making requirements, and greater stress. Young people, a greater number of whom are single, may welcome the traveling and may not mind the longer hours. Older individuals with families, especially women who are mothers, may find the benefits of the promotion outweighed by their presumption that their quality of life will decline. The requirements need not change so long as they are job related. If any individual cannot travel or work longer hours, that person will not get the position. The point is to refrain from stereotyping. Many women with small children may be willing to travel, and some men may not be willing to travel. The Equal Employment Opportunity Act presumes an equal percentage of all groups seek promotions. Overcoming this premise is a difficult task for the employer.

Promotion Criteria

Although not required by law, some companies, to reach a wider source of potential candidates, post job opportunities and promotions as a matter of policy. Posting may also provide a defense to allegations of disparate impact discrimination. The procedure must utilize criteria that are job-related, and the imposition of these criteria must be uniformly applied to every applicant. The managers who are in charge of recommending candidates for promotion must be judged on the basis of their recommendations to determine whether they are acting in conformity with equal employment opportunity guidelines. Finally, the racial, ethnic, and gender composition of the manager will be looked into where a breach of equal opportunity employment occurs.

Nepotism and Promoting from Within

Nepotism is the hiring of family members. Employers should specifically define what constitutes family members. Are in-laws and distant cousins considered family members? Some companies forbid nepotism; others allow it if the employed family member does not take part in the decision process. Still others encourage it wholeheartedly. This approach, as well as the concept of promoting from within, is incestuous because it may discourage diversity. If that is so, discrimination exists. Employers argue that promoting from within allows the company to reward an individual who is known and respected. Although there is substance in that argument, if the result is the creation of a disparate impact against a suspect class, the tradition will be held to be discriminatory and will need to be abandoned.

This case presents two issues: whether nepotism includes in-laws, and whether the nepotism policy was consistently enforced.

Blackburn v. United Parcel Service
179 F.3d 81 (3rd Cir. 1999)

Becker, Chief Judge.

UPS contends that Blackburn was fired for violations of UPS's anti-nepotism, favoritism, integrity, and accountability policies.

UPS has had an anti-nepotism policy in its Policy Book for management employees since 1965.

The 1992 version, in effect during the period in question, states:

We Strictly Limit the Employment of Relatives. . . .

We prohibit hiring—for either full-time or part-time employment—relatives of active employees. . . .

The Policy Book does not define relatives. The favoritism policy states, We Treat Our People Fairly and Without Favoritism. . . . We have the responsibility to avoid any relationship that may result in actual or perceived favoritism. The integrity policy states:

We Insist Upon Integrity in Our People. . . .

We insist on integrity in the preparation and approval of all reports.

When we do discover a dishonest person in our organization, we deal with that individual quickly and firmly.

Finally, the accountability policy states:

We Are All Accountable for Compliance With Our Policies. As individuals, we do not have the authority to change or disregard any of our company's policies. We are expected to follow existing policies, even if not always in complete agreement with them. We must be careful not to misinterpret or violate a policy's spirit and intent. If in doubt, we should check with others for guidance.

Our managers and supervisors set the example for carrying out our policies. . . . They, therefore, are expected to lead the way for other UPS people—by word and action—in living up to our policies.

As a management employee, Blackburn received a copy of the Policy Book and was aware of these policies.

Blackburn married Loren Morrissey in April of 1990. On September 29, 1993, Linda Shepard, Morrissey's sister, applied for a job at UPS's Mahwah facility. Shepard stated on her employment application that she did not have any relatives employed by UPS. In December of 1993, Shepard was hired as a Methods Analyst at Mahwah, and began work in the same building as Blackburn. Blackburn was aware that Shepard had applied for and gotten the job, and at times commuted to work with Shepard and had contact with her during the workday by, for example, meeting her for lunch. At no time before September 1994 did Blackburn disclose his relationship with Shepard to UPS.

At various times after Shepard's hiring, and before September 1994, Blackburn recommended Shepard for other UPS positions without informing those to whom he made the recommendations that Shepard was his sister-in-law.

On September 14, 1994, UPS's Loss Prevention Department received an anonymous complaint, forwarded to Patricia Knowles of UPS's Human Resources Department at Mahwah, that Blackburn was Shepard's brother-in-law. The complaint also expressed concern that Shepard might be promoted because of Blackburn's influence. That same day, Knowles and UPS manager Nigel Watson met with Shepard and questioned her regarding her relationship with Blackburn. After initially denying that Blackburn was her brother-in-law, Shepard eventually admitted that he was married to her sister. However, she gave an incorrect date for Blackburn's marriage to her sister, claiming that they were married in April 1994, after Shepard had been hired by UPS.

After verifying the actual date of Blackburn's marriage (through UPS's Human Resources Department in Atlanta), Knowles confronted Blackburn on September 15, 1994. Blackburn denied that he was related to Shepard but admitted that he was married to her sister. He also expressed disbelief that the relationship was of concern to UPS. On September 16, Knowles met again with Shepard, who claimed that Blackburn was aware that Shepard was interviewing with UPS when she originally sought a job there. On

September 29, 1994, UPS offered Shepard a chance to resign, on the grounds that she had lied on her application (by indicating that she was not related to anyone at UPS) and had lied to Knowles when confronted with this information. Shepard resigned on September 30, 1994.

Also in September, Blackburn's supervisor, Hopwood, was informed of the events surrounding Shepard's hiring and her relationship to Blackburn. Hopwood spoke with Blackburn and, upon learning the identity of Blackburn's sister-in-law, realized that she was the person Blackburn had recommended to him and another manager for openings in the department without informing them that she was his sister-in-law. Blackburn allegedly refused to acknowledge that his conduct was inappropriate, and told Hopkins that UPS would regret it if it pursued the matter.

On September 29, 1994, Hopwood's supervisor Bain and Human Resources manager James Daniels met with Blackburn, who stated that he was not related to Shepard but that he was her brother-in-law. He denied any misconduct in permitting her to be hired, recommending her for positions without revealing the nature of their relationship, and claiming not to be related to her. Bain advised Blackburn that he had violated the anti-nepotism policy and the policies on favoritism, integrity, and accountability. That day, after consultation with Daniels and two Human Resources coordinators, Bain fired Blackburn.

The Ensuing Litigation

In August 1995, Blackburn filed suit in New Jersey state court, claiming that UPS had fired him in violation of CEPA, and seeking compensatory and punitive damages, attorneys' fees, costs, and such other relief as the court might provide. UPS removed the case to the District Court for the District of New Jersey on the basis of diversity jurisdiction.

Following discovery, UPS moved for summary judgment.

The District Court found that Blackburn's conduct was not covered by CEPA, and it therefore granted summary judgment for UPS.

UPS's Stated Reason for the Discharge

UPS's stated reason for firing Blackburn was his violation of the company's anti-nepotism, favoritism, integrity, and accountability policies, which it placed in the record. UPS adduced evidence that Blackburn failed to divulge that Shepard was his relative, and that he recommended her for positions within UPS without disclosing to the relevant decision makers that she was his sister-in-law. UPS also offered evidence that it has consistently enforced its anti-nepotism policy, which supports its proffer that Blackburn's violation of this policy was the actual reason he was discharged. Indeed, Blackburn himself conceded at his deposition that UPS has regularly enforced the anti-nepotism policy (although he offers purported examples of the policy's nonenforcement). Therefore, UPS has met its burden of production at the second step of the burden-shifting analysis.

While Blackburn has suggested that the anti-nepotism policy does not apply to his situation because Shepard is not a blood relation, he does not press this point, relying instead on UPS's purported nonenforcement of the policy. However, UPS alleges that Blackburn's conduct also violated its favoritism, integrity, and accountability policies, and he has offered little evidence in response to this proffer.

Blackburn's Evidence

In order to meet his burden, Blackburn must point to admissible evidence in the record showing that there is a genuine issue for trial. In attempting to show that UPS's stated reason for firing him was pretextual, Blackburn claims that he never hid his relationship with Shepard. Rather, he testified that he regularly commuted to and from work with her, entered the building with her each day, often met her for lunch and breaks, displayed a wedding picture prominently on his desk with Shepard in the wedding party, and was otherwise open about the relationship, including the fact that they shared an address. Similarly, Shepard testified that she told colleagues about the relationship and even inquired about it at her initial interview, and nothing was done. Blackburn also testified that he assumed that the prohibition on the hiring of relatives included only blood relatives.

If the policy actually covered relationships such as Blackburn and Shepard's, and if this (along with the concomitant violations of the other policies) was the real reason that Blackburn was discharged, Blackburn's CEPA case must fail. The record evidence overwhelmingly supports the conclusion that the relevant UPS managers were unaware of Blackburn's relationship with Shepard until the anonymous tip was received in September 1994, at which time immediate action was taken against both Shepard and Blackburn.

Blackburn's stronger argument for pretext—and one that would be sufficient to preclude summary judgment, if supported by adequate admissible evidence—is that UPS did not consistently enforce its anti-nepotism policy, which, according to UPS, was the primary basis for his discharge. If Blackburn has presented admissible evidence that would raise a fact question whether UPS enforced its anti-nepotism policy, it would be for a jury to decide whether UPS's proffered reason for firing him was pretextual. Given our assumption that Blackburn has presented sufficient evidence to meet his prima facie burden under CEPA, we would have to reverse summary judgment in UPS's favor if a fact issue regarding pretext existed.

In support of his pretext argument, Blackburn provides numerous examples of UPS employees who were related to other employees yet allegedly were not disciplined or terminated for this apparent violation of the anti-nepotism policy. His examples include brothers-in-law, siblings, spouses, uncles and nephews, fathers and sons, and intimate relationships between employees who were dating or living together. UPS responds with evidence that, within the last five years, twenty-nine people at Mahwah left UPS in accordance with the anti-nepotism policy, and that no exceptions currently exist there.

Blackburn's testimony regarding UPS employees he believes to be related includes the following: Jackie and Sal Biancardi, a married couple who work at the UPS facility in Morristown; an uncle and nephew working together at a UPS facility; Mark Hopkins and his wife, Beth; Bill, and Art Weyrauch, brothers. Blackburn has no personal knowledge of any of the alleged relationships listed above. Rather, he testified in his deposition that he was told of these relationships by other persons. The alleged relationships are offered for their own truth. Therefore, Blackburn's information is based on hearsay.

We conclude that Blackburn's evidence that UPS decision makers were aware of his relationship to Shepard, and later fired him for his whistle-blowing activity under the pretext of its anti-nepotism policy, is, without more, insufficient to overcome summary judgment. As we have detailed, we find that virtually none of his evidence regarding other UPS employees who were allegedly related would likely be admissible at trial as relevant evidence that

falls within a hearsay exception. We must therefore determine whether Blackburn has offered sufficient evidence to create a genuine issue of material fact regarding UPS's stated reason for firing him. In sum, on this record, we are satisfied that, even assuming that Blackburn has met his prima facie burden under CEPA, he has failed to adequately rebut UPS's proffered reason for his discharge by pointing to sufficient inconsistencies or anomalies that could support an inference that the employer did not act for its stated reasons. The judgment of the District Court will therefore be affirmed.

Case Commentary

The Third Circuit Court suggested Blackburn could have argued that a sister-in-law does not qualify as a relative. UPS does not clearly define this term. Instead, Blackburn focused on whether UPS was consistent in enforcement of its anti-nepotism policy. Blackburn uncovered numerous violations of this policy, but did not have the documentation to prove the violations. Blackburn's argument was based totally on inadmissible hearsay. ■

CASE QUESTIONS

1. Do you believe an in-law qualifies as a relative?
2. Was UPS consistent in enforcement of its anti-nepotism policy?
3. Should Blackburn's evidence of UPS's policy violations have been admissible?

The issue in the following case is whether the employee's romantic involvement with a felon compromises her ability to perform her work.

Ortiz v. Los Angeles Police Relief Association
2002 Cal. App. LEXIS 4192

Mallano, Judge.

Plaintiff Cipriana Ortiz was employed by an association to assist in the processing of insurance benefits for current and former officers of the Los Angeles Police Department (LAPD). In that capacity, Ortiz had access to files containing confidential information about the officers.

Ortiz became romantically involved with a felon who was incarcerated. She planned to marry him. Ortiz's superiors, upon learning of this, concluded that she had a conflict of interest because she had an intimate relationship with an inmate and access to confidential information about law enforcement personnel. Ortiz's employer gave her the choice of ending the relationship or terminating her employment. Ortiz chose the latter and then filed this action.

The principal issue on appeal is whether Ortiz's discharge violated her right to privacy under the state Constitution. We conclude that her employer's enforcement of the conflict of interest policy was a rational response to a legitimate employer interest. Accordingly, we agree with the trial court and affirm.

In California, the right to marry is so fundamental that state legislation and the Constitution protect an *inmate's* right to marry. By statute, "each person [sentenced to imprisonment in a state prison] shall have the following civil rights: . . . To marry."

The invasion of Ortiz's right of privacy was "serious" in every sense of the word. LAPRA vetoed her choice of spouses. If she wanted to keep her job of 11 years, she had to give up her plans to marry Estrada and bring an abrupt halt to their two-year relationship.

In sum, the seriousness of the invasion into Ortiz's right to marry, together with the showing on the other two elements of a constitutional privacy claim, leads to the conclusion that Ortiz's privacy claim is not de minimis.

Further inquiry is necessary. We therefore proceed to balance the parties' competing interests.

[W]e conclude that LAPRA's conflict of interest rule is valid if it is rationally related to a legitimate employer interest.

LAPRA's conflict of interest rule functions much like an antinepotism policy, which may "forc[e] one spouse to attempt to transfer to another department within [a company] or *to leave the [company's] employ altogether*." The conflict of interest rule "is not rendered invalid simply because some persons who might otherwise have married were deterred by the rule or because *some who did marry were burdened thereby*."

LAPRA has a legitimate—indeed, a paramount—interest in preventing the improper disclosure of confidential information about LAPD officers and, more specifically, the disclosure of that information to criminals. As Voge realized, Ortiz's relationship with Estrada could jeopardize the personal safety of the officers. Voge believed, and correctly so, that even if Ortiz did not want to disclose any of the officers' information to Estrada, he or others could attempt to get the information through threats, coercion, deceit, or violence.

The California Legislature has also recognized the need to safeguard personal information about law enforcement personnel. Penal Code section 832.7 provides that, subject to certain exceptions, "[p]eace officer personnel records and records maintained by any state or local agency . . . or information obtained from these records, are confidential and shall not be disclosed by the department or agency that employs the peace officer in any criminal or civil proceeding. . . . " And "[e]very person who maliciously, and with the intent to obstruct justice or the due administration of the laws, . . . discloses the residence address or telephone number of any peace officer . . . or that of the spouse or children of these persons, . . . without the authorization of the employing agency, is guilty of a misdemeanor."

We conclude that LAPRA's conflict of interest rule is a rational means of pursuing its interests. "Reasonable regulations that do not significantly interfere with decisions to enter into the marital relationship may legitimately be imposed." To ensure that Ortiz would not divulge confidential information to inmates and to avoid an appearance of impropriety, LAPRA properly exercised its discretion in terminating Ortiz's employment based on her impending marriage to Estrada.

Finally, Ortiz has not shown that "there were feasible and effective alternatives to LAPRA's conduct which would have had a lesser impact on privacy interests." At her deposition, Ortiz testified that she could have worked in the snack bar or as a receptionist. But Ortiz admitted in discovery that *everyone* employed by LAPRA had access to the officers' confidential files. In fact, Voge and Ortiz discussed whether there were any other positions that did not allow access to the files. Ortiz acknowledged that there were none. And Ortiz never expressed an interest in working as a receptionist or in the snack bar.

In sum, we find that Ortiz's right to marry, as guaranteed by the privacy provision of the California Constitution, was not violated because LAPRA—in response to Ortiz's decision to marry an incarcerated felon—made a rational decision to further legitimate interests: the personal safety and well-being of police officers and their families.

Judgment for LAPRA.

Case Commentary

The California Appellate Court reasoned that the LAPRA exercised proper judgment in discerning that Ortiz's relationship with a felon presented a conflict of interest which would necessitate her discharge. ■

CASE QUESTIONS

1. Are you in agreement with the decision in this case?
2. Are there circumstances that would warrant an exception in this case?
3. What if Ortiz had a relationship with a prisoner out of state?

NEGLIGENT HIRING

Many job applications and résumés contain false representations made by prospective applicants specifically with regard to their employment history and educational background. Many candidates resort to this falsification to improve their prospects of being hired. Employers must be diligent in confirming the authenticity of the offered information. If the individual is hired and causes damage or injury to a third party, the employer will be liable.

The issue in the next case is whether a religious organization owes a duty to a follower victimized by one of its spiritual leaders.

S.H.C. v. Sheng-Yen Lu and Ling Shen Ching Tze Temple, Inc.

2002 Wash. App. Lexis 2228

Cox, A., Chief Judge.

The First Amendment does not provide religious organizations with absolute immunity from liability for tortious conduct. If such liability is predicated on secular conduct and does not involve the interpretation of church doctrine or religious beliefs, there is no violation of the Constitution. Here, S.H.C. claims that the Ling Shen Ching Tze Temple, Inc., (Temple) is vicariously liable under various theories for alleged sexual acts committed by Grandmaster Sheng-Yen Lu (Grandmaster Lu). He is the spiritual leader and founder of the True Buddha religion practiced by followers worshiping at the Temple. Because the Temple did not owe S.H.C. a duty under the facts of this case, there was no breach of fiduciary duty for which the Temple is liable. Moreover, the negligent supervision/retention claim and the business invitee claim are barred by the First Amendment. Finally, this record does not support any claim under the alternative theories of alter ego, ostensible agency, or negligent pastoral counseling. Accordingly, we affirm the order granting summary judgment of dismissal to the Temple.

Grandmaster Lu founded the True Buddha School, a denomination of Buddhism. The Temple is a Buddhist Temple and associated monastic community of the True Buddha School. The practice of the True Buddha School is a combination of Taoism, sectarian Buddhism, and Tantric Buddhism. Grandmaster Lu is recognized by followers of the True Buddha School as a living Buddha.

S.H.C. became a follower of Grandmaster Lu in 1992. Sometime in 1996 she began to go to the Temple to receive blessings because she was not feeling well. During her stays there, she had headaches. According to S.H.C., Grandmaster Lu told her that he could cure the headaches. She also claims that he told her that she would die. According to her, Grandmaster Lu told her that he could save her life and cure her illness by the "Twin Body Blessing."

The "blessing" was, in fact, sexual intercourse, which S.H.C. engaged in with Grandmaster Lu multiple times from 1996 to 1999. She maintains that he assured her that this "blessing" would save her life. Only when she did not die, and after she saw him approach other women in similar ways, did she realize that he had tricked her.

S.H.C. sued Grandmaster Lu for negligent and/or intentional infliction of emotional distress, outrage, breach of fiduciary duty, and negligent pastoral counseling. Her suit against the Temple included claims for breach of fiduciary duty, negligent pastoral counseling, and negligent retention and supervision of Grandmaster Lu.

The Temple moved for summary judgment on all claims against it, and the trial court granted this motion. S.H.C. appeals. We first establish certain parameters of our decision. Although the Temple concedes that factual questions preclude dismissal of Grandmaster Lu, the claims of S.H.C. against him are not presently before us. For purposes of the summary judgment motion of the Temple that is before us, we assume, without deciding, that Grandmaster Lu is liable for one or more of the claims that S.H.C. asserts against him. Our focus here is on the claims against the Temple that the trial court dismissed.

The trial court ruled that S.H.C.'s claim against Grandmaster Lu for negligent pastoral counseling might be sustained if that counseling was essentially secular, not religious. But the trial court noted that it was premature at the summary judgment stage to decide whether the "Twin Body Blessing," the specific conduct at issue in this case, would require the court to choose between competing interpretations of church doctrine with respect to the claims against Grandmaster Lu. We agree with the trial court's assessment, and do not further address the liability of Grandmaster Lu.

NEGLIGENT SUPERVISION

S.H.C. argues that the court erred in dismissing her claim for negligent supervision. Specifically, S.H.C. argues that the First Amendment does not bar review of the claim. We disagree.

"Negligent supervision creates a limited duty to control an employee for the protection of a third person, even when the employee is acting outside the scope of employment." Employer liability for negligent hiring, retention, and supervision arises from this duty. "If an employee conducts negligent acts outside the scope of employment, the employer may be liable for negligent supervision." An employer is not liable for negligent supervision of an employee unless the employer knew, or in the exercise of reasonable care should have known, that the employee presented a risk of danger to others.

The parties dispute whether Grandmaster Lu is an employee of the Temple. They also dispute whether the Temple had knowledge of Grandmaster Lu's alleged acts. We address the second point, and need not address the first. Viewing the evidence in the light most favorable to S.H.C., the nonmoving party, there are genuine issues of fact as to the Temple's notice of improper activities.

S.H.C. testified that Temple officials were aware that her interactions with Grandmaster Lu were "out of the ordinary or unacceptable for interactions by followers." She states that one of the Temple's nuns saw her leave a closed door consultation room after she was alone with Grandmaster Lu. She further states that one of the Temple's monks scolded her for approaching Grandmaster Lu because followers were not supposed to approach and speak with him. She also states that on another occasion several nuns saw Grandmaster Lu approach her in the Temple, take her into an office, and close the door. She states that Temple personnel summoned her to Grandmaster Lu's presence and that masters, monks, and nuns saw her leave Grandmaster Lu's bedroom. Finally, she states that one of the Temple's nuns warned her that they were keeping track of how much time she spent with Grandmaster Lu, that she should stop having consultations with him, and that she should not have consultations with the door locked. This evidence is sufficient to create a factual issue that the Temple was on notice of Grandmaster Lu's activities, subject only to the question of whether the factual issue is material for summary judgment purposes.

The Temple also argues that S.H.C. has failed to show that the Temple had the authority to control Grandmaster Lu. Again, this presents a genuine factual issue. Even if the Temple has no authority to supervise or terminate Grandmaster Lu "in his capacity as Spiritual Leader of the True Buddha religion," as Temple President Master Teck Hui Teng testified, S.H.C. did introduce evidence that the Temple officials had the authority to exclude Grandmaster Lu from the Temple grounds. Thus, on the question of control, there are also genuine issues of fact.

Because there were genuine issues of fact regarding notice and control, we must now turn to the question of whether those factual issues are material. Because the First Amendment bars consideration of this claim, we hold they are not.

Clergy sexual misconduct and the consequences that flow from such misconduct continue to be the subjects of much litigation.

A principle question for religious institutions associated with clergy accused of sexual misconduct is whether the First Amendment bars vicarious liability for such institutions. Resolution of this question has, by no means, been uniform either among or within jurisdictions that have considered the issue.

In Washington, C.J.C. v. Corporation of Catholic Bishop of Yakima presented this question. The state supreme court rejected the argument by a church that the First Amendment barred the court from imposing a duty on the church to take reasonable measures to prevent harm intentionally inflicted on children by a church worker. In that case, the court considered three consolidated cases regarding negligence claims brought against church entities and individual church officials. The defendants included officials who did not themselves directly perpetrate intentional acts of childhood sexual abuse, but who allegedly failed to protect the child victims or otherwise prevent the abuse.

The supreme court then considered whether the claims against the Church were barred by the First Amendment. The court stated that "[t]he First Amendment does not provide churches with absolute immunity to engage in tortious conduct. So long as liability is predicated on secular conduct and does not involve the interpretation of church doctrine or religious beliefs, it does not offend constitutional principles." The court held that because these principles were not offended by the case before it, there was no constitutional bar to the claim.

In C.J.C., the supreme court discussed this state's "strong public policy in favor of protecting children against acts of sexual abuse." The court noted that the Legislature had "made clear that the prevention of child abuse is of 'the highest priority, and all instances of child abuse must be reported to the proper authorities who should diligently and expeditiously take appropriate action. . . . '" The court also noted that the Legislature had made it a criminal offense for some professionals to fail to notify the proper authorities when there is reason to suspect childhood sexual abuse. Concluding that the enforcement of these strong public policies did not offend the First Amendment, the court allowed enforcement of the claim against the church. Here, unlike the case in C.J.C., the court would have to examine the religious doctrine of the True Buddhist faith to determine whether the Temple was negligent in its "supervision and retention" of Grandmaster Lu. That necessarily would involve the "excessive entanglement that First Amendment jurisprudence forbids."

Here, the evidence in the record shows that the Temple and its followers regard Grandmaster Lu as a Living Buddha—one to whom they have an obligation of obedience. These religious followers also believe that they are bound by the 50 stanzas of guru devotion to Grandmaster Lu. Those stanzas state that the follower should "see only good qualities in [Grandmaster Lu], and never any faults." They further state that if [Grandmaster Lu] "acts in a seemingly unenlightened manner" the follower should remember that "your own opinions are unreliable and the apparent faults you see may only be a reflection of your own deluded state of mind."

Moreover, as the trial court noted, the Precepts of the True Buddha School state that:

> If, after taking refuge, one discovers that the Guru is really a phony and without any achievement in Dharma, then one should depart from the Guru and take refuge in another true Guru. With regard to the original Guru, however, . . . , one should not criticize nor slander the former Guru.

If a civil court were to review the conduct of the Temple to determine whether it should have exercised more or better supervision of Grandmaster Lu, that court would necessarily entangle itself in the religious precepts and beliefs set forth above. The truth of the above beliefs is not open to question by civil courts. Should the Temple have been other than "obedient" to Grandmaster Lu under the circumstances of this case? Should the Temple have seen faults in or "criticized" him? Should the Temple have "slandered" him by calling into question the activities of which it had knowledge? We can see no way that a civil court could avoid interpreting the above religious doctrine in determining whether the Temple was liable for negligent supervision and retention. In short, there are no neutral principles of law governing this case that would permit a civil court to resolve the question of liability against the Temple.

Furthermore, it is arguable that in fashioning a "reasonable religious organization" standard for the Temple, there is danger that standard would vary, for example, from a "reasonable Protestant" standard, a "reasonable Catholic" standard, a "reasonable Jewish" standard, or a "reasonable Islamic" standard. In short, entanglement in the doctrine of this church and others would be inevitable.

The trial court correctly concluded that it would have to examine True Buddha School doctrine to determine whether the Temple acted reasonably. Such a determination would excessively entangle the court in the religious doctrine of the Temple, and is barred by the First Amendment.

S.H.C. argues that the cause of action here must be measured against secular concepts of liability. The implication of this argument is that if we do so, she will prevail. But focusing on whether the alleged activity by Grandmaster Lu is secular does not fully address the constitutional issue: whether resolution of the legal issues necessarily would require a civil court to become involved in interpreting church doctrine to determine the Temple's liability. Thus, although the alleged activities of Grandmaster Lu may be secular in this case, that does not address whether a civil court may avoid interpreting doctrine of the True Buddha religion to address whether the Temple is liable for negligent supervision.

S.H.C. further argues that we should rigorously examine First Amendment claims lest we institutionally establish religion by allowing conduct not permitted in secular situations. We have rigorously examined the claim, and conclude that the First Amendment is validly asserted as a bar to the Temple's liability in this case.

As we previously explained in this opinion, in C.J.C., one of the consolidated cases involved claims by three adult sisters against a church based on their sexual molestation by a prominent church member while they were minors. In that connection, the court first addressed whether a church and its officials have a special relationship with either its workers or the children of its congregation giving rise to a duty to take reasonable measures to prevent harm intentionally inflicted on the children by a church worker. The court identified what types of special relationships give rise to a duty to prevent intentional harm to victims:

Thus, for instance, a school has a duty to protect students within its custody from reasonable anticipated dangers, an innkeeper has a duty to protect guests, and a hospital its patients.

The court went on to hold that because the activities of a church are similar to those of a school, the duty of protection of children is the same.

The obvious distinction between this case and C.J.C. is that this case involves allegations by an adult of sexual improprieties. In contrast, C.J.C. involved such improprieties against children, a group protected by criminal statutes and other public policies. Moreover, none of the other relationships between an alleged victim and an entity associated with the accused that our courts have characterized as "special" appears to be analogous to this situation. S.H.C. has not shown that she was a particularly vulnerable victim, like the children abused by the church worker in C.J.C.

Here, the vulnerability on which S.H.C. chiefly appears to base her claim is her belief as a devoted follower of Grandmaster Lu. This approach appears to be outside the scope of the numerous cases defining special relationship that C.J.C. cited in this opinion, and that we have located in this jurisdiction.

In short, present Washington case authority does not support the conclusion that an adult victim of sexual abuse has a special relationship with a religious organization associated with the alleged abuser.

S.H.C. has not shown that such a claim is viable against the Temple in this case. She argues in her briefing that Grandmaster Lu has committed the tort of negligent pastoral counseling. This may be true. But she fails to explain why or how that theory would create liability for the Temple as a result. She states merely that this liability is "examined under traditional tort theories involving an entities liability for conduct of its agent." But, as we have already noted, the state supreme court has rejected the imposition of respondeat superior or strict liability for an employee's intentional sexual misconduct. And we have upheld the trial court's summary judgment of S.H.C.'s other claims that the Temple is vicariously liable here. Accordingly, there is simply no basis for liability on this theory.

Judgment for the Temple.

Case Commentary

The Washington Appellate Court stated that the Buddist temple owed no duty to the plaintiff to protect her from being victimized by one of its spiritual leaders. ■

CASE QUESTIONS

1. Do you agree with the decision in this case?
2. Should the resolution hinge upon whether the temple knew or should have known of its spiritual leaders' proclivities?

3. Should a different rule apply where children are the victims?

Employment Perspective

Dennis Michaelson applied for a position as a resident gynecologist at Fairview Hospital in Brooklyn. According to Dennis's résumé, he had graduated from one of the top medical schools and had an extensive private practice on the Kohala Coast on the big island of Hawaii. Dennis explained that after his wife's recent death, he wanted to return to his roots. Dennis's appearance, demeanor, and expertise convinced the hospital board to retain his services. The hospital was so impressed that it did not check with the medical school or on the references he had submitted. Dennis was at the hospital for 14 months before he was questioned intensively about his diagnosing two cases of ovarian cancer as being benign growths. Dennis suddenly heard the call of the islands and disappeared. Fairview was sued by the two cancer victims as well as countless others who were treated by the fraud. When Fairview investigated, it learned that Dennis was not a licensed physician; he was just a con artist in disguise. Is the hospital liable? Yes! Fairview is liable for negligent hiring.

REFERENCES

References should be consulted for information regarding the character, skill, knowledge, and experience of the applicant.

Many firms refuse to cast aspersions on former employees, preferring to limit their response to position held and dates of service. A few states grant qualified immunity to the prior employer where statements are made without malice.

Employers who choose to refrain from disclosing knowledge of a former employee's theft or violent behavior may run the risk of being sued by a future employer, coworker, or customer who is the victim of theft or a violent act by the employee in question. The prior employer's refusal could amount to negligent misrepresentation. Although some states recognize this as a cause of action, many have not had the occasion to address the issue. On the other hand, employers run the risk of suits for defamation, invasion of privacy, and/or interference with contractual relations where the employee believes the information disclosed was confidential, untrue, or given with the intent to prevent the prior employee from gaining future employment. Employers should obtain a written release from the employee before providing a reference. Employers should provide only the information requested, ensuring that it is accurate and documented.

Regarding the disclosure of information concerning theft, violence, insubordination, or incompetence, an employer should determine whether a qualified immunity exists in the state in which it conducts business. This affords protection when the reference is made in good faith.

WORKPLACE VIOLENCE

Violent acts in the workplace including assaults, rapes, and murders must be guarded against by the employer for the safety of its workers as well as to avoid liability and harm to its reputation. An employer will be civilly liable in tort for the criminal acts of its employee where it knew of the danger presented by the employee. An employer may also be liable where an extensive background check would have revealed the employee's propensity for violence.

Background checks are essential to ensure that the information provided by the applicant is true. An employer must discern whether the individual poses a financial risk through a credit check and a safety risk based on a criminal conviction report. An employer would be wise to limit the investigation to information that is related to the job and constitutes a business necessity. This will avoid invasion of privacy suits. The information requested may differ based on the position, but all individuals applying for the same position should be treated equally. If an applicant is treated differently because of race, sex, or national origin, then discrimination may be claimed.

The issue presented in the following case is whether a business owes a duty to a member of the general public when one of its employees commits a tortious act against an individual.

Stalbosky v. Belew and Three Rivers Trucking Company

205 F.3d 890 (6th Cir. 2000)

Gilman, Circuit Judge.

On April 27, 1995, William Belew was driving a truck through Kentucky on behalf of Three Rivers Trucking Co. Belew picked up a stranded motorist, Myra Stalbosky, at an interstate rest area. He later raped and murdered her in the cab of his truck. Michael Stalbosky, the administrator of Myra Stalbosky's estate, brought suit against both Belew and Three Rivers. He alleged that Three Rivers should be held liable for negligently hiring and retaining Belew because the company knew or should have known that Belew posed an unreasonable risk to members of the general public such as Myra Stalbosky. The district court granted summary judgment against Belew and awarded a two and a half million dollar judgment to Stalbosky. As to Three Rivers, however, the district court granted the company's motion for summary judgment, holding that Stalbosky had not raised a genuine issue of material fact under Kentucky law that would allow recovery in his favor. For the reasons set forth below, we AFFIRM the judgment of the district court.

On February 8, 1991, Belew was convicted of arson in Weakley County, Tennessee and sentenced to three years in prison. After serving 90 days, he was released on probation for the remainder of his term. On September 9, 1991, Patricia Buchanan, a former girlfriend of Belew's, swore out a complaint against him, alleging that he struck her, tied her feet, and pulled her out of her house by the hair while her eight year old son watched. Buchanan's complaint was subsequently dismissed.

Over three and a half years later, Belew was arrested on a charge of aggravated assault. According to the complaint, Belew entered the home of Maureen Revel, another former girlfriend, in the early morning hours on March 21, 1995.

Belew allegedly tried to force Revel out of her residence, and placed a gun to her head when she refused. The complaint states that Belew then attempted to rape Revel, although she was ultimately able to dissuade him.

Upon being arrested,

Belew managed to escape, but was recaptured shortly thereafter and charged with aggravated assault and escape. On April 26, 1995, he pled guilty and was sentenced to 11 months and 29 days of incarceration. The majority of the sentence was suspended, except for 15 days, which were to be served beginning on August 4, 1995. On April 27, 1995, the day after his sentencing, Belew took a driving assignment for Three Rivers, which scheduled him to make a round trip from Paris, Tennessee to East Sparta, Ohio and back. Belew pulled over at a rest area on Interstate 71, in Henry County, Kentucky, where he encountered Myra Stalbosky, an eighteen-year-old motorist who was having car troubles. Myra Stalbosky then rode with Belew to a truck stop, where Belew raped and strangled her in his cab. After his arrest, Belew pled guilty to rape and murder, and is currently serving a life sentence for those crimes.

BELEW'S EMPLOYMENT HISTORY WITH THREE RIVERS

Three Rivers first hired Belew in 1991 for part-time work, washing trucks and working in its shop. On February 9, 1994, Belew was hired as a full-time truck driver. Prior to hiring Belew as a driver, Three Rivers checked with his previous employer, obtained a copy of his driving record, and performed a drug screen. According to Three Rivers, none of these inquiries indicated that Belew was unfit for a position as a truck driver. On his application form, Belew denied that he had ever been convicted of a felony, despite his prior conviction for arson in 1991. Three Rivers has no record of any complaints against Belew in his capacity as one of its employees.

Belew was off work between March 12 and April 2, 1995, during which time he assaulted Revel, was arrested, and was held in jail for four days. The officers of Three Rivers deny any knowledge of this incident prior to Belew's April 27, 1995 road trip. A former Three Rivers employee, however, claims that it was "common knowledge" at the company that Belew's girlfriend had had him arrested and put in jail.

On April 26, 1996, Michael Stalbosky, administrator of Myra Stalbosky's estate, filed suit against Belew and Three Rivers for the wrongful death of Myra Stalbosky, with jurisdiction based on diversity of citizenship. Stalbosky asserted two claims against Three Rivers—respondeat superior and negligent hiring and retention. Three Rivers moved for summary judgment on both claims. On December 20, 1996, the district court dismissed Stalbosky's respondeat superior claim, finding that Belew's actions were not taken in furtherance of his employment. The district court declined to dismiss the negligent hiring and retention claim, however, and ordered the parties to proceed with discovery.

On February 19, 1998, after Stalbosky had received several extensions to conclude his discovery, Three Rivers requested a ruling on its summary judgment motion regarding Stalbosky's negligent hiring and retention claim. The district court granted Three Rivers's motion on April 27, 1998, finding no evidence indicating that the officers of Three Rivers should have foreseen Belew's violent behavior. Stalbosky filed a timely notice of appeal on December 4, 1998, limiting the issue to the grant of summary judgment on his negligent hiring and retention claim.

Under Kentucky law, the two elements of a suit for negligent hiring and retention are that (1) the employer knew or reasonably should have known that the employee was unfit for the job for which he was employed, and (2) the employee's placement or retention at that job created an unreasonable risk of harm to the plaintiff.

The district court granted summary judgment in favor of Three Rivers on the grounds that Stalbosky failed to raise a genuine issue of material fact as to the first element, i.e., whether Three Rivers knew or reasonably should have known that Belew was unfit for his job as a truck driver.

In its analysis, the district court considered whether Sonny and Randy Crutcher, the owners and managers of Three Rivers, had any knowledge of Belew's prior crimes or violent acts before the murder of Myra Stalbosky. It first noted that Belew had lied on his application, denying any prior felony convictions. Turning then to Stalbosky's evidence, the court found that his supporting affidavits on the key issue of the Crutchers' knowledge constituted inadmissible hearsay. The district court concluded that "the plaintiff has not come forth with any affirmative evidence that Three Rivers did in fact know, or should have known, of Belew's unfitness."

Philip Blakeley, a private investigator hired by the Stalbosky family to investigate the circumstances surrounding Myra Stalbosky's death, submitted an affidavit recounting an interview with Belew that took place on April 10, 1997. In that affidavit, Blakeley related Belew's statement that Randy and Sonny Crutcher were both aware of his criminal history, but told him not to worry about it and not to list it on his application.

The district court disregarded this testimony as hearsay. On appeal, Stalbosky argues that Blakeley's statement was admissible under Rule 801(d)(2) of the Federal Rules of Evidence as an admission by Belew, a party-opponent. Belew is a party to this action, but the statements that are at issue here were not offered against Belew, but rather against Three Rivers to establish its knowledge of Belew's prior criminal history. Under Rule 801(d)(2)(A), a party's statement is admissible as non-hearsay only if it is offered against that party. The district court therefore properly refused to consider Blakeley's affidavit.

James Norsworthy, a former driver for Three Rivers, stated in an affidavit dated March 2, 1998 that "it was common knowledge at the company that Chris' girlfriend had him arrested and put in jail." The district court disregarded this part of Norsworthy's testimony on the grounds that it was inadmissible hearsay. In the alternative, the trial court held that Norsworthy's statement "does not definitively show that Sonny and Randy Crutcher knew that Belew had been arrested or that he had a violent disposition."

Regardless of whether Norsworthy's statement is admissible, however, it is too conclusory and vague to successfully counter a motion for summary judgment.

Moreover, as the district court aptly noted, even if it is assumed that Belew's arrest was "common knowledge" at Three Rivers, that does not necessarily indicate that the owners of Three Rivers were aware of this fact.

Glenn Boggs, a detective with the Kentucky State Police, was the lead investigator in the homicide of Myra Stalbosky.

As part of his investigation, he interviewed Sonny Crutcher in July of 1995. Boggs stated in a November 15, 1996 affidavit that Crutcher told him the following:

> I am ashamed at what has happened. This is what happens when you try to give someone a chance. Chris's dad told me that Chris had served some time in prison and had been in quite a bit of trouble over fighting with his former girlfriends. Chris's dad said Chris was trying to straighten up and do what was right, so I gave him a chance.

In Boggs's affidavit, he also quotes Crutcher as saying that Belew's father, Mike Belew, had told him that at a younger age, Chris Belew had been placed in a behavioral health hospital because of a drug addiction and a hot temper that resulted in him attacking other people.

The district court excluded this affidavit as well, ruling without elaboration that it constituted inadmissible hearsay. Stalbosky argues on appeal that Boggs's affidavit is not hearsay because it relates statements made by Sonny Crutcher that are admissions of a party-opponent under Rule 801(d)(2)(D) of the Federal Rules of Evidence. That rule allows for the admission of statements by a party's agent, concerning a matter within the scope of his agency or employment, made during the existence of the relationship.

Three Rivers responds by contending that Sonny Crutcher retired from Three Rivers in February of 1995, and was therefore not speaking as an agent of the company at the time of the interview in July of 1995. The evidence on the record does not support Three Rivers's contention. Sonny Crutcher remains the chairman of the board of Three Rivers and he described himself in September of 1997 as being only "semi-retired." Boggs's recollection of Crutcher's comments is therefore non-hearsay and is admissible as the admission of a party-opponent.

Furthermore, Boggs's statements are also not hearsay because they were not offered to prove the truth of the matter asserted—that Belew had served time in prison or fought with former girlfriends—but solely to prove that Sonny Crutcher was aware of Belew's history.

This error by the district court, however, is not cause for reversal. Viewed in the light most favorable to Stalbosky, the import of Boggs's affidavit is that when Three Rivers hired Belew as a full-time driver in 1994 the company may have known that (1) Belew had been convicted of arson in February of 1991, (2) an assault charge had been filed against him by a former girlfriend in September of 1991 and subsequently dropped, and (3) "at a younger age" Belew had been placed in a behavioral health hospital because of a drug addiction and a hot temper. There is no competent evidence indicating that Three Rivers learned of Belew's March 21, 1995 arrest for assault—which occurred while Belew was on leave—prior to its dispatching Belew on the tragic April 27, 1995 road trip. Even if Three Rivers was aware of the three incidents listed above, we agree with the district court that no reasonable juror could conclude from that information that Three Rivers knew or should have known that Belew was unfit for his job as a long-haul truck driver.

We find the facts in the present case to be distinguishable from the unusual facts presented in Malorney v. B&L Motor Freight, Inc.

In Malorney, a trucking company hired a driver with a history of violent sex-related crimes, including an arrest only a year before he was hired, for aggravated sodomy of two teenage hitchhikers. Based on these facts, the Illinois appellate court denied the trucking company's motion for summary judgment in a suit brought by a hitchhiker who was sexually assaulted by the driver, holding that material issues of fact existed as to whether the company was negligent in entrusting a truck with a sleeping compartment to the driver. In the present case, there is no comparable evidence demonstrating that Three Rivers should have reasonably foreseen that Belew was likely to assault a total stranger while driving for the company.

Belew's position as a long-haul truck driver did not grant him supervisory power over or special access to others, particularly because Three Rivers had an explicit policy prohibiting its drivers from picking up hitchhikers. As Three Rivers observes:

> Belew was not provided, by virtue of his employment, with a unique opportunity to commit a crime against Myra Stalbosky. Indeed, he was in no better position than any other member of the general public. Myra Stalbosky was not an invitee or customer of Three Rivers, rather, Belew happened upon her as a member of the general public.

In sum, the competent proof presented by Stalbosky would at best allow a factfinder to conclude that Three Rivers knew or should have known of Belew's 1991 offenses and his even earlier commitment to a behavioral health hospital. Unlike the factual scenario in Malorney, however, these facts are insufficient to support a conclusion that Three Rivers should have reasonably foreseen that Belew might assault a total stranger while on the road several years later.

Conclusion
For all of the reasons set forth above, we AFFIRM the district court's grant of summary judgment in favor of Three Rivers.

Case Commentary
The Sixth Circuit Court of Appeals implemented a two *tiered* test for determining an employer's liability for negligent hiring. First, the employer knew or should have know that the employee was unfit for the job. Second, hiring the employee for this job, created an unreasonable risk of harm to the plaintiff. The Court concluded that even if Three Rivers Trucking knew or should have know of William *Belew's* past criminal record of assault, arson and his drug addiction, it had no reason to believe that he would assault a stranger while driving the truck.

His employment with Three Rivers did not place him in a better position to accomplish the assault. Three Rivers had a policy against its drivers picking up hitch hikers. Myra Stalbosky voluntarily accepted a ride from Belew. In doing so, she assumed the risk. There was no way Three Rivers could have guarded against this. ∎

CASE QUESTIONS

1. Do you agree with the verdict in this case?
2. Usually murderers do not have many assets, so dependents of the deceased are left without monetary recourse. Should the murderer's employer be absolutely responsible?

3. Is there anything more Three Rivers could have done to prevent this murder?

EMPLOYEE LESSONS

1. Recognize inappropriate questions asked during an interview.
2. Decide prior to an interview how you intend to respond if an inappropriate question is asked.
3. Understand if you take issue with the interviewer that you may not get the job for that reason.
4. Do not expect the interviewer to apologize because he or she may be wrong.
5. Be prepared for a time-consuming and possibly expensive lawsuit to resolve the conflict.
6. Ask what the job qualifications are for the position for which you are applying.
7. Inquire as to the criteria employed and the decision-making process utilized in determining promotions.
8. Learn the employer's policy on nepotism and promoting from within.
9. Appreciate the fact that employers should only inquire into prior criminal convictions that are related to the job.
10. Respond to questions honestly or refuse if inappropriate, but never lie; otherwise, you may be discharged for being dishonest.

SUMMARY

The selection process has become a complicated procedure for employers. They must carefully choose questions based on job qualifications. They risk litigation if they ask inappropriate questions that can be inferred as being discriminatory. Employers must recruit from a diverse pool of candidates. Employers must keep accurate records of these candidates, such as who applied and who was hired. Employers must establish job-related criteria necessary for promotions. Employers must perform background checks on employees to guard themselves against negligent hiring, but these checks are limited to activities or criminal convictions that are job related. Policies with regard to nepotism and promoting from within should also be drafted by the employer. The selection process is a daunting but necessary undertaking for the employer. As most of us know, it is an equally stressful experience for workers.

REVIEW QUESTIONS

1. Is discrimination possible in the selection process?
2. What are the Uniform Guidelines on Employee Selection Procedures?
3. Can an employer be guilty of negligent hiring?
4. Is nepotism permissible?
5. Are promotions from within the company discriminatory?
6. Do firms that recruit at colleges practice discrimination?
7. What records must an employer keep with regard to its employees?
8. Can an employer specify "recent college graduates only" in an employment ad?
9. What procedure should a company follow when a job becomes available that would entail promoting someone from within the company?
10. Does an employer have to be careful where it advertises for potential job applicants to avoid acting in a discriminatory manner?

CASE PROBLEMS

1. The plaintiffs allege that from 1991 to 1993, the city promoted various members of the fire department in the ranks of driver, lieutenant, captain, and deputy chief. Each of the plaintiffs, all of whom are white males, with the exception of plaintiff Wallace J. Graves, who is a Native American, applied for promotions by taking and passing the promotional exam. The plaintiffs were passed over for promotion in favor of lower

ranked individuals. Plaintiffs' complaint asserts that they were passed over solely because of race or gender in an attempt by the city and Dallas Fire Department (DFD) to promote minorities in accordance with the city's affirmative action plan. Plaintiffs allege that these promotions violate the equal protection clause of the U.S. Constitution. The DFD does not hire laterally from other fire departments. Therefore, each rank is composed of those individuals qualified for promotion from the rank below. The promotional goals should be statistically related to the number of qualified applicants in each rank below. The affirmative action goals of the city's 1992 adopted AAP state that annual promotion goals are based on a ratio of African-American and Hispanics in the population of Dallas, Texas, at a level not to exceed 40 percent.

The city argues that because no unqualified candidates were considered for promotion and the plaintiffs were only denied an employment opportunity, they were not deprived of their existing jobs.

Dallas Fire Fighters v. City of Dallas, 885 F.Supp. 915 (N.D. Tex. 1995)

2. Domino's hired Mr. Sturtz in early 1994. On March 7th of that year, he was distributing pizza coupons door-to-door near the college that Ms. Poe attended in Cedar Rapids, Iowa. Ms. Poe was waiting at a bus stop, and Mr. Sturtz approached her, told her she had missed the bus, and offered her a ride. Ms. Poe declined and told him she would wait for the next bus. Mr. Sturtz asked Ms. Poe where she was going and, when she told him, said he was going that way. Mr. Sturtz told Ms. Poe he worked for Domino's; said that it would be okay for her to ride with him; and showed her the coupons he was passing out. Ms. Poe got into the car, and Mr. Sturtz drove to a remote area of Cedar Rapids, where, at knifepoint, he raped Ms. Poe. She alleges negligent hiring and supervision.

Mr. Sturtz had previous convictions for sexual assault and abuse, and when he applied for a job with Domino's, he lied on the application, saying he had never been convicted of a felony. What result?

Poe v. Domino's Pizza, Inc., 139 F.3D 617 (8th Cir. 1998)

3. Ms. Stukey had several experiences in teaching. Ms. Stukey directed educational seminars at Central State University and Antioch College from 1978 until 1981. In addition, Ms. Stukey had conducted seminars on a variety of legal topics, including labor law and housing law. Ms. Stukey had also been managing attorney for the Greene County Legal Aid Office from 1978 until 1981.

In contrast, one successful male candidate had only taught freshman chemistry at the University of Maryland from 1966 to 1967. Nevertheless, the selection committee gave the male candidate substantially more teaching points than Ms. Stukey in the selection committee's evaluation.

Prior to the start of the March 25, 1985, interview, selection committee member Earnest Spitzer spoke with Ms. Stukey. In this conversation, Mr. Spitzer questioned Ms. Stukey about her divorce and her child-care arrangements. Ms. Stukey claimed she was rattled by these questions, which as a labor lawyer, she knew were improper. What was the result? *Stukey v. U.S. Air Force*, 809 F.Supp. 536 (S.D. Ohio 1992)

HUMAN RESOURCE DILEMMAS

1. Treetop Publishing is going to promote a sales rep to regional manager to fill a vacancy. This job requires air travel and extended days away from home; a sales rep usually travels within a 100-mile radius by car. Treetop offers the promotion to Sheila, who is single. They bypass Laura, who is a single mom with two small children, even though she is more qualified. Laura consults with the Moran Legal Advisory Board. As an associate, what is your recommendation?

2. Very Cool Music is a chain that caters to the sale of hip-hop and rap CDs to the youth of the nation. It refuses to hire anyone over the age of 25. When Sparkey, a recently retired and partially deaf senior, applies for a position hoping to supplement his social

security while engaging with the youth of the world, he is summarily rejected. When Sparkey seeks advice, the case is turned over to you. How do you rule?

3. Sandra Hanson is a store manager with Tip Top Hardware, a national chain. Tip Top has a nepotism policy that precludes managers from hiring family members. The definition of "family members" includes cousins. Sandra hires Scott Petersen. Four months later, it is discovered that Sandra and Scott are fifth cousins once removed. Neither of them knew that they were related. Tip Top discharges them both. Sandra and Scott feel that the true meaning of the nepotism policy is being distorted. Do you agree with them?

WEB SITE ASSIGNMENT

Using the following Web sites, construct employment policies with regard to selection procedure, recruitment, promotion, nepotism, and negligent hiring.

www.nolo.com
www.doi.gov/hrm/pmanager/st13d.html
www.employeetrainingguide.com/Employee-Selection-Tips.html
www.lawinfo.com
public.findlaw.com/employment_employer/nolo/ency/94B1A49C-57A1-4B3B-98F
www.bizjournals.com/birmingham/stories/2000/08/14/focus1.html
get2work.borderlink.org/page.php?pid = 175&book = ip
www.ksu.edu/affact/Policies/Interviews.htm
www.wetfeet.com/employer/articles/article.asp?aid = 362
www.besr.org/dvartorah/Devarim.html
www.inc.com/magazine/20030901/ahanft.html
www.saterfiel.com
www.employeetrainingguide.com
www.tabicpro.com/products/employmentselection.html
www.findlaw.com
www.usccr.gov/index.html
sacramento.bcentral.com/sacramento/stories/1997/08/04/smallb6.html
www.poynerspruill.com/infocenter
www.hightechcareers.com/docs/agediscr.html

Chapter 3

Testing

Employment Scenario

In 2 years, The Long and Short of It has grown to three stores with each having at least 1,500 square feet of floor space. L&S employs 48 workers, 42 of whom are employees. Recently, L&S has experienced customer complaints regarding the lack of employee knowledge about some of L&S's clothing lines. In addition, on three occasions, salespeople have lost their cool with indecisive customers, alleging the customers were wasting the salespeople's time. To remedy this, L&S planned to require those applicants selected for employment as salespeople to take written aptitude and psychological tests. Tom and Mark ask Susan North, Esq., for her perspective. How should she advise them?

Employment Scenario

The Long and Short of It experienced a wave of property thefts over a 2-week period. The company estimates that more than $18,000 in clothing was stolen from two of its stores. L&S decides to require all 48 workers to submit to a polygraph test. L&S contacts Susan, but she is away on vacation. Tom and Mark forge ahead rather than wait for her to return. In addition to questions about the $18,000 theft, they propose asking the following: Have you ever stolen anything? Do you ever think of stealing? Have you ever taken drugs and, if so, which drugs? Are you currently taking drugs? How much alcohol do you consume daily? Sarah Michels, a bookkeeper for L&S, refuses to take the polygraph test. L&S immediately terminates her employment and threatens to notify the authorities that it has reason to believe she is a prime suspect if she does not divulge information about the theft and make restitution. Sarah files a complaint with the EEOC. Was L&S's actions justifiable?

Chapter Checklist

➤ *Distinguish among the different tests available to employers.*

➤ *Determine when it is appropriate to use a specific test.*

➤ *Decide whether the test questions are related to the job.*

➤ *Balance the employer's need to know against the worker's desire for privacy.*

➤ *Establish whether the test is being used to deny employment to women and minorities.*

➤ *Understand the ramifications of the Employee Polygraph Protection Act.*

➤ *Identify the exceptions to that Act.*

➤ *Appreciate the employer's concern for restricting employment to workers who do not engage in the use of alcohol and drugs.*

➤ *Be familiar with the Drug-Free Workplace Act.*

➤ *Appreciate the impact that the Fourth Amendment has had on drug testing.*

INTRODUCTION

Employers are seeking to hire qualified workers who will do the best job. Aside from interviewing candidates, evaluating their experience, and checking their references, testing provides the most useful source of information for employers. The tests most often used are aptitude, residency, psychological, honesty, polygraph, and drug tests. Concerns over privacy and discrimination lead to litigation regarding the use of tests. With regard to privacy, the employer's desire to know must be balanced with the employee's right to safeguard his or her personal information. With respect to discrimination, the tests must be designed to determine the ability of the worker to perform the task. The tests themselves must be a business necessity, and the questions must be related to the job. The tests cannot be used for the purpose of refusing employment to women and minorities. With that in mind, an analysis should be undertaken for each position. Job qualifications should be determined. A job description should be written based on the analysis and should include appropriate qualifications. An evaluation should be made to determine if testing is necessary and, if so, what type of testing is required.

Then, a test should be drafted utilizing questions specific to determining whether the worker has the qualifications for the particular job.

HUMAN RESOURCE ADVICE

- Conduct an analysis for each position.
- Identify the qualifications necessary for each job.
- Draft a job description based on those qualifications.
- Evaluate the necessity of commissioning a test to determine those job qualifications.
- Design specific questions to establish those job qualifications.
- Gauge employee morale when testing is introduced.
- Educate the employees as to why testing is necessary.
- Balance the gain in knowledge from testing with the potential loss of employee trust.
- Assure confidentiality with regard to test results.
- Refrain from using test results to discriminate.

APTITUDE TESTS

Employers must justify the use of an aptitude test by showing that the test is job related and, if so, is used for the sole purpose of identifying qualified applicants. If the test is used as a pretext to disqualify members of a suspect classification, then the employer's action is discriminatory.

Opponents of general tests argue that they are biased against women and minorities. Proponents insist that scholarly individuals at impartial testing facilities established these tests. Their use is widespread, and their reliability is reinforced by a long tradition.

The issue is whether the education skills test is a business necessity and job related.

The Association of Mexican-American Educators v. State of California
231 F.3d 572 (9th Cir. 2000)

Graber, Circuit Judge.

Plaintiffs are a class of Mexican-American, Asian-American, and African-American educators and would-be educators in California. They appeal from an adverse judgment in their action against the State of California and its agency, challenging the district court's holding that the California Basic Education Skills Test ("CBEST"), which is a prerequisite to employment in a variety of positions in the California public schools, violates Title VII of the Civil Rights Act of 1964.

FACTUAL AND PROCEDURAL BACKGROUND

Effective February 1, 1983, the California legislature amended the California Education Code to prohibit the California Commission on Teacher Credentialing ("CCTC") from issuing "any credential, permit, certificate, or renewal of an emergency credential to any person to serve in the public schools unless the person has demonstrated proficiency in basic reading, writing, and mathematics skills." At the same time, the legislature authorized the state's Superintendent of Public Instruction to "adopt an appropriate state test to measure proficiency in these basic skills." The Superintendent adopted the CBEST and, in May 1983, CCTC assumed responsibility for administering and revising the test.

The CBEST is a pass-fail examination consisting of three sections: reading, writing, and mathematics.

To pass the CBEST, a candidate must receive a "scaled" score of 123. Accordingly, a candidate passes by averaging 41 points on each of the three sections (out of a score range of 20 to 80). A scaled score of 41 on the reading section translates into a raw score of 28 out of 40 questions correct; on the mathematics section, a scaled score of 41 equates to a raw score of 26 out of 40 correct. Each of the two essays is graded by two readers, who give raw scores of between one and four points per essay. Thus, the range of possible scores for the writing section is between four and 16 points. A raw score of 12 points translates into a scaled score of 41 points. The CBEST employs a "compensatory scoring" model, under which a candidate passes the test with a scaled score lower than 41 on a particular section, so long as his or her total scaled score is at least 123.

A passing score on the CBEST is required for all public elementary and secondary school teachers in California. A passing score also is required for many nonteaching employees of the California public schools, including administrators.

Since the CBEST's inception, minority candidates have disproportionately received failing scores. The named Plaintiffs are three nonprofit organizations that represent the interests of minority educators, and eight individual minority candidates. They brought this action against the State of California and the CCTC to challenge the validity of the test under Title VI and Title VII, on behalf of themselves and all others similarly situated. The district court certified the following class:

> All Latinos, African-Americans and Asians who have sought or are seeking California public school credentials and certificated positions who have been, are being, or will be adversely affected in their ability to obtain credentials and certificated positions by [CBEST] results.

In their complaint, Plaintiffs sought to enjoin the use of the CBEST, alleging that the test has a disproportionate, adverse impact on minority candidates and that Defendants have failed to adopt screening procedures with a less adverse impact.

To summarize, the circumstances here demonstrate a level of control and interference far greater than that in the "mere licensing" cases on which Defendants rely. The State of California exerts a high degree of control over the operation of local public school districts. That control is evidenced both by the record and by California law.

We hold that the CBEST examination is subject to the provisions of Title VII. We turn next to the question whether the CBEST violates the provisions of that Act.

"Discriminatory tests are impermissible unless shown, by professionally acceptable methods, to be predictive of or significantly correlated with important elements of work behavior which comprise or are relevant to the job or jobs for which candidates are being evaluated." In evaluating employment tests that are alleged to have a racially disparate impact, we first consider whether the plaintiff has established a prima facie case by demonstrating that the test causes a disparate impact on the basis of race. Here, the district court concluded that Plaintiffs had established a prima facie case. Defendants do not challenge that conclusion on appeal.

Because Plaintiffs have established a prima facie case, the burden shifts to Defendants to demonstrate that the CBEST was validated properly. In its detailed and careful opinion, the district court concluded that Defendants had met their burden and that the test had been validated properly based on three studies: (1) the 1982 Wheeler and Elias study; (2) the 1985 Practitioners' Review; and (3) the 1995 Lundquist study. Plaintiffs challenge that conclusion.

In cases in which a defendant establishes that a test is validated properly, the burden shifts back to the plaintiff to show the existence of other selection devices that also would "serve the employer's legitimate interest in efficient and trustworthy workmanship," but that are not discriminatory. Here, Plaintiffs' challenge is limited to the validation of the test; they do not attempt on appeal to meet their burden of demonstrating the existence of preferable selection devices, assuming that the CBEST is validated.

To demonstrate that the CBEST was validated properly, Defendants are required to "show that it has 'a manifest relationship to the employment in question.'" In cases in which a scored test, like this one, is challenged, we require that the test be "job related"—that is, "that it actually measures skills, knowledge, or ability required for successful performance of the job." In making a determination about job-relatedness, we follow a three-step approach:

> The employer must first specify the particular trait or characteristic which the selection device is being used to identify or measure. The employer must then determine that the particular trait or characteristic is an important element of work behavior. Finally, the employer must demonstrate by "professionally acceptable methods" that the selection device is "predictive of or significantly correlated" with the element of work behavior identified in the second step.

We will analyze each of those three steps in turn. In addition, we will consider Plaintiffs' argument that the passing score on the writing component of the CBEST is set too high.

1. Specific Traits or Characteristics
The first step of our inquiry is to identify the trait or characteristic that the test is designed to measure. Here, the district court found that the test was being used to measure "basic skills in reading, writing, and mathematics," and Plaintiffs do not dispute that finding.

2. Important Elements of Work Behavior

Next, we consider whether basic skills in reading, writing, and mathematics are "important elements of work behavior," for the public school jobs for which the test is required. The district court found that the tested skills were important to the jobs at issue. Plaintiffs challenge that finding on three grounds. *First*, they argue that the 1985 Practitioners' Review failed to identify *any* particular work behaviors or job duties and thus could not be used to assess whether the CBEST measured important elements of work behavior. *Second*, they argue that Lundquist's 1995 study failed to distinguish "important" skills from skills that are less important. *Third*, they argue that Defendants failed to demonstrate that the CBEST is job-related for the *particular* positions for which it is required. We address each of those arguments in turn.

Plaintiffs first argue that the 1985 Practitioners' Review, conducted by Dr. Richard Watkins, was inadequate because it failed to identify specific job duties to which the CBEST skills could be correlated. We conclude that the district court did not clearly err in finding that the 1985 study adequately identified the "elements of work behavior," that the CBEST is designed to measure.

The district court found that the Review comprised the "pooled judgments" of knowledgeable persons, such as incumbents in the jobs, "about the relevance of the skills tested on the CBEST to the jobs for which it is required, an appropriate form of a job analysis under the professional standards of the time."

Thus, the Practitioners' Review was designed to learn from teachers, administrators, and other school employees the categories of skills that they considered relevant to their own jobs. The skills measured by the study tracked the categories of skills measured by the CBEST, and the skills were described in some detail on the rating forms used by the panel members.

The study's participants were guided by detailed instructions relating to each skill category and were told to rank the importance of each skill for both teaching and non-teaching jobs. The study therefore satisfies the requirement from *Craig* that the employer determine whether a "specific trait or characteristic is an important element of work behavior." The district court did not clearly err in concluding that the 1985 Practitioners' Review was "an appropriate form of a job analysis under the professional standards of the time."

Validation studies "are by their nature difficult, expensive, time consuming and rarely, if ever, free of error." Plaintiffs' argument demonstrates, at most, that Dr. Lundquist's study may not be totally free of error. But the argument does not persuade us that the district court clearly erred in relying on Dr. Lundquist's study.

Finally, Plaintiffs argue that Defendants failed to conduct job-specific studies to determine that the CBEST is "job related for the positions in question." The CBEST is not intended to measure all the skills that are relevant to all the jobs for which it is required. (Indeed, it does not purport to measure *all* the skills of *any* of the jobs for which it is

required.) Rather, the CBEST is intended to establish only a minimum level of competence in three areas of basic educational skills. The question is whether the validation studies in this case have satisfied the requirement that those skills be "job related" for all the positions in question. The district court found that the validation studies adequately analyzed the CBEST in terms of both the teaching and nonteaching jobs for which the test is required. The district court did not clearly err in so finding.

Dr. Lundquist's study classified jobs for which the CBEST is required as either "teacher" or "administrator" and determined that the CBEST was valid for both groups of positions. Accordingly, the 1995 study considered the validity of the CBEST across the range of jobs for which the test is required. The district court accepted the study's conclusions and found that the CBEST had been validated adequately "with respect to teaching and non-teaching jobs." On this record, that finding is not clearly erroneous.

In sum, we hold that the district court did not clearly err in finding that the skills measured by the CBEST are "important elements of work behavior" with regard to the jobs for which the test is required.

3. Actual Measurement of Skills

The final step in this court's three-step analysis from *Craig* is to determine whether Defendants have demonstrated by "professionally acceptable methods that the selection device is predictive of or significantly correlated with the element of work behavior" that it is designed to measure. The district court concluded that "the CBEST actually measures . . . basic skills [in reading, writing, and mathematics]."

In short, there is evidence—even if not overwhelming evidence—that the development and evaluation of the CBEST were appropriate and that the test measures the types of skills that it was designed to measure. We therefore hold that the district court did not clearly err in concluding that the test questions had been shown by professionally acceptable methods to be "predictive of or significantly correlated with the element of work behavior" that they were designed to measure.

In sum, we hold that the district court did not clearly err in concluding that the CBEST was validated properly.

4. Standards for Passing Scores

Plaintiffs also argue that the 12-out-of-16 passing score on the writing section of the CBEST is too high.

An employer is not required to validate separately the selection of particular passing scores on an employment test. Rather, the EEOC's Guidelines more generally provide: "Where cutoff scores are used, they should normally be set so as to be reasonable and consistent with normal expectations of acceptable proficiency within the work force." This court previously has applied that standard.

Here, the district court found that "the passing scores on the CBEST reflect reasonable judgments about the minimum level of basic skills competence that should be required of teachers." The evidence before the court revealed that the California Superintendent of Public Instruction, who was responsible for establishing the cutoff scores, relied on polling data created as part of the Wheeler and Elias study in setting the cutoff for the writing section of the test. As part of that study, 44 readers reviewed approximately 6,800 CBEST essays and made recommendations regarding the cutoff between passing and failing scores. The readers *unanimously* agreed that a raw score of 12 out of 16 was a "passing" score. Approximately 80 percent of the readers agreed that a score of 11 out of 16 could be a "passing" score. On that basis, the Superintendent established a passing score of 12 out of 16, with an absolute minimum of 11 out of 16 under the "compensatory scoring" system.

Those cutoff scores represent a "logical breakpoint" between passing and failing scores. Plaintiffs argue that the breakpoint should have been set at 9 or 10 out of 16, because a majority of the readers opined that 10 out of 16 was a "passing" score. But the Superintendent was not required to set the score at the lowest level that a majority of the readers considered to be "passing." Rather, he was required to set a cutoff

that was logical, reasonable, and consistent with the data before him. He chose to set the cutoff at a level that all the readers agreed was "passing," and to set an absolute minimum at a level that 80 percent of the readers thought was "passing." The district court found that the Superintendent's decision to set the cutoff score at that level was consistent with the EEOC's Guidelines. We conclude that the district court did not clearly err in so finding.

Conclusion
For the reasons stated, we hold that Title VII applies to the CBEST; that the CBEST was validated properly; that the district court permissibly used a technical advisor; and that the district court did not abuse its discretion by refusing to award costs to Defendants. Accordingly, we affirm both the judgment in Defendants' favor and the order denying them costs.

Judgment for State of California.

Case Commentary
The Ninth Circuit Court ruled that the educational skills test was an appropriate measure of whether teachers were proficient at reading, writing, and math. ■

CASE QUESTIONS

1. Are you in agreement with the court's decision?
2. Do you believe the state had an ulterior motive for using this test?
3. Is a test of this nature indicative of whether an individual will be a good teacher?

RESIDENCY TESTS

Cities, towns, counties, and municipalities may require that applicants for civil service positions be residents. This mandate of preference must be clearly stated in a local ordinance.

Residency requirements may not be instituted by state or local governments in public contracts given to private contractors unless they are implemented to alleviate the loss of economic benefits to the state or to alleviate the state's high unemployment rate.

The issue in the case that follows is whether a municipality's use of a residency requirement is constitutional.

Kiel v. City of Kenosha
236 F.3d 814 (7th Cir. 2000)

Coffey, Circuit Judge.

Kiel and his fiance wanted to buy a house in Racine County and live there but could not because, as a Kenosha firefighter, Kiel was required to reside in Kenosha County. On May 19, 2000, Kiel, despite the residency requirement, made an offer on a house in Caledonia, Wisconsin, which is in an adjacent county known as Racine County, and sought a waiver of the residency requirement from the City Administrator, Nick

Arnold. On May 22, 2000, Kiel sent another letter to Arnold informing him that Kiel's offer to purchase the Caledonia property was accepted, but was contingent on Kiel's ability to obtain a waiver of the residency requirement. In a joint letter, Kiser and Grapentine denied Kiel's request for a waiver of the residency requirement. In a separate letter, Arnold also denied Kiel's request. Instead of accepting the City's decision,

Kiel brought this suit and sought a preliminary injunction barring the enforcement of the residency requirement. As stated above, the trial judge denied the motion for a preliminary injunction, holding that Kiel had little chance of succeeding on the merits of his claim. Kiel appeals.

Initially, the Supreme Court recognized the right of municipalities to condition employment with continued residency in the city. As the parties stipulated at oral argument, the City of Kenosha could have enacted an even more stringent residency requirement; that is, one which required its firefighters to live within the city limits of Kenosha rather than within the parameters of Kenosha County.

The City has set forth a plethora of rational justifications for the residency requirement, including improving the City's tax base, increasing interest and participation in Kenosha City and County events, and providing services (through more revenue) which benefit Kenosha City and County residents.

We are of the opinion that these reasons are more than sufficient to provide a rational basis for the City's residency requirement.

It is important to note that all interested parties agree that the City of Kenosha could constitutionally require its firefighters to live within the limits of the City. Given that the City could constitutionally restrict its employees to an area as small as the City of Kenosha, it is obviously constitutional for the City to require its employees to live in Kenosha County, a much larger geographical area.

The decision of the district court is AFFIRMED.

Judgment for the City of Kenosha.

Case Commentary

The Seventh Circuit Court decided that the City of Kenosha's reasons for employing a residency requirement were justifiable. ■

CASE QUESTIONS

1. Do you agree with the court's decision?
2. Can you describe a situation where the use of a residency requirement would be discriminatory?

3. Are residency requirements a subtle form of segregation?

PHYSICAL AND SKILLS TESTS

Physical tests may be employed in those jobs requiring certain physical attributes such as strength, dexterity, quickness, and endurance. Firefighters, police officers, sanitation workers, delivery people, and postal employees who deliver the mail on foot need a combination of certain physical characteristics not needed by office workers.

Skills tests may be required for typists, legal stenographers, electricians, carpenters, and plumbers. As long as the test mimics the actual work performed, the test will be valid.

PERSONALITY AND INTEGRITY TESTS

The use of personality tests to determine character traits essential for a particular job such as "aggressive, outgoing, and persistent" for a sales position satisfies Title VII's requirement of business necessity. If the questions on the specific personality test are related to discerning the character traits necessary for the position, the test will be valid.

The same may be said for integrity tests designed to identify those individuals who have a propensity to steal. The importance of these tests to banks and retail establishments to reduce employee theft is clear.

When the tests create a disparate impact against a specific class such as women and/or minorities, the necessity for requiring the tests or the specific questions asked on the tests will be closely scrutinized. Questions about religion, politics, and sex have no bearing on the job for which the applicant is applying.

Honesty tests are those that measure physiological changes in the person tested. They are usually referred to as lie-detector tests. Polygraphs, voice stress analyzers, and psychological stress evaluators are the most prevalent types. Some employers also attempt to determine veracity through the use of psychological questionnaires of personal judgments.

PSYCHOLOGICAL TESTING

Psychological tests may be administered only where the employer can show a compelling need. Employees are considered to be patients of the physicians conducting the examinations. In that respect, the patients are entitled to examine their medical reports.

Employment Perspective

Excelsior Bank, a specialist in investment banking, established along with a team of psychologists a psychological profile of people who work best under pressure. Every new applicant is required to take the test. The result is a prime determinant as to whether the applicant is given the job. Susan Morgan, who was otherwise qualified, is refused employment as a result of her low score on the psychological profile. Excelsior Bank's employees are overwhelmingly white males. Susan claims the test is not job related and is used as a pretext to discriminate. Is she correct? Yes! Excelsior has not shown a compelling need for the administration of the psychological test. Its use by Excelsior is to eliminate women and minorities from the selection process.

The issue in the following case is whether the use of a psychological test served a compelling need or resulted in improper medical inquiries.

Karraker v. Rent-A-Center, Inc
239 F. Supp. 2d 828 (C.D. ILL. 2003)

McCuskey, District Judge.

Plaintiffs wish to raise a claim under the Americans with Disabilities Act.

Plaintiffs' Amended Complaint sought to initiate a class action lawsuit against Rent-A-Center, Inc. (RAC); J. Ernest Talley, RAC's Chairman of the Board and Chief Executive Officer; and Associated Personnel Technicians (APT). Plaintiffs, current and former employees of RAC, alleged that RAC required all employees or outside applicants seeking management positions to take a battery of written tests, collectively referred to as the Management Test. Several tests included in the Management Test were personality inventories that inquired about personal information including sexual preferences and orientation, religious beliefs and practices, and medical conditions.

APT scored and interpreted the Management Test for RAC, creating a two-page psychological profile about the individuals. RAC distributed this report to the employees' immediate supervisor and placed a copy of it in the employees' personnel file. RAC used the test results in deciding which employees to promote and what additional training to require. Plaintiffs assert that RAC formulated no policy or procedure for keeping the test results confidential.

The ADA claim included in Plaintiffs' proposed Second Amended Complaint alleges that Defendants violated the ADA's prohibition against medical examinations and inquiries for job applicants.

In the context of employment, the ADA prohibits discrimination against "a qualified individual with a disability . . . in regard to job application procedures, the hiring, advancement, or discharge of employees, employee compensation, job training, and other terms, conditions, and privileges of employment." Concerning medical examinations and inquiries, the statute sets forth the general statement that "the prohibition against discrimination as referred to in subsection (a) of this section shall include medical examinations and inquiries." The ADA then outlines separate rules governing examinations and inquiries for job applicants who have not received an offer of employment, applicants who have received an offer of employment but have not yet commenced working for the entity and current employees. For job applicants who have not received an offer of employment, an employer may only ask about the applicant's ability to perform job-related functions, but may not inquire whether the applicant has a disability. After extending an offer of employment to an applicant, an employer may condition that offer on the results of a medical examination provided that all entering employees are subject to the examination and that the results are maintained as confidential medical records. Once the period of employment has commenced, the employer may not inquire whether an employee has a disability unless the examination or inquiry is "job-related and consistent with business necessity."

The crucial issue before this court is whether an individual must be a "qualified individual with a disability" in order to bring a claim that an employer required improper or unauthorized medical inquiries.

The statute refers to "job applicants" and "employees" rather than again using the more restrictive "qualified individual with a disability." Subsection (1), which incorporates the "qualified individual with a disability" language, is only one of the protections afforded and "it is only discrimination itself (and not illegal disclosure) that requires a showing of disability." Accordingly, these courts held that the requirements in (d)(2), (d)(3), and (d)(4) apply to all job applicants and employees, regardless of disability.

"[I]t makes little sense to require an employee to demonstrate that he has a disability to prevent his employer from inquiring as to whether or not he has a disability."

Although the reasoning of the Magistrate Judge is not inherently flawed or entirely unsupported, it appears that the great weight of case law supports the opposite conclusion. [T]he better interpretation does not require that Plaintiffs be qualified individuals with disabilities in order to state a claim.

MENTAL HEALTH AND DEVELOPMENTAL DISABILITIES CONFIDENTIALITY ACT

Plaintiffs assert in their amended complaint that Defendants' conduct violated the rights given them by the Illinois Mental Health and Developmental Disabilities Confidentiality Act (MHDDCA). Defendants argue that Plaintiffs cannot state a claim under the MHDDCA because the communications at issue were not made to a therapist in the context of mental health or developmental disability services. Defendants maintain that the purposes of the MHDDCA—to encourage candor between patient and therapist and to provide motivation to seek treatment—are not served by allowing Plaintiffs' claim.

Plaintiffs admit that their MHDDCA claim presents "a novel question of law," but they assert that Defendants' actions may indeed fall under the mandates of the Act. Specifically, they claim that the Management Tests were "psychological tests" and that the profiles APT provided to RAC prescribed personal growth exercises that the employee must undergo if he wanted a management job. The profiles summarized psychological characteristics of the individual employees and then recommended corrective action, a function of the tests that constituted mental health services.

Although Plaintiffs' characterization of the tests and the MHDDCA are indeed novel, it is perhaps possible for them to develop facts that would establish a claim under the Act. It is, therefore, inappropriate to dismiss their claims at this stage in the proceedings.

INVASION OF PRIVACY

Plaintiffs' Amended Complaint includes an allegation that Defendants' actions violated their right of privacy. Defendants first argue that this claim is barred by the one-year statute of limitations. Plaintiffs rely on the continuing violation doctrine to overcome this hurdle, arguing that Defendants perpetually failed to store the Management Test results in a confidential manner and that they continually used the results of the test in making hiring and promoting decisions. It is unclear given the limited record whether the continuing violation doctrine applies to the facts of this case. Even so, Plaintiffs alleged a set of facts that, if further developed, could support a timely claim for invasion of privacy, and so dismissal is inappropriate at this time.

Defendants also maintain that Plaintiffs have failed to state a claim for any of the four categories of invasion of privacy: intrusion upon the seclusion of another, appropriation of name or likeness of another, publicity given to private life, and publicity placing person in false light. [A] careful reading of their Amended Complaint reveals that they have stated a claim only for disclosure of private facts.

PUBLICITY GIVEN TO PRIVATE LIFE

To state a claim for public disclosure of private facts, Plaintiffs must allege (1) publicity was given to the disclosure of private facts; (2) the facts were private and not public facts; and (3) the matter made public would be highly offensive to a reasonable person. Defendants argue that Plaintiffs failed to allege publicity because the test results were given only to their immediate supervisors and that the facts were not private facts because Plaintiffs voluntarily took the Management Test knowing how the results would be used.

Plaintiffs' Amended Complaint sufficiently states a claim for public disclosure of private facts. They alleged that the test results were in their personnel files and that the managers were free to distribute the results to anyone, even those who had no business reason for viewing the documents. This allegation is sufficient, at this time, to satisfy the publicity requirement. Also, Plaintiffs dispute that they voluntarily took the test because they maintain that it was required by RAC for anyone wishing to be considered for a management position. Again, although not factually developed, this contention is sufficient to survive a motion to dismiss for failure to state a claim.

APT

APT, a Kansas corporation with its principal place of business in Kansas, argues that it has insufficient contacts with Illinois to justify personal jurisdiction. Specifically, APT argues that it does not have an Illinois address or phone number, any employees in Illinois, or an office or agent in Illinois. The president of APT averred in his affidavit that APT does not advertise or solicit customers in Illinois, nor do its employees travel to Illinois to conduct business. APT claims that merely sending the tests to RAC, scoring the tests, and mailing the results back to RAC do not constitute "minimum contacts."

Although APT's relationship with Illinois would be insufficient to warrant general jurisdiction, it is enough for this court to exercise specific jurisdiction over APT. APT mailed the tests to RAC in Illinois. After receiving the test results back from RAC, APT tabulated the score and created a written psychological profile for each individual, which it sent to RAC management (not in Illinois). This lawsuit arises directly out of those contacts with the state, and it is not unreasonable for APT to anticipate being haled into court in Illinois knowing that its work product was being distributed to employees in this state.

APT's motion to dismiss for want of jurisdiction is denied.

Judgment for Karraker.

Case Commentary

The Central District Court of Illinois decided that Karraker presented evidence sufficient to warrant a trial on the merits. ■

CASE QUESTIONS

1. Do you believe this case was correctly decided?
2. Will Karraker win when the case goes to trial?

3. Under what circumstances, if any, could this employer use psychological tests?

MEDICAL EXAMS

Medical exams may be given when an applicant is given a conditional offer of employment. Medical inquiries made prior to a conditional job offer are in violation of the ADA. However, an employer can ask a person whether he or she can perform the essential functions of the job.

The medical exam should be required of all new employees, and it should be designed to determine whether the individual is fit to perform the job. Testing for AIDS is discouraged because it amounts to an invasion of privacy. The determination should be made on whether the worker can perform the job now, not in 5 years' time. Otherwise, individuals with histories of cancer, heart disease, and smoking would be ruled out. The medical results must remain confidential. The physician conducting the exam need only report to the employer whether the individual is fit to perform the job unless the health condition may pose a danger to the individual or those around him or her. Once an employer has been given the opportunity to discern whether an individual is medically fit to perform the job and that individual is employed, no further inquiries may be made about the employee's medical condition unless it becomes a business necessity.

POLYGRAPH TESTS

Polygraphs are a form of lie-detector test. Their use is prohibited in all but a select set of instances because the reliability is questionable and their use amounts to an invasion of privacy.

The lie detector originated in Italy in 1895. Originally, changes in blood pressure were noted as questions involving criminal activity were asked. That same premise is the basis of the polygraph today.

The use of polygraphs became widespread among corporations, particularly those in retail and finance. Polygraph testing was often required of all applicants and employees. Employees were concerned that employers were making employment decisions based on inaccurate conclusions from polygraph readings. Researchers and defense attorneys began to question the polygraph's validity.

In the early 1980s, studies undertaken by Kleinmuntz and Szucko and Barland and Raskin have documented the unreliability of the polygraph. In 1988, protection was finally afforded by the passage of the Employee Polygraph Protection Act.

Employee Polygraph Protection Act of 1988

Under the Employee Polygraph Protection Act, employers cannot directly or indirectly suggest or require an employee to take a lie-detector test, nor can an employer use an employee's results from a lie-detector test. The term "lie detector" encompasses a polygraph, voice-stress analyzer, psychological stress evaluator, or any similar device used to determine the honesty of a person. A fine up to $10,000 is imposed on any employer found to be in breach of this Act. If employee selection or termination is determined by the polygraph, the Secretary of Labor may order employment, promotion, reinstatement, and reimbursement for lost wages and benefits. The employee may also seek these remedies in a private civil action. The Employee Polygraph Protection Act (EPPA) applies to all employers engaged in commerce. It does not apply to the federal government or to any state and local governments. There are other exemptions. Polygraphs may be used by an armored car company, a security alarm system firm, or a security personnel provider with regard to their screening of employee applicants who are being hired to protect any facility impacting on the national health or safety of the United States and any facility supplying electric, nuclear, or public water, shipments of radioactive or other toxic wastes, public transportation, currency, securities, precious commodities, or drug manufacture.

The issue in the next case is whether the use of a polygraph test to identify an individual who committed a theft is justifiable.

Calbillo v. Cavender Oldsmobile
288 F.3d 721 (5th Cir. 2002)

Stewart, Circuit Judge.

Calbillo was employed by Cavender Oldsmobile, Inc. ("Cavender") as a parts counter technician in January 1998. In April 1998, Rohda Smid ("Smid"), the parts manager, began noticing that quantities of Freon were missing. Edward Hollas ("Hollas"), the general manager, confronted several employees, including Calbillo, about the missing Freon. In response to Hollas's questioning, Calbillo claimed that he did not know who was stealing the Freon.

In the fall of 1998, the decision was made by Cavender management to hire Donald Trease ("Trease"), a licensed private investigator and polygraph examiner, who is the principal operator of Allied. When Hollas asked Trease "what could be done" about the missing Freon, Trease recommended that Hollas interview the employees of the parts department. Trease complied with Hollas's request that Trease interview the employees on his behalf instead. Trease came to the dealership, toured the parts department, talked to management, and interviewed all of the employees in the parts department. During Calbillo's interview, he explained that he did not have a key to the cabinet where the Freon was stored. According to Calbillo, Trease told him that the other employees had agreed to take polygraph examinations and Trease asked whether he was willing to take the test as well. Calbillo agreed to take a polygraph examination; however, immediately after the interview, some of Calbillo's co-workers told him that they refused to take a polygraph examination.

Trease gave a verbal report to Hollas regarding the information that he gathered from the employees interviewed, which included other employees' suspicions that Calbillo stole the Freon. Trease also provided Hollas with a three-page standard package about polygraph testing, which included information on the EPPA, rules and regulations pertaining to polygraph examination, and termination of employees. At Hollas's request, Trease spoke with Cavender's attorneys and discussed the EPPA, general procedures involved in a polygraph examination, and information acquired during the employee interviews. Following the employee interviews, Hollas requested that Trease administer a polygraph examination to Calbillo.

Hollas then demanded that Calbillo take a polygraph examination to prove that he was innocent of the theft as a condition of continued employment. Hollas explained that as a result of the investigation, Calbillo was chosen to take a polygraph examination based upon the way he answered Trease's questions. Hollas then gave Calbillo a piece of paper with an appointment time for the polygraph examination, and Calbillo signed it as instructed. According to Calbillo, Hollas also told him not to speak with an attorney or to bring an attorney to the examination.

Calbillo took the polygraph examination on October 6, 1998. He was read his rights relating to the polygraph examination prior to taking the examination. The examination consisted of three sets of twelve questions, with about twenty-five to thirty seconds between the individual questions and a few minutes between the sets of questions. After the first set of questions, Trease told Calbillo that he had "a deception of 99." At the end of the full examination, Trease reported the results to Calbillo and gave him a copy of the results. Calbillo claims that Trease also told him to "tell him who took the Freon" and said that he "was hiding something." Calbillo again responded that he did not know who took the Freon. Further, Trease reported the test results to Hollas. On the morning of October 7, 1998, Hollas informed Calbillo that he was terminated because he did not pass the polygraph examination.

Calbillo sued Cavender and Allied, alleging violations of the EPPA as well as state law claims of negligence and fraud, among other claims. On September 29, 2000, the district court granted Allied's motions for summary judgment and dismissed the case in its entirety. This appeal followed.

THE EMPLOYEE POLYGRAPH PROTECTION ACT

The district court entered summary judgment in favor of Allied on Calbillo's EPPA claims after concluding that Allied was not an employer subject to liability under the EPPA. The court observed that in order for Calbillo to recover under the EPPA, Allied must qualify as an "employer" as defined by the EPPA. The court further adopted the view that the determination of whether a polygraph examiner is an employer under the EPPA requires consideration of whether the examiner exerted control, as a matter of economic reality, over the employer's compliance with the EPPA. After reviewing Calbillo's allegations and the evidence put forth in support thereof, the court noted that most of the allegations concerned actions taken by Trease in his role as a private investigator, not as a polygraph examiner. Placing much emphasis on Hollas's "uncontroverted" affidavit concerning Trease's role, the court concluded that, other than Calbillo's speculation to the contrary, there was no evidence that Trease, acting in his role as investigator or polygraph examiner, exerted control over Cavender's compliance with the EPPA. The court found it compelling that "the decision to polygraph, who to polygraph, and the decision to terminate" were all ultimately made by Cavender.

Calbillo argues that summary judgment on his EPPA claim was inappropriate because a genuine issue of material fact exists as to whether Allied qualified as an employer under the EPPA. Calbillo's appeal thus presents an issue of first impression in this circuit: whether and under what circumstances a polygraph examiner is an "employer" within the meaning of the EPPA's definition of that term. The EPPA makes it illegal for an employer to require or request that an employee take a polygraph examination. Employers are also prohibited from discharging any employee who fails or refuses to take a polygraph examination. Congress created a limited exemption that permits an employer to request an employee to submit to a polygraph examination if it "is administered in connection with an ongoing investigation involving economic loss or injury to the employer's business, such as theft." The EPPA provides for private enforcement by creating a cause of action for employees against "an *employer* who violates [the EPPA] . . . for such legal or equitable relief as may be appropriate." The EPPA defines an "employer" as "any person acting directly or indirectly in the interest of an employer in relation to an employee or prospective employee." Pursuant to the Secretary of Labor's duty to "issue such rules and regulations as may be necessary or appropriate to carry out [the EPPA]," the Secretary promulgated the following regulation:

The term *employer* means any person acting directly or indirectly in the interest of an employer in relation to an employee or prospective employee. A polygraph examiner either employed for or whose services are otherwise retained for the sole purpose of administering polygraph tests ordinarily would not be deemed an employer with respect to the examinees.

Conclusion

We AFFIRM the district court's grant of summary judgment in favor of Allied.

Case Commentary

The Fifth Circuit Court ruled that the EPPA applies to employers. Allied was not Calbillo's employer, but rather was hired by Calbillo's employer. ■

CASE QUESTIONS

1. Are you in favor of the court's reasoning?
2. Why do you believe Calbillo sued Allied?

3. Do you think Cavender is in violation of the EPPA?

A polygraph test may also be administrated to an employee against whom the employer has a reasonable suspicion for believing the employee is involved in a theft of property or information. The lie-detector test may be administrated as part of an investigation. The employer must submit a signed statement setting forth the specific property misappropriated or the damage that may be caused by the transfer of the secret information, the access the employee had to the property or information, and why the employer believes the employee was involved in a theft.

When a polygraph test is administered, the questions must relate to the job and to general matters for the purpose of determining the subject's veracity. Questions about private personal matters unrelated to the business are not permitted.

Employment Perspective

Linda Merrit applies for a job with Bull and Bear Securities Firm. The firm requires Linda to take a polygraph test. She consents. The questions include Linda's religious affiliation, political affiliation, beliefs on race relations, sex life, and labor unions. Linda feels very uncomfortable about divulging her answers to these private matters. Has Bull and Bear conducted the polygraph examination in accord with the EPPA? No! Questions relating to these matters are prohibited by the act.

Polygraph Licensing

The polygraph examiner must be licensed by the state if so required and must post a substantial bond of professional liability coverage. The examiner's conclusion must be derived solely from the polygraph charts and cannot be based on a subjective evaluation. The examiner can give no opinion on whether the employer should hire the person examined. Disclosure of the results of a polygraph may be given only to the employee, employer who commissioned the test, and a court, should the matter arise in the course of litigation. The pertinent provisions of the EPPA must be conspicuously posted in the workplace.

DRUG TESTING

Businesses lose many billions of dollars each year because of employee drug use. Employees using drugs are less productive. The quality of their work is suspect because of impairment to their reasoning capabilities. Drug users may be negligent in the assembly of a product; the driving of a motor vehicle, train, or airplane; the security of documents, currency, office, or other real or personal property; and the preparation of food and beverages. The list goes on and on. Employees who use drugs are have a much higher rate of absenteeism, and they file more workers' compensation claims. Employee drug users may also steal from their company to support their drug habit. Employers wish to safeguard against abuses by drug users that could jeopardize the safety of the company, its employees, and its customers. To do so, many companies beef up security, increase supervision, create drug-rehabilitation programs, propagate the antidrug message, advocate a drug-free work environment through a written policy conspicuously posted in the workplace, and test for drugs.

Fourth Amendment

The use of drug testing is a volatile issue because of concern about privacy. The argument put forth against drug testing because it infringes on a person's privacy is based on the Fourth Amendment. The Fourth Amendment affords individuals the right to be secure in their person, property, and effects; individuals do not have to submit to unreasonable searches and seizures. Opponents of drug testing claim that mandating a person to turn over a sample of his or her urine, blood, saliva, or hair is an infringement on the right of that person to be secure in his or her person, because the bodily fluids and the hair are seized for the purpose of subjecting them to a search for illegal drug contaminants. Proponents of drug testing argue that search and seizure are not unreasonable in light of the pervasiveness of employee theft and the potential harm that may result to the drug user, coworkers, or customers in the work environment.

Reasonable Suspicion Drug Testing

When applying the Fourth Amendment, there must be probable cause to believe that the person committed a crime before a warrant will be issued to conduct a search. The standard for reasonable suspicion drug testing is less strict. It may be justified when an employer can document its reasonable suspicion. Suspicion-based drug testing requires that an employer have a reasonable suspicion that the employee is using drugs before a drug test can be required. A reasonable suspicion exists where a rational inference can be drawn from the facts and circumstances in the employment. Suspicion-based drug testing may be undertaken at any time during the worker's employment upon the satisfaction of the following criteria: reasonable suspicion that the employee is selling or using drugs; is in possession of drugs or alcohol at the workplace; is working under the influence of drugs or alcohol; is exhibiting significant behavioral changes that may be related to the use of drugs or alcohol; is engaging in criminal activity with a connection to the sale or use of drugs or alcohol; or is involved in an accident while operating in an impaired state. The employer must document in writing the circumstances that formed the basis for the reasonable suspicion that led to the requirement of the drug testing. The sources of information must be credible. The legitimate interests of the employer are balanced against the intrusion on an individual's physical solitude. In those cases where random drug testing has been found permissible, the need must overwhelmingly outweigh the unwanted invasion of privacy.

Employment Perspective

Victory College's administrators are arch-conservatives who abhor the use of drugs and alcohol. The college institutes a policy that all faculty and staff submit to drug testing at the beginning of each semester. The faculty and staff claim the drug testing is an invasion of their privacy and that the invasion of privacy is not outweighed by the college's need to know. Who will win? Most likely the faculty and staff. Although the use of drugs always impairs an employee's ability to function, the implementation of a drug-testing program will be allowed where the safety of the public or the security of the workplace is at issue. The college has not shown this to be the case.

The following is the first major drug-testing case dealing with the right to a suspicionless search of employees' blood and urine samples.

Skinner v. Railway Labor Executives' Assn.
489 U.S. 602 (1989)

Justice Kennedy delivered the opinion of the Court.

The Federal Railroad Safety Act of 1970 authorizes the Secretary of Transportation to "prescribe, as necessary, appropriate rules, regulations, orders, and standards for all areas of railroad safety." Finding that alcohol and drug abuse by railroad employees poses a serious threat to safety, the Federal Railroad Administration (FRA) has promulgated regulations that mandate blood and urine tests of employees who are involved in certain train accidents. The FRA also has adopted regulations that do not require, but do authorize, railroads to administer breath and urine tests to employees who violate certain safety rules. The question presented by this case is whether these regulations violate the Fourth Amendment.

I

A

The problem of alcohol use on American railroads is as old as the industry itself, and efforts to deter it by carrier rules began at least a century ago. For many years, railroads have prohibited operating employees from possessing alcohol or being intoxicated while on duty and from consuming alcoholic beverages while subject to being called for duty. More recently, these proscriptions have been expanded to forbid possession or use of certain drugs. These restrictions are embodied in "Rule G," an industry-wide operating rule promulgated by the Association of American Railroads, and enforced, in various formulations, by virtually every railroad in the country. The customary sanction for Rule G violations is dismissal.

Comments submitted in response to this request indicated that railroads were able to detect a relatively small number of Rule G violations, owing, primarily, to their practice of relying on observation by supervisors and co-workers to enforce the rule. At the same time, "industry participants . . . confirmed that alcohol and drug use did occur on the railroads with unacceptable frequency," and available information from all sources "suggested that the problem included 'pockets' of drinking and drug use involving multiple crew members (before and during work), sporadic cases of

individuals reporting to work impaired, and repeated drinking and drug use by individual employees who are chemically or psychologically dependent on those substances." "Even without the benefit of regular post-accident testing," the FRA "identified 34 fatalities, 66 injuries and over $28 million in property damage (in 1983 dollars) that resulted from the errors of alcohol and drug-impaired employees in 45 train accidents and train incidents during the period 1975 through 1983." Some of these accidents resulted in the release of hazardous materials and, in one case, the ensuing pollution required the evacuation of an entire Louisiana community. In view of the obvious safety hazards of drug and alcohol use by railroad employees, the FRA announced in June 1984 its intention to promulgate federal regulations on the subject.

B

After reviewing further comments from representatives of the railroad industry, labor groups, and the general public, the FRA, in 1985, promulgated regulations addressing the problem of alcohol and drugs on the railroads. The regulations prohibit covered employees from using or possessing alcohol or any controlled substance. The regulations further prohibit those employees from reporting for covered service while under the influence of, or impaired by, alcohol, while having a blood alcohol concentration of 0.04 or more, or while under the influence of, or impaired by, any controlled substance. The regulations do not restrict, however, a railroad's authority to impose an absolute prohibition on the presence of alcohol or any drug in the body fluids of persons in its employ, and, accordingly, they do not "replace Rule G or render it unenforceable."

The FRA proposes to place primary reliance on analysis of blood samples, as blood is "the only available body fluid . . . that can provide a clear indication not only of the presence of alcohol and drugs but also their current impairment effects." Urine samples are also necessary, however, because drug traces remain in the urine longer than in blood, and in some cases it will not be possible to transport employees to a medical facility before the time it takes for certain drugs to be eliminated from the bloodstream. In those instances, a "positive urine test, taken with specific information on the pattern of elimination for the particular drug and other information on the behavior of the employee and the circumstances of the accident, may be crucial to the determination of" the cause of an accident. The regulations require that the FRA notify employees of the results of the tests and afford them an opportunity to respond in writing before preparation of any final investigative report. Employees who refuse to provide required blood or urine samples may not perform covered service for nine months, but they are entitled to a hearing concerning their refusal to take the test.

Respondents, the Railway Labor Executives' Association and various of its member labor organizations, brought the instant suit in the United States District Court for the Northern District of California, seeking to enjoin the FRA's regulations on various statutory and constitutional grounds. A divided panel of the Court of Appeals for the Ninth Circuit reversed.

We granted the federal parties' petition for a writ of certiorari, to consider whether the regulations invalidated by the Court of Appeals violate the Fourth Amendment. We now reverse.

II
A

We have long recognized that a "compelled intrusion into the body for blood to be analyzed for alcohol content" must be deemed a Fourth Amendment search.

The Government's interest in regulating the conduct of railroad employees to ensure safety, like its supervision of probationers or regulated industries, or its operation of a government office, school, or prison, "likewise presents 'special needs' beyond normal law enforcement that may justify departures from the usual warrant and probable-cause requirements." The hours of service employees covered by the FRA regulations include persons engaged in handling orders concerning train movements, operating crews, and those engaged in the maintenance and repair of signal systems. It is undisputed that these and other covered employees are engaged in safety-sensitive tasks.

Our cases indicate that even a search that may be performed without a warrant must be based, as a general matter, on probable cause to believe that the person to be searched has violated the law. When the balance of interests precludes insistence on a showing of probable cause, we have usually required "some quantum of individualized suspicion" before concluding that a search is reasonable. We make it clear, however, that a showing of individualized suspicion is not a constitutional floor, below which a search must be presumed unreasonable. In limited circumstances, where the privacy interests implicated by the search are minimal, and where an important governmental interest furthered by the intrusion would be placed in jeopardy by a requirement of individualized suspicion, a search may be reasonable despite the absence of such suspicion.

We believe this is true of the intrusions in question here.

More importantly, the expectations of privacy of covered employees are diminished by reason of their participation in an industry that is regulated pervasively to ensure safety, a goal dependent, in substantial part, on the health and fitness of covered employees. By contrast, the Government interest in testing without a showing of individualized suspicion is compelling. Employees subject to the tests discharge duties fraught with such risks of injury to others that even a momentary lapse of attention can have disastrous consequences.

While no procedure can identify all impaired employees with ease and perfect accuracy, the FRA regulations supply an effective means of deterring employees engaged in safety-sensitive tasks from using controlled substances or alcohol in the first place. The railroad industry's experience with Rule G persuasively shows, and common sense confirms, that the customary dismissal sanction that threatens employees who use drugs or alcohol while on duty cannot serve as an effective deterrent unless violators know that they are likely to be discovered. By ensuring that employees in safety-sensitive positions know they will be tested upon the occurrence of a triggering event, the timing of which no employee can predict with certainty, the regulations significantly increase the deterrent effect of the administrative penalties associated with the prohibited conduct, thereby increasing the likelihood that employees will forgo using drugs or alcohol while subject to being called for duty.

We conclude that the compelling Government interests served by the FRA's regulations would be significantly hindered if railroads were required to point to specific facts giving rise to a reasonable suspicion of impairment before testing a given employee. In view of our conclusion that, on the present record, the toxicological testing contemplated by the regulations is not an undue infringement on the justifiable expectations of privacy of covered employees, the Government's compelling interests outweigh privacy concerns.

In light of the limited discretion exercised by the railroad employers under the regulations, the surpassing safety interests served by toxicological tests in this context, and the diminished expectation of privacy that attaches to information pertaining to the fitness of covered employees, we believe that it is reasonable to conduct such tests in the absence of a warrant or reasonable suspicion that any particular employee may be impaired. We hold that the alcohol and drug tests contemplated by the FRA's regulations are reasonable within the meaning of the Fourth Amendment. The judgment of the Court of Appeals is accordingly reversed.

Judgment for Railway Labor Executives' Assn.

JUSTICE MARSHALL, with whom JUSTICE BRENNAN joins, dissenting.

The issue in this case is not whether declaring a war on illegal drugs is good public policy. The importance of ridding our society of such drugs is, by now, apparent to all. Rather, the issue here is whether the Government's deployment in that war of a particularly Draconian weapon—the compulsory collection and chemical testing of railroad workers' blood and urine—comports with the Fourth Amendment. Precisely because the need for action against the drug scourge is manifest, the need for vigilance against unconstitutional excess is great. History teaches that grave threats to liberty often come in times of urgency, when constitutional rights seem too extravagant to endure.

In permitting the Government to force entire railroad crews to submit to invasive blood and urine tests, even when it lacks any evidence of drug or alcohol use or other wrongdoing, the majority today joins those shortsighted courts which have allowed basic constitutional rights to fall prey to momentary emergencies. The majority holds that the need of the Federal Railroad Administration (FRA) to deter and diagnose train accidents outweighs any "minimal" intrusions on personal dignity and privacy posed by mass toxicological testing of persons who have given no indication whatsoever of impairment. In reaching this result, the majority ignores the text and doctrinal history of the Fourth Amendment, which require that highly intrusive searches of this type be based on probable cause, not on the evanescent cost-benefit calculations of agencies or judges.

The majority purports to limit its decision to postaccident testing of workers in "safety-sensitive" jobs, much as it limits its holding in the companion case to the testing of transferees to jobs involving drug interdiction or the use of firearms. But the damage done to the Fourth Amendment is not so easily cabined. The majority's acceptance of dragnet blood and urine testing ensures that the first, and worst, casualty of the war on drugs will be the precious liberties of our citizens. I therefore dissent.

For the reasons stated above, I find nothing minimal about the intrusion on individual liberty that occurs whenever the Government forcibly draws and analyzes a person's blood and urine. Several aspects of the FRA's testing program exacerbate the intrusiveness of these procedures. Most strikingly, the agency's regulations not only do not forbid, but, in fact, appear to invite criminal prosecutors to obtain the blood and urine samples drawn by the FRA and use them as the basis of criminal investigations and trials. This is an unprecedented invitation, leaving open the possibility of criminal prosecutions based on suspicionless searches of the human body.

Case Commentary
Justices Marshall and Brennan believe suspicionless searches contravene the Fourth Amendment prohibition against unreasonable searches and seizures. They believe a search must be based on probable cause. The majority agrees that probable cause is necessary in criminal cases, but not in civil cases where public safety is at issue. ■

CASE QUESTIONS

1. Are Justices Marshall and Brennan correct in this case?
2. Do you need probable cause in all cases?

3. Why are the dissenting justices opposed to suspicionless drug testing?
4. What are they afraid will happen?

The issue in the following case is whether a suspicionless search is justified for Gubernatorial candidates.

Chandler v. Miller
520 U.S. 305 (1997)

Justice Ginsburg delivered the opinion of the Court.
The Fourth Amendment requires government to respect "the right of the people to be secure in their persons . . . against unreasonable searches and seizures." This restraint on government conduct generally bars officials from undertaking a search or seizure absent individualized suspicion. Searches conducted without grounds for suspicion of particular individuals have been upheld, however, in "certain limited circumstances." These circumstances include brief stops for questioning or observation at a fixed Border Patrol checkpoint, or at a sobriety checkpoint, and administrative inspections in "closely regulated" businesses.

Georgia requires candidates for designated state offices to certify that they have taken a drug test and that the test result was negative. We confront in this case the question whether that requirement ranks among the limited circumstances in which suspicionless searches are warranted. Relying on this Court's precedents sustaining drug testing programs for student athletes, customs employees, and railway employees, the United States Court of Appeals for the Eleventh Circuit judged Georgia's law constitutional. We reverse that judgment. Georgia's requirement that candidates for state office pass a drug test, we hold, does not fit within the closely guarded category of constitutionally permissible suspicionless searches.

The prescription at issue, approved by the Georgia Legislature in 1990, orders that "each candidate seeking to qualify for nomination or election to a state office shall as a condition of such qualification be required to certify that such candidate has tested negative for illegal drugs." Georgia was the first, and apparently remains the only, State to condition candidacy for state office on a drug test.

Under the Georgia statute, to qualify for a place on the ballot, a candidate must present a certificate from a state approved laboratory, in a form approved by the Secretary of State, reporting that the candidate submitted to a urinalysis drug test within 30 days prior to qualifying for nomination or election and that the results were negative. The statute lists as "illegal drugs": marijuana, cocaine, opiates, amphetamines, and phencyclidines. The designated state offices are: "the Governor, Lieutenant Governor, Secretary of State, Attorney General, State School Superintendent, Commissioner of Insurance, Commissioner of Agriculture, Commissioner of Labor, Justices of the Supreme Court, Judges of the Court of Appeals, judges of the superior courts, district attorneys, members of the General Assembly, and members of the Public Service Commission."

Petitioners were Libertarian Party nominees in 1994 for state offices. The Party nominated Walker L. Chandler for the office of Lieutenant Governor, Sharon T. Harris for the office of Commissioner of Agriculture, and James D. Walker for the office of member of the General Assembly. In May 1994, about one month before the deadline for submission of the certificates petitioners Chandler, Harris, and Walker filed this action in the United States District Court for the Northern District of Georgia. They asserted that the drug tests violated their rights under the First, Fourth, and Fourteenth Amendments to the United States Constitution. In June 1994, the District Court denied petitioners' motion for a preliminary injunction. Stressing the importance of the state offices sought and the relative unintrusiveness of the testing procedure, the court found it unlikely that petitioners would prevail on the merits of their claims. Petitioners apparently submitted to the drug tests, obtained the certificates and appeared on the ballot. After the 1994 election, the parties jointly moved for the entry of final judgment on stipulated facts. In January 1995, the District Court entered final judgment for respondents.

A divided Eleventh Circuit panel affirmed. It is settled law, the court accepted, that the drug tests required by the statute rank as searches. We granted the petition for certiorari and now reverse.

To be reasonable under the Fourth Amendment, a search ordinarily must be based on individualized suspicion of wrongdoing. But particularized exceptions to the main rule are sometimes warranted based on "special needs, beyond the normal need for law enforcement." When such "special needs"—concerns other than crime detection—are alleged in justification of a Fourth Amendment intrusion, courts must undertake a context specific inquiry, examining closely the competing private and public interests advanced by the parties. "In limited circumstances, where the privacy interests implicated by the search are minimal, and where an important governmental interest furthered by the intrusion would be placed in jeopardy by a requirement of individualized suspicion, a search may be reasonable despite the absence of such suspicion." In evaluating Georgia's ballot access, drug testing statute—a measure plainly not tied to individualized suspicion—the Eleventh Circuit sought to "'balance the individual's privacy expectations against the State's interests,'" in line with our precedents most immediately in point: Skinner, Von Raab, and Vernonia.

In Von Raab, the Court sustained a United States Customs Service program that made drug tests a condition of promotion or transfer to positions directly involving drug interdiction or requiring the employee to carry a firearm. While the Service's regime was not prompted by a demonstrated drug abuse problem, it was developed for an agency with an "almost unique mission," as the "first line of defense" against the smuggling of illicit drugs into the United States. Work directly involving drug interdiction and posts that require the employee to carry a firearm pose grave safety threats to employees who hold those positions, and also expose them to large amounts of illegal narcotics and to persons engaged in crime; illicit drug users in such high risk positions might be unsympathetic to the Service's mission, tempted by bribes, or even threatened with blackmail. The Court held that the government had a "compelling" interest in assuring that employees placed in these positions would not include drug users. Individualized suspicion would not work in this setting, the Court determined, because it was "not feasible to subject these employees and their work product to the kind of day to day scrutiny that is the norm in more traditional office environments."

Finally, in Vernonia, the Court sustained a random drug testing program for high school students engaged in inter-scholastic athletic competitions. The program's context was critical, for local governments bear large "responsibilities, under a public school system, as guardian and tutor of children entrusted to its care." An "immediate crisis," caused by "a sharp increase in drug use" in the school district, sparked installation of the program. District Court findings established that student athletes were not only "among the drug users," they were "leaders of the drug culture." Our decision noted that "'students within the school environment have a lesser expectation of privacy than members of the population generally.'" We emphasized the importance of deterring drug use by schoolchildren and the risk of injury a drug using student athlete cast on himself and those engaged with him on the playing field.

Turning to those guides, we note, first, that the testing method the Georgia statute describes is relatively noninvasive; therefore, if the "special need" showing had been made, the State could not be faulted for excessive intrusion. Our precedents establish that the proffered special need for drug testing must be substantial—important enough to override the individual's acknowledged privacy interest, sufficiently vital to suppress the Fourth Amendment's normal requirement of individualized suspicion. Georgia has failed to show a special need of that kind.

The statute was not enacted in response to any fear or suspicion of drug use by state officials:

"QUESTION: Is there any indication anywhere in this record that Georgia has a particular problem here with State officeholders being drug abusers?

"COUNSEL FOR RESPONDENTS: No, there is no such evidence. . . . and to be frank, there is no such problem as we sit here today."

A demonstrated problem of drug abuse, while not in all cases necessary to the validity of a testing regime would shore up an assertion of special need for a suspicionless general search program. Proof of unlawful drug use may help to clarify—and to substantiate—the precise hazards posed by such use. Thus, the evidence of drug and alcohol use by railway employees engaged in safety sensitive tasks in *Skinner*, and the immediate crisis prompted by a sharp rise in students' use of unlawful drugs in *Vernonia*, bolstered the government's and school officials' arguments that drug testing programs were warranted and appropriate.

In contrast to the effective testing regimes upheld in *Skinner, Von Raab*, and *Vernonia*, Georgia's certification requirement is not well designed to identify candidates who violate antidrug laws. Nor is the scheme a credible means to deter illicit drug users from seeking election to state office. The test date—to be scheduled by the candidate anytime within 30 days prior to qualifying for a place on the ballot—is no secret. As counsel for respondents acknowledged at oral argument, users of illegal drugs, save for those prohibitively addicted, could abstain for a pretest period sufficient to avoid detection. Moreover, respondents have offered no reason why ordinary law enforcement methods would not suffice to apprehend such addicted individuals, should they appear in the limelight of a public stage.

However well meant, the candidate drug test Georgia has devised diminishes personal privacy for a symbol's sake. The Fourth Amendment shields society against that state action.

We reiterate, too, that where the risk to public safety is substantial and real, blanket suspicionless searches calibrated to the risk may rank as "reasonable"—for example, searches now routine at airports and at entrances to courts and other official buildings. But where, as in this case, public safety is not genuinely in jeopardy, the Fourth Amendment precludes the suspicionless search, no matter how conveniently arranged.

For the reasons stated,
the judgment of the Court of Appeals
for the Eleventh Circuit is *Reversed*.

Case Commentary

This case appears to be at odds with the Sixth Circuit decision in the Knox County Association case. In that case, a suspicionless search of schoolteachers and administrators was justified because of their influence and supervision of children. Here, the Supreme Court appears to believe that the public safety is not in jeopardy. But, the governor has authority over the state police and national guard within the state. Applying the Supreme Court's reasoning to the Knox case would probably lead to a different result. ■

CASE QUESTIONS

1. Is the Supreme Court correct that the public safety would not be endangered if the governor was a drug user?

2. What criteria determine whether to implement suspicionless drug testing?

3. In what occupations do you believe suspicionless drug testing is warranted?

Suspicionless Drug Testing

In 1989, the U.S. Supreme Court legitimized suspicionless drug testing for two distinct classes of workers: railroad employees involved in accidents or who violated safety regulations and customs agents carrying firearms or detecting drug smuggling. In *Skinner v. Railway Labor Executives' Assn.*, there had been a history of substance abuse by railroad workers. The Supreme Court ruled that the public safety interest was so compelling as to warrant the urine test to detect the presence of controlled substances. It further reasoned that the deterrence of drug and alcohol use in railroad operations outweighed the privacy concerns of railroad employees. This balancing test has become a standard.

In *National Treasury Employees Union v. Von Raab*, a suspicionless drug test was challenged by customs agents because they had no history of drug or alcohol abuse. While acknowledging that a search is usually conducted pursuant to a warrant or based on probable cause, the Supreme Court stated that a search may be undertaken where special needs arise that are so compelling as to outweigh the individuals' privacy concerns that are invaded. In *Von Raab*, the Supreme Court invoked a special needs test for national security and protection of U.S. borders. The court decided these special needs could be compromised by drug and alcohol use. However, the urine test provides no protection against customs agents taking bribes or taking possession of drugs for resale. The suspicionless drug test was limited to applications and promotions to jobs involving the detection of drug smuggling or the carrying of a firearm. The Supreme Court stated that each case involving postemployment suspicionless drug testing must be evaluated based on its own special needs.

In 1995, the Supreme Court confronted a random drug-testing policy designed to control rampant drug use by student athletes initiated by the Vernonia School District in a Portland, Oregon, high school. The court acknowledged the support of the local school board and the majority of the parents. The random drug test is limited to the season of the interscholastic sport in which they participate. The court refrained from mandating a national policy. It reasoned that each community should decide what measures need to be taken should a drug problem arise. The court will act as a reviewer balancing the interests of the community against those of the individuals who will be subjected to the suspicionless drug test. The Supreme Court cautioned that each case would be evaluated based on its own circumstances. In 2002, it reached a similar conclusion in the *Board of Education of Pottawatomie County* case.

In 1997, the Supreme Court ruled against requiring candidates for political office to pass a drug test. The court reasoned that the privacy interests of the gubernatorial candidates outweighed the need for drug testing because no compelling reason had been set forth. There was no history of drug use or interaction with drug smugglers.

In 2001, the Supreme Court ruled against a suspicionless drug-testing policy of pregnant women by a hospital in Charleston. The hospital notified the police, who arrested those women who tested positive. The women were threatened with prosecution unless they entered a drug treatment program. The compelling need to deter pregnant women from using drugs was not found to be legitimate because of the circumstances under which the drug tests were taken.

Suspicion-based drug testing is supported by probable cause. Suspicionless drug testing is not. Preemployment drug testing is suspicionless. It has been upheld in most cases. Postemployment drug testing has been granted in limited circumstances (i.e., *Skinner* and *Von Raab*). In these cases, the suspicionless drug test was triggered by a certain event. They were not random.

Postemployment suspicionless drug testing may contain a random component. A number of federal and state courts have upheld this involving police officers, firefighters, airport mechanics, chemical weapons workers, and nuclear power plant engineers. The Supreme Court has never sanctioned this in an employment case. Neither has the court held this was prohibited in private employment. The only situation where the Supreme Court supported random drug testing involved drug use among students in extracurricular activities in the *Vernonia* and the *Board of Education of Pottawatomie County* cases.

Random drug testing presents a greater invasion of privacy than drug testing based upon a reasonable suspicion because everyone in the designated group is a potential candidate for drug testing. However, when a person is required to undergo a drug test based upon a reasonable suspicion, an immediate stigma of guilt attaches, which is not the case with random drug testing.

The issue in the following case is whether schoolteachers should be subject to a suspicionless test of their urine for drugs upon being offered a teaching position and a suspicion-based test of their urine at any other time during their employment because their position of looking after the well-being of children is safety sensitive.

Knox County Education Association v. Knox County Board of Education

158 F.3d 361 (6th Cir. 1998)

Rosen, District Judge.

BACKGROUND

Plaintiff Knox County Education Association ("KCEA"), which represents professional employees in the Knox County School System, initiated this action to challenge drug and alcohol testing procedures adopted by Defendant Knox County Board of Education ("Board"), which is the body responsible for the administration, management, and control of the Knox County School System. In the District Court, KCEA made a facial attack on the Board's "Drug-Free Workplace Substance Abuse Policy," seeking declaratory and injunctive relief. The policy establishes two different levels of testing: (1) suspicionless drug testing for all individuals who apply for, transfer to, or are promoted to, "safety sensitive" positions within the Knox County School system, including teaching positions; and (2) "reasonable suspicion" drug and/or alcohol testing of all school employees. KCEA challenged both testing programs as violative of the Fourth Amendment's prohibition against unreasonable searches and seizures.

Facts

Thirty-two hundred teachers are employed in the Knox County Schools.

1994 Drug Testing Policy The Policy describes its goals and objectives as follows:

1. To establish, promote, and maintain a safe, healthy, working and learning environment for employees and students.
2. To aid the affected employee in locating a rehabilitation program for employees with self-admitted or detected substance abuse problem.
3. To promote the reputation of the Knox County School System and its employees as responsible citizens of public trust and employment.
4. To eliminate substance abuse problems in the workplace.
5. To aid in the reduction of absenteeism, tardiness, and apathetic job performance.
6. To provide a clear standard of job performance for Knox County Schools employees.
7. To provide a consistent model of substance-free behavior for students.

1. *Suspicionless Testing* The Policy allows suspicionless testing for people applying for positions that are "safety sensitive." The Policy defines "safety sensitive" positions as those positions "where a single mistake by such employee can create an immediate threat of serious harm to students and fellow employees." According to the Policy, and consistent with the ruling in KCEA I, this category includes principals, assistant principals, teachers, traveling teachers, teacher aides, substitute teachers, school secretaries and school bus drivers. Applicants for these positions are tested after they are offered a job but before their employment has commenced (i.e., post-offer, pre-employment). They are to be given a copy of the Policy in advance of the physical and are to sign an acknowledgment prior to substance screening, permitting the summary result to be transmitted to the Medical Review Officer ("MRO") and Director of Personnel. An applicant refusing to complete any part of the drug testing procedure will not be considered a valid candidate for employment with the school system, and such refusal will be considered as a withdrawal of the individual's application for employment. If substance screening shows a confirmed positive result for which there is no current physician's prescription, a second confirming test may be requested by the MRO. If the first or any requested second confirming test is positive, any job offer will be revoked.

Current employees attempting to transfer into safety sensitive positions—including those who already hold such positions—are also tested. Employees who test positive for illegal drugs on a promotion/transfer test will no longer be considered an applicant for that position. Employees seeking a transfer or promotion who refuse any portion of the drug testing procedure forfeit the opportunity to transfer to, or advance into, a safety sensitive position and are subject to discipline for insubordination (including termination).

2. *Reasonable Suspicion Testing* Section .05 of the Policy provides for drug and/or alcohol screening based upon reasonable suspicion as follows:

Whenever the Knox County Board of Education, through its Director of Personnel or the person authorized to act as the Director in the Director's absence, and/or the Medical Review Officer, reasonably suspects that an employee's work performance or on-the-job behavior may have been affected in any way by illegal drugs or alcohol, or that an employee has otherwise violated the Knox County Board of Education Drug-Free Workplace Substance Abuse Policy, the employee may be required to submit a breath and/or urine sample for drug and alcohol testing. When a supervisor observes or is notified of behavior or events that lead the supervisor to believe that the employee is in violation of the Drug-Free Workplace Substance Abuse Policy, the Supervisor should notify the Director of Personnel.

An employee who is required to submit to drug/alcohol testing based upon such reasonable suspicion and refuses will be charged with insubordination and subject to the disciplinary sanctions, including possible termination.

Further, an employee testing positive on a reasonable suspicion test will be found to be in violation of the Policy, and such a violation will constitute grounds for termination. The Policy notes that the School System Director of Personnel, or the person authorized to act in that person's absence, or the MRO are the only individuals in the Knox County School System authorized to make a determination that reasonable suspicion, or cause, exists to order a drug screen, and are the only individuals in the School System who may order an employee to submit to a drug screen.

The Policy describes two types of cases for which the reasonable suspicion procedures may be invoked:

(1) Chronic case

Deteriorating job performance or changes in personal traits characteristics where the use of alcohol or drugs may be reasonably suspected as the cause. These cases may develop over a fairly long period of time.

(2) Acute case

Appearing in a specific incident or observation to then be under the present influence of alcohol and/or drugs is reasonably suspected to be a contributing cause. Regardless of previous history, immediate action is necessary.

The Policy further enumerates the circumstances under which substance screening may be considered, which include, but are not limited to, the following:

1. Observed use, possession, or sale of illegal drugs and/or use, possession, sale, or abuse of alcohol and/or the illegal use or sale of prescription drugs.
2. Apparent physical state of impairment of motor functions.
3. Marked changes in personal behavior not attributable to other factors.
4. Employee involvement in or contribution to an accident where the use of alcohol or drugs is reasonably suspected or employee involvement in a pattern of repetitive accidents, whether or not they involve actual or potential injury.
5. Violations of criminal drug law statutes involving the use of illegal drugs, alcohol, or prescription drugs and/or violations of drug statutes.

The above circumstances under which substance screening may be considered "are strictly limited in time and place to employee conduct on duty or during work hours, or on or in Knox County Board of Education property, or at school system-approved or school related functions."

3. *Testing Procedures*   Section .11 of the Policy describes the drug and alcohol abuse testing procedures. The Board has designated a physician as the MRO. The MRO is responsible for reviewing the results of drug tests before they are reported to the Board's Director of Personnel; reviewing and interpreting each confirmed positive test to determine if there is an alternative medical explanation for the positive result; conducting an interview with the individual testing positive; reviewing the individual's medical history and medical records to determine if the positive result was caused by legally prescribed medication; requiring re-test of the original specimen if the MRO deems it necessary; and verifying that the laboratory report and the specimen are correct. The initial test performed on the urine at the laboratory will be an Enzyme-Multiplied Immunoassay Technique (EMIT) screen which will be used to eliminate negative urine specimens from further consideration. All specimens identified as positive on the initial test will then be confirmed using gas chromatography/mass spectrometry (GC/MS) techniques.

ANALYSIS

The Fourth Amendment safeguards the privacy of individuals against arbitrary and unwarranted governmental intrusions by providing that "the right of the people to be secure in their persons, houses, papers, and effects against unreasonable searches and seizures, shall not be violated." However, "the Fourth Amendment does not proscribe all searches and seizures, but only those that are unreasonable." It is now well-settled that drug testing which utilizes urinalysis is a "search" that falls within the ambit of the Fourth Amendment

A. Suspicionless Testing   As a general rule, in order to be reasonable, a search must be undertaken pursuant to a warrant issued upon a showing of probable cause. But particularized exceptions to the main rule are sometimes warranted based on "special needs, beyond the normal need for law enforcement." In evaluating the constitutionality of the Board's drug testing Policy here, we must balance the government's (or public's) interest in testing against the individual's privacy interest.

1. *Public Interest in Testing*   With regard to the government's interest in testing, the Supreme Court has traditionally focused its analysis on two central factors: (1) whether the group of people targeted for testing exhibits a pronounced drug problem; and, if not, whether the group occupies a unique position such that the existence of a pronounced drug problem is unnecessary to justify suspicionless testing; and (2) the magnitude of the harm that could result from the use of illicit drugs on the job.

   In this case, there is little, if any, evidence of a pronounced drug or alcohol abuse problem among Knox County's teachers or other professional employees. The second factor we must consider in the balancing test analysis focuses on the magnitude of harm that could result from the use of illicit drugs in any given set of circumstances. The validity of this argument hinges in large part upon whether or not teachers, principals, and the other school officials covered by the testing actually occupy "safety-sensitive" positions.

The Court believes that a local school district has a strong and abiding interest in requiring that teachers and other school officials be drug-free so that they can satisfy their statutory obligation to ensure the safety and welfare of the children. The fact that the Board has not been able to cite any one specific example in which a teacher or other employee responsible for children has allowed any harm to the children by being in an impaired condition while on the job is certainly not dispositive of the question of whether teachers and administrators hold "safety-sensitive" positions. We do not believe that the Board must wait passively for a disaster to occur before taking preemptive action to minimize the risks of such an occurrence. Indeed, we have no doubt that if a tragedy were to befall one or more of the school children of Knox County that in some manner implicated a teacher or administrator being under the influence of an illegal substance, the members of that community would rightly question why the Board had not taken all efforts possible in advance to prevent such an occurrence.

2. *Privacy Interest of Employees* Having ruled that the public interest in suspicionless testing is very strong, an analysis of the employee's privacy rights is necessary to determine which of the competing values should prevail in this case. As will become evident in the course of this analysis, because teachers' legitimate expectation of privacy is diminished by their participation in a heavily regulated industry and by the nature of their job, the public interest in suspicionless testing outweighs that private interest.

For all of the reasons stated here, we believe that the privacy interest for the employees not to be tested is significantly diminished by the level of regulation of their jobs and by the nature of the work itself. The ultimate inquiry before the Court is whether the search at issue here—the one-time, suspicionless testing of people hired to serve in teaching and administrative positions—is reasonable. On balance, the public interest in attempting to ensure that school teachers perform their jobs unimpaired is evident, considering their unique *in loco parentis* obligations and their immense influence over students. These public interests clearly outweigh the privacy interests of the teacher not to be tested because the drug-testing regime adopted by Knox County is circumscribed, narrowly-tailored, and not overly intrusive, either in its monitoring procedures or in its disclosure requirements. This is particularly so because it is a one-time test, with advance notice and with no random testing component, and because the school system in which the employees work is heavily regulated, particularly as to drug usage.

Therefore, we REVERSE the District Court's finding this portion of the statute unconstitutional.

B. Suspicion-Based Testing The Court now turns to the suspicion-based testing, and finds that this portion of the Policy is also constitutional under the Fourth Amendment.

1. *Drug Testing* The Policy provides for testing of an employee if the Director of Personnel "reasonably suspects" that an employee's work performance or on-the-job behavior may have been affected by illegal drugs or alcohol. The Policy further enumerates the circumstances under which substance screening may be considered. These requirements of "reasonable cause" sufficiently limit the discretion of the officials administering the rule and, because the testing is clearly based upon a finding of individualized suspicion, this portion of the Policy comports with the reasonableness requirement of the Fourth Amendment. Thus, for these reasons and those identified by the District Court, we AFFIRM the District Court's ruling on this aspect of the suspicion-based testing program.

2. *Alcohol Testing* As the District Court noted, the record does not contain any evidence regarding whether the broad range of the alcohol testing and particularly the low threshold is reasonably related to the purpose of the testing, nor does it indicate the amount and timing of consumption that would result in that low level reading. Therefore, it is unclear from the record why the Board believes impairment at the relatively low .02 level is significant, and how that level is related to the purpose of the testing. It may be that there is no such nexus and, if this is so, this portion of the Policy is indeed unconstitutional. However, we cannot conclude that from this record (just as we cannot conclude that there is some relationship between the nature of the test and levels established and the identified need for testing). Therefore, the issue of whether this portion of the test is constitutional is REVERSED AND REMANDED to the District Court to determine whether the .02 level is reasonably related to the purpose of the testing.

Case Commentary

The Sixth Circuit Court decided that suspicionless testing is reasonable when individuals are hired for teaching or administrative positions. The court came to this conclusion even though drug use was not a widespread problem among teachers and staff. The decision is based on the influence teachers have and the supervisory role they play in the lives of their students. Other courts may differ as to the result. ■

CASE QUESTIONS

1. Does the teacher's position alone justify drug testing?
2. Should widespread drug use among teachers be required before drug testing is permitted?
3. Does the level set for alcohol consumption bear any relationship to impairment?
4. Would applying the Supreme Court's logic in *Chandler* lead to a different result in this case?

In the case that follows, the issue is whether suspicionless drug testing and its random testing component for police officers and firefighters satisfies the special needs test.

Anchorage Police Department Employees Association, and International Association of Fire Fighters v. Municipality of Anchorage

24 P.3d 547 (Sup. Ct. Alaska 2001)

Per Curiam.

In September 1994 the Municipality adopted Policy No. 40-24 ("the policy"). The policy provides for substance abuse testing, by urinalysis, of certain municipal employees (1) upon employment application, promotion, demotion, or transfer; (2) following a vehicular accident; (3) on reasonable suspicion; and (4) at random. All employees are subject to post-accident testing. Only employees in "public safety positions" are subject to random testing and to promotion/demotion/transfer testing. A public safety position is defined as "a position in the Police or Fire Department having a substantially significant degree of responsibility for the safety of the public where the unsafe performance of an incumbent could result in death or injury to self or others."

The Municipality policy at issue here requires Police Employees and Fire Fighters members to submit to urinalysis for purposes of disclosing potential substance abuse. The United States Supreme Court has held that urine testing conducted under analogous circumstances qualifies as a "search" for constitutional purposes:

> Because it is clear that the collection and testing of urine intrudes upon expectations of privacy that society has long recognized as reasonable, the Federal Courts of Appeals have concluded unanimously, and we agree, that these intrusions must be deemed searches under the Fourth Amendment.

In the present case, the superior court adopted the Supreme Court's "special needs" analysis as a guide for its own application of the Alaska Constitution's protection against unreasonable searches and seizures.

And as the superior court properly recognized here, "special needs" findings are especially appropriate when employment occurs "in a highly regulated, safety-essential field of work." Workers employed in such fields necessarily expect reduced privacy in their job-related activities and implicitly agree to a diminished level of privacy when they accept employment.

Fire Fighters nevertheless question whether firefighting is a heavily regulated activity, insisting that "Fire Fighters are not pervasively regulated for safety." More pertinent, in our view, is that members of Police Employees and Fire Fighters undeniably hold safety-sensitive positions in extensively regulated fields of activity where they "discharge duties fraught with risks of injury to others that even a momentary lapse of attention can have disastrous consequences." We believe that workers in such positions would reasonably expect that their conditions of employment would subject them to exceptionally close scrutiny.

Police Employees and Fire Fighters further allege that, even if the policy's provisions for suspicionless testing are not per se invalid, the superior court applied an improper privacy analysis in concluding that the policy meets article I, section 14's requirement of reasonableness. Insisting "that its members have a reasonable expectation of privacy in the collection and testing of their urine," Police Employees contends that the Municipality lacks a sufficiently compelling interest to override this privacy interest and that suspicionless urinalysis fails to provide a "close and substantial" means of meeting the Municipality's interest. Fire Fighters echoes these arguments, emphasizing its view that there can be no compelling need for suspicionless testing without proof of an existing substance abuse problem:

> The central objection which the Fire Fighters have to this policy is not one premised upon the intrusiveness of twenty-first century technology or medical science. It is not being subjected to the indignity of compelled urination. It is an objection which has its genesis in the two hundred year old Fourth Amendment: They do not, as individuals or as a group, have a drug problem. There is no "compelling need" which justifies divergence from the Fourth Amendment's main rule that searches must be made pursuant to individualized suspicion.

We find that these arguments are unpersuasive. In *Messerli v. State* we explained that the right to privacy is not absolute, but is subject to balancing against conflicting rights and interests. We concluded that, where a fundamental right is involved, the state must show a compelling state interest justifying its abridgement. More recently we reiterated the *Messerli* test in the following way:

1. does the party seeking to come within the protection of the right to privacy have a legitimate expectation that the materials or information will not be disclosed?

2. is disclosure nonetheless required to serve a compelling state interest?
3. if so, will the necessary disclosure occur in that manner which is least intrusive with respect to the right to privacy?

This test eschews absolute measures of privacy; it prescribes the same kind of flexibility that the Supreme Court described in *Vernonia*:

> It is a mistake, however, to think that the phrase "compelling state interest," in the Fourth Amendment context, describes a fixed, minimum quantum of governmental concern, so that one can dispose of a case by answering in isolation the question: Is there a compelling state interest here? Rather, the phrase describes an interest which appears important enough to justify the particular search at hand, in light of other factors which show the search be relatively intrusive upon a genuine expectation of privacy.

The touchstone of a compelling state interest, then, is simply that "the right to privacy must yield when it interferes in a serious manner with the health, safety, rights and privileges of others or with the public welfare."

We therefore decline to hold that a history of substance abuse problems is invariably necessary to establish a "special need" for suspicionless testing in situations involving heavily regulated, safety-sensitive job duties.

We note that the Supreme Court reached the same conclusion in *Von Raab*, where the Court upheld suspicionless testing of certain Customs Service employees based on the nature of their duties, despite the absence of any documented drug abuse problem among Service employees.

We do not read *Chandler v. Miller* to conflict with this proposition in stating that "*Von Raab* must be read in its unique context." To the contrary, Chandler recognizes that the "special needs" test requires a case-by-case examination of the duties performed by the employees to be tested. In our view, the duties of police officers and firefighters fall far closer to those of Customs Service employees than those of elected public officials.

Applying the flexible *Messerli* standard to the case at hand, moreover, we hold that the superior court did not err, for the most part, in concluding that a "special need" for testing existed here. The superior court found that the Municipality's interest in ensuring public safety is sufficiently compelling to outweigh the relatively modest—though admittedly not insignificant—intrusion on privacy that occurs under the disputed Municipality policy when Police Employees and Fire Fighters members are subjected to suspicionless urine testing upon application for employment, upon promotion, demotion or transfer, or after a vehicular accident. We agree with these findings. We further agree with the superior court's finding that the Municipality's policy reflects a close and substantial means-to-end fit in these situations. In such cases, then—cases when suspicionless testing occurs upon application for employment, upon promotion, demotion or transfer, and after vehicular accidents—we conclude that the balance of individual versus governmental interests tips decidedly in the Municipality's favor.

In our view, however, the balance shifts in the case of an indefinite requirement of random testing. The policy's provision for ongoing random urinalysis testing alters the "special needs" balance between individual privacy interests and competing governmental interests in at least three significant ways.

First, random testing places increased demands on employees' reasonable expectations of privacy. Because the policy's provision for random testing could subject employees to "unannounced" probing throughout the course of their employment, the tests are peculiarly capable of being viewed as "unexpected intrusions on privacy."

Second, random testing is more intrusive: it subjects employees to a greater degree of subjective intrusion. An unannounced test's added element of "fear and surprise," and its "unsettling show of authority," make random drug testing qualitatively more intrusive."

Third, a requirement of random testing impacts the balance between individual and governmental interests by reducing the immediacy of the government's need for the disclosed information. Unlike suspicionless testing occasioned by application, promotion, demotion, transfer, or vehicular accident, the policy's random test provision has no logical nexus to any job-related occurrence. Particularly in the absence of a documented history of substance abuse, then, the Municipality can claim no immediate, job-contextual need to know the results of a randomly drawn urinalysis; it can only claim a more attenuated, institutional interest in checking.

Considering these subtle yet significant attributes of random testing, we conclude that the Municipality has failed to meet its burden of establishing a special need for its random testing provision. In so concluding, we note that the United States Supreme Court has never approved an open ended random-testing regime like the one at issue here. Indeed, *Von Raab* spoke favorably of a suspicionless testing regime that applied only upon transfer or promotion precisely because it lacked a random, unannounced component: Indeed, these procedures significantly minimize the program's intrusion on privacy interests. Only employees who have been tentatively accepted for promotion or transfer to one of the three categories of covered positions are tested, and applicants know at the outset that a drug test is a requirement of those positions. Employees are also notified in advance of the scheduled sample collection, thus reducing to a minimum any "unsettling show of authority."

Conclusion

Except as to the random testing provision, we AFFIRM the superior court's ruling upholding the validity of the disputed Municipality policy. We also AFFIRM the trial court's conclusion that Police Employees and Fire Fighters are public interest litigants. As to the random testing policy, we REVERSE for the reasons stated in this opinion.

Judgment for the Anchorage police and firefighters with regard to the imposition of random drug testing.

CASE QUESTIONS

1. Do you agree with the reasoning of the court?
2. Can you think of a situation that would justify the use of random drug testing?

Case Commentary

The Supreme Court of Alaska ruled that the use of suspicionless searches is permissible upon application for employment, promotion, transfer or an on-the-job accident; however, the use of open-ended random drug testing is prohibited. ■

3. What about the old adage, "If you have done nothing wrong, you have nothing to worry about"?

The issue in the following case is whether students who participate in extracurricular activities should be required to submit to suspicionless drug testing.

Board of Education of Pottawatomie County v. Earls

536 U.S. 822 (2002)

Justice Thomas delivered the opinion of the Court.
The Student Activities Drug Testing Policy implemented by the Board of Education of Independent School District No. 92 of Pottawatomie County (School District) requires all students who participate in competitive extracurricular activities to submit to drug testing. Because this Policy reasonably serves the School District's important interest in detecting and preventing drug use among its students, we hold that it is constitutional.

The city of Tecumseh, Oklahoma, is a rural community located approximately 40 miles southeast of Oklahoma City. The School District administers all Tecumseh public schools. In the fall of 1998, the School District adopted the Student Activities Drug Testing Policy (Policy), which requires all middle and high school students to consent to drug testing in order to participate in any extracurricular activity. In practice, the Policy has been applied only to competitive extracurricular activities sanctioned by the Oklahoma Secondary Schools Activities Association, such as the Academic Team, Future Farmers of America, Future Homemakers of America, band, choir, pom pon, cheerleading, and athletics. Under the Policy, students are required to take a drug test before participating in an extracurricular activity, must submit to random drug testing while participating in that activity, and must agree to be tested at any time upon reasonable suspicion. The urinalysis tests are designed to detect only the use of illegal drugs, including amphetamines, marijuana, cocaine, opiates, and barbitu-

rates, not medical conditions or the presence of authorized prescription medications.

At the time of their suit, both respondents attended Tecumseh High School. Respondent Lindsay Earls was a member of the show choir, the marching band, the Academic Team, and the National Honor Society. Respondent Daniel James sought to participate in the Academic Team. Together with their parents, Earls and James brought a § 1983 action against the School District, challenging the Policy both on its face and as applied to their participation in extracurricular activities. They alleged that the Policy violates the Fourth Amendment as incorporated by the Fourteenth Amendment and requested injunctive and declarative relief. They also argued that the School District failed to identify a special need for testing students who participate in extracurricular activities, and that the "Drug Testing Policy neither addresses a proven problem nor promises to bring any benefit to students or the school."

The District Court noted that the School District's allegations concerning Daniel James called his standing to sue into question because his failing grades made him ineligible to participate in any interscholastic competition. The court noted, however, that the dispute need not be resolved because Lindsay Earls had standing, and therefore the court was required to address the constitutionality of the drug testing policy. Because we are likewise satisfied that Earls has standing, we need not address whether James also has standing.

The respondents did not challenge the Policy either as it applies to athletes or as it provides for drug testing upon reasonable, individualized suspicion.

Applying the principles articulated in *Vernonia School Dist. v. Acton*, (1995), in which we upheld the suspicionless drug testing of school athletes, the United States District Court for the Western District of Oklahoma rejected respondents' claim that the Policy was unconstitutional and granted summary judgment to the School District. The court noted that "special needs" exist in the public school context and that, although the School District did "not show a drug problem of epidemic proportions," there was a history of drug abuse starting in 1970 that presented "legitimate cause for concern." The District Court also held that the Policy was effective because "it can scarcely be disputed that the drug problem among the student body is effectively addressed by making sure that the large number of students participating in competitive, extracurricular activities do not use drugs."

The United States Court of Appeals for the Tenth Circuit reversed, holding that the Policy violated the Fourth Amendment. The Court of Appeals agreed with the District Court that the Policy must be evaluated in the "unique environment of the school setting," but reached a different conclusion as to the Policy's constitutionality. Before imposing a suspicionless drug testing program, the Court of Appeals concluded that a school "must demonstrate that there is some identifiable drug abuse problem among a sufficient number of those subject to the testing, such that testing that group of students will actually redress its drug problem." The Court of Appeals then held that because the School District failed to demonstrate such a problem existed among Tecumseh students participating in competitive extracurricular activities, the Policy was unconstitutional. We granted *certiorari* and now reverse.

The Fourth Amendment to the United States Constitution protects "the right of the people to be secure in their persons, houses, papers, and effects, against unreasonable searches and seizures." Searches by public school officials, such as the collection of urine samples, implicate Fourth Amendment interests. We must therefore review the School District's Policy for "reasonableness," which is the touchstone of the constitutionality of a governmental search.

In the criminal context, reasonableness usually requires a showing of probable cause. The probable-cause standard, however, "is peculiarly related to criminal investigations" and may be unsuited to determining the reasonableness of administrative searches where the "Government seeks to *prevent* the development of hazardous conditions." The Court has also held that a warrant and finding of probable cause are unnecessary in the public school context because such requirements "'would unduly interfere with the maintenance of the swift and informal disciplinary procedures [that are] needed.'"

Significantly, this Court has previously held that "special needs" inhere in the public school context. While schoolchildren do not shed their constitutional rights when they enter the schoolhouse, rights . . . are different in public schools than elsewhere; the "reasonableness' inquiry cannot disregard the schools' custodial and tutelary responsibility for children." In particular, a finding of individualized suspicion may not be necessary when a school conducts drug testing.

In *Vernonia*, this Court held that the suspicionless drug testing of athletes was constitutional. The Court, however, did not simply authorize all school drug testing, but rather conducted a fact-specific balancing of the intrusion on the children's Fourth Amendment rights against the promotion of legitimate governmental interests. Applying the principles of *Vernonia* to the somewhat different facts of this case, we conclude that Tecumseh's Policy is also constitutional.

In any event, students who participate in competitive extracurricular activities voluntarily subject themselves to many of the same intrusions on their privacy as do athletes. Some of these clubs and activities require occasional off-campus travel and communal undress. All of them have their own rules and requirements for participating students that do not apply to the student body as a whole. For example, each of the competitive extracurricular activities governed by the Policy must abide by the rules of the Oklahoma Secondary Schools Activities Association, and a faculty sponsor monitors the students for compliance with the various rules dictated by the clubs and activities. This regulation of extracurricular activities further diminishes the expectation of privacy among schoolchildren. We therefore conclude that the students affected by this Policy have a limited expectation of privacy.

Under the Policy, a faculty monitor waits outside the closed restroom stall for the student to produce a sample and must "listen for the normal sounds of urination in order to guard against tampered specimens and to ensure an accurate chain of custody." The monitor then pours the sample into two bottles that are sealed and placed into a mailing pouch along with a consent form signed by the student. This procedure is virtually identical to that reviewed in *Vernonia*, except that it additionally protects privacy by allowing male students to produce their samples behind a closed stall. Given that we considered the method of collection in *Vernonia* a "negligible" intrusion, the method here is even less problematic.

In addition, the Policy clearly requires that the test results be kept in confidential files separate from a student's other educational records and released to school personnel only on a "need to know" basis.

Moreover, the test results are not turned over to any law enforcement authority. Nor do the test results here lead to the imposition of discipline or have any academic consequences. Rather, the only consequence of a failed drug test is to limit the student's privilege of participating in extracurricular activities. Indeed, a student may test positive for drugs twice and still be allowed to participate in extracurricular activities. After the first positive test, the school contacts the student's parent or guardian for a meeting. The student may continue to participate in the activity if within five days of the meeting the student shows proof of receiving drug counseling and submits to a second drug test in two weeks. For the second positive test, the student is suspended from participation in all extracurricular activities for 14 days, must complete four hours of substance abuse counseling, and must submit to monthly drug tests. Only after a third positive test will the student be suspended from participating in any extracurricular activity for the remainder of the school year, or 88 school days, whichever is longer.

Given the minimally intrusive nature of the sample collection and the limited uses to which the test results are put, we conclude that the invasion of students' privacy is not significant.

Finally, this Court must consider the nature and immediacy of the government's concerns and the efficacy of the Policy in meeting them. This Court has already articulated in detail the importance of the governmental concern in preventing drug use by schoolchildren. The drug abuse problem among our Nation's youth has hardly abated since *Vernonia* was decided in 1995. In fact, evidence suggests that it has only grown worse.

Furthermore, this Court has not required a particularized or pervasive drug problem before allowing the government to conduct suspicionless drug testing. For instance, in *Von Raab* the Court upheld the drug testing of customs officials on a purely preventive basis, without any documented history of drug use by such officials. In response to the lack of evidence relating to drug use, the Court noted generally that "drug abuse is one of the most serious problems confronting our society today," and that programs to prevent and detect drug use among customs officials could not be deemed unreasonable. Likewise, the need to prevent and deter the substantial harm of childhood drug use provides the necessary immediacy for a school testing policy. Indeed, it would make little sense to require a school district to wait for a substantial portion of its students to begin using drugs before it was allowed to institute a drug testing program designed to deter drug use.

Given the nationwide epidemic of drug use, and the evidence of increased drug use in Tecumseh schools, it was entirely reasonable for the School District to enact this particular drug testing policy.

III

Within the limits of the Fourth Amendment, local school boards must assess the desirability of drug testing schoolchildren. In upholding the constitutionality of the Policy, we express no opinion as to its wisdom. Rather, we hold only that Tecumseh's Policy is a reasonable means of furthering the School District's important interest in preventing and deterring drug use among its schoolchildren. Accordingly, we reverse the judgment of the Court of Appeals.

Judgment for the Board of Education.

Case Commentary

The U.S. Supreme Court ruled that the use of suspicionless drug testing by a school board to address a drug problem does not violate the Fourth Amendment of the Constitution. ∎

CASE QUESTIONS

1. Are you in favor of the court's decision?
2. Do you think the same policy could be imposed on college students?

3. Do you believe that individuals under the age of 21 are unfairly discriminated against with regard to drug and alcohol policies?

Drug-Free Workplace Act

The Drug-Free Workplace Act of 1988 applies to contractors that provide more than $25,000 worth of property or services to the federal government and to those employers receiving federal grant monies. Under the Drug-Free Workplace Act, the employer must publish a conspicuous notice in the workplace that drug use is prohibited. This notice must also be sent to all employees. The employer must educate its employees about the dangers of drug use, the availability of counseling and drug treatment programs, and the consequences the employee will suffer if he or she does not seek assistance. Notification must be given to the appropriate federal agency by the employer within 10 days of learning that an employee has been convicted for drug use. Employees must notify their employer if they have been convicted within 5 days of said conviction. The employer must in all respects make a good faith effort to ensure a drug-free workplace.

Job Relatedness

The Fourth Amendment applies to the federal government. Through the due process clause of the Fourteenth Amendment, the Fourth Amendment, along with the rest of the Bill of Rights, was applied to state and local governments. The application to others, including private employers, is essentially based on public policy decisions in court cases. The test applied, which is one of reasonableness, requires that the reason for the drug testing must be significantly job related. Adequate safeguards must be taken, and the intrusion on a person's physical solitude must be minimal. Job relatedness means that the purpose of the test must affect the public safety, the national security, or the safety and security of the workplace. Adequate safeguards must be instituted to assure that the testing is done by a qualified, independent laboratory. As an independent contractor, the lab will be responsible for generating false results or breaches of confidentiality.

Lab Testing

Laboratory drug testing has become a lucrative business. It is important that both the laboratory and the test it performs be reliable. Laboratories conducting drug testing for federal agencies are required to be certified. The initial urine tests, immunoassay, or thin-layer chromatography are usually expeditious and inexpensive to perform. If a positive result is found, a gas chromatography/mass spectrometry test may be used to confirm the finding. This test is more expensive and more reliable than the others.

The examination of blood, saliva, and hair follicles are alternative methods, which are said to provide more detailed information. The collection of the sample is less intrusive, but the results are more intrusive as they provide the quantity and duration of the drug use and genetic information. Each method of testing has certain strengths with regard to identifying specific drugs used, how quickly the drug shows up, and quantity and duration of use. Marijuana accounts for the majority of drug use, with cocaine and heroin placing second and third.

Testing Procedure

It is important that the results be absolutely confirmed before aggressive action is taken. The procedure for gathering the urine specimen should be conducted by an independent source. The process from urination to labeling the vial to transportation to the laboratory to the performance of the actual test itself must be properly controlled. To allow the employer to do it would create a conflict of interest. Employees would find it intrusive and would allege tampering upon the determination of a positive finding. The collection of the urine sample must be observed to verify that the employee has not substituted another person's sample for his or her own. The observer may stand behind the male applicant who is at the urinal. The observer may stand outside the stall while listening for the sound of urination by the female applicant. Then the sample may be temperature checked to guard against substitution. As an alternative, urine samples may be gathered during a medical exam wherein the employee, wearing a medical gown, enters a lavatory to produce a sample. This is another method used to guard against substitution of a drug-free specimen. These methods are not unreasonably intrusive. However, products are available to cleanse the body of drug residue. The consequences of confirming drug use may be a warning, required counseling, admission to a drug treatment program, or termination.

A drug test is not a medical exam, so it can be given prior to employment. However, if a positive result is caused due to prescription medication and the employer asks for an explanation, then the divulging of this information by the individual to clear his or her name may be tantamount to a medical inquiry, which is in violation of the ADA.

The more prudent method would be to condition the job offer on the passing of the drug test.

Drug Treatment Programs

Those employees who are enrolled or have completed an alcohol or drug treatment program are protected under the ADA. Current drug users are not covered. Postemployment drug or alcohol use on the job is grounds for termination unless the employee agrees to enter a drug or alcohol rehabilitation program. If the employee agrees to enter the program and abide by its regulations, then termination is precluded.

Employee Acceptance

Studies have indicated that employees favor drug testing to ensure a safe working environment. Given that, the best approach is for employers to attempt to elicit an acceptance of the program by the employees. This can be accomplished by emphasizing safety, security, and a more productive work environment. The latter translates into greater profits, less theft, and possibly a sharing of this new-found wealth with the employees through better raises or bonuses. Advocating an employer/employee partnership in the fight against drugs will go a long way in easing the implementation of a drug-testing program into the workplace.

EMPLOYEE LESSONS

1. Inquire into the employer's purpose for administering the test: What does the employer hope to achieve?
2. Ask if the test result will be kept confidential.
3. Identify legitimate objections to testing.
4. Distinguish among the different tests available and know when each is appropriate.
5. Query the employer on whether the test questions are job related.
6. Familiarize yourself with the protections afforded by the EPPA.
7. Respect the significance of the Drug-Free Workplace Act.
8. Understand the impact of the Fourth Amendment on drug testing.
9. Appreciate the amount of information gleaned from the hair follicle drug test.
10. Protect your privacy to the best of your ability.

SUMMARY

With respect to information concerning the employee, the employer and the employee are often adversaries. The employer's need to know is at odds with the employee's privacy concerns. That is why courts will often require an employer to establish a compelling interest in the need for information to overrule invasion of privacy concerns. Although they may not eliminate the controversy, employers may reduce the hostility and build trust by sharing with employees the concerns that have driven the employers to want to implement testing. It's not always what you say or do, but how you say or do it.

REVIEW QUESTIONS

1. What is a polygraph?
2. Is the use of polygraphs generally acceptable?
3. When can polygraphs be used?
4. What is the importance of the Fourth Amendment as it relates to testing?
5. Why are employers interested in testing their employees?

6. Are laboratory tests reliable?
7. What is the most informative method of testing for drug use?
8. When is random drug testing permissible?
9. What other types of testing devices can be utilized to determine an employee's honesty?
10. Explain the significance of the Drug-Free Workplace Act of 1988.

CASE PROBLEMS

1. The teachers alleged that the Texas Examination for Current Administrators and Teachers (TECAT), a state-administered examination for teachers that tested basic reading and writing skills, violated Title VI and Title VII of the 1964 Civil Rights Act. Section 13.047 of the TECAT act, which provides for teacher competency testing, is the section at issue on this appeal.
    a. The board shall require satisfactory performance on an examination prescribed by the board as a condition to continued certification for each teacher and administrator who has not taken a certification examination.
    b. The board shall prescribe an examination designed to test knowledge appropriate to teach primary grades and an examination designed to test knowledge appropriate to teach secondary grades. The issue is whether the state may test the competency of its teachers through the administration of aptitude exams. The teachers felt that this was a violation of the Civil Rights Act and the Age Discrimination in Employment Act. *Frazier v. Garrison*, 980 F.2D (5th Cir. 1993)
2. The issue on appeal is whether a Pennsylvania act violates the Privileges and Immunities Clause of the U.S. Constitution by requiring contractors to employ only Pennsylvania residents as laborers and mechanics on Commonwealth-funded public works projects To comply with the act, PennDOT includes in each construction contract a provision that reads:

Residence requirements
Laborers and mechanics to be employed for work under the contract are required by Act 1935-414 to have been residents of the State for at least 90 days prior to their starting work on the contract. Failure to comply with these provisions will be sufficient reason to refuse paying the contract price.

Nevertheless, Blades employed Jeffrey Elliot and Simon Barnes, who were New York residents. In November and December 1994, PennDOT notified Blades that continued employment of nonresident workers could result in withholding contract payments and could affect its prequalification status to do future work in Pennsylvania. Following this notification, Blades fired Elliot and Barnes.

In December 1994, Blades, Elliot, and Barnes brought this action against the Pennsylvania secretary of transportation and other officials. Is residency a permissible requirement for employment? *A. L. Blades & Sons v. Yerusalim*, 121F.3d 865 (3rd Cir. 1997)
3. Respondent Wackenhut Services, Inc. (Wackenhut) is under contract with the U.S. Department of Energy (DOE) to provide security services at the Nevada test site and related nuclear weapons facilities in Nevada. Wackenhut referred Cleghorn to Dr. Hess for psychological testing on May 9, 1982 (preemployment) and again on July 6, 1990. Cleghorn requested copies of his psychological records and test results. Dr. Hess and Wackenhut refused Cleghorn's repeated requests for copies of his psychological test results. Do employees qualify as patients who are entitled to obtain copies of their psychological test results? *Cleghorn v. Hess*, 853 P.2D 1260 (Nev. 1993)
4. In the fall of 1996, Darryl Veazey's employer, LaSalle Telecommunications, Inc., suspected that Veazey, who was employed as an outage coordinator/dispatcher, had left a hostile and threatening anonymous message on the voicemail of another employee at LaSalle.

Despite Veazey's denials, Mason and Burke requested that Veazey read a verbatim transcript of the threatening message into a tape recorder, which would in turn enable LaSalle to create a voice exemplar. Veazey refused to read the verbatim transcript of the message because he was concerned about how the tape might be used and because he thought the message was offensive. In a counteroffer, Veazey agreed to provide a tape-recorded voice exemplar of his reading of a different message. Based on Veazey's continued refusal to provide the requested voice exemplar, Mason discharged him for insubordination. A voice exemplar is simply a recording of a person's utterances used to capture the physical properties of that person's voice.

The issue in this case is whether LaSalle's specific request that Veazey produce a voice exemplar of him reading a transcript of the threatening voicemail message amounts to a "lie detector test" under the EPPA.

Darryl Veazey v. Communications & Cable of Chicago, Inc., 194 F.3d 850 (7th Cir. 1999)

5. On July 7, 1991, Kruse gave birth to her son Kanoa. The next day, the hospital staff found that Kanoa was jittery and easily aroused, and that Kruse's breath smelled of marijuana. A urine test revealed the presence of marijuana in Kanoa's system. A hospital social worker reported the results to Child Protective Services (CPS), a division of Hawaii's Department of Human Services (DHS). That afternoon, Kruse allegedly admitted to a CPS caseworker that she occasionally used marijuana and smoked it once a week during her pregnancy.

The question presented is whether the disclosure of the results of a drug test taken while the employee was in a hospital giving birth is an invasion of privacy. The employee lost her job as a result. Kruse allegedly told Angela Thomas, her employer, that she had used marijuana and was under CPS investigation.

Kruse refused to take a drug test. On August 29, Thomas fired Kruse. The termination letter stated that Kruse was being fired because the in utero transmission of marijuana to a fetus constitutes "abuse and neglect of the child," which disqualifies Kruse from working at a child-care facility. Thomas told (CPS), that she would not rehire Kruse because Kruse's marijuana use had become known in the community, and that this situation could harm the preschool's reputation.

Kruse v. State of Hawaii, 68 F.3d 331 (9th Cir. 1995)

HUMAN RESOURCE DILEMMAS

1. Thompson Medical Supply has been experiencing a theft of medical equipment on the late shift from its Atlanta factory. It decides to polygraph all 35 of its employees who work the late shift. They object, claiming violation of the EPPA. How would you advise them?

2. Superior Teen Baseball League sponsors two travel teams in addition to its regular 12-team league. The travel teams each have three coaches. These coaches are paid a modest salary, unlike the league coaches who volunteer. Superior decides to institute a suspicionless drug test for the travel team coaches only. They complain that they are being treated differently. How would you advise them?

3. Rolling Hills is an affluent town. It borders Flatlands, a Hispanic community that is predominantly Mexican. Rolling Hills has recently passed an ordinance that states that all municipal employees must reside within the town. There is no unemployment problem in Rolling Hills. When a number of Flatlands residents apply to Rolling Hills for positions with the police, fire, and sanitation departments, they are refused for failing to meet the residency requirement. How would you advise them?

4. Yellow Bus Company is considering instituting a suspicionless search with a random component of its bus drivers. No prior history of drug use has been discovered, and the accident rate of the Yellow Bus Company is the envy of the industry. Advise Yellow Bus accordingly.

WEB SITE ASSIGNMENT

Using the following Web sites as well as others, develop policies regarding aptitude testing, residency requirement, psychological testing, physical tests, polygraph tests, and drug testing.

www.drugtesting.com/didyouknow.htm
library.cqpress.com/cqresearcher/document
www.bdtzone.com/drug_testing_4.asp
www.twc.state.tx.us/news/efte/drug_testing_in_the_workplace.html
www.elitedetox.com/workplace_drug_testing.asp
www.passusa.com/html/go-random-drug-screening.shtml
www.globalchange.com/drugtest.htm
www.curtis-arata.com/winart/rsc0169.html
www.reedassoc.com/substance.htm
www.waldentesting.com
www.brgarrison.com
www.employeeselect.com
www.caliperonline.com
www.polygraph.org
www.criminology.fsu.edu/journal/volume1.html
www.passyourdrugtest.com

Chapter 4

Privacy, Theft, and Whistle-Blowing

Employment Scenario

Long and Short phone Susan to inquire as to whether they can ask employees questions about their medical conditions when the employees ask for time off for illness. Long and Short also wish to know if it can share that information when queried by coworkers.

Employment Scenario

L&S thinks it would be great to include in advertising how good Shaquille O'Neal, Kareem Abdul-Jabbar, and Patrick Ewing would look after shopping at The Long and the Short of It (L&S). Long and Short ask Susan whether a life-sized, cardboard cutout photo of Michael Jordan holding Dr. Evil's "Mini Me" (from the Austin Powers movies) with the store's name on it could be placed at its entrance directly above the photo. What response do you believe Susan will give them?

Employment Scenario

Due to a personality conflict with Tom Long, Ray Costello decides to leave L&S. Ray finds a job at giant department store in the men's clothing section. On his employment application form, Ray lists L&S as his prior employer, naming Mark Short as his supervisor. Sam Hong, the men's clothing manager at the giant department store, phones Mark for a reference. Tom answers and explains to Sam that although Ray is a competent salesperson, Ray possesses a bad attitude in his relations with management. Ray's hostility is apparent to other employees and fills the working environment with tension. Tom says, "Sam, Ray will make your life very difficult." Based on Tom's candor, Sam does not hire Ray. Ray believes something is awry. He questions Sam, who denies any bad-mouthing by L&S. Ray sues L&S for interference with Ray's business relations and subpoenas Sam to testify to any conversations Sam had with Tom or Mark. Under oath, Sam testifies as to his conversation with Tom. How would you advise L&S to proceed?

Employment Scenario

Fred Samuels has knowledge that Ruth Gurdon, head buyer for L&S, has been procuring imitation brand-name jeans through the black market, while charging L&S at the rate charged by the brand name merchants. Ruth is pocketing the rest. Fred is afraid to whistle-blow because he knows Ruth is dating Mark Short. Fred does not want to lose his job because of this, but he still wants to do the right thing. Fred asks Tom Long to recommend a competent attorney. Tom suggests Susan North, L&S's attorney. Fred relates the story to Susan. How will Susan advise Fred to proceed?

Employment Scenario

The Long and the Short of It feels it can improve its profits by discouraging employee theft and shoplifting through the conspicuous use of surveillance cameras. L&S is also contemplating tape recording phone conversations to monitor personal phone use, which it believes has become a problem. Finally, L&S wants to prohibit use of its e-mail system for private messages after receiving a complaint from a customer who received a sexual joke from L&S's e-mail. The joke was mistakenly sent to the customer by Rodney Fraizer, an employee, instead of to his friend. But the damage was done. If L&S implements these measures, are the employees' privacy interests violated?

Chapter Checklist
➤ *Understand the employer's motives for invading the privacy of employees.*
➤ *Appreciate the employee's rationale for objecting to invasion of privacy.*
➤ *Familiarize yourself with the safeguards afforded by the Privacy Act, Omnibus Crime Control and Safe Streets Act, Electronic Communications Act, and Fair Credit Reporting Act.*
➤ *Learn whether an employer's actions fall within one of the defined categories of invasion of privacy.*
➤ *Distinguish between an opinion and a defamatory statement.*
➤ *Know when someone is intentionally interfering with a business relationship.*

➤ Appreciate the negative impact employee theft has on business.

➤ Discern when an employer has the right to conduct an office search and whether the parameters of the search are justified.

➤ Be able to define whistle-blowing and the protections afforded by the Whistleblower Protection Act.

➤ Understand the dilemma confronting a potential whistle-blower: the desire to reveal wrongdoing versus possible retaliation.

INTRODUCTION

Freedom and privacy are sacred to Americans. The Bill of Rights safeguards these principles. But the right to privacy is not absolute. In employment law, a balancing test is used. When an employer can show that its need to know outweighs the employee's right to privacy, then an invasion of that employee's privacy will be warranted. Conversely, when an employee's right to privacy is paramount, then it will be protected. Certain situations may be clear-cut, while others are controversial. Surveillance, security guards, tape-recorded conversations, credit checks, and e-mail monitoring may be used by employers. But an employer's rights are not absolute. The employer's need to know must be business related. Listening to personal phone conversations, reading the contents of private e-mails, and installing cameras in employee bathrooms and lounges are not permissible. In any event, an employer must evaluate the benefits to the business from invading employee privacy versus depressing employee morale, creating a lack of trust, and causing employees to leave the business for a competitor who will not infringe upon employee privacy. Employees should be cognizant of privacy intrusions and decide whether to be docile, resign in protest, or object and litigate. The financial and emotional makeup of each employee will dictate the approach taken.

HUMAN RESOURCE ADVICE

- Consider the effect surveillance and security measures have on employee morale.
- Balance that against money lost through theft and slacking off.
- Refrain from listening to the contents of employees' personal telephone calls.
- Never utter statements about employees that are false or damaging to their reputation.
- Protect the privacy of employees by refusing to divulge confidential information.
- Refrain from reading the contents of personal letters or e-mail directed to or sent by an employee.
- Investigate thoroughly and compile evidence before accusing an employee of theft.

- Never accuse an employee of committing any crime in front of others. In case you are wrong, it's defamation.
- Share the problem that is forcing you to implement security measures with your employees.
- Encourage whistle-blowers to come forward with information that, if not disclosed, would result in harm to the business.

PRIVACY ACT OF 1974

The Privacy Act of 1974 was enacted to safeguard private information of federal employees from being disclosed by the federal government. Under the act, no information pertaining to an employee may be released before obtaining prior written consent of the employee. There are many exceptions to this procedure. Other employees of the agency may access the records of a particular worker on a need-to-know basis, if their position so requires. A court, civil or criminal law enforcement agency, Congress, the Census Bureau, or the National Archives may have access to an employee's records for a justifiable reason. Unless exempted under the Privacy Act, the information should be kept in a secure facility that guards against easy access by unauthorized people. Civil and criminal penalties can be imposed for breaches of trust.

Access to Personnel Records

Employee access to personnel files in the private sector is not guaranteed in most states. However, many employers as a matter of company policy do permit employees to review their personnel files.

Employee Phone Conversations

Employers may record the telephone conversations of their employees; however, they may listen only to the contents of the business calls for quality control purposes. Employers may note the frequency and duration of personal use, but they may not listen to the conversation. In California, both parties must be apprised that the conversation is being recorded by a recorded message or a series of beeps.

Title III of the Omnibus Crime Control and Safe Streets Act of 1968 (also known as the *Federal Wiretap Act*) prohibits employers from listening to the private telephone conversations of their employees and/or from publicly disclosing the contents of these conversations. Employers who eavesdrop intentionally when employees are justified in expecting their conversations to be private are in violation of the Act. Employers may ban personal calls and then monitor conversations for violations, but they may not listen to the entire conversation for the purpose of discerning its content. Violators may incur fines up to $10,000.

Employment Perspective

Sheena Whitmore placed a call to her physician concerning the results of a blood test she had taken to determine whether she had contracted a sexually transmitted disease. This call was intercepted by her employer, who then stayed on the line to hear the test results. Is this an invasion of privacy? Yes! The employer's actions are in violation of Title III of the Omnibus Crime Control and Safe Streets Act. Sheena was expecting privacy. Her employer invaded that privacy by listening to her test results.

ELECTRONIC COMMUNICATIONS PRIVACY ACT

The Electronic Communications Privacy Act of 1986 (ECPA) is an amendment to the Omnibus Crime Control and Safe Streets Act. It extended people's privacy protection to e-mail. The focus of ECPA is on interceptions. Once the e-mail is received and stored on a computer belonging to the employer, the employer may peruse it. Unauthorized interceptions are subject to stiff civil and criminal penalties. Federal law also prohibits tampering with e-mail. However, there are three exceptions for employers who want to intercept employees' e-mail: (1) consent by the employee to monitoring (best obtained in writing); (2) where the employer is the provider of the e-mail (this may apply to internal e-mails, but if incoming e-mail arrives through an outside provider such as AOL, this exception does not apply); and (3) ordinary course of business (this may apply only to business e-mails, not personal ones). Employers may monitor e-mail for quality control, and sexual, racial, and abusive language. Employers should not divulge the contents of the e-mail communications. Employees should be on guard when transmitting e-mail because of the limited protection afforded to them.

Most large corporations monitor e-mail and employee Internet use. Many employees spend an hour or more each day surfing the Web and reading and writing e-mail that is not work related. Employees may argue that this is just a substitute for time spent on the phone or at the water cooler. But companies retort that the costs run into the millions for lost productivity. In addition, lawsuits may result from sexual, ethnic, and racial jokes as well as sexually explicit e-mails or computer printouts. In effect, companies may be negligent if they do not have a policy in place and fail to monitor.

The prudent strategy for companies is to create a policy alerting employees that they may be monitored and telling them specifically what is not acceptable. Companies may install a filter to block certain Web sites because they are objectionable or time-consuming. Employees accessing certain sites such as those involving games may slow down the company's computer network. These sites may be freed up during nonworking hours. Employees must remember they are not at home. The computer and phone are all property of the employer. The use of personal cell phones will provide a safe haven from monitoring, but the employer may prohibit excessive use on company time.

Although employees may have some expectation of privacy in the work environment, courts are willing to overcome this for the employer's legitimate business interests. In most cases, requiring an employee password for access to the computer protects the employee's privacy interests with regard to coworkers, but not the employer. Most employers understand that employees need to take care of some personal needs during business hours and that the Internet, e-mail or phone can facilitate the employee's ability to do so. It is the abuse of privilege that most employers seek to guard against. The best method to resolve this is through employer–employee dialogue to develop a policy that addresses the concerns of both parties.

The issue in the case that follows is whether an employer has the right to check an employee's e-mail.

Garrity v. John Hancock Mutual Life Insurance Company

2002 U.S. Dist. Lexis 8343 (Mass.)

Zobel, District Judge.

Plaintiffs Nancy Garrity ("Mrs. Garrity") and Joanne Clark ("Ms. Clark") were employees of John Hancock Mutual Life Insurance Company ("John Hancock") for twelve and two years, respectively, until their termination in July of 1999. According to the defendant, plaintiffs regularly received on their office computers, sexually explicit e-mails from internet joke sites and other third parties, including Mrs. Garrity's husband, Arthur Garrity ("Mr. Garrity"), which they then sent to coworkers. These facts are undisputed: A fellow employee complained after receiving one such e-mail. Hancock promptly commenced an investigation of plaintiffs' e-mail folders, as well as the folders of those with whom they e-mailed on a regular basis. Based upon the information gleaned from this investigation, Hancock determined that plaintiffs had violated its E-Mail Policy, which states, in relevant part:

- Messages that are defamatory, abusive, obscene, profane, sexually oriented, threatening or racially offensive are prohibited.
- The inappropriate use of E-mail is in violation of company policy and may be subject to disciplinary action, up to and including termination of employment.
- All information stored, transmitted, received, or contained in the company's E-mail systems is the property of John Hancock. It is not company policy to intentionally inspect E-mail usage. However, there may be business or legal situations that necessitate company review of E-mail messages and other documents.
- Company management reserves the right to access all E-mail files.

During plaintiffs' employment, defendant periodically reminded its employees that it was their responsibility to know and understand the e-mail policy. In addition, defendant warned them of several incidents in which employees were disciplined for violations. Plaintiffs assert that the e-mail policy is almost impossible to locate on Hancock's intranet system, and even harder to decipher. In addition, they contend that the reminders sent by defendant during plaintiffs' employment did not accurately communicate its e-mail policy. They also dispute defendant's characterization of the e-mails in question as sexually explicit, or in any way in violation of the policy language. Upon review of the e-mails in question, however, there can be no question that they are sexually explicit within the meaning of defendant's e-mail policy. Regardless, plaintiffs assert that Hancock led them to believe that these personal e-mails could be kept private with the use of personal passwords and e-mail folders. Their complaint sets forth claims based on invasion of privacy, unlawful interception of wire communications, wrongful discharge in violation of public policy, wrongful discharge to deprive plaintiffs of benefits, and defamation. Defendant filed a Motion for Summary Judgment on all counts.

INVASION OF PRIVACY

Plaintiffs' opposition states that "it is uncontested . . . that Ms. Garrity, Mr. Garrity and Ms. Clark believed that the personal e-mail correspondence they sent and received was private." While that may be true, the relevant inquiry is whether the expectation of privacy was reasonable. Although there is a dearth of case law on privacy issues with regard to office e-mail, *Smyth v. Pillsbury Co.* is instructive here. In *Smyth*, the court held that *even in the absence* of a company e-mail policy, plaintiffs would not have had a reasonable expectation of privacy in their work e-mail:

> Once plaintiff communicated the alleged unprofessional comments to a second person (his supervisor) over an e-mail system which was apparently utilized by the entire company, any reasonable expectation of privacy was lost. Significantly, the defendant did not require plaintiff, as in the case of urinalysis or personal property search to disclose any personal information about himself. Rather, plaintiff voluntarily communicated the alleged unprofessional comments over the company e-mail system. We find no privacy interests in such communications.

Both Mrs. Garrity and Ms. Clark admit that they knew defendant had the ability to look at e-mail on the company's intranet system, and knew they had to be careful about sending e-mails. Nevertheless, they claim that their e-mails were private because the company had instructed them on how to create passwords and personal e-mail folders. This precise argument was flatly rejected in *McLaren v. Microsoft Corp.*:

> According to (plaintiff), his practice was to store e-mail messages in "personal folders." Even so, any e-mail messages stored in [plaintiff's] personal folders were first transmitted over the network and were at some point accessible by a third party. Given these circumstances, we cannot conclude that [plaintiff], even by creating a personal password, manifested—and [defendant] recognized—a reasonable expectation in privacy in the contents of e-mail messages such that [defendant] was precluded from reviewing the messages.

Even if plaintiffs had a reasonable expectation of privacy in their work e-mail, defendant's legitimate business interest in protecting its employees from harassment in the workplace would likely trump plaintiffs' privacy interests. Both Title VII of the Civil Rights Act of 1964 and M.G.L. c. 151B require employers to take affirmative steps to maintain a workplace free of harassment and to investigate and take prompt and effective remedial action when potentially harassing conduct is discovered. Therefore, once defendant received a complaint about the plaintiffs' sexually explicit e-mails, it was required by law to commence an investigation.

MASSACHUSETTS WIRETAP STATUTE

Plaintiffs claim that, by reading their e-mails, defendant violated M.G.L. c. 272 § 99, which prohibits certain interceptions of wire and oral communications. Because the reading of e-mails, after they have been transmitted to the recipient, does not constitute "interception" within the wiretap statute, plaintiffs' claim fails. (This court has previously) held that the Electronic Communications Privacy Act of 1986 requires that the acquisition of electronic communications occur *during transmission*. That is, the act of "interception" cannot proceed after the e-mail is received as is the case here. Therefore, plaintiffs' wiretap claim fails as a matter of law.

Even if an employer's reading of employee e-mails constituted "interception," within the meaning of the statute, at least one Massachusetts court has held that an automatic e-mail back-up system is protected under the "ordinary business exemption" and therefore "does not constitute an unlawful interception in violation of M.G.L. c. 272 Section 99."

DEFAMATION

The last count asserts that two Hancock supervisors defamed plaintiffs by telling former co-workers, and Hancock employees in other departments, that plaintiffs were terminated for sending and receiving "sexually lewd, harassing and defamatory" and "sexually explicit" e-mails. Even if the statements made by defendant met the required elements of a defamation claim, defendant is entitled to a conditional privilege which insulates it from liability for these statements. The privilege "protects an employer's statements of opinion and facts, and statements that an employer reasonably believes to be true." It also extends to "information which may turn out not to be true concerning an employee when the publication is reasonably necessary to serve the employer's legitimate interest in the fitness of an employee to perform his or her job." In order to defeat the employer's conditional privilege, the employee bears the burden of proving that the employer abused the privilege by recklessly publishing the defamatory facts. Plaintiffs have not done so here. Rather, plaintiffs simply state that "no legitimate business purpose was served by disseminating these statements among such a large group of employees." To the contrary, all Hancock employees are subject to its e-mail policy. Therefore, defendant had an obvious legitimate business purpose, as to *all employees*, if it so chose—to warn them and thereby prevent any recurrence of the events that led to this law suit. Accordingly, defendant's motion for summary judgment is allowed. Judgment may be entered for defendant.

Judgment for John Hancock.

Case Commentary

The Massachusetts District Court decided that an employer has the right to check e-mails once they have been communicated through the company e-mail system. Informing coworkers of the termination of the plaintiffs for violating company e-mail policy does not constitute defamation. ∎

CASE QUESTIONS

1. Do you agree with the court's decision?
2. Is termination for violating an e-mail policy too harsh?

3. Does the employer have the right to explain the reason for an employee's discharge to his or her coworkers?

FAIR CREDIT REPORTING ACT

The Fair Credit Reporting Act (FRCA) of 1970 requires an employer to obtain permission before hiring a third party to conduct a background check of an applicant or an investigation in the workplace involving an employee. After the report is submitted, a copy must be given to the applicant or worker. Notice or permission is not required for investigations conducted by the employer. Background checks can be a consumer report or an investigative report. A consumer report analyzes an applicant's credit history. FCRA allows consumer-reporting agencies to furnish credit reports for employment purposes. These reports contain basic information about the individual and his or her credit worthiness. If the employer wishes to have a more detailed background check done by the consumer-reporting agency or private investigator with regard to interviews of the employee or of the applicant's friends, neighbors, and coworkers, then notice must be given to the individual. In all respects, the employer's reason for doing so must be job related. If the report goes beyond what is considered to be a business necessity, an invasion of privacy suit may ensue. If the individual falls into a suspect classification (race, gender, religion, national origin, age, or disability), then grounds for a discrimination suit may exist.

DEFAMATION

Defamation is a false statement communicated to at least one other person, orally or in a permanent form such as a writing, that causes harm to a third person's reputation. *Libel* is written defamation; *slander* is oral defamation. Libel is actionable without proof of special damages because a writing remains in existence and could be distributed widely. The requirement for libel is a false statement that is published and read by someone other than the one about whom it is written. Slander is usually temporary and limited to the range of a person's voice, except when the oral statement is recorded and continuously broadcast on television, radio, or sound tracks. Slander requires a defamatory statement that is heard by someone other than the person against whom it is directed.

Employment Perspective

Mary Thompson, an employee of Creative Publishing, names Roger Burton, a supervisor, as a reference for a job that will be a major step for her. Mary will be making more money and have a title superior to Roger. Out of jealousy, Roger falsely states in writing that Mary is often uncooperative and belligerent. Mary is not hired because of Roger's statement. Does Mary have a case for libel against Roger and Creative Publishing? Yes! Creative is liable because its employee made a false statement within the scope of his employment that deprived Mary from obtaining a job.

Employment Perspective

Peter J. Roberts is a local attorney who has a well-regarded real estate law practice. Matthew Brady was formerly employed by Roberts as a paralegal. Out of revenge, he tells several real estate brokers who refer clients to Peter J. Roberts that Roberts has cheated his clients in several real estate deals. Even though Brady's statements are false, Roberts's business suffers a severe decline as a result. Does Peter J. Roberts have any recourse? Yes! Roberts may recover general damages for the harm suffered to his business reputation.

Truth and Malice

Truth is an absolute defense when the statement made is fully true. However, the truth must be proved. There is a special rule pertaining to defamatory statements made by the media concerning public figures. Even if the statement cannot be proved to be true, the media will not be liable unless malicious intent can be substantiated. *Malice* is the making of a false statement with the intent to injure another.

Employment Perspective

In the previous situation, assume that Matthew Brady's allegations concerning Peter J. Roberts were the truest words ever spoken but that Brady has no way of proving them to be true. What would be the result? The result would be the same: Roberts will recover general damages. Although truth is an absolute defense, if Roberts meets his initial burden of proof, the burden then shifts to the person who made the statement.

INVASION OF PRIVACY

Personal privacy is protected against invasions causing economic loss or mental suffering. There are four distinct invasions: intrusion on a person's physical solitude; publication of private matters violating ordinary decencies; putting a person in a false position in the public eye by connecting him or her with views he or she does not hold; appropriating some element of a person's personality for commercial use, such as photographs.

Employment Perspective

Statler Beer is introducing a new beer called Sparkling Lite. To market the product, Statler is featuring an unauthorized poster of the Reverend Luther Winthrop advocating the purchase of Sparkling Lite. The Reverend Winthrop is a well-known fundamentalist minister who openly decries the consumption of alcohol. Has Reverend Winthrop any recourse? Yes! He may sue Statler Beer, asserting that the poster was not consented to and that it puts him in a false position in the public eye by connecting him with a view that he does not hold and a product that he does not deem appropriate.

Employment Perspective

Rob Peters is a pension benefits specialist for Americana Insurance Company. One of his assistants, Brad Matthews, informs Rob that he must leave work 2 hours early this Tuesday for medical reasons. Rob asks Brad for specifics, citing company policy. Brad declines at first, but when pressed, Brad admits that he has the HIV virus and is being tested for AIDS. After Brad departs early on Tuesday, Jim Waters, a coworker, asks Rob why Brad left early. Rob responds, "You wouldn't believe it, Jim!" Jim retorts, "Try me." Rob blurts out, "Brad's got AIDS!" Jim responds in astonishment, "No!" Then Jim sends an e-mail message to the other coworkers. Brad's AIDS test comes back negative. Who does Brad have recourse against? Because it was company policy for the manager to inquire about the specific medical condition of the employee, Brad may sue Americana for invasion of privacy. Brad may also sue Rob for slander, because Rob made a false statement about Brad having AIDS. Brad may sue Jim for invasion of privacy and libel, because the false statement was in written form. Rob and Jim may have been motivated by curiosity and gossip, not intent to harm, but the damage to Brad's reputation still occurred.

The issue in this case is whether the searches were motivated by race discrimination.

Wal-Mart, Inc. v. Stewart

990 P.2d 626 (Alaska 1999)

Compton, Justice.

INTRODUCTION

Elvis R. Stewart sued Wal-Mart for violating Alaska's civil rights statute, for invading his common-law right to privacy, and for negligent and intentional infliction of emotional distress. He sought both compensatory and punitive damages. At the close of Stewart's case, Wal-Mart moved for a directed verdict. The court denied the motion. The jury returned a verdict in favor of Wal-Mart on Stewart's civil rights claim, but found for Stewart on his claims of invasion of privacy and intentional infliction of emotional distress. The jury awarded Stewart both compensatory and punitive damages. We affirm.

FACTS AND PROCEEDINGS

A. Facts

In July 1994 Elvis R. Stewart, an African-American, began working for the McDonald's restaurant located inside the Wal-Mart store on Benson Boulevard in Anchorage. Stewart's shift was from 7:30 P.M. until closing, the time of which varied. Stewart also worked at Taco Bell. Stewart's shift at Taco Bell was from 11:30 A.M. until 7:00 P.M. In order to work both shifts, Stewart carried a change of clothes and personal items in a duffel-type bag. He would change out of his Taco Bell uniform, and into his McDonald's uniform, in the Wal-Mart bathroom. He also took the time between shifts to freshen up, i.e., wash himself with soap and a washcloth that he carried in his bag, and brush his teeth. He used the Wal-Mart bathroom, instead of the Taco Bell bathroom, because it was larger and less crowded with customers.

Wal-Mart had a nation-wide policy of stationing a member of its management team at its exits to check for receipts of purchases made by Wal-Mart and McDonald's employees, and to check for stolen items that might be concealed in their personal bags. Management conducted the checks before employees left the store at the end of their shifts.

The first few weeks Stewart worked at McDonald's, he exited the Wal-Mart store at the close of his shift without incident. According to Stewart, sometime during his third week of employment, Hardy stopped Stewart as he was exiting McDonald's at the end of his shift. Hardy asked to search Stewart's bag, and then proceeded to dump the contents of Stewart's bag onto the counter and look through it. According to Stewart, this type of bag search continued until mid-February 1995. Stewart testified that he routinely objected to the searches. On February 15 Stewart was again searched by Hardy. Hardy questioned Stewart about some candy bars in his bag, for which Stewart produced a receipt. After Hardy completed the bag search he allowed Stewart to

leave. The next day Stewart came to McDonald's to speak with Sheila Hay, the wife of the franchise owner of the McDonald's where Stewart worked. It was Stewart's day off. He told Hay that he felt that Hardy was singling him out for bag searches. Hay took Stewart to speak with Mark Divis, the Wal-Mart store manager. Stewart repeated to Divis that he felt that Hardy was singling him out for bag searches. Divis called Hardy into the office. Hardy denied singling out Stewart for searches. Stewart testified that during the meeting Hay asked Hardy who else he searched. Stewart asked Hardy whether he searched certain people because they were black; Hardy answered yes.

On February 23 Stewart wrote a letter to Divis commending him on his "efforts with enforcing Wal-Mart [p]olicy, as it is in regards to the checking of All bags. . . . " But after he had written the letter, Stewart testified that things "drifted back to the same old way that—people started being singled out."

B. Proceedings

Stewart sought compensatory and punitive damages. The jury returned a verdict in favor of Wal-Mart on Stewart's civil rights claim. However, it did conclude that Stewart had proved by a preponderance of the evidence that Wal-Mart intentionally inflicted emotional distress on him, and that it had invaded his privacy. Lastly, the jury concluded that Stewart had proved by clear and convincing evidence that Wal-Mart's conduct warranted punitive damages because it had been "the result of malicious or hostile feelings toward plaintiff Stewart, or was undertaken with reckless indifference to his interests or rights and was outrageous." The jury awarded Stewart $7,800 in compensatory damages and $50,000 in punitive damages.

1. Invasion of privacy We have recognized that all persons are entitled to the common-law "right to be free from harassment and constant intrusion into one's daily affairs." The trial court instructed the jury that [i]n order to recover, plaintiff must prove by a preponderance of the evidence that:

1. One or more defendants intentionally intruded upon the solitude, seclusion or private affairs or concerns of plaintiff Stewart; and
2. A reasonable person would find this a highly offensive intrusion.

Our review of the record discloses sufficient evidence that would allow reasonable minds to conclude that Wal-Mart searched Stewart's bag in an unreasonable manner or for an unlawful reason.

Ample evidence was presented that also would permit reasonable jurors to find that Hardy searched Stewart's bag for an unlawful reason, i.e., because he is an African-American.

The superior court stated: "On the issue of consent, again there is evidence on both sides that Mr. Stewart essentially voiced his dissent numerous times when he was being searched." Specifically, Stewart did not consent to Hardy's vigorous and overly-thorough searches.

Whether consent is implied when a store has a legal bag search policy is irrelevant. Even were we to conclude that a consent is implied when a legal bag search procedure is in effect, Stewart's suit was premised on the notion that he was not searched pursuant to Wal-Mart's legal bag search policy. Rather, Stewart successfully argued at trial that the searches of his bag invaded his privacy because they were done for an unlawful purpose or in an unreasonable manner.

2. Intentional infliction of emotional distress The elements necessary for establishing a prima facie case of IIED are: "(1) the conduct is extreme and outrageous, (2) the conduct is intentional or reckless, (3) the conduct causes emotional distress, and (4) the distress is severe."

We conclude that it was not an abuse of discretion for the superior court to make the threshold determination, based on the evidence presented, that Hardy's conduct was sufficiently outrageous, and Stewart's emotional distress was sufficiently severe, to submit the IIED claim to the jury. The following are examples of this evidence:

1. Stewart testified that Hardy admitted that the reason he searched the people that he did was because they were African-Americans.
2. Stewart testified that he was told to empty his pockets, and that Hardy grabbed his duffel bag off of his shoulder.
3. Numerous witnesses testified that Stewart and other people of color were searched very often, while Caucasians were either allowed to exit the store without being searched or were searched much less frequently.

We AFFIRM the judgment of the superior court.

Case Commentary
The lessons to be learned from this case are to treat all employees alike and to treat them in a humane manner. Do not distinguish between employees on the basis of personal prejudices. ∎

CASE QUESTIONS

1. Could Hardy's searches of only black employees ever be justified?
2. Do you agree with the Alaska Supreme Court's decision?

3. If all employees were searched, would it be an invasion of privacy?

Publication of private matters that are newsworthy is privileged as long as it does not violate ordinary decencies. A false report by the media of a matter of public interest is protected by the First Amendment right of free press, in the absence of proof that it was published with malice.

INTERFERENCE WITH BUSINESS RELATIONS

A person who intentionally interferes in a business relationship through the use of fraudulent inducement or other unethical means that result either in an unfavorable contract or in the loss or breach of a favorable contract is liable for damages. The victim must prove damages, such as the specific loss of a customer, except where the nature of the falsehood is likely to bring about a general decline in business.

Employment Perspective
Phil Murray owns a service station in Mobile, Alabama. The On-The-Spot Car Service Company approaches Phil about maintaining their 12-car fleet. This opportunity would greatly enhance Phil's business. While they are still negotiating, Michael Dean, a former employee who was fired for stealing from the owner, circulates a false rumor that Phil Murray is incompetent and unreliable when it comes to servicing cars. As a result, Phil loses the contract with On-The-Spot Car Service. Thereafter, he discovers that Michael Dean originated the false rumor and sues him for damages. Will Phil be successful? Yes! Michael Dean's intentional

interference with the contractual negotiations between Phil Murray and On-The-Spot Car Service caused Phil to lose the contract. Phil is entitled to the profits that he lost because of Michael Dean's interference.

EMPLOYEE THEFT

Theft by employees accounts for billions of dollars in losses for businesses each year. Employee theft can be narrowly or broadly defined. The narrow definition is the appropriating of personal property belonging to the business for an employee's own personal use. This appropriation can be temporary, but most often it is permanent.

Employment Perspective

Harry Tubbs and Pete Jackson work as a team for Moving On Van Lines. They often make long-distance moves. After being assigned a job, they often complete it in less time by working late hours. Then they use the company van for making short moves from which they derive a profit. Harry and Pete believe that as long as they perform their assigned work within the allotted time, they are doing their job, and the company should not be concerned. Are they guilty of employee theft? Yes! Their theft is temporary, but the consequences are still severe. A van's useful life and maintenance costs will directly correspond to its mileage. Harry's and Pete's ventures are lowering the van's useful life to the company and increasing its maintenance costs. There is no difference between doing this and keeping the equivalent amount of money from a customer's cash payment. Both acts are theft. In addition, if they are in an accident while performing their personal work, the accident could subject Moving On to liability for damages and injuries. If Harry and Pete are injured, most likely Moving On will incur medical expenses, and workers' compensation benefits will be paid out. Harry and Pete are not entitled to any of this because this occurrence happened outside the scope of their employment, but Moving On may have to pay for it if the theft is not known. Some companies will want their employees prosecuted, but most will not because of the bad publicity it would bring. Dismissal with or without restitution is the most likely consequence.

Employment Perspective

When Marge Adams resigned from Pentangel Publishing, everything in her office was intact. That evening, Phil Thomas took the computer, printer, lamp, office supplies, and fax machine from Marge's office home with him. Phil believed his actions were justified because most likely Marge was not going to be replaced. Is Phil's reasoning sound? No! Phil has stolen company property for his own personal aggrandizement.

Conversion

Conversion is the unlawful taking of personal property from the possession of another. It is the converting of another's property for one's own use. Conversion may be made by mistake, but if it is done intentionally, it amounts to criminal theft, which is considered under the headings of larceny, embezzlement, and robbery.

Employment Perspective

Mary Rodgers works as a cashier in Macy's Department Store. She takes a break one afternoon to go to the powder room. She mistakenly leaves her pocketbook at the register. When she returns, her pocketbook is there, but her wallet has been removed. The store detective apprehends Debbie Wilson, a stock clerk, with Mary's wallet in her hand. Has Mary Rodgers any civil recourse for Debbie Wilson's theft? Yes! Mary may sue Debbie in tort for conversion. Debbie may also be criminally prosecuted for the crime of larceny or theft.

Employee theft occurs when a worker, usually a cashier or someone in billing, charges a customer, who is generally a friend, less than the amount owed. Although the employee may not be benefiting directly, the employee is instrumental in making the theft happen. There would be no difference between the preceding example and that of an employee stealing the merchandise and giving it to a friend. Both acts are thefts.

Employment Perspective

Missy Atkins is a waitress at the Busy Body Diner. Missy, who is shy and unassuming, wants to become more popular with the in-crowd at school. Whenever they come in for burgers, fries, and sundaes, Missy charges them only for the sundaes. Missy's popularity is increasing fast, but is she gaining it at Busy Body's expense? Yes! Missy is guilty of employee theft.

Embezzlement

Embezzlement is the fraudulent taking of property during the course of employment.

Padded Payroll

A *padded payroll* is one to which a dishonest employee has added names that are unauthorized and frequently fictitious. Checks are issued to these fictitious payees and endorsed by the dishonest employee. The person or bank receiving the endorsed instrument is not liable if they acted in good faith and exercised ordinary care.

Employment Perspective

Jonathan Rhodes worked as the treasurer for the Whitney and Myers Department Store. There were 92 employees of the store. Rhodes issued 95 checks each week. The three additional checks were issued to Kelly, Paige, and Evan—fictitious employees of the department store who supposedly worked with mannequins. Rhodes endorsed the names of the payees and negotiated the checks to the Williamsburg Savings Bank in return for cash. When the department store discovered Rhodes's scheme, he had left for a permanent vacation in the Bahamas. Has the department store any recourse against the bank? No! The endorsement of

Rhodes, the impostor, is effective against the company as long as the bank acted in good faith.

Theft of Time

The broad definition of employee theft would also include theft of time. This would encompass longer lunch breaks, arriving late, leaving early, conducting personal business on company time, and just goofing off. The old expression "time is money" is true. An employee who commits this theft of time is not giving the employer adequate work in return for the wage bargained for. The employee is wrongfully inflating his or her wage at the employer's expense, which is a form of theft. Theft of time will not result in prosecution but may result in dismissal or demotion.

Employment Perspective

Pamela Hall is a research assistant at Bull and Bear Stockbrokerage. She often spends time in the firm's library researching information on companies that her father, an avid market player, is interested in investing in. Is this act employee theft? Yes! Pamela is guilty of theft of time. What if Pamela had no work assigned? Then she should ask her supervisor for an assignment or educate herself on some aspect of the company's business.

Employment Perspective

Justin Sheldon is a data entry clerk for Miracle Drug Pharmaceutical Company. Justin often spends an hour or two a day making personal calls and running errands. He then works overtime at time-and-a-half to accomplish what he could not do in the 8-hour day. Obviously, Justin is not closely supervised. In any event, is he guilty of employee theft? Yes! Justin is not only stealing time but also charging the company at the overtime rate for the time he spent on personal business.

Fourth Amendment

Employee theft is a very serious problem. It undermines business profitability and gives the unethical employees an unfair advantage over their honest counterparts. Some solutions are closer supervision through time sheets, electronic surveillance, desk and office searches, security guards, and tape-recorded phone lines. Many employees feel that such steps are an invasion of privacy, but what degree of privacy should an employee have at the workplace? The Fourth Amendment to the U.S. Constitution guarantees the right of the people to be secure in their person, property, and effects from unreasonable searches and seizures. In the workplace, absent an overcoat or a briefcase, what personal effects or property belong to the employee? Aren't the office and the desk company property? That would seem to be the case.

Americans have safeguarded their privacy rights since the inception of this nation. Today privacy is a major concern in the workplace. Employees have argued that the Fourth Amendment prohibition against unreasonable searches and seizures should be extended to office searches, e-mail monitoring, tape recording telephone conversations, and drug testing. With the advent of suspicionless searches, employees seem to be slowly losing ground. At the same time, employers feel that employees' reasonable expectations of privacy should give way due to the increase in employee theft and drug use.

SURVEILLANCE

Many companies use time sheets and electronic surveillance. Time sheets require an employee to justify his or her time spent during the workday, but they can be doctored. However, supervisors should be able to distinguish fabrications by comparisons with other similarly engaged employees and from experience with the work habits of the employee in question. Electronic surveillance is often installed by retail companies under the guise of identifying shoplifters, but equally important to the company is the electronic supervision of the work habits of its employees and the recognition of those who steal. Tape-recorded conversations are often used in the securities industry to record conversations between broker and customer for the purpose of verification should a miscommunication occur. Tape-recorded conversations can also discourage an employee from receiving personal calls. The use of polygraphs, otherwise known as *lie-detector tests*, is severely restricted to cases in which the employer has a reasonable suspicion that an employee has committed a theft.

SECURITY

The mere presence of security guards is a deterrent to many employees who would otherwise want to steal. Security guards, though, cannot be everywhere and see everything. They are also expensive when compared with the other alternatives. An additional method would be the use of inventory control. This requires limiting access to inventory to certain employees and instituting accounting controls and physical checks for verification. Inconsistencies can be investigated, and thefts are more easily traceable. When companies are lax in determining the existence of theft, it encourages employees so inclined to steal because there is little chance of detection. When controls are instituted, employees are more wary.

OFFICE SEARCHES

Desk and office searches are often used primarily to locate drug use but also to identify the conducting of work unrelated to the company by the employee while on the job. Many employees find this to be particularly intrusive and an invasion of privacy. Most courts come down on the side of the employer if it has a justifiable business reason. However, employees who have been with an employer for a lengthy period of time develop a reasonable expectation of privacy in at least their desk and file cabinets.

The following case addresses the question of whether the contents of a physician's office can be searched by the hospital that employs him. The resolution revolves around the issue of whether the Fourth Amendment protects the physician's privacy.

O'Connor v. Ortega

480 U.S. 709 (1986)

O'Connor, Justice.

This suit under 42 U.S.C. 1983 presents two issues concerning the Fourth Amendment rights of public employees. First, we must determine whether the respondent, a public employee, had a reasonable expectation of privacy in his office, desk, and file cabinets at his place of work. Second, we must address the appropriate Fourth Amendment standard for a search conducted by a public employer in areas in which a public employee is found to have a reasonable expectation of privacy.

Dr. Magno Ortega, a physician and psychiatrist, held the position of Chief of Professional Education at Napa State Hospital for 17 years, until his dismissal from that position in 1981. As Chief of Professional Education, Dr. Ortega had primary responsibility for training young physicians in psychiatric residency programs.

In July 1981, Hospital officials, including Dr. Dennis O'Connor, the Executive Director of the Hospital, became concerned about possible improprieties in Dr. Ortega's management of the residency program. In particular, the Hospital officials were concerned with Dr. Ortega's acquisition of an Apple II computer for use in the residency program. The officials thought that Dr. Ortega may have misled Dr. O'Connor into believing that the computer had been donated, when in fact the computer had been financed by the possibly coerced contributions of residents. Additionally, the Hospital officials were concerned with charges that Dr. Ortega had sexually harassed two female Hospital employees, and had taken inappropriate disciplinary action against a resident.

Dr. O'Connor selected several Hospital personnel to conduct the investigation, including an accountant, a physician, and a Hospital security officer. Richard Friday, the Hospital Administrator, led this "investigative team." At some point during the investigation, Mr. Friday made the decision to enter Dr. Ortega's office. The petitioners claim that the search was conducted to secure state property. Initially, petitioners contended that such a search was pursuant to a Hospital policy of conducting a routine inventory of state property in the office of a terminated employee. At the time of the search, however, the Hospital had not yet terminated Dr. Ortega's employment; Dr. Ortega was still on administrative leave. Apparently, there was no policy of inventorying the offices of those on administrative leave. Before the search had been initiated, however, petitioners had become aware that Dr. Ortega had taken the computer to his home. Dr. Ortega contends that the purpose of the search was to secure evidence for use against him in administrative disciplinary proceedings.

The resulting search of Dr. Ortega's office was quite thorough. The investigators entered the office a number of times and seized several items from Dr. Ortega's desk and file cabinets, including a Valentine's Day card, a photograph, and a book of poetry, all sent to Dr. Ortega by a former resident physician. These items were later used in a proceeding before a hearing officer of the California State Personnel Board to impeach the credibility of the former resident, who testified on Dr. Ortega's behalf. The investigators also seized billing documentation of one of Dr. Ortega's private patients under the California Medicaid program. The investigators did not otherwise separate Dr. Ortega's property from state property because, as one investigator testified, "trying to sort State from non-State, it was too much to do, so I gave it up and boxed it up." Thus, no formal inventory of the property in the office was ever made. Instead, all the papers in Dr. Ortega's office were merely placed in boxes, and put in storage for Dr. Ortega to retrieve.

Dr. Ortega commenced this action against petitioners in Federal District Court under 42 U.S.C.1983, alleging that the search of his office violated the Fourth Amendment.

The Fourth Amendment protects the "right of the people to be secure in their persons, houses, papers, and effects, against unreasonable searches and seizures. . . . " Our cases establish that Dr. Ortega's Fourth Amendment rights are implicated only if the conduct of the Hospital officials at issue in this case infringed "an expectation of privacy that society is prepared to consider reasonable."

Because the reasonableness of an expectation of privacy, as well as the appropriate standard for a search, is understood to differ according to context, it is essential first to delineate the boundaries of the workplace context. The workplace includes those areas and items that are related to work and are generally within the employer's control. At a hospital, for example, the hallways, cafeteria, offices, desks, and file cabinets, among other areas, are all part of the workplace. These areas remain part of the workplace context even if the employee has placed personal items in them, such as a photograph placed in a desk or a letter posted on an employee bulletin board. Not everything that passes through the confines of the business address can be considered part of the workplace context, however. An employee may bring closed luggage to the office prior to leaving on a trip, or a handbag or briefcase each workday. While whatever expectation of privacy the employee has in the existence and the outward appearance of the luggage is affected by its presence in the workplace, the employee's expectation of privacy in the contents of the luggage is not affected in the same way. The appropriate standard for a workplace search does not necessarily apply to a piece of closed personal luggage, a handbag, or a briefcase that happens to be within the employer's business address.

Within the workplace context, this Court has recognized that employees may have a reasonable expectation of privacy against intrusions by police. As with the expectation of privacy in one's home, such expectations have deep roots in the history of the Amendment.

Given the societal expectations of privacy in one's place of work, we reject the contention made by the Solicitor General and petitioners that public employees can never have a reasonable expectation of privacy in their place of work. Individuals do not lose Fourth Amendment rights merely because they work for the government instead of a private employer. The operational realities of the workplace, however, may make some employees' expectations of privacy unreasonable when an intrusion is by a supervisor rather than a law enforcement official. Public employees' expectations of privacy in their offices, desks, and file cabinets, like similar expectations of employees in the private sector, may be reduced by virtue of actual office practices and procedures, or by legitimate regulation.

The Court of Appeals concluded that Dr. Ortega had a reasonable expectation of privacy in his office, and five Members of this Court agree with that determination. Because the record does not reveal the extent to which Hospital officials may have had work-related reasons to enter Dr. Ortega's office, we think the Court of Appeals should have remanded the matter to the District Court for its further determination. But regardless of any legitimate right of access the Hospital staff may have had to the office as such, we recognize that the undisputed evidence suggests that Dr. Ortega had a reasonable expectation of privacy in his desk and file cabinets. The undisputed evidence discloses that Dr. Ortega did not share his desk or file cabinets with any other employees. Dr. Ortega had occupied the office for 17 years and he kept materials in his office, which included personal correspondence, medical files, correspondence from private patients unconnected to the Hospital, personal financial records, teaching aids and notes, and personal gifts and mementos.

On the basis of this undisputed evidence, we accept the conclusion of the Court of Appeals that Dr. Ortega had a reasonable expectation of privacy at least in his desk and file cabinets.

Judgment for Ortega.

Case Commentary

The U.S. Supreme Court decided that after occupying the same office for 17 years, the employee is entitled to a reasonable expectation of privacy in his desk and file cabinets. Because their decision is specific to this employee, it does not provide guidance for employees who occupy an office for a much shorter period of time or an employee who works in a cubicle or at a desk in an open floor plan with many others. ∎

CASE QUESTIONS

1. Do you agree with the court's decision?
2. Why did the court bother to hear this case if they were not going to make a decision that would provide guidance for employers who want to conduct office searches and for employees who want to know the extent of their privacy?

3. Does the fact that the desk, file cabinets, computer, and office belong to employers give them the right to search their contents?
4. Must notice be given to employees if an employer wants to conduct a search?

The issue in the next case is whether an employee has a right to privacy with the computer files in his office computer.

Muick v. Glenayre Electronics
280 F.3d 741 (7th Cir. 2002)

Posner, Circuit Judge.

Muick, at the time an employee of Glenayre Electronics, was arrested on charges of receiving and possessing child pornography in violation of federal law. At the request of federal law enforcement authorities, Glenayre seized from Muick's work area the laptop computer that it had furnished him for use at work and held it until a warrant to search it could be obtained. He was later convicted and imprisoned. He has now sued his former employer, claiming that Glenayre, acting under color of federal law, seized "proprietary and privileged personal financial and contact data" contained in files in the computer, in violation of the Fourth and Fifth Amendments.

The district judge rightly granted summary judgment to Glenayre on Muick's federal claims. The federal agents wanted Glenayre to give them the laptop right away but it refused until the search warrant was issued (and so it had no choice) because the computer contained confidential corporate information.

Anyway Muick had no right of privacy in the computer that Glenayre had lent him for use in the workplace. Not that there can't be a right of privacy (enforceable under the Fourth Amendment if the employer is a public entity, which Glenayre we have just held was not) in employer-owned equipment furnished to an employee for use in his place of employment. If the employer equips the employee's office with a safe or file cabinet or other receptacle in which to keep his private papers, he can assume that the contents of the safe are private. But Glenayre had announced that it could inspect the laptops that it furnished for the use of its employees, and this destroyed any reasonable expectation of privacy that Muick might have had and so scotches his claim. The laptops were Glenayre's property and it could attach whatever conditions to their use it wanted to. They didn't have to be reasonable conditions; but the abuse of access to workplace computers is so common (workers being prone to use them as media of gossip, titillation, and other entertainment and distraction) that reserving a right of inspection is so far from being unreasonable that the failure to do so might well be thought irresponsible.

Judgment for Glenayre Electronics.

Case Commentary

The Seventh Circuit Court rules that an employer has the right to inspect an office computer or laptop being used by an employee. ■

CASE QUESTIONS

1. Do you find the court's reasoning acceptable?
2. Is there any situation in which an employee can have a privacy interest?

3. Should there be guidelines placed on what an employer may look for when inspecting computer files?

COMPANY POLICY

Establishing a policy against employee theft is an important consideration for a company. The policy should include a definition encompassing all the property that the company feels if taken or allowed to be taken would constitute theft. The policy should spell out what the consequences for thefts will be and whether the company intends to have the employee prosecuted. A statement should be included stipulating that the policy applies to all employees from executives on down. The company must disseminate this policy to all its employees along with conspicuous posting. Finally the company should follow through rigorously, identifying and then enforcing breaches of this policy in a consistent manner.

WHISTLE-BLOWING

Whistle-blowing is the notification by an employee to management about a coworker's unlawful activities or to the appropriate federal and state agencies about the company's illegal activities.

Whistle-blowing is a noble and ethical act that sometimes requires a courageous effort on the part of an employee. Whistle-blowers may be heroes in the movies, but they are often labeled troublemakers and treated with disdain by management and coworkers for the disruption they cause. Although the authorities encourage whistle-blowing, more could be done to protect people who do risk their jobs for the truth to be known.

On the other hand, some workers whistle-blow as an act of spite or revenge. They may fabricate the event or blow it out of proportion. These workers are not acting in an ethical manner.

Whistleblower Protection Act

The Whistleblower Protection Act of 1989 (WPA) was enacted to safeguard workers who report major violations of the law from being discharged or otherwise retaliated against by their employers. To qualify for whistle-blower protection, an employee must provide a written disclosure regarding a violation of state or federal law through (1) mismanagement, (2) abuse of authority, (3) substantial waste of public funds, or (4) danger to public health and/or safety.

False Claims Act

The False Claims Act of 1863, as revised in 1986, protects whistle-blowers against retaliation and encourages whistle-blowers by providing relators (whistle-blowers) with a percentage of the funds recovered from those who defrauded the federal or state government.

Sarbanes-Oxley Act

In 2002, the Sarbanes-Oxley Act was enacted in response to the false accounting reports that enabled Enron and other corporations to perpetrate securities fraud. To ensure enforcement of this act, employees and other individuals are encouraged to disclose information about a company that they reasonably believe is in violation of the federal securities laws or SEC rules and regulations. These whistle-blowers are protected from retaliation by their employer. They are entitled to reinstatement, back pay, attorney's fees, and court costs. Some state statutes also provide punitive damages.

EMPLOYEE LESSONS

1. Familiarize yourself with the protections afforded by law to safeguard your privacy.
2. Question employers who have implemented or are implementing security measures to determine their motives.
3. Decide if you want to work in an environment where your privacy is restricted.
4. Refrain from stealing property from the business.
5. Avoid conducting an inordinate amount of personal business on company time.
6. Do not use company property, such as vehicles or equipment, for personal tasks without consent.
7. Refrain from abusing phone, fax, and copying privileges.
8. Know when you have been subjected to the torts of defamation, invasion of privacy, and interference with business relations.
9. Never justify your immoral or illegal action against the business out of revenge for its ill-treatment toward you.
10. Acquaint yourself with the WPA.
11. Comprehend the ramifications that could befall you for whistle-blowing and evaluate whether your decision to do so is justified.

SUMMARY

Employers and workers have strong opinions on privacy, theft, and whistle-blowing, and most often their interests are adverse. Absent litigation, these conflicts can only be resolved through a thorough understanding of the other party's concerns and the applicable laws governing privacy. Fostering communication is key here. Open or secret retaliation can result in a war zone where sides are drawn. This can only hurt the business. Power struggles and authoritative behavior are ultimately no match for compromise and balance.

REVIEW QUESTIONS

1. Explain the significance of the Privacy Act of 1974.
2. What are the implications of the Omnibus Crime Control and Safe Streets Act of 1968?
3. How has the right to privacy been affected by the Electronic Communications Act of 1986?
4. In what respect has the Fair Credit Reporting Act of 1970 improved the right to privacy?
5. What types of property are encompassed under the heading of employee theft?
6. What types of action have been taken by employers to combat employee theft?
7. Do any of these security actions infringe on an employee's right to privacy?
8. How can both interests be effectively balanced?
9. Is an employer entitled to conduct office searches?

CASE PROBLEMS

1. Jon F. Moran, M.D., former head of the Department of Cardiothoracic Surgery at the University of Kansas Medical Center (KUMC), brought this action against defendants, alleging that they made false and defamatory statements about him and his stewardship of KUMC's heart transplant program. At issue are statements made by KUMC administrators in May 1995.

   The impact of the Kansas City *Star's* May 7 article lay in its pairing of the fact that no heart transplants had been performed at KUMC from early May 1994 to late March 1995 with the paradox that patients continued to be admitted and added to the heart transplant waiting list. In investigating the circumstances, the reporter talked to Moran and Dr. Clay Beggerly, the program's two former surgeons. The account that Moran gave the reporter was that he had complained for many months of a lack of surgeons and qualified nurses. When the complaints produced no changes, Moran asked twice in early June 1994 that the program be suspended. His request was not granted. In early November, he told administrators that he would do no more heart transplants.

   Jon Jackson, an associate administrator of KUMC, was quoted in the Star's article: "There was not any indication given to us that he was not operating a program," said Jon Jackson, an associate administrator, "had Dr. Moran told us that we're not going to do transplants prior to his letter of Nov. 4, we would have made other arrangements for those procedures to take place." What result? *Moran v. State of Kansas*, 985 p.2d 127 (Kan. 1999)

2. The state's evidence at trial showed that Benton had stolen at least $2,300 from her employer. Benton was convicted of felony theft and falsification of business records. On October 25, 1996, Benton was sentenced to probation. She was also ordered to make restitution. The Superior Court aggregated the total theft from the Association by Benton at $5,994.65. The Superior Court also determined that Benton should pay restitution for the following amounts, which reflect a portion of the fees the Association had paid its accountants: $6,660 to ascertain the amount stolen by Benton through the "lapping" scheme; $1,336 in expenses for trial preparation; and $7,460 for restoring the Association's financial records because of the damage done by Benton's falsifications.

   In an amended sentencing order dated August 15, 1997, the Superior Court directed Benton to pay restitution in the total amount of $21,450.65. Prior to the Superior Court's order quantifying Benton's restitution, the Association had received the proceeds of a $10,000 bond under a policy of theft insurance, as a result of Benton's theft. Therefore, the Superior Court divided the restitution. The first $11,450.65 was ordered to be paid to the Association and the remaining $10,000 to the insurer.

The issue is whether an employee who has stolen funds should be liable to make restitution for the funds converted as well as for the expenses the employer incurred to straighten out its accounting records. Benton submits that the maximum amount of restitution she could be ordered to pay is limited to the evidence presented during her criminal trial. Therefore, Benton contends that the Superior Court erred by ordering her to pay an amount of restitution in excess of $2,300. What result? *Benton v. State of Delaware,* 711 A.2d 792 (Del. 1998)

3. Chavira was passing funds embezzled from his employer, ITT, to his friend Tovar's bank account. Tovar was able to extricate himself because he was unaware that this was happening. Tovar sought damages from ITT for infliction of emotional distress. The issue is whether he is entitled damages to relief. *ITT Consumer Financial Corp. v. Tovar,* 932 S.W.2d 147 (Tex. 1996)

4. The Petitioner, Dr. Richard Herman, filed an Individual Right of Action ("IRA") appeal to the Merit Systems Protection Board ("Board" or "MSPB"), alleging that he was reassigned in retaliation for whistle-blowing activities. In September 1997, Dr. Herman was laterally reassigned from the position of Chief Clinical Psychologist, GM-13, at the Federal Prison Camp, Eglin Air Force Base, Florida, to that of Staff Clinical Psychologist, GM-13, at the Federal Correctional Complex, Coleman, Florida. Before the Board, Dr. Herman asserted that the memorandum indicated that failure to have a formal written agreement with the hospital, or have a suicide watch room at the camp itself, potentially posed a substantial and specific danger to the public health and safety within the meaning of the WPA and violated the U.S. Department of Justice/Federal Bureau of Prisons Suicide Prevention Program ("SPP"). Is the disclosure protected under the WPA? *Herman v. Department of Justice,* 193 F.3d 1375 (Fed. Cir. 1999)

HUMAN RESOURCE DILEMMAS

1. Bobby Tucker has been working as a Web designer for Velvet, Inc., for 2 years. During lunch, Maria Brown, a coworker, enters Bobby's cubicle to hand him a file. She is startled when she observes graphic pornography on Bobby's computer. He retorts that he confines his viewing to off-hours. Maria informs human resources. How should human resources respond?

2. Jill Malibu has a new boyfriend, Jack. Jack phones Jill at least three times a day, and each conversation is at least 30 minutes. Jill's employer, "Q" Inc., has been monitoring calls for use and duration. Jill's work performance has been satisfactory to date. How should "Q" respond?

3. Jared Littleton is an accountant for Wilhelm, Dawkins and White. Jared's friends send him e-mail jokes. He usually forwards these to coworkers and superiors. Even Mr. White enjoys receiving them. One day a copy of a racial e-mail joke is lying around. Tyler Matthews comes across it and is horrified by its contents. He notifies Mr. White, unaware that Mr. White is also a recipient. How should Mr. White respond?

WEB SITE ASSIGNMENT

Using the following Web sites as a guide, formulate policies with regard to e-mail, phone use, computer site access, whistle-blower protection, and office searches.

www.epic.org/privacy/consumer/states.html
www.netatty.com/privacy/privacy.html
www.employeetheft.com
www.privacy.gov.au/internet/email/index.htm
www.publaw.com/privacy.html
www.discriminationattorney.com/whistle.html

Chapter

Termination

Employment Scenario

Fred Williams was hired by The Long and the Short of It 3 months ago. His position is market analyst. Fred's function is to anticipate fashion trends and to make purchase recommendations as to the type of clothing, the brand name, and the quantity. Fred has been off the mark on all of his recommendations. Tom Long and Mark Short inform Fred that his work is unsatisfactory and, therefore, he is being discharged. Fred states he should not be judged on one mistake. He begs Tom and Mark to reconsider; otherwise, he will be forced to sue. Tom and Mark consult with Susan North, Esq., concerning their discharge of Fred. What advice should she give them?

Employment Scenario

Tom Long and Mark Short approach Susan with a query about whether L&S should create an employment handbook. What are the advantages and disadvantages?

Chapter Checklist

➤ Understand the significance of at-will employment.

➤ Appreciate the controversy surrounding this topic.

➤ Be aware of the public policy exceptions to at-will employment.

➤ Consider how an employer can vitiate at-will employment through an employee handbook.

➤ Learn how an employee proceeds with an objection to the termination.

➤ Understand the compromise of the Model Employment Termination Act.

➤ Comprehend the impact this Act has on both employer and employee.

➤ Imagine why an employer may retaliate against an employee by discharging him or her.

➤ *Identify when an uncomfortable employment environment transforms itself into constructive discharge.*

➤ *Be familiar with the other reasons for concluding an employment relationship.*

INTRODUCTION

Most employment relationships are oral contracts for an indefinite period of time. As such, these relationships can be ended at the will of either of the parties without a reason. That is how the term "at-will" employment originated. It is a source of major controversy in the field of employment law. Public policy exceptions have been carved into the at-will employment doctrine. Every state has its own list of exceptions, but the major ones are the following: discrimination, retaliation for whistle-blowing, instituting a workers' compensation claim, and filing or testifying in a harassment or discrimination lawsuit against an employer.

HUMAN RESOURCE ADVICE

- Understand the law relating to at-will employment.
- Be careful to identify reasons for termination, because they may compromise at-will employment.
- Use a consistent set of criteria for evaluating employees for discharge.
- Establish a grievance procedure within the company that culminates in arbitration.
- Avoid bad publicity and litigation.
- Refrain from discrimination when terminating employees.
- Do not retaliate against employees when they whistle-blow, file a workers' compensation claim, or initiate or testify in a lawsuit based on discrimination or harassment.
- Avoid acting maliciously toward an employee by making the work environment so intolerable for him or her that it constitutes constructive discharge.

TERMINATION OF EMPLOYMENT

Termination is the discharge of an employee by an employer with or without cause. An employment relationship may terminate in the following ways:

- Employment at will
- Agreement
- Fulfillment of purpose

Employment at will

Employment at will is the employer's right to revoke the worker's authority and to terminate him or her at will.

An employer may dismiss an employee without cause where the employment relationship is considered to be at will. *At will* means either the employer or the employee can terminate the relationship upon giving proper notice. Proper notice is considered to be the duration of the pay period, i.e., 1 week, 2 weeks, or 1 month. (The phrase "2-week notice" is derived from this policy.) Employers feel that if employees are free to leave at will, then employers should be free to discharge employees at will, too. However, some employers state in their employee handbooks that employees will not be dismissed except for cause or in case of layoffs. In this context, the employer has given up its ability to terminate at will.

In the case that follows, the issue is whether an at-will employee is entitled to protection from reprisals and intimidation when he is asked to appear as a witness against superiors.

Haddle v. Garrison
525 U.S. 121 (1998)

Chief Justice Rehnquist delivered the opinion of the Court.

Petitioner Michael A. Haddle, an at-will employee, alleges that respondents conspired to have him fired from his job in retaliation for obeying a federal grand jury subpoena and to deter him from testifying at a federal criminal trial. We hold that such interference with at-will employment may give rise to a claim for damages under the Civil Rights Act.

According to petitioner's complaint, a federal grand jury indictment in March 1995 charged petitioner's employer, Healthmaster, Inc., and respondents Jeanette Garrison and Dennis Kelly, officers of Healthmaster, with Medicare fraud. Petitioner cooperated with the federal agents in the investigation that preceded the indictment. He also appeared to testify before the grand jury pursuant to a subpoena, but did not testify due to the press of time. Petitioner was also expected to appear as a witness in the criminal trial resulting from the indictment.

Although Garrison and Kelly were barred by the Bankruptcy Court from participating in the affairs of Healthmaster, they conspired with G. Peter Molloy, Jr., one of the remaining officers of Healthmaster, to bring about petitioner's termination. They did this both to intimidate petitioner and to retaliate against him for his attendance at the federal-court proceedings.

Petitioner sued for damages in the United States District Court for the Southern District of Georgia, asserting a federal claim and various state-law claims. Petitioner stated two grounds for relief: one for conspiracy to deter him from testifying in the upcoming criminal trial and one for conspiracy to retaliate against him for attending the grand jury proceedings.

Respondents moved to dismiss for failure to state a claim upon which relief can be granted. Because petitioner conceded that he was an at-will employee, the District Court granted the motion on the authority of *Morast v. Lance.* In *Morast,* the Eleventh Circuit held that an at-will employee who is dismissed pursuant to a conspiracy has no cause of

action. The *Morast* court explained that "to make out a cause of action the plaintiff must have suffered an actual injury. Because Morast was an at will employee, . . . he had no constitutionally protected interest in continued employment. Therefore, Morast's discharge did not constitute an actual injury under this statute." Relying on its decision in *Morast,* the Court of Appeals affirmed.

The Eleventh Circuit's rule in Morast conflicts with the holdings of the First and Ninth Circuits. We therefore granted certiorari. At issue is whether petitioner was "injured in his property or person" when respondents induced his employer to terminate petitioner's at will employment as part of a conspiracy prohibited by §1985(2). Section 1985(2), in relevant part, proscribes conspiracies to "deter, by force, intimidation, or threat, any party or witness in any court of the United States from attending such court, or from testifying to any matter pending therein, freely, fully, and truthfully, or to injure such party or witness in his person or property on account of his having so attended or testified." The statute provides that if one or more persons engaged in such a conspiracy "do, or cause to be done, any act in furtherance of the object of such conspiracy, whereby another is injured in his person or property, . . . the party so injured . . . may have an action for the recovery of damages occasioned by such injury . . . against any one or more of the conspirators." Our review in this case is accordingly confined to one question: Can petitioner state a claim for damages by alleging that a conspiracy proscribed by §1985(2) induced his employer to terminate his at-will employment?

We disagree with the Eleventh Circuit's conclusion that petitioner must suffer an injury to a "constitutionally protected property interest" to state a claim for damages under §1985(2). Nothing in the language or purpose of the proscriptions in the first clause of §1985(2), nor in its attendant remedial provisions, establishes such a requirement. The gist of the wrong at which §1985(2) is directed is not deprivation of property, but intimidation or retaliation against witnesses in federal-court proceedings. The terms "injured in his person or property" define the harm that the victim may suffer as a result of the conspiracy to intimidate or retaliate. Thus, the fact that employment at will is not "property" for purposes of the Due Process Clause does not mean that loss of at-will employment may not "injure petitioner in his person or property" for purposes of §1985(2). The kind of interference with at-will employment relations alleged here is merely a species of the traditional torts of intentional interference with contractual relations and intentional interference with prospective contractual relations. This protection against third-party

interference with at-will employment relations is still afforded by state law today. Even though a person's employment contract is at will, he has a valuable contract right which may not be unlawfully interfered with by a third person.

The judgment of the Court of Appeals is reversed, and the case is remanded for further proceedings consistent with this opinion.

Judgment per Haddle.

Case Commentary

Most employment positions are at will. If at-will employees were not protected from intimidation, then practically all employees could be exposed to this harm without recourse. ■

CASE QUESTIONS

1. What do you think of the Eleventh Circuit Court's decision in *Morast?*

2. Do at-will employees deserve any protection?
3. To what measure of damages is Haddle entitled?

Reason for Discharge

Employers may decide to tell employees the real reason for the discharge. The reason should be job related, dealing with performance, attendance, theft, drug use, harassment, negligence, and so forth. Employers should never give a false reason. This may lead to a lawsuit by the employee.

The issue in the case that follows is whether the plaintiff was the victim of intentional discrimination to satisfy the pretext requirement for disparate treatment.

Reeves v. Sanderson Plumbing
530 U.S. 133 (2000)

Justice O'Connor delivered the opinion of the Court.

This case concerns the kind and amount of evidence necessary to sustain a jury's verdict that an employer unlawfully discriminated on the basis of age. Specifically, we must resolve whether a defendant is entitled to judgment as a matter of law when the plaintiff's case consists exclusively of a prima facie case of discrimination and sufficient evidence for the trier of fact to disbelieve the defendant's legitimate, nondiscriminatory explanation for its action. We must also decide whether the employer was entitled to judgment as a matter of law under the particular circumstances presented here.

In October 1995, petitioner Roger Reeves was 57 years old and had spent 40 years in the employ of respondent, Sanderson Plumbing Products, Inc., a manufacturer of toilet seats and covers. Petitioner worked in a department known as the "Hinge Room," where he supervised the "regular line." Joe Oswalt, in his mid-thirties, supervised the Hinge Room's "special line," and Russell Caldwell, the manager of the Hinge Room and age 45, supervised both petitioner and Oswalt. Petitioner's responsibilities included recording the attendance and hours of those under his supervision, and

reviewing a weekly report that listed the hours worked by each employee.

In the summer of 1995, Caldwell informed Powe Chesnut, the director of manufacturing and the husband of company president Sandra Sanderson, that "production was down" in the Hinge Room because employees were often absent and were "coming in late and leaving early." Because the monthly attendance reports did not indicate a problem, Chesnut ordered an audit of the Hinge Room's timesheets for July, August, and September of that year. According to Chesnut's testimony, that investigation revealed "numerous timekeeping errors and misrepresentations on the part of Caldwell, Reeves, and Oswalt." Following the audit, Chesnut, along with Dana Jester, vice president of human resources, and Tom Whitaker, vice president of operations, recommended to company president Sanderson that petitioner and Caldwell be fired. In October 1995, Sanderson followed the recommendation and discharged both petitioner and Caldwell.

In June 1996, petitioner filed suit in the United States District Court for the Northern District of Mississippi, contending that he had been fired because of his age in violation of the Age Discrimination in Employment Act of 1967 (ADEA). At trial, respondent contended that it had fired petitioner due to his failure to maintain accurate attendance records, while petitioner attempted to demonstrate that respondent's explanation was pretext for age discrimination. Petitioner introduced evidence that he had accurately recorded the attendance and hours of the employees under his supervision, and that Chesnut, whom Oswalt described as wielding "absolute power" within the company, had demonstrated age-based animus in his dealings with petitioner.

The District Court accordingly entered judgment for petitioner in the amount of $70,000, which included $35,000 in liquidated damages based on the jury's finding of willfulness. Respondent then renewed its motion for judgment as a matter of law and alternatively moved for a new trial, while petitioner moved for front pay. The District Court denied respondent's motions and granted petitioner's, awarding him $28,490.80 in front pay for two years' lost income.

The Court of Appeals for the Fifth Circuit reversed, holding that petitioner had not introduced sufficient evidence to sustain the jury's finding of unlawful discrimination. After noting respondent's proffered justification for petitioner's discharge, the court acknowledged that petitioner "very well may" have offered sufficient evidence for "a reasonable jury to have found that [respondent's] explanation for its employment decision was pretextual." The court explained, however, that this was "not dispositive" of the ultimate issue—namely, "whether Reeves presented sufficient evidence that his age motivated respondent's employment decision." Addressing this question, the court weighed petitioner's additional evidence of discrimination against other circumstances surrounding his discharge. Specifically, the court noted that Chesnut's age-based comments "were not made in the direct context of Reeves's termination"; there was no allegation that the two other individuals who had recommended that petitioner be fired (Jester and Whitaker) were motivated by age; two of the decisionmakers involved in petitioner's discharge (Jester and Sanderson) were over the age of 50; all three of the Hinge Room supervisors were accused of inaccurate recordkeeping; and several of respondent's management positions were filled by persons over age 50 when petitioner was fired. On this basis, the court concluded that petitioner had not introduced sufficient evidence for a rational jury to conclude that he had been discharged because of his age.

We granted certiorari to resolve a conflict among the Courts of Appeals as to whether a plaintiff's prima facie case of discrimination combined with sufficient evidence for a reasonable factfinder to reject the employer's nondiscriminatory explanation for its decision, is adequate to sustain a finding of liability for intentional discrimination.

II

In this case, the evidence supporting respondent's explanation for petitioner's discharge consisted primarily of testimony by Chesnut and Sanderson and documentation of petitioner's alleged "shoddy record keeping." Chesnut testified that a 1993 audit of Hinge Room operations revealed "a very lax assembly line" where employees were not adhering to general work rules. As a result of that audit, petitioner was placed on 90 days' probation for unsatisfactory performance. In 1995, Chesnut ordered another investigation of the Hinge Room, which, according to his testimony, revealed that petitioner was not correctly recording the absences and hours of employees. Respondent introduced summaries of that investigation documenting several attendance violations by 12 employees under petitioner's supervision, and noting that each should have been disciplined in some manner. Chesnut testified that this failure to discipline absent and late employees is "extremely important when you are dealing with a union" because uneven enforcement across departments would keep the company "in grievance and arbitration cases, which are costly, all the time." He and Sanderson also stated that petitioner's errors, by failing to adjust for hours not worked, cost the company overpaid wages. Sanderson testified that she accepted the recommendation to discharge petitioner because he had "intentionally falsified company pay records."

Petitioner, however, made a substantial showing that respondent's explanation was false. First, petitioner offered evidence that he had properly maintained the attendance records. Most of the timekeeping errors cited by respondent involved employees who were not marked late but who were recorded as having arrived at the plant at 7 A.M. for the 7 A.M. shift. Respondent contended that employees arriving at 7 A.M. could not have been at their workstations by 7 A.M., and therefore must have been late. But both petitioner and Oswalt testified that the company's automated time-clock often failed to scan employees' timecards, so that the timesheets would not record any time of arrival. On these occasions, petitioner and Oswalt would visually check the workstations and record whether the employees were present at the start of the shift. They stated that if an employee arrived promptly but the timesheet contained no time of arrival, they would reconcile the two by marking "7 A.M." as the employee's arrival time, even if the employee actually arrived at the plant earlier. On cross-examination, Chesnut acknowledged that the timeclock sometimes malfunctioned, and that if "people were there at their work stations" at the start of the shift, the supervisor "would write in seven o'clock." Petitioner also testified that when employees arrived before or stayed after their shifts, he would assign them additional work so they would not be overpaid.

Based on this evidence, the Court of Appeals concluded that petitioner "very well may be correct" that "a reasonable jury could have found that respondent's explanation for its employment decision was pretextual." Nonetheless, the court held that this showing, standing alone, was insufficient to sustain the jury's finding of liability: "We must, as an essential final step, determine whether Reeves presented sufficient evidence that his age motivated respondent's employment decision."

And in making this determination, the Court of Appeals ignored the evidence supporting petitioner's prima facie case and challenging respondent's explanation for its decision. The court confined its review of evidence favoring petitioner to that evidence showing that Chesnut had directed derogatory, age-based comments at petitioner, and that Chesnut had singled out petitioner for harsher treatment than younger employees. It is therefore apparent that the court believed that only this additional evidence of discrimination was relevant to whether the jury's verdict should stand. That is, the Court of Appeals proceeded from the assumption that a prima facie case of discrimination, combined with sufficient evidence for the trier of fact to disbelieve the defendant's legitimate, nondiscriminatory reason for its decision, is insufficient as a matter of law to sustain a jury's finding of intentional discrimination.

The ultimate question is whether the employer intentionally discriminated, and proof that "the employer's proffered reason is unpersuasive, or even obviously contrived, does not necessarily establish that the plaintiff's proffered reason . . . is correct." In other words, "it is not enough . . . to *dis*believe the employer; the factfinder must *believe* the plaintiff's explanation of intentional discrimination."

Whether judgment as a matter of law is appropriate in any particular case will depend on a number of factors. Those include the strength of the plaintiff's prima facie case, the probative value of the proof that the employer's explanation is false, and any other evidence that supports the employer's case and that properly may be considered on a motion for judgment as a matter of law. For purposes of this case, we need not—and could not—resolve all of the circumstances in which such factors would entitle an employer to judgment as a matter of law. It suffices to say that, because a prima facie case and sufficient evidence to reject the employer's explanation may permit a finding of liability, the Court of Appeals erred in proceeding from the premise that a plaintiff must always introduce additional, independent evidence of discrimination.

III

Petitioner introduced evidence that Chesnut was the actual decisionmaker behind his firing. Chesnut was married to Sanderson, who made the formal decision to discharge petitioner. Although Sanderson testified that she fired petitioner because he had "intentionally falsified company pay records," respondent only introduced evidence concerning the inaccuracy of the records, not their falsification. A 1994 letter authored by Chesnut indicated that he berated other company directors, who were supposedly his co-equals, about how to do their jobs. Moreover, Oswalt testified that all of respondent's employees feared Chesnut, and that Chesnut had exercised "absolute power" within the company for "as long as he can remember."

In holding that the record contained insufficient evidence to sustain the jury's verdict, the Court of Appeals misapplied the standard of review dictated by Rule 50. Again, the court disregarded critical evidence favorable to petitioner—namely, the evidence supporting petitioner's prima facie case and undermining respondent's nondiscriminatory explanation. The court also failed to draw all reasonable inferences in favor of petitioner. For instance, while acknowledging "the potentially damning nature" of Chesnut's age-related comments, the court discounted them on the ground that they "were not made in the direct context of Reeves's termination." And the court discredited petitioner's evidence that Chesnut was the actual decisionmaker by giving weight to the fact that there was "no evidence to suggest that any of the other decision makers were motivated by age." Moreover, the other evidence on which the court relied—that Caldwell and Oswalt were also cited for poor recordkeeping, and that respondent employed many managers over age 50—although relevant, is certainly not dispositive. In concluding that these circumstances so overwhelmed the evidence favoring petitioner that no rational trier of fact could have found that petitioner was fired because of his age, the Court of Appeals impermissibly substituted its judgment concerning the weight of the evidence for the jury's.

The ultimate question in every employment discrimination case involving a claim of disparate treatment is whether the plaintiff was the victim of intentional discrimination. Given the evidence in the record supporting petitioner, we see no reason to subject the parties to an additional round of litigation before the Court of Appeals rather than to resolve the matter here. The District Court plainly informed the jury that petitioner was required to show "by a preponderance of the evidence that his age was a determining and motivating factor in the decision of respondent to terminate him." The court instructed the jury that, to show that respondent's explanation was a pretext for discrimination, petitioner had to demonstrate "1, that the stated reasons were not the real reasons for petitioner's discharge; *and* 2, that age discrimination was the real reason for petitioner's discharge." Given that petitioner established a prima facie case of discrimination, introduced enough evidence for the jury to reject respondent's explanation, and produced additional evidence of age-based animus, there was sufficient evidence for the jury to find that respondent had intentionally discriminated. The District Court was therefore correct to submit the case to the jury, and the Court of Appeals erred in overturning its verdict.

For these reasons, the judgment of the Court of Appeals is reversed in favor of Reeves.

Case Commentary

The U.S. Supreme Court ruled that Reeves presented sufficient evidence to prove intentional age discrimination, meeting the pretext requirement for disparate treatment. Prior to the Reeves decision, if an employer lied about the reason for termination, the employee would have to prove the real reason was discriminatory. In *Reeves*, the U.S. Supreme Court stated that the employee need only prove the reason was false and let the jury decide if the real reason was discriminatory. ∎

1. Are you in agreement with the court's decision?
2. Do you believe the age-related comments made were sufficient to constitute age discrimination?
3. To prove intentional discrimination is it enough if the employer's reason for termination is not legitimate?

WARN

The Worker Adjustment and Retraining Notification Act (WARN) of 1989 requires employers having 100 or more employees to give 60 days' notice of a substantial layoff or the closing of a plant or office. This gives employees the opportunity to retrain or seek other work. It also gives state agencies that assist the unemployed time to prepare. There are exceptions for unforeseen conditions, acts of God, strikes and layoffs that are anticipated not to exceed 6 months.

Employment Handbooks

The purpose of an employment handbook is to provide a reference guide for employees concerning the employer's policies. This dispels confusion and ignorance, which may arise from lack of information. Company policies should be described in detail, yet the language of an employment handbook must be clear and concise.

Employment handbooks are not considered to be contracts in most states. However, where employers have provided for a written discharge procedure in their handbook, courts in many states may view these procedures as constituting a binding contract by which the employer must abide. In these states, the written discharge procedure mitigates the at-will employment protection afforded to employers. To preserve at-will employment, handbooks should clearly state that employment is at will and may be terminated by either the employer or the employee at any time for any or no reason with or without cause.

The issue in the case that follows is whether the employee was justifiably terminated because of a violation of the company's employment handbook.

Autoliv Asp, Inc. v. Department of Workforce Services
29 P.3d 7 (UT 2001)

Billings, Judge.

Autoliv ASP, Inc. (Autoliv) appeals from a decision of the Workforce Appeals Board (Board) granting Christopher Guzman and Thomas King unemployment benefits. Autoliv argues that Guzman and King were discharged for just cause and are thus ineligible for unemployment benefits. We agree and thus reverse and remand.

BACKGROUND

Autoliv provides its over 6,000 employees with an employee handbook. The policies in the handbook that are relevant here include Autoliv's general rules of conduct, its anti-harassment policy, and its policy regarding computer usage.

Autoliv's general rules of conduct state:

Each employee is required to be familiar with these rules and with additional rules which apply to particular jobs and operations. . . . In addition, each employee is expected to maintain conduct consistent with job efficiency and accepted standards of behavior for a business environment. Deviation from those standards may be cause for disciplinary action.

Disciplinary action may be taken for violation of any single rule or combination of rules, or for other improper conduct or unsatisfactory performance, and may *include* any of the following actions: [1] Employee discussion; [2] Notice of Caution; [3] Involuntary Suspension; [4] *Termination.* . . .

Failure of the company to enforce any rule does not excuse any employee from his other responsibility to comply with the rule, nor will such failure alter the company's right to take disciplinary action thereafter.

Autoliv's anti-harassment policy stated that Autoliv would not "tolerate or permit illegal harassment or retaliation, of any nature within our workforce." Autoliv's policy regarding the use of its computer system specifically prohibited, "use of e-mail for reasons other than transmittal of business related information," and "conduct that reflects unfavorably on the corporation."

In June 1998, Autoliv investigated problems it had experienced with the transmission of e-mail messages through its computer system because of excessive use. It was determined that non-business related messages were contributing to the problems. As a result, a company wide e-mail was sent explaining the problem and reiterating Autoliv's e-mail policy. The e-mail stated, "e-mail is to be used for business only. We do not wish to 'police' the e-mail system, so your cooperation would be appreciated. Please refrain from sending/receiving these types of messages as it is interfering with legitimate business e-mail."

In September 1998, Autoliv's Vice President of Human Resources sent another company wide e-mail which explained Autoliv's policy in more detail and included a warning that failure to adhere to the business only e-mail policy could result in termination.

In January 1999, Autoliv again reiterated its e-mail policy by sending out another company wide e-mail which stated that transmission of chain letters, jokes and stories, and non-business related announcements constituted improper use of the e-mail system. The message instructed employees, "If you receive an inappropriate E-mail, delete it and do not forward it to anyone." Finally, the message warned, "E-mail use is a benefit and abuse could lead to disciplinary action and/or termination."

Autoliv received a complaint from a former employee alleging that she had received offensive and sexually harassing e-mail from current Autoliv employees. Autoliv immediately began an investigation. The investigation revealed that several employees had violated Autoliv's e-mail policy by using e-mail for non- business related messages. Guzman and King were found to have violated the policy including the transmission of sexually oriented and offensive messages.

Specifically, the investigation revealed that Guzman had sent eleven non-business related messages containing jokes, photos, and short videos that were sexually explicit and clearly offensive in nature. King had sent approximately twenty-five non-business related messages containing the same type of sexually explicit and offensive content.

Concerned about the quantity of non-business related e-mail messages and the threat of sexual harassment lawsuits that could result from the sexual and offensive content of the messages, Autoliv terminated Guzman and King for "improper and unauthorized use of company e-mail." After

unsuccessfully seeking reinstatement, Guzman and King filed applications for unemployment benefits with the Department of Workforce Services (Department). The Department found that Guzman and King had been discharged by Autoliv without just cause and thus found them eligible for benefits. Autoliv appealed the decisions of the Department to an Administrative Law Judge (ALJ).

At the hearing before the ALJ, Guzman and King admitted to sending the e-mails. They testified that they had received Autoliv's handbook and were aware of the anti-harassment policy. They also testified they probably had received the three company wide e-mail messages about Autoliv's e-mail policy. However, they claimed they most likely deleted the e-mails before reading them. Thus, both claimants testified they were unaware their conduct could result in immediate termination and did not understand why they were not warned and allowed to change their conduct.

The ALJ upheld the decision of the Department. The ALJ concluded, "abuse of the company e-mail was common among employees, and the employer had an obligation to the claimant[s] to issue a specific warning, maybe even a suspension (not merely a memo) notifying the claimant[s] the conduct would not be tolerated."

Autoliv appealed the ALJ's decisions to the Workforce Appeals Board. The Board adopted the ALJ's findings of fact and, in a 2-1 decision, concluded that while Guzman and King were culpable, the element of "knowledge" was not present and thus there was no just cause for their discharge. The Board reasoned that Autoliv's strict written policy on e-mail use differed from its actual application of that policy. The Board concluded that "because of the difficulty of deciding when an employee's use of the e-mail becomes 'excessive' [Autoliv] had an obligation to notify the claimant that his e-mail use differed significantly in content and extent from that of his co-workers and that continuing to use the e-mail as he was doing would result in a discharge."

Autoliv appeals.

JUST CAUSE TERMINATION

A claimant is ineligible for unemployment benefits if the claimant was discharged for "just cause." To establish "just cause," three elements must be present: culpability, knowledge, and control. The Board concedes the elements of culpability and control. Thus, the only issue is whether Guzman and King had "'knowledge of the conduct which the employer expected.'" There are two ways to establish that a claimant had knowledge: (1) the employer must have provided a clear explanation of the expected behavior or a written policy regarding the same; or (2) "the conduct involved is a 'flagrant violation of a universal standard of behavior.'"

Autoliv need not establish "knowledge" with a clear explanation or written policy and consistent enforcement of that policy if Guzman and King's conduct was "a flagrant violation of a universal standard of behavior." There is a minimum level of behavior an employer has a right to expect from its employees and thus the employer need not specifically communicate that expectation.

Autoliv asserts that, in this day and age of sexual harassment lawsuits, it is "incomprehensible" for the Board to hold that a worker could be unaware of the dangers of having sexually offensive materials, including videos depicting sexual acts sent between co-workers in a company's computer network. We agree. The Board in its opinion states the "content of the materials was sexually explicit and offensive. Such material in the workplace could have subjected the employer to sexual harassment claims." This finding in our view supports a conclusion that the claimants' conduct violated a universal standard of behavior.

E-mail transmission of sexually explicit and offensive material such as jokes, pictures, and videos exposes the employer to sexual harassment and sex discrimination lawsuits. As the Utah Supreme Court stated "our society has ceased seeing sexual harassment in the work place as a playful inevitability that should be taken in good spirits and has awakened to the fact that sexual harassment has a corrosive effect on those who engage in it as well as those who are subjected to it."

We conclude that in today's workplace, the e-mail transmission of sexually explicit and offensive jokes, pictures, and videos constitutes a flagrant violation of a universal standard of behavior. Therefore, we reverse the Board's decision and remand to the Board to enter a decision consistent with our opinion.

Judgment for Autoliv.

Case Commentary

The Utah Supreme Court ruled that the employer had a policy against sexual harassment in its employment handbook. The employees who violated that policy were either aware of it or should have been aware of it because it had been properly communicated to all employees. ∎

CASE QUESTIONS

1. Are you in agreement with the court's reasoning?
2. Is it possible that the employees who were charged with harassment were unaware of the policy?
3. If so, whose fault is it?

Breach of Contract

A *breach of contract* occurs when the employee's reasonable expectations under the contract have not been fulfilled. Breach of contract suits arise in the following situations:

1. When a contract is made for a definite period of time, and the employee is terminated before the expiration of that time period without cause, the employer will be liable for the duration of the contract.
2. When an employer specifies in an interview the reasons why an employee may be terminated, then discharge will be limited to those reasons.
3. When an employment handbook recites a litany of causes for an employee's discharge, then the employer will be bound to what it has stipulated.

In the following case, the issue presented is whether a change in the personnel rules compromised the employer's right to discharge regular employees at will. The employee filed a breach of contract claim as a result of the discharge.

Alaska Housing Finance Corp. v. Salvucci
950 p.2d 1116, (Alaska 1997)

Matthews, Justice.

I. INTRODUCTION

This is an appeal by the Alaska Housing Finance Corporation (AHFC) from certain rulings of the superior court in favor of former AHFC employee Pat Salvucci. The superior court directed a verdict for Salvucci on his breach of contract claim.

Salvucci also was granted prejudgment interest on lost past and future wages and benefits as well as on punitive damages. We remand the award of prejudgment interest on lost past and future wages and benefits, reverse the award of punitive damages, and affirm in all other respects.

II. FACTS AND PROCEEDINGS

In 1989 Salvucci was hired by AHFC as its Internal Auditor. At the time of his hire, Salvucci signed a letter stating that his "employment at AHFC is at all times subject to AHFC Personnel Rules and any future amendments to those rules." The Personnel Rules divided employees into two groups, the "Regular" and "Executive" Service. Personnel Rule, Section 2.01.0. While the former could be terminated only for cause and only following a disciplinary procedure, the latter could be terminated at will by the Executive Director. All Regular Service employees received contractual employment protection, set forth in Rules 4, 11 and 13; only Executive Service employees did not receive the protection afforded by these rules.

The Executive Service became a part of AHFC Personnel Rules in August 1989 when AHFC's Board of Directors adopted Personnel Rule 2, Section 2.03.03. One of the positions designated Executive Service by Section 2.03.03 was the Internal Auditor position. Regular Service was defined as "positions within the Corporation that are not in the executive service."

The AHFC's Audit Charter, authored by Salvucci and adopted in June 1990, defined the duties and role of the Internal Auditor. The Charter set forth the reporting procedure, specifically that the Internal Auditor reported administratively to the chief executive officer and functionally to the Audit Committee of the Board of Directors. Further, it mandated that the Internal Auditor's removal required the concurrence of the Audit Committee.

In 1992 AHFC Personnel Rule 2.03.03 was amended. The amended rule shortened the list of Executive Service positions and omitted the Internal Auditor position from the list of positions in the Executive Service. The definition of Regular Service was not changed.

In July 1993 Will Gay became AHFC's Executive Director. In November Gay placed Salvucci on administrative leave, subject to an approval vote by the Audit Committee. In December the Audit Committee concurred in Gay's decision and Salvucci's employment was terminated. Salvucci was not given any reason for his termination and was not afforded a prior disciplinary process, as required for the termination of Regular Service employees. Salvucci filed a grievance, pursuant to Personnel Rule 13. AHFC refused to consider his grievance and also declined to consider his appeal of the grievance refusal, both instances on the ground that the Personnel Rules were inapplicable to the position of Internal Auditor. After the denial of his internal remedies, Salvucci filed a complaint in superior court alleging breach of contract, breach of the implied covenant of good faith and fair dealing, due process violations, and violation of the Whistleblower Act.

The superior court denied AHFC's motions for summary judgment on Salvucci's claim for punitive damages. The court granted a directed verdict for Salvucci on his breach of contract claim, finding that the 1992 amendment removed the Internal Auditor position from the Executive Service, placing the Internal Auditor within the Regular Service, with its accompanying contractual protections.

The jury awarded Salvucci $43,200 in lost past wages and benefits, $144,234 in lost future wages and benefits, and $500,000 in punitive damages. The superior court awarded Salvucci prejudgment interest on his wage and benefit award and on his punitive damage award, for a total of $62,493.30 in prejudgment interest. The court did not specify what amount of prejudgment interest was awarded for wages and benefits, and what amount of prejudgment interest was awarded for punitive damages.

The Breach of Contract Claim

AHFC contends that the superior court improperly granted a directed verdict for Salvucci on the breach of contract claim. AHFC argues that evidence presented at trial allowed a reasonable jury to conclude either that the Internal Auditor position was never removed from the Executive Service or that the Internal Auditor position enjoyed a unique classification falling outside either the Regular or Executive Service. AHFC argues that the Internal Auditor was a "corporation director" within the meaning of amended Rule 2, Section 2.03.03.

At the time the Audit Charter was passed, the Internal Auditor was an Executive Service position. The Charter did not refer to or alter the Service categorization of the Internal Auditor; rather it created a distinct process of reporting and removal for the Internal Auditor. Pursuant to the Charter, the Executive Director did not have sole discretion to appoint or remove the auditor; any such action required the concurrence of the Board of Director's Audit Committee.

In 1991 Barry Hulin, then Executive Director, proposed amending the Personnel Rules to narrow the categories of positions in the Executive Service. The proposal removed the Internal Auditor from the Executive Service. In presenting the proposal to the Board of Directors, Hulin specifically stated that the amendment took the Internal Auditor out of the Executive Service. Hulin also specifically informed the Board that those persons not in the Executive Service are subject to termination only for a "performance-related cause" and cannot be terminated before receiving "progressive discipline" in accordance with contractual employment protections. In 1992 the amendment was adopted.

All parties agree that the terms of Salvucci's employment contract are governed by his employment letter, the Audit Charter and the Personnel Rules. The text of Section 2.03.03 before and after the amendment makes evident that the Internal Auditor position was included in the Executive Service before the amendment and excluded once the section was amended. Hulin's testimony confirms that one intention of the amendment was to remove the Internal Auditor from the Executive Service, and further confirms that the Board was informed of this intent before it approved the amendment. The record shows that AHFC's Deputy Executive Director and AHFC's Personnel Director were also aware that one purpose of the amendment was to remove the Internal Auditor from the Executive Service.

We have held that when the provisions of a personnel manual create reasonable expectations that employees have been granted certain rights, the employer is bound by the representations contained in those provisions. Similar reasoning applies in this case. AHFC created a reasonable expectation that Salvucci was granted the rights of Regular Service employees after the 1992 amendment.

The employment letter required Salvucci to sign a statement that the Personnel Rules and any subsequent amendments to those rules governed the terms and conditions of his employment. When the Personnel Rules were amended in 1992 to delete the Internal Auditor from the list of Executive Service, Salvucci was bound to accept the amendment and the accompanying obligations or rights imposed by the Personnel Rules. Hulin informed Salvucci that the rules had been changed to remove him from the Executive Service. Salvucci read the transcript of the Board meeting at which the Board was told it was being asked to remove the Internal Auditor from the Executive Service.

As Salvucci reasonably believed that he was a Regular Service employee after the amendment, and as the superior court's analysis of the contract turns largely on his reasonable expectation, based on the binding nature of the employment letter, the clear text of Section 2.03.03 before and after amendment, the absence of any language in the Audit Charter creating a category other than Executive or Regular Service for the Internal Auditor, Hulin's statements of intent to remove the Internal Auditor from the Executive Service to the Board before its passage of the amendment, and Salvucci's reasonable expectations, we hold that in 1993, at the time Salvucci was terminated, the Internal Auditor position was in the Regular Service.

It is undisputed that in November 1993 Gay informed Salvucci that Salvucci would be placed on administrative leave and, subject to approval by the Audit Committee, would be terminated. It is further undisputed that Salvucci was not given any reason by Gay or the Audit Committee for his termination, and that he was not afforded the protection of progressive disciplinary procedures. Given AHFC's failure to afford Salvucci the contractual protections due Regular Service employees, we hold that the superior court correctly directed a verdict in favor of Salvucci on his breach of contract claim.

Judgment for Salvucci.

Case Commentary
The Alaska Supreme Court held that Salvucci was entitled to recover for breach of contract. Salvucci's position was changed from Executive to Regular. AHFC failed to adhere to its procedure for terminating Regular employees only for performance-related reasons and only after they have been disciplined. Here, Salvucci was terminated without reason. ■

CASE QUESTIONS

1. Is the court's decision regarding the breach of contract claim valid?
2. Was AHFC's amendment to the personnel rules the determining factor in Salvucci's victory?
3. Did AHFC's personnel rules compromise its right to terminate Salvucci at will?

An employee's or an independent contractor's authority may be revoked if the duration of the contract is indefinite or if no time limit has been specified. The employer may also revoke an employee's or an independent contractor's authority for cause where the employee or independent contractor has breached one of the duties owed. The employee or independent contractor must be notified that his or her authority is revoked. If the employment contract was in writing, then the revocation must also be in writing. Under other circumstances, it may be oral. This notice is effective when the employee or independent contractor receives it.

Notice of termination by revocation or mutual agreement must also be communicated to third persons who have dealt with the employer through the employee or independent contractor. Otherwise, the employer will be liable to third persons who contract with the employee or independent contractor. The employer's liability is based on apparent authority to act based on prior dealings that the third party is justified in believing. Third parties who have dealt with the employee or independent contractor on prior occasions must be sent actual notice of termination. This becomes effective when the third party receives it. For all other third parties, the employer's duty to notify may be satisfied by publishing a statement regarding termination of authority in a newspaper.

Employment Perspective

Bob Kaufman was the managing agent for the Barons, a singing group that performed at clubs and weddings. When it came time to renew his contract, Kaufman demanded that his commission be increased from 10 percent to 15 percent of the band's gross earnings. Although the Barons told him that they would consider his request, they subsequently told him that they would not accede to his request and terminated his employment. Infuriated by their reply, Kaufman, who was in the process of negotiating with several clubs for bookings, told each of the clubs that the Barons would perform on the dates requested for $250 less than their usual price. Kaufman said, "They're glad to get the work." The Barons were familiar with these particular clubs but never told them of the termination of Kaufman's employment. Are they bound to perform at the club for the lower fee? Yes! The Barons, as employer, have a duty to tell the clubs of Kaufman's termination. Otherwise, as in the case here, the clubs are justified in relying on Kaufman's apparent authority because they have dealt with the Barons through him on past occasions.

Agreement

An employment contract can be terminated, like any other contract, by the mutual agreement of the parties. This termination is valid even if the contract had called for a longer term of employment.

Fulfillment of Purpose

The authority of an employee or an independent contractor hired for a specific term of employment, as in an employee–employer relationship, will terminate upon the expiration of that term. An agency relationship created for the fulfillment of a specific purpose will terminate when that purpose is completed.

Employment Perspective

Jonathan Murrow, a lawyer, was engaged by Marvelous Mini-Bikes, Inc., to represent it in several product liability suits. Murrow hired Timothy Hines, a paralegal, to assist him by researching the numerous cases in point and writing a legal memorandum of the principles of law applicable to the issues presented. Hines was hired for 2 years, by which time Murrow figured the suits would be settled. What is the status of the employment relationships created, and when will they terminate? Jonathan Murrow is an independent contractor hired by Marvelous Mini-Bikes and is free to use his own methods to handle the case. This employment will terminate when all of the product liability suits against Marvelous Mini-Bikes have been settled. Timothy Hines is an employee of Jonathan Murrow. Hines must follow Murrow's instructions with regard to the work he undertakes. This employment relationship will expire at the end of the 2-year term of employment.

MODEL EMPLOYMENT TERMINATION ACT

The Model Employment Termination Act was designed to permit employers to discharge employees only for cause. In turn, employees would have to relinquish their right to sue in favor of arbitration. The advantage to the employer is to forgo the time and expense of litigation. The advantage to the employee is that he or she could no longer be terminated at will. The Model Employment Termination Act has been adopted as law only in the state of Montana. Some companies use it as a reference in setting their own employment guidelines.

An employer may terminate for good cause when the employee has been derelict in his or her duties of loyalty, duty to act in good faith, and duty to account; acting in excess of or without authority; performing work outside the scope of employment; harassing coworkers or subordinates; and engaging in employee theft. The employer may also discharge for good cause when the employer downsizes its workforce because of a consolidation, reorganization, or divestiture.

Under the act, termination refers to dismissal for cause, layoff pursuant to downsizing, and resignation of an employee due to the employer's intolerable actions.

Within 180 days of termination, the employee may file a complaint. The matter will then be arbitrated. After the arbitration hearing, a decision will be rendered within 30 days. If the arbitrator finds for the employee, an award may be made for reinstatement, back pay, reimbursement for benefits lost, or a lump sum if reinstatement is not permissible.

CONTESTING THE TERMINATION

When an employee believes he or she has been terminated for a discriminatory reason, in retaliation for filing a charge of discrimination, or for acting as a witness in a discrimination or harassment suit, he or she may file a claim with the Equal Employment Opportunity Commission (EEOC) for a violation of federal law and the appropriate state division of human rights for a violation of state law. In those cases involving infringements of the Occupational Safety and Health Act, the Fair Labor Standards Act, and the Employee Retirement Income Security Act, the employee may file a claim with the U.S. Department of Labor. An employee raising a tort claim for defamation, invasion of privacy, intentional interference with contractual relations, or breach of implied contract with regard to an employment handbook discharge provision would file a suit in state court. The employer will be afforded the opportunity to settle the claim pursuant to a no-fault agreement. If a settlement cannot be reached, the division of human rights will proceed with its fact-finding investigation. A fact-finding conference may be held, with mandatory attendance required of the employer and the employee. A decision regarding probable cause that a violation has occurred will be made. If the division of human rights finds probable cause, it will attempt to reach a conciliation agreement with the employer regarding damages and/or reinstatement of the employee. If an agreement cannot be reached, a complaint will be filed by the division of human rights within the enforcement arm of the agency. The parties may submit written briefs prior to the hearing. After the hearing, the division of human rights will make its decision and pronounce a remedy. The decision can be appealed to a court of general jurisdiction. The court's function is to determine whether the decision was substantiated by sufficient evidence.

Because downsizing has become a widespread phenomenon among companies, hundreds of thousands of employees have been laid off as a result. When a company downsizes for economic reasons, the employee has no recourse. Economic reasons may encompass a broad spectrum from saving a company from filing for bankruptcy to improving the price of the stock by increasing earnings.

The issue in the next case is whether the termination of an employee who assaulted a coworker was a legitimate reason.

Gray v. Toshiba
263 F.3d 595 (6th Cir. 2001)

Batchelder, Circuit Judge.

Plaintiff-Appellee Connie Gray was employed in Toshiba's Lebanon, Tennessee, plant from 1986 until June 11, 1993. Early in June of 1993, Gray and a Toshiba employee named Tammy Lynch became embroiled in an argument involving another employee, Pam Chapman, and the company's policy on appropriate attire in the workplace. The conflict between Gray and Lynch escalated when Chapman volunteered to Gray that Lynch had been calling Gray a b**ch. According to Chapman, Gray stated that she would confront Lynch, and if the allegations were true, she would hit her. Chapman advised Gray to let the matter lie.

The next day, another employee told Gray that Lynch had called her a b**ch. Gray informed her assistant supervisor, Jackie Harris, about Lynch's derogatory statements, and asked what would happen to her if she hit Lynch. Ms. Harris advised against that course of action, and suggested that Gray simply ignore Lynch. Gray sought a second opinion from Joe Collins, the Plant Manager. Collins also advised against attacking Lynch, and warned Gray that she could be fired for such an act.

By mid-morning, however, Gray had decided to confront Lynch regarding her alleged comments. Gray told fellow employee Audrey Duke that Lynch would not get away with calling her a b**ch. According to Duke, Gray then removed her hair-clip and earrings, and put her hair in a ponytail and left her work station. On her way to see Lynch, Gray passed Joyce Mitchell, Personnel Manager at Toshiba. Gray recounted the statements allegedly made by Lynch, and again, asked what would happen if she hit Lynch in retaliation. Mitchell repeated the company line in regard to hitting fellow employees, warning Gray that she could be fired if she hit Lynch. Gray told Mitchell that she was just going to talk to Lynch to determine if she had in fact called her a b**ch.

During the mid-morning break, Gray approached Lynch, and asked if she had called her a derogatory name, and if so, if Lynch wanted to repeat it to her face. According to Gray, when Lynch accepted the invitation, Gray punched Lynch in the face, breaking her glasses and giving her a black eye. Thus vindicated, Gray returned to her work station and said to Chapman, "I told you I would hit that b**ch if she admitted it." According to supervisor Harris, when asked whether she hit Lynch, Gray admitted to the assault saying, "Yes, I knocked the c**p out of her." Gray was dismissed for the remainder of the day.

The following day, Gray met with Leonard Tyree, Vice-President of General Affairs, Ms. Mitchell from personnel, and Margaret Maynard, a union steward, to discuss the incident. According to Mitchell, although the plaintiff was sorry the incident had happened at Toshiba, she was not sorry she hit Lynch. Mitchell recommended that Gray be terminated because the assault was premeditated and two managers had warned her that she could be fired for hitting a co-worker. Tyree discharged Gray pursuant to Rule B–1 of the Plant Rules, which prohibits "fighting on company property where the employee is determined to be the instigator or aggressor." Rule B–1 provides that Toshiba may discharge or suspend the employee for a violation.

Gray based her gender discrimination claim on the fact that three years prior to her melee with Lynch, two workplace altercations involving male employees had occurred at the Toshiba plant. In both those instances, management elected to suspend rather than discharge the participants.

Here, Toshiba articulated a non-discriminatory reason for firing Gray, namely, that she committed an intentional, premeditated assault on a fellow employee after being warned by several superiors not to do so. Gray, however, has produced no evidence casting doubt on the credibility of this articulated reason. First, there is no evidence in the record that Gray did not commit assault or that she was not warned not to commit it. Hence, there is no evidence that Toshiba's articulated reason has no basis in fact. Second, there is no evidence in the record that committing an intentional, premeditated assault on another employee, having been warned not to do so, is not sufficient to warrant discharge under Toshiba's rules. Gray claims that she presented this evidence—that is, evidence that similarly situated male employees were not disciplined as severely as she was—as the fourth prong of her prima facie case, but it is clear from the record that she did not.

The employees Gray seeks to cast as similarly situated differ from her in several important ways. First, the male employees' conduct was different. Most significantly, Gray's assault on Lynch was premeditated, whereas the record indicates that the prior incidents involving male employees erupted spontaneously. In one of the prior incidents, one employee hit another in the knee with a hammer as an act of workplace horseplay. The employee who had been struck did not see the humor and grabbed his co-worker by the shirt. After other workers intervened, the two ceased hostilities and shook hands. Both employees were suspended without pay for three days on account of the incident. The other incident involving two male employees also occurred spontaneously, with no clear aggressor. Some witnesses claim that actual punches were thrown, while other witnesses dispute this account.

Gray, on the other hand, announced her intentions to several co-workers. She asked management-level employees if she would be subject to discipline for hitting Lynch. According to one co-worker, she removed her earrings and put her hair back in anticipation of a brawl. This intentional and premeditated conduct is more severe, and justifying of harsher discipline than the conduct of the male Toshiba combatants.

Second, the record demonstrates that several management-level employees had put Gray on notice that she could be terminated for attacking a co-worker. Although the male employees were on constructive notice through the company rules—and common sense—that fighting on company premises was forbidden, they had not received the specific warnings that Gray had. Moreover, the warnings Gray received came only hours, and finally moments, before she punched Lynch.

Third, we note that Gray and the male employees are not similarly situated in regard to the company rules in place at the time of the respective incidents, or the rule under which each was disciplined. The men involved in altercations were suspended for violation of Rule C–16, which prohibits fighting and allows for dismissal, but does not differentiate an employee who is involved in a fight from one who instigates a fight. Following those altercations, and prior to Gray's fight with Lynch, Toshiba instituted a stricter policy that permitted the company to terminate an employee if that employee was found to be the instigator of the fight. Gray responds that the sections of the rules were merely re-numbered, and no significant change in policy occurred. Even if this were the case, the rules as they were written at the time of the Gray-Lynch incident permitted the employer to fire an employee who instigated a fight. There is no dispute that, although verbally provoked by Lynch, Gray threw the first, and only punch. This kind of offensive conduct appears to be exactly the type of activity the Toshiba rules were designed to deter.

Gray has not provided any evidence to support a claim that Toshiba's proffered reason for her discharge was not the company's actual motivation for discharging her. The evidence presented in this case did not even support a prima facie showing of gender discrimination, and Gray points to nothing beyond that evidence to support a claim that Toshiba really discharged her because of her gender and not because she deliberately provoked a fight with another employee.

Although we are always hesitant to overturn a jury verdict, we hold that the district court erred as a matter of law in denying Toshiba's Rule 50 motion. The evidence in this record is simply insufficient to permit the jury, even if it chose to disbelieve Toshiba's articulated reason for discharging Gray, to conclude that the true reason for Gray's discharge was discriminatory. To allow an employee who has committed an intentional, premeditated assault on another employee to avoid dismissal on the evidence presented here is to shift the burden of proof from the employee to the employer. Accordingly, we reverse the judgment of the district court.

Judgment for Toshiba.

Case Commentary

The Sixth Circuit Court ruled that an employer who discharges an employee who assaults another is justified where the terminated employee has offered no evidence of discrimination. ■

CASE QUESTIONS

1. Are you in agreement with the court's decision?
2. Should the victim's verbal provocation be taken into account?
3. Because this was an isolated instance of aggressive behavior, should the aggressor have escaped with a warning?

WRONGFUL DISCHARGE

An employer is guilty of wrongful discharge where its motivation for termination is discriminatory. This situation gives the employee the right to sue under Title VII of the Civil Rights Act, the Americans with Disabilities Act (ADA), the Age Discrimination in Employment Act (ADEA), or The Equal Pay Act, to name a few. Furthermore, employees may not be discharged for exercising their constitutional rights such as freedom of speech or freedom of religion.

The case that follows addresses the question of whether an employer can dismiss an employee for his or her political affiliation.

Pierce v. Montgomery County Opportunity Bd., Inc.
884 F.Supp. 965 (E.D.Pa. 1995)

Joyner, District Judge.

This litigation arises out of the termination of Plaintiff Frances Pierce from her position as Executive Director of the Montgomery County Opportunity Board, Inc. (MCOB). Pierce is and has been a Republican Committeewoman at all material times and votes for Republican political candidates. In August, 1990, Pierce was made the Acting Executive Director of MCOB. At some point after August 1990, State Defendants, presumably Democrats, resolved to have Pierce removed from the head of MCOB, allegedly for political reasons. In June 1991, Pierce was appointed MCOB's Executive Director for a 5-year term at a certain salary and with certain benefits.

In November 1991, State Defendants arranged to terminate MCOB's federal funding, allegedly because Pierce's active Republicanism created a prohibited conflict of interest under Federal regulations. In May 1992, MCOB Defendant Harvey Portner was appointed to the MCOB Board and at some point became its President. He apparently asked Pierce to resign as Executive Director, and when she refused, embarked upon a campaign to impugn Pierce's reputation. In August 1992, the MCOB's Defendants (including at least one Republican) joined in a conspiracy with Portner and the State Defendants to remove Pierce from MCOB on account of her Republicanism.

In December 1992, Portner resigned as President of the Board so as to "create an aura of non-involvement," but nonetheless, "maintained effective control over the Opportunity Board." He was replaced by MCOB Defendant Aaron Schell, a Republican.

On December 16, 1992, Schell informed Pierce that the MCOB Board was to meet with the Department of Community Affairs, told Pierce that he did not know the purpose of the meeting, and then did not attend the meeting himself. At this meeting, State Defendants informed the board that they were there to close down MCOB. According to the Amended Complaint, the "purpose of the attendance of defendants Darling and Weisberg was to give a basis for the actions which were planned sub rosa to remove Frances Pierce as Executive Director." One month later the MCOB Board voted to remove Pierce as Executive Director.

In Pennsylvania, an at-will employee can be discharged for any reason or for no reason at all. The exception to this rule is the public policy exception. This provides that when there is no plausible and legitimate reason for a termination, and a clear mandate of public policy is violated by the termination, even an at-will employee has a claim for wrongful discharge. Pennsylvania does not, however, permit a wrongful discharge claim if statutory relief is available to the plaintiff.

Here, Pierce alleges that "The Opportunity Board of Montgomery County, Inc. could not discharge an employee for utilizing the right to freedom of speech in the employee's off hours, such discharge as here complained of, being in violation of the public policy of the Commonwealth of Pennsylvania." Elsewhere in the Amended Complaint, Pierce alleges that she was terminated solely on account of her participation in Republican party politics. As the Third Circuit has held, "an important public policy is in fact implicated wherever the power to hire and fire is utilized to dictate the term of employee political activities." Pierce alleges that she was terminated for engaging in protected First Amendment activities. We find that this states a claim for wrongful discharge, for which, if the allegations are proved, relief can be granted.

Judgment for Pierce.

Case Commentary

The Eastern District Court of Pennsylvania held that a public policy exception to the at-will termination doctrine exists where the employee is engaging in protected First Amendment activities. Here Frances Pierce was discharged for her political affiliation. ■

CASE QUESTIONS

1. Should a person's political affiliation be entitled to protection?
2. Do you believe this was the real reason why she was discharged?
3. What public policy exceptions do you believe should exist to the at-will employment doctrine?

RETALIATORY DISCHARGE

If an employee has made a claim of discrimination or is to appear as a witness in a discrimination investigation, the employer may not take retaliatory action against the employee.

Employment Perspective

Cindy Thomas has filed a gender-based discrimination claim against Star Enterprises for not receiving a promotion. Nicole Robinson will be appearing as a witness on Cindy's behalf. In the interim, Cindy has been discharged, and Nicole has been demoted. Do they have recourse? Yes! Cindy may amend her claim to include the charge of retaliation. Nicole may commence an action for violation of Title VII against Star Enterprises based on its retaliatory behavior.

In addition, it is wrongful when a worker is discharged for filing a workers' compensation claim or blowing the whistle on a company's illegal activity. The employee may bring an action for retaliatory discharge against the employer.

Employment Perspective

Carly Fisher worked the night shift at Top Cat Chemical Corporation. One evening while on a break, she observed several workers emptying barrels into the Pristine River adjacent to the plant. Carly notified the Environmental Protection Agency. Because their investigation revealed that toxic waste had been dumped, the company was fined heavily. One month later, Carly was discharged after a poor performance rating. For 6 years, Carly had received satisfactory ratings. Is this a case of retaliatory discharge? Yes! Top Cat's actions in dismissing Carly were motivated by its desire for revenge against her for whistle-blowing.

CONSTRUCTIVE DISCHARGE

As opposed to outright termination, an employer may make the work environment so intolerable that the employee may be forced to resign. This process amounts to constructive discharge. These actions may be motivated by discrimination, general dislike, or retaliation. The employer may act directly or through the targeted employee's coworkers. The coworkers themselves may act on their own initiative.

The issue in the following case is whether an employee was constructively discharged from her position.

Campos v. City of Blue Springs, Missouri
289 F.3d 546 (8th Cir. 2002)

Heaney, Circuit Judge.

BACKGROUND

In April 1996, Campos was hired as a crisis counselor for the Blue Springs Police Department's Youth Outreach Unit (YOU). At that time, Campos did not have the advanced psychology or social work degree and Missouri licensure required by the written job description for the position.

Campos's immediate supervisor at YOU was Pamela Petrillo. When Campos was hired, Petrillo indicated that Campos needed to complete her Ph.D. dissertation and obtain a Missouri counseling license by February of 1997 to guarantee her continued employment. Petrillo also informed Campos that she would be paid an extra $10,000 per year for support group work, she would be a team leader within three months, and she would be an assistant director within six months of starting her full-time employment.

On October 21, 1996, Campos began working full-time. Initially she enjoyed her work and got along well with co-workers. This apparently changed on October 31, 1996 after she disclosed to Petrillo that she observed tenets of Native American spirituality rather than Christianity. Campos contends that Petrillo treated her differently after this disclosure. For example, Campos alleges that Petrillo's behavior towards her became unfriendly and critical, and that she began to imply that Campos may not have been a good fit for the job. Petrillo also began to exclude Campos from employee meetings, including those during which employees discussed whether YOU should be transformed into a Christian counseling unit.

On November 23, 1996, Campos was injured in a car accident. Because these injuries prevented her from spending time outside of work to complete her Ph.D. dissertation, she was granted an extension of the February deadline. Petrillo testified that she set a June 1, 1997 deadline for Campos to complete her dissertation. Campos denied that a new deadline was established.

On January 6, 1997, Petrillo completed Campos's three month evaluation. The evaluation was largely complimentary. Nevertheless, Campos contends that Petrillo continued to treat her poorly. Campos testified that she was passed over for the team leader position she was promised when she was hired. She also testified that Petrillo told her she was not a good role model and that she needed to find a good Christian boyfriend to teach her to be submissive.

In March 1997, Campos did not receive the $10,000 in extra compensation that Petrillo promised she would earn for conducting support groups. When Campos complained, Petrillo responded that people "sometimes have to give up the things they need most in order to be a good Christian." Campos also testified that she was taken off of counseling assignments because of her refusal to use the scripture, and that she was verbally abused by co-workers at the direction of Petrillo. In May of 1997, Campos was given a favorable six-month evaluation.

By September of 1997, Campos still had not completed her dissertation, so she arranged to meet with her dissertation professor every Monday afternoon during the fall. In order to take time off from work, Campos submitted written requests in advance of her absences. Petrillo did not respond to these requests, nor did she make herself available to meet

with Campos to discuss the absences. After repeated attempts, Campos remained unable to obtain explicit permission from Petrillo to attend her dissertation meetings. Unable to reach Petrillo, Campos went to a meeting without permission. Petrillo responded by accusing Campos of misconduct and informing Campos that she could not grant her permission to attend the meetings without a letter from the university explaining why the meetings were necessary. Although Campos admitted that obtaining such a letter would not have been a problem, she chose to resign. Campos initially cited Petrillo's abusive behavior and intolerable workings conditions as the reasons for her resignation. It was not until Campos's last day of work that she alleged she had been discriminated against because of her religion.

After her resignation, Campos filed suit against the City, alleging that she suffered from employment discrimination based upon her religion, sex, and national origin. The charges of sex and national origin discrimination were eliminated, and the case was submitted to the jury on the theory that Campos was constructively discharged because of her religion. On April 13, 2001, the jury awarded Campos $79,200 for back pay and compensatory damages. The district court denied the City's Motion for Judgment as a Matter of Law, or in the Alternative, for a New Trial, and awarded Campos's attorneys $90,556.20 in fees and $11,825.41 in expenses.

We agree with the district court that Campos presented sufficient evidence to allow the jury to find that she was forced to quit because she was not a Christian. Campos presented evidence that she was subjected to months of harassment and criticism by Petrillo because Petrillo wanted a Christian in Campos's position. Campos also demonstrated that immediately before her resignation Petrillo refused to respond to her request to attend dissertation meetings, which were a prerequisite to her continued employment. Petrillo then accused Campos of insubordination for failing to get permission. The jury had sufficient evidence to find that Petrillo made it nearly impossible for Campos to attend the dissertation meetings because she wanted to replace Campos with a Christian employee. The jury also had sufficient evidence to determine that Campos's resignation was a foreseeable consequence of Petrillo's actions.

Petrillo supervised the City's employees with its approval and had the rank of City Director, which gave her the power to hire and fire City employees. Her statements to Campos constitute direct evidence of discriminatory animus.

Conclusion
For the reasons cited above, the judgment of the district court is affirmed for Campos.

Case Commentary
The Eighth Circuit Court found Campos's supervisor criticisms, a number of which had religious overtones, to constitute harassment, which made it impossible for Campos to perform her work. ■

CASE QUESTIONS

1. Do you agree with the court's decision?
2. Was the harassment severe and pervasive?

3. Do you believe Campos had to resign because the work environment was so intolerable?

Employment Perspective

Sean Stockton works for Premier Motors Manufacturing in their quality control division. He uncovers a scheme to shortcut the process by continuing assembly before the adhesives dry. Sean notifies his superiors, but he is told to ignore the problem. Sean approaches senior management, who appreciate his forthrightness. Sean's superiors and coworkers are severely disciplined. Later, though, he begins to receive threatening notes, his car windshield is smashed, his tires are flattened, and he is demoted. Sean complains to senior management, but they tell him to deal with the problems in his own way. After being assaulted, Sean leaves the company, claiming constructive discharge. Is he correct? Yes! His coworkers and superiors have made the work environment so intolerable that it is no longer conducive to Sean's mental and physical well-being to continue on the job. If the individuals responsible had been discharged because of Sean's whistle-blowing, then Premier's duty to protect Sean and safeguard his property extends only while Sean is on the premises. Once he departs, he is on his own. This is a major risk that a whistle-blower must bear on his or her own. It may not be foreseeable to the whistle-blower that retaliatory acts will be directed against him or her. However, it would be wise for the employee to consider all of the possible ramifications for whistle-blowing and the recourses available for protection.

EMPLOYEE LESSONS

1. Familiarize yourself with the at-will employment doctrine of the state in which you are employed.
2. Read the company's employment handbook if one exists.
3. Focus on any language surrounding the discharge of employees.
4. Determine whether or not the employer has ever given a litany of reasons for discharge.
5. Ask the new employer for a written employment contract guaranteeing your employment for a certain period of time if you are in a strong bargaining position when relocating or giving up a good job.
6. Know your rights upon termination if you have been the subject of discrimination, retaliation, or constructive discharge.
7. Identify whether the company has a grievance procedure that culminates in arbitration.
8. Learn the time constraints in this procedure and abide by them.
9. Identify whether you have been discharged in a manner that is not consistent with the treatment of other employees.

SUMMARY

Generally, employers do not take termination as personally as do employees. However, it can be a difficult process for both sides, especially if the employee believes that the discharge is wrongful.

At-will termination protects the rights of employers to terminate employees. Therefore, employees must evaluate the evidence to discern whether it meets one of the public policy exceptions to the at-will doctrine.

Employers must guard against compromising their protection under the at-will employment doctrine and should not stipulate that employees will be discharged only for cause or list explicit reasons for discharge in an employment handbook or in conversation with an applicant or an employee. Rather employers should state that employees maybe discharged at any time for any reason.

REVIEW QUESTIONS

1. What constitutes a wrongful discharge?
2. Is downsizing a form of discriminatory conduct?
3. What does at-will employment mean?
4. Explain retaliatory discharge.
5. Is retaliatory discharge ever justifiable?
6. How can an employee be constructively discharged?
7. What does it mean to be dismissed for cause?
8. Define termination.
9. Can an employee be dismissed without cause?
10. Explain the significance of the Model Employment Termination Act.
11. How can a termination be contested?

CASE PROBLEMS

1. On March 1, 1993, Ms. Blackwell's supervisor, Steve Duke, told Ms. Blackwell to see a neurologist regarding her back injury. Following her visit to the neurologist, Ms. Blackwell missed approximately 4 months of work because of her injury. Ms. Blackwell continued to receive full salary during her leave of absence. However, Mr. Ridlon told Shelter Mutual to place a "hold" on the merit increase after he received some "strong allegations" against Ms. Blackwell regarding her involvement in the improper handling of salvage vehicles. Apparently Mr. Ridlon learned that several vehicles Ms. Blackwell determined to be total losses were later owned by Ms. Blackwell's son or processed through the business of Ms. Blackwell's husband. According to a company memorandum, Shelter Mutual's legal and human resources department recommended terminating Ms. Blackwell on August 22, 1994, "due to numerous problems." *Blackwell v. Shelter Mutual Insurance Co.*, 109 F.3d 1550 (10th Cir. 1997)

2. In August 1991, a coworker of McKenzie, Marsha McElroy, attended a seminar on wage and hour laws and returned with various informational materials. McElroy gave these materials to McKenzie, who, after reviewing them, became concerned that certain employees of the company were not receiving proper compensation for working overtime. McKenzie discussed the matter with McElroy and then decided to disclose her concerns to the company attorney, Steve Andrew. McKenzie and McElroy met with Andrew on September 4, 1991, and later that same day, McKenzie also discussed the wage and hour problem with Robert Renberg ("Renberg"), the company president. Sixteen days later, on September 20, 1991, McKenzie was terminated by Renberg. *McKenzie v. Renberg's Inc.*, 94 F.3d 1478 (10th Cir. 1996)

3. While driving together, Beall told Budlong that she wanted to stop at the Fairfax Hospital lactation room to use the breast pump. According to Beall, Budlong replied, "'I don't want to stop now, pull your car off the road, get in the back seat of your car and get out your breast pump.'" In a July 1994 field visit to a doctor's office, Beall took offense to a comment Budlong made about Beall's weight loss. Beall claims that Budlong said, "'Get over here and get on this scale, I want to see how much you weigh.'" Beall also alleges that Budlong "frequently spoke to me in a demeaning and condescending tone and yelled at me during our monthly supervisory work visits."

On September 12, 1994, Beall wrote a letter to Maiocco alleging that Budlong had "created a hostile and intimidating work environment" and "inaccurately and unfairly attacked my performance."

On September 26, Maiocco again met with Beall and told her that his investigation did not substantiate her harassment claim.

At the September 26 meeting, Maiocco gave Beall a letter formally placing her on unsatisfactory performance status (USP) for 60 days. The USP letter stated that Beall was being placed on USP because she had the lowest market share in the district for the second quarter of 1994. The defendants contend that, although Beall's district ranking improved to 28th out of 43 Territory Managers (TMs), Beall did not meet the goals of the September 26 letter. In June 1995, Abbott decided to reduce its Ross sales force by eliminating 12 TM positions. According to Ross's policy, the territory of any TM who is on leave for more than 6 months is considered vacant, and a new individual is hired to fill the opening. Beall's 6-month period ended July 10, 1995. Rather than hire a new TM, Ross eliminated or "collapsed" Beall's territory pursuant to its reduction in force on September 27, 1995. *Beall v. Abbott Laboratories*, 130 F.3d 614 (4th Cir. 1997)

4. In 1980, Mintzmyer became the regional director of the Rocky Mountain Region of the National Park Service, a bureau within the U.S. Department of the Interior (agency). As such, she was in the senior executive service working in Denver, Colorado. In October 1991, Mintzmyer and two other directors of different regions were part of a 3-way rotation, in which Mintzmyer was reassigned as regional director of the mid-Atlantic region in Philadelphia, Pennsylvania.

Displeased with her transfer, Mintzmyer filed an Equal Employment Opportunity complaint with the agency, claiming that her reassignment was due to gender and age discrimination and was in retaliation for whistle-blowing. In April 1992, Mintzmyer retired. She then amended her EEO complaint to allege that she had been coerced into retiring for the same reasons. *Mintzmyer v. Department of the Interior*, 84 F.3d 419 (Fed. Cir. 1996)

HUMAN RESOURCE DILEMMAS

1. Professor Padilla has been very critical of the new department chair in European literature. When Padilla receives his course schedule for next semester, he notices he is scheduled to teach Lit 105 from 8:00 to 8:50 A.M. in Moran Hall on the east side of campus and Lit 107 from 9:00 to 9:50 A.M. in Mullins Hall on the north side of campus. It is at least a 20-minute walk from the first classroom to the second. Padilla asks for a room change, which is denied. His solution is to let his first class out 5 minutes early and start the second 5 minutes late. His department chairperson, Ann Fullerton, writes Padilla up for this. Padilla, who is not tenured, is discharged at the end of the academic year. He claims constructive discharge. How would you advise him?

2. In Elliptical Electronics Company's employment handbook, it states in bold, "Employment is at will and can be terminated by either employer or employee at anytime for any reason with or without cause." Later in the handbook, a multiple-step grievance procedure is outlined. Thomas Walker physically assaults a coworker without provocation. The coworker is hospitalized, and Thomas is discharged immediately under the at-will policy. Thomas, who is black, reports that Elliptical violated its employment handbook by not providing him with a hearing as outlined in its grievance procedure. How would you advise Elliptical?

3. Sue Robbins recently testified in a sexual harassment suit brought by colleague Amada Haskins. Now Sue, up for her annual review, is given a 2 percent raise and no bonus. Her coworkers are averaging 8 percent raises and $30,000 bonuses. How would you advise Sue to proceed?

WEB SITE ASSIGNMENT

Using the following Web sites, construct an at-will termination policy, an exit interview form, and a description of what to say to an employee who is being discharged. Consider several different scenarios when completing your description of what to say to a discharged employee.

www.eeoc.gov
www.legal-database.com/laborlaw.htm
www.bloodhoundnetwork.com/employment-law/index.htm
www.legal-term.com/atwillemployment-definition.htm
www.legal-definitions.com/at-will-employment.htm
www.Majlaw.com/terminate.html
www.findlaw.com
sacramento.bcentral.com/sacramento/stories/1996/11/18/smallb3.html
www.gov.on.ca/lab/es/terminae.htm
www.ilrg.com/forms/terminat.html

Chapter

Arbitration

Employment Scenario

L&S has been hit with several wrongful termination suits alleging discriminatory behavior on the part of Tom and Mark. They realize that the sympathy of juries lies with employees. L&S proposes to adopt mandatory arbitration agreements as a condition of employment. They are uncertain as to whether employees' statutory rights under Title VII, ADEA, and ADA can be subject to arbitration. They seek counsel from their attorney, Susan North.

Chapter Checklist
- ➤ *Appreciate the advantages arbitration maintains over the court system.*
- ➤ *Learn the trade-offs involved when arbitration is selected.*
- ➤ *Identify the exceptions to the mandatory use of arbitration.*
- ➤ *Be cognizant of Supreme Court rulings affecting arbitration.*
- ➤ *Realize that on matters where the Supreme Court has not ruled, jurisdictions may differ.*
- ➤ *Discern the future of arbitration.*

INTRODUCTION

Many employers favor the use of arbitration in employment disputes. Arbitration was designed as an alternative to litigation because it is generally considered to be less expensive and less time-consuming. To facilitate the arbitration process, a written agreement must be entered into that provides for the selection of an arbitrator and the legal issues that he or she may deliberate. An *arbitrator* is a mediator who examines documents and listens to testimony. Then he or she grants an award based on a factual determination. An arbitrator must be impartial. The arbitrator's award is binding on both parties and may be overturned by a court only where the arbitrator acted out of self-interest; the decision was procured by fraud or corruption; the arbitrator exceeded his or her powers; or the decision was made with a manifest disregard for the law.[1]

HUMAN RESOURCE ADVICE

- Comprehend the savings in cost and time by adopting an arbitration agreement.
- State the purpose and scope of the arbitration agreement.
- Use simple terms when drafting the arbitration agreement.
- Require employees to acknowledge in writing receipt of notice of arbitration agreement. Understand the benefits of avoiding a jury trial.
- Realize that the EEOC is not bound by an employee's agreement to arbitrate.
- Ensure that an employee's statutory rights are preserved in arbitration.

For an arbitration program to be enforceable, it must be written in simplified terms. The purpose and scope of the arbitration agreement must be clearly stated. An employer must notify employees of the agreement's effective date and of the fact that employees' continued employment beyond the effective date constitutes employees' willingness to be bound by arbitration. Employers should also require the employees to sign an acknowledgment that they received notice. The employer must permit employees to have equal say in the selection of the arbitrator. Consideration of an arbitrator's experience and competence should be taken into account. The arbitration process must be performed in accordance with federal and/or state rules of civil procedure. Arbitrators are given the power to grant awards including costs and legal fees.

However, if an employee can show that the fee-splitting arrangement provided in the arbitration agreement creates a financial hardship that precludes him or her from arbitrating the dispute, a court may invalidate the agreement.[2]

In many instances, an employee's access to court may no longer be available because of mandatory arbitration. The Seventh Amendment assures a jury trial. Some argue this amendment is compromised by arbitration. The main issue surrounding the use of arbitration in employment disputes is whether the employee's statutory rights are adequately protected. Arbitration must preserve all the substantive rights of the employee to be valid. If an arbitration agreement is challenged, a court becomes the proper venue for determining whether arbitration provides an effective forum to discern whether employees' statutory rights have been violated.[3] Employees would prefer to litigate issues involving violations of their statutory rights because of the possibility of huge jury awards; employers prefer to arbitrate to avoid jury awards.

Traditionally, settling disputes involving collective bargaining agreements has been the area of expertise for most arbitrators; resolution of statutes has generally been within the purview of the courts. Arbitrators do not go through the rigorous process to be nominated and confirmed like judges do. The principle of precedence applies to judges, not arbitrators. Arbitration rules out extensive discovery often required in discrimination suits, which are often decided based upon circumstantial or statistical evidence.

Prior to the enactment of the Federal Arbitration Act of 1925 (FAA), courts had frowned upon the enforcement of arbitration agreements. The purpose of the FAA was to raise the credibility of arbitration agreements to the level enjoyed by other contracts. The FAA encouraged the use of voluntary arbitration agreements by providing for court enforcement, but what about mandatory arbitration agreements?

Originally, in the securities field a registration form called the Uniform Application for Securities Industry Registration or Transfer (Form U–4) contained a provision for mandatory arbitration of all employment disputes. Now many other employers require this as a condition to obtaining employment. Some employees argue that forcing individuals to sign as a precondition to employment borders on duress, especially if employees are desperately in need of a job.

In the case of *Gilmer v. Interstate/Johnson Lane Corp.*,[4]Interstate/Johnson Lane Corporation hired Robert Gilmer as a financial services manager. Gilmer was required to register as a securities representative with the New York Stock Exchange (NYSE). The application for registration provided for arbitration for any dispute between employer and employee, which is required under the rules of the NYSE. Gilmer was terminated 6 years later when he was 62 years of age. He filed a claim under the Age Discrimination in Employment Act (ADEA) with the EEOC. The EEOC gave Gilmer permission to sue, and he brought an action in District Court. Interstate filed a motion to dismiss and to compel arbitration. The District Court held for Gilmer, stating that U.S. Congress did not intend to allow a judicial waiver of ADEA claims. The Fourth Circuit Court reversed and the U.S. Supreme Court affirmed.

In *Gilmer*, the Supreme Court stated that the FAA overruled judicial bias against arbitration. The FAA stipulates that "a written provision in any maritime transaction or a contract evidencing a transaction involving commerce to settle by arbitration a controversy thereafter arising out of such contract or transaction . . . shall be valid, irrevocable, and enforceable, save upon such grounds as exist at law or in equity for the revocation of any contract."[5] The Supreme Court acknowledged that as long as due process has been granted to an employee in having his or her Title VII claims decided in arbitration, the statutory protection would be afforded.[6]

In *AT&T Technologies v. Communications Workers*[7], the U.S. Supreme Court set forth the precepts that govern whether an issue may be arbitrated. These rules were originally promulgated in 1960 in three cases known as the *Steelworkers Trilogy*.[8] First, an issue can be arbitrated when both parties have agreed. Second, if it is unclear whether the parties have agreed to arbitrate a particular issue, the court, not the arbitrator, must resolve it. Third, there is a rebuttable presumption to arbitrate. And fourth, the court must refrain from passing judgment on the merits.

In *Mitsubishi Motors Corp. v. Soler Chrysler Plymouth, Inc.*,[9] the U.S. Supreme Court held the employer and employee must agree that arbitration specifically includes employee claims that their statutory rights have been violated and that a resolution of this issue can be adequately obtained through arbitration. If either of these requirements is not met to the court's satisfaction, the dispute cannot be arbitrated.

An employee prior to requesting arbitration should raise concerns over fee-splitting arrangements if the employee believes it will present an undue financial burden. This was the reasoning applied in *Bradford v. Rockwell Semiconductor*[10] by the Fourth Circuit Court. In this case, John Bradford initiated the arbitration, conceded the process was fair, and then claimed that his share of the costs created a financial hardship. The court ruled against Bradford, stating he could not prove a financial burden. The Fourth Circuit Court went on to say that fee splitting of arbitration costs should be decided on a case-by-case basis. An employee who has limited financial resources should request an estimate of the costs and raise any objections prior to commencing arbitration.

In *Green Tree Financial Corp.—Alabama v. Randolph*,[11] the U.S. Supreme Court ruled that an arbitration agreement that does not speak to the employee's responsibility for costs would not fail for indefiniteness. The plaintiff should request information regarding the fee-splitting arrangement and potential costs. Once in hand, the burden is on the plaintiff to prove there is a strong possibility the costs will present an undue financial burden. Here Larketta Randolph failed to establish that she would suffer a financial burden, which she could not bear due to the excessive arbitration costs.

In the movement toward the greater use of mandatory arbitration in employment disputes, only the Ninth Circuit Court has ruled to the contrary in its 1998 decision by Judge Reinhardt in *Duffield v. Robertson, Stephens & Co.*[12] As a condition of employment, Tonyja Duffield was required to sign Form U–4.

Robertson, Stephens & Co. is a member of the NYSE and the National Association of Securities Dealers (NASD). Form U–4 required the applicant to be bound by the rules of these organizations. The NYSE and the NASD both mandate arbitration for the resolution of employment disputes.

Rule 347 of the NYSE states:

> Any controversy between a registered representative and any member or member organization arising out of the employment or termination of employment of such registered representative by and with such member or member organization shall be settled by arbitration, at the instance of any such party, in accordance with the arbitration procedure prescribed elsewhere in these rules.

The NASD code of arbitration procedure as amended in 1993 stipulates:

> Any dispute, claim, or controversy arising out of or in connection with the business of any member of the Association, or arising out of the employment or termination of associated person(s) with any members . . . shall be arbitrated.

Tonyja Duffield did sign Form U–4. She began working as a broker-dealer for Robertson, Stephens & Co. Seven years later, she filed a lawsuit alleging sexual discrimination and sexual harassment in a federal court. The District Court dismissed Duffield's claims.[13]

The arbitration provision is contained in the fifth paragraph of Form U–4.

> I agree to arbitrate any dispute, claim or controversy that may arise between me and my firm, or a customer, or any other person, that is required to be arbitrated under the rules, constitutions, or bylaws of the organizations with which I register, as indicated in item 10 as may be amended from time to time.

On appeal, the Ninth Circuit Court conceded that federal law favors arbitration, but not in all circumstances. Title VII employment claims are the exception. In this case, Tonyja Duffield was not given an option of selecting arbitration or litigation to resolve potential employment disputes, nor after an incident arose, did she voluntarily agree to pursue arbitration. On the contrary, to be gainfully employed with Robertson, Stephens & Co., she had to forego all rights to litigate in court. Duffield believed she was not in a position of equal bargaining power, which would enable her to argue for striking such a clause from the contract.[14]

The Ninth Circuit Court noted that the purpose of the 1991 Civil Rights Act was to both reaffirm and expand the civil rights of employees and widen the avenues available to them in their pursuit of remedies. Encouraging the use of arbitration would be in concert with Congress' intent, but mandating arbitration with the exclusion of all other remedies would not be.[15]

The Ninth Circuit Court held that, with reference to the passage of the 1991 Civil Rights Act, Congress stipulated that parties to a contract could provide for arbitration as a means of dispute settlement of Title VII claims where appropriate and authorized by law.

Congress' intent in enacting the 1991 Civil Rights Act was to restrict the Supreme Court's decision in *Gilmer v. Interstate/Johnson Lane Corp.* to matters other than Title VII–based employment disputes requiring mandatory arbitration.[16]

Seven months after the Duffield decision, the Ninth Circuit Court tackled the question of whether Section 1 of the FAA prohibits agreements to arbitrate in employment contracts in *Craft v. Campbell Soup Company*.[17] Anthony Craft was an employee of Campbell's Soup and a member of the Food Process Workers and Warehouse Men and Helpers Local Union 228. After allegedly being subjected to racial discrimination and harassment, Craft filed a grievance. After the grievance procedure was exhausted, Craft brought a lawsuit in contravention to the arbitration agreement. Section 1 of the FAA in defining commerce excludes employment contracts involving seamen, railroad workers, and workers engaged in interstate and foreign commerce. The Ninth Circuit Court interpreted Section 2 of the FAA broadly as not applying to employment contracts.

The Third Circuit Court in *Seus v. John Nuveen & Co., Inc.*[18] reached a contrary conclusion. Fourteen years after signing Form U–4, Sheila Seus ignored the mandatory provision for arbitration and filed a claim in District Court for discrimination under Title VII. She claimed her statutory rights should not be subject to an arbitration agreement that is a contract of adhesion. The District Court dismissed her case. The Third Circuit Court in affirming the decision stated that arbitration was binding on both parties. It referenced the FAA, which stated that for arbitration to be compelled there must be a contract evidencing a transaction in commerce and not an employment contract. In *Gilmer v. Interstate/Johnson Lane*,[19] the U.S. Supreme Court held that Form U–4 was a contract evidencing a transaction in commerce. Therefore, this case must be submitted for arbitration in accordance with the FAA.

In 1999, the Second Circuit Court announced in *Desiderio v. NASD*[20] that an individual agreement to arbitrate statutory discrimination claims does not violate Title VII. Most circuit courts favor arbitration of employment disputes. Only, the Ninth Circuit Court had ruled to the contrary. This changed in 2001.

In *Circuit City Stores, Inc., v. Adams*,[21] the U.S. Supreme Court overruled the Ninth Circuit decision to interpret the FAA as not pertaining to employment contracts. When Saint Clair Adams sought employment with Circuit City, Adams signed an application, which included an arbitration provision that stated:

> "I agree that I will settle any and all previously unasserted claims, disputes or controversies arising out of or relating to my application or candidacy for employment, employment and/or cessation or employment with Circuit City, *exclusively* by final and binding *arbitration* before a neutral Arbitrator. By way of example only, such claims include claims under federal, state, and local statutory or common law, such as the Age Discrimination in Employment Act, Title VII of the Civil Rights Act of 1964, as amended, including the amendments of the Civil Rights Act of 1991, the Americans with Disabilities Act, the law of contract and the law of tort."[22]

Adams was hired and worked for 2 years in Circuit City's employ. When Adams filed a suit for discrimination in state court, Circuit City sought an injunction from the District Court. It was granted and then overruled by the Ninth Circuit Court.[23]

The U.S. Supreme Court in reinstating the District Court's order queried why a separate exemption exists for transportation employees if the FAA precludes all employment contracts as the Ninth Circuit Court suggested. The term in question—"engaged in commerce"—applies narrowly to those employees working for employers who operate in the flow of interstate commerce—in other words, transportation workers.[24]

The broad interpretation of the Ninth Circuit Court that the exemption includes all companies subject to federal law through the interstate commerce clause is unfounded. This is reinforced by the initial reason for the enactment of the FAA: to ensure enforceability of arbitration agreements, which had previously been subject to judicial hostility. The U.S. Supreme Court concluded that by agreeing to arbitrate, an employee does not forego his or her statutory rights, only the right to a judicial forum.[25]

Duffield v. Robertson Stephens was effectively overturned by the U.S. Supreme Court's decision of *Circuit City v. Adams,* even though the Duffield decision was never actually mentioned. As a follow-up to Circuit City, the Ninth Circuit Court in *EEOC v. Luce*[26] effectively overturned Duffield in September 2002, when it stated employers might be forced to sign arbitration agreements as a precondition to employment.

The issue in the case that follows is whether an employee's statutory rights can be subject to mandatory arbitration.

Circuit City v. Adams
532 U.S. 105 (2001)

Justice Kennedy delivered the opinion of the Court.

Section 1 of the Federal Arbitration Act (FAA) excludes from the Act's coverage "contracts of employment of seamen, railroad employees, or any other class of workers engaged in foreign or interstate commerce." All but one of the Courts of Appeals which have addressed the issue interpret this provision as exempting contracts of employment of transportation workers, but not other employment contracts, from the FAA's coverage. A different interpretation has been adopted by the Court of Appeals for the Ninth Circuit, which construes the exemption so that all contracts of employment are beyond the FAA's reach, whether or not the worker is engaged in transportation. It applied that rule to the instant case. We now decide that the better interpretation is to construe the statute, as most of the Courts of Appeals have done, to confine the exemption to transportation workers.

I

In October 1995, respondent Saint Clair Adams applied for a job at petitioner Circuit City Stores, Inc., a national retailer of consumer electronics. Adams signed an employment application which included the following provision:

"I agree that I will settle any and all previously unasserted claims, disputes or controversies arising out of or relating to my application or candidacy for employment, employment and/or cessation of employment with Circuit City, *exclusively* by final and binding *arbitration* before a neutral Arbitrator. By way of example only, such claims include claims under federal, state, and local statutory or common law, such as the Age Discrimination in Employment Act, Title VII of the Civil Rights Act of 1964, as amended, including the amendments of the Civil Rights Act of 1991, the Americans with Disabilities Act, the law of contract and the law of tort."

Adams was hired as a sales counselor in Circuit City's store in Santa Rosa, California. Two years later, Adams filed

an employment discrimination lawsuit against Circuit City in state court, asserting claims under California's Fair Employment and Housing Act, and other claims based on general tort theories under California law. Circuit City filed suit in the United States District Court for the Northern District of California, seeking to enjoin the state-court action and to compel arbitration of respondent's claims pursuant to the FAA. The District Court entered the requested order. Respondent, the court concluded, was obligated by the arbitration agreement to submit his claims against the employer to binding arbitration. An appeal followed.

While respondent's appeal was pending in the Court of Appeals for the Ninth Circuit, the court ruled on the key issue in an unrelated case. The court held the FAA does not apply to contracts of employment. In the instant case, following the rule announced in *Craft*, the Court of Appeals held the arbitration agreement between Adams and Circuit City was contained in a "contract of employment," and so was not subject to the FAA. Circuit City petitioned this Court, noting that the Ninth Circuit's conclusion that all employment contracts are excluded from the FAA conflicts with every other Court of Appeals to have addressed the question. We granted certiorari to resolve the issue.

II
A

Congress enacted the FAA in 1925. As the Court has explained, the FAA was a response to hostility of American courts to the enforcement of arbitration agreements, a judicial disposition inherited from then-longstanding English practice. To give effect to this purpose, the FAA compels judicial enforcement of a wide range of written arbitration agreements. The FAA's coverage provision, § 2, provides that

"[a] written provision in any maritime transaction or a contract evidencing a transaction involving commerce to settle by arbitration a controversy thereafter arising out of such contract or transaction, or the refusal to perform the whole or any part thereof, or an agreement in writing to submit to arbitration an existing controversy arising out of such a contract, transaction, or refusal, shall be valid, irrevocable, and enforceable, save upon such grounds as exist at law or in equity for the revocation of any contract."

In sum, the text of the FAA forecloses the construction of § 1 followed by the Court of Appeals in the case under review, a construction which would exclude all employment contracts from the FAA.

When the FAA was adopted, moreover, grievance procedures existed for railroad employees under federal law, and the passage of a more comprehensive statute providing for the mediation and arbitration of railroad labor disputes was imminent, see Railway Labor Act of 1926. It is reasonable to assume that Congress excluded "seamen" and "railroad employees" from the FAA for the simple reason that it did not wish to unsettle established or developing statutory dispute resolution schemes covering specific workers.

As for the residual exclusion of "any other class of workers engaged in foreign or interstate commerce," Congress' demonstrated concern with transportation workers and their necessary role in the free flow of goods explains the linkage to the two specific, enumerated types of workers identified in the preceding portion of the sentence. It would be rational for Congress to ensure that workers in general would be covered by the provisions of the FAA, while reserving for itself more specific legislation for those engaged in transportation. Indeed, such legislation was soon to follow, with the amendment of the Railway Labor Act in 1936 to include air carriers and their employees.

III

By requiring arbitration agreements in most employment contracts to be covered by the FAA, the statute in effect preempts those state employment laws which restrict or limit the ability of employees and employers to enter into arbitration agreements. It is argued that States should be permitted, pursuant to their traditional role in regulating employment relationships, to prohibit employees like respondent from contracting away their right to pursue state-law discrimination claims in court.

Furthermore, for parties to employment contracts not involving the specific exempted categories set forth in § 1, it is true here, that there are real benefits to the enforcement of arbitration provisions. We have been clear in rejecting the supposition that the advantages of the arbitration process somehow disappear when transferred to the employment context. Arbitration agreements allow parties to avoid the costs of litigation, a benefit that may be of particular importance in employment litigation, which often involves smaller sums of money than disputes concerning commercial contracts. These litigation costs to parties (and the accompanying burden to the Courts) would be compounded by the difficult choice-of-law questions that are often presented in disputes arising from the employment relationship, and the necessity of bifurcation of proceedings in those cases where state law precludes arbitration of certain types of employment claims but not others. The considerable complexity and uncertainty that the construction of § 1 urged by respondent would introduce into the enforceability of arbitration agreements in employment contracts would call into doubt the efficacy of alternative dispute resolution procedures adopted by many of the Nation's employers, in the process undermining the FAA's proarbitration purposes and "breeding litigation from a statute that seeks to avoid it." The Court has been quite specific in holding that arbitration agreements can be enforced under the FAA without contravening the policies of congressional enactments giving employees specific protection against discrimination prohibited by federal law; "by agreeing to arbitrate a statutory claim, a party does not forgo the substantive rights afforded by the statute; it only submits to their resolution in an arbitral, rather than a judicial, forum."

For the foregoing reasons, the judgment of the Court of Appeals for the Ninth Circuit is reversed, and the case is remanded for further proceedings consistent with this opinion.

Judgment for Circuit City.

Case Commentary
The U.S. Supreme Court stated that employees' claims based on federal statutes may be subject to mandatory arbitration. ■

CASE QUESTIONS

1. Are you in favor of the court's decision?
2. Are the statutory rights of employees adequately protected through arbitration?
3. Was there any merit to the reasoning of the Ninth Circuit Court?
4. What about an employee's right to a jury trial?

State courts appear to be following suit. In *Re Halliburton Company and Brown v. Root Energy Services,*[27] an employee was demoted after an arbitration program's effective date. The employee believed that the demotion was due to his race and age. He filed a complaint with the Texas Commission on Human

Rights. Halliburton filed a motion with the court to dismiss the action and require arbitration. The lower courts held for the employee, but the Texas Supreme Court reversed their decisions. Halliburton's arbitration program was binding.

In *Martindale v. Sandvik, Inc.*,[28] Maureen Martindale signed an agreement as a condition of employment, which waived her right to a jury trial in favor of arbitration.

Subsequently, she filed a complaint in Superior Court of New Jersey, alleging discrimination and violations of The Family and Medical Leave Act (FMLA). Sandvik filed a motion to dismiss the complaint and compel arbitration. The Superior Court granted the motion. On appeal, the New Jersey Supreme Court affirmed, stating Martindale was an educated businesswoman who had ample opportunity to review the arbitration agreement and determine whether it was in her best interest to sign it.

In the Tenth Circuit Court decision of *Dumais v. American Golf*,[29] American Golf's employment handbook permitted it to unilaterally modify any provision except for at-will termination and the agreement to arbitrate. However, in the arbitration provision itself, there was a statement that only at-will termination could not be modified. This ambiguity was construed against American Golf, who stated the employment handbook was a contract. Theresa Dumais, a 3-year employee, claimed discrimination after resigning. She filed with the EEOC, and then District Court. The Tenth Circuit Court affirmed the District Court's ruling in her favor.

In separate actions brought in California state and federal courts, decisions were rendered against Countrywide Home Loan's policy of conditioning employment on the signing of an agreement to arbitrate and the provision allowing the arbitrator to assess all costs relating to the arbitration, including the arbitrator's fee, against the employee if he or she loses. Both courts ruled the policies were unconscionable.[30]

The subsequent decision by the Ninth Circuit Court in *EEOC v. Luce*[31] would appear to overturn its Countrywide Home Loan decision with respect to mandatory signing of arbitration agreements.

In 2002, the Seventh Circuit Court, in *McCaskill v. SCI Management Corp.*,[32] held that an arbitration agreement that prohibits the awarding of attorneys' fees to an employee is unenforceable if it is determined that he or she was discriminated against or harassed. The arbitration provision read, "Each party may retain legal counsel and shall pay its own costs and attorneys' fees, regardless of the outcome of the arbitration." McCaskill asserted females in the work environment were being sexually harassed. She was denied a bonus and then discharged.

In *EEOC v. Waffle House*,[33] the U.S. Supreme Court stated that the FAA provides that a court must stay a proceeding and compel arbitration where the parties have agreed to arbitrate. If a claim is filed with the EEOC, the EEOC has jurisdiction for 180 days. During that period, the employee may request a right to sue letter. If the EEOC decides to file a suit, the employee is precluded from suing on his or her own, but may intervene in the EEOC case. Thus, the EEOC is not bound by an employee's agreement to arbitrate.

In filling out his application for employment, Eric Baker agreed to submit any employment dispute to arbitration. The Waffle House hired Baker as a grill operator. Two weeks after commencing work, Baker had a seizure during work. He was discharged subsequently. The District Court held that Baker's employment contract did not contain an arbitration agreement. The Fourth Circuit Court disagreed. It believed an arbitration agreement was included and that the EEOC's right to litigate paled in favor of the FAA's policy of compelling arbitration where an agreement exists between employer and employee. In reversing, the U.S. Supreme Court stipulated that only those matters referenced in the agreement can be arbitrated, and only those parties who sign the agreement are bound by the arbitration proceeding. If the EEOC brings an action in court when an individual's statutory rights have been violated, the court cannot compel the parties to arbitrate because the EEOC was not a party to the arbitration agreement. This decision will not have a chilling effect on the use of arbitration by employers because the actual number of cases filed by the EEOC is very small.[34]

The issue in the following case is whether a mandatory arbitration provision in an employment contract precludes the EEOC from commencing a lawsuit against an employer.

EEOC v. Waffle House
534 U.S. 279 (2002)

Justice Stevens delivered the opinion of the Court.

The question presented is whether an agreement between an employer and an employee to arbitrate employment-related disputes bars the Equal Employment Opportunity Commission (EEOC) from pursuing victim-specific judicial relief, such as backpay, reinstatement, and damages, in an enforcement action alleging that the employer has violated Title I of the Americans with Disabilities Act of 1990 (ADA).

I

As a condition of employment, all prospective Waffle House employees are required to sign application containing a similar mandatory arbitration agreement. Baker began working as a grill operator at one of respondent's restaurants on August 10, 1994. Sixteen days later he suffered a seizure at work and soon thereafter was discharged. Baker did not initiate arbitration proceedings, nor has he in the seven years since his termination, but he did file a timely charge of discrimination with the EEOC alleging that his discharge violated the ADA.

The agreement states:

"The parties agree that any dispute or claim concerning Applicant's employment with Waffle House, Inc., or any subsidiary or Franchisee of Waffle House, Inc., or the terms, conditions or benefits of such employment, including whether such dispute or claim is arbitrable, will be settled by binding arbitration. The arbitration proceedings shall be conducted under the Commercial Arbitration Rules of the American Arbitration Association in effect at the time a demand for arbitration is made. A decision and award of the arbitrator made under the said rules shall be exclusive, final and binding on both parties, their heirs, executors, administrators, successors and assigns. The costs and expenses of the arbitration shall be borne evenly by the parties."

After an investigation and an unsuccessful attempt to conciliate, the EEOC filed an enforcement action against respondent in the Federal District Court for the District of South Carolina, the ADA, and the Civil Rights Act of 1991. Baker is not a party to the case. The EEOC's complaint alleged that respondent engaged in employment practices that violated the ADA, including its discharge of Baker "because of his disability," and that its violation was intentional, and "done with malice or with reckless indifference to his federally protected rights." The complaint requested the court to grant injunctive relief to "eradicate the effects of [respondent's] past and present unlawful employment practices," to order specific relief designed to make Baker whole, including backpay, reinstatement, and compensatory damages, and to award punitive damages for malicious and reckless conduct.

Respondent filed a petition under the Federal Arbitration Act (FAA), to stay the EEOC's suit and compel arbitration, or to dismiss the action. Based on a factual determination that Baker's actual employment contract had not included the arbitration provision, the District Court denied the motion. The Court of Appeals granted an interlocutory appeal and held that a valid, enforceable arbitration agreement between Baker and respondent did exist. The court then proceeded to consider "what effect, if any, the binding arbitration agreement between Baker and Waffle House has on the EEOC, which filed this action in its own name both in the public interest and on behalf of Baker." After reviewing the relevant statutes and the language of the contract, the court concluded that the agreement did not foreclose the enforcement action because the EEOC was not a party to the contract, and it has independent statutory authority to bring suit in any federal District Court where venue is proper. Nevertheless, the court held that the EEOC was precluded from seeking victim-specific relief in court because the policy goals expressed in the FAA required giving some effect to Baker's arbitration agreement. The majority explained:

"When the EEOC seeks 'make-whole' relief for a charging party, the federal policy favoring enforcement of private arbitration agreements outweighs the EEOC's right to proceed in federal court because in that circumstance, the EEOC's public interest is minimal, as the EEOC seeks primarily to vindicate private, rather than public, interests. On the other hand, when the EEOC is pursuing large-scale injunctive relief, the balance tips in favor of EEOC enforcement efforts in federal court because the public interest dominates the EEOC's action."

But no question concerning the validity of his claim or the character of the relief that could be appropriately awarded in either a judicial or an arbitral forum is presented by this record. Baker has not sought arbitration of his claim, nor is there any indication that he has entered into settlement negotiations with respondent. It is an open question whether a settlement or arbitration judgment would affect the validity of the EEOC's claim or the character of relief the EEOC may seek. The only issue before this Court is whether the fact that Baker has signed a mandatory arbitration agreement limits the remedies available to the EEOC. The text of the relevant statutes provides a clear answer to that question. They do not authorize the courts to balance the competing policies of the ADA and the FAA or to second-guess the agency's judgment concerning which of the remedies authorized by law that it shall seek in any given case.

Moreover, it simply does not follow from the cases holding that the employee's conduct may affect the EEOC's recovery that the EEOC's claim is merely derivative. We have recognized several situations in which the EEOC does not stand in the employee's shoes.

The judgment of the Court of Appeals is reversed, and the case is remanded for further proceedings consistent with this opinion.

Judgment for EEOC.

Case Commentary

The U.S. Supreme Court ruled that the EEOC is not bound by a mandatory arbitration agreement because it was not a party to it. ∎

CASE QUESTIONS

1. Are you in accord with the court's decision?
2. Do you agree that if the decision were otherwise, the power of the EEOC would be undermined?

3. Why did the Fourth Circuit Court not take this into account in making its determination?

Today it appears to be resolved that individual agreements executed between an employer and its employees that include a provision to arbitrate an employee's statutory rights under Title VII, the ADEA, and ADA are enforceable. An action brought in court may be stayed, with the court ordering the parties to arbitrate. The right to mandate arbitration is not absolute where the arbitration provision prohibits the awarding of attorneys' fees, limits a party's remedies, denies due process, or is otherwise unconscionable.

EMPLOYEE LESSONS

1. Realize that arbitration is expensive and expeditious in comparison to a lawsuit.
2. Understand that access to court may no longer be available.
3. Appreciate that arbitration rules out extensive discovery.
4. Comprehend that you do not forego your statutory rights, just your right to a judicial forum.
5. Recognize that an arbitrator's award can be overturned only when it is arbitrary and capricious.
6. Request a fee-splitting arrangement.
7. Know that the burden is on the employee to show that the cost to arbitrate presents a financial hardship.

REVIEW QUESTIONS

1. Define arbitration.
2. What are the duties of an arbitrator?
3. How is an arbitrator selected?
4. Is an arbitrator's award equivalent to a court's judgment?
5. When can an arbitrator's award be overturned?
6. Who is responsible for paying an arbitrator's fee?
7. What was the purpose of the FAA?

8. What is the significance of Form U–4 with respect to arbitration?
9. Can statutory rights be arbitrated?
10. What are the benefits of arbitration?

CASE PROBLEMS

1. Howard Saari was employed by Smith Barney, Harris Upham & Co., Inc., as an account executive beginning in July 1988; he alleges that his work was satisfactory at all times. According to Saari's complaint, on or about December 14, 1988, a "sum of money, supposedly belonging to a client of Smith Barney, was supposedly stolen from the desk of a Smith Barney employee." Saari alleged he was questioned about the theft and was later asked to take a polygraph test concerning the incident, which he refused. Saari claims he was then terminated for his refusal to take the polygraph examination.

   Saari became a registered representative of the NYSE and thereby subject to its Rule 347, which provides that "Any controversy between a registered representative and any member or member organization arising out of the employment or termination of employment of such registered representative by and with such member or member organization shall be settled by arbitration."

   Saari contends that the enforcement provisions of the Employee Polygraph Protection Act show no such flexibility. Is the arbitration requirement in violation of the EPPA? *Saari v. Smith Barney*, 968 F.2d 877 (9th Cir. 1992)
2. Gilmer filed an age discrimination lawsuit against Interstate/Johnson Lane Corp. The company argued that all employment matters were subject to arbitration. Gilmer retorted that an ADEA claim was exempt from that requirement. What was the result? *Gilmer v. Interstate/Johnson Lane Corp.*, 111 S. Ct 1647 (1991)

HUMAN RESOURCE DILEMMAS

1. Aloe Inc. has decided to institute a mandatory arbitration agreement as a condition of employment. One of its employees, Alyssa Jorgenson, an African-American female, refuses to sign it. Aloe wishes to terminate her, but the company is fearful of reprisals. How would you advise Aloe?
2. The law firm of Gilbert, Jones, and Harrington discharged Homer White when he was overheard espousing the attributes of the Reverend Al Sharpton for President. Homer files suit for violation of his First Amendment freedom of speech. The firm files a motion to dismiss, alleging this matter must be arbitrated in line with the mandatory arbitration agreement between the firm and its employees. Can an employee's constitutional rights be subject to mandatory arbitration?
3. Sprinkles, Inc., has a provision in its arbitration agreement that the loser pays the arbitrator's fee. One of its employees, Hilda Rodriguez, refuses to pay, alleging an undue financial burden. After paying the arbitrator, Sprinkles is considering suing Hilda for breach of contract. How would you advise Sprinkles to proceed?

WEB SITE ASSIGNMENT

Draft an arbitration agreement for The Long and the Short of it (L&S) men's clothing store, which appears in the scenario in the beginning of this chapter.

www.dol.gov/sol/media/memos/August9.htm
www.business.com/directory/law/practice_areas/alternative_dispute_resolution/employment_arbitration/
www.smrh.com/publications/pubview.cfm?pubID=127

www.adr.org/index2.1.jsp

www.vault.com/nr/newsmain.jsp?nr_page=3&ch_id=402&article_id=18893&cat_id=1244

ENDNOTES

1. Moran, John Jude. 1995. *Practical Business Law,* Third Edition. Upper Saddle River, NJ: Prentice Hall.
2. *Green Tree Financial Corp.—Alabama v. Randolph,* 531 U.S. 79 (2000).
3. *AT&T Technologies, Inc. v. Communications Workers of America,* 475 U.S. 643 (1986).
4. *Gilmer v. Interstate/Johnson Lane Corp.,* 500 U.S. 20 (1991).
5. 9 U.S.C. Section 2.
6. 500 U.S. 20 (1991).
7. 475 U.S. 643 (1986).
8. 363 U.S. 593 (1960).
9. 473 U.S. 614 (1985).
10. 238 F.3d 549 (4th Cir. 2001).
11. 531 U.S. 79 (2000).
12. 144 F.3d 1182 (9th Cir. 1998).
13. Id.
14. Id.
15. Id.
16. Id.
17. 161 F.3d 1199 (9th Cir. 1998).
18. 146 F.3d 175 (3rd Cir. 1998).
19. 500 U.S. 20 (1991).
20. 191 F.3d 198 (2nd Cir. 1999).
21. 532 U.S. 105 (2001).
22. Id.
23. Id.
24. Id.
25. Id.
26. No. 00–57222 (9th Cir. 2002).
27. 27 SW3d 117 (2002).
28. 173 N.J. 76 (2002).
29. No. 01–2224 (10th Cir. 2002).
30. *Ferguson v. Countrywide Credit Industries, Inc.,* 2002 U.S. App. LEXIS 14739 (9th Cir.).
31. No. 00–57222 (9th Cir. 2002).
32. 2000 U.S. Dist. LEXIS 10317 (N.D.Ill.).
33. 534 U.S. 279 (2002).
34. Id.

Chapter

Civil Rights Act

Employment Scenario

One day during lunch with Susan, Tom Long and Mark Short ask her whether Title VII of the Civil Rights Act applies to The Long and the Short of It. As she digests her grilled salmon and baked sweet potato, Susan replies in the affirmative. L&S has four stores with a total of 62 employees. Growth has been phenomenal. Susan explains that L&S has been subject to Title VII since it hired its fifteenth employee. At that time, Susan reminded Tom and Mark that she sent them a memo detailing the requirement that they keep records regarding their selection process of potential candidates. These records must be made available to the EEOC upon request. Susan advised Tom and Mark to notify her if anyone filed a claim against L&S for discrimination. She also warned them to be consistent in their treatment of employees. She reminded them not to favor or discourage any class of worker. Susan also warned them not to favor the employment of one sex over the other by stereotyping certain jobs. Treating everyone equally is the key to an employer's peaceful coexistence with its employees. What are the ramifications if they do not take Susan's advice?

Employment Scenario

All 62 employees at The Long and the Short of It are white. The customer base is predominantly white, but the four stores are located in neighborhoods that are 40 percent minority. Debbie Brown, a minority, applies for a sales position at an L&S store. She is rejected. A few months later, Debbie accompanies her husband to another L&S store to purchase a new suit. It suddenly dawns on her that the sales staff of both stores she visited is all white. After a perusal of the remaining two stores evidences the same result, Debbie files a disparate impact claim with the EEOC. L&S consults with Susan North, Esq., concerning the viability of Debbie's claim. What advice should Susan give?

Chapter Checklist

➤ *Appreciate the history of events leading up to passage of the Civil Rights Act.*

➤ *Understand the purpose of Title VII of the Civil Rights Act.*

➤ *Comprehend the decisions in Griggs v. Duke Power Co. and McDonnell Douglas Corp. v. Green.*

➤ *Distinguish between disparate impact and disparate treatment.*

➤ *Learn what constitutes business necessity and job relatedness.*

➤ *Understand the issue of whether an employer's decision was a pretext.*

➤ *Appreciate the function of the Equal Employment Opportunity Commission.*

➤ *Be able to explain the 80 percent rule.*

➤ *List the significant features of the Civil Rights Act of 1991.*

➤ *Identify the exemptions to Title VII of the Civil Rights Act.*

INTRODUCTION

Shortly after the conclusion of the Civil War in 1865, the Thirteenth, Fourteenth, and Fifteenth Amendments to the U.S. Constitution were adopted. The Thirteenth Amendment abolished slavery. The Fifteenth Amendment gave black men the right to vote. But, it was the Equal Protection Clause of the Fourteenth Amendment that laid the basis for equal rights in employment. The Equal Protection Clause basically states that all people are entitled to equal protection under the law. A few years after its enactment, the Supreme Court of the United States, in *Plessy v. Ferguson*, interpreted this to mean that separate but equal facilities would satisfy the Fourteenth Amendment requirement. Segregation persisted into the 1970s, but inroads began to be made in the mid-1950s with the *Brown v. Board of Education* decision, which mandated integration in public schools. This decision had a reverberating effect throughout society. In 1964, Congress passed the Civil Rights Act to legislate integration in schools, housing, restaurants, transportation, shopping, and employment. Title VII of the Civil Rights Act speaks to employment. It prohibits discrimination because of religion, race, color, sex, and national origin.

There are two main types of discrimination: disparate impact, which is discrimination against a class of people, and disparate treatment, which is discrimination against an individual. The two major cases defining these forms of discrimination are *Griggs v. Duke Power Co.*, which deals with disparate impact, and *McDonnell Douglas Corp. v. Green*, which deals with disparate treatment. Both of these cases are set forth in this chapter.

- Educate officials, managers, and workers about the Civil Rights Act.
- Persuade officials, managers, and workers to conduct themselves in such a manner as to avoid discrimination.
- Guard against retaliation.
- Keep in mind the 80 percent rule when hiring.
- Maintain records on employee hiring and retention.
- Be familiar with the authority of the Equal Employment Opportunity Commission.
- Understand the different avenues available to an employee in maintaining an action for discrimination.
- Be apprised that compensatory and punitive damages are now available.
- Appreciate the requirements of business necessity and job relatedness when formulating qualifications for a job.
- Be cognizant of the exemptions to the Civil Rights Act.

The question presented in the case that follows is whether separate but equal facilities are discriminatory.

Brown v. Board of Education of Topeka
347 U.S. 483 (1954)

Chief Justice Warren.

The decision in this lawsuit was rendered in response to a number of cases having the same constitutional question concerning the segregation of white and colored children in public schools.

In each case, colored children have made applications to schools attended by white children and in most cases they have been denied admission based on the separate but equal doctrine formulated in 1896. That doctrine provided that equal treatment of races is satisfied when the races are provided separate, but equal facilities. The parties bringing these lawsuits contended that segregated public schools are not "equal."

The issue is whether segregation in public schools is unconstitutional in violation of the Equal Protection clause of the Fourteenth Amendment.

In 1954, the United States Supreme Court held that segregation in public schools was unconstitutional. They cited as their reasoning a finding made by the court in the Kansas case which, although holding segregation to be constitu-tional, declared "Segregation of white and colored children in public schools has a detrimental effect upon the colored children. The impact is greater when it has the sanction of the law; for the policy of separating the races is usually interpreted as denoting the inferiority of the Negro group. A sense of inferiority affects the motivation of a child to learn." The Supreme Court added "In these days, it is doubtful that any child may reasonably be expected to succeed in life if he or she is denied the opportunity of an education. Such an opportunity, where the state has undertaken to provide it, is a right which must be made available to all on equal terms."

Judgment for Brown.

Case Commentary

The U.S. Supreme Court concluded that separate but equal facilities are discriminatory because separating a class of people is tantamount to claiming they are inferior. This was the landmark case for the civil rights movement. ■

CASE QUESTIONS

1. Why did it take almost 90 years for the Supreme Court to abolish the separate but equal doctrine?
2. What solution did the court provide to effectuate integration?
3. Did the court state that all public schools must be integrated, or only those in racially diverse neighborhoods?
4. Was busing the appropriate response to the court's decision?

Ten years later, the Civil Rights Act was introduced to codify existing statutes and case law. Enforcement of the Civil Rights Act continued to wane until the *Griggs v. Duke Power* case of 1971 set forth the criteria for bringing a discrimination suit based on the disparate impact of an employer's selection and promotion procedure.

One year later, the Supreme Court laid out the process for an individual to bring a discrimination action based on disparate treatment in *McDonnell Douglas v. Green*.

Title VII of the Civil Rights Act of 1964 is the main authority governing employment discrimination. Because it is a federal law, it is binding on all employers throughout the United States. An employer is a person or business employing at least 15 individuals for 20 weeks of the year. The employer's business must have some connection with interstate commerce for Title VII to be applicable. Basically, a business is engaged in interstate commerce if it ships goods to a state other than the one in which it is located, performs services in another state, or performs services intrastate for individuals traveling interstate. Interstate commerce has been construed so broadly that it would be difficult for a business to seek exemption from Title VII under the auspices of not participating in interstate commerce.

The main thrust of Title VII is that it is an unlawful practice to discriminate in failing or refusing to hire, train, discharge, promote, compensate, or in any other aspect of the employment relationship because of an individual's religion, race, color, sex, or national origin. Employers may not segregate employees or classify them in such a way as to deprive any of them of employment opportunities or to adversely affect their status as employees.

Employment Perspective

Redeye Truck Stop is located on Interstate 80 in Pennsylvania. It refuses to serve women and minority truckers. Redeye argues that it is not subject to the Civil Rights Act because all of its business is transacted in Pennsylvania. Is this argument valid? No! Although Redeye's business is conducted intrastate, it services truckers who are traveling interstate. Therefore, its business affects interstate commerce.

The term employer includes individuals, partnerships, corporations, associations, unincorporated organizations, and governments. Employment agencies and labor unions are also subject to Title VII. For purposes here, employer will also refer to employment agencies and labor unions where appropriate. It does not include the United States, an American Indian tribe, or a tax exempt, bona fide private membership club. Religious societies and religious educational institutions are also exempt insofar as they have the right to employ only individuals of their religion.

Employment Perspective

George Feinstein, who is Jewish, has just received a college degree in education. Neither the public schools nor the Jewish schools have openings for teachers. George applied to the Catholic Diocese, where positions are readily available. He was turned down because he is not a practicing Catholic. Is this discrimination? No! Catholic schools, as well as any other religious-affiliated institutions, may restrict employment to members of their own particular faith.

Most states have their own laws prohibiting discrimination and a human rights agency to investigate violations. State law will often parallel Federal law and in some instances will exceed it as with affinity orientation. Each state has its own agency to monitor and enforce its employemnt discrimination laws. A violation of state law must be brought in the appropriate state court having jurisdiction. Jurisdiction is the authority to hear and decide a particular legal issue and bind it to the party against whom the lawsuit is brought.

The issue in the following case is whether an employer had the requisite number of employees for the application of Title VII.

Stinnett v. Iron Works Gym/Executive Health SPA

301 F.3d 610 (7th Cir. 2002)

Rovner, Circuit Judge.

The law allowing victims of sexual harassment to sue their employers applies only to those businesses with fifteen or more employees for each working day in each of twenty or more calendar weeks in the current or preceding calendar year. In order to proceed in his sexual harassment claim, Kerry Stinnett was thus required to show that his employer, Iron Works Gym/Executive Health Spa, Incorporated (collectively "Executive Health"), employed at least fifteen persons during 1995, 1996 or 1997. This proved to be an insurmountable task for Stinnett, however, because the Executive Health Spa was a house of prostitution and criminal enterprises rarely keep accurate personnel or payroll records. The district court granted summary judgment in favor of the employer because Stinnett had inadequate evidence to show the number of employees at Executive Health at the relevant time. We affirm.

We construe the facts in a light most favorable to Stinnett, the party opposing summary judgment. Kerry Stinnett was employed as the manager of the Iron Works Gym (the "Gym") from June 1996 through July 1997. The Gym employed nine persons including Stinnett. The Gym, which was a sole proprietorship, was wholly owned by the Executive Health Spa (the "Spa"), another business down the street from the Gym. The Spa was incorporated and its sole shareholder was Stinnett's boss, Kathy Andrews. For reasons we will discuss below, the district court counted the Gym and Spa as a single entity when determining the number of employees. The Gym, so far as the record shows, was actually a gym. The Spa, however, was a house of prostitution providing sexual services to its patrons under the guise of "massage." Not surprisingly, the Spa's payroll records are somewhat sketchy and show that the Spa never employed enough workers to meet the minimum requirement of fifteen, even if the Spa and Gym are counted together and even if the "spa attendants" (a creative euphemism for prostitutes) are counted as employees.

Executive Health does not contest the district court's conclusion that the Spa and the Gym should be treated as a single entity for the purposes of determining the number of employees.

We begin with the deposition of Carrie Lee, one of the spa attendants. Lee had considerable difficulty recalling the dates of her employment at the Spa in part because she quit once and was terminated twice. Ultimately, though, she testified that she last worked at the Spa in 1993. She stated that when she left the Spa for the final time in 1993, there were approximately 20 to 23 women working there. She stated that approximately 10 women worked each of two shifts and that another woman answered phones. Although she also stated that an equal number of women worked at the Spa in 1996 and 1997, she clarified that she had no personal knowledge of this fact and based it on the complaints of a friend who worked at the Spa at that time, and who was annoyed that she had to work with so many other women. Because Lee's personal knowledge ended in 1993, two years before the relevant time, the district court struck Lee's deposition (and presumably would have struck her testimony at trial) because her personal knowledge of the number of workers ended in 1993.

The district court similarly struck the transcript of an audiotape made during a criminal investigation of the Spa in 1999. A woman named Tammy Strawberry, cooperating with local authorities, wore a wire into a meeting with Kathy Andrews. The ostensible purpose of the meeting was that Strawberry was applying for a job as a spa attendant at the Executive Health Spa. In the course of the conversation, Andrews volunteered that "We have what, 25, 30 people that work here." The conversation took place on September 2,

1999, approximately a year and a half after Stinnett terminated his employment at the Gym. The district court struck the transcript because the conversation occurred in 1999 and was not relevant to how many employees worked at Executive Health during 1995, 1996 or 1997. Under the district court's ruling, both the Lee deposition and the Strawberry transcript described the number of employees at times that were too remote to be relevant to the number of employees during 1995, 1996 and 1997.

Stinnett argues that if there were 20 employees before the relevant time and 20 employees after the relevant time, the court must infer that there were at least 15 employees during the relevant time. But we cannot find that the district court abused its discretion in striking these materials from the record on the ground that they were too remote in time to be relevant.

This quandary over the proper status of the spa attendants turns out to be a red herring, though. We have carefully reviewed all of the evidence on which Stinnett relies and none of it shows that there were more than fourteen employees for each working day in each of twenty or more calendar weeks in the relevant calendar years, even if spa attendants are counted as employees rather than independent contractors.

That brings us finally to the ultimate question of whether the district court properly granted summary judgment in favor of Executive Health. Without any admissible evidence showing the requisite number of employees, Stinnett cannot maintain his sexual harassment claim. The court was therefore correct to grant judgment in favor of the employer.

Affirmed.

Case Commentary

The Seventh Circuit Court decided that the 15-employee threshold could not be met in part due to the lack of record keeping by the prostitution branch of the business. ■

CASE QUESTIONS

1. Are you in agreement with the court's reasoning?
2. Is the court saying that it's okay that the lack of record keeping was due to criminal activity?
3. How is it conceivable that the lack of record keeping by a criminal enterprise could render the business immune from Title VII violations?
4. Does an exception to the 15-employee requirement need to be made for criminal enterprises?

DISPARATE TREATMENT

Disparate treatment exists where an employer treats an individual differently because that individual is a member of a particular race, religion, gender, or ethnic group. The complaining party must show that he or she is a member of a particular Title VII class; that the employer in question was seeking applicants for a position; that he or she was rejected; and that the employer continued to seek applicants with similar qualifications.

Employment Perspective

Thomas Johnson, who is black, responded to an advertisement offering a position with the law firm of Mayer, Morgan, and Marconi. The law firm was seeking a person who graduated in the top half of his or her class from an Ivy League law school. Johnson met those qualifications. However, he was told that the position had already been filled. The same advertisement continued to run in the newspaper, though. Johnson claimed disparate treatment. Is he correct? Yes! The law firm lied to Johnson about the position's being filled, because it did not want to hire a black person.

The following case, which set the standard for qualifying for disparate treatment, is a landmark case. To qualify for Title VII protection, a person must show that (1) he or she is a member of a protected class; (2) he or she applied for a position for which he or she was qualified and for which the employer had openings; (3) he or she was rejected; (4) the position remained open. At this point, the burden of proof has been met by the employee or the applicant and then shifts to the employer to establish a justifiable reason for its action. Finally, the employee must prove that the employer's reason was just a pretext for its refusal to hire.

McDonnell Douglas Corp. v. Green

411 U.S. 792 (1972)

Justice Poweli delivered the opinion of the Court.

The case before us raises significant questions as to the proper order and nature of proof in actions under Title VII of the Civil Rights Act of 1964, 42 U.S.C. 2000e.

Petitioner McDonnell Douglas Corp., is an aerospace and aircraft manufacturer headquartered in St. Louis, Missouri, where it employs over 30,000 people. Respondent, a black citizen of St. Louis, worked for petitioner as a mechanic and laboratory technician from 1956 until August 28, 1964 when he was laid off in the course of a general reduction in petitioner's work force. Respondent, a long-time activist in the civil rights movement, protested vigorously that his discharge and the general hiring practices of petitioner were racially motivated. As part of this protest, respondent and other members of the Congress on Racial Equality illegally stalled their cars on the main roads leading to petitioner's plant for the purpose of blocking access to it at the time of the morning shift change. The District Judge described the plan for, and respondent's participation in, the "stall-in."

Some three weeks following the "lock-in" on July 25, 1965, petitioner publicly advertised for qualified mechanics, respondent's trade, and respondent promptly applied for re-employment. Petitioner turned down respondent, basing its rejection on respondent's participation in the "stall-in" and "lock-in." Shortly thereafter, respondent filled a formal complaint with the Equal Employment Opportunity Commission, claiming that petitioner has refused to rehire him because of his race and persistent involvement in the civil rights movement, in violation of 703 (a)(1) and 704 (a) of the Civil Rights Act of 1964. The former section generally prohibits racial discrimination in any employment decision while the latter forbids discrimination against applicants or employees for attempting to protest or correct allegedly discriminatory conditions of employment.

The language of Title VII makes plain the purpose of Congress to assure equality of employment opportunities and to eliminate those discriminatory practices and devices which have fostered racially stratified job environments to the disadvantage of minority citizens.

The complainant in a Title VII trial must carry the initial burden under the statute of establishing a prima facie case of racial discrimination. This may be done by showing (i) that he belongs to a racial minority; (ii) that he applied and was qualified for a job for which the employer was seeking applicants, (iii) that, despite his qualifications, he was rejected; and (iv) that, after his rejection, the position remained open and the employer continued to seek applicants from persons of complainant's qualifications. In the instant case, we agree with the Court of Appeals that respondent proved a prima facie case. Petitioner sought mechanics, respondent's trade, and continued to do so after respondent's rejection. Petitioner, moreover, does not dispute respondent's qualifications and acknowledges that his past work performance in petitioner's employ was "satisfactory."

The burden then must shift to the employer to articulate some legitimate, nondiscriminatory reason for the employer's rejection. We need not attempt in the instant case to detail every matter which fairly could be recognized as a reasonable basis for a refusal to hire. Here petitioner has assigned respondent's participation in unlawful conduct against it as the cause for his rejection. We think that this suffices to discharge petitioner's burden of proof at this stage and to meet respondent's prima facie case of discrimination.

Respondent admittedly had taken part in a carefully planned "stall-in," designed to tie up access to and egress from petitioner's plant at a peak traffic hour. Nothing in Title VII compels an employer to absolve and rehire one who has engaged in such deliberate, unlawful activity against it.

> "We are unable to conclude that Congress intended to compel employers to retain persons in their employ regardless of their unlawful conduct, to invest those who go on strike with an immunity from discharge for acts of trespass or violence against the employer's property."

Petitioner's reason for rejection thus suffices to meet the prima facie case, but the inquiry must not end here. While Title VII does not, without more, compel rehiring of respondent, neither does it permit petitioner to use respondent's conduct as a pretext for the sort of discrimination prohibited by 703(a)(1). On remand, respondent must, as the Court of Appeals recognized, be afforded a fair opportunity to show that petitioner's stated reason for respondent's rejection was in fact pretext. Especially relevant to such a showing would be evidence that white employees involved in acts against petitioner of comparable seriousness to the "stall-in" were nevertheless retained or rehired. Petitioner may justifiably refuse to rehire one who was engaged in unlawful, disruptive acts against it, but only if this criterion is applied alike to members of all races.

In sum, respondent should have been allowed to pursue his claim under 703(a)(1). If the evidence on retrial is substantially in accord with that before us in this case, we think that respondent carried his burden of establishing a prima facie case of racial discrimination and that petitioner successfully rebutted that case. But this does not end the matter. On retrial, respondent must be afforded a fair opportunity to demonstrate that petitioner's assigned reason for refusing to re-employ was a pretext or discriminatory in its application. If the District Judge so finds, he must order a prompt and appropriate remedy. In the absence of such a finding, petitioner's refusal to rehire must stand.

The judgment is vacated and the cause is hereby remanded to the District Court for further proceedings consistent with this opinion.

Judgment for Green.

CASE QUESTIONS

1. Do you think the *McDonnell Douglas* test is appropriate?
2. Are there any changes you would make to the test?

Case Commentary

In *McDonnell Douglas*, the U.S. Supreme Court set forth the requirements for disparate treatment cases. In so doing, they concluded that Green had established a prima facie case of discrimination, which was rebutted by McDonnell Douglas's legitimate nondiscriminatory reason for refusing to rehire him. The case was remanded to the district court where Green will bear the burden of proving McDonnell Douglas's legitimate nondiscriminatory reason was not the real reason, but a mere pretext. ■

3. Will Green be able to prove McDonnell Douglas's reason was pretexual?

The issue in the case that follows is whether the plaintiff must allege sufficient facts to meet the burden of proof in his or her Title VII complaint.

Swierkiewicz v. Sorema N. A.
534 U.S. 506 (2002)

Justice Thomas delivered the opinion of the Court.

This case presents the question whether a complaint in an employment discrimination lawsuit must contain specific facts establishing a prima facie case of discrimination under the framework set forth by this Court in *McDonnell Douglas Corp.* v. *Green.* We hold that an employment discrimination complaint need not include such facts and instead must contain only "a short and plain statement of the claim showing that the pleader is entitled to relief."

I

Petitioner Akos Swierkiewicz is a native of Hungary, who at the time of his complaint was 53 years old. In April 1989, petitioner began working for respondent Sorema N. A., a reinsurance company headquartered in New York and principally owned and controlled by a French parent corporation. Petitioner was initially employed in the position of senior vice president and chief underwriting officer (CUO). Nearly six years later, Francois M. Chavel, respondent's Chief Executive Officer, demoted petitioner to a marketing and services position and transferred the bulk of his underwriting responsibilities to Nicholas Papadopoulo, a 32-year-old who, like Mr. Chavel, is a French national. About a year later, Mr. Chavel stated that he wanted to "energize" the underwriting department and appointed Mr. Papadopoulo as CUO. Petitioner claims that Mr. Papadopoulo had only one year of underwriting experience at the time he was promoted, and therefore was less experienced and less qualified to be CUO than he, since at that point he had 26 years of experience in the insurance industry.

Because we review here a decision granting respondent's motion to dismiss, we must accept as true all of the factual allegations contained in the complaint.

Following his demotion, petitioner contends that he "was isolated by Mr. Chavel . . . excluded from business decisions and meetings and denied the opportunity to reach his true potential at SOREMA." Petitioner unsuccessfully attempted to meet with Mr. Chavel to discuss his discontent. Finally, in April 1997, petitioner sent a memo to Mr. Chavel outlining his grievances and requesting a severance package. Two weeks later, respondent's general counsel presented petitioner with two options: He could either resign without a severance package or be dismissed. Mr. Chavel fired petitioner after he refused to resign.

Petitioner filed a lawsuit alleging that he had been terminated on account of his national origin in violation of Title VII of the Civil Rights Act of 1964 and on account of his age in violation of the Age Discrimination in Employment Act of 1967 (ADEA). The United States District Court for the Southern District of New York dismissed petitioner's complaint because it found that he "had not adequately alleged a prima facie case, in that he had not adequately alleged circumstances that support an inference of discrimination." The United States Court of Appeals for the Second Circuit affirmed the dismissal, relying on its settled precedent, which requires a plaintiff in an employment discrimination complaint to allege facts constituting a prima facie case of discrimination under the framework set forth by this Court in

McDonnell Douglas. The Court of Appeals held that petitioner had failed to meet his burden because his allegations were "insufficient as a matter of law to raise an inference of discrimination." We granted certiorari to resolve a split among the Courts of Appeals concerning the proper pleading standard for employment discrimination cases, and now reverse.

Applying Circuit precedent, the Court of Appeals required petitioner to plead a prima facie case of discrimination in order to survive respondent's motion to dismiss. In the Court of Appeals' view, petitioner was thus required to allege in his complaint: (1) membership in a protected group; (2) qualification for the job in question; (3) an adverse employment action; and (4) circumstances that support an inference of discrimination.

The prima facie case under *McDonnell Douglas*, however, is an evidentiary standard, not a pleading requirement. In *McDonnell Douglas*, this Court made clear that "the critical issue before us concerned the order and allocation *of proof* in a private, non-class action challenging employment discrimination." In subsequent cases, this Court has reiterated that the prima facie case relates to the employee's burden of presenting evidence that raises an inference of discrimination.

This Court has never indicated that the requirements for establishing a prima facie case under *McDonnell Douglas* also apply to the pleading standard that plaintiffs must satisfy in order to survive a motion to dismiss.

In addition, under a notice pleading system, it is not appropriate to require a plaintiff to plead facts establishing a prima facie case because the *McDonnell Douglas* framework does not apply in every employment discrimination case. For instance, if a plaintiff is able to produce direct evidence of discrimination, he may prevail without proving all the elements of a prima facie case. Under the Second Circuit's heightened pleading standard, a plaintiff without direct evidence of discrimination at the time of his complaint must plead a prima facie case of discrimination, even though discovery might uncover such direct evidence. It thus seems incongruous to require a plaintiff, in order to survive a motion to dismiss, to plead more facts than he may ultimately need to prove to succeed on the merits if direct evidence of discrimination is discovered.

Moreover, the precise requirements of a prima facie case can vary depending on the context and were "never intended to be rigid, mechanized, or ritualistic." Given that the prima facie case operates as a flexible evidentiary standard, it should not be transposed into a rigid pleading standard for discrimination cases.

Applying the relevant standard, petitioner's complaint easily satisfies the requirements of Rule 8(a) because it gives respondent fair notice of the basis for petitioner's claims. Petitioner alleged that he had been terminated on account of his national origin in violation of Title VII and on account of his age in violation of the ADEA. His complaint detailed the events leading to his termination, provided relevant dates, and included the ages and nationalities of at least some of the relevant persons involved with his termination. These allegations give respondent fair notice of what petitioner's claims are and the grounds upon which they rest. In addition, they state claims upon which relief could be granted under Title VII and the ADEA.

For the foregoing reasons, we hold that an employment discrimination plaintiff need not plead a prima facie case of discrimination and that petitioner's complaint is sufficient to survive respondent's motion to dismiss. Accordingly, the judgment of the Court of Appeals is reversed, and the case is remanded for further proceedings consistent with this opinion.

Judgment for Swierkiewicz.

Case Commentary

The U.S. Supreme Court ruled that in a Title VII complaint a plaintiff need only set forth a claim upon which relief can be granted. ∎

CASE QUESTIONS

1. Do you believe this case was decided correctly?
2. Does it not make sense for a plaintiff to allege facts sufficient to meet his or her burden of proof?
3. Why do you think the court adopted this reasoning?

DISPARATE IMPACT

Employers may not institute an employment practice that causes a disparate impact on a particular class of people unless they can show that the practice is job related and necessary. If there is intent to discriminate, then proof of business necessity will not save the employer from being in violation of Title VII.

The following case, which established the standard for disparate impact, is a landmark case. When an employer establishes a test or other barrier with the intention of using it to discriminate against a protected class, this act creates a disparate impact against the class. The burden, having been met, shifts to the employer to justify its actions as being job related or a business necessity.

Griggs v. Duke Power Co.

401 U.S. 424 (1971)

Chief Justice Burger delivered the opinion of the Court.

We granted the writ in this case to resolve the question whether an employer is prohibited by the Civil Rights Act of 1964, Title VII, from requiring a high school education or passing of a standardized general intelligence test as a condition of employment in or transfer to jobs when (a) neither standard is shown to be significantly related to successful job performance, (b) both requirements operate to disqualify Negroes at a substantially higher rate than white applicants, and (c) the jobs in question formerly had been filled only by white employees as part of a longstanding practice of giving preference to whites.

The District Court found that prior to July 2, 1965, the effective date of the Civil Rights Act of 1964, the Company openly discriminated on the basis of race in the hiring and assigning of employees at its Dan River plant. The plant was organized into five operating departments: (1) Labor, (2) Coal Handling, (3) Operations, (4) Maintenance, and (5) Laboratory and Test. Negroes were employed only in the Labor Department where the highest paying jobs paid less than the lowest paying jobs in the other four "operating" departments in which only whites were employed. Promotions were normally made within each department on the basis of job seniority. Transfers into a department usually began in the lowest position.

In 1955 the Company instituted a policy of requiring a high school education for initial assignment to any department except Labor, and for transfer from the Coal Handling to any "inside" department (Operations, Maintenance, or Laboratory). When the Company abandoned its policy of restricting Negroes to the Labor Department in 1965, completion of high school also was made a prerequisite to transfer from Labor to any other department. From the time the high school requirement was instituted to the time of trial, however, white employees hired before the time of the high school education requirement continued to perform satisfactorily and achieve promotions in the "operating" departments. Findings on this score are not challenged.

The Company added a further requirement for new employees on July 2, 1965, the date on which Title VII became effective. To qualify for placement in any but the Labor Department it became necessary to register satisfactory scores on two professionally prepared aptitude tests, as well as to have a high school education. Completion of high school alone continued to render employees eligible for transfer to the four desirable departments from which Negroes had been excluded if the incumbent had been employed prior to the time of the new requirement. In September 1965 the Company began to permit incumbent employees who lacked a high school educa-

tion to qualify for transfer from Labor or Coal Handling to an "inside" job by passing two tests—the Wonderlic Personnel Test, which purports to measure general intelligence, and the Bennett Mechanical Comprehension Test. Neither was directed or intended to measure the ability to learn to perform a particular job or category of jobs. The requisite scores used for both initial hiring and transfer approximated the national median for high school graduates.

After careful analysis a majority of that court concluded that a subjective test of the employer's intent should govern, particularly in a close case, and that in this case there was no showing of a discriminatory purpose in the adoption of the diploma and test requirements. On this basis, the Court of Appeals concluded there was no violation of the Act.

Congress did not intend by Title VII, however, to guarantee a job to every person regardless of qualifications. In short, the Act does not command that any person be hired simply because he was formerly the subject of discrimination, or because he is a member of a minority group. Discriminatory preference for any group, minority or majority, is precisely and only what Congress has prescribed. What is required by Congress is the removal of artificial, arbitrary, and unnecessary barriers to employment when the barriers operate invidiously to discriminate on the basis of racial or other impermissible classification.

The Act proscribes not only overt discrimination but also practices that are fair in form, but discriminatory in operation. The touchstone is business necessity. If an employment practice which operates to exclude Negroes cannot be shown to be related to job performance, the practice is prohibited. On the record before us, neither the high school completion requirement nor the general intelligence test is shown to bear a demonstrable relationship to successful performance of the jobs for which it was used. Both were adopted, as the Court of Appeals noted, without meaningful study of their relationship to job-performance ability. Rather, a vice president of the Company testified, the requirements were instituted on the Company's judgment that they generally would improve the overall quality of the work force.

The evidence, however, shows that employees who have not completed high school or taken the tests have continued to perform satisfactorily and make progress in departments for which the high school and test criteria are now used. The promotion record of present employees who would not be able to meet the new criteria thus suggests the possibility that the requirements may not be needed even for the elicited purpose of preserving the avowed policy of advancement within the Company. In the context of this case, it is unnecessary to reach the question whether testing requirements that take into account capability for the next succeeding position or related future promotion might be utilized upon a showing that such long-range requirements fulfill a genuine business need. In the present case the Company has made no such showing.

The Court of Appeals held that the Company had adopted the diploma and test requirements without any "intention to discriminate against Negro employees." We do not suggest that either the District or the Court of Appeals erred in examining the employer's intent; but good intent or absence of discriminatory intent does not redeem employment procedures or testing mechanisms that operate as "built-in headwinds" for minority groups and are unrelated to measuring job capability.

The facts of this case demonstrates the inadequacy of broad and general testing devices as well as the infirmity of using diplomas or degrees as fixed measures of capability. History is filled with examples of men and women who rendered highly effective performance without the conventional badges of accomplishment in terms of certificates, diplomas, or degrees. Diplomas and tests are useful servants, but Congress has mandated the common-sense proposition that they are not to become masters of reality.

The Company contends that its general intelligence tests are specifically permitted by 703 (h) of the Act. That section authorizes the use of "any professionally developed ability test" that is not "designed, intended or used to discriminate because of race. . . ."

The Equal Employment Opportunity Commission, having enforcement responsibility, has issued guidelines interpreting 703(h) to permit only the use of job related tests.

Nothing in the Act precludes the use of testing or measuring procedures; obviously they are useful. What Congress has forbidden is giving these devices and mechanisms controlling force unless they are demonstrably a reasonable measure of job performance. Congress has not commanded that the less qualified be preferred over the better qualified simply because of minority origins. Far from disparaging job qualifications as such, Congress has made such qualifications the controlling factor, so that race, religion, nationality, and sex become irrelevant. What Congress has commanded is that any tests used must measure the person for the job and not the person in the abstract.

The judgment of the Court of Appeals is, as to that portion of the judgment appealed from, reversed.

Judgment for Griggs.

Case Commentary

Duke Power had a policy that prohibited black employees from rising above the Labor Department. After the *Brown v. Board of Education* decision, Duke Power amended its policy to require a high school diploma, knowing that most black people did not graduate from high school. Subsequent to the Civil Rights Act, Duke amended its policy again to require satisfactory scores on two aptitude tests. Duke Power was cognizant of the fact that blacks probably would not score well on these particular tests. The decision in this case was a precursor to the enactment of the Equal Employment Opportunity Act, which provided for court-ordered affirmative action programs to remedy disparate impact situations created by employers such as Duke Power. The Supreme Court also set forth the requirements for the validation of an employment test: business necessity and job relatedness. ■

CASE QUESTIONS

1. Are the business necessity and job-relatedness requirements appropriate?
2. Was Duke Power ethical in its treatment of blacks?

3. Were the standards set by Duke Power a façade to keep black workers in the Labor Department?

Employment Perspective

Skyscraper Construction Company was awarded a contract by the Detroit Downtown Redevelopment Agency with the provision that all of the workers used in the project must live within the city of Detroit. In response to the company's advertisement, two-thirds of the applicants were minorities. Skyscraper, afraid that it would have to hire mostly minorities, instituted a standardized achievement test as a prerequisite to the job, knowing that on average, whites score higher than do minorities. As a result of selecting workers by the test scores, 75 percent of those hired were white. Is this disparate impact? Yes! The use of the standardized test could not be proven to constitute a business necessity, because it was not related to performance on the job. Although the test may be indiscriminate, the purpose for which it was used was to discriminate intentionally against minorities, a protected class.

The "80 Percent Rule"

The EEOC issued the *80 percent rule* as a statistical measure to ascertain when an employment practice has had a disparate impact on a minority group. The selection rate of minorities must be within 80 percent of the selection rate of nonminorities; otherwise, the selection procedure utilized is discriminatory.

Employment Perspective

In 1993, 1,000 people applied for a position with Zip, Inc., and 230 people were selected.

Group	Applied	Selected	Selection Rate
Minorities	200	30	15%
Nonminorities	800	200	25%

Minorities selection rate 15% divided by nonminorities selection rate 25% = 60%.

Is this selection procedure discriminatory? Yes! This shows only a 60 percent selection rate, which falls short of the 80 percent rule. Therefore, Zip's selection procedure has an adverse impact on minorities. Zip, Inc., must enact a plan to remedy this.

EQUAL EMPLOYMENT OPPORTUNITY COMMISSION

The Equal Employment Opportunity Commission (EEOC) was established in 1972 when the Equal Employment Opportunity Act amended Title VII of the Civil Rights Act of 1964. It is composed of five members, no more than three of which may be Republican or Democrat. The President of the United States shall appoint these members with the advice and consent of the U.S. Senate for a period of 5 years. Although the Civil Rights Act of 1964 is the cornerstone of the movement against employment discrimination, it is important to understand that legislative policy on employment discrimination has developed over time through the enactment of several different laws.

The commission's responsibility is to enforce the provisions of Title VII against unlawful employment practices. A person claiming a violation of Title VII has 180 days to file the complaint with the EEOC. There is no cost to file.

Violations of Title VII are brought before the Equal Employment Opportunity Commission. Upon receipt of the complaint, the EEOC determines whether there is a possibility that mediation may help resolve the conflict between the parties. In the majority of cases, parties are notified in writing of the offer to mediate. If both parties voluntarily accept within 10 days, mediation will occur within 60 days. Otherwise, the EEOC notifies the employer and conducts an investigation that entails questioning employees and/or obtaining physical evidence. A determination must be made by the EEOC. If there is a reasonable cause to believe that the charges are true, the EEOC will attempt to persuade the offender to change its practices. None of these proceedings are made public. The offender has 30 days to comply. If the violation is charged against a government or one of its agencies, the EEOC shall refer the matter to the Attorney General of the United States, who may then proceed in federal district court. There are 98 federal district courts located throughout the United States. These are the general trial courts in the federal court system. Appeals from them go to one of the 11 Circuit Courts of Appeals and then to the U.S. Supreme Court.

If a state or local law exists prohibiting the unlawful employment practice, the complainant must first proceed within the state or locality before filing with the EEOC. After 60 days of instituting the suit with the state, the time limit for filing with the EEOC shall be extended to the earlier of 300 days or 30 days after the state or local action has been resolved.

If, at the time of filing, the EEOC or Attorney General's office believes that irreparable harm will result if the employer's unlawful employment practices are not immediately halted, they can apply for a temporary restraining order or a preliminary injunction against the employer.

After the initial investigation, the EEOC will determine whether there is a reasonable basis to believe that the allegation is true. If the EEOC believes that there is no basis, the complaining party is informed and is given a right-to-sue letter. He or she is free to proceed with a civil suit in a federal district court within 90 days of notification.

The district court may enter a permanent injunction against the employer to refrain from engaging in the unlawful employment practice cited in the complaint. Furthermore, the court may authorize the employer to hire the individual or individuals issuing the charge, reinstate them if they have been discharged, reimburse them with back pay, promote them, or give them any other type of equitable relief that the court deems necessary. The court may also allow the prevailing party reasonable fees for attorney representation, as well as for expert testimony. The charge for discrimination under Title VII is limited to race, color, religion, national origin, or sex. Discrimination for age and disability are covered under separate acts discussed later.

CIVIL RIGHTS ACT OF 1991

The Civil Rights Act of 1991 amended in part the Civil Rights Act of 1964. Jury trials are permitted. Juries are primarily comprised of workers who may be more sympathetic to the plight of employees with whom they can identify. Compensatory and punitive damages are now recoverable. Individuals who are covered by the Americans with Disabilities Act of 1990 and the Rehabilitation Act of 1973 are now covered by the Civil Rights Act of 1964 for the purpose of recovering compensatory and punitive damages. Punitive damages are recoverable when the employer has acted with malice or in reckless disregard of an individual's civil rights.

Compensatory and Punitive Damages

Compensatory damages include emotional pain and suffering, mental anguish, loss of enjoyment of life, inconvenience, as well as other nonpecuniary losses. Punitive damages are awarded to punish the party who has committed the wrong. Compensatory and punitive damages are awarded where there has been intentional discrimination on the part of the employer. These damages are granted in addition to back pay, which is still recoverable under the Civil Rights Act of 1964. The total of compensatory and punitive damages may not exceed $50,000 for employers with 15 to 100 employees; $100,000 for employers with 101 to 200 employees; $200,000 for employers with 201 to 500 employees; and $300,000 for employers with more than 500 employees. The employee claiming the violation may request a jury trial. The term *complaining party* now encompasses a disabled person as well as a member of a minority race, religion, sex, and national origin. Attorney fees may also be granted in the courts discretion.

Business Necessity

The Civil Rights Act of 1991 adopted the concepts of "business necessity" and "job related" as enunciated by the Supreme Court in *Griggs vs. Duke Power Co.* (1971). The test for business necessity is not met where the employment practice that excludes a particular class is not job related. In such a case, the practice is prohibited.

It shall be an unlawful practice to adjust scores, establish different cutoff scores, or alter scores on employment-related tests for a particular race, religion, gender, or national origin.

Glass Ceiling

Congress has found that barriers still exist to the advancement of women and minorities in the workplace. They remain underrepresented in management decision-making positions. Under the Civil Rights Act of 1991, Congress established the Glass Ceiling Commission to rectify this problem. The commission must consider how prepared women and minorities are for advancement, what opportunities are available, and what policies businesses follow in making such promotions. The commission also makes comparisons with businesses that have actively promoted women and minorities to determine their reasons for success.

The issue in the case that follows is in what circumstances is the granting of punitive damages under Title VII of the Civil Rights Act appropriate.

Kolstad v. American Dental Association
527 U.S. 526 (1999)

Justice O'Connor delivered the opinion of the Court.

Under the terms of the Civil Rights Act of 1991 (1991 Act), punitive damages are available in claims under Title VII of the Civil Rights Act of 1964 (Title VII), and the Americans with Disabilities Act of 1990 (ADA). Damages are limited, however, to cases in which the employer has engaged in intentional discrimination and has done so "with malice or with reckless indifference to the federally protected rights of an aggrieved individual." Here we consider the circumstances under which punitive damages may be awarded in an action under Title VII.

I

A

In September 1992, Jack O'Donnell announced that he would be retiring as the Director of Legislation and Legislative Policy and Director of the Council on Government Affairs and Federal Dental Services for respondent, American Dental Association (respondent or Association).

Petitioner, Carole Kolstad, was employed with O'Donnell in respondent's Washington, D.C., office, where she was serving as respondent's Director of Federal Agency Relations. When she learned of O'Donnell's retirement, she expressed an interest in filling his position. Also interested in replacing O'Donnell was Tom Spangler, another employee in respondent's Washington office. At this time, Spangler was serving as the Association's Legislative Counsel, a position that involved him in respondent's legislative lobbying efforts. Both petitioner and Spangler had worked directly with O'Donnell, and both had received "distinguished" performance ratings by the acting head of the Washington office, Leonard Wheat.

Both petitioner and Spangler formally applied for O'Donnell's position, and Wheat requested that Dr. William Allen, then serving as respondent's Executive Director in the Association's Chicago office, make the ultimate promotion decision. After interviewing both petitioner and Spangler, Wheat recommended that Allen select Spangler for O'Donnell's post. Allen notified petitioner in December 1992 that he had, in fact, selected Spangler to serve as O'Donnell's replacement. Petitioner's challenge to this employment decision forms the basis of the instant action.

B

After first exhausting her avenues for relief before the Equal Employment Opportunity Commission, petitioner filed suit against the Association in Federal District Court, alleging that respondent's decision to promote Spangler was an act of employment discrimination proscribed under Title VII. In petitioner's view, the entire selection process was a sham. Counsel for petitioner urged the jury to conclude that Allen's stated reasons for selecting Spangler were pretext for gender discrimination, and that Spangler had been chosen for the position before the formal selection process began. Among the evidence offered in support of this view, there was testimony to the effect that Allen modified the description of O'Donnell's post to track aspects of the job description used to hire Spangler. In petitioner's view, this "preselection" procedure suggested an intent by the Association to discriminate on the basis of sex. Petitioner also introduced testimony at trial that Wheat told sexually offensive jokes and that he had referred to certain prominent professional women in derogatory terms. Moreover, Wheat allegedly refused to meet with petitioner for several weeks regarding her interest in O'Donnell's position. Petitioner testified, in fact, that she had historically experienced difficulty gaining access to meet with Wheat. Allen, for his part, testified that he conducted informal meetings regarding O'Donnell's position with both petitioner and Spangler, although petitioner stated that Allen did not discuss the position with her.

The District Court denied petitioner's request for a jury instruction on punitive damages. The jury concluded that respondent had discriminated against petitioner on the basis of sex and awarded her backpay totaling $52,718. Although the District Court subsequently denied respondent's motion for judgment as a matter of law on the issue of liability, the court made clear that it had not been persuaded that respondent had selected Spangler over petitioner on the basis of sex, and the court denied petitioner's requests for reinstatement and for attorney's fees. Petitioner appealed from the District Court's decisions denying her requested jury instruction on punitive damages and her request for reinstatement and attorney's fees. Respondent cross-appealed from the denial of its motion for judgment as a matter of law. In a split decision, a panel of the Court of Appeals for the District of Columbia Circuit reversed the District Court's decision denying petitioner's request for an instruction on punitive damages. In so doing, the court rejected respondent's claim that punitive damages are available under Title VII only in " 'extraordinarily egregious cases.' " The panel reasoned that, "because 'the state of mind necessary to trigger liability for the wrong is at least as culpable as that required to make punitive damages applicable,' " the fact that the jury could reasonably have found intentional discrimination meant that the jury should have been permitted to consider punitive damages. The court noted, however, that not all cases involving intentional discrimination would support a punitive damages award. Such an award might be improper, the panel reasoned, in instances where the employer justifiably believes that intentional discrimination is permitted or where an employee engages in discrimination outside the scope of that employee's authority. Here, the court concluded, respondent "neither attempted to justify the use of sex in its promotion decision nor disavowed the actions of its agents."

We granted certiorari, to resolve a conflict among the Federal Courts of Appeals concerning the circumstances under which a jury may consider a request for punitive damages.

II

A

Prior to 1991, only equitable relief, primarily backpay, was available to prevailing Title VII plaintiffs; the statute provided no authority for an award of punitive or compensatory damages. With the passage of the 1991 Act, Congress provided for additional remedies, including punitive damages, for certain classes of Title VII and ADA violations.

The 1991 Act limits compensatory and punitive damages awards, however, to cases of "intentional discrimination"—that is, cases that do not rely on the "disparate impact" theory of discrimination. Section 1981a(b)(1) further qualifies the availability of punitive awards:

"A complaining party may recover punitive damages under this section against a respondent (other than a government, government agency or political subdivision) if the complaining party demonstrates that the respondent engaged in a discriminatory practice or discriminatory practices with malice or with reckless indifference to the federally protected rights of an aggrieved individual."

The very structure of § 1981a suggests a congressional intent to authorize punitive awards in only a subset of cases involving intentional discrimination. There will be circumstances where intentional discrimination does not give rise to punitive damages liability under this standard. In some instances, the employer may simply be unaware of the relevant federal prohibition. There will be cases, moreover, in which the employer discriminates with the distinct belief that its discrimination is lawful. The underlying theory of discrimination may be novel or otherwise poorly recognized, or an employer may reasonably believe that its discrimination satisfies a bona fide occupational qualification defense or other statutory exception to liability.

B

The inquiry does not end with a showing of the requisite "malice or . . . reckless indifference" on the part of certain individuals, however. The plaintiff must impute liability for punitive damages to respondent.

We have concluded that an employer's conduct need not be independently "egregious" to satisfy § 1981a's requirements for a punitive damages award, although evidence of egregious misconduct may be used to meet the plaintiff's burden of proof. We leave for remand the question whether petitioner can identify facts sufficient to support an inference that the requisite mental state can be imputed to respondent. The parties have not yet had an opportunity to marshal the record evidence in support of their views on the application of agency principles in the instant case, and the en banc majority had no reason to resolve the issue. Although trial testimony established that Allen made the ultimate decision to promote Spangler while serving as petitioner's interim executive director, respondent's highest position, it remains to be seen whether petitioner can make a sufficient showing that Allen acted with malice or reckless indifference to petitioner's Title VII rights. Even if it could be established that Wheat effectively selected O'Donnell's replacement, moreover, several questions would remain, e.g., whether Wheat was serving in a "managerial capacity" and whether he behaved with malice or reckless indifference to petitioner's rights. It may also be necessary to determine whether the Association had been making good faith efforts to enforce an antidiscrimination policy. We leave these issues for resolution on remand.

CASE QUESTIONS

1. Do you agree with the decision in this case?
2. Is egregious conduct the appropriate standard for awarding punitive damages?

For the foregoing reasons, the decision of the Court of Appeals is vacated, and the case is remanded for proceedings consistent with this opinion.

Judgment for the American Dental Association.

Case Commentary

The U.S. Supreme Court decided that the granting of punitive damages is contingent upon proving the employer's conduct was so egregious as to warrant punishment to dissuade the employer from acting in the same vein in the future. ■

3. Did Carole Kolstad meet this criterion?

EXEMPTIONS

There are a number of classifications that are exempt from the Civil Rights Act. In these situations, discrimination would be permissible.

Bona Fide Occupational Qualification

Employers may discriminate because of religion, gender, and national origin if they can establish that there is a bona fide occupational qualification. This condition does not generally apply to race and color, except for the casting of certain actors in the movies and theatre.

Employment Perspective

Mary Jacobs applied for a position as a rest-room attendant at the Nautilus Health and Fitness Club. A total of seven women, but no men, applied for the position. After another woman was selected for the position of attendant to the female locker-room, Mary asserted that she should be considered for attendant to the male locker-room. Nautilus refused on the ground that Mary is a woman. Is this discrimination? No! Gender is bona fide occupational qualification in the selection of a locker-room attendant.

Communists

Title VII does not apply to individuals who are members of the Communist party of the United States.

Employment Perspective

Igor Musnovec, a Communist party member, applied for a job as a checkout clerk at a local Foodway supermarket. His application was not considered because he is a Communist. Is this discrimination? No! It is lawful to discriminate against a Communist.

Drug Addicts

It is lawful for an employer to refuse to hire individuals who are using illegal drugs as long as this practice was not adopted intentionally to discriminate against a particular class.

Employment Perspective

Julio Gonzalez, who is currently participating in drug rehabilitation, has applied for a job as a clerk at the Save Mart Department Store. Save Mart refuses to hire Julio because of his drug addiction. Does Julio have any recourse? No! Julio's only recourse would be if he could prove that Save Mart had instituted the stipulation with the intention of enforcing it only against Hispanics.

Merit Pay

Employers may compensate individuals differently on the basis of merit, seniority, quality or quantity of work performed, or location of employment. It is understood that employers cannot discriminate under the guise of the protected categories of the Civil Rights Act. If it turns out that discrimination is the employer's intention, then the employer will be in violation of Title VII. Professionally developed ability tests may be designed and administered to determine hiring and promoting as long as the test is job related, not intended to discriminate.

EMPLOYEE LESSONS

1. Familiarize yourself with the protections afforded to you under the Civil Rights Act.
2. Be apprised of the types of damages recoverable and the monetary caps.
3. Be aware of the exemptions to the Civil Rights Act.
4. Know what rights are available to you under state law.
5. Understand the functions of the Equal Employment Opportunity Commission.
6. Discern whether the employer has retaliated against you.
7. Know what the deadlines are for filing discrimination claims.

SUMMARY

In hindsight, the Civil Rights Act of 1964, along with subsequent amendments, has had the most profound impact on employment since the proliferation of unions. The Civil Rights Act opened the door to employment opportunities and promotions for minorities and women. These two groups comprise more than half the workforce. Neglecting them for so long was an egregious mistake. Forgetting them in the future would be economically disastrous.

Securing a well-paying job is the main step for an individual to increase his or her standard of living and to secure better housing. Without employment opportunities, women and minorities are relegated to welfare, unemployment, or ministerial positions with low pay. In turn, minorities and women providing sole support for a family have the lowest economic status. Making ends meet is a day-to-day goal. The Civil Rights Act, although not a panacea, provided an area of opportunity for those on the lowest levels of society. Women and minorities are now significantly represented in professional and graduate school programs. They are also present in middle-level management positions. Attaining upper-level positions is much harder to realize because it is easier for decision makers to integrate those departments that are beneath them than it is to integrate their own.

Also, though it takes time for qualified candidates to work their way up through the ranks, that moment is at hand because enough time has passed for these candidates to emerge. It is now that access to the executive level and the boardroom should begin to increase. It will likely remain a slow process, though, for these positions involve sizable amounts of pay and, more importantly, power.

Societies should not be judged on the basis of their most wealthy citizens. If they were, Mexico and certain Arabian countries would score very high. The average standard of living is not the most satisfactory basis either, because great wealth can give the average an upward bias. Instead, societies should be judged on how well their poor are doing. The greater the number of people in this classification, the more likely the society has failed to serve the needs of all of its people. When a society can boast that even the least of its members has a job that provides the means for a satisfactory subsistence, then a society has achieved its greatest goal.

The Civil Rights Act has provided an impetus for achieving this goal. Raising the bottom up is its underlying purpose. However, improvements in education, life at home, and the community have not kept pace with the advancement made in employment opportunities. Employment opportunities are the goal for a young person who has honed his or her intellect and been brought up in a stable community, with a family oriented toward principles and values. When education and environment leave a lot to be desired, employment opportunities are difficult to take advantage of. In order for the Civil Rights Act to fulfill its main purpose of lifting the lower echelon of society to a more suitable level, similar strides must take place in education and the community and family environment.

REVIEW QUESTIONS

1. Explain the significance of the Civil Rights Act of 1964.
2. Who is covered under the Civil Rights Act?
3. What changes were made by the 1991 Civil Rights Act?
4. What is a bona fide occupational qualification?
5. Are Communists covered by the Civil Rights Act?
6. Is the use of merit pay permissable?
7. What is the difference between disparate treatment and disparate impact?
8. Give an example of the 80 percent rule.
9. Does the employee have recourse if the employer retaliates?
10. May drug addicts be discriminated against?
11. What is the function of the EEOC?
12. What is the purpose of the Glass Ceiling Commission?
13. When are punitive damages awarded?
14. What is the test for business necessity?
15. Does the EEOC have the right to access employment records regarding the makeup of a company's employees?
16. Is the 80 percent rule ethical?

CASE PROBLEMS

1. The question is whether an employer "has" an employee on any working day on which the employer maintains an employment relationship with the employee, or only on working days on which the employee is actually receiving compensation from the employer.

Darlene Walters filed a charge with the Equal Employment Opportunity Commission (EEOC), claiming that Metropolitan had discriminated against her on account of her sex in failing to promote her to the position of credit manager. Soon after that, Metropolitan fired her.

During most of 1990, Metropolitan had between 15 and 17 employees on its payroll on each working day; but in only 9 weeks of the year was it actually compensating 15 or more employees on each working day (including paid leave as compensation). The difference resulted from the fact that Metropolitan had two part-time hourly employees who ordinarily skipped 1 working day each week.

The issue concerns whether employees who work part-time or who are hired midweek count for the purposes of fulfilling the 15-employee threshold of the Civil Rights Act. *Walters v. Metropolitan Educational Enterprises*, Inc. 519 U.S. 202 (1997)

2. At various times, the EEOC notified each appellant that his or her charge of age discrimination was dismissed. Receipt of such notice triggers the statute of limitations for bringing a civil action in court, and the plaintiff must then file suit within 90 days. This 90-day limitations period is tolled, however, while the plaintiff is a putative member of a class action. Twenty-eight of the 31 appellants opted into *Carmichael v. Martin Marietta Corp.*, an age discrimination class action. The Carmichael court, therefore, certified a plaintiff class that did not include as members the appellants in the instant case. The court then dismissed the claims of appellants.

On October 11, 1994, more than 90 days after the Carmichael court's partial denial of class certification, the 31 appellants and 14 additional plaintiffs filed the complaint that commenced the instant action in the district court.

The question in this case is whether the plaintiffs' lawsuit was filed within the time constraints provided by the Civil Rights Act. *Armstrong, et al. V. Martin Marietta Corp.*, 138 F.3d 1374 (11th Cir. 1998)

3. Michael Gibson filed a complaint with the Department of Veterans Affairs, charging that the department had discriminated against him by denying him a promotion on the basis of his gender. The EEOC, however, subsequently found in Gibson's favor and awarded the promotion plus back pay. The department then voluntarily complied with the EEOC's order, but it continued to oppose Gibson's claim for compensatory damages. The issue in this case is whether the EEOC has the power to award compensatory damages. *West, Secretary of Veterans Affairs v. Gibson*, 527 U.S. 212 (1999)

HUMAN RESOURCE DILEMMAS

1. Mustapha Khalid, who is Muslim, applies to the Alphabet Cereal Corporation for work. He is denied employment. Mustapha is qualified for the position. He possesses excellent references, having worked for Galaxy Cereals for a number of years. He files a lawsuit alleging religious and national origin discrimination in violation of Title VII of the Civil Rights Act. He has a prima facie case. Alphabet alleges that Mustapha's membership in a right-wing fundamentalist group several years ago is a legitimate reason for not hiring him. Is that justifiable?

2. Marshall Whitman, who is African-American, applies for a position with Bull and Bear Brokerage House. He is denied employment. Marshall is able to establish a prima facie case. Bull and Bear raise the fact that because Marshall was arrested for drunk driving 7 years ago, this is a legitimate reason for not hiring him. Marshall retorts that this is a mere pretext. How would you advise him?

3. Emmanuel Abrams is a craftsman specializing in woodcarvings. He employs 16 people. Emmanuel sells his wood sculptures from a gift shop in Flatbush, which is located in the center of state Z. Locally grown products and homemade jams are also sold at the shop. Emmanuel does not advertise, and his customers are locals. Hector Martinez applies for a job, but Emmanuel refuses to hire Mexicans. Hector brings a lawsuit alleging violation of Title VII. Emmanuel believes his actions are justified. How would you advise him?

WEB SITE ASSIGNMENT

Compare and contrast Title VII of the Civil Rights Act with employment discrimination laws in foreign countries.

www.eeoc.gov
www.findlaw.com
www.westbuslaw.com
www.usccr.gov/index.html
www.watson.org/~lisa/blackhistory/early-civilrights/

Chapter 8

Affirmative Action

Employment Scenario

Tom and Mark consult with Susan about the handling of Debbie Brown's disparate impact claim (discussed in Chapter 7). Tom and Mark resent the allegation that their actions may be viewed as prejudicial. Susan retorts that they must put aside their personal feelings and view the claim objectively. She suggests that L&S voluntarily adopt an affirmative action program to recruit and hire minorities. Tom and Mark are perturbed. What are the advantages and disadvantages of following Susan's advice?

Chapter Checklist

➤ *Understand the origin of the concept of affirmative action.*

➤ *Appreciate the role of affirmative action in accomplishing the goals of the Civil Rights Act of 1964.*

➤ *Distinguish between voluntary and court-ordered affirmative action programs.*

➤ *Discern the difference between an affirmative action plan and a quota.*

➤ *Reconcile the decisions of the U.S. Supreme Court in United Steelworkers of America v. Weber and University of California Regents v. Bakke.*

➤ *Be able to explain the significance of reverse discrimination.*

➤ *Understand the significance of the Equal Employment Opportunity Act.*

➤ *Consider whether affirmative action is still needed.*

➤ *Comprehend the impact of California's Proposition 209.*

➤ *Understand the ramifications of the settlement reached in Taxman v. School Board of Piscataway.*

INTRODUCTION

Affirmative action attempts to achieve equal employment opportunity by actively selecting minorities and women where they have been underrepresented in the workforce. Although affirmative action programs are considered temporary, many remain in force for a long time until equilibrium is achieved. To determine whether an affirmative action program is needed, a number of factors must be considered: the minority population of the area and their percentage of the total population in the area; the number of minorities employed and unemployed, together with their respective percentages; the skills of the minority; the labor pool; the amount of training the employer can reasonably undertake; and the availability of other minorities or women in the organization who can be promoted or transferred. The same criteria are considered in determining the need for an affirmative action program for women. After procedures are in place, the goals must be achieved following reasonable timetables. The rate of success must be measured.

HUMAN RESOURCE ADVICE

- Understand the history of affirmative action.
- Appreciate the significance of the Equal Employment Opportunity Act.
- Conduct a voluntary self-audit of your business to determine if it has adequate representation of women and minorities.
- If it does not, determine how and why your company created this disparate impact.
- Recognize that affirmative action is in a state of transition.
- Familiarize yourself with the *Gratz* and *Grutter* cases.
- Learn the status of affirmative action in the state in which your business is located.
- Formulate an affirmative action plan only if it is remedial in purpose and does not have an adverse effect on the current workforce.
- Appreciate the difference between a quota and an affirmative action plan.
- Guard against instituting a plan that will result in reverse discrimination.

HISTORY OF AFFIRMATIVE ACTION

Equal employment opportunity had its roots in a series of executive orders and acts. In 1940, President Roosevelt issued Executive Order 8587, which prohibited the denial of public employment based on race. Several orders and acts followed that were designed to prohibit other forms of discrimination in public employment, such as on the basis of religion and color. The emphasis was on what the administrative agencies could *not* do. There was no mandate as to what they *should* do.

The beginning of a transformation from passive to active programs began in 1955. In Executive Order 10050, President Eisenhower stipulated, " . . . it is the policy of the United States Government that equal opportunity be afforded all qualified persons, consistent with law, for employment in the Federal Government." Equal employment opportunity was formally recognized and confirmed by President Kennedy in 1961; Executive Order 10925 called for " . . . positive measures for the elimination of any discrimination, direct or indirect, which now exist."

The concept of affirmative action first arose out of an executive order promulgated by President Lyndon Johnson in 1964. It provided that contractors who were supplying goods or services to the federal government be required to take an affirmative action; that employees should be hired without regard to race, color, religion, sex, or national origin; and that once selected, promotion, compensation, training, and termination should be made without discrimination. Subcontractors hired by federal contractors were held to the same standards.

Those federal contractors whose employees were underrepresented with regard to women and minorities were forced to correct that injustice by developing an affirmative action plan designed to hire and/or promote more women and minorities.

Employment Perspective

Blackwell Enterprises, a federal contractor that employs 100 workers, 10 of whom are minorities, is located in the city of Atlanta. The minority population of the city of Atlanta is approximately 50 percent. Will Blackwell jeopardize its federal contracts because of the underrepresentation of minorities in its workforce? Yes, unless it establishes an affirmative action plan designed to increase the number of minorities hired! How should this plan be designed? Blackwell may create a plan that for every three new positions that become open, two must be filled by qualified minorities. Thus, when the first position becomes available, if there is a qualified minority applicant, he or she will receive the job. With the second position, if there are no qualified minority applicants, a white person may be hired, but then preference will be given to the minority applicant for the third position.

In 1965, President Johnson, through Executive Order 11246, placed the responsibility for equal employment opportunity with the Civil Service Commission. Johnson followed that in 1967 with Executive Order 11375, which added sex discrimination. However, it was not until 1969 that affirmative action was used to address the problem of those seeking employment as well as those stuck in low-level positions.

President Nixon's Executive Order 11478 issued in 1969 provided that equal employment opportunity " . . . applies to and must be made an integral part of every aspect of personnel policy and practice in the employment, development, advancement and treatment of civilian employees of the Federal Government." It also set forth the procedure for affirmative action, as well as the requirement for training programs to enable low-level employees to gain the experience necessary to be eligible for upper-level positions.

The executive order resulted in the Equal Employment Opportunity Act of 1972.

What if an employer is having difficulty finding qualified minority candidates? The employer must make every effort to locate potential candidates through advertisements in newspapers that are likely to be read by minorities. The employer must also contact employment agencies that service minority job-seekers. The burden is on the employer to put the word out in the minority community.

Employment Perspective

The CPA firm of Glick, Worthington, and Sutherland has 50 accountants and 150 staff members. The latter includes administrative assistants, typists, and file clerks. During tax season, the firm's accountants and staff put in

80-plus–hour workweeks. For this reason, the firm refuses to hire women during their childbearing years. Young women who are refused employment claim this provision creates a disparate impact. Is this correct? Yes! The court will impose an order on the CPA firm to establish an affirmative action plan to hire females, including those who are in their childbearing years. If females make up 40 percent of accountants, then a plan to hire two out of three will suffice. Does the firm have to discharge men and replace them with women? No! The entire injustice does not have to be remedied immediately, as long as the process begins in a timely manner. As long as an affirmative action plan is implemented as the accounting firm expands or as existing accountants leave, justice is served.

TITLE VII VIOLATORS

Those employers who have intentionally discriminated or who have been guilty of creating an employee environment where a disparate impact exists against a class of people of race, color, religion, sex, or national origin may receive a court order to establish an affirmative action plan to remedy the discrimination.

Employment Perspective

Fredericks Meat Packing in Kansas City has 150 managers and 500 workers. Minority employees consist of 400 workers and no managers, although the population of Kansas City is approximately one-third minority. A claim is registered with the EEOC against Fredericks for discrimination. The EEOC files suit in federal district court and secures a judgment. How will the court remedy this injustice? The district court will issue a court order mandating Fredericks to establish an affirmative action plan to increase the number of minority managers to reflect more adequately the percentage of minorities in the Kansas City population. This plan may be achieved either through recruitment or promotion.

Voluntary Action

Rather than wait for potential lawsuits to force the correction of Title VII violations, many employers have created their own voluntary plans. In many instances, quotas were instituted to increase the number of women and minorities; the quotas require a set number of women and minorities to be hired. In effect, if qualified applicants cannot be found, unqualified ones must be hired. Quotas are not mandated by law and are thought to be necessary only where the racial imbalance is severe and has been intentionally disregarded. Although the word *quota* sparks controversy, it seems that every plan designed must have a goal of some fraction or percentage, allocating two out of three or 60 percent of new hirings or promotions. This would appear to be equivalent to a quota, but strictly speaking it is not.

Affirmative action plans require that only qualified women and minorities have to be hired, unlike quotas, where the hiring is done without regard to qualification. If there are no qualified women or minorities, white males may be hired in their place. But as mentioned earlier, the employer must make every effort to attempt to locate qualified women and minority applicants.

Affirmative action plans are designed to address manifest imbalances in the racial makeup of the workforce. Once the imbalance is eradicated, the affirmative action plan will be discontinued. Affirmative action plans are not designed to remain indefinitely to maintain equilibrium. If a discrepancy occurs in the future, then the affirmative action plan can be put into effect again.

Affirmative action plans do not place existing employees in jeopardy regarding termination or disciplinary action, which must be applied equally to all employees. However, it is lawful for an employer to hire qualified women and minorities over white men who are more qualified. The key is that the women and minorities must be qualified.

Employment Perspective

Express Airlines requires that applicants who wish to be considered for the job of pilot must have completed 750 hours of flight training. Currently, Express employs 100 pilots, none of whom are women or minorities. Express then implements an affirmative action program. The next five openings are filled by two women, two minorities, and one white male. There were 15 qualified applicants. The women and minorities chosen were among them. Although the women and minorities selected were not among the top five persons most qualified, they were chosen to fulfill the affirmative action plan. Is this lawful? Yes, because they were qualified! If they had not been qualified, Express would have been justified in hiring all white male employees, as long as its requirement met the strict standard of being a business necessity. In this situation, Express Airlines might be persuaded to initiate a training program for women and minorities to enable them to become pilots.

The following case addresses the question of whether a private employer and a union can in a collective bargaining agreement provide for an affirmative action plan. The plan reserved 50 percent of the openings for black applicants until the racial makeup of the workplace was indicative of the local community.

United Steelworkers of America v. Weber
443 U.S. 193 (1978)

Justice Brennan delivered the opinion of the Court.

Challenged here is the legality of an affirmative action plan—collectively bargained by an employer and a union—that reserves for black employees 50 percent of the openings in an in-plant craft-training until the percentage of black craftworkers in the plant is commensurate with the percentage of blacks in the local labor force. The question for decision is whether Congress in Title VII of the Civil Rights Act of 1964, left employers and unions in the private sector free to take such race-conscious steps to eliminate manifest racial imbalances in traditionally segregated job categories. We hold that Title VII does not prohibit such race-conscious affirmative action plans. In 1974, petitioner United Steelworkers of America (USWA) and petitioner Kaiser Aluminum & Chemical Corp. (Kaiser) entered into a master collective-bargaining agreement covering terms and conditions of employment at 15 Kaiser plants. The agreement contained an affirmative

action plan designed to eliminate conspicuous racial imbalances in Kaiser's then almost exclusively white craftwork forces. Black crafthiring goals were set for each Kaiser plant equal to the percentage of blacks in the respective local labor forces. To enable plants to meet these goals, on-the-job training programs were established to teach unskilled production workers—black and white—the skills necessary to become craftworkers. The plan reserved for black employees 50 percent of the openings in these newly created in-plant training programs.

This case arose from the operation of the plan at Kaiser's plant in Gramercy, La. Until 1974, Kaiser hired as craft-workers for that plant only persons who had had prior craft experience. Because blacks had long been excluded from craft unions, few were able to present such credentials. As a consequence, prior to 1974 only 1.83 percent (5 out of 273) of the skilled craftworkers at the Gramercy plant were black, even though the work force in the Gramercy area was approximately 39 percent black.

Pursuant to the national agreement Kaiser altered its craft-hiring practice in the Gramercy plant. Rather than hiring already trained outsiders, Kaiser established a training program to train its production workers to fill craft openings. Selection of craft trainees was made on the basis of seniority, with the proviso that at least 50 percent of the new trainers were to be black until the percentage of black skilled craftworkers in the Gramercy plant approximated the percentage of blacks in the local labor force.

During 1974, the first year of the operation of the Kaiser-USWA affirmative action plan, 13 craft trainees were selected from Gramercy's production work force. Of these, seven were black and six white. The most senior black selected into the program had less seniority than several white production workers whose bids for admission were rejected. Thereafter one of those white production workers, respondent Brian Weber (hereafter respondent), instituted this class action in the United States District Court for the Eastern District of Louisiana.

The complaint alleged that the filling of craft trainee positions at the Gramercy plant pursuant to the affirmative action program had resulted in junior black employees' receiving training in preference to senior white employees, thus discriminating against respondent and other similarly situated white employees in violation of Section 703 (a) and (d) of Title VII. The District Court entered a judgment in favor of the plaintiff class, and granted a permanent injunction prohibiting Kaiser and the USWA "from denying plaintiffs, Brian F. Weber and all other members of the class, access to on-the-job training programs on the basis of race." A divided panel of the Court of Appeals for the Fifth Circuit affirmed, holding that all employment preferences based upon race, including those preferences incidental to bona fide affirmative action plans, violated Title VII's prohibition against racial discrimination in employment. We granted certiorari. We reverse.

We emphasize at the outset the narrowness of our inquiry. Since the Kaiser-USWA plan does not involve state action, this case does not present an alleged violation of the Equal Protection Clause of the Fourteenth Amendment. Further, since the Kaiser-USWA plan was adopted voluntarily, we are not concerned with what Title VII requires or with what a court might order to remedy a past proved violation of the Act. The only question before us is the narrow statutory issue of whether Title VII forbids private employers and unions from voluntarily agreeing upon bona fide affirmative action plans that accord racial preferences in the manner and for the purpose provided in the Kaiser-USWA plan.

Congress' primary concern in enacting the prohibition against racial discrimination in Title VII of the Civil Rights Act of 1964 was with "the plight of the Negro in our economy." Before 1964, blacks were largely relegated to "unskilled and semi-skilled jobs." Because of automation the number of such jobs was rapidly decreasing. As a consequence, "the relative position of the Negro worker was steadily worsening. In 1947 the nonwhite unemployment rate was 64 percent higher than the white rate; in 1962 it was 124 percent higher." As Senator Humphrey explained to the Senate:

"What good does it do a Negro to be able to eat in a fine restaurant if he cannot afford to pay the bill? What good does it do him to be accepted in a hotel that is too expensive for his modest income? How can a Negro child be motivated to take full advantage of intergrated educational facilities if he has no hope of getting a job where he can use that education?

"Without a job, one cannot afford public convenience and accommodations. Income from employment may be necessary to further a man's education, or that of his children. If his children have no hope of getting a good job, what will motivate them to take advantage of educational opportunities?"

These remarks echoed President Kennedy's original message to Congress upon the introduction of the Civil Rights Act in 1963:

"There is little value in a Negro's obtaining the right to be admitted to hotels and restaurants if he has no cash in his pocket and no job."

Accordingly, it was clear to Congress that the crux of the problem was to open employment opportunities for Negroes in occupations which have been traditionally closed to them and it was to this problem that Title VII's prohibition against racial discrimination in employment was primarily addressed.

Clearly, a prohibition against all voluntary, race conscious, affirmative action efforts would disserve these ends. We therefore hold that Title VII's prohibition in section 703 (a) and (d) against racial discrimination does not condemn all private, voluntary, race-conscious affirmative action plans.

We need not today define in detail the line of demarcation between permissible and impermissible affirmative action plans. It suffices to hold that the challenged Kaiser-USWA affirmative action plan falls on the permissible side of the line. The purposes of the plan mirror those of the statute. Both were designed to break down old patterns of racial segregation and hierarchy. Both were structured to "open employment opportunities for Negroes in occupations which have been traditionally closed to them."

At the same time, the plan does not unnecessarily trammel the interest of the white employees. The plan does not require the discharge of white workers and their replacement. Nor does the plan create an absolute bar to the advancement of white employees; half of those trained in the program will be white. Moreover, the plan is a temporary measure; it is not intended to maintain racial balance, but simply to eliminate a manifest racial imbalance.

Judgment for United Steelworkers of America.

Case Commentary

The U.S. Supreme Court set forth a 4-prong test to determine whether an affirmative action plan is in violation of Title VII's prohibition against race discrimination: The plan must be remedial in purpose; it must have a limited duration; the minority workers hired under the plan must be qualified; and current white employees must not be discharged to provide positions for minorities. Here, Weber, who is white, was not hired even though he was more qualified than several black candidates who were selected. The court upheld the affirmative action plan because it met all of the requirements. ■

CASE QUESTIONS

1. Do you agree with the Supreme Court's decision?
2. Is the 4-prong test set forth in *Weber* the most accurate method for justifying an affirmative action program?

3. Should the most qualified individual be entitled to the job?

EQUAL EMPLOYMENT OPPORTUNITY ACT OF 1972

This was the first major amendment to Title VII of the 1964 Civil Rights Act. The act provided the Civil Service Commission with the power to address all federal employment issues and to remedy injustices with reinstatement and back pay. Each agency director was required to apply the law. The Equal Employment Opportunity Act of 1972 states that all employment decisions " . . . shall be made free from any discrimination based on race, creed, color, religion, sex, or national origin."

To insure compliance, evaluation will be made and record keeping will be required on the employment of women and minorities. " . . . nothing contained in the act shall relieve any Government agency or official of its or his primary responsibility to assure non-discrimination in employment as required by the Constitution and statutes or its or his responsibility under Executive Order 11478 relating to equal employment opportunity in the Federal Government."

Each administrative agency, as well as each department within the agency, was required to set forth an affirmative action plan. This was even required to be done on a regional basis to help the Civil Service Commission identify areas in need of particular attention. Agencies were required to develop education and training programs geared to aiding its employees achieve their greatest potential. To implement these programs, agencies were required to secure qualified personnel to administer these programs. Program content and personnel size and competency were both subject to scrutiny by the Civil Service Commission. On-site inspections were conducted routinely. After annual review, the Civil Service Commission would publish reports on each agency's progress. Employees were encouraged to file complaints if they had not been afforded an equal employment opportunity. The commission would reach a resolution after investigation. If dissatisfied with the resolution, access to the courts was now available to an aggrieved employee. Court decisions over time have developed a body of case law, which now provides legal precedent in certain areas of employment discrimination (i.e., the U.S. Supreme Court decisions of *Griggs v. Duke Power Co.* and *McDonnell Douglas Corp. v. Green*).

Agencies were required to administer skill utilization surveys to identify the skill that each employee had and to determine whether those skills were being utilized. Nonutilization of a skill may be grounds for an adaptation of the current job or a transfer or a promotion of that employee to a job in which the skill will be more fully utilized. An illustrative questionnaire was given to all employees for purposes of eliciting meaningful responses regarding their skills. Then the supervisors were asked to evaluate each response to determine whether the skills were being utilized in the current job and whether they could be utilized there or at another position within the agency.

Many deficiencies were noted by the Civil Service Commission in reviewing the affirmative action plans of the administrative agencies. These included lack of specificity in the development of employment opportunities, failure to file timely reports, refusal to set timetables for achievement of plan goals, designating inadequate and inexperienced personnel to the plan, and relegating employment and supervision to human resource departments rather than integrating them throughout the agency.

The Civil Service Commission redefined its mandate to correct these deficiencies. In developing the plan, the commission called for agencies to file an assessment report to single out departments where access had been denied or rarely given to women and minorities. Consultation with women and minority groups was strongly suggested for the valuable input they could give. Next, specific remedies were required to address the problems identified in the assessment report. Each department was to tailor the plan to meet its respective needs. Timetables were then required to be attached to each plan of action to monitor progress and ultimately resolution. Although the plans permitted flexibility, movement toward the goal was necessary. These plans would then be reviewed by the commission annually, and agency directors would be called to explain noncompliance.

A breakdown of the composition of women and minorities for each department and each grade level in the administrative agency should be an integral part of the assessment. The percentage of women and minorities in maintenance, clerical, managerial, technical, and professional areas should also be included. Once jobs become available, each agency should endeavor to discover those women and minorities in their workforce who have the capability for advancement. In addition, agencies should seek out potential recruiting venues for women and minority employment candidates.

Discriminatory complaints must be grouped according to job category and grade level. Solutions should be proposed for reoccurring complaints, while unique dilemmas should be handled on an ad hoc basis. The goal of an affirmative action plan is not an instantaneous resolution, but one of constant movement toward the accomplishment of equal opportunity in employment for all.

With the assessment report in hand, specific actions can be taken. Expeditious resolution of discriminatory complaints is the key toward ensuring that women and minorities continue to have faith in the system. Advertising job opportunities in promotional mediums that are earmarked specifically toward recruiting women and minorities is imperative to secure greater applicants from that cohort. Instituting programs in the community to enhance the potential pool of prospective employees is a proactive step. These might include helping an employee find adequate housing, aiding the community in establishing day-care centers or providing on-site day-care centers instead, and fostering relations with women and minority groups. The designing of proficient training programs will enable women and minority employees to become the most qualified they can be. Self-evaluation of the affirmative action program's proficiency is an important tool when future reassessment is made.

AFFIRMATIVE ACTION PLAN GUIDELINES FOR THE PRIVATE SECTOR

The key to establishing an affirmative action plan is to garner the commitment of management. Once committed, management can emphasize its importance and lead by example. An assessment must be made of the number of women and minorities and their current status within the organization. This data will prove invaluable as a benchmark against which the program's progress can be measured. Once the problem areas are identified, then recruitment and promotion issues must be addressed. A critical look at the current methods utilized must be taken, and a plan must be instituted to remedy its deficiencies. To bolster recruitment, notification should be sent to the placement offices of schools with significant or exclusive women or minority populations. Women and minority organizations can also be advised of the need for prospective candidates. Advertisements in newspapers, magazines, radio, and television designed for women and minorities will enable a company to tap into that particular circle. Company tours for students and community groups are also beneficial. Relying solely on referrals and traditional recruitment techniques will only reinforce discrimination.

Career counseling to direct women and minorities toward career paths and training programs to help them realize these accomplishments must be created or embellished. The fact that counseling and training programs exist is not sufficient. They must be made available or specifically developed with women and minorities in mind.

Job descriptions must also be perused for possible barriers against women and minorities. If found, the descriptive narration must be rethought. All requirements must be job-related. Any that are not should be eliminated, especially unnecessary education or experience; otherwise, discrimination will continue. Testing should also be restricted to when it is absolutely necessary and its reality and job-relatedness can be proved. The assignment of grade levels to jobs must also be reviewed for bias in favor of men. If discovered, such bias must be readjusted. Interviewers must be indoctrinated to no longer believe that women and minorities can perform only certain jobs—those involving routine ministerial tasks. They must avoid asking women and minorities personal questions about marital status, other sources of income, number of children, criminal record, and other issues that are not job-related and are not routinely asked of white men.

Job categories, job descriptions, promotional materials, and in-house rules and regulations must be redrafted to be gender-neutral, both in written communications and pictorials.

Employment Perspective

In an advertisement brochure, Sunshine Chemicals states that the men in its employ are the most qualified in the industry. Several pages of pictorials of white men follow. Is this material discriminatory toward the women and minorities who are employed there? Yes! The language is not gender-neutral, and the pictorials are neither gender- nor racially-neutral.

The affirmative action plan should be in written form and distributed throughout the company. A director should be appointed to administer the plan. A letter from the director as well as the CEO should confirm that it is the company's intention to refrain from discrimination both maliciously as well as accidentally and that the company expects all of its employees to act accordingly or face disciplinary measures. Lip service will not be tolerated.

The director should be developing company-wide goals for recruitment, training, promotion, and termination; company-wide applies to top management equally. There can be no exceptions or else a good example will not be set, and the plan will fail because of selective application. Each of the goals should be tailored appropriately to work within individual departments. Discussions should be held at all levels to explain the reasoning behind the plan. Getting as much support as possible from top to bottom will thwart divisiveness, prejudice, and subversion. Unions should be encouraged to embrace and promote the plan. Whenever a positive attribute of the plan is realized, it should be publicized throughout the company as well as externally. It is wise to clear up any misunderstanding or resentment about the purpose of the plan by counseling those feeling so inclined. Educating employees goes a long way to resolving prejudice and conflict. The director should have an open-door policy for all employees and should communicate periodically with the CEO.

REVERSE DISCRIMINATION

Reverse discrimination exists when the affirmative action plan is unfair to white males in that it selects unqualified women and minorities over them, establishes mandatory quotas, or bars the selection of white males completely. Often, reverse discrimination is claimed when qualified women and minorities are given preference over higher-qualified white males. Although there have been conflicting cases, it is generally agreed that this is an acceptable practice when a racial imbalance exists.

Employment Perspective

Oakville is going to employ 20 new police officers. Oakville has very few women and minority police officers. A score of 70 on the police exam is required to be qualified. Oakville plans to hire 10 minorities and five women, if they are qualified. The 10 minorities selected scored 74 to 90. The five women selected scored 78 to 87. Jim Newman, a white male, scored 94 but was not selected because five other white males scored higher. He sues Oakville, claiming reverse discrimination. Will he win? Most likely not. The issue is not who is more qualified, but whether the individuals selected are qualified. As long as they are qualified, as is the case here, the affirmative action plan will be upheld. If they were not qualified, then Jim's claim of reverse discrimination would be granted, and he would be given a position.

Without affirmative action plans, it is unlikely that women and minorities would have the opportunity of obtaining certain jobs, especially those involving managerial positions.

The following case addresses the issue of whether a school can set aside a definitive number of seats for minority applicants. A white applicant argued that race should not be the determining factor in making an admissions decision.

University of California Regents v. Bakke
438 U.S. 265 (1977)

Justice Powell announced the judgment of the Court.

This case presents a challenge to the special admissions program of the petitioner, the Medical School of the University of California at Davis, which is designed to assure the admission of a specified number of students from certain minority groups. The Superior Court of California sustained respondent's challenge, holding that petitioner's program violated the California Constitution, Title VII of the Civil Rights Act of 1964, and the Equal Protection Clause of the Fourteenth Amendment. The court enjoined petitioner from considering respondent's race or the race of any other applicant in making admissions decisions.

Following the interviews, each candidate was rated on a scale of 1 to 100 by his interviewers and four other members of the admissions committee. The rating embraced the interviewers' summaries, the candidate's overall grade point average, grade point average in science courses, scores on the Medical College Admissions Test (MCAT), letters of recommendation, extracurricular activities, and other biographical data. The ratings were added together to arrive at each candidate's "benchmark" score. Since five committee members rated each candidate in 1973, a perfect score was 500; in 1974, six members rated each candidate, so that perfect score was 600. The full committee then reviewed the file and scores of each applicant and made offers of admission on a "rolling" basis. The chairman was responsible for placing names on the waiting list. They were not placed in strict numerical order; instead, the chairman had discretion to include persons with "special skills."

The special admissions program operated with a separate committee, a majority of whom were members of minority groups. On the 1973 application form, candidates were asked to indicate whether they wished to be considered as "economically and/or educationally disadvantaged" applicants; on the 1974 form the question was whether they wished to be considered as members of a "minority group," which the Medical School apparently viewed as "Blacks," "Chicanos," "Asians," and "American Indians." If these questions were answered affirmatively, the application was forwarded to the special admissions committee. No formal definition of "disadvantaged" was ever produced, but the chairman of the special committee screened each application to see whether it reflected economic or educational deprivation. Having passed this initial hurdle, the applications then were rated by the special committee in a fashion similar to that used by the general admissions committee, except that special candidates did not have to meet the 2.5 grade point average cutoff applied to regular applicants. About one-fifth of the total number of special applicants were invited for interviews in 1973 and 1974. Following each interview, the special committee assigned each special applicant a benchmark score. The special committee then presented its top choices to the general admissions committee. The latter did not rate or compare the special candidates against the general applicants, but could reject recommended special candidates for failure to meet course requirements or other specific deficiencies. The special committee continued to recommend special applicants until a number prescribed by faculty vote were admitted. While the overall class size was still 50, the prescribed number was 8; in 1973 and 1974, when the class size had doubled to 100, the prescribed number of special admissions also doubled, to 16.

Allan Bakke is a white male who applied to the Davis Medical School in both 1973 and 1974. In both years Bakke's application was considered under the general admissions program, and he received an interview. His 1973 interview was with Dr. Theodore C. West, who considered Bakke "a very desirable applicant to the medical school." Despite a strong benchmark score of 468 out of 500, Bakke was rejected. His application had come late in

the year, and no applicants in the general admissions process with scores below 470 were accepted after Bakke's application was completed. There were four special admissions slots unfilled at that time, however, for which Bakke was not considered. After his 1973 rejection, Bakke wrote to Dr. George H. Lowrey, Associate Dean and Chairman of the Admissions Committee, protesting that the special admissions program operated as a racial and ethnic quota.

Bakke's 1974 application was completed early in the year. His student interviewer gave him an overall rating of 94, finding him "friendly, well tempered, conscientious and delightful to speak with." His faculty interviewer was, by coincidence, the same Dr. Lowrey to whom he had written in protest of the special admissions program. Dr. Lowrey found Bakke "rather limited in his approach" to the problems of the medical profession and found disturbing Bakke's "very definite opinions which were based more on his personal viewpoints than upon a study of the total problem." Dr. Lowrey gave Bakke the lowest of his six ratings, at 86; his total was 549 out of 600. Again, Bakke's, application was rejected. In neither year did the chairman of the admissions committee, Dr. Lowrey, exercise his discretion to place Bakke on the waiting list. In both years, applicants were admitted under the special program with grade point averages, MCAT scores, and benchmark scores significantly lower than Bakke's.

After the second rejection, Bakke filed the instant suit in the Superior Court of California. He sought mandatory, injunctive, and declaratory relief compelling his admission to the Medical School. He alleged that the Medical School's special admissions program operated to exclude him from the school on the basis of his race, in violation of his rights under the Equal Protection Clause of the Fourteenth Amendment. The University cross-complained for a declaration that its special admissions program was lawful.

Applicants admitted under the special program also had benchmark scores significantly lower than many students, including Bakke. Bakke was rejected under the general admissions program, even though the special rating system apparently gave credit for overcoming "disadvantage."

The special admissions program is undeniably a classification based on race and ethnic background. To the extent that there existed a pool of at least minimally qualified minority applicants to fill the 16 special admissions seats, white applicants could compete only for 84 seats in the entering class, rather than the 100 open to minority applicants. Whether this limitation is described as a quota or a goal, it is a line drawn on the basis of race and ethnic status.

The guarantees of the Fourteenth Amendment extend to all persons. Its language is explicit: "No State shall . . . deny to any person within its jurisdiction the equal protection of the laws." The guarantee of equal protection cannot mean one thing when applied to one individual and something else when applied to a person of another color. If both are not accorded the same protection, then it is not equal.

If petitioner's purpose is to assure within its student body some specified percentage of a particular group merely because of its race or ethnic origin, such a preferential purpose must be rejected not as insubstantial but as facially invalid. Preferring members of any one group for no reason other than race or ethnic origin is discrimination for its own sake. This the Constitution forbids.

In such an admissions program, race or ethnic background may be deemed a "plus" in a particular applicant's file, yet it does not insulate the individual from comparison with all other candidates for the available seats. The file of the particular black applicant may be examined or his potential contribution to diversity without the factor of race being decisive when compared, for example, with that of an applicant identified as an Italian-American if the latter is thought to exhibit qualities more likely to promote beneficial educational pluralism. Such qualities could include exceptional personal talents, unique work or service experience, leadership potential, maturity, demonstrated compassion, a history of overcoming disadvantage, ability to communicate with the poor, or other qualifications deemed important. In short, an admissions program operated in this way is flexible enough to consider all pertinent elements of diversity in light of the particular qualifications of each applicant, and to place them on the same footing for consideration, although not necessarily according them the same weight. Indeed, the weight attributed to a particular quality may vary from year to year depending upon the "mix" both of the student body and the applicants for the incoming class.

This kind of program treats each applicant as an individual in the admissions process. The applicant who loses out on the last available seat to another candidate receiving a "plus" on the basis of ethnic background will not have been foreclosed from all consideration for that seat simply because he was not the right color or had the wrong surname. It would mean only that his combined qualifications, which may have included similar nonobjective factors, did not outweigh those of the other applicant. His qualifications would have been weighed fairly and competitively, and he would have no basis to complain of unequal treatment under the Fourteenth Amendment.

It had been suggested that an admissions program which considers race only as one factor is simply a subtle and more sophisticated—but no less effective—means of according racial preference than the Davis program. A facial intent to discriminate, however, is evident in petitioner's preference program and not denied in this case. No such facial infirmity exists in an admissions program where race or ethnic background is simply one element—to be weighed fairly against other elements—in the selection process.

In summary, it is evident that the Davis special admissions program involves the use of an explicit racial classification never before countenanced by this Court. It tells applicants who are not Negro, Asian, or Chicano that they are totally excluded from a specific percentage of the seats in an entering class. No matter how strong their qualifications, quantitative and extracurricular, including their own potential for contribution to educational diversity, they are never afforded the chance to compete with applicants from the preferred groups for the special admissions seats. At the same time, the preferred applicants have the opportunity to compete for every seat in the class.

The fatal flaw in petitioner's preferential program is its disregard of individual rights as guaranteed by the Fourteenth Amendment. Such rights are not absolute. But when a State's distribution of benefits or imposition of burdens hinges on ancestry or the color of a person's skin, that individual is entitled to a demonstration that the challenged classification is necessary to promote a substantial state interest. Petitioner has failed to carry this burden. For this reason, that portion of the California court's judgment holding petitioner's special admissions program invalid under the Fourteenth Amendment must be affirmed.

In enjoining petitioner from ever considering the race of any applicant, however, the courts below failed to recognize that the State has a substantial interest that legitimately may be served by a properly devised admissions program involving the competitive consideration of race and ethnic origin. For this reason, so much of the California court's judgment as enjoins petitioner from any consideration of the race of any applicant must be reversed.

With respect to respondent's entitlement to an injunction directing his admission to the Medical School, petitioner has conceded that it could not carry its burden of proving that, but for the existence of its unlawful special admissions program, respondent still would not have been admitted. Hence, respondent is entitled to the injunction, and that portion of the judgment must be affirmed.

Judgment for Bakke.

Case Commentary

The Supreme Court of the United States decided the medical school's admission policy was discriminatory toward white applicants because it was based on a quota. A certain number of seats were reserved exclusively for minorities. This amounted to reverse discrimination in violation of the Civil Rights Act of 1964's prohibition against race discrimination. ■

CASE QUESTIONS

1. Do you agree with the decision in this case?
2. What is the difference between a quota and an affirmative action program?

3. Should a school have a lower set of criteria for minorities?

The most qualified standard applies only to candidates of the same race; where candidates are of different races, being qualified is sufficient. Thus, the fact that the black workers were not the most qualified is immaterial because they were qualified. Both Bakke and Weber were denied admission because they were not the most qualified candidates within their racial classification (white). When selecting among candidates of different races, being qualified is all that matters. But, when deciding among people of the same race, being the most qualified is the deciding factor.

Requirements of An Affirmative Action Plan

An affirmative action plan will be upheld if it is remedial in nature. A remedial purpose can be determined by the following criteria:

1. The plan creates a balance in the workforce that would not have existed absent discrimination.
2. The plan's duration is limited to the achievement of its objective.
3. Only qualified applicants will be hired.
4. White candidates are not barred from being hired.

The issue in the case that follows is whether race can be taken into account when a school is formulating its admissions procedure.

Hopwood v. State of Texas
21 F.3d 603 (5th Cir. 1996)

Smith, Circuit Judge.

With the best of intentions, in order to increase the enrollment of certain favored classes of minority students, the University of Texas School of Law ("the law school") discriminates in favor of those applicants by giving substantial racial preferences in its admissions program. The beneficiaries of this system are blacks and Mexican Americans, to the detriment of whites and non-preferred minorities. The question we decide today is whether the Fourteenth Amendment permits the school to discriminate in this way.

We hold that it does not. The law school has presented no compelling justification, under the Fourteenth Amendment or Supreme Court precedent, that allows it to continue to elevate some races over others, even for the wholesome purpose of correcting perceived racial imbalance in the student body. "Racial preferences appear to 'even the score' . . . only if one embraces the proposition that our society is appropriately viewed as divided into races, making it right that an injustice rendered in the past to a black man should be compensated for by discriminating against a white."

As a result of its diligent efforts in this case, the district court concluded that the law school may continue to impose racial preferences. We reverse and remand, concluding that the law school may not use race as a factor in law school admissions. Further, we instruct the court to reconsider the issue of damages in accordance with the legal standards we now explain.

I.

A.

The University of Texas School of Law is one of the nation's leading law schools, consistently ranking in the top twenty. Accordingly, admission to the law school is fiercely competitive, with over 4,000 applicants a year competing to be among the approximately 900 offered admission to achieve an entering class of about 500 students. Many of these applicants have some of the highest grades and test scores in the country. Numbers are therefore paramount for admission. In the early 1990's, the law school largely based its initial admissions decisions upon an applicant's so-called Texas Index ("TI") number, a composite of undergraduate grade point average ("GPA") and Law School Aptitude Test ("LSAT") score. The law school used this number as a matter of administrative convenience in order to rank candidates and to predict, roughly, one's probability of success in law school. Moreover, the law school relied heavily upon such numbers to estimate the number of offers of admission it needed to make in order to fill its first-year class.

Of course, the law school did not rely upon numbers alone. The admissions office necessarily exercised judgment in interpreting the individual scores of applicants, taking into consideration factors such as the strength of a student's undergraduate education, the difficulty of his major, and significant trends in his own grades and the undergraduate grades at his respective college (such as grade inflation). Admissions personnel also considered what qualities each applicant might bring to his law school class. Thus, the law school could consider an applicant's background, life experiences, and outlook. Not surprisingly, these hard-to-quantify factors were especially significant for marginal candidates.

Because of the large number of applicants and potential admissions factors, the TI's administrative usefulness was its ability to sort candidates. For the class entering in 1992—the admissions group at issue in this case—the law school placed the typical applicant in one of three categories according to his TI scores: "presumptive admit," "presumptive deny," or a middle "discretionary zone." An applicant's TI category determined how extensive a review his application would receive.

Blacks and Mexican Americans were treated differently from other candidates, however. First, compared to whites and non-preferred minorities, the TI ranges that were used to place them into the three admissions categories were lowered to allow the law school to consider and admit more of them. In March 1992, for example, the presumptive TI admission score for resident whites and non-preferred minorities was 199. Mexican Americans and blacks needed a TI of only 189 to be presumptively admitted. The difference in the presumptive-deny ranges is even more striking. The presumptive denial score for "nonminorities" was 192; the same score for blacks and Mexican Americans was 179.

While these cold numbers may speak little to those unfamiliar with the pool of applicants, the results demonstrate that the difference in the two ranges was dramatic. According to the law school, 1992 resident white applicants had a mean GPA of 3.53 and an LSAT of 164. Mexican Americans scored 3.27 and 158; blacks scored 3.25 and 157. The category of "other minority" achieved a 3.56 and 160.

These disparate standards greatly affected a candidate's chance of admission. For example, by March 1992, because the presumptive denial score for whites was a TI of 192 or lower, and the presumptive admit TI for minorities was 189 or higher, a minority candidate with a TI of 189 or above almost certainly would be admitted, even though his score was considerably below the level at which a white candidate almost certainly would be rejected. Out of the pool of resident applicants who fell within this range (189–192 inclusive), 100% of blacks and 90% of Mexican Americans, but only 6% of whites, were offered admission.

The stated purpose of this lowering of standards was to meet an "aspiration" of admitting a class consisting of 10% Mexican Americans and 5% blacks, proportions roughly comparable to the percentages of those races graduating from Texas colleges. The law school found meeting these "goals" difficult, however, because of uncertain acceptance rates and the variable quality of the applicant pool. In 1992, for example, the entering class contained 41 blacks and 55 Mexican Americans, respectively 8% and 10.7% of the class.

In addition to maintaining separate presumptive TI levels for minorities and whites, the law school ran a segregated application evaluation process. Upon receiving an application form, the school color-coded it according to race. If a candidate failed to designate his race, he was presumed to be in a nonpreferential category. Thus, race was always an overt part of the review of any applicant's file.

The law school reviewed minority candidates within the applicable discretionary range differently from whites. Instead of being evaluated and compared by one of the various discretionary zone subcommittees, black and Mexican American applicants' files were reviewed by a minority subcommittee of three, which would meet and discuss every minority candidate. Thus, each of these candidates' files could get extensive review and discussion. And while the minority subcommittee reported summaries of files to the admissions committee as a whole, the minority subcommittee's decisions were "virtually final."

Finally, the law school maintained segregated waiting lists, dividing applicants by race and residence. Thus, even many of those minority applicants who were not admitted could be set aside in "minority-only" waiting lists. Such separate lists apparently helped the law school maintain a pool of potentially acceptable, but marginal, minority candidates.

B.

Cheryl Hopwood, Douglas Carvell, Kenneth Elliott, and David Rogers (the "plaintiffs") applied for admission to the 1992 entering law school class. All four were white residents of Texas and were rejected.

The plaintiffs were considered as discretionary zone candidates. Hopwood, with a GPA of 3.8 and an LSAT of 39 (equivalent to a three-digit LSAT of 160), had a TI of 199, a score barely within the presumptive-admit category for resident whites, which was 199 and up. She was dropped into the discretionary zone for resident whites (193 to 198), however, because Johanson decided her educational background overstated the strength of her GPA. Carvell, Elliott, and Rogers had TI's of 197, at the top end of that discretionary zone. Their applications were reviewed by admissions subcommittees, and each received one or no vote.

II.

The plaintiffs sued primarily under the Equal Protection Clause of the Fourteenth Amendment; they also claimed derivative statutory violations of 42 U.S.C. 1981 and 1983 and of title VI of the Civil Rights Act of 1964, 42 U.S.C. 2000d ("title VI"). The plaintiffs' central claim is that they were subjected to unconstitutional racial discrimination by the law school's evaluation of their admissions applications.

III.

The central purpose of the Equal Protection Clause "is to prevent the States from purposefully discriminating between individuals on the basis of race. It seeks ultimately to render the issue of race irrelevant in governmental decisionmaking."

Accordingly, discrimination based upon race is highly suspect. "Distinctions between citizens solely because of their ancestry are by their very nature odious to a free people whose institutions are founded upon the doctrine of equality," and "racial discriminations are in most circumstances irrelevant and therefore prohibited. . . . " Hence, "preferring members of any one group for no reason other than race or ethnic origin is discrimination for its own sake. This the Constitution forbids." These equal protection maxims apply to all races.

In order to preserve these principles, the Supreme Court recently has required that any governmental action that expressly distinguishes between persons on the basis of race be held to the most exacting scrutiny.

Indeed, the purpose of strict scrutiny is to "smoke out" illegitimate uses of race by assuring that the legislative body is pursuing a goal important enough to warrant use of a highly suspect tool. The test also ensures that the means chosen "fit" this compelling goal so closely that there is little or no possibility that the motive for the classification was illegitimate racial prejudice or stereotype.

Under the strict scrutiny analysis, we ask two questions: (1) Does the racial classification serve a compelling government interest, and (2) is it narrowly tailored to the achievement of that goal?

Finally, when evaluating the proffered governmental interest for the specific racial classification, to decide whether the program in question narrowly achieves that interest, we must recognize that "the rights created by . . . the Fourteenth Amendment are, by its terms, guaranteed to the individual. The rights established are personal rights." Thus, the Court consistently has rejected arguments conferring benefits on a person based solely upon his membership in a specific class of persons.

With these general principles of equal protection in mind, we turn to the specific issue of whether the law school's consideration of race as a factor in admissions violates the Equal Protection Clause.

We agree with the plaintiffs that any consideration of race or ethnicity by the law school for the purpose of achieving a diverse student body is not a compelling interest under the Fourteenth Amendment. Finally, the classification of persons on the basis of race for the purpose of diversity frustrates, rather than facilitates, the goals of equal protection. Within the general principles of the Fourteenth Amendment, the use of race in admissions for diversity in higher education contradicts, rather than furthers, the aims of equal protection. Diversity fosters, rather than minimizes, the use of race. It treats minorities as a group, rather than as individuals. It may further remedial purposes but, just as likely, may promote improper racial stereotypes, thus fueling racial hostility.

The use of race, in and of itself, to choose students simply achieves a student body that looks different. Such a criterion is no more rational on its own terms than would be choices based upon the physical size or blood type of applicants. Thus, the Supreme Court has long held that governmental actors cannot justify their decisions solely because of race.

While the use of race per se is proscribed, state-supported schools may reasonably consider a host of factors some of which may have some correlation with race in making admissions decisions. The federal courts have no warrant to intrude on those executive and legislative judgments unless the distinctions intrude on specific provisions of federal law or the Constitution. A university may properly favor one applicant over another because of his ability to play the cello, make a downfield tackle, or understand chaos theory. An admissions process may also consider an applicant's home state or relationship to school alumni. Law schools specifically may look at things such as unusual or substantial extracurricular activities in college, which may be atypical factors affecting undergraduate grades. Schools may even consider factors such as whether an applicant's parents attended college or the applicant's economic and social background.

For this reason, race often is said to be justified in the diversity context, not on its own terms, but as a proxy for other characteristics that institutions of higher education value but that do not raise similar constitutional concerns. Unfortunately, this approach simply replicates the very harm that the Fourteenth Amendment was designed to eliminate.

The assumption is that a certain individual possesses characteristics by virtue of being a member of a certain racial group. This assumption, however, does not withstand scrutiny. "The use of a racial characteristic to establish a presumption that the individual also possesses other, and socially relevant, characteristics, exemplifies, encourages, and legitimizes the mode of thought and behavior that underlies most prejudice and bigotry in modern America."

Plaintiff Hopwood is a fair example of an applicant with a unique background. She is the now-thirty-two-year-old wife of a member of the Armed Forces stationed in San Antonio and, more significantly, is raising a severely handicapped child. Her circumstance would bring a different perspective to the law school. The school might consider this an advantage to her in the application process, or it could decide that her family situation would be too much of a burden on her academic performance.

We do not opine on which way the law school should weigh Hopwood's qualifications; we only observe that "diversity" can take many forms. To foster such diversity, state universities and law schools and other governmental entities must scrutinize applicants individually, rather than resorting to the dangerous proxy of race.

In sum, the use of race to achieve a diverse student body, whether as a proxy for permissible characteristics, simply cannot be a state interest compelling enough to meet the steep standard of strict scrutiny. These latter factors may, in fact, turn out to be substantially correlated with race, but the key is that race itself not be taken into account. Thus, that portion of the district court's opinion upholding the diversity rationale is reversibly flawed.

In sum, the law school has failed to show a compelling state interest in remedying the present effects of past discrimination sufficient to maintain the use of race in its admissions system. Accordingly, it is unnecessary for us to examine the district court's determination that the law school's admissions program was not narrowly tailored to meet the compelling interests that the district court erroneously perceived.

IV.

In summary, we hold that the University of Texas School of Law may not use race as a factor in deciding which applicants to admit in order to achieve a diverse student body, to combat the perceived effects of a hostile environment at the law school, to alleviate the law school's poor reputation in the minority community, or to eliminate any present effects of past discrimination by actors other than the law school. Because the law school has proffered these justifications for its use of race in admissions, the plaintiffs have satisfied their burden of showing that they were scrutinized under an unconstitutional admissions system. The plaintiffs are entitled to reapply under an admissions system that invokes none of these serious constitutional infirmities. The judgment is REVERSED and REMANDED for further proceedings in accordance with this opinion.

Judgment for Hopwood.

Case Commentary

The Fifth Circuit Court held that race should not be a factor in the admissions process where there has been no past evidence of discrimination on the part of the school that is seeking to implement the affirmative action plan. ■

CASE QUESTIONS

1. Do you agree with the Court's decision?
2. Where there is inadequate representation of minorities, should entrance requirements be lowered to increase minority enrollment?

3. How would the U.S. Supreme Court have decided this case?

In the following case, the questions presented are whether the affirmative action program was remedial in nature and whether it had a deleterious effect on white employees.

Taxman v. Board of Education of the Township of Piscataway
91 F.3d 1547 (3rd Cir. 1996)

Mansmann, Circuit Judge.

In this Title VII matter, we must determine whether the Board of Education of the Township of Piscataway violated that statute when it made race a factor in selecting which of two equally qualified employees to lay off. Specifically, we must decide whether Title VII permits an employer with a racially balanced work force to grant a non-remedial racial preference in order to promote "racial diversity."

It is clear that the language of Title VII is violated when an employer makes an employment decision based upon an employee's race. The Supreme Court determined in *United Steelworkers v. Weber*, however, that Title VII's prohibition against racial discrimination is not violated by affirmative action plans which first, "have purposes that mirror those of the statute" and second, do not "unnecessarily trammel the interests of the non-minority employees."

We hold that Piscataway's affirmative action policy is unlawful because it fails to satisfy either prong of Weber. Given the clear antidiscrimination mandate of Title VII, a non-remedial affirmative action plan, even one with a laudable purpose, cannot pass muster. We will affirm the district court's grant of summary judgment to Sharon Taxman.

I.

In 1975, the Board of Education of the Township of Piscataway, New Jersey, developed an affirmative action policy applicable to employment decisions. The Board's affirmative action policy did not have "any remedial purpose"; it was not adopted "with the intention of remedying the results of any prior discrimination or identified underrepresentation of minorities within the Piscataway Public School System." At all relevant times, Black teachers were neither "underrepresented" nor "underutilized" in the Piscataway School District work force. Indeed, statistics in 1976 and 1985 showed that the percentage of Black employees in the job category which included teachers exceeded the percentage of Blacks in the available work force.

A.

In May, 1989, the Board accepted a recommendation from the Superintendent of Schools to reduce the teaching staff in the Business Department at Piscataway High School by one. At that time, two of the teachers in the department were of equal seniority, both having begun their employment with the Board on the same day nine years earlier. One of those teachers was intervenor plaintiff Sharon Taxman, who is White, and the other was Debra Williams, who is Black. Williams was the only minority teacher among the faculty of the Business Department.

Decisions regarding layoffs by New Jersey school boards are highly circumscribed by state law; nontenured faculty must be laid off first, and layoffs among tenured teachers in the affected subject area or grade level must proceed in reverse order of seniority. Seniority for this purpose is calculated according to specific guidelines set by state law. Thus, local boards lack discretion to choose between employees for layoff, except in the rare instance of a tie in seniority between the two or more employees eligible to fill the last remaining position.

The Board determined that it was facing just such a rare circumstance in deciding between Taxman and Williams. In prior decisions involving the layoff of employees with equal seniority, the Board had broken the tie through "a random process which included drawing numbers out of a container, drawing lots or having a lottery." In none of those instances, however, had the employees involved been of different races.

In light of the unique posture of the layoff decision, Superintendent of Schools Burton Edelchick recommended to the Board that the affirmative action plan be invoked in order to determine which teacher to retain. Superintendent Edelchick made this recommendation "because he believed Ms. Williams and Ms. Taxman were tied in seniority, were equally qualified, and because Ms. Williams was the only Black teacher in the Business Education Department."

While the Board recognized that it was not bound to apply the affirmative action policy, it made a discretionary decision to invoke the policy to break the tie between Williams and Taxman. As a result, the Board "voted to terminate the employment of Sharon Taxman, effective June 30, 1988. . . . "

B.

Following the Board's decision, Taxman filed a charge of employment discrimination with the Equal Employment Opportunity Commission. Attempts at conciliation were unsuccessful, and the United States filed suit under Title VII against the Board in the United States District Court for the District of New Jersey. Taxman intervened, asserting claims

under both Title VII and the New Jersey Law Against Discrimination (NJLAD).

A trial proceeded on the issue of damages. By this time, Taxman had been rehired by the Board and thus her reinstatement was not an issue. The court awarded Taxman damages in the amount of $134,014.62 for backpay, fringe benefits and prejudgment interest under Title VII. A jury awarded an additional $10,000 for emotional suffering under the NJLAD.

The Board appealed, contending that the district court erred in granting Taxman summary judgment as to liability.

The Board admits that it did not act to remedy the effects of past employment discrimination. The parties have stipulated that neither the Board's adoption of its affirmative action policy nor its subsequent decision to apply it in choosing between Taxman and Williams was intended to remedy the results of any prior discrimination or identified underrepresentation of Blacks within the Piscataway School District's teacher workforce as a whole. Nor does the Board contend that its action here was directed at remedying any de jure or de facto segregation. Even though the Board's race-conscious action was taken to avoid what could have been an all-White faculty within the Business Department, the Board concedes that Blacks are not underrepresented in its teaching workforce as a whole or even in the Piscataway High School.

Rather, the Board's sole purpose in applying its affirmative action policy in this case was to obtain an educational benefit which it believed would result from a racially diverse faculty. While the benefits flowing from diversity in the educational context are significant indeed, we are constrained to hold, as did the district court, that inasmuch as "the Board does not even attempt to show that its affirmative action plan was adopted to remedy past discrimination or as the result of a manifest imbalance in the employment of minorities," the Board has failed to satisfy the first prong of the Weber test.

We turn next to the second prong of the Weber analysis. This second prong requires that we determine whether the Board's policy "unnecessarily trammels . . . nonminority interests. . . . " Under this requirement, too, the Board's policy is deficient.

The affirmative action plans that have met with the Supreme Court's approval under Title VII had objectives, as well as benchmarks which served to evaluate progress, guide the employment decisions at issue and assure the grant of only those minority preferences necessary to further the plans' purpose. By contrast, the Board's policy, devoid of goals and standards, is governed entirely by the Board's whim, leaving the Board free, if it so chooses, to grant racial preferences that do not promote even the policy's claimed purpose. Indeed, under the terms of this policy, the Board, in pursuit of a "racially diverse" work force, could use affirmative action to discriminate against those whom Title VII was enacted to protect. Such a policy unnecessarily trammels the interests of nonminority employees.

Moreover, valid affirmative action plans are "temporary" measures that seek to "'attain,'" not "maintain" a "permanent racial . . . balance." The Board's policy, adopted in 1975, is an established fixture of unlimited duration, to be resurrected from time to time whenever the Board believes that the ratio between Blacks and Whites in any Piscataway School is skewed. On this basis alone, the policy contravenes Weber's teaching.

Finally, we are convinced that the harm imposed upon a nonminority employee by the loss of his or her job is so substantial and the cost so severe that the Board's goal of racial diversity, even if legitimate under Title VII, may not be pursued in this particular fashion. This is especially true where, as here, the nonminority employee is tenured. In Weber, when considering whether nonminorities were unduly encumbered by affirmative action, the Court found it significant that they retained their employment.

Accordingly, we conclude that under the second prong of the Weber test, the Board's affirmative action policy violates Title VII. In addition to containing an impermissible purpose, the policy "unnecessarily trammels the interests of the nonminority employees."

While we have rejected the argument that the Board's non-remedial application of the affirmative action policy is consistent with the language and intent of Title VII, we do not reject in principle the diversity goal articulated by the Board. Indeed, we recognize that the differences among us underlie the richness and strength of our Nation. Our disposition of this matter, however, rests squarely on the foundation of Title VII. Although we applaud the goal of racial diversity, we cannot agree that Title VII permits an employer to advance that goal through non-remedial discriminatory measures.

Having found that the district court properly concluded that the affirmative action plan applied by the Board to lay off Taxman is invalid under Title VII, and that the district court did not err in calculating Taxman's damages or in dismissing her claim for punitive damages, we will affirm the judgment of the district court.

Judgment for Taxman.

Case Commentary
The tests for determining whether an affirmative action program is enforceable are whether the enactment of the plan was in response to a disparate impact against minorities, and whether the implementation of the plan will have an adverse effect on white employees. The Piscataway Board of Education's plan failed in both respects. There were a sufficient number of minorities employed; therefore, remediation was unnecessary, and a white employee, Sharon Taxman, suffered the loss of her job because of the implementation of the plan. ∎

CASE QUESTIONS

1. Do you agree with the decision in this case?
2. Does this mark the end of affirmative action?

3. How would the U.S. Supreme Court have decided this case?

The question presented in the case that follows is whether a state referendum approved by the voters disbanding affirmative action programs is in violation of the Fourteenth Amendment's Equal Protection Clause.

The Coalition v. Pete Wilson
122 F.3d 692 (9th Cir. 1997)

O'Scannlain, Judge.
We must decide whether a provision of the California Constitution prohibiting public race and gender preferences violates the Equal Protection Clause of the United States Constitution.

On November 5, 1996, the people of the State of California adopted the California Civil Rights Initiative as an amendment to their Constitution. The initiative, which appeared on the ballot as Proposition 209, provides in relevant part that the state shall not discriminate against, or grant preferential treatment to, any individual or group on the basis of race, sex, color, ethnicity, or national origin in the operation of public employment, public education, or public contracting.

The California Legislative Analyst's Office portrayed Proposition 209 to the voters as a measure that would eliminate public race-based and gender-based affirmative action programs. The California Ballot Pamphlet explained to voters that: A YES vote on Proposition 209 means: The elimination of those affirmative action programs for women and minorities run by the state or local governments in the areas of public employment, contracting, and education that give "preferential treatment" on the basis of sex, race, color, ethnicity, or national origin.

A NO vote on this measure means State and local government affirmative action programs would remain in effect to the extent they are permitted under the United States Constitution.

The Ballot Pamphlet also included arguments by proponents and opponents of Proposition 209. Proponents urged a "yes" vote, arguing that: A generation ago, we did it right. We passed civil rights laws to prohibit discrimination. But special interests hijacked the civil rights movement. Instead of equality, governments imposed quotas, preferences, and set-asides. And two wrongs don't make a right! Today, students are being rejected from public universities because of their RACE. Job applicants are turned away because their RACE does not meet some "goal" or "timetable." Contracts are awarded to high bidders because they are of the preferred RACE.

That's just plain wrong and unjust. Government should not discriminate. It must not give a job, a university admission, or a contract based on race or sex. Government must judge all people equally, without discrimination! And, remember, Proposition 209 keeps in place all federal and state protections against discrimination!

Opponents of Proposition 209 urged a "no" vote, responding that: California law currently allows tutoring, mentoring, outreach, recruitment, and counseling to help ensure equal opportunity for women and minorities. Proposition 209 will eliminate affirmative action programs like these that help achieve equal opportunity for women and minorities in public employment, education and contracting. Instead of reforming affirmative action to make it fair for everyone, Proposition 209 makes the current problem worse. . . .

The initiative's language is so broad and misleading that it eliminates equal opportunity programs including: tutoring and mentoring for minority and women students; affirmative action that encourages the hiring and promotion of qualified women and minorities; outreach and recruitment programs to encourage applicants for government jobs and contracts; and programs designed to encourage girls to study and pursue careers in math and science.

Proposition 209 passed by a margin of 54 to 46 percent; of nearly 9 million Californians casting ballots, 4,736,180 voted in favor of the initiative and 3,986,196 voted against it.

On the day after the election, November 6, 1996, several individuals and groups ("plaintiffs") claiming to represent the interests of racial minorities and women filed a complaint in the Northern District of California against several officials and political subdivisions of the State of California ("the State").

The complaint, brought under 42 U.S.C. S 1983, alleges that Proposition 209, first, denies racial minorities and women the equal protection of the laws guaranteed by the Fourteenth Amendment, and, second, is void under the Supremacy Clause because it conflicts with Titles VI and VII of the Civil Rights Act of 1964, and Title IX of the Educational Amendments of 1972. As relief, plaintiffs seek a declaration that Proposition 209 is unconstitutional and a permanent injunction enjoining the State from implementing and enforcing it.

With their complaint, plaintiffs filed an application for a temporary restraining order ("TRO") and a preliminary injunction. The district court entered a TRO on November 27, 1996, and granted a preliminary injunction on December 23, 1996. The preliminary injunction enjoins the State, pending trial or final judgment, "from implementing or enforcing Proposition 209 insofar as said amendment to the Constitution of the State of California purports to prohibit or affect affirmative action programs in public employment, public education or public contracting."

We may now address the merits.

In granting the preliminary injunction, the district court first concluded that plaintiffs have demonstrated a likelihood of success on their claim that Proposition 209 violates the Equal Protection Clause of the Fourteenth Amendment. As a matter of "conventional" equal protection analysis, there is simply no doubt that Proposition 209 is constitutional. The Equal Protection Clause provides that "no State shall . . . deny to any person within its jurisdiction the equal protection of the laws." The central purpose of the Equal Protection Clause "is the prevention of official conduct discriminating on the basis of race." The Fourteenth Amendment forbids such conduct on the principle that "distinctions between citizens solely because of their ancestry are by their very nature odious to a free people whose institutions are founded upon the doctrine of equality."

Racial distinctions "threaten to stigmatize individuals by reason of their membership in a racial group and to incite racial hostility."

The ultimate goal of the Equal Protection Clause is "to do away with all governmentally imposed discrimination based on race." Therefore, "whenever the government treats any person unequally because of his or her race, that person has suffered an injury that falls squarely within the language and spirit of the Constitution's guarantee of equal protection." The Equal Protection Clause also protects against classifications based on gender. "Without equating gender classifications, for all purposes, to classifications based on race or national origin, the Court . . . has carefully inspected official action that closes a door or denies opportunity to women or to men." The standard of review under the Equal Protection Clause does not depend on the race or gender of those burdened or benefited by a particular classification.

Any governmental action that classifies persons by race is presumptively unconstitutional and subject to the most exacting judicial scrutiny. To be constitutional, a racial classification, regardless of its purported motivation, must be narrowly tailored to serve a compelling governmental interest, an extraordinary justification. When the government classifies by gender, it must demonstrate that the classification is substantially related to an important governmental interest, requiring an "exceedingly persuasive" justification.

Plaintiffs challenge Proposition 209 not as an impediment to protection against unequal treatment but as an impediment to receiving preferential treatment. The controlling words, we must remember, are "equal" and "protection." Impediments to preferential treatment do not deny equal protection. It is one thing to say that individuals have equal protection rights against political obstructions to equal treatment; it is quite another to say that individuals have equal protection rights against political obstructions to preferential treatment. While the Constitution protects against obstructions to equal treatment, it erects obstructions to preferential treatment by its own terms.

The alleged "equal protection" burden that Proposition 209 imposes on those who would seek race and gender preferences is a burden that the Constitution itself imposes. The Equal Protection Clause, parked at our most "distant and remote" level of government, singles out racial preferences for severe political burdens—it prohibits them in all but the most compelling circumstances. It is well-settled that "all governmental action based on race—a group classification long recognized as in most circumstances irrelevant and therefore prohibited—should be subject to detailed judicial inquiry to ensure that the personal right to equal protection of the laws has not been infringed." That is because "there is simply no way of determining what classifications are 'benign' or 'remedial' and what classifications are in fact motivated by illegitimate notions of racial inferiority or simple racial politics." The Constitution permits the people to grant a narrowly tailored racial preference only if they come forward with a

compelling interest to back it up. Proposition 209, the district court relied on an erroneous legal premise in concluding that plaintiffs are likely to succeed on the merits of their pre-emption claims.

With no likelihood of success on the merits of their equal protection or pre-emption claims, plaintiffs are not entitled to a preliminary injunction.

Assuming all facts alleged in the complaint and found by the district court to be true, and drawing all reasonable inferences in plaintiffs' favor, we must conclude that, as a matter of law, Proposition 209 does not violate the United States Constitution. With no constitutional injury on the merits as a matter of law, there is no threat of irreparable injury or hardship to tip the balance in plaintiffs' favor.

Preliminary injunction VACATED.

Judgment for Wilson.

Case Commentary

The Ninth Circuit Court held that granting preferential treatment based on race in school admissions, contracts with the state, and state jobs was prohibited by voter-approved Proposition 209. The court further held that Proposition 209 does not violate the Equal Protection Clause of the Fourteenth Amendment. ■

CASE QUESTIONS

1. Should the voters have the right to decide this issue or should it be left to the courts or the legislature?
2. Do you agree with the decision in this case?

3. Where does this decision leave women and minorities? Are they on an equal footing?
4. Is this the death knell for affirmative action?

The issue in the following case is whether the use of race in the law school admissions process is in violation of the Equal Protection Clause of the Fourteenth Amendment.

Grutter v. Bollinger

123 S. Ct. 2325 (2003)

Justice O'Connor delivered the opinion of the Court.

This case requires us to decide whether the use of race as a factor in student admissions by the University of Michigan Law School (Law School) is unlawful.

I

A

The Law School ranks among the Nation's top law schools. It receives more than 3,500 applications each year for a class of around 350 students. Seeking to "admit a group of students who individually and collectively are among the most capable," the Law School looks for individuals with "substantial promise for success in law school" and "a strong likelihood of succeeding in the practice of law and

contributing in diverse ways to the well-being of others." More broadly, the Law School seeks "a mix of students with varying backgrounds and experiences who will respect and learn from each other." In 1992, the dean of the Law School charged a faculty committee with crafting a written admissions policy to implement these goals. In particular, the Law School sought to ensure that its efforts to achieve student body diversity complied with this Court's most recent ruling on the use of race in university admissions. Upon the unanimous adoption of the committee's report by the Law School faculty, it became the Law School's official admissions policy.

The hallmark of that policy is its focus on academic ability coupled with a flexible assessment of applicants' talents, experiences, and potential "to contribute to the learning of those around them." The policy requires admissions officials to evaluate each applicant based on all the information available in the file, including a personal statement, letters of recommendation, and an essay describing the ways in which the applicant will contribute to the life and diversity of the Law School. In reviewing an applicant's file, admissions officials must consider the applicant's undergraduate grade point average (GPA) and Law School Admissions Test (LSAT) score because they are important (if imperfect) predictors of academic success in law school. The policy stresses that "no applicant should be admitted unless we expect that applicant to do well enough to graduate with no serious academic problems."

The policy makes clear, however, that even the highest possible score does not guarantee admission to the Law School. Nor does a low score automatically disqualify an applicant. Here, the policy requires admissions officials to look beyond grades and test scores to other criteria that are important to the Law School's educational objectives. So-called "'soft' variables" such as "the enthusiasm of recommenders, the quality of the undergraduate institution, the quality of the applicant's essay, and the areas and difficulty of undergraduate course selection" are all brought to bear in assessing an "applicant's likely contributions to the intellectual and social life of the institution."

The policy aspires to "achieve that diversity which has the potential to enrich everyone's education and thus make a law school class stronger than the sum of its parts." The policy does not restrict the types of diversity contributions eligible for "substantial weight" in the admissions process, but instead recognizes "many possible bases for diversity admissions." The policy does, however, reaffirm the Law School's long-standing commitment to "one particular type of diversity," that is, "racial and ethnic diversity with special reference to the inclusion of students from groups which have been historically discriminated against, like African-Americans, Hispanics and Native Americans, who without this commitment might not be represented in our student body in meaningful numbers." By enrolling a "'critical mass' of [underrepresented] minority students," the Law School seeks to "ensure their ability to make unique contributions to the character of the Law School."

The policy does not define diversity "solely in terms of racial and ethnic status." Nor is the policy "insensitive to the competition among all students for admission to the Law School." Rather, the policy seeks to guide admissions officers in "producing classes both diverse and academically outstanding, classes made up of students who promise to continue the tradition of outstanding contribution by Michigan Graduates to the legal profession."

B

Petitioner Barbara Grutter is a white Michigan resident who applied to the Law School in 1996 with a 3.8 grade point average and 161 LSAT score. The Law School initially placed petitioner on a waiting list, but subsequently rejected her application. In December 1997, petitioner filed suit in the United States District Court for the Eastern District of Michigan against the Law School. Petitioner alleged that respondents discriminated against her on the basis of race in violation of the Fourteenth Amendment; Title VI of the Civil Rights Act of 1964.

Petitioner further alleged that her application was rejected because the Law School uses race as a "predominant" factor, giving applicants who belong to certain minority groups "a significantly greater chance of admission than students with similar credentials from disfavored racial groups." Petitioner also alleged that respondents "had no compelling interest to justify their use of race in the admissions process." Petitioner requested compensatory and punitive damages, an order requiring the Law School to offer her admission, and an injunction prohibiting the Law School from continuing to discriminate on the basis of race.

Dennis Shields, Director of Admissions when petitioner applied to the Law School, testified that he did not direct his staff to admit a particular percentage or number of minority students, but rather to consider an applicant's race along with all other factors. Shields testified that at the height of the admissions season, he would frequently consult the so-called "daily reports" that kept track of the racial and ethnic composition of the class (along with other information such as residency status and gender). This was done, Shields testified, to ensure that a critical mass of underrepresented minority students would be reached so as to realize the educational benefits of a diverse student body. Shields stressed, however, that he did not seek to admit any particular number or percentage of underrepresented minority students.

Erica Munzel, who succeeded Shields as Director of Admissions, testified that "'critical mass'" means "'meaningful numbers'" or "'meaningful representation,'" which she understood to mean a number that encourages underrepresented minority students to participate in the classroom and not feel isolated. Munzel stated there is no number, percentage, or range of numbers or percentages that constitute critical mass. Munzel also asserted that she must consider the race of applicants because a critical mass of underrepresented minority students could not be enrolled if admissions decisions were based primarily on undergraduate GPAs and LSAT scores.

The current Dean of the Law School, Jeffrey Lehman, also testified. Like the other Law School witnesses, Lehman did not quantify critical mass in terms of numbers or percentages. He indicated that critical mass means numbers such that underrepresented minority students do not feel isolated or like spokespersons for their race. When asked about the extent to which race is considered in admissions, Lehman testified that it varies from one applicant to another.

Ibid. In some cases, according to Lehman's testimony, an applicant's race may play no role, while in others it may be a "'determinative'" factor.

In an attempt to quantify the extent to which the Law School actually considers race in making admissions decisions, the parties introduced voluminous evidence at trial. Relying on data obtained from the Law School, petitioner's expert, Dr. Kinley Larntz, generated and analyzed "admissions grids" for the years in question (1995–2000). These grids show the number of applicants and the number of admittees for all combinations of GPAs and LSAT scores. Dr. Larntz made "'cell-by-cell'" comparisons between applicants of different races to determine whether a statistically significant relationship existed between race and admission rates. He concluded that membership in certain minority groups "'is an extremely strong factor in the decision for acceptance,'" and that applicants from these minority groups "'are given an extremely large allowance for admission'" as compared to applicants who are members of nonfavored groups. Dr. Larntz conceded, however, that race is not the predominant factor in the Law School's admissions calculus.

Dr. Stephen Raudenbush, the Law School's expert, focused on the predicted effect of eliminating race as a factor in the Law School's admission process. In Dr. Raudenbush's view, a race-blind admissions system would have a "'very dramatic,'" negative effect on underrepresented minority admissions. He testified that in 2000, 35 percent of underrepresented minority applicants were admitted. Dr. Raudenbush predicted that if race were not considered, only 10 percent of those applicants would have been admitted. Under this scenario, underrepresented minority students would have comprised 4 percent of the entering class in 2000 instead of the actual figure of 14.5 percent.

In the end, the District Court concluded that the Law School's use of race as a factor in admissions decisions was unlawful. Applying strict scrutiny, the District Court determined that the Law School's asserted interest in assembling a diverse student body was not compelling because "the attainment of a racially diverse class . . . was not recognized as such by *Bakke* and is not a remedy for past discrimination." The District Court went on to hold that even if diversity were compelling, the Law School had not narrowly tailored its use of race to further that interest. The District Court granted petitioner's request for declaratory relief and enjoined the Law School from using race as a factor in its admissions decisions. The Court of Appeals entered a stay of the injunction pending appeal.

Sitting en banc, the Court of Appeals reversed the District Court's judgment and vacated the injunction. The Court of Appeals also held that the Law School's use of race was narrowly tailored because race was merely a "potential 'plus' factor."

II

A

Since this Court's splintered decision in *Bakke*, Justice Powell's opinion announcing the judgment of the Court has served as the touchstone for constitutional analysis of race-conscious admissions policies. Public and private universities across the Nation have modeled their own admissions programs on Justice Powell's views on permissible race-conscious policies.

First, Justice Powell rejected an interest in "'reducing the historic deficit of traditionally disfavored minorities in medical schools and in the medical profession'" as an unlawful interest in racial balancing. Second, Justice Powell rejected an interest in remedying societal discrimination because such measures would risk placing unnecessary burdens on innocent third parties "who bear no responsibility for whatever harm the beneficiaries of the special admissions program are thought to have suffered." Third, Justice Powell rejected an interest in "increasing the number of physicians who will practice in communities currently underserved," concluding that even if such an interest could be compelling in some circumstances the program under review was not "geared to promote that goal."

Justice Powell approved the university's use of race to further only one interest: "the attainment of a diverse student body." With the important proviso that "constitutional limitations protecting individual rights may not be disregarded," Justice Powell grounded his analysis in the academic freedom that "long has been viewed as a special concern of the First Amendment." Justice Powell emphasized that nothing less than the "'nation's future depends upon leaders trained through wide exposure' to the ideas and mores of students as diverse as this Nation of many peoples." In seeking the "right to select those students who will contribute the most to the 'robust exchange of ideas,'" a university seeks "to achieve a goal that is of paramount importance in the fulfillment of its mission." Both "tradition and experience lend support to the view that the contribution of diversity is substantial."

Justice Powell was, however, careful to emphasize that in his view race "is only one element in a range of factors a university properly may consider in attaining the goal of a heterogeneous student body." For Justice Powell, "it is not an interest in simple ethnic diversity, in which a specified percentage of the student body is in effect guaranteed to be members of selected ethnic groups," that can justify the use of race. Rather, "the diversity that furthers a compelling state interest encompasses a far broader array of qualifications and characteristics of which racial or ethnic origin is but a single though important element."

More important, for the reasons set out below, today we endorse Justice Powell's view that student body diversity is a compelling state interest that can justify the use of race in university admissions.

B

We have held that all racial classifications imposed by government "must be analyzed by a reviewing court under strict scrutiny." This means that such classifications are constitutional only if they are narrowly tailored to further compelling governmental interests. "Absent searching judicial inquiry into the justification for such race-based measures," we have no way to determine what "classifications are 'benign' or 'remedial' and what classifications are in fact motivated by illegitimate notions of racial inferiority or simple racial politics." We apply strict scrutiny to all racial classifications to "'smoke out' illegitimate uses of race by assuring that government is pursuing a goal important enough to warrant use of a highly suspect tool."

III
A

With these principles in mind, we turn to the question whether the Law School's use of race is justified by a compelling state interest. Before this Court, as they have throughout this litigation, respondents assert only one justification for their use of race in the admissions process: obtaining "the educational benefits that flow from a diverse student body." Brief for Respondents Bollinger et al. In other words, the Law School asks us to recognize, in the context of higher education, a compelling state interest in student body diversity.

It is true that some language in those opinions might be read to suggest that remedying past discrimination is the only permissible justification for race-based governmental action. But we have never held that the only governmental use of race that can survive strict scrutiny is remedying past discrimination. Nor, since *Bakke*, have we directly addressed the use of race in the context of public higher education. Today, we hold that the Law School has a compelling interest in attaining a diverse student body.

The Law School's educational judgment that such diversity is essential to its educational mission is one to which we defer. The Law School's assessment that diversity will, in fact, yield educational benefits is substantiated by respondents. Our scrutiny of the interest asserted by the Law School is no less strict for taking into account complex educational judgments in an area that lies primarily within the expertise of the university. Our holding today is in keeping with our tradition of giving a degree of deference to a university's academic decisions, within constitutionally prescribed limits.

We find that the Law School's admissions program bears the hallmarks of a narrowly tailored plan. As Justice Powell made clear in *Bakke*, truly individualized consideration demands that race be used in a flexible, nonmechanical way. It follows from this mandate that universities cannot establish quotas for members of certain racial groups or put members of those groups on separate admissions tracks. Nor can universities insulate applicants who belong to certain racial or ethnic groups from the competition for admission. Universities can, however, consider race or ethnicity more flexibly as a "plus" factor in the context of individualized consideration of each and every applicant.

We are satisfied that the Law School's admissions program does not operate as a quota. Properly understood, a "quota" is a program in which a certain fixed number or proportion of opportunities are "reserved exclusively for certain minority groups." Quotas "'impose a fixed number or percentage which must be attained, or which cannot be exceeded,'" and "insulate the individual from comparison with all other candidates for the available seats." In contrast, "a permissible goal . . . requires only a good-faith effort . . . to come within a range demarcated by the goal itself," and permits consideration of race as a "plus" factor in any given case while still ensuring that each candidate "competes with all other qualified applicants."

The Law School's current admissions program considers race as one factor among many, in an effort to assemble a student body that is diverse in ways broader than race. Because a lottery would make that kind of nuanced judgment impossible, it would effectively sacrifice all other educational values, not to mention every other kind of diversity. So too with the suggestion that the Law School simply lower admissions standards for all students, a drastic remedy that would require the Law School to become a much different Institution and sacrifice a vital component of its educational mission. The United States advocates "percentage plans," recently adopted by public undergraduate institutions in Texas, Florida, and California to guarantee admission to all students above a certain class-rank threshold in every high school in the State. The United States does not, however, explain how such plans could work for graduate and professional schools. Moreover, even assuming such plans are race-neutral, they may preclude the university from conducting the individualized assessments necessary to assemble a student body that is not just racially diverse, but diverse along all the qualities valued by the university. We are satisfied that the Law School adequately considered race-neutral alternatives currently capable of producing a critical mass without forcing the Law School to abandon the academic selectivity that is the cornerstone of its educational mission.

We acknowledge that "there are serious problems of justice connected with the idea of preference itself." Narrow tailoring, therefore, requires that a race-conscious admissions program not unduly harm members of any racial group. Even remedial race-based governmental action generally "remains subject to continuing oversight to assure that it will work the least harm possible to other innocent persons competing for the benefit." To be narrowly tailored, a race-conscious admissions program must not "unduly burden individuals who are not members of the favored racial and ethnic groups."

In summary, the Equal Protection Clause does not prohibit the Law School's narrowly tailored use of race in admissions decisions to further a compelling interest in obtaining the educational benefits that flow from a diverse student body. Consequently, petitioner's statutory claims based on Title VI also fail. The judgment of the Court of Appeals for the Sixth Circuit, accordingly, is affirmed.

Judgment for Bollinger.

Case Commentary

The U.S. Supreme Court decided that the use of race as one of the characteristics in the admissions process does not violate the Fourteenth Amendment. ■

CASE QUESTIONS

1. Are you in favor of the Court's resolution?
2. Should race be allowed to be one factor in the admissions process?

3. Should race be the deciding factor?

The issue in the case that follows is whether the awarding of points for race in the admissions process is justifiable.

Gratz v. Bollinger et al.
123 S. Ct. 2411 (2003)

Chief Justice Rehnquist delivered the opinion of the Court.

We granted certiorari in this case to decide whether the University of Michigan's use of racial preferences in undergraduate admissions violates the Equal Protection Clause of the Fourteenth Amendment, Title VI of the Civil Rights Act of 1964. Because we find that the manner in which the University considers the race of applicants in its undergraduate admissions guidelines violates these constitutional and statutory provisions, we reverse that portion of the District Court's decision upholding the guidelines.

A

Petitioners Jennifer Gratz and Patrick Hamacher both applied for admission to the University of Michigan's (University) College of Literature, Science, and the Arts (LSA) as residents of the State of Michigan. Both petitioners are Caucasian. Gratz, who applied for admission for the fall of 1995, was notified in January of that year that a final decision regarding her admission had been delayed until April. This delay was based upon the University's determination that, although Gratz was "'well qualified,'" she was "'less competitive than the students who had been admitted on first review.'" Gratz was notified in April that the LSA was unable to offer her admission. She enrolled in the University of Michigan at Dearborn, from which she graduated in the spring of 1999.

Hamacher applied for admission to the LSA for the fall of 1997. A final decision as to his application was also postponed because, though his "'academic credentials were in the qualified range, they were not at the level needed for first review admission.'" Hamacher's application was subsequently denied in April 1997, and he enrolled at Michigan State University

In October 1997, Gratz and Hamacher filed a lawsuit in the United States District Court for the Eastern District of Michigan against the University of Michigan. Petitioners' complaint was a class-action suit alleging "violations and threatened violations of the rights of the plaintiffs and the class they represent to equal protection of the laws under the Fourteenth Amendment and for racial discrimination." Petitioners sought compensatory and punitive damages for past violations, declaratory relief finding that respondents violated petitioners' "rights to nondiscriminatory treatment," an injunction prohibiting respondents from "continuing to discriminate on the basis of race in violation of the Fourteenth Amendment," and an order requiring the LSA to offer Hamacher admission as a transfer student.

Bollinger was the president of the University when Hamacher applied for admission. He was originally sued in both his individual and official capacities, but he is no longer the president of the University.

The District Court granted petitioners' motion for class certification after determining that a class action was appropriate pursuant to Federal Rule of Civil Procedure

23(b)(2). The certified class consisted of "those individuals who applied for and were not granted admission to the College of Literature, Science and the Arts of the University of Michigan for all academic years from 1995 forward and who are members of those racial or ethnic groups, including Caucasian, that defendants treated less favorably on the basis of race in considering their application for admission."

The University has changed its admissions guidelines a number of times during the period relevant to this litigation, and we summarize the most significant of these changes briefly. The University's Office of Undergraduate Admissions (OUA) oversees the LSA admissions process. In order to promote consistency in the review of the large number of applications received, the OUA uses written guidelines for each academic year. Admissions counselors make admissions decisions in accordance with these guidelines.

OUA considers a number of factors in making admissions decisions, including high school grades, standardized test scores, high school quality, curriculum strength, geography, alumni relationships, and leadership. OUA also considers race. During all periods relevant to this litigation, the University has considered African-Americans, Hispanics, and Native Americans to be "underrepresented minorities," and it is undisputed that the University admits "virtually every qualified . . . applicant" from these groups.

During 1995 and 1996, OUA counselors evaluated applications according to grade point average combined with what were referred to as the "SCUGA" factors. These factors included the quality of an applicant's high school (S), the strength of an applicant's high school curriculum (C), an applicant's unusual circumstances (U), an applicant's geographical residence (G), and an applicant's alumni relationships (A). After these scores were combined to produce an applicant's "GPA 2" score, the reviewing admissions counselors referenced a set of "Guidelines" tables, which listed GPA 2 ranges on the vertical axis, and American College Test/Scholastic Aptitude Test (ACT/SAT) scores on the horizontal axis. Each table was divided into cells that included one or more courses of action to be taken, including admit, reject, delay for additional information, or postpone for reconsideration.

In both years, applicants with the same GPA 2 score and ACT/SAT score were subject to different admissions outcomes based upon their racial or ethnic status. For example, as a Caucasian in-state applicant, Gratz's GPA 2 score and ACT score placed her within a cell calling for a postponed decision on her application. An in-state or out-of-state minority applicant with Gratz's scores would have fallen within a cell calling for admission.

In 1997, the University modified its admissions procedure. Specifically, the formula for calculating an applicant's GPA 2 score was restructured to include additional point values under the "U" category in the SCUGA factors. Under this new system, applicants could receive points for underrepresented minority status, socioeconomic disadvantage, or attendance at a high school with a predominantly underrepresented minority population, or underrepresentation in the unit to which the student was applying (for example, men who sought to pursue a career in nursing). Under the 1997 procedures, Hamacher's GPA 2 score and ACT score placed him in a cell on the in-state applicant table calling for postponement of a final admissions decision. An underrepresented minority applicant placed in the same cell would generally have been admitted.

Beginning with the 1998 academic year, the OUA dispensed with the Guidelines tables and the SCUGA point system in favor of a "selection index," on which an applicant could score a maximum of 150 points. This index was divided linearly into ranges generally calling for admissions dispositions as follows: 100–150 (admit); 95–99 (admit or postpone); 90–94 (postpone or admit); 75–89 (delay or postpone); 74 and below (delay or reject).

Each application received points based on high school grade point average, standardized test scores, academic quality of an applicant's high school, strength or weakness of high school curriculum, in-state residency, alumni relationship, personal essay, and personal achievement or leadership. Of particular significance here, under a "miscellaneous" category, an applicant was entitled to 20 points based upon his or her membership in an underrepresented racial or ethnic minority group. The University explained that the "'development of the selection index for admissions in 1998 changed only the mechanics, not the substance of how race and ethnicity were considered in admissions.'"

In all application years from 1995 to 1998, the guidelines provided that qualified applicants from underrepresented minority groups be admitted as soon as possible in light of the University's belief that such applicants were more likely to enroll if promptly notified of their admission. Also from 1995 through 1998, the University carefully managed its rolling admissions system to permit consideration of certain applications submitted later in the academic year through the use of "protected seats." Specific groups—including athletes, foreign students, ROTC candidates, and underrepresented minorities—were "protected categories" eligible for these seats. A committee called the Enrollment Working Group (EWG) projected how many applicants from each of these protected categories the University was likely to receive after a given date and then paced admissions decisions to permit full consideration of expected applications from these groups. If this space was not filled by qualified candidates from the designated groups toward the end of the admissions season, it was then used to admit qualified candidates remaining in the applicant pool, including those on the waiting list.

During 1999 and 2000, the OUA used the selection index, under which every applicant from an underrepresented racial or ethnic minority group was awarded 20 points. Starting in 1999, however, the University established an

Admissions Review Committee (ARC), to provide an additional level of consideration for some applications. Under the new system, counselors may, in their discretion, "flag" an application for the ARC to review after determining that the applicant (1) is academically prepared to succeed at the University, (2) has achieved a minimum selection index score, and (3) possesses a quality or characteristic important to the University's composition of its freshman class, such as high class rank, unique life experiences, challenges, circumstances, interests or talents, socioeconomic disadvantage, and underrepresented race, ethnicity, or geography. After reviewing "flagged" applications, the ARC determines whether to admit, defer, or deny each applicant.

B

Petitioners alternatively argue that even if the University's interest in diversity can constitute a compelling state interest, the District Court erroneously concluded that the University's use of race in its current freshman admissions policy is narrowly tailored to achieve such an interest. Respondents reply that the University's current admissions program *is* narrowly tailored and avoids the problems of the Medical School of the University of California at Davis program (U. C. Davis) rejected by Justice Powell (*Bakke*).

To withstand our strict scrutiny analysis, respondents must demonstrate that the University's use of race in its current admission program employs "narrowly tailored measures that further compelling governmental interests." Because "racial classifications are simply too pernicious to permit any but the most exact connection between justification and classification," our review of whether such requirements have been met must entail "'a most searching examination.'" We find that the University's policy, which automatically distributes 20 points, or one-fifth of the points needed to guarantee admission, to every single "underrepresented minority" applicant solely because of race, is not narrowly tailored to achieve the interest in educational diversity that respondents claim justifies their program.

In *Bakke*, Justice Powell reiterated that "preferring members of any one group for no reason other than race or ethnic origin is discrimination for its own sake." He then explained, however, that in his view it would be permissible for a university to employ an admissions program in which "race or ethnic background may be deemed a 'plus' in a particular applicant's file." He explained that such a program might allow for "the file of a particular black applicant to be examined for his potential contribution to diversity without the factor of race being decisive when compared, for example, with that of an applicant identified as an Italian-American if the latter is thought to exhibit qualities more likely to promote beneficial educational pluralism." Such a system, in Justice Powell's view, would be "flexible enough to consider all pertinent elements of diversity in light of the particular qualifications of each applicant."

Justice Powell's opinion in *Bakke* emphasized the importance of considering each particular applicant as an individual, assessing all of the qualities that individual possesses, and in turn, evaluating that individual's ability to contribute to the unique setting of higher education. The admissions program Justice Powell described, however, did not contemplate that any single characteristic automatically ensured a specific and identifiable contribution to a university's diversity. Instead, under the approach Justice Powell described, each characteristic of a particular applicant was to be considered in assessing the applicant's entire application.

The current LSA policy does not provide such individualized consideration. The LSA's policy automatically distributes 20 points to every single applicant from an "underrepresented minority" group, as defined by the University. The only consideration that accompanies this distribution of points is a factual review of an application to determine whether an individual is a member of one of these minority groups. Moreover, unlike Justice Powell's example, where the race of a "particular black applicant" could be considered without being decisive, see *Bakke*, the LSA's automatic distribution of 20 points has the effect of making "the factor of race . . . decisive" for virtually every minimally qualified underrepresented minority applicant.

Also instructive in our consideration of the LSA's system is the example provided in the description of the Harvard College Admissions Program, which Justice Powell both discussed in, and attached to, his opinion in *Bakke*. The example was included to "illustrate the kind of significance attached to race" under the Harvard College program. It provided as follows:

> "The Admissions Committee, with only a few places left to fill, might find itself forced to choose between A, the child of a successful black physician in an academic community with promise of superior academic performance, and B, a black who grew up in an inner-city ghetto of semi-literate parents whose academic achievement was lower but who had demonstrated energy and leadership as well as an apparently abiding interest in black power. If a good number of black students much like A but few like B had already been admitted, the Committee might prefer B; and vice versa. If C, a white student with extraordinary artistic talent, were also seeking one of the remaining places, his unique quality might give him an edge over both A and B. Thus, the critical criteria are often individual qualities or experience *not dependent upon race but sometimes associated with it.*"

This example further demonstrates the problematic nature of the LSA's admissions system. Even if student C's "extraordinary artistic talent" rivaled that of Monet or Picasso, the applicant would receive, at most, five points under the LSA's system. At the same time, every single underrepresented minority applicant, including students A and B, would automatically receive 20 points for submitting an application. Clearly, the LSA's system does not offer applicants the individualized selection process described in Harvard's example. Instead of considering how the differing backgrounds, experiences, and characteristics of students A, B, and C might benefit the University, admissions counselors reviewing LSA applications would simply award both A and B 20 points because their applications indicate that they are African-American, and student C would receive up to 5 points for his "extraordinary talent."

Respondents emphasize the fact that the LSA has created the possibility of an applicant's file being flagged for individualized consideration by the ARC. We think that the flagging program only emphasizes the flaws of the University's system as a whole when compared to that described by Justice Powell. Again, students A, B, and C illustrate the point. First, student A would never be flagged. This is because, as the University has conceded, the effect of automatically awarding 20 points is that virtually every qualified underrepresented minority applicant is admitted. Student A, an applicant "with promise of superior academic performance," would certainly fit this description. Thus, the result of the automatic distribution of 20 points is that the University would never consider student A's individual background, experiences, and characteristics to assess his individual "potential contribution to diversity," Instead, every applicant like student A would simply be admitted.

It is possible that students B and C would be flagged and considered as individuals. This assumes that student B was not already admitted because of the automatic 20-point

distribution, and that student C could muster at least 70 additional points. But the fact that the "review committee can look at the applications individually and ignore the points," once an application is flagged is of little comfort under our strict scrutiny analysis. The record does not reveal precisely how many applications are flagged for this individualized consideration, but it is undisputed that such consideration is the exception and not the rule in the operation of the LSA's admissions program. Additionally, this individualized review is only provided *after* admissions counselors automatically distribute the University's version of a "plus" that makes race a decisive factor for virtually every minimally qualified underrepresented minority applicant.

We conclude, therefore, that because the University's use of race in its current freshman admissions policy is not narrowly tailored to achieve respondents' asserted compelling interest in diversity, the admissions policy violates the Equal Protection Clause of the Fourteenth Amendment. We further find that the admissions policy also violates Title VI. Accordingly, we reverse that portion of the District Court's decision granting respondents summary judgment with respect to liability and remand the case for proceedings consistent with this opinion.

Case Commentary

The U.S. Supreme Court ruled that an admissions process that awards points for being a minority such that race becomes the deciding factor in the admissions process is not justifiable. ■

CASE QUESTIONS

1. Are you in accord with the Court's reasoning?
2. What is the difference in the admissions process in this case and the prior one?

3. What effect do these two cases have on affirmative action in employment?

EMPLOYEE LESSONS

1. Take advantage of the opportunities afforded by affirmative action programs if you are a woman or a minority.
2. Appreciate why these programs were instituted.
3. Be aware of current decisions that may jeopardize the future of affirmative action.
4. Understand that affirmative action programs must be remedial in their purpose.
5. Be cognizant that affirmative action plans must not adversely affect current employees.
6. Know that affirmative action plans must be discontinued once their purpose has been achieved.
7. Recognize that you must be qualified to be hired under an affirmative action plan.
8. Learn that if a quota system is employed, as in the *Bakke* case, it will result in reverse discrimination.
9. Appreciate the argument that the existence of a disparate impact against a class of people because of race or sex can only be obliterated through an affirmative action program.
10. Understand the opposing position that giving preferential treatment to people because of their race or sex is in violation of the Equal Protection Clause of the Fourteenth Amendment.

In 1977, the *Bakke* decision cast doubt over the merits of affirmative action. These doubts were quickly set aside the following year by the U.S. Supreme Court's reaffirmation of affirmative action in *Weber*. In that case, criteria were set forth to justify the implementation of affirmative action programs: remedial purpose, limited duration, qualified applicants, and no adverse consequences to current employees. Since 1996, some affirmative action plans have been falling short of these requirements. The Fifth Circuit Court in the *Hopwood* case and the Third Circuit Court in the *Taxman* case both ruled against affirmative action programs, deciding they were not remedial in purpose and that their implementation affected white people adversely. Both *Hopwood* and *Taxman* indicate that affirmative action plans will be subject to more intensive scrutiny in the future. As a result, more plans will fail to meet the requirements set forth in *Weber*. Whereas before many private employers, state and local governments, and federal agencies formulated affirmative action plans to avoid litigation, they will now have to reevaluate their plans to see if they are in strict compliance with *Weber* requirements. If the criteria have not been met, the affirmative action plan will have to be discontinued or these employers will risk litigation with the opposition, which will cite the courts' interpretation of the *Weber* requirements in the *Hopwood* and *Taxman* cases.

The U.S. Supreme Court agreed to hear the *Taxman* case; however, before they did, the case was settled for an amount greatly exceeding what Sharon Taxman originally requested. Proponents of affirmative action feared the Supreme Court might require strict scrutiny of the *Weber* criteria in all affirmative action cases. This would have been a death knell for affirmative action.

Meanwhile, California's voter-approved Proposition 209 went beyond strictly scrutinizing existing affirmative action plans to eliminating them for all state jobs, for all businesses contracting with the state, and for all state schools. Private employers were not affected. In *Grutter* and *Gratz*, it seems as if there is a return to the *Bakke* and *Weber* era. Affirmative action plans are acceptable where they are crafted in such a way to be a factor in the hiring or admissions process, but not the determining factor. Some states are considering a 10 percent rule where the top 10 percent of each high school graduating class will be guaranteed admission to the state university. Clearly, affirmative action is in a state of transition.

As proponents of human rights, Americans should be solving our own problems and teaching other nations through the good examples of promoting equality among peoples. To accomplish this, the majority does not have to give handouts to the disenfranchised. All that is required is to remove the obstacles in their path to job hiring and subsequent promotions. Let them be judged on their content rather than on their cover. Equal opportunity is the answer. The pendulum was stuck on one side. Swinging it to the other side is not the answer. Stopping it in the middle is. Giving women and minorities preference may cause a backlash and undermine the progress already made. With multinationals downsizing workforces and relocating them to foreign countries, American jobs can only be saved by ability. Successful businesses will not survive by employing minimally qualified people; they must employ the most qualified people. The players in the National Football League are qualified, but the most successful teams are the ones that have employed the most qualified players. This is the philosophy that will rule in the world of global business. Helping women and minorities to be the most qualified they can be should be the philosophy adopted. The American business that will not hire women or minorities may end up losing business to a competitor who will hire diverse candidates. Discrimination will be phased out in favor of ability. The most qualified will rule.

1. What is affirmative action?
2. When did this concept first arise?
3. How is a quota different from an affirmative action plan?
4. Why would a company voluntarily institute an affirmative action plan?
5. What is meant by equal employment opportunity?
6. Explain the affirmative action plan guidelines for the private sector.
7. Explain the concept of reverse discrimination.
8. How can the EEOC enforce its ruling against an employer who refuses to comply?
9. Are affirmative action plans ethical?
10. Once an affirmative action plan is implemented, can it remain indefinitely?

CASE PROBLEMS

1. In the instant case, the OHA's (Office of Housing Administration) affirmative action plan is designed to increase over a 5-year period and, by varying specific percentages, the numbers of women and minorities who are ALJs (Administrative Law Judges) through "reaching out to inform potential applicants about ALJ employment opportunities at OHA."

    The government's latest statistics indicate that five of every six ALJs nationwide are white males. The question presented is whether sufficient statistical facts have been introduced to show the plan has a reverse discrimination effect on white males. *Hannon v. Chater,* 887 F. Supp. 1303 (N.D. Cal. 1995)

2. Mr. Lawson served as coordinator for the security department of the Central Louisiana State Hospital (CLSH) for 6 months during the illness of the previous police chief. When applications for the vacancy were accepted, Mr. Lawson ranked first on the promotional certificate of eligibles issued by the Department of State Civil Service and third on the probational certificate.

    Mr. Lawson also notes that he was interviewed by a 5-member, all-white committee appointed by the hospital's associate administrator and that the committee was not refereed according to the hospital's affirmative action plan. It is undisputed that in the hospital's affirmative action plan, the position of DHH police chief falls within Group 4-A, specialty staff consisting of one black male, one white female, and nine white males. The group bears the label "underutilization of minority employees."

    Acknowledging that the affirmative action plan was not considered, the commission, through its referee, concluded that appellant presented no evidence that racial bias or prejudice affected the results of the selection process for police chief. The referee pointed out that appellant neither alleged nor proved that the questions asked during the interview were designed to disadvantage a minority applicant such as himself, nor that any member of the selection committee exhibited a predisposition against him either before, during, or after the interview. What was the result? *Lawson v. Dept. of Health and Hospitals,* 618 So.2d 1002 (La.App. 1 Cir. 1993)

3. Miller, who was unfamiliar with the new affirmative action plan (AAP), interviewed Stock for the open position on September 9, 1991. Miller told Stock he was impressed with Stock's qualifications and arranged for Stock to be interviewed the next day by the plant manager, Allan Brethauer ("Brethauer"). After this second interview, Miller again told plaintiff that everything "looked good," and Miller began arranging for a physical examination for Stock.

    It then came to the attention of Dennis Cassidy, the assistant plant manager, that Miller had interviewed an applicant before the position had been publicly advertised. Cassidy contacted Miller and informed him of the AAP's requirements. Miller in turn told Stock that the company needed to advertise and interview more applicants to comply with its affirmative action plan, but that Miller was still very impressed by plaintiff's qualifications.

Tyrone Anderson ("Anderson") was interviewed and subsequently hired by Universal for the maintenance vacancy. Anderson, who is black, had vocational training from a respected school and had production line equipment experience. His former employer gave him an unqualified recommendation and expressed disappointment that he was leaving. Despite his admitted prejudice against minorities, Miller was impressed by Anderson's qualifications and decided Universal should hire him. What was the result? *Stock v. Universal Foods Corp.*, 817 F.Supp. 1300 (D.Md. 1993)

4. Mr. Kelsay's statement of claim is repeated below in its entirety:

As a Limited Term Employee at MATC (Milwaukee Area Technical College), I was entitled to retain the teaching position to which I had been appointed until such time as a permanent hiring took place. Instead, at the beginning of the second semester of the 1990–91 school year MATC transferred a black male NON-APPLICANT into this position in violation of the Collective Bargaining Agreement then in effect between the teachers, union AFT (of which I am a member) and the administration of MATC. I filed a grievance and was reinstated but lost wages as a result of this incident.

Mr. Kelsay is a white male. That addendum also states that Carol Brady, a black female, was hired by MATC on August 26, 1991, to fill the permanent paralegal instructor position that Mr. Kelsay had applied for on August 1, 1990, and was qualified for, and had filled for MATC as a limited-term employee from August 1990 through May 1991. What was the result? *Kelsay v. Milwaukee Area Technical College*, 825 F. Supp. 215 (E.D. Wis. 1993)

HUMAN RESOURCE DILEMMAS

1. Starbright Computers voluntarily instituted an affirmative action policy 15 years ago. Every June, during its primary hiring season, 30 percent of its new employees must be minorities. This reflects the percentage of minorities in the surrounding community. Anthony Mazzaro, who is white, applies for a position, but he is refused. After learning of Starbright's policy, Anthony brings a lawsuit claiming violation of Title VII. Starbright says their policy is justified and argues that Anthony is not protected under Title VII because he is a white male.

2. Delicious Supermarkets currently has 34 stores in 8 states. It employs 812 workers. Recently, it adopted an affirmative action program in response to complaints from its 354 minority employees, none of whom hold a store manager or assistant store manager position. The program stipulates that at least 50 percent of the vacant assistant manager positions be offered to qualified minority candidates. Luke Simpson, who has superior qualifications in comparison to the minority candidates who were promoted, claims the program is actually a quota, which smacks of reverse discrimination. How would you advise him?

3. Rocco's Pizzeria and Restaurant employs 24 workers. Todd Jackson and Mike Holmes, both of whom are African-American, apply for work and are denied. The neighborhood in which Rocco's Pizzeria is located is now 20 percent African-American. Todd and Mike claim a disparate impact exists. The EEOC agrees and attempts to reason with Rocco to change his hiring process. Rocco refuses. How would you advise Todd and Mike to proceed?

WEB SITE ASSIGNMENT

Using the Web, explore the future of affirmative action in light of the recent Supreme Court cases cited in the chapter. Do any foreign countries have laws relating to affirmative action? If so, compare and contrast those laws with the laws in the United States.

www.feminist.org/other/ccri/aafact2.html
www.now.org/nnt/08–95/affirmhs.html
www.affirmativeaction.com
www.washingtonpost.com/wp-srv/politics/special/affirm/affirm.htm
aad.english.ucsb.edu/
www.diversityinc.com/public/register.cfm?hpage = department16.cfm
www.commerce-database.com/legal-terms/affirmative-action.htm
www.newspaperarchive.com/Search.aspx?Search = affirmative%20action
www.feminist.org/other/ccri/cahome.html

Racial Discrimination

The Long and the Short of It advertise for four new employees. Tim Jackson sees the ad and tells three of his friends, "Wouldn't it be great if we could all work together?" Tim and his friends are black. When Tom Long and Mark Short are confronted by four black men looking for employment, Tom abruptly responds that three of the positions have been filled, but they would be interested in considering one person for the fourth position. Tim is eventually selected. After gaining employment, he learns that L&S is still interviewing for the three positions that were supposed to have been filled. Tim confronts Tom and Mark about this issue. Tom and Mark put Tim off until they can consult with their attorney, Susan North. Tom explains they did not mind hiring a black person for one of four vacancies, but filling all four slots with black people would have been overwhelming. Susan asks Tom and Mark if all four black applicants were qualified. Mark responds, "Yes, but that's not the point." What advice should Susan give them?

Chapter Checklist
- ➤ *Learn the meaning of race discrimination.*
- ➤ *Understand that white people can be the victims of race discrimination.*
- ➤ *Know the importance of treating all workers equally.*
- ➤ *Appreciate the fact that an employer usually invites litigation when it treats people differently.*
- ➤ *If you are white, imagine that you are of another race before forming an opinion on race discrimination.*
- ➤ *Be aware of what constitutes racial harassment.*
- ➤ *Be able to define color discrimination.*
- ➤ *Be apprised of the parameters of the Reconstruction Era Act.*

INTRODUCTION

Racial discrimination exists where employees of one race are favored by the employer over another. Usually, it is the white race favored over the black race, but there are also many instances of Hispanics, Orientals, Asians, and American Indians being subjected to racial discrimination. There are even isolated instances of white people being victimized as well.

HUMAN RESOURCE ADVICE

- Apprise yourself of the proportion of minority groups in the area from which you hire your workers.
- Treat all workers equally.
- Do not discriminate because of race.
- Be color blind in making employment decisions.
- Judge applicants, employees, and independent contractors on their qualifications.
- Do not participate in, encourage, or condone racial harassment.
- Establish a company policy against race and color discrimination and racial harassment.
- Define each of these suspect classifications explicitly in your company policy.
- Teach employees to understand why race and color discrimination and racial harassment are hurtful to the victims as well as damaging to the company.

Employment Perspective

Mary Jones, who is black, and Martha Thomas, who is white, were both salespersons for the Fashion Boutique, a women's apparel store. In concert, they stole over $4,000 worth of merchandise. Upon discovery, Martha was terminated, but Mary was not. Fashion Boutique felt that if Mary was terminated, she might file a complaint with the EEOC, claiming discrimination because she was the only black employee. Martha filed a claim for racial discrimination. Is she correct? Yes! Although both could be terminated for the theft, by choosing one race over the other, the employer racially discriminated against Martha. The argument that Title VII does not cover white people is without merit. It applies to all races.

The issue in the following case is whether an African-American female did not receive her promotion to full professor because of race discrimination.

Bickerstaff v. Vassar College
196 F.3d 435 (2nd Cir. 1999)

McAvoy, Chief District Judge.

Plaintiff Joyce Bickerstaff appeals from a final judgment of the United States District Court for the Southern District of New York, dismissing her complaint alleging that defendant Vassar College ("Vassar") denied her request for promotion to full professor because of her race and sex, in violation of Title VII of the Civil Rights Act of 1964 ("Title VII"). The district court granted summary judgment dismissing the complaint on the ground that Vassar had presented a sufficiently supported nondiscriminatory reason for denying Bickerstaff promotion and Bickerstaff had not produced evidence that the reason advanced was pretextual. On appeal, Bickerstaff contends that summary judgment was improper because the district court overlooked and misconstrued a vast array of evidence establishing genuine issues of material fact as to whether Vassar's decision to deny her promotion to full professor was race and sex-based. Finding no basis for reversal, we affirm.

I. BACKGROUND

The facts of this case, taken in the light most favorable to Bickerstaff as the party against whom summary judgment was granted, are as follows.

Vassar is a private educational institution, chartered in 1863, and located in Poughkeepsie, New York. Dr. Bickerstaff, an African-American female, was hired by Vassar as a lecturer with a joint appointment in the Africana Studies Program and the Education Department in 1971. Her joint appointment was originally allocated two-thirds to the Department of Education and one-third to the Africana Studies Program. That allocation was later reversed. Upon earning a Ph.D. in 1975, Bickerstaff received the rank of Assistant Professor at Vassar. In 1978, Vassar promoted Bickerstaff to the rank of Associate Professor and granted her tenure.

In 1989, Bickerstaff sought promotion to full professor, which Vassar denied. Bickerstaff appealed to Vassar's Appeal Committee ("VAC"), which rejected her challenge. No litigation ensued. Between 1989 and 1994, Bickerstaff published no scholarly articles. Bickerstaff spent the entire 1990–91 and 1991–92 academic years on leave as a visiting professor at Berea College. In 1994, Bickerstaff again sought promotion to full professor, which Vassar denied. The present litigation ensued concerning the denial in 1994 only. We thus review Vassar's procedures for promotion and the events surrounding Bickerstaff's application in 1994 for full professor.

A. Vassar's Criteria and Procedures for Promotion to Full Professor

To achieve promotion to full professor, the Vassar Faculty Handbook requires a candidate to meet the following posted criteria:

Continued demonstration of sound scholarship or significant artistic activity and teaching of a high quality will be required. It is necessary that marked distinction will have been reached in scholarship or teaching, preferably in both.

An additional important consideration will be academic leadership, which may be evidenced by participation in professional activities outside the College, service on committees within the College, or contributions to educational innovation or policy making at both the departmental and college levels. Vassar's procedures for promotion are established in its bylaws and are set forth in the Faculty Handbook. For a candidate such as Bickerstaff with a joint appointment, the review is a diffusive process that involves several steps and multiple recommenders. First, "two members of rank higher than that of the member under consideration each from the home department (e.g., the chair and one other) and from the multidisciplinary program . . . meet to evaluate the professional qualifications of the candidate." Second, members of the program and the department confer and "make a written report of their deliberations," which is transmitted to the program, the department, the college-wide Faculty Appointments and Salary Committee ("FASC"), the Dean of the Faculty, and the President. Third, "the program and the department . . . take this report into consideration in making their own separate recommendations to FASC, the Dean and the President." Fourth, FASC and the Dean, upon consideration of the departmental and program recommendations, the teaching evaluation of the Student Advisory Committee ("SAC"), the committee reports of the department and the program, and the reports of the outside evaluators, make separate recommendations to the President. Lastly, the President submits her final recommendation to the Board of Trustees. In instances "when the department or the program has fewer than two members of rank higher then that of the person under consideration, an ad hoc committee is formed in each case." These procedures "are designed to accommodate recommendations from both the department and program." An appeal is available to VAC, comprised exclusively of members of the Vassar faculty.

B. Bickerstaff's Review for Promotion to Full Professor in 1994–1995

At issue is Bickerstaff's review for promotion to full professor over the 1994–95 academic year. On November 14, 1994, SAC, which is charged with reviewing student Course Evaluation Questionnaires ("CEQs") and issuing its analysis and recommendation on promotional applications, issued a 5–0 (with one abstention) recommendation against promotion for Bickerstaff. SAC stated that it was alarmed by Bickerstaff's recently "remarkably low" CEQs and that "the only identified trend is a steady decline in evaluations."

On November 28, 1994, a group consisting of the ad hoc Education Committee ("Education Committee") and the ad hoc Africana Studies Committee ("AS Committee") met to discuss Bickerstaff's qualifications for promotion. On December 2, 1994, the three-member AS Committee unanimously recommended Bickerstaff for promotion to full professor. In terms of Bickerstaff's classroom teaching, however, the AS Committee did find "problems" as reflected in her CEQs. Thus, it urged her to "refocus and reinvigorate her efforts in the classroom." In the end, the AS Committee concluded that Bickerstaff had made "distinctive contributions to scholarship" and that she had "a constant and consistent educational vision through all of her work as educator, scholar, and consultant."

In unanimously recommending against promotion, the Education Committee concluded that Bickerstaff's scholarly activities, while "creditable," did not exhibit "marked distinction" and that her teaching fell short of "marked distinction by a rather wide margin."

On December 7, 1994, the three-member FASC issued its report unanimously recommending against Bickerstaff for promotion, stating that the members found that "she did not meet the stated criteria for promotion." Dean Kalin recommended against promotion for Bickerstaff because she did not meet the posted criteria of marked distinction in teaching. In his affidavit, he states that "her teaching evaluations are among the poorest he has seen in a promotional review for full professor."

On February 8, 1995, the President of Vassar wrote to Bickerstaff and informed her that she would not be recommending her for promotion to the rank of full professor. Vassar "requires the achievement of 'marked distinction' in at least teaching or scholarship, a standard which has not yet been met." The President concluded that "while service is certainly important, it cannot alone compensate for limitations in both these areas."

In the academic year 1994–95, Vassar considered eight applications for promotion to full professor. Of the six successful candidates, five were women. At present, Bickerstaff continues to teach at Vassar as a tenured associate professor.

C. The Present Action

Following the denial of her request in 1994 for promotion to full professor, Bickerstaff filed charges of race and sex-based discrimination with the Equal Employment Opportunity Commission.

After receiving a right-to-sue letter, on November 29, 1996, Bickerstaff timely filed a complaint against Vassar in the United States District Court for the Southern District of New York. The complaint claimed that she was denied promotion to full professor in 1994 because of her race and sex, in violation of Title VII of the Civil Rights Act of 1964. It also alleged that Vassar denied her promotion in 1994 in retaliation for her internal appeal of the denial of her promotion to full professor; and that Vassar paid her less than male professors of comparable rank, in violation of the Equal Pay Act. The complaint sought monetary damages and an order granting her the rank of full professor at Vassar.

After discovery, Vassar moved for summary judgment on all of Bickerstaff's claims. On January 26, 1998, the district court granted Vassar's motion for summary judgment and dismissed the complaint in its entirety.

II. DISCUSSION

A violation of Title VII can be shown by either direct, statistical or circumstantial evidence. Title VII suits fall into two basic categories: "single issue motivation" and "dual issue motivation" cases. In single issue motivation cases, "the single issue is whether an impermissible reason motivated the adverse action," which courts analyze under the framework first set forth in *McDonnell Douglas Corp. v. Green*. In dual issue motivation cases, the determination involves "both the issue of whether the plaintiff has proved that an impermissible reason motivated the adverse action and the additional issue of whether the defendant has proved that it would have taken the same action for a permissible reason."

As a single issue motivation case, we apply the three-step, burden-shifting paradigm set forth in *McDonnell Douglas*. Applying the paradigm to the present case, we too shall assume in Bickerstaff's favor a prima facie case of sex and race discrimination. Vassar, in turn, has satisfied its burden of production by proffering admissible evidence of a legitimate, nondiscriminatory reason for denying Bickerstaff promotion to full professor—namely, that she did not meet the posted criteria. Thus, the central question presented on this appeal is whether Bickerstaff has presented sufficient admissible evidence from which a rational finder of fact could infer that more likely than not she was the victim of intentional discrimination. We now turn to consider whether Bickerstaff's evidence is sufficient to create an issue of material fact as to whether she was the victim of discrimination.

Shamba Donovan

She thus asserts that the unfavorable SAC Report, which formed part of the materials reviewed by Vassar's decision makers in evaluating her teaching, was impermissibly tainted with race bias. We recognize that the impermissible bias of a single individual at any stage of the promoting process may taint the ultimate employment decision in violation of Title VII. We find that there is insufficient evidence to raise a reasonable inference that such occurred in this case.

Alleged Incidences of Disparate Treatment

Bickerstaff has not shown that the creation of two ad hoc committees in her case was a procedural irregularity or, more importantly, that it was either race-related or motivated by retaliation.

Bickerstaff has not presented evidence that an illegal discriminatory motive played a motivating role in Vassar's decision to deny her promotion. Instead, the evidence overwhelmingly supports Vassar's explanation that it denied Bickerstaff promotion for the legitimate, nondiscriminatory reason that she did not satisfy the posted criteria for promotion.

In the final analysis, in response to the evidence that Vassar denied Bickerstaff promotion to full professor because she did not satisfy the criteria for promotion, Bickerstaff does not present sufficient rebuttal evidence from which a rational finder of fact could infer that more likely than not Vassar intentionally discriminated against Bickerstaff because of her race or sex. The district court thus properly granted summary judgment to Vassar College and dismissed Bickerstaff's Title VII and section 1981 claims. Bickerstaff's Equal Pay Act claim, which relies on the statistical evidence that we have already discussed and found that the district court properly discounted, was also properly dismissed.

CONCLUSION

We have considered all of Bickerstaff's arguments on appeal and have found them to be without merit. The judgment of the district court dismissing the complaint is affirmed.

CASE QUESTIONS

1. Was Bickerstaff entitled to the full professorship?
2. What do you think about the differences in the student evaluations in the African Studies classes and the Education classes?

Case Commentary

The Second Circuit Court of Appeals concluded that Professor Bickerstaff did not meet Vassar's job-related requirements for promotion to full professor because student evaluations of her teaching were not of the high caliber required of a full professor. Furthermore, the court held that the alleged racial prejudice of one student on the Student Advisory Committee was not proven. Finally, the statistical evidence introduced by Bickerstaff was not probative of whether Vassar had discriminated against Bickerstaff and denied her equal pay. ∎

3. Was there evidence of race discrimination?
4. Did a violation of the Equal Pay Act exist?

Employment Perspective

Fisher Oil Drilling Equipment prides itself on being an equal opportunity employer because it has numerous employees of all races. However, the minority employees are all factory workers. Each time a minority worker applies for a managerial position, he or she is rejected. Fisher feels that it is better that the minorities work among their own kind. Is this racial discrimination? Yes! Fisher Oil is prejudicing the ability and competence of its minority workers on the basis of the color of their skin or of their origin. Fisher Oil may know that its white managers may feel uncomfortable with minorities working with them rather than underneath them, but this privilege of racial dominance can no longer be sustained. Everyone must be given an equal opportunity.

Employment Perspective

Marshall Jackson, who is black, has been a sales representative for Tucker Machinery Corp. for 20 years. His district has a predominantly black population. He has applied for promotion to sales manager. Although his credentials are superior to those of the other candidates, Jackson is overlooked because management feels that he will not command the respect of the sales force, which is overwhelmingly white. Is this employment discrimination? Yes! Tucker Machinery has violated Title VII because the sole reason that Jackson was not selected was because he was black. Jackson would be entitled to the promotion, together with the pay differential from the date when he should have been selected.

In the case that follows, a black male claimed he was discharged from his position as a disc jockey because of his race. He satisfied his initial burden under the *McDonnell Douglas* test. The employer, in turn, met its burden of justifiable action. The question presented is whether the employer's reason for discharge was a pretext.

Thompson v. Price Broadcasting Co.
817 F. Supp. 1538 (D. Utah 1993)

Anderson, District Judge.

Wayne Thompson (hereafter "Thompson") brought this race discrimination action against his former employer, Price Broadcasting Company KCPX (hereafter referred to as "Price" or "KCPX"), for allegedly discharging him in violation of Title VII of the 1964 Civil Rights Act.

Thompson is a 36-year-old African male who has worked since 1980 in the broadcasting industry. During that time Thompson has worked in radio production, and has acted as a radio personality ("Jockey"). As a Disk Jockey, Thompson is aware that listeners develop listening habits and loyalty to radio stations because of the particular personalities involved. Thus, radio stations require their Disk Jockeys to make every effort possible to be at work in sufficient time to go "on the air" for assigned time slots.

On October 14, 1988, Thompson was hired by Price to work part time as a KCPX Jockey for the Sunday afternoon time slot 2:00 P.M. to 9:00 P.M. Prior to working for Price, Thompson worked as a Disk Jockey for Radio Station KDAB in Ogden, Utah, where Thompson resided. KCPX is located in Salt Lake City, Utah, and Thompson agreed to provide his own transportation to and from work on Sundays.

Shortly after going to work for Price, Thompson brought a Title VII lawsuit against his former employer KDAB for allegedly firing him because of his race. This lawsuit was publicized in the local newspapers, and a copy of an article relating to the suit was cut out by an unknown employee of Price, and placed on the desk of supervisor David Leppink, whose radio name is Morgan Evans (hereafter "Evans"). Evans acknowledged seeing the article, but testified that it played no part in his decision making with regard to Thompson.

A few days after the local newspapers publicized Thompson's suit against KDAB, a snow storm hit the northern parts of Utah. By 4:00 P.M., Mountain Standard Time, on Saturday, November 26, 1988, driving conditions in the Ogden area became hazardous as a result of snowy and icy roads. Thompson, being concerned about the driving conditions, telephoned Evans' home at 4:43 P.M. to inform Evans that he would not be coming into KCPX the next day for his radio slot. Evans was not home, and Thompson left a message on Evans' answering machine.

When Evans returned home at approximately 4:50 P.M. he listened to the telephone message from Thompson and telephoned Thompson's house. Mrs. Thompson answered the telephone, and informed Evans that her husband was not at home, and was at Lionel Playworld in Ogden where he had a second job. Evans informed Mrs. Thompson that roads in Salt Lake City were not too bad, and that he expected Thompson to be at work at 2:00 P.M. the next day. Evans further informed

Mrs. Thompson that she should contact her husband to tell him that he was expected to report to work, and that if there was a problem Thompson should call Evans to talk about it.

Mrs. Thompson did as she was instructed and telephoned Evans' home thirty minutes later with her husband's reply. Evans had gone out, however, and Mrs. Thompson had to leave another message on Evans answering machine. She stated that her husband still felt the same way, and that he would not be coming into work the next day. Five hours later, when Evans returned home and listened to his messages, Evans telephoned Mrs. Thompson to get Thompson's telephone number at Lionel Playworld.

When Evans spoke with Thompson at Lionel Playworld, he asked Thompson what the problem was. Thompson responded that KCPX did not pay him enough to risk his life driving down to Salt Lake City to do a shift. Evans responded that he needed someone he could count on every Sunday, regardless of the weather. When Thompson stated he would not be coming down to Salt Lake City the next day for the 2:00 P.M. shift, Evans fired him.

Following his firing by KCPX, Thompson brought race discrimination claims against Price before the Anti-Discrimination Division of the Industrial Commission of Utah ("ICU") and the Equal Opportunity Commission of the United States ("EEOC"). The ICU and EEOC found no basis for Thompson's discrimination charges.

There are two theories of employment discrimination under Title VII: disparate treatment and disparate impact. The disparate treatment theory focuses on the employer's intent to discriminate. Disparate impact, on the other hand, requires no proof of discriminatory intent. Rather, a plaintiff need only show that the employer's practices are "discriminatory in operation."

At trial, Thompson only sought relief for disparate treatment under Title VII, specifically, discriminatory discharge and retaliatory discharge. Consequently, Thompson needed to show discriminatory intent on the part of Price. Thompson failed to do so.

Title VII of the 1964 Civil Rights Act makes it unlawful for an employer to discharge any individual, or to otherwise discriminate against any individual . . . because of such individual's race.

To establish a prima facie case for discrimination under Title VII, the plaintiff must show that: (1) he belongs to a protected group; (2) he was qualified for his job; (3) he was terminated despite his qualifications; and (4) after his termination, the employer hired someone or sought applicants for the plaintiff's vacated position, whose qualifications were no better than the Plaintiff's.

The court is persuaded that Thompson met the burden of establishing a prima facie case of discriminatory discharge. In that regard, Thompson, an African-American, is a member of a protected class. Further, Price did not dispute that Thompson was qualified for the Disk Jockey job. Price conceded that Thompson has been involved in the radio broadcast industry for a number of years, and had performed his job at KCPX for six weeks without complaint from management as to his performance. Despite being qualified for the job, Thompson was discharged. Finally, while there was a dispute between the parties as to who took over Thompson's radio time slot, there is no question that someone handled the air time.

The Court is also persuaded that Thompson met his burden to establish a prima facie cause of action for retaliatory discharge under Title VII of the 1964 Civil Rights Act. The Act provides:

It shall be unlawful . . . for an employer to discriminate against any of his employees . . . because the employee has made a charge, testified, assisted, or participated in any manner in an investigation, proceeding, or hearing under this subchapter.

The Tenth Circuit Court of Appeals has held that in order for a plaintiff to establish a prima facie cause of action for retaliation, the plaintiff must show by a preponderance of the evidence that: (1) Plaintiff engaged in protected opposition to discrimination or participation in a proceeding arising out of discrimination; (2) adverse action by the employer subsequent to the protected activity; and (3) a causal connection between the employee's activity and the adverse action.

Thompson established that he was engaged in a protected activity at the time of his discharge from KCPX. In that regard, although there exists no business relationship between KDAB, the station against whom Thompson brought his discrimination suit and KCPX, the law does not require such a relationship. If a relationship between employers was required, claimants would be discouraged from filing discrimination claims against former employers because of the fear that their present employers, upon learning of the claims, would fire them. The purposes of Title VII would, therefore, be frustrated.

Thompson also established the second requirement of a retaliation claim, by showing that subsequent to his filing of a suit against KDAB, he was fired by Price. Termination of employment clearly constitutes an "adverse action by the employer subsequent to the protected activity."

Finally, Thompson established, as a result of the timing of his discharge by KCPX and the filing of the claim against KDAB, that a causal connection existed between the protected activity and the adverse action, at least for purposes of proving a prima facie case.

A "causal connection may be demonstrated by the proximity of the adverse action to the protected activity, provided, the employer . . . had knowledge of the plaintiff's protected activity."

Having found a prima facie case for Thompson's discriminatory discharge claim and retaliatory discharge claim, the burden of production shifts to Price to show "a legitimate non-discriminatory reason for terminating the employee."

In meeting its burden, Price need not prove that it was actually motivated by its non-discriminatory reason.

As noted by the United States Supreme Court:

"The burden that shifts to the defendant, therefore, is to rebut the presumption of discrimination by producing evidence that the plaintiff was rejected . . . for a legitimate, nondiscriminatory reason. The defendant need not persuade the court that it was actually motivated by the proffered reasons. . . . It is sufficient if the defendant's evidence raises a genuine issue of fact as to whether it discriminated against the plaintiff. To accomplish this, the defendant must clearly set forth, through the introduction of admissible evidence the reasons for the plaintiff's rejection. The explanation must be legally sufficient to justify a judgment for the defendant.

The question of Price's actual motivation is only addressed after Price shows a legitimate nondiscriminatory reason for termination, and the burden of proof shifts back to Thompson under *McDonnell Douglas*.

At trial, Price presented credible evidence that on the day before Thompson was to report to work, Thompson telephoned his superior at KCPX, Morgan Evans, to inform Evans that he was not going to come to work because of adverse weather conditions. Evans informed Thompson that the weather was not that bad, and that he expected him to report to work. When Thompson continued to refuse to come to work, he was fired.

A refusal to work is a legitimate nondiscriminatory reason for terminating an employee. In *E.E.O.C. v. Wendy's of Colorado Springs, Inc.*, the reason for terminating the employee that Defendant articulated was that he "refused to work necessary time periods necessary to meet store needs." Refusal to work the time periods necessary to meet the demands of business demonstrates a lack of qualification for the job. Lack of qualifications is a legitimate, nondiscriminatory reason for terminating an employee.

In the radio broadcast industry, management is constantly concerned with the concept of "listener expectation." That concept is that listeners have expectations that when they tune to a certain radio station at a certain time, a particular music or news format will be in the process of being presented, and that a certain disk jockey will be on the air. By consistently fulfilling the listener's expectations, the radio station keeps the listener's loyalty, and can ask advertisers to pay for the privilege of broadcasting their messages to the listener. For this reason, broadcast employers legitimately expect their Disk Jockeys to make every effort possible to be on the air when scheduled. Thompson was unable to satisfy Price that he would make that effort. The Court determines, therefore, that Price had a legitimate reason to terminate Thompson.

Price did not discuss the KDAB suit with Thompson and did not look for an excuse to fire Thompson after finding out about the lawsuit. On the contrary, the evidence shows that when Evans was first informed by Thompson that Thompson was not coming in to work the next day, Evans did not fire Thompson but, rather, gave Thompson an opportunity to say that he would be coming into work. The Court is convinced that if Thompson had simply informed Evans on November 26, 1988, that he would be at the radio station for his assigned time slot on Sunday, Thompson would not have been fired. Even if Evans "had in mind" the KDAB lawsuit at the time that he fired Thompson, and there is no direct evidence that he did, Thompson's Title VII claim would still fail.

As noted by the Tenth Circuit Court of Appeals:

Once a plaintiff in a Title VII case shows that an illegitimate reason played a motivating part in an employment decision, the defendant may avoid a finding of liability only by proving that it would have made the same decision even if it had not allowed the improper motive to play such a role.

The Court finds that Price would have discharged Thompson on November 21, 1988, even if no lawsuit had been filed by Thompson against his former employer, KDAB. Price needed Disk Jockeys that it could count on to make every reasonable effort possible to make their assigned shifts regardless of the weather. Thompson was not willing to make that effort.

While Thompson established a prima facie case under Title VII on both his retaliatory discharge and discriminatory discharge claims, he was unable to show by a preponderance of the evidence that Price's legitimate nondiscriminatory reason for discharge was a pretext. No violation of Title VII was shown and judgment will be entered for the defendant.

Judgment for Price Broadcasting.

Case Commentary

The District Court of Utah determined that Thompson's discharge for not arriving at work due to a snowstorm was not evidence of discrimination due to race. ■

CASE QUESTIONS

1. Do you agree with the Court's decision?

2. Was the snowstorm a legitimate excuse?

RACIAL HARASSMENT

Racial harassment in the workplace exists when conduct by coworkers, superiors, or the company itself has created a hostile work environment in which the victimized employee's ability to do his or her job has been impaired. Evidence of the severity of the incidents is equally as important as the frequency.

When an employee claims that he or she is being racially harassed by a coworker, the employee must notify the employer. The employer must not condone this activity and must investigate the complaint in a timely fashion. If the employer finds a reasonable basis for believing that the harassment exists, it must take corrective action immediately or otherwise it will be held liable. When the harassment originates with the employer itself, then no notification is needed. The employer will be held liable.

Employment Scenario

One day, Greg, Sam, and Bill, all white employees, were exchanging racial jokes during their break. Mark Short, while passing by, stopped to listen, then joined in, telling a few racial jokes of his own. Tim Jackson, a black employee, overheard the laughter and listened in. He became visibly upset and approached Mark with his concerns. Mark put his arm around Tim's shoulder and dismissed the jokes as harmless fun. Mark told Tim to ignore the jokes and to take a walk around the block. These episodes continued to occur, and Tom and Mark continued to ignore Tim's complaints of a hostile work environment. Tim filed a racial harassment complaint with the EEOC. When they learned that the EEOC intended to investigate Tim's allegations, Tom and Mark sought Susan North's counsel. Susan responded that their cavalier attitude toward employment law had once again embroiled them in a conflict unrelated to the business of selling clothing. Susan recommended a full apology to Tim by those concerned; an educational seminar for all employees on race discrimination and harassment, which she would facilitate; and a company policy, which she would draft, defining discrimination and harassment affecting race and its prohibition during the scope of employment. Susan said she hoped this would appease Tim and the EEOC, and serve as a strong lesson to Tom, Mark, and the participating employees that racial harassment would not be tolerated and that the consequences for any reoccurrence would be severe. Susan believed these steps would serve as an impetus for modifying the behavior of the participants.

Employment Perspective

Todd Washington was hired as a management trainee in Bulls and Bears Brokerage House. He was the first black person in a managerial position in the Jackson, Mississippi, office. Toward the end of the first week, he found his desk covered by a white sheet with a burnt cross lying across it. Washington complained to his superiors, who told him that the boys just have a warped sense of humor. Similar incidents followed. Does this constitute racial harassment? Yes! Todd Washington was harassed by his coworkers. He made a timely complaint to his employer, which made no attempt to investigate and took no corrective action. For its failure to act, Bulls and Bears is liable.

The issue in the case that follows is whether the Pacific Maritime Association can be held liable for the racially harassing acts of employees of the companies it represents.

Anderson v. Pacific Maritime Association
336 F.3d 924 (9th Cir. 2003)

Tallman, Circuit Judge.

This case presents a cause of action in search of a defendant. The Plaintiffs, a group of longshoremen working on the docks in Seattle and Tacoma, allege that they were subject to a racially hostile work environment in violation of Title VII of the Civil Rights Act of 1964 as well Washington's Law Against Discrimination. But the sole defendant left before us on appeal, Pacific Maritime Association ("PMA"), is not the employer of any of the Plaintiffs. Rather, PMA is a non-profit association of the stevedoring and shipping companies that do employ the Plaintiffs. The district court granted summary judgment to PMA, holding that PMA could not be liable for discrimination because PMA was not the Plaintiffs' employer. We agree and affirm.

The Plaintiffs are all African-American. They allege that they were subjected to a racially hostile work environment while employed on the waterfront in Seattle and Tacoma. For purposes of reviewing a summary judgment order, we assume these facts could be established in favor of the Plaintiffs. Their allegations paint a horrific and pervasive picture of racial animosity and discrimination on the waterfront of the Pacific Northwest.

For instance, the Plaintiffs allege that they have been referred to as "n***er," "sp**k," "n***er gang," "boy," and "son," as well as other racial slurs. They assert that racial innuendos and jokes are common on the docks. Furthermore, they allege that longshoremen training materials employ terms such as "n***er lips" and "n***er heads." The Plaintiffs allege that they were even subject to direct, racially charged physical threats.

The members of PMA ("member-employers") are the various companies that employ the longshoremen. The Board of Directors of PMA is primarily composed of executives from these stevedoring companies. The member-employers grant PMA the authority to establish and negotiate labor contracts and policies with the International Longshoremen's and Warehousemen's Union ("Union").

PMA, as the bargaining agent for the member-employers, entered into a Collective Bargaining Agreement ("CBA") with the Union, as bargaining agent for its local affiliates. Under the CBA, the member-employers and their walking bosses and foremen—but not PMA—have the responsibility to "supervise, place or discharge men and to direct the work and activities of longshoremen on the job in a safe, efficient and proper manner." The member-employers—but not PMA—also retain the right to discipline any longshoreman for "in-competence, insubordination or failure to perform the work as required in conformance with the provisions of [the CBA]." The CBA lays out an extensive system for maintaining discipline, safety, and conformity with the master labor agreement on the docks, but these provisions place the burden of meeting these standards on the longshoremen, the Union, and the member-employers and their supervisors—not PMA.

Specifically, the CBA prohibits illegal discrimination, and provides a detailed procedure for reporting and curing alleged discrimination. Under this procedure, all grievances regarding discrimination must first be referred to a longshoreman's supervisor. If the supervisor cannot settle the grievance, it is referred to one official designated by the Union and one official designated by the member-employers. If the grievance still is not settled, it is referred to a Joint Committee made up of six members. Three members of the Joint Committee are appointed by the Union and three are appointed by the member-employers. If the Joint Committee fails to resolve the dispute, the CBA provides for binding arbitration.

Although PMA has the general responsibility for ensuring that member-employers comply with the terms of the CBA, PMA has no direct role in this formal procedure for resolving discrimination complaints. Under the CBA, PMA is not responsible for handling, collecting, or investigating grievances, let alone mediating or resolving the grievances. Those tasks, under the plain terms of the CBA, are left to managers employed by the member-employers and the Joint Committee appointed by the member-employers and the Union.

In 1997, the Union and PMA agreed to an expedited grievance procedure to address both discrimination and the problems associated with the length of time needed to complete the formal procedure. This expedited procedure is a supplement to, and not a replacement of, the formal grievance procedure described in the CBA. Under this new expedited procedure, a longshoreman alleging racial or sexual discrimination is required to fill out a form—copies of which are posted around the work site—describing the discrimination. The longshoreman is then required to send a copy of the form to the area manager of PMA and to the president of the local chapter of the Union. Both the PMA area manager and the local-chapter president then have the discretion to call for a meeting or series of meetings in order to mediate the dispute. If this is unsuccessful, the worker can then require that the parties enter into arbitration.

PMA also performs a variety of other organizational tasks for its member companies. Together with the Union, it operates a dispatch hall where longshoremen receive their work assignments from the member-employers. It also provides a payroll service for its member-employers. PMA keeps track of where everyone works each day, but the member-employers actually pay the longshoremen.

Equally important to our analysis is what PMA does not control. It does not supervise the longshoremen. It has no power to hire or fire longshoremen. It has no power to discipline longshoremen. It does not supervise the work sites of its member-employers. It is undisputed that the monitoring and control over those sites, as well as the control of the employees, is within the *sole* province of the member-employers.

Below, the Plaintiffs hinged the viability of their hostile work environment claim against PMA on the applicability of the "integrated enterprise" test. We apply this four-part test to determine if two or more employers are so interrelated that they form an integrated enterprise.

The Plaintiffs argued that PMA is an integrated enterprise with its member-employers and therefore liable for the hostile work environment at the member-employers work sites. The district court, noting the likely inapplicability of the test to this case, nevertheless found that PMA is not an integrated enterprise with its member-employers.

PMA's status as an employer in its own right does not mean that a claim by the Plaintiffs, who were not PMA's employees, is cognizable under Title VII.

When we apply the principles articulated in these precedents to the case before us, it is clear that PMA cannot be liable to the Plaintiffs under Title VII. Here, on the other hand, the hostile work environment did not occur at any facility controlled by PMA, but instead at the docks and waterfront facilities controlled by the member-employers that actually employ and supervise the Plaintiffs and their putative harassers on the job site.

The Plaintiffs may have been the victims of severe racial discrimination and rightly sought to redress their wrongs in federal court. Their employers and the Union were the obvious defendants and were initially named in the Plaintiffs' complaint. The Plaintiffs' decision to drop the employers and the Union as defendants from this case is a mystery to us. All that remains, a cause of action alleging a hostile work environment against PMA, is not cognizable against this defendant under Title VII. PMA was not the one illegally discriminating; PMA did not exercise control over the waterfront work environment the Plaintiffs claim was hostile; and PMA's purported failure to remedy the situation on the docks did not amount to interference with the Plaintiffs' *employment* relationship with the stevedoring and shipping companies. The district court properly granted summary judgment in favor of PMA.

Case Commentary

The Ninth Circuit Court held that a trade association cannot be held liable for the racial harassment perpetrated by employees of companies that it represents even though the executives of those companies sit on its board. ∎

CASE QUESTIONS

1. Do you agree with the Court's decision?
2. Why did the plaintiffs drop their case against their employer and the union?
3. Why would the plaintiffs want to sue the association?
4. Does the fact that the executives of the companies in question sit on the board of the association affect your judgment?

The issue in the following case is whether the racial statements made were severe and pervasive enough to warrant a finding of racial harassment.

Marvelli v. CHAPS Community Health Center
193 F. Supp. 2d 636 (E.D. NY 2002)

Gershon, District Judge.

Plaintiffs Catherine Marvelli, Denise Mattox, Lillian Morales, Seon Mickle, and Tanisha Gardner bring this action against defendants CHAPS Community Health Center, Staten Island University Hospital ("SIUH"), Municipal Training Center ("MTC"), Duncan Huie, and Mark Appel alleging racial harassment.

1. MATTOX AND MARVELLI'S EMPLOYMENT HISTORY:

Mark Appel founded CHAPS in January 1998 as an outpatient healthcare facility, and managed the company for a year. Originally, there were four employees. There were two doctors, Dr. Denise Mattox and Dr. Cheryl Brown-Murray, as well as an Administrator, Karen Bronstein, and a Receptionist, Donna Samuels. In June 1998, Bronstein resigned and Appel hired Duncan Huie as CHAPS' Administrator. Huie began working in July 1998, and Catherine Marvelli began work as an intern shortly thereafter.

In late 1998, Appel negotiated with SIUH for SIUH to acquire corporate sponsorship over CHAPS for $2.5 million. Pursuant to the transfer of sponsorship between CHAPS and SIUH dated December 28, 1998, SIUH became the sole member/sponsor of CHAPS, effective January 1, 1999. It is undisputed that at all times CHAPS and SIUH were two "separate entities." They had separate operations, payrolls, employee handbooks, employment practices and procedures, offices, locations, and bank accounts. After the transfer of sponsorship, Appel was no longer affiliated with either CHAPS or SIUH in any manner.

Based on its deficits and lack of patients, Walsh made the decision to restructure CHAPS and terminate Brown-Murray, Mattox, and Marvelli. In March 1999, CHAPS contracted with the University Physicians Group ("UPG"), which is affiliated with SIUH, to run CHAPS.

It is undisputed that neither Huie nor Appel were involved in any manner with Walsh's decision to contract with UPG and terminate Mattox and Marvelli. Walsh terminated Brown-Murray, Mattox, Marvelli at a meeting on March 16, 1999.

2. HUIE'S ALLEGED HARASSMENT OF MATTOX AND MARVELLI

Marvelli, who is part African American, claims that Huie often made racist and sexist jokes about her having large buttocks. Huie would draw pictures of Marvelli's buttocks. Marvelli never showed this picture to Appel. He also said "'you are big in the back like a black chick. You have a black butt.'" Huie made other racist comments. On one occasion, when rap music was playing in the office where Marvelli was working, and rock music was playing in the office where Huie was working, Huie said to Marvelli that she "would appreciate the rock music because I have white blood in me and don't need the n***er rap music." At another point, Huie told Marvelli that she looked like a "rasta" when she had braids in her hair.

Marvelli claims that Huie also made racist and sexist comments about other people. Huie "constantly" referred to Morales, who is Puerto Rican, as a "wetback." She claims Huie called Morales "stupid, illiterate, a worthless Mexican and dozens of similar comments. Again, this was on a daily basis." He also made comments about Gardner's dark skin and made sexually derogatory comments about her. The student interns also testified that Huie made these comments.

Mattox claims that Huie showed her pictures of male private parts on his computer screen, and sent her a picture of a women with dogs painted on her bare breasts. He would also tell Mattox about the strippers he was dating. Mattox testified that she also thought Huie was being racist and sexist when he called her "shortie." Mattox also claims that Huie "often" told jokes about Jewish people. The specific joke that Mattox remembers is "what happens to a Jewish man with a h**d-on when he runs into a wall? He breaks his nose." He also referred to Brown-Murray, who is African American, as an ape and drew a picture of her as a monkey. Finally, Mattox claims that he would "do parodies of black people, you know, like shuck-and-jive talk." For example, Huie would say "hey, Hommey, I'm down with it." Gardner claims that she heard Huie call Brown-Murray a gorilla.

Huie denies all the allegations of Mattox and Marvelli. There is no evidence that Mattox ever complained to Appel about Huie.

Marvelli claims that after SIUH acquired CHAPS on January 1, 1999, no one supervised Huie. Marvelli claims that no one from SIUH ever introduced themselves and they did not know who to talk to about Huie. After SIUH acquired CHAPS, Marvelli claims that Huie complained to her that he had bought his girlfriend an expensive Christmas present, and he had not received "p***y" in return. After complaining about his sex life, Huie told Marvelli that Huie was going to rape his girlfriend. Marvelli claims that she became frightened and vomited because she had been raped. Marvelli claims that that evening she called Appel and told him she worried that Huie might be a rapist. Marvelli claims that Appel responded with a joke, saying that he had Huie "pegged more as a child molester than a rapist." When Marvelli said she was serious, she claims Appel apologized for leaving Huie at the clinic, but that he was working with SIUH to get him terminated. According to Marvelli, no action was ever taken.

The entire staff of CHAPS confronted Huie about his behavior. Huie broke down in tears and acknowledged that he behaved inappropriately. He stated he was having a breakdown because of the stress he was under.

The following day, which was a Friday, Huie showed up to work drunk and began arguing with Brown-Murray. Brown-Murray and Marvelli faxed SIUH requesting an immediate meeting. That following Monday, Mattox went to SIUH to try and speak with Joe Pasani, an officer of SIUH who had helped to acquire CHAPS, but Pasani refused to see her. The next day, February 16, 1999, the five plaintiffs and Brown-Murray went to SIUH corporate offices without a meeting to complain about Huie's behavior. They met with Gerald Ferlisi, Vice President of Finance, and Caryl Mahoney, Senior Vice President of Human Resources. This was the first time any of the plaintiffs complained to SIUH.

The next day, February 17, 1999, Ferlisi and Mahoney met Huie to discuss the allegations. At that meeting, it was decided that Huie would resign as administrator of CHAPS.

3. APPEL'S ALLEGED HARASSMENT OF MATTOX

Mattox, who is African American, also claims that Appel suggested that he was interested in a sexual relationship because he "made it very clear" that he had a "preference for Black women" by bringing his girlfriends, who Mattox claims were always young black women, to the clinic and commenting that they slept at his apartment. On one occa-

sion, Mattox claims Appel asked her, "can you tell me why black women sleep so bad? This morning I woke up with a big black butt in my face."

MATTOX'S AND MARVELLI'S HOSTILE WORK ENVIRONMENT CLAIMS

To "withstand summary judgment a plaintiff must demonstrate either that a single incident was extraordinarily severe, or that a series of incidents were sufficiently continuous and concerted to have altered the conditions of her working environment." The Supreme Court has established a non-exhaustive list of factors relevant to the determination whether conduct is so severe or pervasive to support a hostile work environment claim. These include 1) the frequency of the discriminatory conduct; 2) its severity; 3) whether the conduct was physically threatening or humiliating, or mere offensive utterance; 4) whether the conduct unreasonably interfered with plaintiff's work; and 5) what psychological harm, if any, resulted.

MATTOX AND MARVELLI'S FEDERAL HOSTILE WORK ENVIRONMENT CLAIM

Against Huie and Appel Individually:

a. Marvelli's Hostile Work Environment (Racial) Claim Against Huie: Viewing the evidence in a light most favorable to plaintiffs, Marvelli has failed to meet her burden of demonstrating that Huie created a racially hostile work environment. Marvelli describes only three instances involving racial comments directed at her, as opposed to a "steady barrage of opprobrious racial comments. First, Marvelli claims that Huie often would make jokes about her having large buttocks, but only one time was this framed in racial terms by saying" "you are big in the back like a black chick. You have a black butt." On another occasion, Huie told Marvelli that she would like rock music because she has white blood, and that she did not need the "n***er rap" music. Third, when Marvelli put braids in her hair, he said that she looked "rasta."

Marvelli also claims that Huie would constantly refer to Morales, who is Puerto Rican, as a "wetback" or a "Mexican." Although she claims that Huie often referred to Morales in derogatory terms, she does not indicate how often the rude comments he made about Morales were racial. These comments, directed towards a different minority, although of limited probative value, cannot be ignored on summary judgment. Even considering the incidents Marvelli experienced more directly in light of these incidents, a reasonable jury could not conclude that this "series of incidents was sufficiently continuous and concerted to have altered the conditions of Marvelli's working environment."

b. Mattox's Hostile Work Environment (Racial) Claim Against Huie: Mattox has failed to show that Huie created a racially hostile work environment. Mattox points to two allegedly racist comments that Huie directed at her. She claims that Huie engaged in racial harassment when he called her "shortie" and did a "parody" of African Americans by saying, "hey, Hommey, I'm down with it." To the extent that a reasonable jury could conclude that these comments are racist, they are of limited severity. The racial comments that Huie directed at other people were more severe. Huie referred to Brown-Murray as an ape and a monkey, and made jokes about Jews. Nevertheless, Huie's racial slurs, which occurred over the approximately 8 months he worked at CHAPS, were sporadic rather than a steady barrage of opprobrious racial comments.

c. Marvelli's Hostile Work Environment Claim (Racial) Against Appel: Marvelli does not claim that Appel directly harassed her. Rather, she claims that Appel is liable for Huie's conduct as his supervisor. However, as discussed above, a reasonable jury could not conclude that Huie racially harassed Marvelli. Therefore, the claim against Appel must be dismissed as well. Even if Marvelli could state a claim against Huie, Appel could not be held liable because, while § 1981 provides for individual liability, "a plaintiff must demonstrate some affirmative link to causally connect the actor with the discriminatory action." Marvelli never claims that she complained to Appel about Huie's racial comments, and, even if she did, she

would have to show more than negligence on Appel's part in maintaining CHAP's anti-discrimination policy; she would have to show personal involvement.

d. Mattox's Hostile Work Environment (Racial) Claim Against Appel: For the same reasons discussed above, Appel is not liable under § 1981 as Huie's supervisor for any racial harassment by Huie against Mattox. Nor has Mattox shown that Appel created a racially hostile environment directly. Mattox's hostile work environment claim against Appel consists of only one allegedly offensive comment. Mattox claims Appel asked her "can you tell me why black women sleep so bad? This morning I woke up with a big black butt in my face." This single offensive utterance over the approximately 14 months that Appel and Mattox worked together, while inappropriate, was not severe enough to altered the conditions of her working environment.

Judgment for Chaps.

Case Commentary

The Eastern District of New York concluded that although the comments made by Huie were racially insensitive, they were not severe or pervasive enough to constitute racial harassment. ∎

CASE QUESTIONS

1. Do you agree with the Court's reasoning?
2. If this had been publicized in the press, would the outcome have been different?

3. Do you believe racial statements are a matter of interpretation that may vary among judges?

The issue in the following case is whether an employee of Hawaiian ancestry was a victim of ethnic and racial harassment.

Aloia v. Eastman Kodak Company

No. 96-4113 (10th Cir. 1997)

Before Porfilio, Circuit Judge, Lucero, Circuit Judge, and McWilliams, Senior Circuit Judge.

Patrick H. Aloia ("Aloia") was hired by Eastman Kodak Company ("Kodak") on August 8, 1988, and, after training, was assigned to Kodak's Salt Lake City, Utah, office as a Customer Product Sales Representative. Kodak terminated Aloia's employment on April 29, 1993. On December 8, 1993, Aloia brought suit against Kodak in the United States District Court for the District of Utah, charging Kodak with breach of contract, retaliatory termination, racial discrimination, intentional inflection of emotional distress, and defamation.

On May 22, 1996, the district court entered a formal order granting summary judgment in favor of Kodak and against Aloia on all of his claims. Aloia appeals. We affirm.

In his complaint, Aloia described himself as being "a person of Hawaiian/Pacific Island parentage and ancestry." In this connection, Aloia in his deposition stated that he was born in the United States, as were his parents, and that his mother was of Irish ancestry and his father of Italian ancestry. Further, according to Aloia, his paternal grandmother was Italian and his biological paternal grandfather was of Portuguese and Polynesian ancestry.

Aloia alleged that in terminating his employment Kodak was "motivated by reasons of race and national origin" in violation of Title VII for which he sought damages in an unspecified amount.

As indicated, Aloia's claim was a Title VII claim of racial harassment in the work place. In granting summary judgment the district court relied primarily on *Bolden v. PRC, Inc.*

In *Bolden*, we spoke as follows:

For Mr. Bolden's harassment claim to survive summary judgment, his facts must support the inference of a racially hostile environment, and support a basis for liability. Specifically, it must be shown that under the totality of the circumstances (1) the harassment was pervasive or severe enough to alter the terms, conditions, or privilege of employment, and (2) the harassment was racial or stemmed from racial animus. General harassment if not racial or sexual is not actionable. The plaintiff must show "'more than a few isolated incidents of racial enmity.'" Instead of sporadic racial slurs, there must be a steady barrage of opprobrious racial comments.

As indicated, in granting summary judgment on Aloia's claim of racial harassment, the district court, citing *Bolden*, held that the epithets directed to Aloia, such as "coconut head," the "throwin' Samoan," "Aloha," "Island Boy," and the like, were "occasional" and not pervasive, and that, in any event, the terms and conditions of his employment with Kodak were not in any wise altered by such name calling. In his deposition, Aloia said that any name calling by his co-workers did not interfere with his job performance, that he did a good job for Kodak, and "enjoyed the h**l out of his job with Kodak. It was a great job."

Aloia's termination "was not motivated by racial bias," notwithstanding the fact that in his complaint Aloia alleged that he was terminated "by reasons of race and national origin." The fact that it is now conceded that Aloia's termination was not the result of race or national origin takes much of the steam out of his Title VII claim. In any event, all things considered, the district court did not err in granting summary judgment for Kodak on Aloia's claim of racial harassment.

CASE QUESTIONS

1. Do you agree with the Court's decision?
2. Do you consider the epithets directed at Aloia to be severe and pervasive?
3. If you say no, what would you consider to be severe and pervasive?

Aloia worked as a sales representative with Kodak from 1988 until his termination on April 29, 1993. Although there were occasional complaints about Aloia from customers and co-workers along the way, he apparently was a good salesman and his record of sales was good. As indicated, Aloia did have some "run-ins" along the road, he, at times, evidencing a rather short temper and was "confrontational" with co-workers and others. In this connection, Aloia had been given several warnings about his conduct.

The straw that broke the camel's back occurred on April 6, 1993, after a sales meeting which took place in Salt Lake City. Stanley Sukalski, a co-worker at Kodak in Salt Lake City, was 20 minutes late for the meeting, which, for some reason, extremely irritated Aloia, who was also attending the meeting. At the conclusion of the meeting, Aloia confronted Sukalski and publicly berated him, at length. Various obscenities were used, Aloia calling Sukalski, an ignorant SOB. Aloia, in his deposition, denied calling Sukalski a "dumb Polack," although Sukalski, when deposed, testified that Aloia had, indeed, called him a "dumb Polack," more than once. This confrontation resumed in the hallway outside Kodak's offices within earshot of Liberty Mutual, which had offices on the same floor as Kodak. Later, Aloia and Sukalski figuratively "shook hands" and agreed to drop the matter. However, Kodak later took statements from its employees, and conferred with both Aloia and Sukalski. The upshot of all this was that Kodak terminated Aloia on April 29, 1993.

Judgment affirmed for Eastman Kodak.

Case Commentary
The Tenth Circuit Court ruled that Aloia was not the victim of racial harassment and was properly dismissed. The conduct Aloia complained of was not so severe and pervasive as to constitute a hostile work environment. ■

4. Do you believe Aloia instituted this lawsuit as a result of being terminated because of his conflict with Sukalski?

COLOR DISCRIMINATION

Title VII prohibits discrimination against color in addition to race. Color could apply to people of mixed races, as well as to the different color of pigmentation of people of the same race. In Europe, white people from southern Europe have darker pigmentation than white people from northern Europe. Black, Asian, and Hispanic people have different shades of pigmentation.

Employment Perspective

Rachel Blake, who is a dark-skinned black woman, is employed as a teller in the Bank of Los Angeles. Dena Perry, a light-skinned black woman, is the bank manager. For 8 years Rachel has been passed over for promotions by whites and light-skinned blacks. Rachel claims that she has been discriminated against by her superior. Dena disagrees, claiming that discrimination cannot exist where both parties are of the same race. Who is correct? Rachel! Dena has discriminated against Rachel because of the color of her skin and not because of her race.

RECONSTRUCTION ERA ACT

Following the abolition of slavery with the passage of the Thirteenth Amendment to the Constitution, Congress passed the Reconstruction Era Act in 1866. The act provided blacks with the right "to make and enforce contracts . . . as enjoyed by white citizens." The right to make and enforce contracts includes employment contracts. The Civil Rights Act of 1991 has amended and incorporated this act within it. There are several distinctions between bringing a claim under the Reconstruction Act and under Title VII.

Title VII applies to employers with 15 or more employees. The Reconstruction Act applies to all employees. Title VII has a statute of limitations for filing. The Reconstruction Act does not. Title VII places monetary limitations on the recovery of compensatory and punitive damages. The Reconstruction Act has no such limitations.

The availability of the Reconstruction Act is limited to race, color, and national origin. It does not apply to sex, religion, disability, or age. The reason that not all claims for racial discrimination are filed under the Reconstruction Act is that there is a more stringent requirement for proving intentional discrimination. Under Title VII, proving intentional discrimination is not required—only that a disparate impact exists.

Employment Perspective

The Beanery, a cafeteria-style restaurant, required that all employees be clean-shaven and free of facial hair. Because Edward Jordan refused to shave his beard, he was discharged. Jordan sued under the Reconstruction Act. His claim was based on the fact that many black men have a facial skin condition that becomes very irritated when they shave. To require them to do so is discriminatory. Will he win? No! Jordan will be unable to prove that the Beanery's requirement was intended to discriminate purposely against black men. He would be better off instituting a claim for disparate impact under Title VII, where no intent on the part of the employer is required. If Jordan sued under Title VII, he would most likely win. However, if more than 180 days from the date of his discharge has elapsed, he will be barred from proceeding under Title VII because of its statute of limitations.

U.S. CONSTITUTION

The Fifth Amendment to the U.S. Constitution provides that no person shall be deprived of "life, liberty or property, without due process of the law." This amendment, which originally applied only to the federal government, was later applied to the states through the Fourteenth Amendment. The Fourteenth Amendment also guarantees to all persons "the equal protection of the laws." Bringing an action under the Constitution does not relieve a party from the statute of limitations under Title VII. The amendments only embellish the validity of the argument against discrimination.

The following case addresses the question of whether the equal protection clause is applicable to black applicants who were equally qualified with the white applicants selected for the position in question.

Sims v. Montgomery County Com'n

887 F. Supp. 1479 (M.D.Ala. 1995)

Thompson, Chief Judge.

This litigation consists of two consolidated class-action lawsuits . . . a class of black employees sought relief from the Montgomery County Sheriff's Department's racially discriminatory employment practices.

On December 15 and 16, 1993, the Sheriff's Department made its selections for promotion to sergeant and lieutenant from among the candidates in band A, the highest band, certified for each rank. Ten white males, one African-American male, and one African-American female scored in the sergeant's band A certification, and two white males, one white female, and one African-American female scored in the lieutenant's band A certification. Because there were no court-approved guidelines to govern the choice of candidates considered equally qualified within a band, the department's selections "were made with consideration of any adverse impact as to race or gender and thereafter, based upon seniority first as to 'time in grade' and second as to time served as a deputy sheriff." The department selected two white males, Robert L. Ingram and Mark C. Thompson, for promotion to sergeant and lieutenant in the enforcement division.

On December 21, 1993, the Sims plaintiffs and the Scott intervenors objected to the selection of two white males, and moved to enjoin the selections. They alleged, among other things, that the Sheriff's Department's selections from within the bands was "unaided by any judicially approved guidelines and was based on seniority, as the determining factor . . . , thereby perpetuating the Department's proven policy and practice of discriminating against African-Americans, who were not even employed in the enforcement division until 1988 and

remain woefully under-represented in the 'rank' positions of Sergeant and Lieutenant."

On October 20, 1994, the Sims plaintiffs, the Scott intervenors, and the defendants moved for approval of an agreement settling the Sims plaintiffs' and the Scott intervenors' objection to the 1993 selections for promotion to sergeant and lieutenant. Under the agreement, in addition to the two whites selected for promotion to sergeant and lieutenant, the department must select two African-Americans from the top scoring band of most qualified candidates.

Under the equal protection clause, this court must apply strict scrutiny to race conscious relief voluntarily implemented by a public employer. . . . The Sims plaintiffs, the Scott intervenors, and the defendants contend that strict scrutiny analysis is not required because all those in the sergeant and lieutenant bands from which the African-Americans are to be selected are equally qualified, that is, African-Americans were not selected over more qualified whites. The court agrees with the Sims plaintiffs, the Scott intervenors, and the defendants that African-Americans were not selected over more qualified whites. The record is clear that all those in band A for both the sergeant and lieutenant positions were equally qualified.

Judgment for Sims.

Case Commentary

In *Sims*, the Middle District Court of Alabama decided that the black employees selected were not less qualified than the white employees who were passed over. Therefore, the selection process was not in violation of the Equal Protection Clause of the Fourteenth Amendment. ■

CASE QUESTIONS

1. Do you believe the Court decided this case correctly?
2. Is the selection of equally qualified black candidates sufficient to satisfy the Equal Protection Clause?

3. How is it possible that all of the candidates in band A were equally qualified?

EMPLOYEE LESSONS

1. Be cognizant of race in the selection, compensation, and promotion process.
2. Apprise yourself of the proportion of minority groups in the area from which you hire your workers.
3. Treat all workers equally.
4. Do not discriminate because of race.
5. Be color blind in making employment decisions.
6. Judge applicants, employees, and independent contractors on their qualifications.
7. Do not participate in, encourage, or condone racial harassment.
8. Establish a company policy against race and color discrimination and racial harassment.
9. Define each of these suspect classifications explicitly in your company policy.
10. Teach employees to understand why race and color discrimination and racial harassment are hurtful to the victims as well as damaging to the company.
11. Know what constitutes race and color discrimination under the Civil Rights Act of 1964.
12. Be aware of the requirements and usefulness of Reconstruction Era Act.
13. Think before you speak, especially if your statement has racial overtones.
14. Treat your coworkers equally.
15. Guard against participating in, encouraging, or condoning racial harassment.
16. Do not judge coworkers or superiors by their race or color lest they judge you in the same way.
17. Be apprised of company policy dealing with race and color discrimination and racial harassment.

SUMMARY

When baseball finally opened its doors to blacks and Hispanics, their numbers proliferated. The same situation may be true in the future for Asian baseball players. Blacks have also flourished in basketball and football. The integration of minorities into sports has not caused a decline; instead, sports are growing at unprecedented rates because people want to see the best players compete. The same is true in the business arena. If businesses give minorities the opportunity to work but with their jobs contingent upon performance, then minorities will have the impetus to perform to the highest potential to which they are capable. Only opportunities can be guaranteed, not lifetime jobs. In sports, minorities must perform up to their potential or otherwise be released. It is rare to hear of a player suing for racial discrimination. In turn, businesses must act like sports teams and hire the most qualified. They must also be color blind.

The population of the United States is a number too formidable in size to be ignored. This country must embrace the fact that it is racially diverse. There are strengths in this situation that must be recognized. People who come from different backgrounds and cultures have different viewpoints, work habits, traits, traditions, and decision-making methods that they bring to the workplace. These must be exploited, not suppressed. In addition, workers often rise to the level of an employer's expectations. If the expectation is low, the result will be, too. Employers need to present a common color-blind-gender-blind level for their workers.

Leading by example is very important. Businesses can do this, and so can successful businesspeople in the minority community. Minorities that become successful must not abdicate their community in favor of white ones and then allege that white people discriminate. They must do their part in being role models. Communicating the message that education enables people to become the best that they can be is essential. Education, like a career, is something to be embraced for life.

In a global world, every country is a team, and every person on the team must be a player. There can be no benchwarmers. If there are, the team will be operating at a disadvantage in the global league. This will be the fault of the team for not giving these nonparticipatory members the opportunity and encouragement to become team players with the goal of enabling these individuals to make a significant contribution to the team's success. Teams that meet the challenge will have a successful quest in the global bowl.

REVIEW QUESTIONS

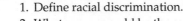

1. Define racial discrimination.
2. What groups could be the subject of racial discrimination?
3. Explain the difference between color discrimination and racial discrimination.
4. Define racial harassment.
5. What impact has the Reconstruction Act had on racial discrimination?
6. Can a bona fide occupational qualification ever exist with regard to race?
7. What effect does the U.S. Constitution have with respect to race?
8. Why is it preferable to sue under Title VII rather than the Reconstruction Act?
9. In what situation must a victim of racial discrimination sue under the Reconstruction Act because Title VII is unavailable?
10. Are the tensions involving racial discrimination decreasing?
11. Are minorities as racist as whites? In other words, if minorities had equal power as whites, would they be equally racist?
12. Should white people be afforded the same protection under the Equal Protection Clause as minorities?
13. Are pretexts often used to cover up discriminatory behavior?
14. When poor performance and racist behavior are both involved, what takes precedence?

CASE PROBLEMS

1. Jiminez produced no scholarly work. Although he was somewhat excused from this requirement while working on his Ph.D., he did not complete his Ph.D. in the prescribed time. Jiminez applied for an assistant professorship in the Department of Economics at MWC on March 4, 1989. In connection with his application, Jiminez represented that he would receive his doctorate degree in economics in June 1989 from the University of New Mexico. The department was split in its decision to offer Jiminez a position because he garnered inauspicious evaluations at the University of New Mexico. Despite this knowledge, MWC offered Jiminez the position because the college was seeking to increase the number of blacks on its faculty. To a degree, therefore, Jiminez was hired because he was black. By letter dated August 3, 1989, William Anderson, president of MWC, notified Jiminez of MWC's offer, expressly explaining that Jiminez' appointment was "contingent upon his being granted his Ph.D. by August 16, 1989." The college claimed it was justified in denying tenure because of a failure to produce scholarly work. The professor claimed the college's argument was just a pretext in order to racially discriminate.
   Jiminez v. Mary Washington College, 57 F.3d 369 (4th Cir. 1995)
2. Marva Brown is an African-American who has worked as a receptionist in Coach's Human Resource Department at its headquarters in Manhattan since 1988. In this charge, she claimed that despite repeated requests to be promoted, Coach had refused to promote her and had instead promoted dozens of nonminority employees and

"scarcely any" minorities. She also claimed that one of her coemployees at Coach told her that she looked "black like a real n***er" when she returned from a vacation, a comment for which the employee was not sanctioned, and that she was routinely excluded from business meetings and holiday parties held by her department.

Brown asserted that she was told repeatedly by supervisors that she was "too valuable in her current position to promote." Brown alleged that she was told by her supervisors that Coach "seeks to hire and promote people who have a 'Coach look'— the examples to whom her supervisors referred were young non-minority persons." The question presented in the case is whether racial comments made by coworkers were severe and pervasive, thus rendering the employer guilty of condoning a hostile work environment based on racial harassment.
*Brown v. Coach Stores, Inc.,*163 F.3d 706 (2nd Cir. 1998)

3. Plaintiff's claim is based on the promotion of Danny Mott, an African-American, to the position of deputy director of Emergency Ambulance Bureau (EAB) of the DCFD in March 1988. Plaintiff alleges that the selection was made on the basis of race. Plaintiff also alleges that defendants Barry, Coleman, and Thornton preselected Mott for the position in October 1987. Mott was "acting" deputy director at the time and remained in the "acting" position until the official announcement of his selection after a purported competitive selection process in March 1988.

Defendants argue that the plaintiff's claim is time-barred because he alleges that the actual selection occurred in October 1987. Plaintiff's claim as to the March 1988 selection process was filed within the 3-year statute of limitations. What was the result? *Zervas v. District of Columbia*, 817 F.Supp. 148 (D.D.C. 1993)

HUMAN RESOURCE DILEMMAS

1. Sidney Green is an assistant branch manager at the Valley Creek Savings Bank. Although Sidney has had favorable reviews for the past 15 years, she has been passed over for branch manager on three occasions by white employees with fewer credentials. Sidney has complained to the regional manager, but has been put off. How would you advise her?

2. Sung Loo Chan has been hired as a sales rep with Rockwell Pharmaceuticals. Sung Loo has been subjected to Asian jokes, name calling, and caricatures over the past 4 months. He complained on several occasions to his manager, to no avail. How would you advise Sung Loo?

3. Reggie Kelly, who is African-American, applies in person for a position as a salesperson with Epitome Realty, which offers homes for sale only in elite neighborhoods. Epitome has only 12 employees. Marcus Bradbury's response is "What? Are you kidding?" Reggie queries Marcus on the meaning of his response. Marcus retorts, "Well, it is obvious." Reggie wishes to proceed under Title VII.

WEB SITE ASSIGNMENT

Using the following Web sites as a guide, construct a policy regarding race discrimination and racial harassment in the workplace.

www.naacp.org
www.discriminationattorney.com/race.html
www.aclu.org/news/n092795a.html
www.eeoc.gov/facts/fs-race.html
www.findlaw.com
www.un.org/WCAR
www.geocities.com/rcdis
www.legal-definitions.com/discriminination.htm
www.legal-term.com/discriminate-definition.htm

Chapter 10

Sex Discrimination

Employment Scenario

Meg Johnson and Stacy Roberts are friends who have children in the Grasmere Elementary School. They would both like to work part-time during school hours. Meg and Stacy apply to The Long and the Short of It, which has advertised part-time sales positions. Tom and Mark interview Meg and Stacy, but decide not to hire them. Mark says to Tom, "We don't want school moms who are looking to earn extra spending cash. They don't fit our image." Subsequently, Tom and Mark hire two men without experience for the positions. Two weeks later, Meg and Stacy tell Laurie, another mother with school-age children, that they were disappointed L&S did not hire them. Laurie seems surprised. She remarks that her brother-in-law, Fred, who has not worked in 6 months, was hired on the spot. Meg and Stacy inquire as to Fred's experience in sales, and Laurie replies that he has none. Meg and Stacy visit four of the L&S stores, and to their astonishment they find no women working in sales. Meg and Stacy file a claim for sex discrimination against L&S. Tom Long and Mark Short, copresidents of L&S, consult with their attorney, Susan North, Esq. They argue that hiring men exclusively to work as salespeople in a men's clothing store is a bona fide occupational qualification. Is their argument valid?

Chapter Checklist

➤ Understand the need for a prohibition against sex discrimination to counteract historical stereotypes.
➤ Learn that men are also protected against sex discrimination.
➤ Appreciate that women are often discriminated against not solely because they are women, but also because they have small children or elderly parents, i.e., sex plus discrimination.
➤ Be aware of the limited exceptions for bona fide occupational qualifications.
➤ Be apprised of potential violations of the Equal Pay Act.
➤ Be familiar with the impracticability of comparable worth.

> ➤ Appreciate the wide latitude given to employers in setting dress codes and grooming standards.

> ➤ Learn that customer preferences are not a valid reason to discriminate on the basis of sex.

INTRODUCTION

In the past, sex was considered a bona fide occupational qualification. Stereotypes ruled. Men were physicians, lawyers, construction workers, and policemen. Women were nurses, flight attendants, secretaries, and teachers. This arrangement had the effect of discriminating against men and women in certain job classifications. The effect on women, particularly with regard to higher-paying positions, was noticeable. Women and men must be treated equally in all aspects of employment, hiring, compensation, training, transfer, and promotions. Prescribing limits for lifting or carrying weight or for working before or after childbirth is prohibited. Any provisions or benefits must be provided to both sexes. Job requirements must be the same for male and female candidates.

HUMAN RESOURCE ADVICE

- Formulate grooming standards and dress codes.
- Treat men and women in a consistent manner.
- Eliminate stereotypes when employing and/or assigning men and women to particular jobs.
- Identify instances of sex plus discrimination.
- Pay women an amount equal to men when the qualifications needed and the work performed are similar.
- Know that bona fide occupational qualifications exist only in a very limited number of instances, such as for bathroom or locker-room attendants.
- Realize that customer preferences cannot dictate your hiring selections with regard to sex.
- Learn that comparable worth has never been implemented in employment.
- Encourage women to realize their full potential in the workplace.
- Understand that men may also be victims of sex discrimination.

Employment Perspective

Eric Freeman is a vice president at Bulls and Bears, Inc., an investment banking firm. There is an opening for an assistant vice president to work directly underneath Freeman. There are two in-house candidates: Tom Folino, a competent securities trader with 2 years of experience, and Mary Michaels, a senior bond trader with 7 years of experience. Mary's experience and competence are clearly superior, but Freeman selects Tom because they have common interests. They go to the hockey games after work and have a few beers together. Eric and Tom are both single, whereas Mary is married with children. Eric and Mary have nothing in common outside of work. Does this qualify as sexual discrimination? Yes! Eric's decision is not based on job performance, but rather on personal interests he shares with one candidate.

The issue in this case is whether prohibiting women from admission to Virginia Military Institute is sex discrimination.

United States v. Virginia
518 U.S. 515 (1996)

Justice Ginsburg delivered the opinion of the Court.

Virginia's public institutions of higher learning include an incomparable military college, Virginia Military Institute (VMI). The United States maintains that the Constitution's equal protection guarantee precludes Virginia from reserving exclusively to men the unique educational opportunities VMI affords. We agree.

Founded in 1839, VMI is today the sole single-sex school among Virginia's 15 public institutions of higher learning. VMI's distinctive mission is to produce "citizen-soldiers," men prepared for leadership in civilian life and in military service. VMI pursues this mission through pervasive training of a kind not available anywhere else in Virginia. Assigning prime place to character development, VMI uses an "adversative method" modeled on English public schools and once characteristic of military instruction. VMI constantly endeavors to instill physical and mental discipline in its cadets and impart to them a strong moral code. The school's graduates leave VMI with heightened comprehension of their capacity to deal with duress and stress, and a large sense of accomplishment for completing the hazardous course.

VMI attracts some applicants because of its reputation as an extraordinarily challenging military school, and "because its alumni are exceptionally close to the school." "Women have no opportunity anywhere to gain the benefits of the system of education at VMI."

In 1990, prompted by a complaint filed with the Attorney General by a female high-school student seeking admission to VMI, the United States sued the Commonwealth of Virginia and VMI, alleging that VMI's exclusively male admission policy violated the Equal Protection Clause of the Fourteenth Amendment.

In the two years preceding the lawsuit, the District Court noted, VMI had received inquiries from 347 women, but had responded to none of them. "Some women, at least," the court said, "would want to attend the school if they had the opportunity." The court further recognized that, with recruitment, VMI could "achieve at least 10% female enrollment"—"a sufficient 'critical mass' to provide the female cadets with a positive educational experience." And it was

also established that "some women are capable of all of the individual activities required of VMI cadets." In addition, experts agreed that if VMI admitted women, "the VMI ROTC experience would become a better training program from the perspective of the armed forces, because it would provide training in dealing with a mixed-gender army."

The heightened review standard our precedent establishes does not make sex a proscribed classification. Supposed "inherent differences" are no longer accepted as a ground for race or national origin classifications. Physical differences between men and women, however, are enduring: "The two sexes are not fungible; a community made up exclusively of one sex is different from a community composed of both."

"Inherent differences" between men and women, we have come to appreciate, remain cause for celebration, but not for denigration of the members of either sex or for artificial constraints on an individual's opportunity. Sex classifications may be used to compensate women "for particular economic disabilities they have suffered," to "promote equal employment opportunity," to advance full development of the talent and capacities of our Nation's people. But such classifications may not be used, as they once were, to create or perpetuate the legal, social, and economic inferiority of women.

Measuring the record in this case against the review standard just described, we conclude that Virginia has shown no "exceedingly persuasive justification" for excluding all women from the citizen-soldier training afforded by VMI. We therefore affirm the Fourth Circuit's initial judgment, which held that Virginia had violated the Fourteenth Amendment's Equal Protection Clause. Because the remedy proffered by Virginia—the Mary Baldwin VWIL program—does not cure the constitutional violation, i.e., it does not provide equal opportunity, we reverse the Fourth Circuit's final judgment in this case.

Judgment for the United States.

Case Commentary

The U.S. Supreme Court decided that a renowned military college such as VMI cannot discriminate against women by denying them admission. ■

CASE QUESTIONS

1. Was the Court's decision correct?
2. Female colleges do exist. Why can't VMI be limited to males?

3. Has allowing women to serve in the armed forces been a good idea?

The issue in the following case is whether the plaintiff was terminated because she is a woman.

Mann V. Mass. Correa Electric

2002 U.S. Dist. LEXIS 949 (S.D. NY 2002)

Cote, District Judge.

Defendant Mass Correa Electric, J.V. ("Mass") has moved for summary judgment on all claims brought in this employment discrimination action by Barbara Mann (("Mann"), a female electrician fired from her employment at the World Trade Center in 1998. For the following reasons, the motion is granted in part.

BACKGROUND

The following facts are undisputed or as alleged by the plaintiff. In 1987, Mann began working at the World Trade Center ("Center") as an employee of Hatzel & Buehler, Inc., a company under contract to the Port Authority of New York and New Jersey (the "Port Authority"), the owner of the Center, to provide services for the operation and maintenance of the Center's electrical systems. Hatzel & Buehler eventually assigned Mann to the "off/night" shift from midnight to 8:00, which she preferred to the day shift because it best accommodated her responsibilities at home and her desire to continue to get an education. In 1994, the Port Authority rebid the contract for services relating to the Center's electrical systems. Mass won the bid on the new contract, took over the operation of the electrical systems at the Center, and became Mann's employer.

From 1991 to the date of her termination in 1998, Mann's foreman at the Center was John Fox ("Fox").

In November of 1995, Mann complained to Mass that Fox gave her "all the dirty jobs", talked down to her and favored the male electricians.

Shortly thereafter, in March 1996, a lewd photograph was left in the women's locker room used by Mann. In response to this incident, Mass distributed a memorandum to all employees stating that it would not tolerate such behavior and that anyone involved would be immediately terminated and prosecuted to the full extent allowed by law.

In March or April 1996, Fox and another employee loudly banged on the bathroom door while Mann was in the bathroom. Fearing an emergency, she opened the door while not fully clothed and found the two employees laughing at her. At a meeting held to discuss this incident, the two men denied that it had occurred. Mass accepted their denials without also questioning Mann at the meeting.

In 1997, Mann signed a list indicating her desire to become a weekend supervisor. A male employee with more seniority but in poor physical condition, with less education and with less relevant experience than the plaintiff was given the appointment.

In September 1997, Mann was verbally warned that her excessive absences, if continued, would lead to her being fired. On June 9, 1998, Mann called in sick, due to a back sprain she suffered off the job. She sent in a doctor's note indicating that she had been told to take from one to two weeks of bed rest. On June 12, Waffenschmidt sent Mann a notice that she was fired for excessive absenteeism after the Port Authority concurred in the decision to fire Mann because of her absenteeism.

In order to establish a prima facie case of discrimination, a plaintiff must show (1) that she was within a protected group; (2) that she was qualified for her position; (3) that she suffered an adverse employment action; and (4) that the adverse action occurred in circumstances giving rise to an inference of discrimination on the basis of her membership in the protected class. Once the plaintiff has demonstrated a prima facie case, "the burden of production shifts to the employer who must defeat a rebuttable presumption of discrimination by articulating a legitimate, non-discriminatory reason" for the adverse employment action. If the employer meets its burden, the plaintiff must then show that the employer intentionally discriminated against the employee.

Mann has presented sufficient evidence of gender discrimination in the failure to promote her in 1997. She has described sufficient reasons for inferring that the promotion of a male employee more senior to her was nonetheless, in the context of the specific job to which he was appointed, discriminatory. Through unrefuted evidence, she has raised issues of fact regarding whether he was qualified for the position to which he was promoted. While the evidence regarding any discriminatory motive for Mass's decision is slim, it is sufficient to permit this claim to survive.

Mann has presented evidence to support a claim of discrimination based on the termination of her employment in 1998. In addition to presenting prima facie evidence of discrimination, she has also presented sufficient evidence to raise a question of fact about Mass's reasons for firing her, specifically whether the decision was motivated by Mann's absenteeism or gender discrimination. Mann has presented some evidence that men with problems with illness were not fired, but were given light duty. While it is undisputed that the Port Authority ordered Mass to terminate Mann's employment,

Mass has presented no legal authority for the proposition that any discriminatory action it took can be excused by the fact that its customer or client ordered it to take the action or suffer adverse financial consequences. In this regard, it is particularly noteworthy that there is some evidence that the decision to fire Mann was initially taken by Mass and not the Center. Finally, it is undisputed that the loss of Mann's employment was an adverse action even though Mass agreed to rehire Mann at another location should a position become available.

Conclusion

For the reasons discussed above, Mass's motion for summary judgment is denied with respect to plaintiff's claims of discriminatory failure to promote, discriminatory termination.

Case Commentary

The Southern District Court of New York ruled that a triable issue has been presented by the plaintiff as to whether her discharge was due to her gender. ■

CASE QUESTIONS

1. Do you agree with the Court's reasoning?
2. Would she have been treated differently if she were a man?

3. At trial, do you believe the evidence the plaintiff will be able to present will be enough to render a verdict in her favor?

In the case that follows, the issue is whether United's motive for rejecting the employee's request to be promoted to line pilot/flight officer was motivated by disparate treatment, disparate impact, retaliation, or the statute of limitations.

Bullington v. United Air Lines, Inc.
186 F.3d 1301 (10th Cir. 1997)

Brorby, Circuit Judge.

United Airlines, Inc. ("United") interviewed and rejected Ms. Bullington for the position of line pilot/flight officer on three separate occasions. Ms. Bullington brought this action pursuant to Title VII of the Civil Rights Act of 1964, and the Age Discrimination in Employment Act ("ADEA"), claiming United refused to hire her because of her gender, her age and in retaliation for complaining about alleged discrimination during the interview process. Ms. Bullington further claims United breached an implied contract or an otherwise enforceable promise by refusing to hire her. The district court granted United's motion for partial dismissal and United's subsequent motion for summary judgment, and Ms. Bullington appeals. We affirm in part and reverse in part.

I. BACKGROUND

Ms. Bullington, a female over the age of forty, currently works for United as a ground school academic instructor. Over a two-year period, Ms. Bullington sought but was denied a position as line pilot with United on three occasions. United's application and selection process for flight officers involves three phases. In the initial phase, United accepts applications from individuals meeting certain minimum qualifications including 350 hours of flight experience, commercial pilot certification, a high school diploma, and other physical and medical requirements. United then ranks

eligible applicants according to aeronautical experience. Those applicants ranked at the top of the list advance to the second phase of the selection process. Because female applicants typically have less aeronautical experience than male applicants, United ranks male and female applicants separately. United then selects a proportionate number of males and females to proceed to the second phase. At the second phase, applicants must complete a simulator flight and a formal interview. Based on the applicant's performance, a review board then decides whether to reject the applicant or to extend a conditional offer. If United extends a conditional offer, the candidate moves on to the third phase, which includes a medical exam and background check. Ms. Bullington objects to the formal interview portion of the selection process.

Two United employees conduct the formal interview, an employment representative and a flight operations representative. These individuals assess the applicant in seven broad categories or "dimensions" including: industry motivation, decision making/problem solving, compliance and conformity, leadership, interpersonal skills, technical evaluation, and appearance/presentation. Each dimension is broken down into a set of attributes or "anchors" United deems desirable in a flight officer. Interviewers ask applicants questions from a suggested list and, based on the applicant's response, evaluate whether the applicant meets United's set standards for each attribute.

Based on those attribute evaluations, the interviewers give the applicant a numerical score for each dimension, ranging from a low of "1" to a high of "5." The dimension scores are then averaged to arrive at the applicant's overall score. An applicant must have an overall score of "3" or better to be recommended for a flight officer position. However, if an applicant scores a "2" or lower on any one dimension, her overall score will also be a "2," and the interviewers will not recommend her for a flight officer position.

United interviewed Ms. Bullington for a flight officer position three times—January 1993, March 1995 and May 1995. Each time, Ms. Bullington received an overall score of "2," thereby disqualifying her from further consideration. After her first unsuccessful interview in January 1993, Ms. Bullington spoke with Ms. Nancy Stuke, United's Manager of Flight Officer Employment, and expressed her concerns that one of her interviewers was biased against her. Ms. Bullington claims Ms. Stuke failed to adequately address her complaints. After unsuccessfully interviewing a second and third time, Ms. Bullington filed suit alleging: (1) United failed to hire her on all three occasions because of her sex and age, (2) United failed to hire her in 1995 in retaliation for her complaints to Ms. Stuke in 1993, and (3) United's failure to hire her breached an implied contract or otherwise enforceable promise for career advancement.

United moved to dismiss Ms. Bullington's claims to the extent they were based on Ms. Bullington's January 1993 rejection because those claims were barred by the statute of limitations. The district court agreed and granted United's motion. United then moved for summary judgment on Ms. Bullington's remaining claims. The district court granted that motion as well, concluding Ms. Bullington failed to establish a prima facie case of age or sex discrimination under either a disparate impact or disparate treatment theory, failed to establish a prima facie case of retaliation, and failed to present sufficient evidence of an enforceable contract or promise.

II. STATUTE OF LIMITATIONS

In Colorado, ADEA and Title VII complainants must file a charge of discrimination with the Equal Employment Opportunity Commission ("EEOC") within 300 days after the alleged unlawful discriminatory practice occurred. This filing is a prerequisite to a civil suit under either statute. In this case, United first rejected Ms. Bullington for the position of flight officer in January 1993. In March 1993, Ms. Bullington complained to Ms. Stuke that she suspected one of her interviewers discriminated against her. In order for a claim based on this conduct to be timely, Ms. Bullington was required to file an EEOC charge within 300 days after the March 1993 incident. However, Ms. Bullington waited almost three years, until February 6, 1996, to file her charge.

Ms. Bullington attempts to avoid this apparent untimeliness by invoking the continuing violation doctrine. Under that doctrine, a plaintiff may recover for incidents which occurred outside the statutory time limit if at least one instance of the alleged discriminatory practice occurred within the limitations period and the earlier acts are part of a "continuing pattern of discrimination." To determine whether alleged incidents of discrimination constitute a continuing violation, a court considers three factors: (i) subject matter—whether the violations constitute the same type of discrimination; (ii) frequency; and (iii) permanence—whether the nature of the violations should trigger an employee's awareness of the need to assert her rights and whether the consequences of the act would continue even in the absence of a continuing intent to discriminate.

Applying these factors, the district court determined that the events arising in 1993 and the later events in 1995 did not constitute a continuing violation. Instead, the court concluded the 1993 non-hire was an isolated event and, moreover, Ms. Bullington had reason to believe she was a victim of discrimination as early as 1993. As such, the court found application of the continuing violation doctrine inappropriate and Ms. Bullington's claims, to the extent they relied on the 1993 conduct, untimely. The court therefore dismissed those claims for failure to state a claim upon which relief may be granted. We review de novo the district court's dismissal for failure to state a claim upon which relief can be granted. We uphold a dismissal "only when it appears that the plaintiff can prove no set of facts in support of the claims that would entitle her to relief, accepting the well-pleaded allegations of the complaint as true and construing them in the light most favorable to the plaintiff."

The continuing violation doctrine "is premised on the equitable notion that the statute of limitations should not begin to run until a reasonable person would be aware that his or her rights have been violated." Thus, a continuing violation claim will likely fail if the plaintiff knew, or through the exercise of reasonable diligence would have known, she was being discriminated against at the time the earlier events occurred. We agree with the district court's conclusion that, although the 1993 conduct is of the same general type as the 1995 conduct, the 1993 decision was a discrete and salient event that put Ms. Bullington on notice that United violated her rights. The allegations contained in Ms. Bullington's Amended Complaint clearly indicate that after United declined to hire her in January 1993, she spoke to Ms. Stuke in March 1993 and expressed her opposition to "what she believed . . . to have been sex and age discrimination by United in not selecting her for the position of line pilot." Because Ms. Bullington was, at the very least, on inquiry notice of the alleged discrimination as early as 1993, she had a duty to assert her rights at that time and she cannot rely on a continuing violation theory to avoid the statutory time bar.

Ms. Bullington also argues for a continuing violation based on her statistical evidence of a pattern and practice of discrimination. It is true that a continuing violation may be based on either a series of related acts taken against a single individual or the maintenance of a company-wide policy or practice of discrimination. However, Ms. Bullington's argument below focused entirely on the specific acts taken against her and did not contend that a company-wide policy of discrimination existed before and after the limitations period. Moreover, she did not present her statistical evidence until well after the district court issued its order granting partial dismissal. The district court properly dismissed Ms. Bullington's discrimination claims for events arising in 1992/1993 as time barred.

III. DISPARATE IMPACT

Ms. Bullington argues United's interview process caused a significant disparate impact on women. As is typical in disparate impact cases, Ms. Bullington relies on statistical evidence to establish her prima facie case. Her statistics compare the "pass rates" of male and female applicants who interviewed for United flight officer positions. The "pass rate," as defined by Ms. Bullington's expert, represents the number of applicants who received an overall score of "3" or better on the interview.

For interviews conducted after 1994, the pass rate for women was 27.9% while the pass rate for men was 46.6%. As such, the women's pass rate is equal to only 60% of the pass rate for men—a statistically significant disparity under EEOC guidelines (stating that a selection rate for a protected group which is less than 80% or 4/5 of the selection rate for the majority group is generally regarded as evidence of adverse impact). This disparity, Ms. Bullington argues, is significant enough to establish a prima facie case of disparate impact discrimination.

The district court disagreed. It determined Ms. Bullington's statistics did not establish a prima facie case because they failed to compare similarly situated individuals.

After examining the facts and circumstances of this case, we find Ms. Bullington's statistical data sufficiently reliable to raise a genuine issue of material fact regarding the existence of a statistical disparity. Her analysis identified a specific employment practice (the interview) and identified two relevant populations for impact comparison—persons who interviewed for flight officer positions and persons who received a passing score on the interview. Her analysis focused on the specific position at issue, namely flight officer. In addition, her applicant pool was appropriately limited to persons who sought out and were at least minimally qualified for the position of flight officer. In fact, each member of the applicant pool not only applied for the at-issue position, as is the usual case with applicant flow data, but actually interviewed for the at-issue position. Based on United's interview eligibility requirements,

we can therefore assume each member of the applicant pool was, at the very least, a certified pilot with a high school diploma and at least 350 hours of flight experience. The relative homogeneity of the applicant pool reassures us that its members are not so diverse as to render her statistics totally meaningless.

This is not to say Ms. Bullington's statistics are without fault. As the district court noted, her analysis fails to account for differences in male and female interviewees' aeronautical experience—a potentially non-discriminatory explanation for the disparate impact. However, we do not believe that fault renders Ms. Bullington's statistics incapable of raising a genuine issue of material fact. We emphasize that Ms. Bullington's burden as the nonmovant is to set forth specific facts establishing a genuine issue for trial. The issue of material fact, here the existence of a significant statistical disparity, need not be resolved conclusively in Ms. Bullington's favor. We simply conclude the district court's basis for granting summary judgment was insufficient, and United has not shown an absence of issues of material fact with respect to Ms. Bullington's prima facie case.

IV. DISPARATE TREATMENT

If she establishes a prima facie case, the burden shifts to United to articulate a legitimate, nondiscriminatory reason for the adverse employment decision. If United offers a legitimate, nondiscriminatory reason for its actions, the burden reverts to Ms. Bullington to show United's proffered reason was a pretext for discrimination.

The only remaining issue, then, is whether Ms. Bullington has shown "that there is a genuine dispute of material fact as to whether the employer's proffered reason for the challenged action is pretextual."

To establish pretext a plaintiff must show either that "a discriminatory reason more likely motivated the employer or . . . that the employer's proffered explanation is unworthy of credence." Plaintiff may accomplish this by demonstrating "such weaknesses, implausibilities, inconsistencies, incoherencies, or contradictions in the employer's proffered legitimate reasons for its action that a reasonable factfinder could rationally find them unworthy of credence." However, the plaintiff's "mere conjecture that her employer's explanation is a pretext for intentional discrimination is an insufficient basis for denial of summary judgment."

In this case, Ms. Bullington bases her pretext argument on the following evidence: disputes regarding things she said and did during the interview, the interviewers' use of gender and age stereotypes, a comparison of her qualifications with those of successful flight officer interviewees, and statistical evidence. We conclude that, even viewing this evidence in the light most favorable to Ms. Bullington, it fails to demonstrate a genuine issue of fact as to whether United's reasons for not hiring her were pretextual.

First, Ms. Bullington lists numerous disputes she has with the notes and summaries prepared by her interviewers. We disagree.

A review of the record shows that the vast majority of the "factual disputes" alleged by Ms. Bullington are in reality her opinion that the interviewers were wrong in their assessment of her qualifications.

However, her own opinions about her qualifications do not give rise to a material fact dispute.

Ms. Bullington's argument merely takes issue with what she believes is an incorrect assessment of her communication skills, goals, and motivation level. As discussed above, Ms. Bullington's opinion about the fairness or accuracy of the interviewers' evaluation is not evidence of pretext.

Next, Ms. Bullington offers a comparison of her qualifications with those of seven other male and/or younger individuals that United interviewed and hired as flight officers. She claims United hired these individuals despite the fact many were less qualified than her or, in many cases, had the same deficiencies identified during her interview. However, we emphasize that an employer does not violate Title VII by choosing between equally qualified candidates, so long as the decision is not based on unlawful criteria. Therefore, pretext cannot be shown simply by identifying minor differences between plaintiff's qualifications and those of successful applicants.

A comparison of Ms. Bullington's qualifications with those of the other interviewees in this case gives us no reason to question United's explanation for its hiring decision. Ms. Bullington's evidence does not show that she was overwhelmingly better qualified than the other candidates. At most, the seven other candidates were similarly qualified and the fact that United chose between them is not evidence of pretext.

V. RETALIATION

Ms. Bullington claims United retaliated against her based on a conversation she had in March 1993 with Ms. Stuke, United's Manager of Flight Officer Employment. During this conversation, Ms. Bullington allegedly informed Ms. Stuke of her "strong concerns" that one of her interviewers in the 1993 interview was biased against her. Because of this complaint, Ms. Bullington claims Ms. Stuke retaliated against her by influencing the interviewers' hiring decisions in her 1995 interviews. As proof of Ms. Stuke's animus towards her, Ms. Bullington points to a conversation which occurred shortly before her March 1995 interview between Ms. Stuke and Mr. H. Jeffery Bartels about a recommendation Mr. Bartels submitted in support of Ms. Bullington's flight officer application. In his affidavit, Mr. Bartels states that Ms. Stuke asked him if he was sure he wanted to submit a recommendation for Ms. Bullington and told him that Ms. Bullington acted like a "real airhead" and "held a troll doll for good luck" during her previous interview.

To establish a prima facie case of retaliation, Ms. Bullington must show: "1) she was engaged in protected opposition to Title VII or ADEA discrimination; 2) she was subjected to adverse employment action; and 3) a causal connection existed between the protected activity and the adverse employment action." The causal connection may be shown by producing "evidence of circumstances that justify an inference of retaliatory motive, such as protected conduct closely followed by adverse action." In other words, Ms. Bullington must present some evidence that her employer undertook the adverse employment action for the purpose of retaliation.

The district court concluded summary judgment in favor of United was appropriate because Ms. Bullington failed to establish a nexus or causal connection between her 1993 complaint to Ms. Stuke and the interviewers' hiring selections in 1995. We agree. The interviewers' decisions in 1995 were remote in time from Ms. Bullington's 1993 complaint, thus undercutting an inference of retaliatory motive.

Judgment for United Airlines.

Case Commentary

Ms. Bullington applied for line pilot once in 1993 and twice in 1995. The Tenth Circuit Court concluded Ms. Bullington's 1993 discrimination claim was not filed in a timely manner. Ms. Bullington's attempt to apply the continuous violation rule failed for lack of continuity. The Tenth Circuit Court concluded that Ms. Bullington's disparate impact claim was viable because the women's pass rate was only 60 percent of the men's pass rate, in violation of the 80 percent rule. The Tenth Circuit Court dismissed the disparate treatment claim because there was no evidence of pretext on United's part. Ms. Bullington's retaliation claim was also dismissed because the retaliation occurred in 1995; the alleged event leading to the retaliation happened in 1993. This was too remote. ■

CASE QUESTIONS

1. Was the Court's decision correct?
2. Do you think the retaliation claim was too remote?
3. Do you think the women's 60 percent pass rate created a disparate impact?
4. If so, how do you think the court will resolve this?

The issue in the case that follows is whether the pressure placed on a regional sales manager by her general manager to hire a sales associate who was attractive constitutes sex discrimination.

Yanowitz v. L'Oreal USA
2003 Cal. App. LEXIS 342

Gemello, J.

Elysa Yanowitz joined L'Oreal's predecessor in 1981. She was promoted from sales representative to regional sales manager for Northern California and the Pacific Northwest in 1986. At one time or another, Yanowitz's region included stores in California, Oregon, Washington, Idaho, Alaska, Hawaii, Arizona, Utah, Colorado, Texas, and Minnesota. Yanowitz was responsible for managing L'Oreal's sales force and dealing with accounts, i.e., department and specialty stores that sold L'Oreal's fragrances.

During her first 10 years as a regional sales manager, Yanowitz's performance was consistently reviewed as "Above Expectation" and in some instances fell just short of "Outstanding," the highest possible rating. In early 1997, Yanowitz was named L'Oreal's Regional Sales Manager of the Year for her performance during 1996. She received a Cartier watch and a congratulatory note complimenting her on her ability to inspire team spirit and her demonstration of leadership, loyalty, and motivation.

Shortly after the restructure, John (Jack) Wiswall, general manager for the new Designer Fragrance Division, and Yanowitz toured the Ralph Lauren installation at a Macy's store in San Jose. After the tour, Wiswall told Yanowitz there needed to be a change because the female sales associate was "not good looking enough." Wiswall instructed Yanowitz to have the sales associate fired, and directed her to "get me somebody hot," or words to that effect.

On a return trip to the store, Wiswall discovered that the sales associate had not been dismissed. He reiterated to Yanowitz that he wanted the associate fired and complained that she had not done so. He passed "a young attractive blonde girl, very sexy," on his way out, turned to Yanowitz, and told her, "G** d**n it, get me one that looks like that." The sales associate, in contrast, was dark-skinned. Yanowitz asked Wiswall for an adequate justification before she would fire the associate.

Yanowitz never carried out Wiswall's order. Wiswall asked her whether the associate had been dismissed on several subsequent occasions. Yanowitz again asked Wiswall to provide adequate justification for dismissing her. Yanowitz never complained to the Human Resources Department (Human Resources), nor did she tell Wiswall that his order was discriminatory; he was her boss, and she did not want to inflame him.

In March 1998, Yanowitz learned that the sales associate was among the top sellers of men's fragrances in the Macy's West chain. Also in March 1998, a member of Yanowitz's sales force learned that Wiswall had issues with Yanowitz and now wanted to get rid of her.

In June 1998, Yanowitz met with Wiswall, Roderick, and various account executives and regional sales managers responsible for the Macy's account. Wiswall screamed at Yanowitz, told her he was "sick and tired of all the f***ups" on the Macy's account, and said that Yanowitz could not get it right.

During the meeting, Roderick imposed a new travel schedule on Yanowitz, a schedule that regulated precisely how often she should visit each market in her territory. Two days after the meeting, Yanowitz went out on disability leave due to stress. She did not return, and L'Oreal replaced her in November 1998.

Yanowitz filed a discrimination charge with the Department of Fair Employment and Housing (DFEH) on June 25, 1999. She alleged that L'Oreal had discriminated against her on the basis of sex, age (Yanowitz was 53), and religion (Yanowitz is Jewish). She also alleged that L'Oreal had retaliated against her for refusing to fire the female employee Wiswall considered unattractive.

We consider only her claim for unlawful retaliation.

First, the employee must make out a prima facie case of retaliation. This requires proof of three elements: the employee "must show that [she] engaged in a protected activity, [the] employer subjected her to adverse employment action, and there is a causal link between the protected activity and the employer's action." Second, if the employee meets this burden, the burden shifts to the employer to articulate a legitimate nonretaliatory reason for any adverse employment action. Finally, after the employer produces a legitimate business justification, the employee must produce substantial responsive evidence that demonstrates the employer's reason for the adverse employment action was untrue or pretextual, or evidence that the employer acted with a retaliatory animus, or a combination of the two, such that a reasonable trier of fact could conclude the employer engaged in unlawful retaliation.

Evidence before the trial court established the following facts, undisputed by either side. In the fall of 1997, Jack Wiswall, Yanowitz's superior, ordered Yanowitz to have a female sales associate at a Macy's West store in her region fired. As justification, Wiswall explained that the associate "was not good looking enough." The associate had dark skin; Wiswall preferred fair-skinned blondes. Wiswall told Yanowitz, "Get me somebody hot," or words to that effect. Yanowitz did not carry out Wiswall's order. When Wiswall asked her whether the associate had been dismissed on subsequent occasions, Yanowitz requested adequate justification for firing her. Yanowitz did not complain to Human Resources, nor did she tell Wiswall that his order was discriminatory.

The trial court found that on these facts, Yanowitz had failed to establish she engaged in any protected activity. On appeal, L'Oreal argues that Yanowitz's actions are not protected because physical appearance is not a protected category under FEHA and because Yanowitz failed to expressly complain.

L'Oreal's argument misframes the first issue. The issue is not whether physical appearance is a protected category. Though protection against discrimination on this basis has been suggested, the FEHA does not proscribe discrimination on the basis of appearance. While courts have interpreted another antidiscrimination statute, the Unruh Act, to proscribe discrimination on many bases not expressed in the statute including physical appearance—no such latitude exists with regard to the FEHA. We are not free to read into the FEHA a category not included by the Legislature, and we do not address whether Wiswall's order was prohibited physical appearance discrimination. Instead, the issue is one of sex discrimination: May a male executive insist that a female subordinate be terminated because she is not sexually appealing to him, when no similar orders are issued with respect to male employees?

Sex discrimination in the workplace comes in many guises. In a most basic form, it involves outright exclusion of women, solely by reason of their sex. Even where women have gained access to the workplace, sex discrimination may persist in other forms, for example, through identification of particular jobs as "man-only" or "woman-only" jobs, through perpetuation of a glass ceiling that ensures women will only rise so high on the corporate ladder, or through the unwritten establishment of two sets of rules for success: for men, based on performance, and for women, based on appearance.

The notion that an employer may not insist on only attractive women employees has long been established. Southwest Airlines defended its policy that only attractive women could be hired as flight attendants and ticket agents. Southwest argued that female sex appeal was a bona fide occupational qualification (BFOQ) under Title VII because it wanted to project a "sexy image and fulfill its public promise to take passengers skyward with 'love.'" Because Southwest was not in a business where "vicarious sex entertainment is the primary service provided," the district court rejected Southwest's defense.

Just as an employer may not impose broad rules that regulate men and women differently based on their appearance or sexual desirability, so an employer may not discriminate against specific individuals on these bases. For example, an employer demoted a cocktail waitress who refused to wear sexually suggestive attire. The court recognized this as unlawful sex discrimination. The employer insisted that a female office building lobby attendant wear a sexually revealing uniform. When the employee refused, she was dismissed. The court concluded that the employee was required to wear the revealing uniform because she was a woman, and that she had made out a prima facie case of sex discrimination.

We find Wiswall's actions analogous. An explicit order to fire a female employee for failing to meet a male executive's personal standards for sexual desirability is sex discrimination. Yanowitz's evidence permits the inference that Wiswall would not have ordered the employee fired if she had been a man, simply because a man's physical attractiveness would not have been an issue. Moreover, we note that Yanowitz did not have to prove that Wiswall's order was discriminatory; she needed only to show a good faith, reasonable belief that it was. She did so here.

http://web.lexis-nexis.com/universe/- refpt_CA23 L'Oreal argues that Yanowitz's claim still must fail because Yanowitz failed to alert L'Oreal that its actions were discriminatory. That requirement does not apply to this case, which is not a grievance case. Here, an employer directed an employee to engage in discriminatory conduct, conduct for which the employer has offered no legitimate business purpose. The refusal to carry out a discriminatory order is protected whether or not the employee explains to the employer the unlawfulness of the conduct.

http://web.lexis-nexis.com/universe/- refpt_CA26b Applying this test at the summary adjudication stage, we hold that a reasonable jury could conclude that the criticisms Yanowitz received, the memos that were written about her, and the inquiries to subordinates seeking negative feedback were all part of a single course of conduct designed to punish her for her inaction on Wiswall's request. A jury could conclude that these actions were similar in kind, closely connected temporally, and had not culminated in a permanent act—such as dismissal—that would have put Yanowitz on notice that further conciliatory efforts would be futile. Consequently, Yanowitz is not barred from relying on pre-June 25, 1998, acts at this stage when trying to prove adverse action.

The judgment is reversed on Yanowitz's FEHA claim for retaliation, and this case is remanded for further proceedings on that claim. In all other respects, the judgment is affirmed. Yanowitz shall recover her costs on appeal.

Case Commentary
The California Appellate Court ruled that pressuring a subordinate to fire a worker for failing to meet the superior's idea of someone who is sexually desirable is tantamount to sex discrimination. ■

CASE QUESTIONS

1. Are you in agreement with the decision of the Court?
2. Was there any justification for Wiswall's actions?

3. Do you believe that Wiswall's conduct rises to the level of sex discrimination because Yanowitz was not the object of Wiswall's comments?

Men are also protected against gender discrimination under Title VII. Although men are not victimized as often as women, there are occasions when men have been treated unfavorably because of their gender.

The issue in the next case is whether an employee who was terminated for sexually harassing comments can claim sex discrimination because the comments were not severe and pervasive.

Gonsalves v. Nissan Motor Corporation in Hawaii, Ltd

58 P.3d 1196 (HI 2002)

Opinion by: Ramil, J.

BACKGROUND

On February 27, 1998, after working for about ten months at Nissan as a service department manager, Gonsalves was fired. On November 6, 1998, Gonsalves filed a complaint against Nissan, alleging (1) sex discrimination, (2) defamation, (3) promissory estoppel, and (4) intentional and negligent infliction of emotional distress.

At trial, Neldine Torres testified that Gonsalves made sexual comments to her, (The comments included "I like to look at you," "You're my honey," "I wouldn't mind getting caught with my pants down depending on who it was with," and "You smell good, you make me hungry.") blew on her neck, poked her sides near her bra-line, and touched her between her knee and thigh. There was testimony that Kevin Kualapai, who replaced Gonsalves as a service manager, made inappropriate comments to Torres, and Torres did not report him for sexual harassment. (Torres stated that Kualapai asked her, while she was counting money, "How much did you make on Hotel Street last night?" Kualapai testified that he once told Torres, who had one leg on her desk, that she should "put her legs down because the flies were getting dizzy.") In addition, a male employee had passed out lingerie calendars to other employees, with no objection.

Gonsalves testified that, in January 1998, Wayne Suehisa, vice president, administrator, and treasurer of Nissan Motor Corporation in Hawai'i, Ltd., informed him of Torres's sexual harassment allegations against him. Gonsalves denied the complaints. Suehisa admitted telling Gonsalves that he would get a "thorough and fair investigation," that he did not "need to get a lawyer," and that "because [Nissan was] planning on continuing to do an investigation at that point in time, Suehisa wasn't planning on terminating Gonsalves." Gonsalves testified that Suehisa also apprised him that he "didn't have to worry about losing his job."

Suehisa hired Linda Kreis to investigate Torres's allegations. Kreis testified that she interviewed and prepared statements for ten employees, including Torres and Gonsalves. After interviewing the witnesses, Kreis prepared a report summarizing the results of her investigation. She concluded that Gonsalves's "behavior . . . at the time of writing the report already could be construed as creating a hostile environment" and recommended that Gonsalves "be counseled about his unacceptable behavior and disciplined in a manner to assure there's no reoccurrence." Because Kreis had not received all of the signed statements, she termed this report an "interim report of investigation."

On February 21, 1998, Kreis sent the interim report to Suehisa. Suehisa responded to the report with "major disappointment":

> You know, here we had a manager that I guess was performing our game plan, like I had mentioned, who had a game plan to grow the business, he was executing on that. He seemed to be going in the right direction operationally. And, you know, as I had said earlier this morning, we were trying to, well, what I was hoping for was that we could come to a different resolution. But as you read each paragraph, as you came to find out that allegation after allegation was being corroborated by not only one witness but a number of witnesses, and that those witnesses were also bringing up things that they saw, they heard, it was very disappointing. It was disheartening, actually.

On February 24, 1998, Suehisa decided to terminate Gonsalves. Given the evidence already adduced from various witnesses, Suehisa determined that he did not need the final report. At the time of Suehisa's decision, four of the affidavits, including one from Torres, had not yet been signed. One of the later-received signed affidavits was actually supportive of Gonsalves.

On February 27, 1998, Nissan terminated Gonsalves. Suehisa explained that he waited until February 27, 1999 because he wanted to see whether receipt of any of the outstanding statements would "substantially change" the facts already established. The termination letter articulated that "based on Ms. Torres's allegations and the corroborating statements of the witnesses, [Nissan had] concluded that Gonsalves's conduct toward Ms. Torres could be construed as sexual harassment and warrants disciplinary action." The letter further expounded that Gonsalves had retaliated against Torres and other employees, contrary to Nissan's harassment and discrimination policy. On cross-examination, Gonsalves admitted that he had received a copy of Nissan's Policies and Guidelines Manual.

Gonsalves testified that he applied for about forty to fifty jobs after being terminated by Nissan, but was rejected from each one. On the applications, he was required to explain the reasons for his termination by Nissan.

On January 13, 2000, the court sent the case to the jury. On January 25, 2000, the jury returned its special verdict in favor of Gonsalves on the discrimination, promissory estoppel, and implied contract claims, and in favor of Nissan on the defamation and intentional infliction of emotional distress claims. The circuit court awarded the following amounts for a grand total of $ 2,918,249.59:

Special Damages (for discrimination, promissory estoppel, and implied contract claims)	$ 1,090,597.00
Punitive Damages (for discrimination claim)	$ 875,000.00
General Damages (for promissory estoppel claim)	$ 140,000.00
Costs (for discrimination, promissory estoppel, and implied contract claims)	$ 76,346.93
Attorney's Fees (maximum awarded under discrimination claim)	$ 708,649.80
Tax on Fees and Costs	$ 32,655.86
Less discovery sanction awarded against Gonsalves	$ 5,000.00

On June 8, 2000, Nissan filed a notice of appeal. On June 21, 2000, Gonsalves filed his notice of cross-appeal.

1. Differential treatment of "similarly situated" employees

First, Gonsalves alleges that Nissan discriminated against him on the basis of sex in that a similarly-situated female employee, Torres, was not subjected to the same treatment as he was.

Gonsalves, unlike Torres, was a supervisor and could be considered Nissan's agent. Once Nissan had notice of Torres's allegations against Gonsalves, Nissan was potentially liable for future sexual harassment. Indeed, Gonsalves's complaint acknowledges that he was responsible for enforcing Nissan's written policies, such as the one addressing sexual harassment, with regard to Torres and other subordinates. Thus, Gonsalves and Torres were not "similarly situated" employees.

Accordingly, Gonsalves is unable to demonstrate a claim of sex discrimination based on differential treatment of similarly situated employees.

2. Differential treatment for similar conduct

Second, Gonsalves contends that Nissan discriminated against him on the basis of sex in that he was "treated differently than others in the work place who engaged in similar conduct."

Yet, Gonsalves cited instances where male employees made comments sexual in nature to female employees, or touched female employees inappropriately, and were not disciplined. Indeed, Gonsalves's evidence actually indicates that male employees may have been treated leniently. Thus, Gonsalves's allegations of inconsistent treatment are not based on sex and are therefore irrelevant to a sex discrimination claim. Accordingly, Gonsalves does not state a cognizable claim of sex discrimination based on differential treatment for similar conduct.

3. Retaliation

Finally, Gonsalves claims that Nissan discriminated against him on the basis of sex in that Nissan illegally retaliated against himself and Nakamura.

In the present case, Gonsalves wrote a memorandum to Morrison and Suehisa regarding the "hostile work environment" he faced:

In 1980 the EEOC promulgated that, "If such conduct of an employee has the purpose of effect or unreasonably interfering with an individual's work performance or creating an intimidating hostile or offensive working environment," it is defined as just cause for a hostile working environment.

Please be aware that Neldine Torres's attitude and conduct along with her daily performance, actions, insubordination of her daily job description, duties, responsibilities, and company policies, is causing a hostile working environment for myself and members of my staff. Not to mention the emotional distress caused by defamation. This emotional distress is being caused by Neldine informing members of the staff that are not involved with the allegations or were unaware of the charges filed against me. This alone is a breach of INMS company rules, "unauthorized release of confidential information."

I do respect the wishes of the company, "being patient until this is resolved," but due to the daily effect it has on me and my staff, I feel that the matter described above should be addressed as soon as possible. This hostile working environment is unwelcome and is substantially affecting the work environment of reasonable persons.

The actual allegations described by Gonsalves in the second paragraph do not involve any discrimination based on sex. In fact, Gonsalves clarified that Torres's conduct created a hostile work environment for not only him, but also his staff, which included both males and females. As a result, Gonsalves does not have a claim for retaliation.

We conclude that Gonsalves was, as a matter of law, unable to maintain a sex discrimination claim based on (a) differential treatment of "similarly situated" employees, (b) differential treatment of similar conduct, or (c) retaliation. Accordingly, we hold, with respect to Gonsalves's sex discrimination claim, that the circuit court erred by denying Nissan's (1) motion for summary judgment, (2) two motions for judgment as a matter of law, and (3) renewed motion for judgment as a matter of law.

Conclusion

Because Gonsalves is unable to establish and maintain his sex discrimination, implied contract, and promissory estoppel claims, we remand for entry of a judgment in favor of Nissan with respect to the discrimination, promissory estoppel, and implied contract claims. Gonsalves's claims raised on appeal are without merit.

Judgment for Nissan.

Case Commentary

The Supreme Court of Hawai'i declared that Gonsalves's discrimination claim had no bearing on his sex. ∎

CASE QUESTIONS

1. Are you in agreement with the Court's decision?
2. Should Gonsalves be entitled to damages since the sexual harassment complaint filed against him was not severe and pervasive?
3. If not, can you imagine a set of circumstances where an individual accused of harassment should be entitled to damages if the requirements of severity and pervasiveness are not met?

SEX PLUS DISCRIMINATION

Discrimination may occur against an individual not solely because of his or her gender, but that fact coupled with another may be its cause. Women with small children, women in childbearing years, and women taking care of elderly parents are all examples.

As part of their interview process, some companies endeavor to discover if a female applicant has small children. It has been their experience that mothers are preoccupied with worrying about their children. In addition, many employers believe if the child becomes ill or gets hurt, the mother will leave work immediately. This behavior can be disruptive to the workplace. For that reason, the company may nonchalantly ask the female applicant where her children go to school. The response will indicate whether the woman has children and, if so, what their ages are. The company can then generally refuse her or deny her for another reason. This is discriminatory behavior.

BONA FIDE OCCUPATIONAL QUALIFICATION (BFOQ)

The bona fide occupational qualification (BFOQ) operates as a defense to a suit for discrimination with regard to religion, national origin, gender, and age. The first three defenses are found in Title VII, while the age BFOQ is found in the Age Discrimination in Employment Act. The courts have narrowly construed this defense, limiting it to job requirements that are essential to the job or are at the core purpose of the business. Mere job relatedness is not sufficient.

Employment Perspective

Nancy Hartwick attended Podunk University, where she was a star basketball player. She later became a women's basketball coach at Premier College, where she won the national championship four times. When a vacancy arose for the men's basketball coach at her alma mater, she applied. Although Podunk's administration had fond affection for Hartwick, they refused her application after consulting the school's students, players, and alumni. The students and alumni said that they would boycott the games. The players said they would have no confidence in her ability. Nancy claimed sex discrimination. Podunk argued that requiring a man to fill the position of men's basketball coach is a BFOQ. Are they correct? No! The preference of the constituents of Podunk does not qualify as a BFOQ. Nancy Hartwick's qualification must be judged in its face alone. Gender preference may not play a part.

Employment Perspective

Gail Dudack is a sports reporter for the *Minnesota Moon*, an evening daily newspaper. Gail had been covering women's sporting events, but now with the retirement of Charlie Scofield, she has been elevated to the major team sports. Her first assignment is a pro basketball game. During the game, Shorty Williams scores his 25,000th point. After the contest, all the reporters are rushing into the locker room to interview Shorty. Gail is refused entry because the men are changing and showering and she is a woman. Gail files a claim with the EEOC, alleging pro basketball is discriminating against women reporters. The team argues that the closed-door policy toward women is a BFOQ. Is her claim viable? Yes! The locker-room policy makes it impossible for a woman to be a first-rate reporter. Either the team must allow unrestricted entry or forbid all reporters from the locker room and conduct all interviews in the pressroom where equal access can be given.

Employment Perspective

Roger Bishop is a registered nurse at Sumner County Hospital. Roger is on duty one evening when Mildred Dirkson calls for assistance. When Roger attempts to assist Mildred, she admonishes him that she called for a nurse. Roger explains that he is a nurse, but she wants no part of him. Roger queries Mildred about the fact that if he were a physician, she would have no problem having him touch her. The next day Mildred's family complains to the hospital administration, and Roger is assigned to an all-male ward. The hospital justifies its action by asserting it is a BFOQ. Roger claims that this behavior is discriminatory because female nurses are not confined to servicing exclusively female patients. Who is correct? Roger! The hospital's action was not justified. BFOQs do not apply to one sex but not the other. Hospitals cannot discriminate in deference to their patients' preferences. The patients must accept the hospital staff as long as they are qualified. What if Mildred's request concerned applying medication to or washing the genital area? Every accommodation should be made in this regard if there are female nurses available. Respecting privacy is important. But patients who are hospitalized must have physicians on duty, who are predominantly male, view their private parts if the need arises and their private physician is not available. So, too, with nurses.

EQUAL PAY

The Equal Pay Act of 1963 is an amendment to the Fair Labor Standards Act, which regulates child labor, minimum wage, and overtime pay. The Equal Pay Act prohibits the payment of different wages to men and women who are performing the same job. This Act covers all types of job categories from clerical to executive. The jobs must be equal with regard to skill, knowledge, or experience, and the conditions under which the work is performed must be similar. For example, a person working overseas is entitled to a pay differential for the same job performed domestically.

The issue in the following case is whether the job of a prison guard requires a bona fide occupational qualification.

Carl v. Angelone
883 F.Supp. 1433 (D.Nev. 1995)

Reed, Jr., District Judge.

Plaintiff alleges that Mr. Angelone is the director of Nevada Department of Prisons (NDOP). Plaintiffs are Correctional Officers (C/Os within NDOP). They allege that Mr. Angelone intentionally discriminated against them on the basis of their gender.

Plaintiffs allege that Mr. Angelone transferred Plaintiff male C/Os out of two women's correctional facilities and transferred plaintiff female C/Os from other correctional facilities to fill the vacancies. Mr. Angelone concedes that he did this and that he did so based on the plaintiff's gender: i.e., Mr. Angelone admits he made the transfers because he wanted female correctional officers at the women's correctional facilities and therefore transferred the male officers out because they were men and transferred the female officers in because they were women.

Qualified immunity protects government officials from civil liability for actions taken in the performance of discretionary functions when their actions do not violate clearly established statutory or constitutional rights of which a reasonable person should have known. However, no official can in good faith impose discriminatory burdens on a person or group by reason of a racial or ethnic animus against them. The constitutional right to be free from such invidious discrimination is so well established and so essential to the preservation of our constitutional order that all public officials must be charged with knowledge of it.

In cases involving intentional discrimination there can be no qualified immunity defense, and the dispositive issue of the defendant's intent merge. If the plaintiff fails to establish that the discrimination was intentional, the claim fails. If the plaintiff does establish such intent, there can be no qualified immunity. Thus, it seems simpler to say that qualified immunity is not a defense in such cases rather than that the defense prevails where proof of intentional discrimination is not established.

There is substantial evidence that the motivating factor for Mr. Angelone's actions was the gender of each of the individual plaintiffs. Mr. Angelone not only admits that he took the challenged actions solely on the basis of gender. Mr. Angelone contends that because he thought his actions were legal and appropriate responses, . . . his actions were non-discriminatory.

Mr. Angelone's belief that his actions were legal and appropriate . . . does not remove discriminatory intent from his actions. This raises the affirmative defense of bona fide occupational qualification (BFOQ) in which a defendant admits the discriminatory intent motivating the actions, but claims that such actions were otherwise necessary.

The BFOQ is an affirmative defense in itself. To allow defendants to elevate it into a qualified immunity appears improper for several reasons. First, the BFOQ is an affirmative defense to liability. No good reason is presented why qualified immunity should flow from the assertion of an affirmative defense on which defendant has the burden of proof. This would in essence reverse the burden of proof, requiring plaintiff to demonstrate that defendant could not have reasonably believed the BFOQ defense applied, even though the defendant would bear the burden of proving the BFOQ defense.

Where discrimination on the basis of gender exists, the employer bears the burden of proving:

1) that the job qualification or function justifying the discrimination is reasonably necessary to the essence of the defendant's particular business; and 2) that gender is a legitimate proxy for the qualification or function because (a) there is a substantial basis for believing that all or nearly all employees of the affected gender lack the qualification or ability to perform that function, or (b) it is impossible or highly impractical for the defendant to insure by individual testing that its employees will have qualifications for the job.

A defendant Prison must demonstrate why it cannot reasonably rearrange job responsibilities within the prison to minimize the clash between the privacy interests of the inmates and the safety of the Prison employees on the one hand and the non-discriminatory requirement of Title VII on the other, before the prison will be entitled to the bfoq exception.

First, Mr. Angelone argues a per se rule making it illegal for male correctional officers to conduct routine or random body searches of female prisoners. If that were so, such a rule would be binding upon Mr. Angelone. . . .

... there is no per se rule upon which Mr. Angelone may rely which would permit him to take the challenged actions. There is no per se rule providing a substantial basis for believing that male C/Os lack the legal ability to perform random or routine body searches of female inmates.

Judgment for Carl.

CASE QUESTIONS

1. Do you agree with the Court's decision?
2. Do you believe male correction officers should be employed in female prisons?
3. Should male correction officers be allowed to conduct body searches on female inmates if

these inmates are uncomfortable with this procedure?
4. Should the BFOQ have been implemented in this case?

Case Commentary

The District Court of Nevada decided that employing only female correction officers in a female prison is not a bona fide occupational qualification. This policy is discriminatory toward male correction officers. ■

In the following case, a female veterinarian claimed that her employer paid her less than similarly experienced male colleagues. The issue is whether the employer discriminated against her in violation of the Equal Pay Act.

McMillan v. Massachusetts Soc. of Cruelty to Animals

880 F. Supp. 900 (D. Mass. 1995)

Stearns, District Judge.

Dr. Marjorie McMillan began her career as Director of Radiology at Angell in 1981. She worked continuously until December of 1983, when she took a leave of absence lasting through 1985. Angell maintains some twenty veterinarians on staff who provide direct care as well as instructional guidance to interns and post-graduate residents. McMillan's salary complaint dates from her return as Director of Radiology in 1985.

Until 1989, Thornton served as Angell's Chief of Staff. In that position, he was responsible for setting salary levels for new employees and determining annual increases. In 1989, Thornton became President of the MSPCA and Gambardella designed and implemented a salary system which assigned a grade to every veterinarian and awarded annual increases in pay based on performance evaluations and ranges within each grade. In the year following the implementation of this new pay system, McMillan's salary jumped from $58,295 to $72,000. Notwithstanding this increase, it is undisputed that from 1985 until the termination of her employment on November 26, 1991, McMillan was paid less than any other Director/Department Head, while her job description was for all practical purposes indistinguishable from that of her male colleagues.

McMillan first discovered the pay disparity in August of 1989. She filed a gender discrimination claim with the MCAD in October of 1989. In January of 1990, McMillan entered into negotiations with Angell over the purchase of Windhover, a private aviary practice established by

McMillan in Walpole, Mass. McMillan sought to rent space at Angell to carry on the new practice.

To establish a prima facie case under the Equal Pay Act, a plaintiff must show: 1. that her employer is subject to the Act; 2. that discrimination regarding wages occurred within the same working establishment; 3. that she performed work in a position requiring equal skill, effort and responsibility under similar working conditions; and 4. that she was paid less than a comparable employee of the opposite sex. The plaintiff is not required to show that the compared jobs are identical, only that they are "substantially equal." Once a prima facie case is made out under the Equal Pay Act, the employer must resort to the Act's statutory defenses, that is, that pay differentials can be explained by seniority, merit, quantity or quality of production or by "any other factor other than sex."

The affirmative defenses of the Equal Pay Act were incorporated by Congress into Title VII by way of the so-called Bennett Amendment. The Amendment is intended to prevent plaintiffs from using Title VII to circumvent the Equal Pay Act when the pay difference at issue can be justified by one or more of the Equal Pay Acts' affirmative defenses. However, as construed by the Supreme Court, the Amendment does not confine Title VII sex-based wage discrimination claims to the four corners of the Equal Pay Act. The Court's concern was with the "equal work" requirement of the Act. If strictly applied in the Title VII context, "this requirement would mean that a woman who is discriminatorily underpaid could obtain no relief—no matter how egregious the discrimination might be—unless her employer also employed a man in an equal job in the same establishment, at a higher rate of pay." Equal Pay Act litigation, therefore, has been structured to permit employers to defend against charges of discrimination where their pay differentials are based on a bona fide use of facts other than sex.

EQUAL PAY

The MSPCA argues that because McMillan as Director/ Department Head of Radiology did not have the same supervisory, budgetary, or administrative responsibilities as did other Directors/ Department Heads (that is, her job was not "substantially equivalent"), she cannot establish a prima facie case under the Equal Pay Act. Thornton and Gambardella also deny that gender formed the basis of any

of their salary decisions. They justify the significant salary differential between McMillan and the others by asserting that her job was less time consuming, produced less revenue for the MSPCA, and involved fewer functions. Specifically, they point to the fact that Radiology had the smallest staff and no actual responsibility for interns or residents.

Because a material dispute of fact exists concerning the comparability of McMillan's position with that of other department heads, the defendant's motion for summary judgment must be denied with respect to a claim of a violation of the Equal Pay Act.

Judgment for McMillan.

Case Commentary

The District Court of Massachusetts held that the Equal Pay Act is at issue. McMillan will be given the opportunity to prove her case at trial. ∎

CASE QUESTIONS

1. Do you agree with the Court's decision?
2. Do you believe McMillan will triumph?

3. Are there any instances where women do not deserve equal pay?

COMPARABLE WORTH

Comparable worth is an attempt to assign values to male-dominated and female-dominated jobs based on worth. Where the values are equated, equal pay would be required. The theory behind this doctrine was that most female-dominated jobs pay less than male-dominated jobs. This argument has not found favor with the courts because assigning values is arbitrary and interferes with payments based on supply and demand.

Employment Perspective

Gary Josephson is a construction worker. Jessica Tremont is a stenographer. He earns $36,000. She earns $22,000. Jessica argues that both jobs have comparable worth and that she should earn the same as Gary. Is she correct? No! Although her argument is based on comparable worth, the courts have decided not to enforce this doctrine.

GROOMING

When employers attempt to regulate grooming, i.e., length of hair, beards, and mustaches, courts have usually found in favor of the employer. Their reasoning is that grooming codes are more closely related to the manner in which an employer decides to operate its business than to equal opportunity. Good grooming standards have always been required in the business world. Imagine walking into a bank and seeing a long-haired branch manager who has not shaved or showered, wearing jeans and a wrinkled shirt. This kind of appearance is not allowed because it would not be a good business policy. Customers may lose confidence in the bank and move their accounts elsewhere.

Arguments against grooming codes have come in the form of the First Amendment's rights of speech through personal expression, the Fourteenth Amendment Equal Protection Clause, and Title VII's provision regarding terms and conditions of employment.

Employment Perspective

Richard Masters is 29, and he is becoming bald. He is very self-conscious, so he has started wearing a hat all the time. Richard works as a bond trader for Bulls and Bears, Inc. Although his manager empathizes with Richard's dilemma, Richard is told to remove the hat while in the office. Richard objects, claiming that baldness is a disability, and files a claim with the EEOC. Will he win? Probably not! Richard is not being subjected to discrimination because of his disability. If Richard is harassed by coworkers, he may register a complaint for harassment. That is not the problem here, though. It revolves around Richard's vanity and his own perception of himself. This reasoning cannot outweigh Bulls and Bears' maintenance of dress codes as the way it conducts its business.

Employment Perspective

Mary Jo Worthington, a longtime customer at Grasmere Bank, is informed by Felix Farnsworth that he will be leaving the branch for a new position. On Monday, his replacement will begin. When Mary Jo enters the bank on Monday, she is horrified to see a long-haired man who has neither showered nor shaved, wearing jeans, cowboy boots, and a T-shirt, sitting behind Felix's old desk. The scruffy man smiles and then introduces himself as Jesse Mickelson, new branch manager. Mary Jo dashes out of the bank and calls its customer service department, reporting what she saw. Mickelson is informed of the bank's grooming policy and is told never to be seen like that again. The next day, Mickelson looks the same and, therefore, is immediately terminated. He files a Title VII claim with the EEOC, asserting that his actions are protected by freedom of speech through personal expression. Jesse also claims that the grooming policy as a term and condition of employment is discrimination. Is he correct? Most likely not! Although there have been conflicting cases, the bank will be able to enforce its grooming policy because it is requiring of Mickelson only what is considered to be the norm in American business. He is not being deprived of an equal opportunity. He is only being asked to conform to the generally accepted standards of our society.

Employment Perspective

Sonja Hendricks was a trader at First Financial in Buffalo. The company dress code requires women to wear skirts, dresses, or suits with skirts. In the winter, the temperature is often below freezing. Sonja wore pants to keep her legs warm. First Financial dismissed her for being uncooperative. She claimed that the dress code manifested sex discrimination because it forced women to show their legs and to be subjected to the cold weather. Is she correct? Probably! This restriction places an undue burden on women in that it does not give them the choice to protect themselves from the cold during the winter months. First Financial's business reasons are not paramount to a woman's health. However, First Financial may suggest that women wear leg warmers or tights under their skirts or dresses and then remove then upon arriving at work. There is no definitive answer to this scenario.

In the next case, a female contests an employer's dress code as being discriminatory in that the women's attire is demeaning as compared with the men's attire. The women were suspended when they wore the same business attire as the men.

O'Donnell v. Burlington Coat Factory Warehouse

706 F. Supp. 263 (S.D. Ohio 1987)

Spiegel, District Judge.

In this sex discrimination action, plaintiffs, female sales clerks at defendants' retail store, challenge defendants' dress code as being violative of Title VII of the Civil Rights Act of 1964. The dress code in question requires female sales clerks to wear a "smock," while male sales clerks only are required to wear business attire consisting of slacks, shirt and a necktie. The smocks are supplied to the female sales clerks at no cost. After complaining that the smock requirement for women is discriminatory, plaintiffs refused to wear the smocks and instead wore regular business attire. Plaintiffs filed sex discrimination charges with the EEOC on August 18, 1983. Thereafter, plaintiffs reported for work wearing a blouse and tie and each day they were suspended. On August 30, 1983, plaintiffs were discharged when they refused to wear smocks. Plaintiffs filed charges with the EEOC claiming their discharge was sex discrimination and retaliation. Subsequently, the EEOC determined that there was reasonable cause to believe that the charge was true. After attempts at conciliation proved futile, plaintiffs commenced the present action in this Court. Both parties agree that the issue before this Court on summary judgment is whether defendants' dress code requiring female sales clerks to wear a smock while allowing male sales clerks to wear a shirt and tie is discriminatory under Title VII. The defendants' contend that distinctions between the sexes that do not adversely effect the terms and conditions of employment or employment opportunities do not violate Title VII. In *Barker*, the Court upheld an employer's grooming code which mandated shorter hair lengths for men than for women. Importantly, this grooming code set standards for both sexes: it regulated the length of men's hair and the styles for women's hair. According to defendants, the question we must decide is whether the differences in treatment created disadvantages for women in their compensation, terms, conditions or privileges of employment or employment opportunities. Because plaintiffs stipulated that wearing the smocks had no effect on their salary, benefits, hours of employment, raises, employment evaluations or any other term or condition of employment, defendants argue that the distinction in question is not discriminatory. Analogizing the dress requirement here to the grooming code in *Barker*, defendants claim both sexes

had equal burdens with respect to their dress requirements: female employees had to wear a smock and male employees had to wear a shirt and tie. Plaintiffs acknowledge that Title VII does not prohibit all differences in treatment between the sexes but claim that a rule requiring only women to wear a smock does violate Title VII. In support of the position, plaintiffs claim that the instant case should not be governed by the "hair length/grooming" line of decisions cited by defendants. Rather, plaintiffs direct our attention to cases directly addressing "uniform" requirements that mandate different dress standards for male and female employees. In the lead case of *Carroll v. Talman Fed. Sav. & Loan*, a bank required its female tellers, officers and managerial employees to wear a uniform while male employees working in the same positions were required only to wear customary business attire. Unlike the case at bar, the female employees in *Talman* incurred the initial cost of their uniforms as well as subsequent cleaning and maintenance expenses. The employer expressly maintained that the purpose of the uniform requirement was to reduce fashion competition among women. Since men do not engage in such competition, they do not need a uniform requirement.

The Seventh Circuit held that personal appearance regulations with differing requirements for men and women do not violate Title VII as long as there is "some justification in commonly accepted social norms and are reasonably related to the employer's business needs." However, an employer who imposes separate dress requirements for men and women performing the same jobs will violate Title VII when one sex can wear regular business attire and the other must wear a uniform. Finding the uniform requirement demeaning to women, the *Talman* Court stated; "while there is nothing offensive about uniforms per se, when some employees are uniformed and others are not there is a natural tendency to assume that the uniformed women have lesser professional status than their colleagues." Even though defendants have expressed no discriminatory motive for the "smock" rule, we find that the blatant effect of such a rule is to perpetuate sexual stereotypes. We believe the cornerstone of the *Talman* decision is that it is demeaning for one sex to wear a uniform when members of the other sex holding the same positions are allowed to wear professional business attire. In contrast to the "hair length" standards for male employees, the smock requirement finds no justification in accepted social norms. Moreover, as plaintiffs point out, defendants have several non-discriminatory alternatives for achieving the goal of sales clerk identification: both sexes could wear the smock, a distinguishing blazer or identifying badges on their professional attire. Thus, we find that the smock rule creates disadvantages to the conditions of employ- ment of females sales clerks and hence, is a violation of Title VII.

Judgment for O'Donnell.

Case Commentary

The Southern District Court of Ohio ruled that requiring women to wear smocks, while men wore business attire, constituted sex discrimination because the requirement was demeaning to women. ■

CASE QUESTIONS

1. Do you agree with the Court's decision?
2. Why do you think the company had different requirements for men and women?

3. If you were representing the company, what argument would you make on its behalf?

CUSTOMER PREFERENCES

Although we are in an age in which customer service and satisfaction rules, acceding to customer preferences for service exclusively by one gender to the exclusion of the other is contradictory to Title VII's prohibition against gender discrimination.

Employment Perspective

Tooters, a sports bar and restaurant chain known for its voluptuous female servers, has recently received applications from Ken, Frank, and Nick, who seek employment as servers. Tooters polls its clientele, who resoundingly state that they will no longer frequent the premises if male servers appear. Tooters denies the position to Ken, Frank, and Nick because of their gender. Ken, Frank, and Nick sue for sex discrimination arguing, as long as they were otherwise qualified, they cannot be refused employment on the basis of their gender. Is the customer always right and will they be toiling at Tooters? Tooters would have to prove that its business is primarily entertainment, which requires females to dress provocatively. This issue has been left in doubt in light of a settlement in a case involving a similar situation against Hooters Restaurant.

Job selection cannot be based on customer preference for a particular gender; otherwise, it is discriminatory.

Employment Perspective

Thomas Stockwell applies for a position with "Workouts for Women Only," a health club exclusively for women. He is denied employment because he is a man. The proprietors are concerned with respecting the privacy rights of women. They argue that requiring only women employees is a bona fide occupational qualification. Thomas argues that assisting women with fitness instruction, teaching aerobics, and performing desk duties do not qualify as a BFOQ. Besides, he adds there are female employees available for locker-room maintenance. Is he correct? Yes! The preference of women customers to refrain from working out in front of men does not qualify as a BFOQ sufficient enough to override perpetuating discrimination against men by requiring their exclusion from employment.

Employee Lessons

1. Know what constitutes sex discrimination.
2. Learn the requirement for filing a sex discrimination claim.
3. Ascertain whether as a woman you are being paid a salary comparable to a man with similar experience for the same job.
4. Do not let stereotypes hinder your realization of your true potential.
5. Appreciate why the enactment of the Equal Pay Act and the Civil Rights Act of 1964 was needed to protect women's rights.
6. Understand that under certain limited circumstances, your sex may disqualify you from being hired because of a bona fide occupational qualification.
7. Realize that the doctrine of comparable worth was never implemented because supply and demand renders it impractical.
8. Demand that you be treated in a manner consistent with the opportunities afforded to employees of the opposite sex.
9. Be cognizant of situations where you are discriminated against not only based on sex, but also because you have small children, are pregnant, or care for elderly parents, i.e., sex plus discrimination.
10. Be aware of grooming and dress code requirements and adhere to them where they are consistent and reasonable.

Summary

In the past, American society excluded women from many positions in the labor market because they could afford to do so. The American society was the most affluent in the world while its economy was flourishing almost exclusively at the hands of men. In today's global environment, no brain can be left untapped. Women should be encouraged by men to realize their potential in the workplace. Some men fear that employing women in business will reduce the number of positions for them. Their fear is misdirected. "Us against them" should not mean men against women. It should mean keeping the jobs in the United States as opposed to them outsourcing overseas. If the power of each American male and female is not used to its fullest to become innovators and entrepreneurs to develop newer, faster, cheaper, and better products, services, and technologies, then the positions that men are trying to safeguard from women will be lost to overseas competitors. The key is that the number and quality of jobs are elastic and can expand or contract, depending upon how well we perform.

Review Questions

1. Define sex discrimination.
2. What is sex plus discrimination?
3. Explain the significance of the Equal Pay Act.
4. Define comparable worth.
5. Is comparable worth in effect today?
6. Are grooming standards permissible?
7. Can a man be discriminated against because of his gender?
8. Why is a BFOQ a defense to a gender discrimination suit?
9. Ethically, should women tennis players be paid the same as the men in the U.S. Open, even though the women play 2 out of 3 sets in comparison to the 3 out of 5 sets played by the men?
10. Are employers justified in practicing sex discrimination in hiring because of customer preferences?
11. Should grooming codes be the same for men as for women?
12. Is the Equal Pay Act helping women to achieve equality in pay?

13. Is there any reason why women should not be paid at the same rate as men?
14. What must a plaintiff prove to establish a prima facie case under the Equal Pay Act?

CASE PROBLEMS

1. Mary Buhrmaster was initially hired in 1984 by Charles Littleton, the manager of Overnite's Dayton Terminal. For the next 7 1/2 years, she had a relatively successful career there. There was apparently widespread discontent among Overnite's employees concerning Buhrmaster's management style. The employees complained to Littleton about these problems several times both individually and en masse, but nothing was done. The employees then complained to the home office in Richmond, Virginia, precipitating a visit from Ray Laughrum, an executive with the company. After meeting with various employees, Laughrum advised Littleton, and, according to Overnite, Littleton decided to fire Buhrmaster. Littleton replaced Buhrmaster with another woman.

   Because there was no direct evidence of discrimination, Buhrmaster attempted to prove her case circumstantially by claiming that she had been treated differently from similarly situated men who had engaged in similar conduct. At trial, she produced evidence showing that a number of supervisors had also engaged in some form of misconduct and had not been fired. The issue in this case is whether there should be a presumption against discrimination where the person who is discharging the employee is the same person who hired her. *Buhrmaster v. Overnite Transportation Company*, 61 F.3d 461 (6th Cir. 1995)

2. Becerra alleged that Pallas traded sexual favors with her superiors, especially Muller and Captain Roland Saenz, commander of Task Force 168, to achieve her success. Becerra argues that he was the victim of sexual discrimination and sexual harassment. Becerra claims that there is evidence of a sexually hostile environment wherein Pallas was trading sexual favors for promotional opportunities to Becerra's career detriment. Becerra relies on 29 C.F.R. § 1604.11(g) to establish this definition of sexual harassment:

   Other related practices: Where employment opportunities or benefits are granted because of an individual's submission to the employer's sexual advances or requests for sexual favors, the employer may be held liable for unlawful sex discrimination against other persons who are qualified but denied that employment opportunity or benefit. The issue is whether a superior who promotes a female lover has sexually discriminated against male employees who would otherwise have been in line for the promotion. *Becerra v. Dalton, Secretary of the Navy*, 94 F.3d 145 (4th Cir. 1996)

3. At issue in this case are the equitable remedies awarded to the plaintiff, Mary Jane Kerr Selgas ("Kerr Selgas"), in a sex discrimination suit against her employer, American Airlines ("American"). A jury awarded Kerr Selgas a lump sum award in that suit that included an unspecified amount for front pay. American maintains in this appeal that front pay and reinstatement are mutually exclusive equitable remedies, and that the court therefore erred in allowing both to Kerr Selgas. The question presented is whether an employee can be entitled to both reinstatement and front pay under Title VII of the Civil Rights Act of 1964. *Kerr Selgas v. American Airlines*, 104 F.3d 9 (1st Cir. 1997)

4. In November 1988, West told her supervisor, James Laufenberg, that she was planning to marry an Atlanta resident in June 1989. West advised that she wanted to remain with Marion but, following the marriage, would need to relocate to Atlanta or to Marion in Kansas City, where her new husband could relocate. West hoped that she would be promoted to regional manager for the Wound Care Division in Kansas City, but Laufenberg was "not particularly positive" that she would attain that position.

   On August 29, West met with both Laufenberg and Gianini. Laufenberg advised that there was no opening in the Wound Care Division in Atlanta. Gianini advised that he had looked but was unable to find her an Atlanta position elsewhere in the company. West then wrote a lengthy letter to Laufenberg on September 2, and she filed a charge of retaliation discrimination on September 5. Alternatively, Marion's Prescription Products Division "will provide you with a rover position in Field Sales. . . . This will permit you to move to Atlanta and remain with Marion at no loss in base pay while we wait for a regular opening to develop" in Atlanta.

After receiving Laufenberg's September 21 letter, West declined all of the positions offered and resigned on September 30. What result? *West v. Marion Merrell Dow, Inc.*, 34 F.3d 493 (8th Cir. 1995)

5. Dr. Anderson brought this suit against various state entities and officers, alleging violations of the EPA. She alleges that since 1984, she has been paid less than male faculty of similar rank at SUNY New Paltz, despite her equivalent or superior qualifications, record, and workload. She began complaining to responsible officials at SUNY New Paltz in 1991, and she contends that she was denied a merit increase in salary in January 1993 as a result of such complaints. This case presents the issue of whether the Equal Pay Act infringes upon the states' rights to sovereign immunity. *Anderson v. Suny College at New Paltz*, 169 F.3d117 (2d Cir. 1999)

HUMAN RESOURCE DILEMMAS

1. Lenore Wilkenson is shopping for a new dress at Oak Valley Department Store. When she decides to try a few on to see how they look, Lenore is confronted by Derek Sanders, who is safeguarding the changing area. Lenore complains to the store manager that she refuses to use the changing area with a male at its entrance. This is the seventh complaint in Derek's first month of work. Oak Valley discharges him. Derek believes this conduct to be unfair. How would you advise him?

2. Tammy Dale works as an administrative assistant for Southeast Trucking Company. Tammy learns from Melissa in payroll that the male drivers make $15,000 more than the predominantly female administrative assistants on average. Tammy wishes to file a complaint alleging violation of Equal Pay Act and the Comparable Work Doctrine. How would you advise her to proceed?

3. Amy Goldstein is an assistant vice president at Reliable Insurance. When her superior retires, Amy is passed over for a subordinate. Amy asks for an explanation. Vice president Bruce Wilson explains that this position involves working long hours, extended business trips, and attendance at numerous weekend corporate functions. Because it is common knowledge that Amy's mother, who lives with her, is bedridden, Amy could not possibly fulfill the responsibilities that come with the promotion. What would your advice to Amy be?

WEB SITE ASSIGNMENT

Assume you are a consultant brought in to advise a large company about employment discrimination. Using the Web sites that follow as a guide, how would you convince an all-male senior management team to hire qualified women in the senior ranks as positions become available?

www.findlaw.com
www.westlaw.com
www.eeoc.gov/facts/fs-sex.html
workers.labor.net.au/26/news9_sex.html
www.pfc.org.uk/legal/sda-gr.htm
www.info.gov.hk/hab/sdo.htm
www.nationalpartnership.org
www.geocities.com/sxdsc
www.legal-definitions.com/discriminination.htm
www.legal-term.com/discriminate-definition.htm
www.ed.gov/policy/rights/guid/ocr/sex.html
www.aclu.org/WorkplaceRights/WorkplaceRightslist.cfm?c=182

Chapter 11

Sexual Harassment

Employment Scenario

Tom Long has been walking on air since the arrival of Jenn Smiley, the new inventory control analyst. Jenn has been currying favor with Tom, hoping it pays off with a raise and promotion down the road. Tom sees things differently. He believes Jenn is infatuated with him. This makes Tom think that, at age 47, he still has what it takes. This could not be further from the truth. When Tom puts the moves on Jenn, inviting her for the weekend to his ski chalet, Jenn rebuffs his advances. Jenn's flirtatious behavior was just a façade. Tom was furious. His initial reaction was to fire Jenn on the spot. When he discussed this with coowner Mark Short, Mark suggested Tom talk this over with L&S's attorney, Susan North. What advice should Susan give them?

Employment Scenario

Edward Fantry, Chris Mendam, and Roy McDonald are all salespeople at The Long and the Short of It. One stormy Monday morning, while business is slow, they are conversing about their weekend sexual exploits. Their recounting of the details of their sexual relations is vivid and demeaning toward women. All of this is transpiring within earshot of the cashier, Sandra Jacoby. Sandra is visibly upset by their language, and she asks them to knock it off. They are unrelenting and reply in tandem to Sandra to buzz off. Sandra files a complaint with L&S for hostile work environment. Tom Long and Mark Short seek Susan North's advice on how to handle this. What course of action should Susan recommend?

Chapter Checklist

➤ *Identify what constitutes sexual harassment.*

➤ *Learn the distinction between the two types of sexual harassment: quid pro quo and hostile work environment.*

➤ *Know that sexual harassment must be severe and pervasive to be actionable.*

➤ *Understand that terms such as babe, sweetheart, and honey are not severe, but may violate company policy.*

➤ *Appreciate that sexual harassment must be based on sex.*

➤ *Be aware that harassment that is neither sexual nor covered under any suspect classification is not protected under the Civil Rights Act of 1964.*

➤ *Be cognizant of the fact that victims of harassment may sue the perpetrator under tort law in state court.*

➤ *Be apprised of the fact that sexual harassment suits are brought only against the company.*

➤ *Understand that the sexual harassment must have occurred within the scope of employment.*

➤ *Know that employers are generally liable only where they have failed to investigate and/or take appropriate action.*

➤ *Become familiar with your employer's sexual harassment policy and conduct yourself accordingly.*

INTRODUCTION

Sexual harassment encompasses the request for sexual favors as well as touching, joking, commenting, or distributing material of a sexual nature that an employee has not consented to and finds offensive. The aggrieved individual may initiate a lawsuit against the individual personally or may proceed against the company. If there was unpermitted touching, this gives rise to the torts of civil assault and battery. If sexual comments were made with a particular individual in mind, that would constitute slander. If sexual comments were written or sexual pictorials were drawn, it would be libel. If generic comments were made that degraded the gender, an individual could claim the tort of infliction of emotional distress.

HUMAN RESOURCE ADVICE

- Draft a sexual harassment policy.
- Educate managers and employees about what constitutes sexual harassment.
- Understand the difference between *quid pro quo* and hostile work environment.
- Investigate complaints expeditiously and thoroughly.
- Determine how you will deal with employees who are guilty of harassment.
- Instruct managers to avoid favoritism, because this may lead to the perception of harassment.
- Acknowledge that harassment may be perpetrated against employees of the same sex.
- Appreciate that a comment, joke, or pictorial must be sexual in nature.

- Realize that sexual harassment must be severe and pervasive.
- Address only those instances of sexual harassment committed during the scope of employment.

Requirements

There are six requirements that must be satisfied for sexual harassment to exist:

1. The victimizing employee alleging sexual harassment must be a member of a protected class, that is, a man or a woman.
2. The complaint must be gender related, for example, a female must assert there would have been no harassment if she were not a woman.
3. The employee must not have consented to the sexual advances or participated in the hostile work environment.
4. The harassment must be based on sex.
5. The conduct complained of must have had a deleterious effect on the employee's job.
6. Vicarious liability exists, that is, the harassment must have occurred during the scope of employment, thus making the employer liable for the sexual harassing conduct of its employees.

The issues in this case are whether hostile work environment is an actionable form of sexual harassment and whether an employer is absolutely liable for sexual harassment whether it knows about it or not.

Meritor Savings Bank v. Vinson

477 U.S. 57 (1986)

Justice Rehnquist delivered the opinion of the Court.

This case presents important questions concerning claims of workplace "sexual harassment" brought under Title VII of the Civil Rights Act of 1964.

I

In 1974, respondent Mechelle Vinson met Sidney Taylor, a vice president of what is now petitioner Meritor Savings Bank (bank) and manager of one of its branch offices. When respondent asked whether she might obtain employment at the bank, Taylor gave her an application, which she completed and returned the next day; later that same day Taylor called her to say that she had been hired. With Taylor as her supervisor, respondent started as a teller-trainee, and thereafter was promoted to teller, head teller, and assistant branch manager. She worked at the same branch for four years, and it is undisputed that her advancement there was based on merit alone. In September 1978, respondent notified Taylor that she was taking sick leave for an indefinite period. On November 1, 1978, the bank discharged her for excessive use of that leave.

Respondent brought this action against Taylor and the bank, claiming that during her four years at the bank she had "constantly been subjected to sexual harassment" by Taylor in violation of Title VII. She sought injunctive relief, compensatory and punitive damages against Taylor and the bank, and attorney's fees.

At the 11-day bench trial, the parties presented conflicting testimony about Taylor's behavior during respondent's employment. Respondent testified that during her probationary period as a teller-trainee, Taylor treated her in a fatherly way and made no sexual advances. Shortly thereafter, however, he invited her out to dinner and, during the course of the meal, suggested that they go to a motel to have sexual relations. At first she refused, but out of what she described as fear of losing her job she eventually agreed. According to respondent, Taylor thereafter made repeated demands upon her for sexual favors, usually at the branch, both during and after business hours; she estimated that over the next several years she had intercourse with him some 40 or 50 times. In addition, respondent testified that Taylor fondled her in front of other employees, followed her into the women's restroom when she went there alone, exposed himself to her, and even forcibly raped her on several occasions. These activities ceased after 1977, respondent stated, when she started going with a steady boyfriend.

Taylor denied respondent's allegations of sexual activity, testifying that he never fondled her, never made suggestive remarks to her, never engaged in sexual intercourse with her, and never asked her to do so. He contended instead that respondent made her accusations in response to a business-related dispute. The bank also denied respondent's allegations and asserted that any sexual harassment by Taylor was unknown to the bank and engaged in without its consent or approval.

The District Court denied relief, but did not resolve the conflicting testimony about the existence of a sexual relationship between respondent and Taylor. It found instead that

> "if respondent and Taylor did engage in an intimate or sexual relationship during the time of respondent's employment with the bank, that relationship was a voluntary one having nothing to do with her continued employment at the bank or her advancement or promotions at that institution.

The court ultimately found that respondent "was not the victim of sexual harassment and was not the victim of sexual discrimination" while employed at the bank. Although it concluded that respondent had not proved a violation of Title VII, the District Court nevertheless went on to address the bank's liability. After noting the bank's express policy against discrimination, and finding that neither respondent nor any other employee had ever lodged a complaint about sexual harassment by Taylor, the court ultimately concluded that "the bank was without notice and cannot be held liable for the alleged actions of Taylor."

The Court of Appeals for the District of Columbia Circuit reversed. The court stated that a violation of Title VII may be predicated on either of two types of sexual harassment: harassment that involves the conditioning of concrete employment benefits on sexual favors, and harassment that, while not affecting economic benefits, creates a hostile or offensive working environment.

As to the bank's liability, the Court of Appeals held that an employer is absolutely liable for sexual harassment practiced by supervisory personnel, whether or not the employer knew or should have known about the misconduct. The court relied chiefly on Title VII's definition of "employer" to include "any agent of such a person." The court held that a supervisor is an "agent" of his employer for Title VII purposes, even if he lacks authority to hire, fire, or promote, since "the mere existence—or even the appearance—of a significant degree of influence in vital job decisions gives any supervisor the opportunity to impose on employees."

We granted certiorari and now affirm but for different reasons.

II

In defining "sexual harassment," the EEOC Guidelines first describe the kinds of workplace conduct that may be actionable under Title VII. These include "unwelcome sexual advances, requests for sexual favors, and other verbal or physical conduct of a sexual nature." Relevant to the charges at issue in this case, the Guidelines provide that such sexual misconduct constitutes prohibited "sexual harassment," whether or not it is directly linked to the grant or denial of an economic quid pro quo, where "such conduct has the purpose or effect of unreasonably interfering with an individual's work performance or creating an intimidating, hostile, or offensive working environment."

Since the Guidelines were issued, courts have uniformly held, and we agree, that a plaintiff may establish a violation of Title VII by proving that discrimination based on sex has created a hostile or abusive work environment.

Of course, not all workplace conduct that may be described as "harassment" affects a "term, condition, or privilege" of employment within the meaning of Title VII ("mere utterance of an ethnic or racial epithet which engenders offensive feelings in an employee" would not affect the conditions of employment to sufficiently significant degree to violate Title VII). For sexual harassment to be actionable, it must be sufficiently severe or pervasive "to alter the conditions of the victim's employment and create an abusive working environment." Respondent's allegations in this case—which include not only pervasive harassment but also criminal conduct of the most serious nature—are plainly sufficient to state a claim for "hostile environment" sexual harassment.

In sum, we hold that a claim of "hostile environment" sex discrimination is actionable under Title VII, that the District Court's findings were insufficient to dispose of respondent's hostile environment claim, and that the District Court did not err in admitting testimony about respondent's sexually provocative speech and dress. As to employer liability, we conclude that the Court of Appeals was wrong to entirely disregard agency principles and impose absolute liability on employers for the acts of their supervisors, regardless of the circumstances of a particular case.

Accordingly, the judgment of the Court of Appeals reversing the judgment of the District Court is affirmed, and the case is remanded for further proceedings consistent with this opinion.

Case Commentary

The U.S. Supreme Court held in *Meritor* that an employer will be liable for a hostile work environment where the employer knew or should have known that the behavior complained of was severe and pervasive. This was the major case establishing hostile work environment as a form of sexual harassment under Title VII. ■

CASE QUESTIONS

1. Do you agree with the Court's decision?
2. Why is the employer not absolutely liable for all severe and pervasive employee behavior that leads to a hostile work environment claim?
3. Do you believe Taylor's conduct was severe and pervasive?

The issue in the following case is whether an employee must have suffered harm to her psychological well-being in order for her to claim hostile work environment.

Harris v. Forklift Systems, Inc.
510 U.S. 17 (1993)

Justice O'Connor delivered the opinion of the Court.

In this case, we consider the definition of a discriminatorily "abusive work environment" (also known as a "hostile work environment") under Title VII of the Civil Rights Act of 1964.

I

Teresa Harris worked as a manager at Forklift Systems, Inc., an equipment rental company, from April, 1985, until October, 1987. Charles Hardy was Forklift's president.

The Magistrate found that, throughout Harris' time at Forklift, Hardy often insulted her because of her gender and often made her the target of unwanted sexual innuendos. Hardy told Harris on several occasions, in the presence of other employees, "You're a woman, what do you know" and "We need a man as the rental manager"; at least once, he told her she was "a dumb a** woman." Again in front of others, he suggested that the two of them "go to the Holiday Inn to negotiate Harris' raise." Hardy occasionally asked Harris and other female employees to get coins from his front pants pocket. He threw objects on the ground in front of Harris and other women, and asked them to pick the objects up. He made sexual innuendos about Harris' and other women's clothing.

In mid-August, 1987, Harris complained to Hardy about his conduct. Hardy said he was surprised that Harris was offended, claimed he was only joking, and apologized. He also promised he would stop, and, based on this assurance Harris stayed on the job. But in early September, Hardy began anew: While Harris was arranging a deal with one of Forklift's customers, he asked her, again in front of other employees, "What did you do, promise the guy . . . some sex Saturday night?" On October 1, Harris collected her paycheck and quit.

Harris then sued Forklift, claiming that Hardy's conduct had created an abusive work environment for her because of her gender. The United States District Court for the Middle District of Tennessee, adopting the report and recommendation of the Magistrate, found this to be "a close case," but held that Hardy's conduct did not create an abusive environment. The court found that some of Hardy's comments "offended Harris, and would offend the reasonable woman," but that they were not "so severe as to be expected to seriously affect Harris' psychological well-being." A reasonable woman manager under like circumstances would have been offended by Hardy, but his conduct would not have risen to the level of interfering with that person's work performance.

"Neither do I believe that Harris was subjectively so offended that she suffered injury. . . . Although Hardy may at times have genuinely offended Harris, I do not believe that he created a working environment so poisoned as to be intimidating or abusive to Harris."

In focusing on the employee's psychological well-being, the District Court was following Circuit precedent.

We granted certiorari to resolve a conflict among the Circuits on whether conduct, to be actionable as "abusive work environment" harassment (no quid pro quo harassment issue is present here), must "seriously affect an employee's psychological well-being" or lead the plaintiff to "suffer injury."

II

Title VII of the Civil Rights Act of 1964 makes it "an unlawful employment practice for an employer . . . to discriminate against any individual with respect to his compensation, terms, conditions, or privileges of employment, because of such individual's race, color, religion, sex, or national origin." As we made clear in *Meritor Savings Bank v. Vinson*, this language is not limited to "economic" or "tangible" discrimination. The phrase "terms, conditions, or privileges of employment" evinces a congressional intent "to strike at the entire spectrum of disparate treatment of men and women in employment," which includes requiring people to work in a discriminatorily hostile or abusive environment. When the workplace is permeated with "discriminatory intimidation, ridicule, and insult," that is "sufficiently severe or pervasive to alter the conditions of the victim's employment and create an abusive working environment," Title VII is violated.

This standard, which we reaffirm today, takes a middle path between making actionable any conduct that is merely offensive and requiring the conduct to cause a tangible psychological injury. As we pointed out in *Meritor*, "mere utterance of an . . . epithet which engenders offensive feelings in a employee," does not sufficiently affect the conditions of employment to implicate Title VII. Conduct that is not severe or pervasive enough to create an objectively hostile or abusive work environment—an environment that a reasonable person would find hostile or abusive—is beyond Title VII's purview. Likewise, if the victim does not subjectively perceive the environment to be abusive, the conduct has not actually altered the conditions of the victim's employment, and there is no Title VII violation.

But Title VII comes into play before the harassing conduct leads to a nervous breakdown. A discriminatorily abusive work environment, even one that does not seriously affect employees' psychological well-being, can and often will detract from employees' job performance, discourage employees from remaining on the job, or keep them from advancing in their careers. Moreover, even without regard to these tangible effects, the very fact that the discriminatory conduct was so severe or pervasive that it created a work environment abusive to employees because of their race, gender, religion, or national origin offends Title VII's broad rule of workplace equality. The appalling conduct alleged in *Meritor*, and the reference in that case to environments "so heavily polluted with discrimination as to destroy completely the emotional and psychological stability of minority group workers," merely present some especially egregious examples of harassment. They do not mark the boundary of what is actionable.

We therefore believe the District Court erred in relying on whether the conduct "seriously affected plaintiff's psychological well-being" or led her to "suffer injury." Such an inquiry may needlessly focus the factfinder's attention on concrete psychological harm, an element Title VII does not require. Certainly Title VII bars conduct that would seriously affect a reasonable person's psychological well-being, but the statute is not limited to such conduct. So long as the environment would reasonably be perceived, and is perceived, as hostile or abusive, there is no need for it also to be psychologically injurious.

This is not, and by its nature cannot be, a mathematically precise test. But we can say that whether an environment is "hostile" or "abusive" can be determined only by looking at all the circumstances. These may include the frequency of the discriminatory conduct; its severity; whether it is physically threatening or humiliating, or a mere offensive utterance; and whether it unreasonably interferes with an employee's work performance. The effect on the employee's psychological well-being is, of course, relevant to determining whether the plaintiff actually found the environment abusive. But, while psychological harm, like any other relevant factor, may be taken into account, no single factor is required.

III

Forklift, while conceding that a requirement that the conduct seriously affect psychological well-being is unfounded, argues that the District Court nonetheless correctly applied the *Meritor* standard. We disagree. Though the District Court did conclude that the work environment was not "intimidating or abusive to Harris," it did so only after finding that the conduct was not "so severe as to be expected to seriously affect plaintiff's psychological well-being," and that Harris was not "subjectively so offended that she suffered injury," The District Court's application of these incorrect standards may well have influenced its ultimate conclusion, especially given that the court found this to be a "close case."

We therefore reverse the judgment of the Court of Appeals, and remand the case for further proceedings consistent with this opinion.

Judgment for Harris.

Case Commentary

The U.S. Supreme Court held that an employee's psychological well-being does not have to be adversely affected for there to be grounds for her claim of hostile work environment. It may be a factor to be considered, but it is enough if the conduct complained of is severe and pervasive. ■

CASE QUESTIONS

1. Do you agree with the Court's decision?
2. Do you believe the conduct complained of was severe and pervasive?

3. Should there be a universal standard for what constitutes a hostile work environment?

Employment Perspective

George Miles works as an insurance underwriter. In the office, he has openly stated his view that women are good only for sex and do not belong in the workplace because they are always crying about PMS. Susan cringes when she hears these remarks and tries to hide from George lest she become a target. George continues to fondle Amanda's backside when she has repeatedly admonished him. He photo-stated a caricature of Debbie, a coworker, as a naked woman with large breasts. George speaks about the pornographic films that he has viewed and describes them in detail. He also has commented that he is due for a promotion after having sex with Margaret, the vice president for operations. What recourse do these women have against George? Amanda may sue George for the tort of battery because the fondling was unpermitted touching that she has found offensive and embarrassing. Margaret may sue for slander because George's remarks are untrue and damaging to her reputation. Debbie may sue for libel because the sexually offensive drawing has been distributed. Susan may sue for infliction of emotional distress because his comments, although not directed at her personally, are degrading to her because she is a woman.

The majority of the victims who are harassed seek recovery from the company, the rule of thumb being to sue the deepest pocket.

The following case addresses the question of whether an employee can sue her supervisor individually for sexual harassment.

Parsons v. Nationwide Mutual Ins. Co.
899 F. Supp. 465 (M.D. Fla. 1995)

Kovachevich, Judge.

Plaintiffs (Parsons, Selph and MacDonald) were employed on the office staff at Nationwide Mutual Insurance. Defendant Walker was also employed by Nationwide, and during the scope of this employment Defendant Walker alleged orally published "rude and offensive remarks" about Plaintiffs' sexual practices, gave detailed accounts of his own sexual exploits, made unwelcome sexually suggestive comments to Plaintiffs and generally created a sexually graphic and offensive work environment. After the occurrence of the alleged events, each of the Plaintiffs was discharged from employment at Nationwide. As a result of these supposed actions, Plaintiffs brought suit against Defendants Walker and Nationwide.

Plaintiffs allege that defendants (hereinafter "Walker" and "Nationwide") are joint employers of plaintiffs because of Nationwide's "exercise of substantial control of the business of Defendant Walker including ownership of accounts, equipment and contracts, the interrelationship of operations, and the centralized control of labor relations and common management." However, plaintiffs fail to specifically allege in the complaint what Walker's role is within Nationwide. Further, there is no mention of Walker's official capacity or job title at Nationwide; it may only be inferred that Walker held some form of supervisory control over Plaintiffs.

Walker moves to dismiss the sexual harassment and retaliation claims against him because he alleges that he is being sued in his individual capacity as a result of his employment at Nationwide.

The court professed that, "The relief granted under Title VII is against the employer, not individual employees whose actions constitute a violation of the Act," and "the proper method for a plaintiff to recover under Title VII is by suing the employer, either by naming the supervisory employees, as agents of the employer or by naming the employer directly." The crux . . . is that, even though Congress defined "employer" to include any "agent" this provision does not impose individual liability but only holds the employer accountable for the acts of its individual agents. Even though such a definition might be construed so as to impose liability on individual employees as "agents" the Eleventh Circuit Court has held that agents of employers who violate Title VII provisions only trigger an action against the employer, and not an action against the individual agent/employee. Moreover, the law in the Eleventh Circuit has been settled that there is no individual liability under Title VII. "If Congress had envisioned individual liability under Title VII for compensatory or punitive damages, it would have included individuals in this litany of limitations and would have discontinued the exemption for small employers."

Judgment for Nationwide.

Case Commentary

The Florida Middle District Court ruled that Title VII does not provide for individual liability in cases of sexual harassment. Parsons could sue Walker individually under tort law in state court. ∎

CASE QUESTIONS

1. Do you agree with the Court's decision?
2. Why do you think Parsons sued Walker individually?
3. Do you believe individuals should be liable for sexual harassment?

The predominant number of instances of sexual harassment have been men harassing women, but there are occasions when men have been harassed by women or other men and when women have been harassed by other women. These instances are equally unacceptable.

Employment Perspective

Phil Thomas is a construction worker who lives with his mother. After work every day, he rushes home to tend to her needs. When he won't join them for a few beers, his coworkers taunt him continually, claiming that he's a momma's boy, a wimp tied to his mother's apron strings. This taunting happens continually throughout the day. The coworkers leave notes and photostat caricatures, and openly make remarks. Is this sexual harassment? Probably not! Phil's coworkers are inflicting emotional distress upon him. But this isolated instance of teasing alone is not sufficient to constitute sexual harassment.

The question presented in the following case is whether a victim of same-sex sexual harassment has a viable claim under Title VII of the Civil Rights Act.

Oncale v. Sundowner Offshore Services, Inc.
523 U.S. 75 (1998)

Justice Scalia delivered the opinion of the Court.

This case presents the question whether workplace harassment can violate Title VII's prohibition against "discriminat[ion] . . . because of . . . sex," when the harasser and the harassed employee are of the same sex.

I

The District Court having granted summary judgment for respondent, we must assume the facts to be as alleged by petitioner Joseph Oncale. The precise details are irrelevant to the legal point we must decide, and in the interest of both brevity and dignity we shall describe them only generally. In late October 1991, Oncale was working for respondent Sundowner Offshore Services on a Chevron U. S. A., Inc., oil platform in the Gulf of Mexico. He was employed as a roustabout on an eight-man crew which included respondents John Lyons, Danny Pippen, and Brandon Johnson. Lyons, the crane operator, and Pippen, the driller, had supervisory authority. On several occasions, Oncale was forcibly subjected to sex related, humiliating actions against him by Lyons, Pippen and Johnson in the presence of the rest of the

crew. Pippen and Lyons also physically assaulted Oncale in a sexual manner, and Lyons threatened him with rape.

Oncale's complaints to supervisory personnel produced no remedial action; in fact, the company's Safety Compliance Clerk, Valent Hohen, told Oncale that Lyons and Pippen "picked on him all the time too," and called him a name suggesting homosexuality. Oncale eventually quit—asking that his pink slip reflect that he "voluntarily left due to sexual harassment and verbal abuse." When asked at his deposition why he left Sundowner, Oncale stated "I felt that if I didn't leave my job, that I would be raped or forced to have sex."

Oncale filed a complaint against Sundowner in the United States District Court for the Eastern District of Louisiana, alleging that he was discriminated against in his employment because of his sex. Relying on the Fifth Circuit's decision in *Garcia v. Elf Atochem North America*, the district court held that "Mr. Oncale, a male, has no cause of action under Title VII for harassment by male co-workers." On appeal, a panel of the Fifth Circuit concluded that Garcia was binding Circuit precedent, and affirmed. We granted certiorari.

II

Title VII's prohibition of discrimination "because of . . . sex" protects men as well as women and in the related context of racial discrimination in the workplace we have rejected any conclusive presumption that an employer will not discriminate against members of his own race. "Because of the many facets of human motivation, it would be unwise to presume as a matter of law that human beings of one definable group will not discriminate against other members of that group." In *Johnson v. Transportation Agency, Santa Clara Cty.* a male employee claimed that his employer discriminated against him because of his sex when it preferred a female employee for promotion. Although we ultimately rejected the claim on other grounds, we did not consider it significant that the supervisor who made that decision was also a man. If our precedents leave any doubt on the question, we hold today that nothing in Title VII necessarily bars a claim of discrimination "because of . . . sex" merely because the plaintiff and the defendant (or the person charged with acting on behalf of the defendant) are of the same sex. Courts have had little trouble with that principle in cases like *Johnson*, where an employee claims to have been passed over for a job or promotion. But when the issue arises in the context of a "hostile environment" sexual harassment claim, the state and federal courts have taken a bewildering variety of stances. Some, like the Fifth Circuit in this case, have held that same-sex sexual harassment claims are never cognizable under Title VII. Other decisions say that such claims are actionable only if the plaintiff can prove that the harasser is homosexual (and thus presumably motivated by sexual desire). Still others suggest that workplace harassment that is sexual in content is always actionable, regardless of the harasser's sex, sexual orientation, or motivations.

We see no justification in the statutory language or our precedents for a categorical rule excluding same-sex harassment claims from the coverage of Title VII. As some courts have observed, male-on-male sexual harassment in the workplace was assuredly not the principal evil Congress was concerned with when it enacted Title VII. But statutory prohibitions often go beyond the principal evil to cover reasonably comparable evils, and it is ultimately the provisions of our laws rather than the principal concerns of our legislators by which we are governed. Title VII prohibits "discriminat[ion] . . . because of . . . sex" in the "terms" or "conditions" of employment. Our holding that this includes sexual harassment must extend to sexual harassment of any kind that meets the statutory requirements.

We have emphasized, moreover, that the objective severity of harassment should be judged from the perspective of a reasonable person in the plaintiff's position, considering "all the circumstances." In same-sex (as in all) harassment cases, that inquiry requires careful consideration of the social context in which particular behavior occurs and is experienced by its target. A professional football player's working environment is not severely or pervasively abusive, for example, if the coach smacks him on the buttocks as he heads onto the field—even if the same behavior would reasonably be experienced as abusive by the coach's secretary (male or female) back at the office. The real social impact of workplace behavior often depends on a constellation of surrounding circumstances, expectations, and relationships which are not fully captured by a simple recitation of the words used or the physical acts performed. Common sense, and an appropriate sensitivity to social context, will enable courts and juries to distinguish between simple teasing or roughhousing among members of the same sex, and conduct which a reasonable person in the plaintiff's position would find severely hostile or abusive.

III

Because we conclude that sex discrimination consisting of same-sex sexual harassment is actionable under Title VII, the judgment of the Court of Appeals for the Fifth Circuit is reversed, and the case is remanded for further proceedings consistent with this opinion.

Judgment for Oncale.

Case Commentary

The U.S. Supreme Court stated that sexual harassment under Title VII encompasses a hostile work environment involving employees of the same sex. ■

CASE QUESTIONS

1. Do you agree with the decision of this case?
2. Do you believe same-sex sexual harassment should apply only where one employee is homosexual?
3. Should Oncale have been left to handle this himself?

Employment Perspective

Steve Hart is a happily married man with three children. His superior, Linda Evert, finds him very attractive. She invites him to dinner, a show, and her apartment. Steve politely declines each time. Linda stresses to Steve that if he wants to get promoted, he must have a close, intimate relationship with her. Is this sexual harassment? Yes! It is an unwelcome sexual advance.

There are two distinct situations for which the company may be liable: vicarious liability (formerly *quid pro quo*) and hostile work environment.

Sexual harassment can be divided into two categories: instances involving supervisors (vicarious liability) and instances involving coworkers (hostile work environment). The difference lies in the supervisor's ability to affect the employee's job through a tangible employment action. A tangible employment action involves situations in which a superior is demanding sexual favors from a subordinate in return for hiring, transfer, promotion, raise, bonus, workload, termination, avoidance, etc. This will inflict direct economic harm on the employee. If a supervisor says, "Sleep with me if you want to keep your job," then the supervisor is threatening to make a tangible employment decision, which may cost the victimized employee his or her job for refusing. Annoying or spiteful acts not rising to these levels are not considered to be sexual harassment unless they become so severe and/or pervasive and permeate the atmosphere as to amount to constructive discharge. A supervisor's threat to terminate an employee who does not engage in sex with him or her (*quid pro quo*) has serious employment consequences; whereas, a coworker's demand for sex, however bothersome, does not have such consequences unless it is so continuous as to constitute a hostile work environment.

Employers are vicariously liable for their supervisors' tangible employment actions undertaken in return for sex with a subordinate or for a subordinate's refusal to engage in sex. However, in the absence of a tangible employment action, an affirmative defense is available to the employer. An affirmative defense can be raised by an employer where it exercised reasonable care to guard against and properly address sexually harassing behavior by instituting a procedure for filing complaints and where the victimized employee failed to take advantage of it.

A copy of the sexual harassment policy must be disseminated to each employee. It must be posted conspicuously throughout the company and it must provide a procedure for a person who believes he or she is victimized to follow. The procedure should provide names and/or titles of high-ranking individuals to whom a complaint may be made. The human resources department would seem the logical choice for companies that have one; otherwise, the director of personnel, office manager, or any senior officer will do. Alternative contact people or departments may be provided.

When no tangible employment action is threatened, an employer will be liable for sexually harassing behavior:

1. Where it failed to institute preventive measures such as a sexual harassment policy
2. Where it condones the sexually harassing behavior
3. Where upon learning of sexually harassing behavior, it fails to promptly investigate and take corrective action

Therefore, upon learning of a sexual harassment complaint, a company must promptly investigate and take appropriate–action i.e. suspension, demotion, termination, etc., depending upon the severity of the harassment. An employee who has failed to file a complaint in accordance with the company's sexual harassment policy will forfeit his or her claim unless he or she can establish retaliation in the form of a tangible employment action. Once a tangible employment action is established, the affirmative defense is no longer available and the employer is absolutely liable.

The U.S. Supreme Court promulgated this reform to employer liability for supervisor's sexual harassment in the *Faragher v. City of Boca Raton* and the

Burlington Industries v. Ellerth cases in 1998. These opinions modified *quid pro quo* sexual harassment by limiting absolute liability to those situations involving a tangible employment act. Because sexual harassment is a form of sex discrimination, Title VII applies to only those employers with 15 or more employees. An employee wishing to bring a sexual harassment complaint against an employer with fewer than 15 workers would have to consult state or local law to determine if protection is provided. If not, then the aggrieved employee would have to bring a tort action in state court against the individual harasser. Specific tort actions were set forth earlier in this chapter. The procedures laid out here have also been applied to harassment in the other suspect categories.

Reasonable Person Standard

The standard by which sexual harassment will be judged is a reasonable person standard. A reasonable person must believe that the conduct complained of must have substantially interfered with the victim's ability to work or created an environment that was intimidating and offensive.

The issue in the following case is whether an employer is liable for a supervisor's threatening sexual advances where the employee has suffered no adverse effects to her job.

Burlington Industries, Inc. v. Ellerth
524 U.S. 742 (1998)

Justice Kennedy delivered the opinion of the Court.

We decide whether, under Title VII of the Civil Rights Act of 1964, as amended, an employee who refuses the unwelcome and threatening sexual advances of a supervisor, yet suffers no adverse, tangible job consequences, can recover against the employer without showing the employer is negligent or otherwise at fault for the supervisor's actions.

I

Summary judgment was granted for the employer, so we must take the facts alleged by the employee to be true. The employer is Burlington Industries, the petitioner. The employee is Kimberly Ellerth, the respondent. From March 1993 until May 1994, Ellerth worked as a salesperson in one of Burlington's divisions in Chicago, Illinois. During her employment, she alleges, she was subjected to constant sexual harassment by her supervisor, one Ted Slowik.

In the hierarchy of Burlington's management structure, Slowik was a mid-level manager. Burlington has eight divisions, employing more than 22,000 people in some 50 plants around the United States. Slowik was a vice president in one of five business units within one of the divisions. He had authority to make hiring and promotion decisions subject to the approval of his supervisor, who signed the paperwork. According to Slowik's supervisor, his position was "not considered an upper-level management position," and he was "not amongst the decision-making or policy-making hierarchy." Slowik was not Ellerth's immediate supervisor. Ellerth worked in a two-person office in Chicago, and she answered to her office colleague, who in turn answered to Slowik in New York.

Against a background of repeated boorish and offensive remarks and gestures which Slowik allegedly made, Ellerth places particular emphasis on three alleged incidents where Slowik's comments could be construed as threats to deny her tangible job benefits. In the summer of 1993, while on a business trip, Slowik invited Ellerth to the hotel lounge, an invitation Ellerth felt compelled to accept because Slowik was her boss. When Ellerth gave no encouragement to remarks Slowik made about her breasts, he told her to "loosen up" and warned, "you know, Kim, I could make your life very hard or very easy at Burlington."

In March 1994, when Ellerth was being considered for a promotion, Slowik expressed reservations during the promotion interview because she was not "loose enough." The comment was followed by his reaching over and rubbing her knee. Ellerth did receive the promotion; but when Slowik called to announce it, he told Ellerth, "you're gonna be out there with men who work in factories, and they certainly like women with pretty butts/legs."

In May 1994, Ellerth called Slowik, asking permission to insert a customer's logo into a fabric sample. Slowik responded, "I don't have time for you right now, Kim—unless you want to tell me what you're wearing." Ellerth told Slowik she had to go and ended the call. A day or two later, Ellerth called Slowik to ask permission again. This time he denied her request, but added something along the lines of, "are you wearing shorter skirts yet, Kim, because it would make your job a whole heck of a lot easier."

A short time later, Ellerth's immediate supervisor cautioned her about returning telephone calls to customers in a prompt fashion. In response, Ellerth quit. She faxed a letter giving reasons unrelated to the alleged sexual harassment we have described. About three weeks later, however, she sent a letter explaining she quit because of Slowik's behavior.

During her tenure at Burlington, Ellerth did not inform anyone in authority about Slowik's conduct, despite knowing Burlington had a policy against sexual harassment. In fact, she chose not to inform her immediate supervisor (not Slowik) because "'it would be his duty as my supervisor to report any incidents of sexual harassment.'" On one occasion, she told Slowik a comment he made was inappropriate.

In October 1994, after receiving a right-to-sue letter from the Equal Employment Opportunity Commission (EEOC), Ellerth filed suit in the United States District Court for the Northern District of Illinois, alleging Burlington engaged in sexual harassment and forced her constructive discharge, in violation of Title VII. The District Court granted summary judgment to Burlington. The Court found Slowik's behavior, as described by Ellerth, severe and pervasive enough to create a hostile work environment, but found Burlington neither knew nor should have known about the conduct. There was no triable issue of fact on the latter point, and the Court noted Ellerth had not used Burlington's internal complaint procedures. Although Ellerth's claim was framed as a hostile work environment complaint, the District Court observed there was a *quid pro quo* "component" to the hostile environment. Proceeding from the premise that an employer faces vicarious liability for *quid pro quo* harassment, the District Court thought it necessary to apply a negligence standard because the *quid pro quo* merely contributed to the hostile work environment. The District Court also dismissed Ellerth's constructive discharge claim.

The Court of Appeals en banc reversed in a decision which produced eight separate opinions and no consensus for a controlling rationale. The judges were able to agree on the problem they confronted: Vicarious liability, not failure to comply with a duty of care, was the essence of Ellerth's case against Burlington on appeal. The judges seemed to agree Ellerth could recover if Slowik's unfulfilled threats to deny her tangible job benefits was sufficient to impose vicarious liability on Burlington.

At the outset, we assume an important proposition yet to be established before a trier of fact. It is a premise assumed as well, in explicit or implicit terms, in the various opinions

by the judges of the Court of Appeals. The premise is: a trier of fact could find in Slowik's remarks numerous threats to retaliate against Ellerth if she denied some sexual liberties. The threats, however, were not carried out or fulfilled. Cases based on threats which are carried out are referred to often as *quid pro quo* cases, as distinct from bothersome attentions or sexual remarks that are sufficiently severe or pervasive to create a hostile work environment. The terms *quid pro quo* and hostile work environment are helpful, perhaps, in making a rough demarcation between cases in which threats are carried out and those where they are not or are absent altogether, but beyond this are of limited utility.

Section 703(a) of Title VII forbids

"an employer—

"(1) to fail or refuse to hire or to discharge any individual, or otherwise to discriminate against any individual with respect to his compensation, terms, conditions or privileges of employment, because of such individual's . . . sex." "*Quid pro quo*" and "hostile work environment" do not appear in the statutory text. The terms appeared first in the academic literature; found their way into decisions of the Courts of Appeals; and were mentioned in this Court's decision in *Meritor Savings Bank, FSB v. Vinson*.

In *Meritor*, the terms served a specific and limited purpose. There we considered whether the conduct in question constituted discrimination in the terms or conditions of employment in violation of Title VII. We assumed, and with adequate reason, that if an employer demanded sexual favors from an employee in return for a job benefit, discrimination with respect to terms or conditions of employment was explicit. Less obvious was whether an employer's sexually demeaning behavior altered terms or conditions of employment in violation of Title VII. We distinguished between *quid pro quo* claims and hostile environment claims and said both were cognizable under Title VII, though the latter requires harassment that is severe or pervasive. The principal significance of the distinction is to instruct that Title VII is violated by either explicit or constructive alterations in the terms or conditions of employment and to explain the latter must be severe or pervasive.

We must decide, then, whether an employer has vicarious liability when a supervisor creates a hostile work environment by making explicit threats to alter a subordinate's terms or conditions of employment, based on sex, but does not fulfill the threat. We turn to principles of agency law, for the term "employer" is defined under Title VII to include "agents." In express terms, Congress has directed federal courts to interpret Title VII based on agency principles.

A

Section 219(1) of the Restatement sets out a central principle of agency law:

"A master is subject to liability for the torts of his servants committed while acting in the scope of their employment."

An employer may be liable for both negligent and intentional torts committed by an employee within the scope of his or her employment. Sexual harassment under Title VII presupposes intentional conduct. While early decisions absolved employers of liability for the intentional torts of their employees, the law now imposes liability where the employee's "purpose, however misguided, is wholly or in part to further the master's business."

The general rule is that sexual harassment by a supervisor is not conduct within the scope of employment.

B

Scope of employment does not define the only basis for employer liability under agency principles. In limited circumstances, agency principles impose liability on employers even where employees commit torts outside the scope of employment. The principles are set forth in the much-cited § 219(2) of the Restatement:

"(2) A master is not subject to liability for the torts of his servants acting outside the scope of their employment, unless:

"(a) the master intended the conduct or the consequences, or

"(b) the master was negligent or reckless, or

"(c) the conduct violated a non-delegable duty of the master, or

"(d) the servant purported to act or to speak on behalf of the principal and there was reliance upon apparent authority, or he was aided in accomplishing the tort by the existence of the agency relation."

Subsection (a) addresses direct liability, where the employer acts with tortious intent, and indirect liability, where the agent's high rank in the company makes him or her the employer's alter ego. None of the parties contend Slowik's rank imputes liability under this principle.

When a supervisor makes a tangible employment decision, there is assurance the injury could not have been inflicted absent the agency relation. A tangible employment action in most cases inflicts direct economic harm. As a general proposition, only a supervisor, or other person acting with the authority of the company, can cause this sort of injury. A co-worker can break a co-worker's arm as easily as a supervisor, and anyone who has regular contact with an employee can inflict psychological injuries by his or her offensive conduct. But one co-worker (absent some elaborate scheme) cannot dock another's pay, nor can one co-worker demote another. Tangible employment actions fall within the special province of the supervisor. The supervisor has been empowered by the company as a distinct class of agent to make economic decisions affecting other employees under his or her control.

Tangible employment actions are the means by which the supervisor brings the official power of the enterprise to bear on subordinates. A tangible employment decision requires an official act of the enterprise, a company act. The decision in most cases is documented in official company records, and may be subject to review by higher level supervisors. For these reasons, a tangible employment action taken by the supervisor becomes for Title VII purposes the act of the employer. Whatever the exact contours of the aided in the agency relation standard, its requirements will always be met when a supervisor takes a tangible employment action against a subordinate. In that instance, it would be implausible to interpret agency principles to allow an employer to escape.

An employer is subject to vicarious liability to a victimized employee for an actionable hostile environment created by a supervisor with immediate (or successively higher) authority over the employee. When no tangible employment action is taken, a defending employer may raise an affirmative defense to liability or damages, subject to proof by a preponderance of the evidence. The defense comprises two necessary elements: (a) that the employer exercised reasonable care to prevent and correct promptly any sexually harassing behavior, and (b) that the plaintiff employee unreasonably failed to take advantage of any preventive or corrective opportunities provided by the employer or to avoid harm otherwise. While proof that an employer had promulgated an anti-harassment policy with complaint procedure is not necessary in every instance as a matter of law, the need for a stated policy suitable to the employment circumstances may appropriately be addressed in any case when litigating the first element of the defense. And while proof that an employee failed to fulfill the corresponding obligation of reasonable care to avoid harm is not limited to showing any unreasonable failure to use any complaint procedure provided by the employer, a demonstration of such failure will normally suffice to satisfy the employer's burden under the second element of the defense. No affirmative defense is available, however, when the supervisor's harassment culminates in a tangible employment action, such as discharge, demotion, or undesirable reassignment.

IV

Relying on existing case law which held out the promise of vicarious liability for all *quid pro quo* claims, Ellerth focused all her attention in the Court of Appeals on proving her claim fit within that category. Given our explanation that the labels *quid pro quo* and hostile work environment are not controlling for purposes of establishing employer liability, Ellerth should have an adequate opportunity to prove she has a claim for which Burlington is liable.

Although Ellerth has not alleged she suffered a tangible employment action at the hands of Slowik, which would deprive Burlington of the availability of the affirmative defense, this is not dispositive. In light of our decision, Burlington is still subject to vicarious liability for Slowik's activity, but Burlington should have an opportunity to assert and prove the affirmative defense to liability.

For these reasons, we will affirm the judgment of the Court of Appeals, reversing the grant of summary judgment against Ellerth.

The judgment of the Court of Appeals is affirmed.

CASE QUESTIONS

1. Did Slowik's actions occur within the scope of employment?
2. Must sexual harassment result in adverse job consequences to the victim?

Case Commentary

The U.S. Supreme Court decided that Kimberly Ellerth should have the opportunity to prove that Burlington Industries is vicariously liable for the sexually harassing actions of its supervisor. ■

3. Was Ellerth at fault for not reporting Slowik's behavior to the company?

The question presented in the case that follows is whether an employer is vicariously liable for a supervisor's creation of a hostile work environment where the employer was unaware of such conduct.

Faragher v. City of Boca Raton
524 U.S. 775 (1998)

Justice Souter delivered the opinion of the Court.

This case calls for identification of the circumstances under which an employer may be held liable under Title VII of the Civil Rights Act of 1964, for the acts of a supervisory employee whose sexual harassment of subordinates has created a hostile work environment amounting to employment discrimination. We hold that an employer is vicariously liable for actionable discrimination caused by a supervisor, but subject to an affirmative defense looking to the reasonableness of the employer's conduct as well as that of a plaintiff victim.

Between 1985 and 1990, while attending college, petitioner Beth Ann Faragher worked part time and during the summers as an ocean lifeguard for the Marine Safety Section of the Parks and Recreation Department of respondent, the City of Boca Raton, Florida (City). During this period, Faragher's immediate supervisors were Bill Terry, David Silverman, and Robert Gordon. In June 1990, Faragher resigned.

In 1992, Faragher brought an action against Terry, Silverman, and the City, asserting claims under Title VII and Florida law. So far as it concerns the Title VII claim, the complaint alleged that Terry and Silverman created a "sexually hostile atmosphere" at the beach by repeatedly subjecting Faragher and other female lifeguards to "uninvited and offensive touching," by making lewd remarks, and by speaking of women in offensive terms. The complaint contained specific allegations that Terry once said that he would never promote a woman to the rank of lieutenant, and that Silverman had said to Faragher, "Date me or clean the toilets for a year." Asserting that Terry and Silverman were agents of the City, and that their conduct amounted to discrimination in the "terms, conditions, and privileges" of her employment,

Faragher sought a judgment against the City for nominal damages, costs, and attorney's fees.

Following a bench trial, the United States District Court for the Southern District of Florida found that throughout Faragher's employment with the City, Terry served as Chief of the Marine Safety Division, with authority to hire new lifeguards (subject to the approval of higher management), to supervise all aspects of the lifeguards' work assignments, to engage in counseling, to deliver oral reprimands, and to make a record of any such discipline. Silverman was a Marine Safety lieutenant from 1985 until June 1989, when he became a captain. Gordon began the employment period as a lieutenant and at some point was promoted to the position of training captain. In these positions, Silverman and Gordon were responsible for making the lifeguards' daily assignments, and for supervising their work and fitness training.

The lifeguards and supervisors were stationed at the city beach and worked out of the Marine Safety Headquarters, a small one-story building containing an office, a meeting room, and a single, unisex locker room with a shower. Their work routine was structured in a "paramilitary configuration," with a clear chain of command. Lifeguards reported to lieutenants and captains, who reported to Terry. He was supervised by the Recreation Superintendent, who in turn reported to a Director of Parks and Recreation, answerable to the City Manager. The lifeguards had no significant contact with higher city officials like the Recreation Superintendent.

In February 1986, the City adopted a sexual harassment policy, which it stated in a memorandum from the City Manager addressed to all employees. In May 1990, the City revised the policy and reissued a statement of it. Although the City may actually have circulated the memos and statements to some employees, it completely failed to disseminate its policy among employees of the Marine Safety Section, with the result that Terry, Silverman, Gordon, and many lifeguards were unaware of it.

From time to time over the course of Faragher's tenure at the Marine Safety Section, between 4 and 6 of the 40 to 50 lifeguards were women. During that 5-year period, Terry repeatedly touched the bodies of female employees without invitation, would put his arm around Faragher, with his hand on her buttocks, and once made contact with another female lifeguard in a motion of sexual simulation. He made crudely demeaning references to women generally, and once commented disparagingly on Faragher's shape. During a job interview with a woman he hired as a lifeguard, Terry said that the female lifeguards had sex with their male counterparts and asked whether she would do the same.

Silverman behaved in similar ways. He once tackled Faragher and remarked that, but for a physical characteristic he found unattractive, he would readily have had sexual relations with her. Another time, he pantomimed an act of oral sex. Within earshot of the female lifeguards, Silverman made frequent, vulgar references to women and sexual matters, commented on the bodies of female lifeguards and beachgoers, and at least twice told female lifeguards that he would like to engage in sex with them.

Faragher did not complain to higher management about Terry or Silverman. Although she spoke of their behavior to Gordon, she did not regard these discussions as formal complaints to a supervisor but as conversations with a person she held in high esteem. Other female lifeguards had similarly informal talks with Gordon, but because Gordon did not feel that it was his place to do so, he did not report these complaints to Terry, his own supervisor, or to any other city official. Gordon responded to the complaints of one lifeguard by saying that "the City just doesn't care."

In April 1990, however, two months before Faragher's resignation, Nancy Ewanchew, a former lifeguard, wrote to Richard Bender, the City's Personnel Director, complaining that Terry and Silverman had harassed her and other female lifeguards. Following investigation of this complaint, the City found that Terry and Silverman had behaved improperly, reprimanded them, and required them to choose between a suspension without pay or the forfeiture of annual leave.

On the basis of these findings, the District Court concluded that the conduct of Terry and Silverman was discriminatory harassment sufficiently serious to alter the conditions of Faragher's employment and constitute an abusive working environment. The District Court then ruled that there were three justifications for holding the City liable for the harassment of its supervisory employees. First, the court noted that the harassment was pervasive enough to support an inference that the City had "knowledge, or constructive knowledge" of it. Next, it ruled that the City was liable under traditional agency principles because Terry

and Silverman were acting as its agents when they committed the harassing acts. Finally, the court observed that Gordon's knowledge of the harassment, combined with his inaction, "provides a further basis for imputing liability on the City." The District Court then awarded Faragher one dollar in nominal damages on her Title VII claim.

A panel of the Court of Appeals for the Eleventh Circuit reversed the judgment against the City. Although the panel had "no trouble concluding that Terry's and Silverman's conduct . . . was severe and pervasive enough to create an objectively abusive work environment," it overturned the District Court's conclusion that the City was liable. The panel ruled that Terry and Silverman were not acting within the scope of their employment when they engaged in the harassment, that they were not aided in their actions by the agency relationship, and that the City had no constructive knowledge of the harassment by virtue of its pervasiveness or Gordon's actual knowledge.

A "master is subject to liability for the torts of his servants committed while acting in the scope of their employment." Restatement §219(1). This doctrine has traditionally defined the "scope of employment" as including conduct "of the kind a servant is employed to perform," occurring "substantially within the authorized time and space limits," and "actuated, at least in part, by a purpose to serve the master," but as excluding an intentional use of force "unexpectable by the master."

The rationale for placing harassment within the scope of supervisory authority would be the fairness of requiring the employer to bear the burden of foreseeable social behavior, and the same rationale would apply when the behavior was that of co-employees. The employer generally benefits just as obviously from the work of common employees as from the work of supervisors; they simply have different jobs to do, all aimed at the success of the enterprise. As between an innocent employer and an innocent employee, if we use scope of employment reasoning to require the employer to bear the cost of an actionably hostile workplace created by one class of employees (i.e., supervisors), it could appear just as appropriate to do the same when the environment was created by another class (i.e., co-workers).

We therefore agree with Faragher that in implementing Title VII it makes sense to hold an employer vicariously liable for some tortious conduct of a supervisor made possible by abuse of his supervisory authority. The agency relationship affords contact with an employee subjected to a supervisor's sexual harassment, and the victim may well be reluctant to accept the risks of blowing the whistle on a superior. When a person with supervisory authority discriminates in the terms and conditions of subordinates' employment, his actions necessarily draw upon his superior position over the people who report to him, or those under them, whereas an employee generally cannot check a supervisor's abusive conduct the same way that she might deal with abuse from a co-worker. When a fellow employee harasses, the victim can walk away or tell the offender where to go, but it may be difficult to offer such responses to a supervisor, whose "power to supervise—which may be to hire and fire, and to set work schedules and pay rates—does not disappear . . . when he chooses to harass through insults and offensive gestures rather than directly with threats of firing or promises of promotion." Recognition of employer liability when discriminatory misuse of supervisory authority alters the terms and conditions of a victim's employment is underscored by the fact that the employer has a greater opportunity to guard against misconduct by supervisors than by common workers; employers have greater opportunity and incentive to screen them, train them, and monitor their performance.

The requirement to show that the employee has failed in a coordinate duty to avoid or mitigate harm reflects an equally obvious policy imported from the general theory of damages, that a victim has a duty "to use such means as are reasonable under the circumstances to avoid or minimize the damages" that result from violations of the statute.

Applying these rules here, we believe that the judgment of the Court of Appeals must be reversed. The District Court found that the degree of hostility in the work environment rose to the actionable level and was attributable to Silverman and Terry. It is undisputed that these supervisors "were granted virtually unchecked authority" over their subordinates, "directly controlling and supervising all aspects of Faragher's day-to-day activities." It is also clear that Faragher and her colleagues were "completely isolated from the City's higher management."

While the City would have an opportunity to raise an affirmative defense if there were any serious prospect of its presenting one, it appears from the record that any such avenue is closed. The District Court found that the City had entirely failed to disseminate its policy against sexual harassment among the beach employees and that its officials made no attempt to keep track of the conduct of supervisors like Terry and Silverman. The record also makes clear that the City's policy did not include any assurance that the harassing supervisors could be bypassed in registering complaints. Under such circumstances, we hold as a matter of law that the City could not be found to have exercised reasonable care to prevent the supervisors' harassing conduct. Unlike the employer of a small workforce, who might expect that sufficient care to prevent tortious behavior could be exercised informally, those responsible for city operations could not reasonably have thought that precautions against hostile environments in any one of many departments in far-flung locations could be effective without communicating some formal policy against harassment, with a sensible complaint procedure.

The judgment of the Court of Appeals for the Eleventh Circuit is reversed, and the case is remanded for reinstatement of the judgment of the District Court.

Case Commentary

The U.S. Supreme Court ruled that the City of Boca Raton was liable for the sexual harassment perpetrated by its supervisors against Beth Ann Faragher. The city failed to apprise the supervisors concerning its sexual harassment policy and to train them to act in accordance with this policy. Faragher's complaint to Gordan, a supervisor, went unheeded. The city's argument that it lacked knowledge of the sexual harassment was due in part to the city's failure to monitor its supervisors. Employers cannot expect that all instances of sexual harassment will be reported because of employee's justifiable fear of reprisal. ∎

CASE QUESTIONS

1. Should Faragher have reported the sexual harassment to a higher authority in the city?
2. Do you agree with the decision of the Court?

3. Should an employer be liable for sexually harassing conduct of which it is unaware?

Employment Perspective

Clarence Conklin, a hospital administrator, approaches one of the nurse's aides and tells her that he can arrange a schedule change from nights, weekends, and holidays to day work if she is willing to sleep with him. Is this *quid pro quo*? Yes! The hospital is liable for the sexual harassment of its employee because a benefit was denied to the nurse's aide unless she agreed to have sex.

There are also instances in which a person uses sex to gain advancement, sometimes called "sleeping the way to the top."

Employment Perspective

Christine Wiley was an administrative assistant at Bay Ridge Publishing when she met Joe Flanagan, the president, at a company picnic. Joe immediately became infatuated with Christine, and they began an affair. During the next 2 years, she was promoted seven times, eventually to vice president of corporate affairs. Her skills were not particularly impressive. Every other vice president had been in a managerial position at least 14 years before attaining the position of vice president. Is this sexual harassment? Yes! In the opposite direction, though. The employees who were passed over for promotion have been sexually harassed because of the favoritism exhibited to Christine.

In some cases, sexual harassment can be used as a threat against management, in that an employee may demand a promotion or else will file a claim against the management.

Employment Perspective

It was obvious to everyone at Parker Management Co. that Charlie Harris was very fond of Marie Copley, a marketing research assistant. He would compliment her every day and often bring her flowers. One day Marie learned of an opening for a sales representative within the company. Marie was tired of doing research—she wanted to earn commissions and work with people. This would be tantamount to a transfer and promotion. Marie approached Charlie, who was vice president of marketing, and asked him to grant her request. Charlie informed Marie that although he was fond of her, he could not grant the request because she was not qualified. Marie told Charlie that unless he granted her wish, she would file a complaint against him, alleging that he demanded sex for the promotion. What should Charlie do? This action is blackmail. Charlie is in a delicate situation because his conduct, although not constituting sexual harassment, has laid the foundation for a false claim to be leveled against him. Charlie should seek the advice of upper management and legal counsel. Ethically, Marie's request should not be granted because it is false. Practically, it may be granted by Charlie or the company to avoid future public embarrassment and litigation. If Charlie adopts an ethical viewpoint and refuses Marie's request and the company is sued, Charlie must be prepared to be severely reprimanded at best or to lose his job at worst as a consequence of the damage done to the company.

HOSTILE WORK ENVIRONMENT

Hostile work environment is intimidating and offensive conduct perpetrated by a superior or coworker against an employee. The hostile action must be severe and pervasive so as to interfere with the performance of the employee's work. Touching, joking, commenting, and distributing material of a sexual nature all fall within the confines of a hostile work environment.

Employment Perspective

Dawn West, an employee of Bull and Bear Stockbrokers, appeared one Monday morning with a new hairstyle and wearing a royal blue dress. Jack Olsen, a coworker, couldn't take his eyes off Dawn. Finally, he said, "Boy don't you look fantastic." Dawn, embarrassed in front of her coworkers, filed a claim for sexual harassment. Will she be successful? No! This incident was not severe nor did it reoccur. It was an isolated occurrence. What if Jack's behavior is repeated on a daily basis? The answer would depend upon whether Dawn communicated to

Jack her distaste for his conduct or whether it was blatantly obvious from Dawn's reaction each day that she did not welcome Jack's behavior.

Employment Perspective

Susan Jennings is speaking to Jessica Randolph in the latter's cubicle about the terrible cramps she is experiencing this month. John Woods, a coworker, happens to overhear their conversation and interjects, "Why don't you let Dr. John have a look down there and see what the problem is? You know I have magic fingers not to mention. . . . " "No thanks, John, now take a walk," was their response. Later, they filed a sexual harassment claim against John. Will they win? Again, this is an isolated occurrence during which the women made clear to John that they did not appreciate his comments. By filing the complaint, they are putting the company on notice that they will not tolerate further harassment from John. The company should investigate their complaint and upon satisfying itself about its accuracy, notify John that future misbehavior will result in suspension or dismissal.

Employment Perspective

Kay Stevens was 5 feet tall and weighed 250 pounds at the age of 32. She worked in a meat-packing plant, where she was subjected to constant criticisms by her coworkers: "You're eating the company's profits," "No man would sleep with you because he could not fit in the bed," and "Your mother thought she was having twins, then you appeared." For many years, Kay endured the belittling behavior because she was ashamed to repeat what had been said. She has been very depressed. Should Kay file a complaint? Yes! If she does not, the harassment will never stop. By filing a complaint, Kay is putting the onus on the company to stop what she cannot end herself.

The case that follows presents the question of whether the presentation of a sexual gift to a female employee for her birthday constitutes sexual harassment. Furthermore, the case addresses the issue of whether the complainant's acceptance of the gift and participation in the event preclude her from winning the lawsuit.

Hansen v. Dean Witter Reynolds, Inc.

887 F. Supp. 669 (S.D.N.Y. 1995)

Baer, District Judge.

PLAINTIFF'S HOSTILE WORK ENVIRONMENT CLAIM

Plaintiff focused primarily on three incidents in her effort to show that defendant maintained a hostile work environment. Two of them involved sexually explicit birthday cakes, while the other concerned what a female employee, Lynn Jerome, described as an "act of terrorism" perpetrated against her by a male Dean Witter manager. As explained below, I find that the birthday cake incidents are not attributable to defendant Dean Witter; the incident that Jerome called an act of "terrorism," meanwhile, is at best an exaggeration and at worst calls into question Jerome's judgment generally.

One of the birthday cakes in question was presented to plaintiff in 1986 by several co-workers. The cake was in the shape and color of a black man's penis, was filled with Devil Dog cream, and bore the dubious greeting, "Happy Birthday, B**ch." Hansen did not file a complaint or otherwise report this incident to management. In fact, there was testimony by a former co-worker that Hansen was so proud to receive the cake that she stored the remaining portion in her freezer and brought it to her parents' home for their July 4th barbecue.

While food for thought, it is unnecessary to decide whether Hansen considered the cake an insult or a joke. There was evidence that she partook enthusiastically in the event, and there was testimony that she was proud of being referred to as the "b**ch" and that the name was in fact a self-professed title as she considered herself "a tough cookie." The fact is that she failed to inform any supervisory personnel, and thus there is nothing on which to base a determination that Dean Witter tolerated, prohibited, or encouraged such activity. There was, however, a similar situation that was reported to management; Dean Witter's reaction left no doubt as to its stance towards such cakes. In 1982, Ms. Jerome received a cake from co-workers "in the shape of a man's anatomy." Upon being made aware of the nature of the cake, Dean Witter's Chairman issued a memorandum stating that such behavior would not be tolerated and that any persons involved in such activity would be terminated. In light of this response, there is hardly support that the birthday cake incident is indicative of a sanctioned hostile work environment for women at Dean Witter.

The same is true of the event that Jerome referred to at trial as an act of terrorism. Jerome stated during her initial testimony that she had complained about "sexual matters" in 1989 based on her being "called in and terrorized" at Dean Witter. When asked to provide greater detail, Jerome offered, "It's very strong male intimidation to the point of, without touching a person, there is a physical reaction by the strength of the words."

When asked to what she was referring regarding the 1989 complaint, Jerome testified to only one event, an incident where she and a male colleague were called into a conference room by Ray Anderson, a Dean Witter manager. Jerome and her colleague had been reading newspapers on the trading floor. According to Jerome, Anderson "rose himself up in an intimidating male stature." Jerome conceded that Anderson never got within three and one-half feet of her, nor did he make any sexist or off-color remarks. Finally, as Jerome acknowledged, no adverse personnel action resulted, notwithstanding Anderson's statement that if Jerome and her colleague "had nothing better to do than read the paper, he wanted their resignations." Jerome then pointed out that Anderson had made the statement "in an extremely loud tone of voice." It is beyond peradventure that one would be hard pressed to consider this an act of terrorism.

Judgment for Dean Witter.

Case Commentary

The Southern District of New York held that an employee who participates in what would normally constitute a hostile work environment would be precluded from instituting a claim. ■

CASE QUESTIONS

1. Do you believe this decision is correct?
2. Why do you believe she brought the claim after participating?
3. Should an employee be precluded from suing because she participated?

The composition of sexual harassment will vary among different types of employment. Conduct and language that is accepted in certain manual labor jobs may be regarded as offensive in an office environment. Each employment environment will have a different set of standards. These will be determined by company policy and female employees themselves. If employees participate, encourage, or accept what would otherwise constitute sexual harassment, they will be precluded from claiming such behavior was intimidating and offensive to them.

The issue in the case that follows is whether the manager's sexually harassing behavior was malicious enough to warrant damages for emotional distress.

Hoffmann-La Roche v. Zeltwanger
69 S.W.3d 634 (Tex. App. 2002)

John G. Hill, Justice.

Joan Zeltwanger, now Joan Zeltwanger Gonzales, testified that she was hired by Hoffmann-La Roche, Inc., a pharmaceutical company, in November 1990, as a sales representative. In order to prevent any confusion caused by her change of names, we will refer to her throughout this opinion as Joan. Joan said that initially her sales manager was Betty Turicchi, with whom she enjoyed working. According to Joan, Turicchi gave her a very good job rating. Joan stated that in 1992, due to realignment, Webber became her sales manager.

Joan related that she started having problems with Webber within the first three or four months of the change, with Webber telling a lot of jokes, making sexual connotations, and not really listening to her. She said that Turicchi was not surprised when she told her the type of behavior he was exhibiting. Joan indicated that Turicchi told her that was how Webber was, that was his personality, and that was how he conducted his business in the work group. Joan related that Turicchi gave her pointers as to how to deal with it, but did not tell her about any complaint procedures nor urge her to take any other action. In fact, according to Joan, Turicchi told her that she would not want that in her file in the company headquarters, because once she complained it would be difficult to get any kind of promotion or anything else within the company.

Joan stated that she talked to Turicchi again in 1993 before filing her complaint with Roche. She said that Turicchi gave her pointers on how to handle and document everything that was happening. Joan filed a sexual harassment complaint with Roche in August 1994. She testified that Webber: (1) continually told dirty jokes; (2) he talked about topless dancers; (3) with thirty people present at a division meeting, he danced up to her with $5 in his teeth and knelt down in front of her and delivered it that way; (4) he talked about the girls he "screwed" in college and how his car was called the "Snatchmobile;" (5) while standing at the trunk of her car, he told about the couples he and his wife still knew and how his goal was to do them all; (6) while on a field trip the previous winter, he made inappropriate references to his "ding-dong" and how he had whipped it out when he was at school; (7) about every time he rode with her he went into explicit details about sexual encounters, and, when she asked him not to, he kept on talking and laughed it off; (8) while he was at her home checking on samples, she caught him going through her underwear.

Joan related that after she filed her complaint, she was scheduled for a performance review that was scheduled at Webber's home, since Roche did not maintain regional offices. She indicated that she requested that it be postponed or not held at Webber's home. She relates that at her request Betty Turicchi appeared as an observer at the review.

Joan stated that, from the beginning of the review, Webber was screaming and yelling at her. She said that he had pages and pages of false accusations against her in her territory and that he ripped apart everything she had done in the territory and that she had done as a person. She indicated that whenever she tried to respond with her data he would come back screaming and yelling at her. She testified that she left the review crying after Webber gave her an "H" rating, which at Roche was an unacceptable rating.

Joan testified that she was notified in September that Roche, following an investigation, had fired Webber. Joan indicated she was notified a month later that, based upon the "H" review that Webber had given her, she was terminated. She stated that her worst fear about making a complaint was that she would be fired. She related that the unfairness of being fired based on the "H" review she received from Webber entered into the distress it was causing. She said that, as a result, she became severely depressed, had a lot of insomnia, and had nightmares. She indicated that there were rumors that Webber was going to come after her because she had filed a complaint. According to Joan, her psychiatrist reported that she was suffering from depression resulting from extreme stress from sexual harassment in the work place and loss of job, that she felt hopeless, had low energy,

reduced concentration, insomnia and other symptoms of depression. Joan acknowledged that Webber never asked her out on a date. She also indicated that in the summer of 1994 she knew that a merger was a possibility.

Dr. James Grubbs, a physician whom Joan was required to see on behalf of Roche with respect to Joan's claim for disability, reported that she was unable to perform the material duties of her regular employment, although he did not feel that she was totally disabled. He said that she could not perform the duties of any occupation other than something part-time that she could do from home.

Both Webber and Roche urge that Webber's acts of sexual harassment do not constitute the outrageous conduct required in order to sustain a claim of intentional infliction of emotional distress. Even if this were so, the acts constituting outrageous conduct are not limited to sexual harassment on Webber's part, but also include acts of Roche in fostering a corporate culture that allowed such conduct on Webber's part; Roche's initial failure to respond to Joan's concerns; Roche's callousness in requiring Joan to appear at a review at Webber's home, thereby allowing him to surmise that she had filed a complaint when she requested another manager to appear with her; Roche's action in not allowing its observer to prevent Webber's hostile behavior at the review; and Roche's terminating Joan, after Webber had recommended that she be terminated, in part based upon the use of the "H" rating Webber gave Joan in connection with her last performance review.

The jury could reasonably have found that Webber and Roche both individually and collectively engaged in this conduct and that the conduct of each was outrageous. Rather than acknowledging any impropriety on its part and asserting that its conduct was not outrageous, Roche merely asserts that Webber's conduct was not outrageous. Roche urges that it is not responsible for Webber's actions of sexual harassment, but it does not address a lack of responsibility for its own actions which were instrumental in inflicting severe emotional distress upon Joan.

Roche argues in issue two that its liability for any emotional distress should be limited to the $30,000 which the jury assessed as the damages awarded Joan as a result of Webber's conduct. This argument is based upon Roche's mistaken assumption that it did not, by itself, act outrageously. We disagree, as previously noted.

We hold that appellants' conduct, as we have previously outlined it, constitutes sufficient evidence to support the jury's finding of malice. Appellants contend that there is no evidence that Webber was guilty of malice because there is no evidence that he intended to harm Joan by his sexual harassment and there is no evidence that he had subjective awareness of the risk involved. The conduct involved here is not solely the numerous acts involving sexual harassment to which appellants refer. Having reviewed all of the evidence, we do not find the jury's verdict finding malice on the part of Webber to be so contrary to the overwhelming weight of the evidence as to be clearly wrong and unjust.

Appellants urge that there is no evidence that Roche acted with malice and that there is no legal basis for imputing Webber's malice to it. This argument again ignores Roche's own actions that we have previously outlined. We hold that Roche's actions by themselves support the jury's finding of malice. Roche contends it could not have had malice because it terminated Webber and discouraged sexual harassment, but such actions on its part are not necessarily inconsistent with the conclusion that, with respect to its other conduct as we have related, it acted with malice.

The judgment is affirmed for Zeltwanger.

Case Commentary

The Texas Appellate Court determined that Roche's awareness of Webber's actions along with their delay in addressing them constituted sexual harassment. ■

CASE QUESTIONS

1. Are you in accord with the Court's decision?
2. Do you believe Webber's actions were severe and pervasive?
3. What do you think was Roche's reasons for not addressing Zeltwanger's concerns on a timely basis?

Severe and Pervasive

The sexual harassment complained of must be severe enough to create an abusive work environment and to disrupt the victim's employment. Casual comments or insignificant events that are isolated or happen only intermittently are not sufficient. In order to come to a determination, the accused's conduct must be viewed in light of all of the circumstances, including the victim's behavior. If the victim consented to, participated in, or initiated the hostile work environment, then that will severely mitigate the victim's claim. If the work environment becomes intolerable because the employer refuses to remedy the situation, thus forcing the victim to resign, the victim can claim constructive discharge. The victim must resign in response to the sexual harassment. If the resignation is for another reason, constructive discharge will not apply.

The issue in the case that follows is whether the plaintiff's allegations are severe and pervasive enough to warrant a determination that a hostile work environment exists.

Shoemaker v. National Management Resources Corp.

(10th Cir. 1997)

Baldock, Ebel, and Murphy, Circuit Judges.

Appellant Carla Shoemaker brought this suit against her former employer, National Management Resources Corporation (NMRC), and former immediate supervisor, Gerald Matheny, alleging that she was sexually harassed by Matheny and discharged by NMRC in retaliation for complaining about the harassment, both in violation of Title VII. Plaintiff also asserted state law claims for intentional infliction of emotional distress, discrimination under the Oklahoma Discrimination in Employment Act, wrongful discharge in violation of Oklahoma public policy, and negligent hiring. She appeals from the district court's grant of summary judgment in favor of defendants on all of her claims. We have jurisdiction and reverse.

Plaintiff was employed by defendant NMRC from March 1994 until March 15, 1995. On February 5, 1995, defendant Matheny was hired as plaintiff's supervisor. He immediately began a campaign of sexual harassment against her. He asked her out to dinner on his first day at work, and gave her his motel room number and telephone number the next day, assuring her that nobody else had those numbers.

He repeatedly told her he wanted to develop a close 'working relationship' with her. He continuously called her at home to see if she wanted to go out with him, and when she told him she had a boyfriend, he repeated that he wanted only a close working relationship with her. He would sit in front of her desk and stare at her for perhaps fifteen minutes at a time, and moved the copy machine into his office so that she would have to stand with her back to him to make copies. He once slammed a book shut in her face while she was reading, barely missing her nose. Matheny cornered plaintiff in private to tell her a story about how big he thought his penis was until he unwrapped the complimentary condom in his motel room, and then realized the condom was actually a shower cap. He also privately told her a story about a friend of his having sex with a woman who was screaming, but it turned out she was having an asthma attack.

He privately told her about getting a b*** job from a beautiful woman for only $10.00 at the motel where he was staying. Matheny admitted that he told a joke about getting a penguin job for $20.00; that is, he dropped his pants for a b*** job, but the woman took off with his money. Plaintiff felt belittled and intimidated by Matheny's conduct, but was afraid of his temper and afraid to complain.

Matheny once cornered plaintiff against a wall for ten or fifteen minutes. She was so terrified that she could not even recall what was said.

Matheny once called her home and asked her boyfriend if she was upset about something that had happened at work.

Matheny asked plaintiff to do push-ups for him on at least two occasions. Once, when she was carrying aerobic tights through the office on her way to change clothes in the restroom, Matheny told her it looked like she needed Vaseline to help put her tights on and asked her if she needed any help.

He patted her on her behind once after asking her to get up and retrieve a file for him.

He also harassed another female employee by pulling on the breast pocket of her jacket where a button was missing and making a comment that he had one of those back in Wisconsin.

Plaintiff said that she suffered anguish, uneasiness, fear, belittlement, intimidation, depression, and stress due to Matheny's conduct.

She sometimes broke down crying at work, and changed from an outgoing, energetic, bubbly person to one who kept to herself, kept quiet, did her job; and barely spoke.

Plaintiff finally wrote a letter to the president of NMRC about Matheny's conduct. She asked for a paid leave of absence while the company investigated her complaint, but upper management's initial reaction was that she must not be doing her job. NMRC's president and Matheny's district manager discussed the matter and decided that plaintiff would be more easily replaced than Matheny.

NMRC management never interviewed the other employees plaintiff said she had confided in, and management gave her the option only to tolerate Matheny's conduct or quit her job. When she told NMRC management that she could no longer tolerate Matheny's harassment, they terminated her on the spot.

The district court erred in granting summary judgment to defendant NMRC on plaintiff's hostile work environment claim.

For sexual harassment to be actionable, it must be sufficiently severe or pervasive to alter the conditions of the victim's employment and create an abusive working environment.

Moreover, except for the book-slamming incident, the incidents alleged by plaintiff are either overtly sexual or could reasonably be construed as sexual. Her allegations are considerably more than enough to create a triable factual dispute as to the existence of a hostile work environment due to sexual harassment. There is no need to go into the nuances in this case.

Therefore, plaintiff's retaliation claim must be reinstated for further proceedings.

The judgment of the United States District Court for the Western District of Oklahoma is REVERSED, and the case is REMANDED for additional proceedings consistent with this order and judgment.

Judgment for Shoemaker.

Case Commentary

The Tenth Circuit Court held that Carla Shoemaker's allegations of sexual harassment were more than sufficient to evidence a hostile work environment. ∎

CASE QUESTIONS

1. Do you agree with the decision in this case?
2. Were Matheny's actions severe and pervasive?
3. What do you think about upper management's reaction?

The issue in the case that follows is whether an isolated comment that had sexual overtones is sufficient to constitute sexual harassment liability for an employer.

Clark County School District v. Breeden
532 U.S. 268 (2001)

Per Curiam.

On October 21, 1994, respondent's male supervisor met with respondent and another male employee to review the psychological evaluation reports of four job applicants.

The report for one of the applicants disclosed that the applicant had once commented to a co-worker, "I hear making love to you is like making love to the Grand

Canyon." At the meeting respondent's supervisor read the comment aloud, looked at respondent and stated, "I don't know what that means." The other employee then said, "Well, I'll tell you later," and both men chuckled. Respondent later complained about the comment to the offending employee, to Assistant Superintendent George Ann Rice, the employee's supervisor, and to another assistant superintendent of petitioner. Her first claim of retaliation asserts that she was punished for these complaints.

Title VII forbids actions taken on the basis of sex that "discriminate against any individual with respect to his compensation, terms, conditions, or privileges of employment." Just three Terms ago, we reiterated, what was plain from our previous decisions, that sexual harassment is actionable under Title VII only if it is "so 'severe or pervasive' as to 'alter the conditions of the victim's employment and create an abusive working environment.'" Workplace conduct is not measured in isolation; instead, "whether an environment is sufficiently hostile or abusive" must be judged "by 'looking at all the circumstances,' including the 'frequency of the discriminatory conduct; its severity; whether it is physically threatening or humiliating, or a mere offensive utterance; and whether it unreasonably interferes with an employee's work performance.'" Hence, "a recurring point in our opinions is that simple teasing, offhand comments, and isolated incidents (unless extremely serious) will not amount to discriminatory changes in the 'terms and conditions of employment.'"

No reasonable person could have believed that the single incident recounted above violated Title VII's standard. The ordinary terms and conditions of respondent's job required her to review the sexually explicit statement in the course of screening job applicants. Her co-workers who participated in the hiring process were subject to the same requirement, and indeed, in the District Court respondent "conceded that it did not bother or upset her" to read the statement in the file. Her supervisor's comment, made at a meeting to review the application, that he did not know what the statement meant; her co-worker's responding comment; and the chuckling of both are at worst an "isolated incident" that cannot remotely be considered "extremely serious," as our cases require. The holding of the Court of Appeals to the contrary must be reversed.

Besides claiming that she was punished for complaining to petitioner's personnel about the alleged sexual harassment, respondent also claimed that she was punished for filing charges against petitioner with the Nevada Equal Rights Commission and the Equal Employment Opportunity Commission (EEOC) and for filing the present suit. Respondent filed her lawsuit on April 1, 1997; on April 10, 1997, respondent's supervisor, Assistant

Superintendent Rice, "mentioned to Allin Chandler, Executive Director of plaintiff's union, that she was contemplating transferring plaintiff to the position of Director of Professional Development Education," and this transfer was "carried through" in May, Brief in Opposition 8. In order to show, as her defense against summary judgment required, the existence of a causal connection between her protected activities and the transfer, respondent "relied wholly on the temporal proximity of the filing of her complaint on April 1, 1997 and Rice's statement to plaintiff's union representative on April 10, 1997 that she was considering transferring plaintiff to the new position." The District Court, however, found that respondent did not serve petitioner with the summons and complaint until April 11, 1997, one day after Rice had made the statement, and Rice filed an affidavit stating that she did not become aware of the lawsuit until after April 11, a claim that respondent did not challenge. Hence, the court concluded, respondent "had not shown that any causal connection exists between her protected activities and the adverse employment decision."

The Court of Appeals reversed, relying on two facts: The EEOC had issued a right-to-sue letter to respondent three months before Rice announced she was contemplating the transfer, and the actual transfer occurred one month after Rice learned of respondent's suit. The latter fact is immaterial in light of the fact that petitioner concededly was contemplating the transfer before it learned of the suit. Employers need not suspend previously planned transfers upon discovering that a Title VII suit has been filed, and their proceeding along lines previously contemplated, though not yet definitively determined, is no evidence whatever of causality.

First, there is no indication that Rice even knew about the right-to-sue letter when she proposed transferring respondent. And second, if one presumes she knew about it, one must also presume that she (or her predecessor) knew *almost two years earlier* about the protected action (filing of the EEOC complaint) that the letter supposedly disclosed. (The complaint had been filed on August 23, 1995, and both Title VII and its implementing regulations require that an employer be given notice within 10 days of filing). The cases that accept mere temporal proximity between an employer's knowledge of protected activity and an adverse employment action as sufficient evidence of causality to establish a prima facie case uniformly hold that the temporal proximity must be "very close." Action taken (as here) 20 months later suggests, by itself, no causality at all.

In short, neither the grounds that respondent presented to the District Court, nor the ground she added on appeal, nor even the ground the Court of Appeals developed on its own, sufficed to establish a dispute substantial enough to withstand the motion for summary judgment. The District Court's granting of that motion was correct. The judgment of the Court of Appeals is reversed.

CASE QUESTIONS

1. Are you in agreement with the Court's reasoning?
2. Do you believe the comment was severe?

3. Should the company reprimand the individual who made the comment?

Case Commentary
The U.S. Supreme Court reasoned that an isolated comment having sexual overtones but lacking sexual language was insufficient to hold the employer liable. ∎

The issue in the next case is whether an employer who knows or should have known be responsible for taking preventive measures to insure that company property is not being used by employees to sexually harass coworkers.

Blakey v. Continental Airlines, Inc.
751 A.2d 538 (NJ 2000)

O'Hern, J.

In this employment discrimination case against Continental Airlines and certain of its employees, one way of framing the issues is whether:

1. Should an employer, having actual or constructive knowledge that co-employees are posting harassing, retaliatory, and sometimes defamatory, messages about a co-employee on a bulletin board used by the company's employees, have a duty to prevent the continuation of such harassing conduct?
2. Should employees of Continental Airlines reasonably expect to be subject to the personal jurisdiction of New Jersey when (a) they have published in that forum defamatory statements that are intended or are foreseeably likely to injure the co-employee in the exercise of her protected rights to be free from discrimination, and (b) they have done so in retaliation for a co-employee having sought in that forum, where her work activities were centered, the protection of the forum's laws against discrimination?

The case appears to have proceeded on the thesis that there could be no liability if the harassment by co-employees did not take place within the workplace setting at a place under the physical control of the employer. Although the electronic bulletin board may not have a physical location within a terminal, hangar or aircraft, it may nonetheless have been so closely related to the workplace environment and beneficial to Continental that a continuation of harassment on the forum should be regarded as part of the workplace. As applied to this hostile environment workplace claim, we find that if the employer had notice that co-employees were engaged on such a work-related forum in a pattern of retaliatory harassment directed at a co-employee, the employer would have a duty to

remedy that harassment. We find that the record is inadequate to determine whether the relationship between the bulletin board and the employer establishes a connection with the workplace sufficient to impose such liability on the employer.

Concerning the issue of personal jurisdiction, we find that defendants who published defamatory electronic messages, with knowledge that the messages would be published in New Jersey and could influence a claimant's efforts to seek a remedy under New Jersey's Law Against Discrimination, may properly be subject to the State's jurisdiction.

A.

Tammy S. Blakey, a pilot for Continental Airlines since 1984, appears from the record to be a highly qualified commercial airline pilot. In December 1989, Blakey became that airline's first female captain to fly an Airbus or A300 aircraft (A300). The A300 is a widebody twin-engine jet aircraft seating 250 passengers. Plaintiff was one of five qualified A300 pilots in the service of Continental Airlines. Shortly after qualifying to be a captain on the A300, Blakey complained of sexual harassment and a hostile working environment based on conduct and comments directed at her by male co-employees. From 1990 to 1993, Blakey was based in Newark, New Jersey, but lived in Arlington, Washington. According to Blakey, in February 1991, she began to file systematic complaints with various representatives of Continental about the conduct of her male co-employees. Specifically, Blakey complained to Continental's management concerning pornographic photographs and vulgar gender-based comments directed at her that appeared in the workplace, specifically in her plane's cockpit and other work areas.

In February 1993, Blakey filed a charge of sexual discrimination and retaliation in violation of Title VII of the Civil Rights Act of 1964 and the Civil Rights Act of 1991 against Continental with the Equal Employment Opportunity Commission in Seattle, Washington, her home state. She simultaneously filed a complaint in the United States District Court in Seattle, Washington, against Continental for its failure to remedy the hostile work environment. Because Blakey's major flight activities had been out of Newark International Airport, the United States District Court granted Continental's motion to transfer the action to the United States District Court for the District of New Jersey. Continental requested the transfer to New Jersey because Blakey was based in Newark, her allegations were predicated on unlawful employment practices that took place in New Jersey and the Continental personnel responsible for investigating Blakey's complaints also were based in Newark. Continental's motion to transfer was granted on May 13, 1993. At her own request, Blakey transferred to Houston in May 1993. To be relieved of the continuing stress that she had experienced in Newark, Blakey assumed a voluntary unpaid leave of absence beginning in August 1993.

B.

In the midst of that federal litigation, her fellow pilots continued to publish a series of what plaintiff views as harassing gender-based messages, some of which she alleges are false and defamatory. From February to July 1995, a number of Continental's male pilots posted derogatory and insulting remarks about Blakey on the pilots' on-line computer bulletin board called the Crew Members Forum ("Forum"). The Forum is accessible to all Continental pilots and crew member personnel through the Internet provider, CompuServe. When Continental employees access CompuServe, one of the menu selections listed in the "Continental Airlines Home Access" program includes an option called "Continental Forum."

The question in this more complex case is whether the Crew Members Forum is the equivalent of a bulletin board in the pilots' lounge or a work-related place in which pilots and crew members continue a pattern of harassment. The trial court correctly perceived the role of the Forum when it asked:

So what's the difference? What's the critical difference now we've taken it off this wood and whatever it is, cork material, that a bulletin board is made out of, and now we've electronically put it on the Internet. Now, what are the critical differences that now take it out of something that Continental could be responsible for as a workplace, or work-related item.

This Court has recognized that harassment by a supervisor that takes place outside of the workplace can be actionable. In *American Motorists*, the Court "noted that whether specific acts of harassment or discrimination took place outside of the workplace, such as harassing telephone calls . . . , is of no consequence because such conduct nevertheless would have arisen out of the employment relationship between the plaintiff and the defendant corporation."

Thus, standing alone, the fact that the electronic bulletin board may be located outside of the workplace (although not as closely affiliated with the workplace as was the cockpit in which similar harassing conduct occurred), does not mean that an employer may have no duty to correct off-site harassment by co-employees. Conduct that takes place outside of the workplace has a tendency to permeate the workplace. A worker need not actually hear the harassing words outside the workplace so long as the harassment contributes to the hostile work environment.

Although an employer's liability for sexual harassment of which the employer knew or should have known can be seen to flow from agency law, it also can be understood as direct liability. When an employer knows or should know of the harassment and fails to take effective measures to stop it, the employer has joined with the harasser in making the working environment hostile. The employer, by failing to take action, sends the harassed employee the message that the harassment is acceptable and that the management supports the harasser. "Effective" remedial measures are those reasonably calculated to end the harassment. The "reasonableness of an employer's remedy will depend on its ability to stop harassment by the person who engaged in harassment."

The Second, Sixth and Tenth Circuits have held that "an employer can be liable for co-workers' retaliatory harassment."

Plaintiff alleges that she gave notice to Continental as early as March 1995 by forwarding copies of the offending "threads" to Continental's counsel as notice of the continuing harassment. If such notice was given, Continental's liability will depend on whether the Crew Members Forum was such an integral part of the workplace that harassment on the Crew Members Forum should be regarded as a continuation or extension of the pattern of harassment that existed in the Continental workplace.

Our common experience tells us how important are the extensions of the workplace where the relations among employees are cemented or sometimes sundered. If an "old boys' network" continued, in an after-hours setting, the belittling conduct that edges over into harassment, what exactly is the outsider (whether black, Latino, or woman) to do? Keep swallowing the abuse or give up the chance to make the team? We believe that severe or pervasive harassment in a work-related setting that continues a pattern of harassment on the job is sufficiently related to the workplace that an informed employer who takes no effective measures to stop it, "sends the harassed employee the message that the harassment is acceptable and that the management supports the harasser."

To repeat, employers do not have a duty to monitor private communications of their employees; employers do have a duty to take effective measures to stop co-employee harassment when the employer knows or has reason to know that such harassment is part of a pattern of harassment that is taking place in the workplace and in settings that are related to the workplace. Besides, it may well be in an employer's economic best interests to adopt a proactive stance when it comes to dealing with co-employee harassment. The best defense may be a good offense against sexual harassment. "We have afforded a form of a safe haven for employers who promulgate and support an active, anti-harassment policy." Effective remedial steps reflecting a lack of tolerance for harassment will be "relevant to an employer's affirmative defense that its actions absolve it from all liability." Surely an anti-harassment policy directed at any form of co-employee harassment would bolster that defense.

The more difficult issue in this case is that of personal jurisdiction over the pilots who are alleged to have defamed the plaintiff in apparent retaliation for her assertion of rights protected under New Jersey's Law Against Discrimination.

The parties have viewed the case as presenting novel issues of Internet jurisdiction. "Sexual harassment is not new, but the expansion of computer networks has seen a new form of communication develop that current law is ill-equipped to confront."

The test for "due process requires only that in order to subject a defendant to a judgment in personam, if he [or she] be not present within the territory of the forum, he or she have certain minimum contacts with it such that the maintenance of the suit does not offend 'traditional notions of fair play and substantial justice.'"

(1) Did defendants have the requisite "minimum contacts" with New Jersey?

In this case, the question is whether the harassment was expected or intended to cause injury in New Jersey.

If this case had arisen just a few years ago and the offending communications had been placed in *The New York Times* or *U.S.A. Today*, with the expectation or intent that the publications would affect the pursuit of Blakey's LAD claims in New Jersey, we would have little difficulty in exercising jurisdiction over the defamatory statements. The messages would have been published in New Jersey,

albeit in print versus electronic form. A claimant who was in the process of vindicating her rights in a forum in New Jersey would surely feel the effect here. It would be a paradox if electronic communications, with their instantaneous messaging, would lessen the jurisdictional power of a state.

Because defamation was alleged to be part of the harassing conduct that took place on the Crew Members Forum, it would be fair to posit jurisdiction where the effects of the harassment were expected or intended to be felt. The center of gravity of this employment dispute was in Newark, New Jersey. Early in the federal case, Continental had claimed that "the evidence of a hostile environment in locations other than Newark was irrelevant to Plaintiff's claim." The effect of retaliatory falsehoods on the worker could reasonably influence the antidiscrimination policies of the forum by deterring her resolve. In these circumstances, we do not believe that it is unfair that the forum where the discrimination took place should exercise jurisdiction over the allegations of defamatory retaliatory harassment.

However, in fairness to defendants, we cannot determine whether they knew that at the time of their defamatory statements plaintiff was actually pursuing this action in New Jersey. We find no indication that discovery from the individual defendants has been obtained. Under the second prong of *International Shoe*, it may simply not be fair to invoke the jurisdiction of the State of New Jersey. Questions to be answered are whether the pilots knew that plaintiff was seeking to vindicate her rights in New Jersey and whether they knew that their messages would be published in the forum.

Finally, we would hope that an employer who cherishes its reputation for caring for its customers would use its good offices to resolve this long simmering disagreement among its key employees, whose harmony would appear crucial not only to efficient flight operations but to general public safety as well. The judgment of the Appellate Division is reversed.

Judgment for Blakey.

Case Commentary

The New Jersey Supreme Court ruled that an employer would be liable if the retaliatory comments made around the country could be shown to have had an effect on Blakey and the litigation she was pursuing in New Jersey. ■

CASE QUESTIONS

1. Do you agree with the Court's ruling?
2. Were the comments severe and pervasive?

3. How should a court determine jurisdiction of sexually harassing and retaliatory comments made via the Internet?

The issue in the following case is whether an employer's ignoring of allegations by employees who were raped by a coworker constitutes sexual harassment.

Ferris v. Delta Air Lines, Inc.

277 F.3d 128 (2nd Cir. 2001)

Leval, Circuit Judge.

In March 1998, Penny Ferris and Michael Young, both Delta flight attendants, were employed together on the crew of a Delta flight from New York City to Rome, Italy. When the flight arrived in Rome on March 17, the crew (including Ferris and Young) boarded a Delta bus to be driven to the Savoy Hotel, where Delta had reserved and paid for a block of rooms to be used by the crew until their return flight to New York on March 18. That afternoon, Ferris and Young had shopped together for wine for Ferris to bring home as a present. Young told her he had brought a bottle of a vintage Ferris was considering and offered to let her taste it in his room when they returned to the hotel. Upon their return, Ferris went to Young's room, where he had a glass of wine ready for her. After drinking about half a glass, Ferris felt faint. She tried to return to her room, but could not make her legs move. She blacked out. While she was unconscious, Young took off her clothes and raped her vaginally, orally, and anally. She partially regained consciousness intermittently during the multiple rapes, at one point telling Young to stop before blacking out again.

That night, at dinner with the other flight attendants, Ferris was in shock and confusion. During the dinner, she began to feel nauseous, and went to the bathroom and vomited. The following day, she flew back to New York, serving as crew together with Young.

On March 30, 1998—about two weeks after the rape—Ferris recounted what had happened to Vanessa Bray, who had been the "On-Board Leader" (the lead flight attendant) on the March 16–18 flights. She told Bray that she thought that she might have been drugged because she was unable to do anything about what was happening to her. Ferris then asked Bray not to repeat what she had said, and Bray did not.

On April 11, 1998—about three weeks after the rape—Ferris reported the rape to Anne Estall, the Delta Duty Supervisor. In the course of a one-hour meeting, Ferris informed her that she had been raped by a flight attendant who was an Italian speaker on a March 1998 flight to Rome. Ferris refused to give Young's name. Using the Delta computer system, Estall narrowed the suspects down to two male, Italian-speaking flight attendants who had been on the March 16–18 flights. She then set up a meeting between Ferris and Maritza Biscaino, the Delta Base Manager at John F. Kennedy International Airport (JFK) for six days later.

At the meeting on April 17, 1998, Ferris told Biscaino about the rape in an interview that lasted approximately two hours. Biscaino requested a written report and the rapist's name, both of which Ferris refused to give her. In follow-up conversations with Ferris around May 4, 1998, Biscaino eventually persuaded Ferris to disclose her assailant's name.

On May 5, 1998, Biscaino and her co-base-manager Kevin Grimes interviewed Michael Young for approximately two hours. He said that, upon arriving in Rome, he had gone to the gym, returned to his room for a nap, and spent the night with another flight attendant, Jaycee Kantz. The same day, he provided a written statement to this effect. Biscaino interviewed Kantz shortly after, and Kantz confirmed that Young had spent the night with her.

Sometime in early June 1998, flight attendant Carolyn Gordon overheard a conversation between Young and another flight attendant in which Young said that he had been accused of drugging and raping a Delta flight attendant. This prompted Gordon to handwrite a memo to Delta on June 22, 1998, which recounted an experience that Gordon had had with Young in December, 1997. Gordon had accepted Young's invitation to come to his room during a layover in Rome for a glass of wine. When she got there, two glasses of wine were already poured on the nightstand. Gordon's memo implied that the wine Young gave her may have been drugged and that he took advantage of her drugged state to have sex with her, although she acknowledged that she may have suffered an adverse reaction between the wine and anti-depressant medications she had been taking.

On June 25, 1998, Ferris gave Biscaino her first written report of the incident. Ferris's written report repeated the events as previously recounted to Vanessa Bray, Estall, and Biscaino. On June 29, 1998, Biscaino and Grimes again met with Young, confronting him with the information in Ferris's written report. At the conclusion of the meeting, Biscaino and Grimes suspended Young and removed his Delta workplace identification. Delta continued to investigate Ferris's claims over the next several months, while Young was on suspension. Young refused to cooperate with the investigation, and was recommended for termination on November 5, 1998. At some point, Young submitted a handwritten resignation to Delta.

A. DELTA'S PRIOR NOTICE OF YOUNG'S SEXUALLY ABUSIVE CONDUCT WITH CO-WORKERS

a. Kathleen Ballweg

At Christmas time, 1993, Kathleen Ballweg and Young were flight attendants together on a Delta flight from New York to Milan. During the flight, Young invited several flight attendants to accompany him to see the Christmas Eve service in Florence. Several agreed, but changed their minds by the time the plane arrived in Florence, leaving Ballweg as the only flight attendant accompanying Young to Florence. Young raped Ballweg in her hotel room in Florence.

Upon returning to the United States, Ballweg reported the incident to a Delta supervisor at JFK. She said the supervisor should know about somebody who is potentially dangerous, and she identified Young by name. She told the supervisor that she wanted to be anonymous, and the supervisor replied that Delta could do nothing about it unless Ballweg made a written, formal complaint, which Ballweg did not want to do.

Ballweg flew with Young only one more time after the phone calls in Frankfurt. Whenever she was flying to Rome or Milan, she would check the flight attendant list to see if Young was on the flight, and tried to avoid assignment to a flight if she saw that Young would be working on it.

Delta took no action in response to Ballweg's reports.

b. Aileen Feingold

In March 1995, Delta flight attendant Aileen Feingold visited Young in Dallas for sightseeing. Young had invited her to stay at his house, telling her she would have a separate bedroom. On the night that Feingold spent at Young's house, Young entered the bedroom where she was sleeping and raped her while she was asleep.

Feingold was so distraught after the rape that she failed a training test that she took the next day. Delta subsequently cancelled one of Feingold's scheduled trips so that she could re-take the test.

Feingold later warned several Delta flight attendants that Young was a rapist. About four months after the rape, Feingold contacted Young about a suitcase that she had left at his house. Young emailed her, telling her that it was her problem to take care of her things, that he had heard that she was talking negatively about him, and that she had better stop because Young had friends that could get her in a lot of trouble, specifically mentioning Delta supervisor Nancy Ruhl, who was manager of in-flight service for JFK. Young also left messages at her home, telling her to shut her mouth, or he would take care of her.

Feingold then contacted Ruhl, the Delta supervisor that Young had mentioned. Feingold told Ruhl about the rape. Feingold also read Ruhl the emails that she had received, and offered to bring her file of Young's emails by Ruhl's office. Ruhl said that that would not be necessary. Feingold said that she believed she was not the first person that Young had raped, as it seemed to her that Young had a method of operation that was down pat. Feingold offered to write up a report to put in Young's file to document her allegations. She told Ruhl that she wanted to do something so that Young would not rape anyone else. Ruhl told Feingold that she would talk to Young and that she would take care of the situation, and that it was not necessary for Feingold to provide a written report.

The next day, Ruhl called Feingold and told her that she had talked to Young, that he would not bother her again, and that she had taken care of everything. She instructed Feingold never to talk to Young, and not to talk to anyone about what had happened.

Delta took no action in response to Feingold's report.

c. Michelle Zachry

Michelle Zachry, another Delta flight attendant, had also reported to Delta that Young had behaved hostilely and aggressively toward her during their work on a flight after she refused to go out to dinner with him.

Zachry flew with Young to Rome in July 1997. During the flight, Young made sexual comments to her, told her about his illegal steroid use, told her that he was involved in a sexual affair with another flight attendant, and invited Zachry to go to dinner. Later, Young called Zachry in her hotel room to ask her to go to dinner, and after she turned him down, called her back and became belligerent.

After landing from the return flight from Rome, Young came up to Zachry and began cursing and screaming at her. Passengers turned around to look at him, and another flight attendant eventually interposed himself between Young and Zachry and told Young that he needed to "chill out."

Zachry reported this incident to a supervisor. She did not give Young's name, but told the supervisor that a flight attendant had gone crazy because she would not go out to dinner with him. The supervisor did not ask any questions of her, and did not make a formal report.

In the meantime, Zachry had spoken with the flight attendant that Young had said he was having an affair with. About one week later, Zachry encountered Young on a Delta tram in the Dallas airport. Young called Zachry obscene names, and threatened to kill her. Zachry feared that Young might physically attack her.

After the incident on the tram, Zachry told Cheryl Merit, a Delta supervisor, that she was going to report an incident. Merit then accompanied Zachry to the office of Kathy Goldberger, a Delta supervisor. This time, Zachry identified Michael Young by name, and told Goldberger what had happened on the plane, on the tram, and how Young had boasted of his illegal steroid use. Goldberger asked Zachry to make a written report, telling her that they could not do anything unless Zachry made a written report, and Goldberger told Zachry that Delta "did not have anything on Young." Zachry was not willing to make a written report. Afterwards, Zachry would not fly to Rome because of her fear of encountering Michael Young.

Delta took no action in response to Zachry's report.

B. THE DISTRICT COURT'S DECISION

Judgment was entered on July 20, 2000. On this appeal, Ferris argues the district court erred in granting summary judgment to Delta on her sexual harassment claim and on her claims for negligent supervision and retention of Young.

DISCUSSION

A. Sexual harassment claims

1. Young's rape of Ferris during the layover in Rome

The district court granted summary judgment to Delta on Ferris's claim based on the rape in Rome. Because Young had no supervisory authority over Ferris and she associated voluntarily with him, and there was no evidence that Delta had affirmatively encouraged flight attendants to visit each other's rooms, the court concluded that the attack in Young's hotel room could not, as a matter of law, be found to have occurred in a "work environment."

Although we think the question is close, we respectfully disagree with the district court's conclusion. In our view, the rape could be found to have occurred in a work environment within the meaning of Title VII. The circumstances that surround the lodging of an airline's flight crew during a brief layover in a foreign country in a block of hotel rooms booked and paid for by the employer are very different from those that arise when stationary employees go home at the close of their normal workday. The flight crew members repeatedly spend brief layovers in a foreign country with little opportunity to develop private lives in that place. Most likely they do not speak the local language. In all likelihood, they do not have family, friends, or their own residences there. Although it is not mandatory for them to do so, they generally stay in a block of hotel rooms that the airline reserves for them and pays for. The airline in addition provides them as a group with ground transportation by van from the airport to the hotel on arrival, and back at the time for departure. It is likely furthermore in those circumstances that the crew members will have no other acquaintances in this foreign place and will band together for society and socialize as a matter of course in one another's hotel rooms. Even though the employer does not direct its employees as to how to spend their off-duty hours, the circumstances of the employment tend to compel these results. In view of the special set of circumstances that surround such a foreign layover, we disagree with the district court's conclusion. A jury could properly find on these facts that Young's hotel room was a part of Ferris's work environment within the terms of Title VII.

A reasonable factfinder might conclude that Delta's negligence made it responsible for Ferris's rape. Delta had notice of Young's proclivity to rape co-workers. The fact that Young's prior rapes were not of Ferris but of other co-workers is not preclusive. If an employer is on notice of a likelihood that a particular employee's proclivities place other employees at unreasonable risk of rape, the employer does not escape responsibility to warn or protect likely future victims merely because the abusive employee has not previously abused those particular employees.

Supervisory personnel at Delta had been notified that Young had twice raped female co-workers and had engaged in other abusive, sexually hostile conduct toward the rape victims and a third co-worker. Not only did Delta do nothing about it, but a Delta supervisor (Ruhl) took affirmative steps to prevent the filing of a formal complaint that might have resulted in protective steps and even to prevent a prior victim (Feingold) from informally spreading cautionary words among the flight attendants about Young. Given all the circumstances, a reasonable factfinder could find that Delta was negligent in failing to take steps that might have protected Ferris from Young's proclivity to rape female co-workers.

The more egregious the abuse and the more serious the threat of which the employer has notice, the more the employer will be required under a standard of reasonable care to take steps for the protection of likely future victims. The district court may have been correct that Delta's ability to investigate was curtailed by the fact that the Feingold and Ballweg rapes occurred off-duty. It does not follow, however, that the off-duty nature of the rapes absolved Delta of all responsibility to take reasonable care to protect co-workers, much less justified a supervisor's affirmative steps to prevent a victim from filing a written complaint and warning co-workers.

2. Ferris's subsequent distress at the prospect of encountering Young at Delta once she was back in New York.

Because Ferris did not work with Young again after their return to New York, the district court granted summary judgment to Delta with respect to Ferris's fear of further encounters with Young on the ground that "such trepidation, standing alone, is too hypothetical and speculative to support a contention that there was an objectively hostile or abusive work environment." We think the evidence, viewed in the light most favorable to Ferris, showed that she suffered real emotional trauma from her fear of seeing Young again while both were working as flight attendants. Ferris endeavored to keep abreast of Young's work schedule in efforts to ensure that she would not ever work on a flight he was on. But she suffered anxiety attacks at work due to her fear that she might again encounter Young, sought psychiatric help and took antidepressants. Under the circumstances, we do not think that Ferris's fear of encountering her rapist at her workplace is too hypothetical and speculative to sustain an award of damages. We do not rule out, however, that Ferris may be chargeable with partial, or even full, responsibility for this later injury or its duration by reason of her failure to mitigate her damages when she delayed reporting the event to Delta and naming her assailant.

Conclusion

The district court's grant of summary judgment in Delta's favor as to Ferris's federal sexual harassment claims is vacated and the case remanded for further proceedings.

Judgment for Ferris.

CASE QUESTIONS

1. Are you in agreement with the Court's reasoning?
2. Is Delta guilty of any criminal conduct for continuing to employ Young?
3. Does Delta have a duty to report Young to the police?

Case Commentary

The Second Circuit Court concluded that Young's rape of Ferris in a hotel in Rome could be considered to have occurred within the scope of employment. ■

4. Would the court's decision have been different if Young had not raped others before Ferris?

The incidents of sexual harassment must be at the workplace or otherwise work related. If the sexual harassment has no connection with work, then action against the employer is without merit. A criminal harassment complaint against the accused may be more appropriate.

Economic dependence has long placed women in vulnerable positions with their fathers, husbands, and employers. A feeling of inferiority has long caused women to have inadequate self-esteem. On the job, verbal and physical sexual abuse is rampant. Almost every woman will be subject to an incident of this during her working career. Most women accept this conduct begrudgingly because they have felt powerless in an employment environment where men are powerful. They fear reporting sexual harassment because of subtle reprisals. Instances of sexual harassment at work often make women feel anxious, embarrassed, and insecure. Their emotional distress and mental anguish interfere with their ability to perform well at work.

In an age in which women are exercising greater freedom in the control of their bodies, they should not submit to unwarranted sexual comments and advances. Women should stand firm in their refusal to accept this treatment and be proactive in seeking a resolution from the company. However, this will happen only when women feel more secure in protecting themselves. Men must be admonished that they have no right to mistreat women, expect sexual gratification at work, and use their positions to extort sex from women in return for promotions, raises, easier work schedules, or just allowing them to keep their jobs. Companies should be educated that permitting the harassment of women results in their decreased performance on the job and the possibility of a long, protracted, and expensive law suit.

Respect for women means more than just paying lip service to them. It means speaking to them as a man would speak to his mother, sister, wife, or daughter. Building women's self-esteem on the job will enable women to become more productive in the work environment.

Sexual harassment complaints are no longer confined to the workplace. Children also face harassment from other students and teachers at school. It is important that schools investigate these incidents as soon as they come to their attention. Schools are usually not liable where they lack knowledge of the sexual harassment.

The issue in the following case involves whether a student is entitled to money damages from a Board of Education because of their indifference to her pleas for the Board to take action against another student who had been sexually harassing her.

Davis v. Monroe County Board of Education
526 U.S. 629 (1999)

Justice O'Connor delivered the opinion of the Court.

Petitioner brought suit against the Monroe County Board of Education and other defendants, alleging that her fifth-grade daughter had been the victim of sexual harassment by another student in her class. Among petitioner's claims was a claim for monetary and injunctive relief under Title IX of the Education Amendments of 1972 (Title IX). The District Court dismissed petitioner's Title IX claim on the ground that "student-on-student," or peer, harassment provides no ground for a private cause of action under the statute. The Court of Appeals for the Eleventh Circuit, sitting en banc, affirmed. We consider here whether a private damages action may lie against the school board in cases of student-on-student harassment. We conclude that it may, but only where the funding recipient acts with deliberate indifference to known acts of harassment in its programs or activities. Moreover, we conclude that such an action will lie only for harassment that is so severe, pervasive, and objectively offensive that it effectively bars the victim's access to an educational opportunity or benefit.

I

A

Petitioner's minor daughter, LaShonda, was allegedly the victim of a prolonged pattern of sexual harassment by one of her fifth-grade classmates at Hubbard Elementary School, a public school in Monroe County, Georgia. According to petitioner's complaint, the harassment began in December 1992, when the classmate, G. F., attempted to touch LaShonda's breasts and genital area and made vulgar statements such as "'I want to get in bed with you'" and "'I want to feel your boobs.'" Similar conduct allegedly occurred on or about January 4 and January 20, 1993. LaShonda reported each of these incidents to her mother and to her classroom teacher, Diane Fort. Petitioner, in turn, also contacted Fort, who allegedly assured petitioner that the school principal, Bill Querry, had been informed of the incidents. Petitioner contends that, notwithstanding these reports, no disciplinary action was taken against G. F.

G. F.'s conduct allegedly continued for many months. In early February, G. F. purportedly placed a door stop in his pants and proceeded to act in a sexually suggestive manner toward LaShonda during physical education class. LaShonda reported G. F.'s behavior to her physical education teacher, Whit Maples. Approximately one week later, G. F. again allegedly engaged in harassing behavior, this time while under the supervision of another classroom teacher, Joyce Pippin. Again, LaShonda allegedly reported the incident to the teacher, and again petitioner contacted the teacher to follow up.

Petitioner alleges that G. F. once more directed sexually harassing conduct toward LaShonda in physical education class in early March, and that LaShonda reported the incident to both Maples and Pippen. In mid-April 1993, G. F. allegedly rubbed his body against LaShonda in the school hallway in what LaShonda considered a sexually suggestive manner, and LaShonda again reported the matter to Fort.

The string of incidents finally ended in mid-May, when G. F. was charged with, and pleaded guilty to, sexual battery for his misconduct. The complaint alleges that LaShonda had suffered during the months of harassment, however; specifically, her previously high grades allegedly dropped as she became unable to concentrate on her studies, and, in April 1993, her father discovered that she had written a suicide note. The complaint further alleges that, at one point, LaShonda told petitioner that she "'didn't know how much longer she could keep G. F. off her.'" Nor was LaShonda G. F.'s only victim; it is alleged that other girls in the class fell prey to G. F.'s conduct. At one point, in fact, a group composed of LaShonda and other female students tried to speak with Principal Querry about G. F.'s behavior. According to the complaint, however, a teacher denied the students' request with the statement, "'If Querry wants you, he'll call you.'"

Petitioner alleges that no disciplinary action was taken in response to G. F.'s behavior toward LaShonda. In addition to her conversations with Fort and Pippen, petitioner alleges that she spoke with Principal Querry in mid-May 1993. When petitioner inquired as to what action the school intended to take against G. F., Querry simply stated, "'I guess I'll have to threaten him a little bit harder.'" Yet, petitioner alleges, at no point during the many months of his reported misconduct was G. F. disciplined for harassment. Indeed, Querry allegedly asked petitioner why LaShonda "'was the only one complaining.'"

Nor, according to the complaint, was any effort made to separate G. F. and LaShonda. On the contrary, notwithstanding LaShonda's frequent complaints, only after more than three months of reported harassment was she even permitted to change her classroom seat so that she was no longer seated next to G. F. Moreover, petitioner alleges that, at the time of the events in question, the Monroe County Board of Education (Board) had not instructed its personnel on how to respond to peer sexual harassment and had not established a policy on the issue.

B

On May 4, 1994, petitioner filed suit in the United States District Court for the Middle District of Georgia against the Board, Charles Dumas, the school district's superintendent, and Principal Querry. The complaint alleged that the Board is a recipient of federal funding for purposes of Title IX, that "the persistent sexual advances and harassment by the student G. F. upon LaShonda interfered with her ability to attend school and perform her studies and activities," and that "the deliberate indifference by Defendants to the unwelcome sexual advances of a student upon LaShonda created an intimidating, hostile, offensive and abusive school environment in violation of Title IX." The complaint sought compensatory and punitive damages, attorney's fees, and injunctive relief.

As for the Board, the court concluded that Title IX provided no basis for liability absent an allegation "that the Board or an employee of the Board had any role in the harassment." Petitioner appealed the District Court's decision dismissing her Title IX claim against the Board, and a panel of the Court of Appeals for the Eleventh Circuit reversed.

We granted certiorari in order to resolve a conflict in the Circuits over whether, and under what circumstances, a recipient of federal educational funds can be liable in a private damages action arising from student-on-student sexual harassment There is no dispute here that the Board is a recipient of federal education funding for Title IX purposes. Nor do respondents support an argument that student-on-student harassment cannot rise to the level of "discrimination" for purposes of Title IX. Rather, at issue here is the question whether a recipient of federal education funding may be liable for damages under Title IX under any circumstances for discrimination in the form of student-on-student sexual harassment.

Petitioner urges that Title IX's plain language compels the conclusion that the statute is intended to bar recipients of federal funding from permitting this form of discrimination in their programs or activities. She emphasizes that the statute prohibits a student from being "subjected to discrimination under any education program or activity receiving Federal financial assistance." Here, however, we are asked to do more than define the scope of the behavior that Title IX proscribes. We must determine whether a district's failure to respond to student-on-student harassment in its schools can support a private suit for money damages

Here, petitioner attempts to hold the Board liable for its own decision to remain idle in the face of known student-on-student harassment in its schools. We thus conclude that recipients of federal funding may be liable for "subjecting" their students to discrimination where the recipient is deliberately indifferent to known acts of student-on-student sexual harassment and the harasser is under the school's disciplinary authority.

We stress that our conclusion here—that recipients may be liable for their deliberate indifference to known acts of peer sexual harassment—does not mean that recipients can avoid liability only by purging their schools of actionable peer harassment or that administrators must engage in particular disciplinary action. We thus disagree with respondents' contention that, if Title IX provides a cause of action for student-on-student harassment, "nothing short of expulsion of every student accused of misconduct involving sexual overtones would protect school systems from liability or damages."

While it remains to be seen whether petitioner can show that the Board's response to reports of G. F.'s misconduct was clearly unreasonable in light of the known circumstances, petitioner may be able to show that the Board "subjected" LaShonda to discrimination by failing to respond in any way over a period of five months to complaints of G. F.'s in-school misconduct from LaShonda and other female students.

The most obvious example of student-on-student sexual harassment capable of triggering a damages claim would thus involve the overt, physical deprivation of access to school resources. Consider, for example, a case in which male students physically threaten their female peers every day, successfully preventing the female students from using a particular school resource—an athletic field or a computer lab, for instance. District administrators are well aware of the daily ritual, yet they deliberately ignore requests for aid from the female students wishing to use the resource. The district's knowing refusal to take any action in response to such behavior would fly in the face of Title IX's core principles, and such deliberate indifference may appropriately be subject to claims for monetary damages. It is not necessary, however, to show physical exclusion to demonstrate that students have been deprived by the actions of another student or students of an educational opportunity on the basis of sex. Rather, a plaintiff must establish sexual harassment of students that is so severe, pervasive, and objectively offensive, and that so undermines and detracts from the victims' educational experience, that the victim-students are effectively denied equal access to an institution's resources and opportunities. Indeed, at least early on, students are still learning how to interact appropriately with their peers. It is thus understandable that, in the school setting, students often engage in insults, banter, teasing, shoving, pushing, and gender-specific conduct that is upsetting to the students subjected to it. Damages are not available for simple acts of teasing and name-calling among school children, however, even where these comments target differences in gender. Rather, in the context of student-on-student harassment, damages are available only where the behavior is so severe, pervasive, and objectively offensive that it denies its victims the equal access to education that Title IX is designed to protect.

The drop-off in LaShonda's grades provides necessary evidence of a potential link between her education and G.F.'s misconduct, but petitioner's ability to state a cognizable claim here depends equally on the alleged persistence and severity of G. F.'s actions, not to mention the Board's alleged knowledge and deliberate indifference.

Applying this standard to the facts at issue here, we conclude that the Eleventh Circuit erred in dismissing petitioner's complaint. Petitioner alleges that her daughter was the victim of repeated acts of sexual harassment by G. F.

over a 5-month period, and there are allegations in support of the conclusion that G. F.'s misconduct was severe, pervasive, and objectively offensive. The harassment was not only verbal; it included numerous acts of objectively offensive touching, and, indeed, G. F. ultimately pleaded guilty to criminal sexual misconduct. Moreover, the complaint alleges that there were multiple victims who were sufficiently disturbed by G. F.'s misconduct to seek an audience with the school principal. Further, petitioner contends that the harassment had a concrete, negative effect on her daughter's ability to receive an education. The complaint also suggests that petitioner may be able to show both

actual knowledge and deliberate indifference on the part of the Board, which made no effort whatsoever either to investigate or to put an end to the harassment.

Accordingly, the judgment of the United States Court of Appeals for the Eleventh Circuit is reversed, and the case is remanded for further proceedings consistent with this opinion.

Case Commentary
The U.S. Supreme Court held that a student may recover from a school board for their deliberate indifference to her sexual harassment complaint. ■

CASE QUESTIONS

1. Do you agree with the decision in this case?
2. What was the reason for the inaction on the part of the principal and teachers?

3. Do you think G. F.'s actions created a severe and pervasive environment?

The question presented in the following case is whether a school district will be liable when a teacher sexually harasses a student where the school district lacks knowledge of the harassment.

Gebser v. Lago Vista Indep. School Dist.
524 U.S. 274 (1998)

Justice O'Connor delivered the opinion of the Court.
The question in this case is when a school district may be held liable in damages in an implied right of action under Title IX of the Education Amendments of 1972 for the sexual harassment of a student by one of the district's teachers. We conclude that damages may not be recovered in those circumstances unless an official of the school district who at a minimum has authority to institute corrective measures on the district's behalf has actual notice of, and is deliberately indifferent to, the teacher's misconduct.

I

In the spring of 1991, when petitioner Alida Star Gebser was an eighth-grade student at a middle school in respondent Lago Vista Independent School District (Lago Vista), she joined a high school book discussion group led by Frank Waldrop, a teacher at Lago Vista's high school. Lago Vista received federal funds at all pertinent times. During the book discussion sessions, Waldrop often made sexually suggestive comments to the students. Gebser entered high school in the fall and was assigned to classes taught by Waldrop in both semesters. Waldrop continued to make inappropriate remarks to the students, and he began to direct more of his suggestive comments toward Gebser, including during the substantial amount of time that the two were alone in his classroom. He initiated sexual contact with Gebser in the spring, when, while

visiting her home ostensibly to give her a book, he kissed and fondled her. The two had sexual intercourse on a number of occasions during the remainder of the school year. Their relationship continued through the summer and into the following school year, and they often had intercourse during class time, although never on school property.

Gebser did not report the relationship to school officials, testifying that while she realized Waldrop's conduct was improper, she was uncertain how to react and she wanted to continue having him as a teacher. In October 1992, the parents of two other students complained to the high school principal about Waldrop's comments in class. The principal arranged a meeting, at which, according to the principal, Waldrop indicated that he did not believe he had made offensive remarks but apologized to the parents and said it would not happen again. The principal also advised Waldrop to be careful about his classroom comments and told the school guidance counselor about the meeting, but he did not report the parents' complaint to Lago Vista's superintendent, who was the district's Title IX coordinator. A couple of months later, in January 1993, a police officer discovered Waldrop and Gebser engaging in sexual intercourse and arrested Waldrop. Lago Vista terminated his employment, and subsequently, the Texas Education Agency revoked his teaching license. During this time, the district had not promulgated or distributed an official grievance procedure for lodging sexual harassment complaints; nor had it issued a formal anti-harassment policy.

Gebser and her mother filed suit against Lago Vista and Waldrop in state court in November 1993, raising claims against the school district under Title IX, and state negligence law, and claims against Waldrop primarily under state law. They sought compensatory and punitive damages from both defendants. After the case was removed, the United States District Court for the Western District of Texas granted summary judgment in favor of Lago Vista on all claims, and remanded the allegations against Waldrop to state court. In rejecting the Title IX claim against the school district, the court reasoned that the statute "was enacted to counter policies of discrimination . . . in federally funded education programs," and that "only if school administrators have some type of notice of the gender discrimination and fail to respond in good faith can the discrimination be interpreted as a policy of the school district." Here, the court determined, the parents' complaint to the principal concerning Waldrop's comments in class was the only one Lago Vista had received about Waldrop, and that evidence was inadequate to raise a genuine issue on whether the school district had actual or constructive notice that Waldrop was involved in a sexual relationship with a student.

Unquestionably, Title IX placed on the Gwinnett County Public Schools the duty not to discriminate on the basis of sex, and 'when a supervisor sexually harasses a subordinate because of the subordinate's sex, that supervisor "discriminates" on the basis of sex.' We believe the same rule should apply when a teacher sexually harasses and abuses a student.

Applying those principles here, we conclude that it would "frustrate the purposes" of Title IX to permit a damages recovery against a school district for a teacher's sexual harassment of a student based on principles of respondeat superior or constructive notice, i.e., without actual notice to a school district official. Because Congress did not expressly create a private right of action under Title IX, the statutory text does not shed light on Congress' intent with respect to the scope of available remedies.

As a general matter, it does not appear that Congress contemplated unlimited recovery in damages against a funding recipient where the recipient is unaware of discrimination in its programs. When Title IX was enacted in 1972, the principal civil rights statutes containing an express right of action did not provide for recovery of monetary damages at all, instead allowing only injunctive and equitable relief. It was not until 1991 that Congress made damages available under Title VII, and even then, Congress carefully limited the amount recoverable in any individual case, calibrating the maximum recovery to the size of the employer.

That contractual framework distinguishes Title IX from Title VII, which is framed in terms not of a condition but of an outright prohibition. Title VII applies to all employers without regard to federal funding and aims broadly to "eradicate discrimination throughout the economy." Thus, whereas Title VII aims centrally to compensate victims of discrimination, Title IX focuses more on "protecting" individuals from discriminatory practices carried out by recipients of federal funds. If a school district's liability for a teacher's sexual harassment rests on principles of constructive notice or respondeat superior, it will likewise be the case that the recipient of funds was unaware of the discrimination. It is sensible to assume that Congress did not envision a recipient's liability in damages in that situation.

The number of reported cases involving sexual harassment of students in schools confirms that harassment unfortunately is an all too common aspect of the educational experience. No one questions that a student suffers extraordinary harm when subjected to sexual harassment and abuse by a teacher, and that the teacher's conduct is reprehensible and undermines the basic purposes of the educational system. The issue in this case, however, is whether the independent misconduct of a teacher is attributable to the school district that employs him under a specific federal statute designed primarily to prevent recipients of federal financial assistance from using the funds in a discriminatory manner. Our decision does not affect any right of recovery that an individual may have against a school district as a matter of state law or against the teacher in his individual capacity under state law or under 42 U.S.C. § 1983. Until Congress speaks directly on the subject, however, we will not hold a school district liable in damages under Title IX for a teacher's sexual harassment of a student absent actual notice and deliberate indifference.

We therefore affirm the judgment of the Court of Appeals.

Case Commentary

The U.S. Supreme Court reasoned that under Title IX school districts should be liable for the conduct of their teachers only where the school district has knowledge of the behavior. This decision is contrary to *Faragher v. City of Boca Raton*. ∎

CASE QUESTIONS

1. Do you agree with the Court's decision?
2. How do you reconcile this case with *Faragher*?

3. If school districts are not liable for their teachers' conduct absent knowledge, what incentive is there for them to monitor the behavior of their teachers?

Companies and schools should draft a sexual harassment policy and have it well publicized throughout the workplace. The policy should clearly define the types of sexual harassment as well as set forth examples of verbal and physical abuse that will not be tolerated. Investigations should be thorough and the consequences severe.

A MODEL SEXUAL HARASSMENT POLICY

Sexual harassment is defined as (1) a sexual advance or request for sexual favor made by one employee to another that is unwelcome and not consented to; and (2) touching, joking, commenting, or distributing material of a sexual nature that an employee has not consented to and finds offensive.

Sexual advance may be defined as embracing, touching, cornering, or otherwise restricting an individual's freedom to move with the intent of pursuing sexual intimacy.

Request for sexual favors may be defined as asking an individual to engage in some type of sexual behavior such as but not limited to sexual intercourse, oral sex, intimate touching, and kissing.

Touching may be defined as placing hands on or rubbing against some part of another individual's body that is unwelcome and not consented to. The part of the person's body includes not only the breast, genitals, and buttocks, but also leg, knee, thigh, arm, shoulder, neck, face, and hair.

Joking may be defined as encouraging, participating, or telling sexual jokes that are offensive and demeaning.

Commenting may be defined as passing remarks of a sexual nature and that are offensive and demeaning about an individual's anatomy, sex life, or personality or about that individual's gender.

Distributing material of a sexual nature encompasses pornography, photostatic sheets that depict sexual cartoons or sexual jokes, or libelous statements about an individual's sex life.

Although the court-appointed test for determining what constitutes sexual harassment is a reasonable person standard and what is reasonable may vary depending on the work environment, it is the purpose of this policy on sexual harassment to avoid litigation, not to win lawsuits. Therefore, employees are forewarned that the use of the terms *babe, broad, b**ch,* and *chick* when spoken either alone or coupled with "hot," "foxy," "dumb," "stupid," and like words may give rise to a woman's filing a sexual harassment complaint and are therefore prohibited.

If a complaint is filed with the company's human resources department on any of these allegations, it will be investigated immediately. The investigation shall consist of questioning the complainant, alleged perpetrator, coworkers, superiors, and subordinates. If a determination is made that a valid complaint had been issued against an employee, that employee will be entitled to a hearing to which he or she may be assisted by outside counsel. If a conclusion is reached that the conduct complained of meets one of the aforementioned criteria, then the employee shall be dismissed forthwith.

Furthermore, the victim will be afforded counseling services, if needed. Every effort will be made by the company to aid the victimized employee in overcoming the emotional trauma of the unfortunate ordeal.

Finally, the company will sponsor in-house workshops explaining this policy on sexual harassment, warning employees against engaging in it, and encouraging those affected by sexual harassment to come forward with the details of their encounter with it in order for the company to investigate and resolve the dilemma and service the needs of the victimized employee.

Mitisubishi Motor Company has agreed to settle a claim June 10, 1998, which was brought against them by the Equal Employment Opportunity Commission. Mitsubishi agreed to pay $34 million in compensation for at least 350 women who were employed at a Normal, Illinois, plant since 1990. The women were allegedly subjected to a pattern of sexual harassment that led to the filing of a civil class action prior to the EEOC suit.

The following case presents the settlement agreement reached in the Mitsubishi case.

EEOC v. Mitsubishi Motor
Case No. 96-1192 (C.Dist. Ill. 1998)

McDade, Judge.

CONSENT DECREE

1. This Consent Decree (the "Decree") is made and entered into by and between Plaintiff United States Equal Employment Opportunity Commission (hereinafter referred to as the "Commission" or "EEOC") and Defendant Mitsubishi Motor Manufacturing of America, Inc., formerly known as "Diamond Star Motors," (hereinafter referred to as "MMMA") (EEOC and MMMA are collectively referred to herein as "the Parties").

Now, therefore, the Court having carefully examined the terms and provisions of this Consent Decree, and based on the pleadings, record and stipulations of the Parties, it is ordered, adjudged and decreed that.

General Injunctive Provisions

15. Sexual Harassment. MMMA and its officers, agents, management (including supervisory employees), successors and assigns, and all those in active concert or participation with them, or any of them, are hereby enjoined from: (i) discriminating against women on the basis of sex; (ii) engaging in or being a party to any action, policy or practice that is intended to or is known to them to have the effect of harassing or intimidating any female employee on the basis of her gender; and/or (iii) creating, facilitating or permitting the existence of a work environment that is hostile to female employees.

16. Retaliation. MMMA and its officers, agents, management (including supervisory employees), successors and assigns, and all those in active concert or participation with them, or any of them, are hereby enjoined from engaging in, implementing or permitting any action, policy or practice with the purpose of retaliating against any current or former employee of MMMA because he or she opposed any practice of sex discrimination, sexual harassment or sex-based harassment made unlawful under Title VII; filed a Charge of Discrimination alleging any such practice; testified or participated in any manner in any investigation (including, without limitation, any internal investigation undertaken by MMMA), proceeding, or hearing in connection with this case and/or relating to any claim of sex discrimination, sexual harassment or sex-based harassment; was identified as a

possible witness in this action; asserted any rights under this Decree; or sought and/or received any monetary and/or non-monetary relief in accordance with this Decree.

Monetary Relief

ESTABLISHMENT OF SETTLEMENT FUND

17. MMMA shall pay the gross sum of thirty-four million dollars ($34,000,000.00) (hereinafter referred to as the "Settlement Fund") to be distributed among all "Eligible Claimants" (as that term is defined in paragraph 20 herein), all in accordance with the provisions of this Decree. None of the amounts paid to Eligible Claimants shall be for back pay.

22. Eligible Claimants shall include only those claimants who satisfy each and all of the following criteria:

(i) the claimant was either: (a) employed by MMMA at any time between January 1, 1987 and the date of entry of this Decree; or (b) worked at MMMA's Normal, Illinois facility pursuant to a contract between MMMA and her direct employer at any time during such time period and has been identified by EEOC, prior to entry of this Decree, as a potential victim.

(ii) EEOC timely received from such claimant, in accordance with the procedures set forth in this Decree, a Claim Form and a Release in the form of Exhibits B and D attached to this Decree; and (iii) EEOC received evidence credible to EEOC that the individual was (a) subjected to sexual harassment or sex-based harassment, or (b) retaliated against because she opposed sexual harassment or participated in any proceeding relating to a complaint of sexual harassment, sex-based harassment or retaliation.

Non-Monetary Relief

43. MMMA affirms the following "Statement of Zero-Tolerance Policy and Equality Objectives": Mitsubishi Motor Manufacturing of America, Inc. is firmly committed to developing and maintaining a zero-tolerance policy concerning sexual harassment, sex-based harassment and retaliation against individuals who report harassment in the company's workplace; to swiftly and firmly responding to any acts of sexual or sex-based harassment or retaliation of which the

company becomes aware; to implementing a disciplinary system that is designed to strongly deter future acts of sexual or sex-based harassment or retaliation; to eradicating any vestiges of a work environment that is hostile to women; and to actively monitoring its workplace in order to ensure tolerance, respect and dignity for all people. This paragraph does not create any contractual causes of action or other rights that would not otherwise exist.

Specific Non-Monetary Relief

44. In order to effectuate the objectives embodied in MMMA's Statement of Zero-Tolerance Policy and Equality Objectives and this Decree, MMMA shall make whatever specific modifications are necessary to its existing policies, procedures and practices in order to ensure that the following policies, procedures and practices are in effect:

(a) Sexual Harassment Policy. MMMA agrees that it shall revise its sexual harassment policy, as necessary, in order to: (i) provide examples to supplement the definitions of sexual harassment and sex-based harassment; (ii) include strong non-retaliation language with examples to supplement the definition of retaliation, and provide for substantial and progressive discipline for incidents of retaliation; (iii) eliminate the "false accusation" provision contained in its current sexual harassment policy; (iv) provide that complaints of sexual harassment, sex-based harassment and/or retaliation will be accepted by MMMA in writing and orally; (v) provide a timetable for reporting harassment, for commencing an investigation after a complaint is made or received and for remedial action to be taken upon conclusion of an investigation; and (vi) indicate that, promptly upon the conclusion of its investigation of a complaint, MMMA will communicate to the complaining party the results of the investigation and the remedial actions taken or proposed, if any.

(b) Complaint Procedures.

(i) MMMA agrees that it shall revise its complaint procedure as necessary in order to ensure that it is designed to encourage employees to come forward with complaints about violations of its sexual harassment policy. As part of this policy, MMMA agrees that it shall provide its employees with convenient, confidential and reliable mechanisms for reporting incidents of sexual harassment, sex-based harassment and retaliation. MMMA agrees that it shall designate at least two employees from the department charged with investigating such issues as persons who may be contacted, and their names, responsibilities, work locations and telephone numbers shall be routinely and continuously posted. Also as part of its procedure, MMMA agrees that it shall keep its 24-hour Complaint hotline in place, and shall take seriously anonymous complaints received on the hotline. Additionally as part of its complaint procedure, MMMA agrees that it shall maintain in the plant the presence of personnel charged with handling complaints of sexual harassment, sex-based harassment and retaliation.

(ii) MMMA agrees that it shall revise its policies as necessary to enable complaining parties to be interviewed by MMMA about their complaints in such a manner that permits the complaining party, at such party's election, to remain inconspicuous to all of the employees in such party's work area. MMMA agrees that its complaint procedure shall not impose upon individuals seeking to make a complaint alleging sexual harassment, sex-based harassment and/or retaliation any requirements that are more burdensome than are imposed upon individuals who make other complaints of comparable gravity. (iii) MMMA agrees that it shall revise its complaint handling and disciplinary procedures as necessary to ensure that all complaints of sexual harassment, sex-based harassment and/or retaliation are investigated and addressed promptly. Specifically, MMMA agrees that it shall make best efforts to investigate all complaints of sexual harassment, sex-based harassment and/or retaliation promptly and to complete investigations within three (3) weeks. MMMA will further make best efforts to prepare its written findings of the results of each investigation and the remedial actions proposed within seven (7) days after completion of the investigation, and shall thereupon promptly communicate to the complaining party the results of the investigation and the remedial actions taken or proposed, if any.

(iv) MMMA agrees that it shall make best efforts to ensure that appropriate remedial action is taken to resolve complaints and to avoid the occurrence of further incidents of sexual harassment, sex-based harassment and/or retaliation. MMMA specifically agrees that its complaint procedure shall include the power, in MMMA's sole discretion, to order, during the pendency of the investigation, the immediate transfer of persons accused of having violated MMMA's sexual harassment policy or of persons who claim to have been victims of such violations, as well as the power to order the permanent transfer of employees found to have violated such policy, and, upon the request of the complaining party, the permanent transfer of any complaining party who is found to have been the victim of a violation of MMMA's sexual harassment policy. Where possible, transfer will be in line with seniority. MMMA further agrees that it shall revise its progressive discipline policy to provide for substantial discipline short of termination—including, but not limited to, suspensions without pay—as a possible consequence for violations of its sexual harassment policy.

(c) Policies Designed To Promote Supervisor Accountability.

(i) MMMA agrees that it shall impose substantial discipline—up to and including termination, suspension without pay or demotion—upon any supervisor or manager who engages in sexual harassment or sex-based harassment or permits any such conduct to occur in his or her work area or among employees under his or her supervision, or who retaliates against any person who complains or participates in any investigation or proceeding concerning any such conduct. MMMA shall communicate this policy to all of its supervisors and managers.

(ii) MMMA agrees that it shall continue to advise all managers and supervisors of their duty to actively monitor their work areas to ensure employees' compliance with the company's sexual harassment policy, and to report any incidents and/or complaints of sexual harassment, sex-based harassment and/or retaliation of which they become aware to the department charged with handling such complaints.

(iii) MMMA agrees that it will complete its current revision of the supervisor appraisal process to include performance evaluations for the handling of equal employment opportunity ("EEO") issues as an element in supervisor appraisals, and to link such evaluations directly to supervisor salary/bonus structure.

(iv) MMMA agrees that it shall include "commitment to equal employment opportunity" as a criterion for qualification for supervisory positions.

(d) Sexual Harassment Training.

(i) MMMA agrees that it shall continue to provide mandatory annual sexual harassment training to all supervisors; to provide mandatory sexual harassment training to all new employees during employee orientation; to provide mandatory sexual harassment training to all senior management officials; to provide mandatory sexual harassment training for all employees of Mitsubishi Motors Corporation who are assigned to work at MMMA's facility in Normal, Illinois, prior to their commencing employment at MMMA's facility in Normal, Illinois; and to provide training to all persons charged with the handling of complaints of sexual harassment, sex-based harassment and/or retaliation related thereto conducted by experienced sexual harassment educators and/or investigators to educate them about the problems of sexual harassment in the workplace and the techniques for investigating and stopping it.

(ii) MMMA agrees that it shall require a senior management official to introduce all sexual harassment training to communicate MMMA's commitment to its Statement of Zero-Tolerance Policy and Monitoring of Complaints.

58. In addition to the functions and purposes described above, the Decree Monitors shall also have the responsibility for overseeing the investigation of all sexual and sex-based harassment and related retaliation complaints reported to MMMA. The Chairperson shall be initially designated as the person who will be responsible for monitoring such complaints (such designated person is hereinafter referred to as the "Complaint Monitor").

59. MMMA shall transmit to the Complaint Monitor a copy of each such written complaint reported to MMMA as soon as practicable and, in any event, no later than the close of the next business day after MMMA receives any such complaint.

60. The Complaint Monitor will oversee the investigation and, where appropriate, may make recommendations to MMMA concerning the conduct of the investigation of each such complaint. MMMA shall make a good faith best effort to follow any recommendations made by the Complaint Monitor concerning the conduct of the investigation. The Complaint Monitor may also interview the complaining party, if the Complaint Monitor deems it appropriate.

61. Upon completion of the investigation, MMMA shall promptly prepare and provide the Complaint Monitor with a copy of a written report summarizing the investigation undertaken and any remedial actions taken or proposed by MMMA, and shall also promptly communicate to the complaining party the results of the investigation and the remedial actions taken or proposed, if any, and shall further inform the complaining party of her right to appeal MMMA's finding to the Complaint Monitor.

62. If, upon receiving and reviewing an appeal from an individual complainant or upon its own initiative, the Complaint Monitor believes that the remedial action proposed by MMMA is inconsistent with MMMA's Statement of Zero-Tolerance Policy and Equality Objectives or with the terms of this Decree, the Complaint Monitor shall first attempt to resolve the disagreement with MMMA. If MMMA and the Complaint Monitor are unable to reach a resolution of their disagreement to the satisfaction of the Complaint Monitor, the Complaint Monitor shall report to EEOC any such inconsistency.

Case Commentary

The Central District Court of Illinois presided over the settlement agreement reached in the Mitsubishi case. Mitsubishi agreed to pay $34 million in settlement of the female employees' sexual harassment claims. Mitsubishi was enjoined from retaliating against any of the victims of sexual harassment. It agreed to start a sexual harassment training program for its managers and employees. Mitsubishi also agreed to provide a complaint monitor to oversee the workplace. ■

CASE QUESTIONS

1. Does this consent decree adequately address the injustices perpetrated upon the female employees?
2. Can you think of anything else that should have been included?

3. Why do you think Mitsubishi management allowed these conditions to continue?

Damages

The 1991 Amendment to the Civil Rights Act has now made compensatory and punitive damages available to Title VII plaintiffs including those victimized by sexual harassment. These damages are capped at $300,000.

EMPLOYEE LESSONS

1. Realize that the harassment must be sexual.
2. Understand that as a victim of harassment, you must not have consented to or participated in the hostile work environment.
3. Do not engage in sexual joke telling, using sexual language, or distributing sexual pictorials.
4. Appreciate that the sexual harassment must occur within the scope of employment.
5. Guard against giving the perception of creating a hostile work environment.
6. Realize that although *sweetheart*, *babe*, and *honey* are not sexually harassing terms, they may be against company policy.
7. Learn that the harassing behavior must make it difficult for you to perform your job.
8. Realize that men can be victims of sexual harassment.
9. Know that people of the same sex may be victims of sexual harassment.
10. Report instances of sexual harassment to human resources in a timely fashion.

SUMMARY

In the competitive global environment in which businesses operate, employees should be instructed that their work hours should be spent productively, not taking time for idle chatter, much less for abusing coworkers and subordinates. The team concept should be promoted, and personal favoritism should be discarded for the success of the team. Encouragement and a willingness to help one another should displace personal aggrandizement at the expense of demeaning one's coworkers. Employees who embrace these concepts will make positive contributions to the firm in a future in which employees will be judged not only on their positive contributions but also on what their negative actions are likely to cost the company.

REVIEW QUESTIONS

1. Define sexual harassment.
2. Explain hostile work environment.
3. Define the concept of *quid pro quo*.
4. What should be included in a company policy on sexual harassment?
5. Can sexual harassment be directed against management?
6. Is it possible for a man to be a victim of sexual harassment?
7. Can sexual harassment occur outside the work environment?
8. Does using the term *babe* constitute sexual harassment?
9. Can sexual harassment involve an aggressor and a victim of the same sex?
10. In situations involving sexually harassing comments, is truth an absolute defense?
11. Should the plaintiff's acquiescence in a relationship preclude him from recovery?
12. If off-color jokes are acceptable to everyone, should an employer still prohibit this type of behavior?
13. If an employee has participated in the offensive behavior, can he or she later claim hostile work environment?
14. Was a company ethical for being indifferent to the employees' affair until such time as the female employee became pregnant, at which time both she and her lover were discharged?

1. Fredette was a waiter at BVP's restaurant, and Mr. Sunshine, who is homosexual, was the maitre d' or manager. Fredette proffered evidence from which a fact finder could conclude that Fredette's supervisor, Mr. Sunshine, repeatedly propositioned him, offering employment benefits in exchange for Fredette's providing sexual favors to Mr. Sunshine. When Fredette refused to comply and later reported the matter to management, Mr. Sunshine retaliated against Fredette in various work-related ways.

   The single issue presented in this appeal is whether, under the circumstances of this case, the sexual harassment of a male employee by a homosexual male supervisor is actionable under Title VII. *Fredette v. BVP Management Associates*, 112 F.3d 1503 (11th Cir. 1997)

2. In April 1994, plaintiff Roger Fleenor filed a complaint against defendant Hewitt Soap Company and several other defendants who were employed by Hewitt. The complaint alleged that for a 2-week period in August 1992, he was subjected to "repeated and unwelcome sexual advances and harassment" by two coworkers, defendants Hatmaker and Wallet. He alleged specifically that defendant Hatmaker exposed his genitals to plaintiff, threatened to force plaintiff to engage in oral sex with him, and "stuck a ruler up Plaintiff's buttocks" against plaintiff's will. In September 1992, the company reprimanded Hatmaker for his behavior.

   We have defined the standard for sexual harassment by coworkers and supervisors in a similar way. When a plaintiff alleges harassment by coworkers, we have defined the test as whether the employer "knew or should have known of the charged sexual harassment and failed to implement prompt and appropriate corrective action."

   The question presented is whether the employer is liable even though it took the appropriate steps to address the hostile work environment. *Fleenor v. Hewitt Soap Company*, 81 F.3d 48 (6th Cir. 1996)

3. Gross has not asserted that she was subjected to sexual harassment, in the form of "unwelcome sexual advances, requests for sexual favors, and other verbal or physical conduct of a sexual nature."

   It is undisputed that Gross was laid off on October 2, 1990, because Burggraf no longer needed the services of a water truck driver on the Jenny Lake Project. Gross claimed her supervisor created a hostile work environment when he used profane language in her presence and directed some of it at her. In determining whether Gross has established a viable Title VII claim, we must first examine her work environment. In the real world of construction work, profanity and vulgarity are not perceived as hostile or abusive. Indelicate forms of expression are accepted or endured as normal human behavior. As is clear from Gross' deposition testimony, she contributed to the use of crude language on the job site:

   Q. As a construction worker, you had occasion to use profane or obscene language, didn't you?
   A. [Gross] Yes.
   Q. You were not offended by the use of profanity on the construction site, were you?
   A. No.
   Q. Did you in fact tell off-color jokes at the construction site?
   A. I can't recall specifics, but I told jokes similar to the same jokes that I was hearing.

   Anderson's Reference to a Portion of Gross' Body
   One afternoon at 4:00 P.M., Anderson yelled at Gross: "What the h**l are you doing? Get your a** back in the truck and don't you get out of it until I tell you."
   Anderson's Use of Demeaning Terms
   Gross maintains that Anderson referred to her as "dumb." Gross did not present any evidence that he characterized her as "dumb" when she was present.

The question presented is whether the profanity must contain language relating to the female gender to be actionable. *Gross v. Burggraf Construction Co.*, 53 F.3d 1531 (10th Cir. 1995)

4. A female employee sued her employer for sexual harassment, claiming that a supervisor referred to her as a "dumb f***ing broad" and a" f***ing c**t." The employer argued that the supervisor's alleged abuse was not gender-oriented in that he treated men the same way. What was the result? *Steiner v. Showboat Operating Co.*, 25 F.3d 1459 (9th Cir. 1994)

5. Byron Brown, a senior counselor at a drug rehabilitation facility, engaged in sexual intercourse with Kimberly Bunce, a patient. This happened several times with her consent. Thereafter, she sued Brown in civil court for sexual assault, battery, and malpractice. Brown argued that consent is a defense. What was the result? *Bunce v. Parkside Lodge of Columbus*, 596 N.E. 2d 1106 (Ohio App. 10 Dist. 1991)

6. Plaintiff testified that after she began working on the main floor of the factory, Oslac, the 65-year-old owner, talked to her about sex, showed her pictures from *Penthouse* magazine, tried to get her to go out with him, and invited her to his apartment on the top floor of the factory to watch pornographic movies. She said that she did not say "no" outright because she was afraid of losing her job. Rather, she would decline his advances with one reason or another and try to change the subject.

   In the spring of 1982, plaintiff appeared nude in *Easy Riders In the Wind* magazine. In April 1983, she appeared nude in *Easy Riders* magazine. The magazine circulated throughout the plant, and employees saw them. In these photographs, she had ornaments or earrings attached to her nipples. One picture revealed a tattoo in the pelvic region. Her father had pierced her nipples and had taken the photographs in her brother's presence.

   On July 19, 1984, plaintiff walked off the job following a work dispute with Eugene Ottaway. Plaintiff testified she got upset, left, and that weekend decided to quit her job.

   Plaintiff did not see Oslac in the plant during the last 4 to 6 weeks of her employment with McGregor Electronics. What was the result? *Burns v. McGregor Electronic Industries, Inc.*, 807 F.Supp. 506 (N.D.Iowa 1992)

HUMAN RESOURCE DILEMMAS

1. Michelle Rosen is a sales rep with Viva Pharmaceuticals, a small foreign firm, which has recently begun doing business in the United States. In her district, Michelle is the only woman among 16 reps. They subject her to verbal sexual taunts, fondling, and vulgar language. Michelle has complained to her district manager, but he has told her it's harmless fun. When her complaints turned to threats of a lawsuit, she was terminated. Viva has no sexual harassment policy in place. How would you advise her?

2. Roger Hummel is very attracted to his coworker Regina Nelson. Finally, he gets the courage to ask her to accompany him on a ski weekend. Regina is shocked by his request, adamantly refuses, and files a sexual harassment complaint. Roger is up for a promotion and loses it. Furthermore, he is reprimanded. What course of action should he follow?

3. In her interview for a job at Carefree Cosmetics, Kristen Hamilton admitted how desperate she was to find a job because she was a single parent. Her plea found a sympathetic ear in Paul Winston. One month after Kristen was hired, Paul began hitting on her. When Kristen rebuffed him, Paul reminded her he gave her a break and that because she was on probation she should accept his invitations. Finally, Kristen, acting out of despair, gave into Paul's sexual advances without reporting him. But when his sexual demands became deviate in her mind, she quit. Paul had been to a sexual harassment training session and had no prior complaints against him. Carefree stated

it had a sexual harassment policy in place. Included in that policy was a directive to report all complaints to the human resource department. Kristen was made aware of the policy. How would you advise her to proceed?

WEB SITE ASSIGNMENT

Referring to the Mitsubishi Settlement Agreement in this chapter, construct a policy to insure against sexual harassment in the future for this company.

www.aclu.org/news/w111097d.html
www.nydailynews.com/archive/97_05/051897/news/22177.htm
www.eeoc.gov/facts/fs-sex.html
www.commerce-database.com/legal-terms/sexual-harassment.htm
www.legal-term.com/sexualharassment-definition.htm
www.legal-database.com/laborlaw.htm

Chapter 12

Family Leave and Pregnancy Discrimination

Employment Scenario

Amanda Summers is planning to give birth in the next few weeks. Her employer, L&S has advised her of her right to 12 weeks of FMLA unpaid leave. Amanda wants to take the time, but as a single parent she cannot afford to do so. Amanda requests the use her 4 weeks' vacation and asks L&S to give her paid leave for the remaining 8 weeks. How would you advise L&S to proceed?

Chapter Checklist
➤ *Learn the requirements for taking family and medical leave.*
➤ *Define serious health condition.*
➤ *Understand that health benefits are maintained during family and medical leave.*
➤ *Appreciate that certification of the serious health condition by a health care provider may be required.*
➤ *Know that medical leave may be granted on an intermittent or consecutive basis.*
➤ *Realize that family leave applies to fathers as well as mothers for the birth of a child.*
➤ *Be aware that adoptive parents are entitled to family leave.*
➤ *Understand the purpose of the Pregnancy Discrimination Act.*
➤ *Be apprised of why some employers do not want to employ pregnant workers.*
➤ *Be cognizant of the existence of fetal protection policies.*

INTRODUCTION

Pregnancy most often leads to the birth of a child. Although a child is precious, its birth may temporarily halt the employment of the mother and the father because of the love and care required by the newborn. This raises two issues.

First, a woman must not be discriminated against because of her desire to become pregnant, her pregnancy, or because she has a child. The Pregnancy Discrimination Act of 1978 protects women against these forms of discrimination. There is no doubt that an employee's pregnancy may be disruptive to the workplace. But with regard to employment, pregnancy is a temporary disability and, as such, is no more disruptive to the workplace than disability due to sickness, accident, or injury.

Second, to accommodate the parents' desire to bond with their newborn, 12 weeks of unpaid family leave must be granted to the mother and father if they have worked for a company with 50 or more employees for 1 year and have accrued at least 1,250 hours of work time during that year. The Family and Medical Leave Act of 1991 guarantees this. The act also extends that guarantee when a serious health condition befalls a spouse, child, or parent.

HUMAN RESOURCE ADVICE

- Realize that some employees may try to take advantage of the medical leave policy.
- Determine whether an employee has a serious health condition.
- Require certification of the serious health condition by a health care provider.
- Be aware of when your company reaches the 50-employee threshold.
- Demand 30 days' notice for family leave definitely, and for medical leave where practical.
- Refrain from discouraging eligible employees from taking family and medical leave.
- Do not ask women if they intend to become pregnant.
- Do not discourage women from becoming pregnant.
- Treat pregnant women the same as other employees.
- Refrain from instituting a fetal protection policy.
- Reassign women whose fetuses may be in danger to positions with comparable pay, overtime, and promotion opportunities.

FAMILY LEAVE

The Family and Medical Leave Act of 1991 permits an employee in any 12-month period to take up to 12 weeks of unpaid leave for the birth or adoption of a child; for the care of a spouse, child, or parent who has a serious health condition; or because of a serious health problem that makes the employee unable to work.

The issue in the case that follows is whether an employer who has consolidated positions in an employee's FMLA absence is justified.

Brenlla v. Lasorsa Buick

2002 U.S. Dist. LEXIS 9358 (S.D. NY)

Francis IV, Judge.

BACKGROUND

In March 1997, Mr. LaSorsa hired Ms. Brenlla to be the comptroller at his car dealership, LaSorsa Buick Pontiac Chevrolet, Inc. She was paid $1,100 a week and was given a company car as a fringe benefit. There were three other women who worked in the back office with Ms. Brenlla: the office manager, Dolores O'Gorman, and two clerical workers, Parvati Brijmahal, and Koowarie, who was only identified by her first name.

In October 1998, Ms. Brenlla underwent a quadruple bypass operation. Subsequent to her discharge from the hospital, she had to be readmitted after suffering congestive heart failure with atrial fibrillation. Ms. Brenlla's daughter informed Mr. LaSorsa that the plaintiff would be out of work for some time. Three months after she had initially taken medical leave, and after she was given medical clearance by her doctor, Ms. Brenlla indicated to Mr. LaSorsa that she was ready to come back to work on a part-time basis. During her absence, Ms. O'Gorman, the office manager, assumed most of Ms. Brenlla's responsibilities.

Starting the week of January 18, 1999, Ms. Brenlla came to work for a few hours a day, but was not paid for her services. On January 22, she notified Mr. LaSorsa that she wanted to return to full-time employment. The following Monday, January 25, when Ms. Brenlla was to resume her position, Mr. LaSorsa fired her.

Mr. LaSorsa claimed that it was during a meeting he had with Ms. Brenlla on January 25 that he decided to terminate her and to consolidate the positions of office manager and comptroller. According to Mr. LaSorsa, Ms. Brenlla complained during this meeting that none of the employees were coming to her for financial information. Mr. LaSorsa testified that "the employees weren't going to her, especially the management, for information, from what she told me, and I had time to reflect and to realize that the office ran smoothly for the time that she was out, and at that moment I decided to combine those two positions." He further maintained that he did not think about consolidating the office manager and comptroller positions until this meeting, although Ms. O'Gorman testified that Mr. LaSorsa had told her that he was considering combining the two positions prior to January 25.

Ms. Brenlla countered that she never made any complaint to Mr. LaSorsa about employees not asking her for financial information and that it was prohibited for employees to disclose such information other than to Mr. LaSorsa. She also stated that Mr. LaSorsa told her that he was discharging her because he was combining the office manager and comptroller jobs

On February 14, 2002, the jury returned a verdict in favor of the plaintiff only with regard to the FMLA claims. It awarded her $150,000 in back pay and benefits, $70,000 in front pay, and $100,000 in liquidated damages.

FMLA CLAIMS

The defendants move for a new trial or judgment as a matter of law on the FMLA claims. The jury found that the defendants had violated two provisions of the FMLA: first, that they had failed to reinstate Ms. Brenlla to an equivalent position and second, that they had retaliated against her for exercising her rights under the FMLA.

Denial of Benefits

To have made out a prima facie case for the denial of benefits, the plaintiff must have demonstrated:

(1) that she is an "eligible employee" under the FMLA; (2) that defendants constitute an employer under the FMLA; (3) that she was entitled to leave under the FMLA; (4) that she gave notice to defendants of her intention to take leave; and (5) that defendants denied her benefits to which she was entitled by the FMLA.

There are several provisions of the statute that prescribe benefits. For example, covered employers must grant employees who have worked for twelve months up to twelve weeks leave each year for "a serious health condition that makes the employee unable to perform the functions of the position of such employee." The benefit at issue here is set forth in 29 U.S.C. § 2614(a)(1), which requires that an employee who takes FMLA-covered leave "be restored by the employer to the position of employment held by the employee when the leave commenced; or . . . to an equivalent position with equivalent employment benefits, pay, and other terms and conditions of employment." Despite this provision, the FMLA does not entitle employees out on leave to unqualified reinstatement; termination ends the right to reinstatement, provided that the employee would have been discharged had she not taken leave.

Section 825.216 reads:

Are there any limitations on an employer's obligation to reinstate an employee?

(a) An employee has no greater right to reinstatement or to other benefits and conditions of employment than if the employee had been continuously employed during the FMLA leave period. An employer must be able to show that an employee would not otherwise have been employed at the time reinstatement is requested in order to deny restoration to employment. For example:

(1) If an employee is laid off during the course of taking FMLA leave and employment is terminated, the employer's responsibility to continue FMLA leave, maintain group health plan benefits and restore the employee cease at the time the employee is laid off, provided the employer has no continuing obligations under a collective bargaining agreement or otherwise. An employer would have the burden of proving that an employee would have been laid off during the FMLA leave period and, therefore, would not be entitled to restoration.

The defendants argue that Ms. Brenlla could not be reinstated because the comptroller position no longer existed and there was no other comparable position available. They maintain that legitimate business concerns motivated consolidation of the responsibilities of the comptroller with those of the office manager, all of which were being performed by Ms. O'Gorman while Ms. Brenlla was on leave.

There was ample evidence to support the jury's conclusion that Ms. Brenlla's termination and the consolidation of positions were not motivated by legitimate business concerns. First, although the defendants claim that the termination arose from their desire to "save the plaintiff's salary, it is unclear what if any financial benefits the defendants reaped from the consolidation."

Second, even if Mr. LaSorsa reduced the payroll by replacing a managerial position with a clerical one, there is no evidence that this was part of any business plan or that this restructuring would have taken place had Ms. Brenlla not taken leave.

Third, if the plaintiff's firing had been part of a legitimate business plan, some consideration would have gone into deciding who was best suited for the new consolidated position. There was no evidence that any assessment of Ms. Brenlla's or any other employee's qualifications ever took place. Nor was there any indication that her past performance was deficient.

Because the jury verdict with regard to liability for denial of benefits under the FMLA is neither seriously erroneous nor against the weight of the evidence, the defendants' motion for judgment as a matter of law or for a new trial is denied.

ATTORNEYS' FEES, COSTS, AND EXPENSES

Finally, Ms. Brenlla moves for attorneys' fees, costs, and expenses as follows:

Under the FMLA, a successful plaintiff is entitled to a "reasonable attorney's fee, reasonable expert witness fees, and other costs of the action to be paid by the defendant." To determine reasonable attorneys' fees, the court first calculates the "lodestar" amount by multiplying the number of hours reasonably expended by the appropriate hourly rates for attorneys. "The district court should exclude excessive, redundant or otherwise unnecessary hours." While the lodestar can then be adjusted in light of factors such as the results obtained, "there is . . . a strong presumption that the lodestar figure represents a reasonable fee."

Conclusion

For the reasons stated above, the defendants' motion for judgment as a matter of law or a new trial on the FMLA claims is denied. Their motion to set aside or reduce the award of front pay and the plaintiff's motion to increase this award are both denied, and the jury's finding on front pay is

Attorney	Hours Expended	Hourly Rate	Total
Michael J. Volpe	98.69	$ 345	$ 34,048.05
George F. Brenlla	62.01	$ 270	$ 16,742.70
Daniel C. Moreland	16.67	$ 270	$ 4,500.90
Shaffin A. Datoo	126.20	$ 175	$ 22,085.00
Total			$ 77,376.65

Cost/Expense Incurred	Amount
Filing Fee for Complaint	$ 150.00
Photocopies	$ 546.24
Messenger Service	$ 12.50
Transcripts	$ 1,244.40
Secretarial Overtime	$ 87.11
Computerized Legal Research	$ 493.67
Defendants' Financial Report	$ 112.00
Witness and Subpoena Fees	$2,920.00
Total	$ 5,560.92

adopted. The plaintiff's motion for prejudgment interest on the back pay award is granted. Her motion for attorneys' fees and costs is granted in the amount of $97,056.15, and her motion for judgment as a matter of law or a new trial on the ADA, the NYSHRL, and the NYCHRL claims is denied.

Judgment for Brenlla.

CASE QUESTIONS

1. Are you in favor of the Court's judgment?
2. Is there any way an employer can justify a consolidation where one employee is out on FMLA?

Case Commentary

The Southern District Court of New York determined that LaSorsa had violated the FMLA for discharging an employee who had just returned from 12 weeks' leave after bypass surgery. ■

3. Were the requested attorney fees excessive?

The issue in the case that follows is whether a biological father who is seeking to adopt his own child is entitled to family leave.

Kelley v. Crosfield Catalysts
135 F.3d 1202 (7th Cir. 1998)

Flaum, Circuit Judge.

Dwayne Kelley allegedly received authorization from his employer, Crosfield Catalysts ("Crosfield"), to travel to New York in order to "seek custody of a young girl for foster care or adoption." Kelley's trip for this purpose caused him to miss four days of scheduled work. Crosfield terminated Kelley on his next work day on account of this four-day absence; Kelley claims that the dismissal was pretextual and in violation of the Family and Medical Leave Act (FMLA). The district court dismissed Kelley's Second Amended Complaint. We disagree with the district court's characterization of the Second Amended Complaint, and we therefore reverse the dismissal and remand the case for further proceedings.

BACKGROUND

Dwayne Kelley began working for Crosfield as a laboratory technician on August 1, 1992. This position required Kelley to work twelve-hour shifts for four consecutive days followed by three consecutive "off" days. Kelley was scheduled to begin a four-day work rotation on October 22, 1993, when he unexpectedly received a phone call from his mother. His mother informed him that the Brooklyn Bureau of Child Welfare was preparing to take custody of Shaneequa Forbes, an eleven-year-old girl. Shaneequa was born into the marriage of Barbara and Michael Forbes, but—although this information was not contained in his Second Amended Complaint—Kelley had reason to believe that he might be the girl's biological father. He told his supervisors at Crosfield that Shaneequa was his

daughter. Kelley missed four scheduled workdays while attending to this matter in New York. On his first day back at work, October 29, Crosfield terminated Kelley's employment.

The parties' pleading maneuvers constitute the focus of this appeal. Kelley filed a pro se complaint on October 26, 1995, which alleged that his termination violated the FMLA because he took leave from work in order to "obtain custody of my kids." Crosfield filed a motion to dismiss this complaint arguing that seeking custody of one's own children was not covered by the FMLA. Before the district court ruled on Crosfield's motion, Kelley filed an amended pro se complaint on April 25, 1996. The amended complaint stated only that the child "grew up" with Kelley, and it referenced Shaneequa's birth certificate on which Barbara and Michael Forbes are listed as the girl's biological parents.

The parties discussed the matter of Shaneequa's parentage at a status hearing regarding the amended complaint five days after it was filed. Kelley admitted there was some confusion about whether he was Shaneequa's father. He stated, "Your Honor, I was told—there is nothing in any records showing that I am the father. I was told that I was the father. So I took this as I'm being the father. But as of late, I found out that I might not even be the father. On record, I am not the father." Based on this colloquy, Crosfield moved to dismiss the amended complaint for failure to state a claim, arguing that obtaining custody of one's own child was not a protected activity under the FMLA.

DISCUSSION

The Family and Medical Leave Act of 1993 affords flexibility in employment for medical or family emergencies to anyone working at least 1250 hours per year at a business employing fifty or more people for at least twenty weeks of the year. Congressional hearings revealed that the FMLA was needed to help balance the demands of work and family, as well as to ease the burden of caretaking among individual family members. The provision of the FMLA most relevant to the instant appeal is 29 U.S.C. sec. 2612(a)(1)(B), which provides that eligible employees may receive twelve weeks of excused leave per year "because of the placement of a son or daughter with the employee for adoption or foster care."

Kelley's Second Amended Complaint did not make any reference to Shaneequa's biological parentage. It only stated that he traveled to New York to "seek custody of Shaneequa for foster care or adoption." Thus, based on the allegations of the Second Amended Complaint alone, the issue of Kelley's biological connection to Shaneequa was not before the district court. It is apparent, however, that the court considered Shaneequa's biological parentage by concluding that Kelley's emergency trip to New York did not fit within the meaning of the FMLA.

The same principle applies in the instant case. Any facts that Kelley had pleaded in his first two complaints were effectively nullified for 12(b)(6) purposes when he filed his Second Amended Complaint, which did not reference those facts.

In addition, we think it is important to note that Kelley could have stated a viable FMLA claim even if his Second Amended Complaint had declared that he was the biological father of Shaneequa. The district court believed that the "usual sense" of the relevant FMLA terms "adoption" and "foster care" did not encompass a situation in which a biological father takes custody of his own child. Indeed, the Department of Labor has defined the term "adoption" as used in the FMLA as the "legal process in which an individual becomes the legal parent of another's child." The court

seemed to fear that allowing one to adopt one's own child or to take the child into foster care would grant FMLA coverage to run-of-the-mill custody disputes.

This is not just another custody case, though, and we believe that Kelley could state a valid claim under the FMLA. The FMLA defines "son or daughter" as "a biological, adopted, or foster child, a stepchild, a legal ward, or a child of a person standing in loco parentis." Thus, in light of this definition, the FMLA expressly protects leaves taken "because of the placement of a biological child with an employee for adoption or foster care." Furthermore, Kelley was not Shaneequa's father of record—unlike the usual situation in custody disputes—and he would have sought leave to take custody of a child who (according to public record) was "another's child."

It will indeed be unusual to encounter a situation in which a biological parent takes a leave from work in order to adopt or take into foster care his own child. This situation may be rare, but Kelley has proven that it is not entirely impossible. In a case such as this in which a biological parent has no custodial rights over a child and is not listed as the child's parent as a matter of record, it may be possible for that parent to adopt his own child. Thus, regardless of whether he was the biological father, Kelley could state a claim under the FMLA.

Conclusion

Discovery may reveal Kelley's claims to be meritless. The face of the complaint, however, does not establish this conclusion because Crosfield failed to prove that there is no set of facts that would entitle Kelley to relief. Dismissal, therefore, was unwarranted. For the foregoing reasons, we reverse the district court's dismissal of Kelley's Second Amended Complaint and remand the cause for further proceedings

Judgment for Kelly.

Case Commentary

The Seventh Circuit Court ruled that a person seeking to adopt a child may be covered under the FMLA even if it turns out that he is the biological father. ■

CASE QUESTIONS

1. Do you agree with the decision of Court?
2. How can a biological father adopt his own child?

3. Why should the FMLA protect him in these unusual circumstances?

To be eligible, the employee must have worked for the employer for at least 1 year and must have earned 1,250 hours of service during the previous 12 months. The Family and Medical Leave Act applies only to employers who have 50 or more employees who have worked for each day during 20 weeks of the current or preceding calendar year.

Effective July 2004, California has approved paid leave for six of the twelve weeks of family medical leave for employees of private employers.

The issue in the following case is whether a company with fewer than 50 employees at a work site can voluntarily consent to coverage of its employees under the FMLA.

Douglas v. E. G. Baldwin
150 F.3d 604 (6th Cir. 1998)

Rosen, District Judge.

INTRODUCTION

Plaintiff Sheila R. Douglas initiated this action against her employer, Defendant E. G. Baldwin and Associates Baldwin, claiming she was not offered an equivalent position when she returned from her maternity leave, in violation of the Family and Medical Leave Act. Although Baldwin did not employ the requisite number of employees to fall with the ambit of the Act itself, the District Court ruled that Baldwin had, through its conduct and representations, modified its at-will employment relationship with Plaintiff by effectively adopting the terms of the Act and the corresponding obligations, thereby exposing Baldwin to potential liability for breach of contract. Although not raised by the parties, the threshold question raised by this appeal is whether federal question jurisdiction exists where an employer who does not employ a sufficient number of employees to come within the ambit of the Family and Medical Leave Act has nevertheless explicitly adopted its policies as its own. For the following reasons, we find that it does not, and that the District Court erred by failing to recognize that because Baldwin did not fall within the statutory definition of employer under the Family and Medical Leave Act, federal question jurisdiction over the case did not exist. Therefore, we dismiss the case for lack of subject matter jurisdiction.

FACTS

Defendant E. G. Baldwin & Associates, Inc. is an Ohio corporation which sells and services medical diagnostic imaging equipment and supplies. Baldwin's corporate headquarters are located in Cleveland, Ohio, and it has several division offices, including one in Holland, Ohio. On August 3, 1992, Plaintiff Sheila R. Douglas began working at Baldwin's Holland office as a sales secretary. At the time the events giving rise to this action occurred, Baldwin employed 29 people in its Holland office. When Baldwin hired Mrs. Douglas, she was given an Employee Handbook that set forth personnel policy statements and outlined performance requirements. After Congress enacted the Family and Medical Leave Act FMLA, Baldwin formally adopted the provisions of the FMLA by adding a new policy to its Employee Handbook, effective January 1, 1994. The policy stated:

Employees who have worked for the Company for at least twelve (12) months and at least 1,250 hours during the prior twelve (12) months may take up to twelve (12) weeks of unpaid Family and Medical Leave (hereinafter leave).

On December 19, 1994, Mrs. Douglas, having by this time been promoted to the position of image processing coordinator, requested a leave of absence from work due to her impending child birth. Upon Douglas' return from leave, Defendant Baldwin informed her that the image processing coordinator position had been eliminated pursuant to a corporate restructuring, and offered her three alternative positions: sales secretary, receptionist, and customer service representative. Plaintiff claimed that none of these positions were equivalent to the position she held at the commencement of her leave, as required by the Act.

DISTRICT COURT'S DECISION

The District Court determined that although Defendant did not technically come within the statutory ambit of the Act, Defendant had voluntarily agreed to abide by the terms of the Act in its employment contract with Plaintiff.

ANALYSIS

In this case, the FMLA specifies that the Act shall only apply to companies that employ 50 or more employees. Consequently, Congress specifically defined the coverage of the Act to exclude coverage for any employee of an employer who is employed at a work site at which such employer employs less than 50 employees if the total number of employees employed by that employer within 75 miles of that work site is less than 50. In this case, although Baldwin employed far more than 50 employees nationwide, it only employed 29 employees at or within 75 miles of the Holland office at the time the events giving rise to this suit took place. Therefore, the plain language of the FMLA excludes Baldwin's Holland office from coverage under the Act.

Whatever the rationale behind this limitation, be it Congress' desire not to burden small businesses by requiring them to operate without employees for an extended period of time or their determination that the effect upon commerce from the small companies is de minimis, is not for us to question and, in any event, is immaterial to our jurisdictional determination. For a federal court to exercise subject matter jurisdiction in a statutory scheme such as the FMLA, the defendant-company must meet the statutory definition of employer.

If the Court were to exercise jurisdiction where the employer does not meet the statutory prerequisite, it would effectively be expanding the scope of the Act, and the scope of our limited jurisdiction as defined by Congress, by judicial decree. This we do not have the power to do.

The fact that the parties contracted to incorporate the terms and responsibilities of the FMLA into their employment relationship does not bring them within the Act itself.

Judgment for Baldwin.

CASE QUESTIONS

1. Do you agree with the Court's decision?
2. Why can't an employer voluntarily agree to cover its employees under the FMLA?

Case Commentary

The Sixth Circuit Court held that an employer who lacks the requisite number of employees for the FMLA to be applicable cannot voluntarily agree to provide leave under the act. ■

3. Do you believe it was Congress's intent to prohibit a large company like Baldwin from granting its employees FMLA coverage at one of its work sites where there are fewer than 50 employees?

Serious Health Condition

Serious health condition means that the person is in a hospital, hospice, or nursing home or requires continuous medical treatment. Biological, adopted, foster, and stepchildren are covered by the act.

The issue in the following case is whether caring for a sick father who has just suffered the loss of his murdered daughter constitutes a serious health condition under the FMLA.

Scamihorn v. General Truck Drivers
282 F.3d 1078 (9th Cir. 2002)

Fisher, Circuit Judge.

This case concerns the construction and application of the Family and Medical Leave Act ("FMLA"). Adopted by Congress in 1993 to address conflicts facing working men and women confronted with their or their family members' serious health problems, the FMLA under certain conditions guarantees employees an amount of unpaid leave each year to deal with such problems. It provides that employees returning from such leave must be returned to the same or an equivalent position. Joseph Scamihorn, Jr. ("Scamihorn") faced such a conflict after his sister was murdered by her ex-husband, causing Scamihorn's 73-year-old father, Joseph Sr., to fall into a deep depression. After discussions with his employer, Albertson's, Scamihorn left his job as a truck driver for several months to provide assistance and comfort to his ailing father. When he sought to return to work, Scamihorn found he had to start over as a probationary employee with no seniority. Scamihorn contends his circumstances fell under the protection of the FMLA, so Albertson's was required to treat his absence as an unpaid leave and to reinstate him in his previous job and seniority level based on his original start date.

The district court, although recognizing Scamihorn's altruistic motives and actions on behalf of his father, granted summary judgment for Albertson's, holding that Scamihorn did not qualify for FMLA protection because he had not" cared for" his father within the meaning of the Act. Albertson's also argued that Scamihorn failed to show that

his father suffered from a "serious health condition," another FMLA requirement; but the district court did not reach that issue.

THE FMLA

Congress enacted the FMLA to allow workers flexibility in scheduling time off to deal with family and medical problems and alleviate some of the tension created by the competing demands of work and family in modern society. The legislative history articulates the rationale for the FMLA:

> Private sector practices and government policies have failed to adequately respond to recent economic and social changes that have intensified the tensions between work and family. This failure continues to impose a heavy burden on families, employees, employers and the broader society. The FMLA provides a sensible response to the growing conflict between work and family by establishing a right to unpaid family and medical leave for all workers covered under the act.

The FMLA does not replace traditional employer-established sick and personal leave policies; rather it provides leave for uncommon and often stressful events such as caring for a family member with a serious health condition. The FMLA provides that "an eligible employee shall be entitled to a total of 12 workweeks of leave during any 12 month period . . . (c) in order to care for the spouse, or a son, daughter, or parent, of the employee, if such spouse, son, daughter, or parent has a serious health condition." At the conclusion of the qualified leave period, the employee is entitled to reinstatement to the position the employee previously held or to an equivalent one with the same terms and benefits that existed prior to the exercise of leave. It is undisputed that Scamihorn was an "eligible employee." Therefore, for his leave to qualify under the terms of the FMLA, Scamihorn must demonstrate that his father had a "serious health condition" and that he needed to "care for" his father.

Although the language of the FMLA provides little guidance on the meaning of the phrases "care for" and "serious health condition," the Department of Labor has issued both interim and final regulations addressing the meaning of these phrases pursuant to an express delegation of authority to the Secretary of Labor to promulgate regulations "necessary to carry out" the FMLA.

"Serious Health Condition"

The FMLA's definition of serious health condition includes a "mental condition" that involves . . . (B) continuing treatment by a health care provider." The FMLA's legislative history noted that "the definition of' 'serious health condition' . . . is broad and intended to cover various types of physical and mental conditions." Albertson's does not dispute that Joseph Sr. suffered from a legitimate mental illness.

The interim regulations specifically define what qualifies as a serious health condition:

For purposes of FMLA, "serious health condition" means an illness, injury, impairment, or physical or mental condition that involves . . . (2) any period of incapacity requiring absence from work, school, or other regular daily activities, of more than three calendar days, that also involves continuing treatment by (or under the supervision of) a health care provider.

Additionally, the regulations discuss the conditions necessary to meet the definition of "continuing treatment by a health care provider." The condition relevant to this case states:

The employee or family member in question is treated two or more times for the injury or illness by a health care provider. Normally this would require visits to the health care provider or to a nurse or physician's assistant under direct supervision of the health care provider.

Therefore, to meet the requirements established by the FMLA and the accompanying regulations, Scamihorn must prove that his father's depression resulted in an incapacity—absence from work or other daily activities—of more than three consecutive days and that he was receiving continuing treatment by a health care provider.

CONTINUING TREATMENT

Specifically, the continuing treatment must have consisted of treatment two or more times by a health care provider.

Dr. Brannon testified that her talks with Joseph Sr. began informally and over time evolved into formal counseling sessions to deal with his grief. When Joseph Sr. indicated he wanted to spend more time talking with Dr. Brannon after their initial informal discussions, she "made that very clear that that would have to be in a psychotherapeutic realm and that we would have to set up a treatment plan and it would be a part of his record." She treated him for approximately seven months. Joseph Sr. was treated more than two times by Dr. Brannon alone and these formal counseling sessions qualify as "continuing treatment by a health care provider."

INCAPACITY

Albertson's points out that when Joseph Sr. worked out of his office at the Veterans Medical Center, he often drove himself the 52 miles each way. Furthermore, in his deposition, Joseph Sr. testified he did not miss any days of work between September 1, 1994 and March 1, 1995. However, in his declaration, he clarified that in actuality he "missed additional days of work due to my daughter's murder that may not be reflected on my attendance record because I am allowed to work at home and my wife works out of the same office as me."

With all inferences taken in Scamihorn's favor, there exists a genuine question of whether he met all statutory requirements to show that his father suffered from "a" serious health condition."

"To Care For"

Although the FMLA does not define the phrase "to care for," the final regulations clarify that the concept of "care" includes providing psychological comfort to those "receiving inpatient or home care." The legislative history of the FMLA underscores the significance of this type of care:

The phrase "to care for" . . . is intended to be read broadly to include both physical and psychological care. Parents provide far greater psychological comfort and reassurance to a seriously ill child than others not so closely tied to the child. In some cases there is no one other than the child's parents to care for the child. The same is often true for adults caring for a seriously ill parent or spouse.

Albertson's argues that under the regulations, "'caring for' a [family member] with a 'serious health condition' involves some level of participation in ongoing treatment of that condition." Scamihorn moved to Reno precisely to be a part of that treatment. Scamihorn does not claim to have personally attended any of Joseph Sr.'s counseling sessions with Dr. Brannon or Dr. Fox, but he participated in the treatment through both his daily conversations with his father about Misty and the grief associated with her death and his constant presence in his father's life. Both Dr. Brannon and Dr. Fox emphasized this fact.

The regulations clearly contemplate not only the physical but, just as important, also the psychological care that seriously ill parents often require from their care-giving children. There is evidence in the record that Joseph Sr. at times was unable to complete daily tasks and it was necessary for his son to assist and comfort him.

Conclusion

Scamihorn experienced first-hand the tension between his job and his father's psychological well-being. The purpose of the FMLA is to relieve some of this tension by giving employees time off without pay to care for relatives who suffer from serious health conditions.

Admittedly, there are gaps and uncertainties in the record here that suggest Scamihorn may be unable ultimately to prove that he meets the criteria established by the Department of Labor regulations. For instance, it appears that because Joseph Sr. worked in the Veterans Medical Center, he was able to obtain treatment without officially taking time off from work and completing insurance and other medical forms to document and authorize the treatment. He also was able to work from home and thereby avoid taking sick leave when he felt too depressed to go to his office. The mere lack of formalities alone, however, would not justify the exclusion of FMLA coverage here. Viewing the evidence in the light most favorable to Scamihorn, as we must, we conclude that he set forth sufficient evidence to create genuine issues of disputed material fact to be resolved in a trial.

For the reasons stated, we reverse the district court's grant of summary judgment to Albertson's and remand for further proceedings.

Judgment for Scamihorn.

Case Commentary

The Ninth Circuit Court ruled that psychological care is included under the FMLA's serious health condition. ■

CASE QUESTIONS

1. Do you agree with the Court's reasoning?
2. Was the father's condition really that serious to warrant constant care?

3. Should the determining factor of whether the son is entitled to FMLA leave be a subjective one or an objective one?

In cases of birth or adoption, the employee is required to provide the employer with at least 30 days' notice of his or her intent to request family leave. When a serious health condition is foreseeable, the employee must provide 30 days' notice and take into consideration the employer when scheduling treatment, if this is practicable.

Employment Perspective

Joseph Woodward is an accountant with Bean, Brower, and Boseman, CPA firm. In early December, his father had been advised to undergo a cataract operation within the next 6 months. The recovery period is up to 3 months. Joseph, dreading the upcoming tax season, schedules his father's operation for mid-January and gives the required 30 days' notice of his intent to take 12 weeks' leave. Is Joseph acting in good faith? No! He has violated the provision of making a reasonable effort to schedule the leave with his employer in mind. Moreover, the operation could have been scheduled in April, thus being in accord with the physician's directive and lessening the burden on his employer.

If the employee has unused paid leave in the form of vacation, personal days, or sick time, he or she may elect, or the employer may require, that time be used toward the 12-week family and medical leave. Use of sick time would apply only to medical leave for the employee himself or herself or for a family member.

Employment Perspective

Henry Marceni's 5-year-old daughter has been diagnosed with leukemia and has to be hospitalized immediately. Henry tells his employer, Apple Valley Bank, that he must take 12 weeks' leave. Henry currently has 10 vacation days, 4 personal days, and 5 sick days remaining. He asks Apple Valley to apply those 19 days of paid leave to the 12 weeks. Apple Valley agrees except for the sick time, asserting that this may only be used when he is sick. Is Apple Valley's reasoning correct?

No! The use of sick time may be applied when leave is taken for a serious health condition of a family member.

Maintenance of Health Benefits

When an employee takes family and medical leave, he or she is entitled to the maintenance of health benefits while on leave. If an employee does not return, he or she may be charged by the employer for the health care premiums while on leave, unless it is due to a continuation of the serious health problem. With regard to pension, life insurance, and other employment benefits, these may be suspended during the period of the leave but must be restored immediately upon the return of the employee.

Employment Perspective

Two months before giving birth, Jessica McCormick applied for family leave for the 12-week period after the birth of her child. At the expiration of the 12-week period, Jessica has decided to resign her position and stay home with her child. Can she be charged for the health care premiums paid on her behalf? Yes! In not returning to work, it was as though she resigned when she gave birth. There is no indication in the act for how long a period of time she must return.

Employment Perspective

Christie Wesley, a financial analyst with Magnificent Mutual Funds, was a senior member of her department. While Christie was on family leave, Kurt Walker was promoted to department manager on the basis of being the senior member at the time that the promotion was made. Christie claimed that she did not forfeit her position of seniority while on family leave. Is she correct? Yes! Although she did not accrue time toward seniority while on leave, she must be accorded her status as senior member even though she is not there.

Certification of a serious health problem may be required by an employer. The health care provider must provide the date when the condition began, its likely duration, and a medical explanation of the condition. If the request for leave is to care for a spouse, child, or parent, then a statement by the health care provider is required, stating that the employee's services are needed and indicating the amount of time likely to be expended. If the employer doubts the validity of the certification, it can, at its own expense, require the employee to get a second opinion. If that opinion is in conflict, the employer may again, at its own expense, request a third opinion, which will be the final arbitrator.

If the employee requests intermittent leave, then a certification of the medical necessity must be presented. The employer may temporarily transfer the employee to another position of equal pay and benefits that is less disruptive to the employer's work environment.

Employment Perspective

Pamela Whalen's daughter Julia has cancer. She is required to go for treatments 3 days a week during the afternoon. Pamela requests medical leave on an intermittent basis for 3 afternoons a week. In this manner, her 12-week unpaid leave can be taken over a much longer period. Is this situation acceptable? Yes!

In 1978, discrimination on the basis of pregnancy became illegal in the United States, with passage of the Pregnancy Discrimination Act, an amendment to Title VII of the 1964 Civil Rights Act.

Pregnant women must be treated the same as other applicants or employees. They must be judged by their ability to perform rather than on their physical condition.

Pregnant Women in the Workplace

One-half of all women who give birth each year return to their jobs before the child is 1 year old. An increasing number of women choose to remain at their jobs until they give birth. These women are working well into their ninth month.

In the next case, an unmarried teacher in a religiously affiliated school became pregnant. The church discharged her because that behavior was not in accord with its theology. She claimed that the church discriminated against her because of her pregnancy.

Boyd v. Harding Academy of Memphis, Inc.
887 F. Supp. 157 (W.D.Tenn. 1995)

McCalla, District Judge.

Plaintiff, who is unmarried, was employed by defendant Harding Academy of Memphis, Inc., ("Harding Academy"), in January of 1992 as a teacher in a preschool facility known as Little Harding. Harding Academy is a religious school affiliated with the Church of Christ, and as such, expects that its teachers will adhere to the religious tenets it supports. All faculty members are required to be Christians with a preference given to Church of Christ members. Harding Academy uses as its religious tenets the teachings of the New Testament, and one of the religious principles embodied therein is that sex outside of marriage is proscribed. Plaintiff knew that Harding Academy was a church-related school and indicated on her employment application that she had a Christian background and believed in God.

In early February, 1993, Brenda Rubio, the director of the Little Harding program, was told by her assistant Sharon Cooper that plaintiff may be pregnant. That information, if true, would inequivocally establish that plaintiff had engaged in sex outside of marriage. Upon receiving this information, Brenda Rubio reported the information through her superior to Dr. Harold Bowie, the President and Chief Executive Officer of Harding Academy. Dr. Bowie required that the information be confirmed by direct conversation with plaintiff, and further directed that plaintiff be terminated if the information was true. At trial, Dr. Bowie testified that he determined to terminate plaintiff

if it were verified that plaintiff was pregnant and unmarried, not because of the pregnancy per se, but because the facts would indicate that plaintiff engaged in sex outside of marriage.

At Dr. Bowie's instruction, a meeting was scheduled between plaintiff, Brenda Rubio, and Sharon Cooper. At that meeting, plaintiff admitted that she was pregnant. Plaintiff was then informed that she would be terminated but that she would be eligible for re-employment if she were to marry the father of the child. During this meeting, Brenda Rubio used words to the effect that plaintiff was being terminated because she was "pregnant and unwed." Plaintiff relies on the statements made by Brenda Rubio at this meeting in support of her allegations that her discharge from Harding Academy under the circumstances of her out of wedlock pregnancy constitutes impermissible gender discrimination. However, Brenda Rubio's testimony at trial also indicates that in explaining the reason for plaintiff's termination, Brenda Rubio used the phrase "pregnant and unwed" to mean plaintiff engaged in sex outside of marriage in violation of the religious principles subscribed to by Harding Academy. It is not disputed that Brenda Rubio did not have the power or authority to terminate plaintiff or any other employee of Harding Academy.

It is also undisputed that Dr. Bowie is the only person with the authority to terminate the employment of teachers at Harding Academy. Throughout Dr. Bowie's tenure as the chief administrative officer of Harding Academy, Dr. Bowie has discharged teachers, both male and female, for engaging in acts of sex outside of marriage, whether or not pregnancy resulted from the proscribed sexual conduct. No deviation from this doctrine-based policy was shown to the Court under circumstances where knowledge of an employee's sexual activity outside of marriage was made known to Dr. Bowie. Furthermore, it was not shown that women employees at Harding Academy are terminated solely on the basis of pregnancy. In fact, the testimony at trial demonstrated that many married women have become pregnant while working at Harding Academy and have remained employed during and after their pregnancies.

CONCLUSIONS OF LAW

Title VII of the Civil Rights Act of 1964 prohibits employment discrimination based on sex. Section 2000e-2 (a) states that:

[i]t shall be an unlawful employment practice for any employer—
   (1) to fail or refuse to hire or to discharge any individual, or otherwise to discriminate against any individual with respect to his compensation, terms, conditions, or privileges of employment, because of such individual's race, color, religion, sex or national origin.

   Title VII further defines sex discrimination as follows:

The terms "because of sex" or "on the basis of sex" include, but are not limited to, because of or on the basis of pregnancy, childbirth, or related medical conditions; and women affected by pregnancy, childbirth, or related medical conditions shall be treated the same for all employment-related purposes. . . .
   Section 2000e (k), referred to as the Pregnancy Discrimination Act, makes clear that sex discrimination includes any adverse employment decision based upon pregnancy.
   (a) Inapplicability of subchapter to certain aliens and employees of religious entities
   This subchapter shall not apply to . . . a religious corporation, association, educational institution, or society with respect to the employment of individuals of a particular religion to perform work connected with the carrying on by such corporation, association, educational institution, or society of its activities.

   Although this provision permits religious organizations to discriminate based on religion, religious employers are not immune from liability for discrimination based on race, sex, or national origin. In order for the religious entities exemption in Title VII to apply, a religious employer must make its employment decision upon a religious basis or criteria. In the present case, defendant Harding Academy asserts that plaintiff's termination was based on her violation of the religious tenet proscribing sex outside of marriage, which was evidenced by the fact of her out of wedlock pregnancy. Plaintiff, however, contends that the religious reason cited by defendant for her termination is simply a pretext for sex discrimination.

   If the defendant can show a legitimate nondiscriminatory reason for its employment decision, the plaintiff must then show that the defendant's proffered reason is just a pretext for discrimination. In the present case, plaintiff asserts that she was terminated because she was pregnant, not because she violated Harding Academy's proscription against sex outside of marriage and that defendant's proffered reason for her termination is merely pretext for unlawful gender discrimination.

   In support of this contention, plaintiff relies upon statements made to her by her supervisor, Brenda Rubio, on February 10, 1993, when plaintiff was terminated. During this meeting, Brenda Rubio used words to the effect that plaintiff was being terminated because she was "pregnant and unwed." Plaintiff asserts that such statements by Brenda Rubio demonstrate that her discharge from Harding Academy was based solely on her pregnancy and therefore constitutes impermissible gender discrimination.

   At trial, Dr. Bowie's testimony clearly established that he did not receive information regarding plaintiff's prior miscarriage and that if he had received such information and it was confirmed then plaintiff would have been terminated according to Harding Academy's doctrine-based policy. Dr. Bowie also testified that plaintiff was terminated not because of her pregnancy per se, but because her pregnancy indicated that plaintiff engaged in sex outside of marriage as proscribed by Harding Academy. Dr. Bowie was a very credible witness and was not materially impeached in any respect. Based on Dr. Bowie's testimony, the fact that Dr. Bowie was the only person with the authority to terminate plaintiff, and the fact that Harding Academy has consistently discharged both male and female employees who engaged in sex outside of marriage, whether or not pregnancy resulted from the conduct, the Court finds that plaintiff has failed to show that defendant's proffered nondiscriminatory reason for plaintiff's termination was mere pretext for gender discrimination. Plaintiff having failed to sustain her burden of proof in this case, plaintiff's claim of gender discrimination under Title VII must be DENIED, and a judgment must be entered in favor of the defendant.
   Judgment for Harding Academy of Memphis.

Case Commentary

The Western District Court of Tennessee ruled that the decision to terminate Boyd was based on the fact that she had engaged in sex outside of marriage, not on the fact that she was pregnant. ■

CASE QUESTIONS

1. Do you agree with Court's decision?
2. Are female employees at Harding Academy being treated as equals with their male counterparts?
3. How would Harding Academy know if men were engaging in sex outside of marriage?

4. Would Harding Academy have preferred that Boyd have an abortion to eliminate the pregnancy before it became recognizable?

The issue in the following case is whether a club designed to provide positive role models for teenage girls may bar single pregnant workers. The employee in this case was dismissed because of her pregnancy. The club maintained that it was justified in doing so.

Chambers v. Omaha Girls Club, Inc.
840 F.2d 583 (8th Cir. 1988)

Lay, Chief Judge.

The Omaha Girls Club's termination of its arts and crafts teacher because of her pregnancy is the most blatant form of sex discrimination that can exist. In my judgment the Girls Club's pregnancy-based discrimination constitutes a per se violation of Title VII of the Civil Rights Act of 1964. The proffered reasons for the discharge of Crystal Chambers are entirely inconsistent with Congress' avowed intent to "ensure that working women are protected against *all* forms of employment discrimination" and with its "unmistakable reaffirmation that sex discrimination includes discrimination based on pregnancy."

The action of the Girls Club is contrary to the letter of the law under the Pregnancy Discrimination Act of 1978 (PDA), the spirit of equal treatment for pregnant women intended by Congress under that Act, and decisions both of this court and of the Supreme Court of the United States.

The district court found that Chambers "was fired solely because of her pregnancy," but did not discuss the enactment of the PDA in 1978. Even prior to passage of the PDA such a finding was sufficient in this circuit to establish a prima facie violation of Title VII.

The district court found that the Girls Club had articulated a neutral reason for its rule barring single pregnant workers: to provide positive role models for the teenagers with whom the Girls Club worked. The court then shifted the burden back to the plaintiff to show that "the rule was a pretext for discriminating against *black women or single black women*." The difficulty I have with this analysis is that when a court finds as a fact, as the district court did, that a plaintiff was fired "solely" because of membership in a protected class, the inquiry should be ended, unless the employer can establish that non-membership in the protected class is a BFOQ. There can be no issue of pretext—whether an alleged nondiscriminatory reason masks a discriminatory reason—when the employer openly admits

the reason for the discharge was solely because of the employee's membership in a protected class. The issue of pretext is not involved. When this occurs we mistakenly substitute our judgment for that of the district court and attempt to make such judgment under standards the district court did not even consider.

In its discussion of Chambers's disparate *impact* claim, the district court stated that because the Girls Club "met its burden on the basis of business necessity, it was not necessary to determine whether the evidence would satisfy a BFOQ, although presumably it would." Nonetheless the panel decides, based on the district court's findings with respect to the business necessity defense, that a BFOQ was shown. The Girls Club raised the business necessity defense to Chambers's *race* discrimination claim, however, which was not based on the disparate impact of the Girls Club role model rule on blacks. I respectfully submit that a business necessity defense to a race-based disparate impact claim is simply not equivalent to a BFOQ defense to a sex-based disparate treatment claim; the factual findings relevant to one defense are not necessarily relevant to or sufficient to sustain the other defense.

The BFOQ defense in a pregnancy discrimination case thus invokes only an extremely narrow inquiry: (1) what are the requirements of the *particular* job in question; and (2) is there objective and compelling proof that the excluded woman is unable to perform the duties that constitute the essence of that job because of her pregnancy.

The PDA and its legislative history contain numerous indications that Congress intended pregnancy to be a relevant consideration in an employer's decision to fire a worker only when the pregnancy affects the woman's physical capabilities such that the employer would fire *anyone* who was similarly physically affected. The language of the PDA itself suggests that Congress so intended:

The terms "because of sex" or "on the basis of sex" include, but are not limited to, because of or on the basis of pregnancy, childbirth, or *related medical conditions*; and women *affected by* pregnancy, childbirth, or related medical conditions shall be treated the same for all employment-related purposes, including receipt of benefits under fringe benefit programs, as other persons not so affected *but similar in their ability or inability to work*. Its use of the terms "related medical conditions" and "affected by" suggests that Congress thought of pregnancy as a physical condition that, like gender, is unrelated to job capabilities except in the narrowest of circumstances.

Moreover, by requiring employers to treat pregnant employees the same as other employees "not so affected but similar in their ability or inability to work," Congress must have been referring to *physical* ability to work; there is no other ability-to-work basis on which all pregnant women as a class can be compared to all non-pregnant persons. Congress clearly stated that pregnant women must be treated the same as those similarly situated, which presupposes that there are other workers who are in some sense similarly situated. Yet by treating pregnancy as a distasteful

component of a negative "role model" rather than as a physical condition that may or may not affect one's ability to work, the employer here has relegated pregnant women to a class by themselves, incapable of being "similarly situated" to anyone. Such segregation is exactly the type of invidious discrimination that Congress intended to eradicate when it enacted the PDA.

As one commentator has stated:

"Accidents of the body," such as one's female sex and thus one's capacity to become pregnant, are not to be criteria for differentiation. Instead all employees, regardless of bodily differences, shall be judged on their ability to perform on the job. That the cause of disability is pregnancy becomes, like one's race or eye color, irrelevant to how one is treated.

Judgment for Chambers.

Case Commentary

The Eighth Circuit Court held that discharging a female employee who is pregnant because she represents a poor role model for the teenage girls in the club amounts to pregnancy discrimination. ∎

CASE QUESTIONS

1. Do you agree with the Court's decision?
2. Are role models important?
3. Can Chambers be a positive role model even though she is pregnant and unwed?
4. Who should make the determination of what constitutes a positive role model, and what standards should he or she use?

5. How do you reconcile this case with the *Boyd v. Harding Academy* case?

FETAL PROTECTION POLICIES

Companies that research, manufacture, warehouse, transport, and use hazardous chemicals and toxic waste are concerned from a liability standpoint about the effect these chemicals may have on their workers, particularly female workers in their childbearing years. Although no adult is immune from the harmful effects of hazardous chemicals and toxic waste, exposure of a fetus to toxic waste could result in deformities, diseases, brain dysfunction, and cancer. The fetus's future quality of life may be severely jeopardized.

From an ethical viewpoint, companies should not want this to happen. From a liability perspective, companies do not want to become embroiled in expensive, time-consuming lawsuits that they will not win and that will result in a public-relations nightmare. To resolve this dilemma, fetus protection policies have been adopted by certain companies that prohibit women in their childbearing years from working in an environment with hazardous chemicals and toxic waste. This places an economic burden on women who cannot find another position paying the same wages. Some companies will arrange transfers, but often the compensation is lower or without the benefit of overtime. This arrangement is not an adequate accommodation. Women claim that this action is discriminatory because their childbearing state has no impact on their job performance and therefore should not be a reason for exclusion.

In the next case, an employer attempted to exclude fertile women from the workplace to avoid damage to fetuses. Female employees claimed this policy was an attempt to discriminate against pregnant women and women who potentially could become pregnant.

UAW v. Johnson Controls, Inc.

499 U.S. 187 (1991)

Justice Blackmun delivered the opinion of the Court.

In this case we are concerned with an employer's gender-based fetal-protection policy. May an employer exclude a fertile female employee from certain jobs because of its concern for the health of the fetus the woman might conceive?

Before the Civil Rights Act of 1964 became law, Johnson Controls did not employ any woman in a battery-manufacturing job. In June 1977, however, it announced its first official policy concerning its employment of women in lead-exposure work:

"Protection of the health of the unborn child is the immediate and direct responsibility of the prospective parents. While the medical profession and the company can support them in the exercise of this responsibility, it cannot assume it for them without simultaneously infringing their rights as persons."

I

" . . . Since not all women who can become mothers wish to become mothers (or will become mothers), it would appear to be illegal discrimination to treat all who are capable of pregnancy as though they will become pregnant." Consistent with that view, Johnson Controls "stopped short of excluding women capable of bearing children from lead exposure," but emphasized that a woman who expected to have a child should not choose a job in which she would have such exposure. The company also required a woman who wished to be considered for employment to sign a statement that she had been advised of the risk of having a child while she was exposed to lead. The statement informed the woman that although there was evidence "that women exposed to lead have a higher rate of abortion," this evidence was "not as clear . . . as the relationship between cigarette smoking and cancer," but that it was, "medically speaking, just good sense not to run that risk if you want children and do not want to expose the unborn child to risk, however small. . . . "

Five years later, in 1982, Johnson Controls shifted from a policy of warning to a policy of exclusion. Between 1979 and 1983, eight employees became pregnant while maintaining blood lead levels in excess of 30 micrograms per deciliter. This appeared to be the critical level noted by the Occupational Health and Safety Administration (OSHA) for a worker who was planning to have a family. The company responded by announcing a broad exclusion of women from jobs that exposed them to lead: " . . . It is Johnson Controls' policy that women who are pregnant or who are capable of bearing children will not be placed into jobs involving lead exposure or which could expose them to lead through the exercise of job bidding, bumping, transfer or promotion rights."

The policy defined "women . . . capable of bearing children" as "all women except those whose inability to bear children is medically documented." It further stated that an unacceptable work station was one where, "over the past year," an employee had recorded a blood lead level of more than 30 micrograms per deciliter or the work site had yielded an air sample containing a lead level in excess of 30 micrograms per cubic meter.

II

In April 1984, petitioners filed in the United States District Court for the Eastern District of Wisconsin a class action challenging Johnson Controls' fetal-protection policy as sex discrimination that violated Title VII of the Civil Rights Act of 1964. Among the individual plaintiffs were petitioners Mary Craig, who had chosen to be sterilized in order to avoid losing her job, Elsie Nason, a 50-year-old divorcee, who had suffered a loss in compensation when she was transferred out of a job where she was exposed to lead, and Donald Penney, who had been denied a request for a leave of absence for the purpose of lowering his lead level because he intended to become a father. Upon stipulation of the parties, the District Court certified a class consisting of "all past, present and future production and maintenance employees" in United Auto Workers bargaining units at nine of Johnson Controls' plants "who have been and continue to be affected by the employer's Fetal Protection Policy implemented in 1982."

The District Court granted summary judgment for defendant-respondent Johnson Controls. Applying a three-part business necessity defense derived from fetal-protection cases in the Courts of Appeals for the Fourth and Eleventh Circuits, the District Court concluded that while "there is a disagreement among the experts regarding the effect of lead on the fetus," the hazard to the fetus through exposure to lead was established by "a considerable body of opinion"; that although "expert opinion has been provided which holds that lead also affects the reproductive abilities of men and women . . . and that these effects are as great as the effects of exposure of the fetus . . . a great body of experts are of the opinion that the fetus is more vulnerable to levels of lead that would not affect adults"; and that petitioners had "failed to establish that there is an acceptable alternative policy which would protect the fetus." The court stated that, in view of this disposition of the business necessity defense, it did not "have to undertake a bona fide occupational qualification's (BFOQ) analysis."

The Court of Appeals for the Seventh Circuit, sitting en banc, affirmed the summary judgment by a 7-to-4 vote. The majority held that the proper standard for evaluating the fetal-protection policy was the defense of business necessity; that Johnson Controls was entitled to summary judgment under that defense; and that even if the proper standard was a BFOQ, Johnson Controls still was entitled to summary judgment.

The Court of Appeals first reviewed fetal-protection opinions from the Eleventh and Fourth Circuits. Those opinions established the three-step business necessity inquiry: whether there is a substantial health risk to the fetus; whether transmission of the hazard to the fetus occurs only through women; and whether there is a less discriminatory alternative equally capable of preventing the health hazard to the fetus. The Court of Appeals agreed with the Eleventh and Fourth Circuits that "the components of the business necessity defense the courts of appeals and the EEOC have utilized in fetal protection cases balance the interests of the employer, the employee and the unborn child in a manner consistent with Title VII." The court further noted that, under *Wards Cove Packing Co. v. Atonio*, the burden of persuasion remained on the plaintiff in challenging a business necessity defense, and—unlike the Fourth and Eleventh Circuits—it thus imposed the burden on the plaintiffs for all three steps.

Applying this business necessity defense, the Court of Appeals ruled that Johnson Controls should prevail. Specifically, the court concluded that there was no genuine issue of material fact about the substantial health-risk factor because the parties agreed that there was a substantial risk to a fetus from lead exposure. The Court of Appeals also concluded that, unlike the evidence of risk to the fetus from the mother's exposure, the evidence of risk from the father's exposure, which petitioners presented, "is, at best, speculative and unconvincing."

The en banc majority ruled that industrial safety is part of the essence of respondent's business, and that the fetal-protection policy is reasonably necessary to further that concern.

III

The bias in Johnson Controls' policy is obvious. Fertile men, but not fertile women, are given a choice as to whether they wish to risk their reproductive health for a particular job. Section 703 (a) of the Civil Rights Act of 1964, 42 U.S.C. 2000e-2(a), prohibits sex-based classifications in terms and conditions of employment, in hiring and discharging decisions, and in other employment decisions that adversely affect an employee's status. Respondent's fetal-protection policy explicitly discriminates against women on the basis of their sex. The policy excludes women with childbearing capacity from lead-exposed jobs and so creates a facial classification based on gender. Respondent assumes as much in its brief before this Court.

First, Johnson Controls' policy classifies on the basis of gender and childbearing capacity, rather than fertility alone. Respondent does not seek to protect the unconceived children of all its employees. Despite evidence in the record about the debilitating effect of lead exposure on the male reproductive system, Johnson Controls is concerned only with the harms that may befall the unborn offspring of its female employees.

Our conclusion is bolstered by the Pregnancy Discrimination Act of 1978 (PDA). Congress explicitly provided that, for purposes of Title VII, discrimination "on the basis of sex" includes discrimination "because of or on the basis of pregnancy, childbirth, or related medical conditions." "The Pregnancy Discrimination Act has now made clear that, for all Title VII purposes, discrimination based on a woman's pregnancy is, on its face, discrimination because of her sex." In its use of the words "capable of bearing children" in the 1982 policy statement as the criterion for exclusion, Johnson Controls explicitly classifies on the basis of potential for pregnancy. Under the PDA, such a classification must be regarded, for Title VII purposes, in the same light as explicit sex discrimination. Respondent has chosen to treat all its female employees as potentially pregnant; that choice evinces discrimination on the basis of sex.

We concluded above that Johnson Controls' policy is not neutral because it does not apply to the reproductive capacity of the company's male employees in the same way as it applies to that of the females. Moreover, the absence of a malevolent motive does not convert a facially discriminatory policy into a neutral policy with a discriminatory effect. Whether an employment practice involves disparate treatment through explicit facial discrimination does not depend on why the employer discriminates but rather on the explicit terms of the discrimination.

In sum, Johnson Controls' policy "does not pass the simple test of whether the evidence shows 'treatment of a person in a manner which but for that person's sex would be different.'" We hold that Johnson Controls' fetal-protection policy is sex discrimination forbidden under Title VII unless respondent can establish that sex is a "bona fide occupational qualification."

IV

Under Title VII, an employer may discriminate on the basis of "religion, sex, or national origin in those certain instances where religion, sex, or national origin is a bona fide occupational qualification reasonably necessary to the normal operation of that particular business or enterprise." 42 U.S.C. 2000e-2 (e) (1). We therefore turn to the question whether Johnson Controls' fetal-protection policy is one of those "certain instances" that come within the BFOQ exception.

The BFOQ defense is written narrowly, and this Court has read it narrowly.

The wording of the BFOQ defense contains several terms of restriction that indicate that the exception reaches only special situations. The statute thus limits the situations in which discrimination is permissible to "certain instances" where sex discrimination is "reasonably necessary" to the "normal operation" of the "particular" business. Each one of these terms—certain, normal, particular—prevents the use of general subjective standards and favors an objective, verifiable requirement. But the most telling term is "occupational"; this indicates that these objective, verifiable requirements must concern job-related skills and aptitudes.

The unconceived fetuses of Johnson Controls' female employees, however, are neither customers nor third parties whose safety is essential to the business of battery manufacturing. No one can disregard the possibility of injury to future children; the BFOQ, however, is not so broad that it transforms this deep social concern into an essential aspect of batterymaking.

Our case law, therefore, makes clear that the safety exception is limited to instances in which sex or pregnancy actually interferes with the employee's ability to perform the job. This approach is consistent with the language of the BFOQ provision itself, for it suggests that permissible distinctions based on sex must relate to ability to perform the duties of the job. Johnson Controls suggests, however, that we expand the exception to allow fetal-protection policies that mandate particular standards for pregnant or fertile women. We decline to do so. Such an expansion contradicts not only the language of the BFOQ and the narrowness of its exception but the plain language and history of the Pregnancy Discrimination Act.

The PDA's amendment to Title VII contains a BFOQ standard of its own: unless pregnant employees differ from others "in their ability or inability to work," they must be "treated the same" as other employees "for all employment related purposes." 42 U.S.C. 2000e(k). This language clearly sets forth Congress' remedy for discrimination on the basis of pregnancy and potential pregnancy. Women who are either pregnant or potentially pregnant must be treated like others "similar in their ability . . . to work." In other words, women as capable of doing their jobs as their male counterparts may not be forced to choose between having a child and having a job.

We conclude that the language of both the BFOQ provision and the PDA which amended it, as well as the legislative history and the case law, prohibit an employer from discriminating against a woman because of her capacity to become pregnant unless her reproductive potential prevents her from performing the duties of her job.

V

We have no difficulty concluding that Johnson Controls cannot establish a BFOQ. Fertile women, as far as appears in the record, participate in the manufacture of batteries as efficiently as anyone else. Johnson Controls' professed moral and ethical concerns about the welfare of the next generation do not suffice to establish a BFOQ of female sterility. Decisions about the welfare of future children must be left to the parents who conceive, bear, support, and raise them rather than to the employers who hire those parents. Congress has mandated this choice through Title VII, as amended by the Pregnancy Discrimination Act. Johnson Controls has attempted to exclude women because of their reproductive capacity. Title VII and the PDA simply do not allow a woman's dismissal because of her failure to submit to sterilization.

VI

Our holding today that Title VII, as so amended, forbids sex-specific fetal-protection policies is neither remarkable nor unprecedented. Concern for a woman's existing or potential offspring historically has been the excuse for denying women equal employment opportunities. Congress in the PDA prohibited discrimination on the basis of a woman's ability to become pregnant. We do no more than hold that the Pregnancy Discrimination Act means what it says.

It is no more appropriate for the courts than it is for individual employers to decide whether a woman's reproductive role is more important to herself and her family than her economic role. Congress has left this choice to the woman as hers to make.

The judgment of the Court of Appeals is reversed and the case is remanded for further proceedings consistent with this opinion.

It is so ordered.

Judgment for UAW.

Case Commentary

The U.S. Supreme Court decided that Johnson Controls' attempt to exclude pregnant women from certain jobs that could have potentially damaged their fetuses amounted to sex discrimination. ■

CASE QUESTIONS

1. Do you agree with the decision in this case?
2. Why do women have the right to work in a job that may damage their fetuses?
3. Should the company close the plant if it cannot be made safe?

In *United Auto Workers v. Johnson Controls, Inc.*, the Supreme Court ruled that fetal protection policies were a form of gender discrimination. This decision places companies in a catch-22 situation. If they exclude women, they are guilty of sex discrimination. If they permit women to work and their offspring are born defective or with a life-threatening illness, they will be held strictly liable for the injuries. A possible benefit could occur if exposure to the hazardous chemicals and toxic waste is minimized or eliminated as a result of the development of protective equipment and gear or the modification of the plant and working environment.

If that solution is impossible or not economically feasible, companies will either close down the plants or move them offshore where there will be no resulting liability for damage to the fetus. Although the latter may be unethical, it is a realistic and practical solution. In any event, both actions will result in a loss of jobs for all workers, something that the women were initially trying to guard against.

The issue in the following case is whether the termination of a pregnant employee during the probationary period constitutes pregnancy discrimination.

Stout v. Baxter Healthcare
282 F.3d 856 (5th Cir. 2002)

Garwood, Circuit Judge.

Stout, who was pregnant during the probationary period, received positive performance reviews and maintained a perfect attendance record during her first two months. But, beginning on August 14, 1998, Stout was absent for more than three days of work after she experienced early labor and suffered a miscarriage that rendered her medically unable to work for over two weeks. Stout notified her supervisor of her condition immediately, and provided a medical excuse a week later, but Baxter terminated Stout on August 21 because her absenteeism was clearly in excess of that permitted during the probationary period.

After receiving a right-to-sue letter from the Equal Employment Opportunity Commission (EEOC), Stout sued Baxter claiming pregnancy discrimination under the PDA and alleging that she was fired "because of" her pregnancy and that Baxter's probationary attendance policy has a disparate impact on pregnant employees.

The PDA amended Title VII by explicitly including discrimination based on pregnancy and related medical conditions within the definition of sex discrimination:

"The terms 'because of sex' or 'on the basis of sex' include, but are not limited to, because of or on the basis of pregnancy, childbirth, or related medical conditions; and women affected by pregnancy, childbirth, or related medical conditions shall be treated the same for all employment-related purposes . . . as other persons not so affected but similar in their ability or inability to work. . . . "

Stout alleged that she was the victim of two types of discrimination prohibited by Title VII: disparate treatment and disparate impact.

DISPARATE TREATMENT

Stout's claim of disparate treatment has no merit. She argues that she was fired "because of" her pregnancy. But, to the contrary, *all* of the evidence in the record indicates that she "was fired because of her absenteeism, not because of her pregnancy." There is no evidence she would have been treated differently if her absences had been due to some reason unrelated to pregnancy or if she had been absent the same amount but not pregnant. Baxter's policy does not in any way mention or focus on pregnancy, childbirth or any related medical condition.

DISPARATE IMPACT

The Supreme Court has explained disparate impact in the following way: "[Disparate impact claims] involve employment practices that are facially neutral in their treatment of different groups but that in fact fall more harshly on one group than another and cannot be justified by business necessity." To establish a *prima facie* case of disparate impact, a plaintiff must both identify the employment practice that has the allegedly disproportionate impact and establish causation by offering statistical evidence to show that the practice in question has resulted in prohibited discrimination.

There is no evidence that Stout (or any other pregnant probationary employee) was treated any differently than any other probationary employee who missed work. In fact, Stout repeatedly asserts in her brief that Stout was treated exactly the same as any other employee who was unable to work. Stout's focus is on the policy itself; Stout claims that the policy affects all pregnant women and that therefore she has provided sufficient evidence to prove a *prima facie* disparate impact case.

Stout has provided expert testimony that no pregnant woman who gives birth will be able to work for at least two weeks. We agree with Stout that this does constitute evidence that "all or substantially all" pregnant women who give birth during the probationary period will be terminated.

It is the nature of pregnancy and childbirth that at some point, for a limited period of time, a woman who gives birth will be unable to work. *All* job requirements,

regardless of their nature, affect "all or substantially all pregnant women." The PDA does not require preferential treatment of pregnant employees and does not require employers to treat pregnancy related absences more leniently than other absences.

The plaintiff's only challenge is that the amount of sick leave granted to employees is insufficient to accommodate the time off required in a typical pregnancy. To hold otherwise would be to transform the PDA into a guarantee of medical leave for pregnant employees, something we have specifically held that the PDA does not do. Such a rule would also be distinctly at odds with the language of the statute, which requires that pregnant employees be treated *the same* for *all* employment related purposes as other employees with respect to their ability or inability to work. We therefore reject Stout's argument that she proved a *prima facie* disparate impact case simply by showing that Baxter's policy affected all or substantially all pregnant women who would give birth during or near to their probationary period.

In the end, Stout's claim in this case is simply that she should have been granted medical leave that is more generous than that granted to non-pregnant employees. This the PDA does not require.

Conclusion

The order of the district court granting summary judgment for Baxter is AFFIRMED.

Case Commentary

The Fifth Circuit Court held that pregnant employees should be treated the same as all other employees who suffer a temporary illness. ■

CASE QUESTIONS

1. Are you in agreement with the court's decision?
2. Do you believe that pregnant employees should be given preferential treatment?

3. What type of preferential treatment was Stout requesting in this case?

Pregnancy disability must not be viewed any differently than any other disability. Pregnant women must be viewed based on their ability to perform the essential functions of the job.

The question in the next case is whether protection is afforded against pregnancy discrimination under the state statute.

Badih v. Myers
43 Cal. Rptr.2d 229 (Cal. App. 1 Dist. 1995)

Dossee, Associate Justice.

On June 25, 1990, Badih filed a complaint against Myers alleging, among other things, that Myers had discriminated

against her on the basis of race and pregnancy. The complaint also alleged that Badih had attempted to file a complaint with the Department of Fair Employment and Housing (FEHA) but that the department had refused to accept the complaint because Myers employed less than five people.

At trial, Badih gave the following testimony: In January 1987, Badih, a recent immigrant from the West African nation of Sierra Leone, began working as a medical assistant in the offices of Myers, a medical doctor. About nine months later, she started dating Constantine Kalaveras. Myers, who disapproved of interracial relationships, referred to Kalaveras as "the White guy."

In December 1988, Badih married Kalaveras. When Badih told Myers about the marriage, "he slapped on the table, stood up, and started yelling and hollering about what a mistake I've made, how much I'm going to regret this, and how disappointed he is in me, that he's never seen an African that . . . came to this country and started, you know, doing things I did, you know, hanging—marrying my husband and all that, having a White boyfriend and finally marrying him. And he gave me long lectures how marriages like that don't last and how they end up in tragedy and it's very bad, especially if children get involved and all that, and he just got so upset."

On September 6, 1989, Badih told Myers that she was pregnant. According to Badih, Myers replied, "'I just can't believe you. I just don't know what to say to you anymore. It seems like everything I ever told you just went right in vain. First you introduce me to this White guy, and then you marry him, and then you're having his baby. What's next? I can't take this anymore. If you told me you were going to get married and have babies, I wouldn't have hired you in the first place. I need an office girl when I need her, not a person that has responsibilities the way you do now. And . . . I am just so sorry, but I don't think I can take this anymore. You're going to have to go.'" Badih asked Myers whether he was serious. He told her that he was and that her last day would be September 15. On September 13, Myers threatened to call security if Badih did not leave immediately. Badih complied.

Myers denied that he had fired Badih because she was pregnant. According to Myers, Badih quit her job.

Following its deliberations, the jury found that Myers had not terminated Badih's employment on the basis of race but that he had terminated her employment on the basis of pregnancy. The jury awarded $20,226 in damages to Badih. The trial court subsequently granted Badih's motion for attorney fees. Myers has filed timely notices of appeal from both the judgment and the attorney fees order.

Badih argues that pregnancy discrimination in employment is a form of sex discrimination and, as such, is prohibited not only by the FEHA but also by article I, section 8 of

the California Constitution. For the reasons discussed below, we agree.

The question of whether pregnancy discrimination in employment is a form of sex discrimination is not without controversy. In *Geduldig v. Aiello* the United States Supreme Court, in the context of the equal protection clause of the United States Constitution, concluded that "while it is true that only women can become pregnant, it does not follow that every legislative classification concerning pregnancy is a sex-based classification. . . . Normal pregnancy is an objectively identifiable physical condition with unique characteristics. Absent a showing that distinctions involving pregnancy are mere pretexts designed to effect an invidious discrimination against the members of one sex or the other, lawmakers are constitutionally free to include or exclude pregnancy from the coverage of legislation such as this on any reasonable basis, just as with respect to any other physical condition. The lack of identity between the excluded disability pregnancy and gender as such under this insurance program becomes clear upon the most cursory analysis. The program divides potential recipients into two groups—pregnant women and non-pregnant persons. While the first group is exclusively female, the second includes members of both sexes. The fiscal and actuarial benefits of the program thus accrue to members of both sexes." In *General Electric Co. v. Gilbert*, the court extended the reasoning of *Geduldig* to employment discrimination cases brought under Title VII of the Civil Rights Act of 1964.

Both the California Legislature and the United States Congress reacted swiftly to the *Gilbert* decision. In 1978, the California Legislature amended the Fair Employment Practices Act (later recodified as the FEHA) to add a provision specifically prohibiting pregnancy discrimination in employment. The provision states that it "shall not be construed to affect any other provision of law relating to sex discrimination or pregnancy." Also in 1978, the United States Congress amended Title VII to provide that "the terms 'because of sex' or 'on the basis of sex' include, but are not limited to, because of or on the basis of pregnancy, childbirth, or related medical conditions." "When Congress amended Title VII in 1978, it unambiguously expressed its disapproval of both the holding and the reasoning of the Court in the Gilbert decision."

With this background in mind, we turn to the question at hand—namely, whether pregnancy discrimination is a form of sex discrimination under article I, section 8 of the California Constitution.

In short, we conclude that pregnancy discrimination is a form of sex discrimination under article I, section 8 of the California Constitution. Since article I, section 8 expresses a fundamental public policy against sex discrimination in employment, Badih was properly allowed to maintain her cause of action for wrongful discharge in contravention of public policy.

Judgment for Badih.

CASE QUESTIONS

1. Do you agree with the decision in this case?
2. Why was Badih successful when Myers only had five employees?

3. Should employers have the right to involve themselves in the personal lives of their employees?

Some employers have instituted prenatal counseling programs to give medical and emotional assistance. This reduces absenteeism, minimizes complications during the pregnancy, and otherwise helps a woman to work longer and more productively during the pregnancy.

With employer-sponsored programs, women are learning that morning sickness and fatigue are ailments common to pregnant women. They are adjusting their workdays to perform their most important tasks at the time of the day when they are most likely going to feel well.

Some companies have nurses and counselors on call to respond to their pregnant employees' needs. The results of these programs mean better health for pregnant female employees and their babies and minimal loss of employee efficiency. Some employers are contributing a portion of the increased savings to more comprehensive obstetrics care coverage.

The plight of pregnant women and mothers with small children, which in past times had been neglected, has now received the attention it deserves. Attitudes concerning their employment capability are changing with time. Whereas before it could be said that they needed the companies, as the labor shortage increases, it is turning out that companies need them. The greatest thing that can happen to these women is to be needed, wanted, and employed.

EMPLOYEE LESSONS

1. Discover whether your employer grants family and medical leave.
2. Learn what is meant by a *serious health condition*.
3. Appreciate that health benefits will be continued during family and medical leave.
4. Realize that fathers are entitled to family leave as well as mothers.
5. Understand that a 30-day notice is required for family leave and for medical leave when the condition is foreseeable.
6. Know that an employer may require certification of a serious health condition by a health care provider.
7. Become familiar with the protection afforded by the Pregnancy Discrimination Act.
8. Be aware of any questions asked by an employer regarding your intentions of having children.
9. Be cognizant of your rights when your employer has adopted a fetal protection policy.

SUMMARY

Under the Pregnancy Discrimination Act, pregnant women cannot be refused employment or be removed from employment due to their temporary disability unless they are unable to perform the essential functions of the job. Pregnant women should not be looked down upon; they should be revered, because procreation enables society to flourish through the birth of children, who will become future workers.

The birth of a child is a life-changing event. A newborn requires a great amount of time. Indefinite unpaid leave is not practical, but family leave is guaranteed for 3 months in companies with 50 or more employees. Smaller companies are not required to provide family leave because the burden of adjusting to the employee's lengthy absence may be too great. Medical leave is also available to employees who must care for a family member with a serious health condition.

Addressing the family and medical concerns of employees is a huge under-taking for employers. But it is another step forward in the advancement of working conditions where employees are treated as worthwhile human beings who have problems that need solutions other than resignation or termination.

REVIEW QUESTIONS

1. Explain the significance of the Family Medical Leave Act.
2. What are the eligibility requirements?
3. For what duration may family or medical leave be taken?
4. Define *serious health condition*.
5. Is the employee entitled to health benefits while on leave?
6. What percentage of women return to the job within 1 year of giving birth?
7. Is pregnancy a disability?
8. Explain the significance of the Pregnancy Disability Act.
9. With whom should pregnant women file complaints of discrimination?
10. Can pregnancy ever be considered a bona fide occupational qualification?
11. Should an employer have to accommodate a pregnant worker even though the accom-modation is disruptive to the workplace?
12. Must an applicant disclose the fact that she is pregnant?
13. Is it acceptable for an employer to ask all female applicants if they are pregnant?
14. Is there any justifiable reason to deny a pregnant employee maternity leave?

CASE PROBLEMS

1. Vivian Martyszenko was working as a cashier at Safeway grocery store in Ogallala, Nebraska, when she received a call indicating that police believed her two children might have been sexually molested. On the basis of this information, Dennis Davis, Martyszenko's supervisor at Safeway, permitted Martyszenko 2 weeks' vacation leave to care for her children.

Davis offered to schedule Martyszenko around her son Kyle's appointments. Martyszenko then left Safeway permanently. She did not report to work as scheduled and she did not contact Davis.

Dr. Sullivan evaluated Kyle on August 14. He reported:

Kyle is not expressing any issues that he has been sexually abused or had any sexual contact.

In October 1995, Safeway twice wrote Martyszenko and advised her that she could return to her position at Safeway with full reinstatement of benefits and no loss in seniority. In January 1996, Safeway provided Martyszenko a check in the amount she would have received as compensation had she remained at work.

Martyszenko rejected the offer to return but cashed the check. The issue presented is whether the diagnosis of the plaintiff's son qualified as a serious health condition under the Family and Medical Leave Act. *Martyszenko v. Safeway, Inc.*, 120 F.3d 120 (8th Cir. 1997)

2. Clay has a degenerative disk disease causing severe back pain, which required her to take several medical leaves. She took her last medical leave from July 7, 1994, through August 8, 1994, receiving hospital treatment and then convalescing at home. On her August 9 return, defendant Erlinda Tzirides, deputy commissioner of administration for the Department of Health, and Kean met with her and told her they wanted Michael Sulewski, who had replaced Clay during her leave, to continue as acting director of human resources because he had worked so effectively during Clay's absence. They told Clay that they would have her work on special projects until she found employment elsewhere.

   On December 19, 1994, after having given Clay 5 months' notice to find another job, Tzirides advised Clay that her discharge would be effective December 31, 1994. Because of many observed deficiencies in her performance, Tzirides had earlier decided to terminate Clay. The hiring forms prepared by her office were defective, and she did not submit request to hire forms with screening criteria under official city job requirements. The question presented is whether the plaintiff was terminated for taking medical leave or for poor performance. *Clay v. City of Chicago Dept. of Health*, 143 F.3d 1092 (7th Cir. 1998)

3. Plaintiff's claim that her discharge from Dean Witter resulted from sex and pregnancy discrimination relied heavily on Dean Witter's decision to retain Melvin Relova, a man, on its TFU desk at the time of plaintiff's discharge. Plaintiff attempted in her case-in-chief to show that Relova was less qualified than she and, therefore, that her termination from Dean Witter must have been discriminatory. Plaintiff proffered as evidence of her pregnancy discrimination claim isolated statements made by Ian Bernstein, a Dean Witter manager, about how difficult it was to raise children in New York. His testimony included the fact that he himself had twins. Dean Witter's consistent policy permitted pregnant employees to retain their position at Dean Witter following their pregnancies, including plaintiff herself following her 1987 pregnancy.

   Bernstein testified that Relova was the best qualified to staff the TFU desk. He based that assessment on "having worked with those individuals for several years in the capital markets area, as well as having supervised them for a period of time." The question is whether an employee's termination was based on her pregnancy. The employer argued that it was based on her competency. She retorted that it was a pretext used to disguise the discriminatory intent of her employer. *Hansen v. Dean Witter Reynolds, Inc.*, 887 F. Supp. 669 (S.D.N.Y. 1995)

HUMAN RESOURCE DILEMMAS

1. South Hill High for Girls is an Ivy League prep school. Theresa Windworth, a social studies instructor, becomes pregnant. South Hill tells Theresa she must resign due to the fact that she would be setting a poor example for the students. When Theresa refuses, she is discharged. What advice would you give to her?

2. Brad Peters and his wife adopt a baby. Brad applies for 12-week family leave. He is denied because his wife did not give birth. How would you advise him to proceed?

3. Ryan's Express is a dry-cleaning establishment with 47 employees working in 6 stores. Maggie Brown's mom must undergo triple-bypass surgery. Maggie applies for medical leave under the FMLA to care for her mom when she is released from the hospital. Maggie's request is denied. How would you advise her to proceed?

Using the following Web sites, prepare arguments for and against paid FMLA leave. Then compare and contrast the U.S. FMLA leave policy with that in other countries.

www.findlaw.com
www.unlv.edu/Human_Resources/Benefits/fmla.html
www.babybag.com/articles/laws.htm
www.legal-database.com/laborlaw.htm
www.pfclaw.com/downloads/pregnancy%20discimination%20email.htm
www.afscme.org/wrkplace/wrfaq06.htm
www.eeoc.gov/types/pregnancy.html

Chapter 13

Sexual Orientation

Employment Scenario

L&S learns that two of its employees, Alyssa Morris and Sarah Jacobs are deciding whether to apply for a marriage license in Massachusetts or a civil union in Vermont. Tom and Mark wish to terminate them because they do not want to be associated with condoning gay marriage. What course of action should Susan recommend?

Chapter Checklist
➤ *Know that protection under the Civil Rights Act does not extend to sexual orientation.*
➤ *Learn that certain states and cities do provide sexual orientation protection.*
➤ *Realize that homosexuals with AIDS or sexually transmitted diseases will be safeguarded under the Americans with Disabilities Act.*
➤ *Appreciate that homosexuals can cover their partners under their health plan in a small but growing number of companies.*
➤ *Understand that gays and lesbians may serve in the military.*
➤ *Recognize that schoolteachers should not be judged by their sexual orientation, but on their ability to teach and follow the course curriculum.*
➤ *Be cognizant of the arguments presented for those advocating gay rights in employment and those against it.*
➤ *Be careful about judging others whose lifestyle may not conform to yours, lest they judge you in the same way.*

INTRODUCTION

Title VII of the Civil Rights Act does not prohibit employers from refusing to hire or subsequently firing someone because he or she is homosexual. Although there is no federal law, state and local laws do exist in select jurisdictions. The terms most commonly used are *sexual affinity* or *sexual orientation*. Many cities also prohibit discrimination on the basis of sexual orientation, but only a few of them extend it to employment.

There is also no federal law protecting transsexuals and those undertaking gender-corrective surgery.

HUMAN RESOURCE ADVICE

- Discover whether state or local protection for sexual orientation exists.
- Choose whether to allow homosexuals to cover their partners under the health plan you provide.
- Decide whether you will take sexual orientation into account in your employment decisions.
- Be cognizant of the power of the gay and lesbian lobby.
- Learn from the judicial overruling of the Colorado referendum outlawing protection for homosexuals.
- Distinguish between homosexuals, transsexuals, and transvestites in determining company policy.
- Realize that the Americans with Disabilities Act extends to homosexuals with AIDS or sexually transmitted diseases.
- Be aware of the trend to provide more protection to gays and lesbians by public and private employers.

Available Protection

Gays and lesbians working pursuant to employment contracts or employee handbooks may be protected by a clause in the agreement requiring that an employee may be discharged only for cause. In such a case, sexual orientation would not qualify as cause, and the homosexual employee could not be terminated absent just cause. Some courts have overruled dismissal of gay employees based on public policy considerations. Other courts have stated that dismissing an individual because of affinity or sexual orientation violates the implied covenant of good faith and fair dealing that exists between employer and employee.

The issue in the case that follows is whether harassment of an individual because of his sexual orientation is protected under Title VII.

Simonton v. Runyon

225 F.3d 122 (2nd Cir. 2000)

Walker, JR., Circuit Judge.

Plaintiff-appellant Dwayne Simonton sued the Postmaster General and the United States Postal Service (together "defendants") under Title VII of the Civil Rights Act of 1964 ("Title VII"), 42 U.S.C. § 2000e et seq., for abuse and harassment he suffered by reason of his sexual orientation. The United States District Court for the Eastern District of New York dismissed Simonton's complaint for failure to state a claim, reasoning that Title VII does not prohibit discrimination based on sexual orientation. We agree.

Simonton's sexual orientation was known to his co-workers who repeatedly assaulted him with such comments as "go f*** yourself, f*g" "suck my d***," and "so you like it up the a**?" Notes were placed on the wall in the employees' bathroom with Simonton's name and the name of celebrities who had died of AIDS. Pornographic photographs were taped to his work area, male dolls were placed in his vehicle, and copies of *Playgirl* magazine were sent to his home. Pictures of an erect penis were posted in his work place, as were posters stating that Simonton suffered from mental illness as a result of "b*** hole disorder." There were repeated statements that Simonton was a "f***ing f****t."

There can be no doubt that the conduct allegedly engaged in by Simonton's co-workers is morally reprehensible whenever and in whatever context it occurs, particularly in the modern workplace. Nevertheless, as the First Circuit recently explained in a similar context, "we are called upon here to construe a statute as glossed by the Supreme Court, not to make a moral judgment." When interpreting a statute, the role of a court is limited to discerning and adhering to legislative meaning. The law is well-settled in this circuit and in all others to have reached the question that Simonton has no cause of action under Title VII because Title VII does not prohibit harassment or discrimination because of sexual orientation.

The Equal Employment Opportunity Act of 1972 extended Title VII's protections to certain federal employees, including U.S. postal service employees. See 42 U.S.C. § 2000e-16(a). Section 2000e-16(a) provides, in part, that all personnel actions affecting covered employees "shall be made free from any discrimination based on race, color, religion, sex, or national origin." Simonton argues that discrimination based on "sex" includes discrimination based on sexual orientation. We disagree.

In *Oncale*, the Supreme Court rejected a per se rule that same-sex sexual harassment was non-cognizable under Title VII. The Court reasoned that "nothing in Title VII necessarily bars a claim of discrimination' 'because of . . . sex' merely because the plaintiff and the defendant (or person charged with acting on behalf of the defendant) are of the same sex." *Oncale* did not suggest, however, that male harassment of other males always violates Title VII. *Oncale* emphasized that every victim of such harassment must show that he was harassed because he was male.

Simonton has alleged that he was discriminated against not because he was a man, but because of his sexual orientation. Such a claim remains non-cognizable under Title VII.

Simonton also argues that discrimination because of sexual orientation is discrimination based on sex because it disproportionately affects men. We decline to adopt a reading of Title VII that would also "achieve by judicial 'construction' what Congress did not do and has consistently refused to do on many occasions." Therefore, this argument is unavailing.

Other courts have suggested that gender discrimination—discrimination based on a failure to conform to gender norms—might be cognizable under Title VII. ("Just as a woman can ground an action on a claim that men discriminated against her because she did not meet stereotyped expectations of femininity, a man can ground a claim on evidence that other men discriminated against him because he did not meet stereotypical expectations of masculinity.")

The same theory of sexual stereotyping could apply here. Simonton argues that the harassment he endured was based on his failure to conform to gender norms, regardless of his sexual orientation. The Court in Price Waterhouse implied that a suit alleging harassment or disparate treatment based upon nonconformity with sexual stereotypes is cognizable under Title VII as discrimination because of sex. This would not bootstrap protection for sexual orientation into Title VII because not all homosexual men are stereotypically feminine, and not all heterosexual men are stereotypically masculine. But it would plainly afford relief for discrimination based upon sexual stereotypes.

We do not reach the merits of this issue, however, as Simonton has failed to plead sufficient facts for our consideration of the issue. We do not have sufficient allegations before us to decide Simonton's claims based on stereotyping because we have no basis in the record to surmise that Simonton behaved in a stereotypically feminine manner and that the harassment he endured was, in fact, based on his non-conformity with gender norms instead of his sexual orientation.

We have considered Simonton's remaining arguments and find them to be without merit. For the reasons set forth above, the judgment of the district court is AFFIRMED.

Judgment for Runyon.

Case Commentary

The Second Circuit Court ruled that same-sex sexual orientation is protected under Title VII if it is based on the victim's gender, not sexual orientation. ∎

CASE QUESTIONS

1. Do you agree with the Court's decision?
2. Would it not be difficult to determine whether the harassment was based on gender or sexual orientation? Is there not some overlap?
3. Can this case be distinguished from the *Oncale* case in Chapter 11?
4. Would the U.S. Supreme Court affirm this decision?

The question presented in the following case is whether a state amendment prohibiting protection from being granted to homosexuals in employment, housing, and so forth, is in violation of the Fourteenth Amendment's Equal Protection Clause.

Roy Romer, Governor of Colorado v. Evans
116 S.Ct. 1620 (1996)

Justice Kennedy delivered the opinion of the Court.

The enactment challenged in this case is an amendment to the Constitution of the State of Colorado, adopted in a 1992 statewide referendum. The parties and the state courts refer to it as "Amendment 2," its designation when submitted to the voters. The impetus for the amendment and the contentious campaign that preceded its adoption came in large part from ordinances that had been passed in various Colorado municipalities. For example, the cities of Aspen and Boulder and the City and County of Denver each had enacted ordinances which banned discrimination in many transactions and activities, including housing, employment, education, public accommodations, and health and welfare services. What gave rise to the statewide controversy was the protection the ordinances afforded to persons discriminated against by reason of their sexual orientation Amendment 2 repeals these ordinances to the extent they prohibit discrimination on the basis of "homosexual, lesbian or bisexual orientation, conduct, practices or relationships."

Yet Amendment 2, in explicit terms, does more than repeal or rescind these provisions. It prohibits all legislative, executive or judicial action at any level of state or local government designed to protect the named class, a class we shall refer to as homosexual persons or gays and lesbians. The amendment reads: "No Protected Status Based on Homosexual, Lesbian, or Bisexual Orientation. Neither the State of Colorado, through any of its branches or departments, nor any of its agencies, political subdivisions, municipalities or school districts, shall enact, adopt or enforce any statute, regulation, ordinance or policy whereby homosexual, lesbian or bisexual orientation, conduct, practices or relationships shall constitute or otherwise be the basis of or entitle any person or class of persons to have or claim any minority status, quota preferences, protected status or claim of discrimination. This Section of the Constitution shall be in all respects self executing."

Soon after Amendment 2 was adopted, this litigation to declare its invalidity and enjoin its enforcement was commenced in the District Court for the City and County of Denver. Among the plaintiffs (respondents here) were homosexual persons, some of them government employees. They alleged that enforcement of Amendment 2 would subject them to immediate and substantial risk of discrimination on the basis of their sexual orientation. Other plaintiffs (also respondents here) included the three municipalities whose ordinances we have cited and certain other governmental entities which had acted earlier to protect homosexuals from discrimination but would be prevented by Amendment 2 from continuing to do so. Although Governor Romer had been on record opposing the adoption of Amendment 2, he was named in his official capacity as a defendant, together with the Colorado Attorney General and the State of Colorado.

The trial court granted a preliminary injunction to stay enforcement of Amendment 2, and an appeal was taken to the Supreme Court of Colorado. Sustaining the interim injunction and remanding the case for further proceedings, the State Supreme Court held that Amendment 2 was subject to strict scrutiny under the *Fourteenth Amendment* because it infringed the fundamental right of gays and lesbians to participate in the political process. On remand, the State advanced various arguments in an effort to show that Amendment 2 was narrowly tailored to serve compelling interests, but the trial court found none sufficient. It enjoined enforcement of Amendment 2, and the Supreme Court of Colorado, in a second opinion, affirmed the ruling. We granted certiorari and now affirm the judgment, but on a rationale different from that adopted by the State Supreme Court.

The State's principal argument in defense of Amendment 2 is that it puts gays and lesbians in the same position as all other persons. So, the State says, the measure does no more than deny homosexuals special rights. This reading of the amendment's language is implausible. We rely not upon our own interpretation of the amendment but upon the authoritative construction of Colorado's Supreme Court. The state court, deeming it unnecessary to determine the full extent of the amendment's reach, found it invalid even on a modest reading of its implications. The critical discussion of the amendment is as follows: "The immediate objective of Amendment 2 is, at a minimum, to repeal existing statutes, regulations, ordinances, and policies of state and local entities that barred discrimination based on sexual orientation."

Homosexuals, by state decree, are put in a solitary class with respect to transactions and relations in both the private and governmental spheres. The amendment withdraws from homosexuals, but no others, specific legal protection from the injuries caused by discrimination, and it forbids reinstatement of these laws and policies.

We have attempted to reconcile the principle with the reality by stating that, if a law neither burdens a fundamental right nor targets a suspect class, we will uphold the legislative classification so long as it bears a rational relation to some legitimate end.

Amendment 2 fails, indeed defies, even this conventional inquiry. First, the amendment has the peculiar property of imposing a broad and undifferentiated disability on a single named group, an exceptional and, as we shall explain, invalid form of legislation. Second, its sheer breadth is so discontinuous with the reasons offered for it that the amendment seems inexplicable by anything but animus toward the class that it affects; it lacks a rational relationship to legitimate state interests.

The primary rationale the State offers for Amendment 2 is respect for other citizens' freedom of association, and in particular the liberties of landlords or employers who have personal or religious objections to homosexuality. Colorado also cites its interest in conserving resources to fight discrimination against other groups. The breadth of the Amendment is so far removed from these particular justifications that we find it impossible to credit them. We cannot say that Amendment 2 is directed to any identifiable legitimate purpose or discrete objective. It is a status based enactment divorced from any factual context from which we could discern a relationship to legitimate state interests; it is a classification of persons undertaken for its own sake, something the Equal Protection Clause does not permit.

We must conclude that Amendment 2 classifies homosexuals not to further a proper legislative end but to make them unequal to everyone else. This Colorado cannot do. A State cannot so deem a class of persons a stranger to its laws Amendment 2 violates the Equal Protection Clause, and the judgment of the Supreme Court of Colorado is affirmed.

Justice Scalia, *with whom*

The Chief Justice and Justice Thomas *join, dissenting.*

In holding that homosexuality cannot be singled out for disfavorable treatment, the Court contradicts a decision, unchallenged here, pronounced only 10 years ago and places the prestige of this institution behind the proposition that opposition to homosexuality is as reprehensible as racial or religious bias. Whether it is or not is *precisely* the cultural debate that gave rise to the Colorado constitutional amendment (and to the preferential laws against which the amendment was directed). Since the Constitution of the United States says nothing about this subject, it is left to be resolved by normal democratic means, including the democratic adoption of provisions in state constitutions. This Court has no business imposing upon all Americans the resolution favored by the elite class from which the Members of this institution are selected, pronouncing that "animosity" toward homosexuality is evil. I vigorously dissent.

But though Coloradans are, as I say, *entitled* to be hostile toward homosexual conduct, the fact is that the degree of hostility reflected by Amendment 2 is the smallest conceiv-

able. The Court's portrayal of Coloradans as a society fallen victim to pointless, hate-filled "gay bashing" is so false as to be comical. Colorado not only is one of the 25 States that have repealed their antisodomy laws, but was among the first to do so. But the society that eliminates criminal punishment for homosexual acts does not necessarily abandon the view that homosexuality is morally wrong and socially harmful; often, abolition simply reflects the view that enforcement of such criminal laws involves unseemly intrusion into the intimate lives of citizens.

There is a problem, however, which arises when criminal sanction of homosexuality is eliminated but moral and social disapprobation of homosexuality is meant to be retained. The Court cannot be unaware of that problem; it is evident in many cities of the country, and occasionally bubbles to the surface of the news, in heated political disputes over such matters as the introduction into local schools of books teaching that homosexuality is an optional and fully acceptable "alternate life style." The problem (a problem, that is, for those who wish to retain social disapprobation of homosexuality) is that, because those who engage in homosexual conduct tend to reside in disproportionate numbers in certain communities, have high disposable income, and of course care about homosexual rights issues much more ardently than the public at large, they possess political power much greater than their numbers, both locally and statewide. Quite understandably, they devote this political power to achieving not merely a grudging social toleration, but full social acceptance, of homosexuality.

By the time Coloradans were asked to vote on Amendment 2, their exposure to homosexuals' quest for social endorsement was not limited to newspaper accounts of happenings in places such as New York, Los Angeles, San Francisco, and Key West. Three Colorado cities—Aspen, Boulder, and Denver—had enacted ordinances that listed "sexual orientation" as an impermissible ground for discrimination, equating the moral disapproval of homosexual conduct with racial and religious bigotry. The phenomenon had even appeared statewide: the Governor of Colorado had signed an executive order pronouncing that "in the State of Colorado we recognize the diversity in our pluralistic society and strive to bring an end to discrimination in any form," and directing state agency heads to "ensure non discrimination" in hiring and promotion based on, among other things, "sexual orientation." I do not mean to be critical of these legislative successes; homosexuals are as entitled to use the legal system for reinforcement of their moral sentiments as are the rest of society. But they are subject to being countered by lawful, democratic countermeasures as well.

That is where Amendment 2 came in. It sought to counter both the geographic concentration and the disproportionate political power of homosexuals by (1) resolving the controversy at the statewide level, and (2) making the election a single issue contest for both sides. It put directly, to all the citizens of the State, the question: Should homosexuality be given special protection? They answered no. The

Court today asserts that this most democratic of procedures is unconstitutional. Lacking any cases to establish that facially absurd proposition, it simply asserts that it must be unconstitutional, because it has never happened before.

Amendment 2 identifies persons by a single trait and then denies them protection across the board. The resulting disqualification of a class of persons from the right to seek specific protection from the law is unprecedented in our jurisprudence. The absence of precedent for Amendment 2 is itself instructive . . . .

The United States Congress, by the way, *required* the inclusion of these anti polygamy provisions in the constitutions of Arizona, New Mexico, Oklahoma, and Utah, as a condition of their admission to statehood. I cannot say that this Court has explicitly approved any of these state constitutional provisions; but it has approved a territorial statutory provision that went even further, depriving polygamists of the ability even to achieve a constitutional amendment, by depriving them of the power to vote.

It remains to be explained how sect. 501 of the Idaho Revised Statutes was not an "impermissible targeting" of polygamists, but (the much more mild) Amendment 2 is an "impermissible targeting" of homosexuals. Has the Court concluded that the perceived social harm of polygamy is a "legitimate concern of government," and the perceived social harm of homosexuality is not?

I strongly suspect that the answer to the last question is yes.

Today's opinion has no foundation in American constitutional law, and barely pretends to. The people of Colorado have adopted an entirely reasonable provision which does not even disfavor homosexuals in any substantive sense, but merely denies them preferential treatment. Amendment 2 is designed to prevent piecemeal deterioration of the sexual morality favored by a majority of Coloradans, and is not only an appropriate means to that legitimate end, but a means that Americans have employed before. Striking it down is an act, not of judicial judgment, but of political will. I dissent.

Case Commentary

The U.S. Supreme Court ruled that the Colorado Amendment violated the Equal Protection Clause of the Fourteenth Amendment because it specifically treated homosexuals in a way that was not equal. The dissenting opinion focused upon the fact that many people believe homosexuality is morally wrong. The dissent reasoned that the fact that homosexuals have to be tolerated does not mean that they have to be accepted. ■

CASE QUESTIONS

1. Do you agree with the decision of the Court?
2. Should homosexuals be a suspect classification entitled to be protected from discrimination?

3. Who should decide this: courts or the people? In this case, the people decided this issue and lost.

The issue in the case that follows is whether an individual claiming harassment based on sexual orientation is protected under the FEHA.

Murray v. Oceanside Unified School District
2000 Cal. App. LEXIS 298 (Cal. 1st App. Ct.)

Huffman, J.

Plaintiff Dawn Murray filed a complaint against her employer, Oceanside Unified School District (Oceanside), alleging she suffered harassment on the basis of her sexual orientation (lesbian) at her place of work, Oceanside High School, where she has taught high school biology and biotechnology since 1983. She alleges that contrary to the protections afforded her under former Labor Code section 1102.1, school officials failed to investigate the incidents and inflicted retaliatory discipline on her when she complained about them. She also contends the school officials' conduct on behalf of her employer amounted to intentional infliction of emotional distress by Oceanside.

Following extensive pretrial motion activity, the trial court granted a defense motion to exclude evidence of all the incidents she alleged except one, as not falling within the protective coverage of Labor Code section 1102.1. The trial court further ruled that her remaining claim, failure to promote, was untimely, based on the administrative tort claims filed. Judgment was entered for Oceanside on both causes of action and Murray appeals.

Accordingly, further proceedings are required to flesh out the nature and scope of the activities which allegedly occurred that remain actionable as part of the anti-harassment law or as a common law tort, and that are timely made in light of the administrative claims made and the applicable limitations periods. We reverse the judgment and remand for further proceedings.

FACTUAL AND PROCEDURAL BACKGROUND

Murray has been employed by Oceanside for many years and has taught at Oceanside High School since 1983. She is acknowledged to be an excellent teacher who has consistently received good evaluations. She continues to work as a teacher at the high school. We will summarize the course of conduct that she claims amounts to sexual harassment based on sexual orientation, after outlining the formalities of this litigation.

Beginning on November 13, 1995, Murray filed three government tort claims with Oceanside, alleging workplace harassment on the basis of her sexual orientation. The second and third claims were filed March 15, 1996, and June 19, 1996, respectively. All were rejected. Her complaint was filed in superior court on June 25, 1996, seeking damages for discrimination in violation of Labor Code section 1101 et seq. and for the tort of intentional infliction of emotional distress. Oceanside answered the complaint and extensive law and motion activity ensued. Oceanside brought two summary judgment motions and several reconsideration motions, which were denied. The matter was set for trial.

1. In the spring of 1993, Oceanside failed to promote Murray to the position of student activities director, even though she was the top candidate (once another candidate withdrew), based on its disapproval of her lifestyle;

2. From September 1993 through October 1994 she endured various insults, criticism, suggestive remarks concerning sex or alleging sexual activity on campus, and rumor mongering by various fellow employees, and a consequent failure to investigate or take corrective action by Oceanside administrative officials. Murray was told if she pursued her complaints about these incidents, she would suffer adverse job consequences;

3. In December 1994, January 1995 and February 1996 harassing and obscene graffiti was painted outside her classroom by unknown persons, and Oceanside administrators failed to investigate the problems even though the police were called;

4. In January 1995 she was verbally harassed at a school in-service meeting when the principal mentioned Murray's sexual orientation to the audience, some of whom were unaware of this; harassing comments by coworkers ensued without proper management or preventative action by the administration;

5. Although Murray received a prestigious statewide teaching award for biology in June 1995, the school district failed to accord her any appropriate recognition, which she believed was due to her sexual orientation; and

6. In April 1996, September 1996, and June 1997 she had a class unfairly canceled and received unfair and retaliatory disciplinary measures, based on complaints by a parent and a fellow teacher, which were inappropriate and motivated by harassment.

The matter went to trial in January 1998 beginning with motions by Oceanside to exclude all evidence pertaining to all claims by Murray except for the failure to achieve promotion. The trial court granted these motions, on the theory that only discriminatory conduct was prohibited by the Labor Code sections relied upon such as hiring, firing and other employment decisions. The court rejected Murray's claims that she could plead the occurrence of other damaging actions in the workplace, creating a hostile environment, as actionable under the referenced statutes.

Murray appealed.

DISCUSSION

To determine if the trial court correctly concluded that these allegations of a hostile work environment, based on harassment on the basis of sexual orientation, fell outside the scope of coverage of Labor Code section 1102.1, we are required to set forth the evolution of the Labor Code statutory scheme, dealing with political freedom in the workplace, in which Labor Code section 1102.1 appears. We are then required to account for the effect of the Legislature's 1999 decision to repeal Labor Code section 1102.1 and place its protections within the FEHA instead, as part of Government Code. Because of that enactment, FEHA now deals with sexual orientation as a prohibited subject of workplace harassment, in addition to many other enumerated categories, such as race, national origin, sex and so forth.

As now amended in 1999, section 12940, subdivision (h) provides: "It shall be an unlawful employment practice, unless based upon a bona fide occupational qualification, or, except where based upon applicable security regulations established by the United States or the State of California: For an employer, labor organization, employment agency, apprenticeship training program or any training program leading to employment, or any other person, *because of* race, religious creed, color, national origin, ancestry, physical disability, mental disability, medical condition, marital status, sex, age, *or sexual orientation, to harass an employee, an applicant, or a person providing services pursuant to a contract. Harassment of an employee, an applicant, or a person providing services pursuant to a contract by an employee other than an agent or supervisor shall be unlawful if the entity, or its agents or supervisors, knows or should have known of this conduct and fails to take immediate and appropriate corrective action. An entity shall take all reasonable steps to prevent harassment from occurring. Loss of tangible job benefits shall not be necessary in order to establish harassment.*"

Based on this recent amendment, FEHA now clearly contains a prohibition of workplace harassment based on the protected category of sexual orientation. The definition of that quality now includes heterosexuality, homosexuality and bisexuality. This is consistent with the political freedom of expression protections which are at the root of Labor Code section 1101 et seq. Labor Code section 1102.1 has also been interpreted to cover discrimination in any aspect of employment based on actual or perceived sexual orientation. Murray has requested in her supplemental briefing that her statutory cause of action be found viable not only under

Labor Code section 1101 et seq., as originally pled, but also be deemed valid under FEHA as recently amended, because the amendment amounted to a clarification of existing law rather than a change in the law. We agree that both questions must be addressed to fully dispose of the issues on review.

To the extent Murray has alleged discrimination took place against her on the basis of sexual orientation, we may be guided by *Meritor Savings Bank v. Vinson*, which held that hostile environment sexual harassment violates federal law affording employees the right to work in an environment free from discriminatory intimidation, ridicule, and insult, where it affects a term, condition, or privilege of employment. That is, severe or pervasive sexual harassment alters the conditions of the victim's employment and creates an abusive working environment. These principles have now been incorporated into FEHA, as applicable to sexual orientation discrimination.

Moreover, the law as to sexual orientation harassment is not far behind. "Sections 1101 and 1102 prohibit *discrimination or different treatment in any aspect of employment* or opportunity for employment based on actual or perceived sexual orientation." Murray has alleged a number of instances in which she was allegedly treated differently than other employees might have been, chiefly or entirely because of her known or perceived sexual orientation. Under a plain language reading of the Labor Code statutes, section 1101 et seq., it was error to dismiss her action.

Judgment for Murray.

Case Commentary
The First Appellate Court of California ruled that the FEHA does extend protection to individuals discriminated against in employment for their sexual affinity. ■

CASE QUESTIONS

1. Do you believe this case was decided correctly?
2. Why is the FEHA at odds with Title VII?

3. Is it a matter of time before affinity orientation will be protected under Title VII?

A woman discharged because she is a lesbian may argue that her sexual orientation was the real reason for her termination and that any reason proffered by the employer was mere pretext. Arguing gender discrimination places a lesbian in a protected class, but she will be protected only as far as her womanhood is the issue and not her homosexuality. Gays and lesbians have been trying to have sex discrimination enlarged to encompass sexual orientation, but so far most courts and legislatures do not agree.

Homosexuals who have the AIDS virus or other sexually transmitted diseases will be protected under the Americans with Disabilities Act because they are operating under a disability. Homosexuals who are promoting gay rights may not be discharged in some states for espousing their political beliefs.

Gays and lesbians have been fired for flaunting their relationships. While this may sound egregious, it is no different from a heterosexual speaking about his or her amorous relationship. Treatment should be similar. If heterosexuals may display pictures of loved ones, so should homosexuals. Buttons espousing political beliefs such as "Support Gay Rights" or "It's OK to Be Gay" may be disallowed if the company has a policy disallowing the visible expression of political viewpoints at the workplace.

The issue in the next case is whether a male employee may have long hair and wear facial jewelry. The employee argued that the company's imposition was discriminatory. The company claimed it had the right to uphold its image.

Lockhart v. Louisiana-Pacific Corp.
795 P.2d 602 (OR. App. 1990)

Richardson, Presiding Judge.
Plaintiff was discharged by Louisiana-Pacific Corporation (employer), after he refused to comply with the requirement of a dress and grooming rule that male employees not wear facial jewelry while on the job. The rule allows female employees to wear jewelry that is not "unusual or overly-large." Plaintiff contends that the rule is sexually discriminatory, and that he

was discharged for "resisting" the discriminatory policy. He brought this action for wrongful discharge against his employer and for interference with contractual relations against his supervisor, Montel Work (Work). The trial court dismissed the wrongful discharge claim for failure to state a claim and allowed Work's motion for summary judgment on the interference claim. Plaintiff appeals and assigns error to both rulings. We affirm.

"The recent federal cases hold that a private employer's promulgation and enforcement of reasonable grooming regulations that restrict the hair length of male employees only is not forbidden by the sex discrimination provisions of the federal act. Only those distinctions between the sexes which are based on immutable, unalterable, or constitutionally protected personal characteristics are forbidden."

" . . . The federal statute was never intended to prohibit sex-based distinctions inherent in a private employer's personal grooming code for employees which do not have a significant effect on employment and which can be changed easily by the employee. . . . The enforcement of a reasonable hair length policy is permissible since such a policy is not used to inhibit equal access to employment opportunities between males and females, is not an employer's attempt to deny employment to a particular sex, and is not a significant employment advantage to either sex."

Perhaps no facet of business life is more important than a company's place in public estimation. That the image created by its employees dealing with the public when on company assignment affects its relations is so well known that we may take judicial notice of an employer's proper desire to achieve favorable acceptance. Good grooming regulations reflect a company's policy in our highly competitive business environment. Reasonable requirements in furtherance of that policy are an aspect of managerial responsibility. Congress has said that no exercise of that responsibility may result in discriminatory deprivation of equal opportunity because of immutable race, national origin, color, or sex classification.

It is not a purpose of the federal statute to accommodate a male employee's desire to wear his hair longer than a private employer's appearance policy allows.

It is unnecessary in this case for us to address the full sweep of the Washington court's reasoning. Plaintiff advances the argument that employer may not prohibit him from wearing an earring, if it allows female employees to wear jewelry. As his argument is cast, plaintiff cannot demonstrate impermissible discrimination unless every difference in dress or grooming requirements for men and women under an employer's rules is impermissibly discriminatory. We reject that argument. The trial court was correct in dismissing the wrongful discharge claim.

Judgment for Louisiana-Pacific Corp.

Case Commentary

The Oregon Appellate Court concluded that the First Amendment of the United States Constitution does not protect male employees who wish to wear facial jewelry in violation of company dress and grooming rules. ■

CASE QUESTIONS

1. Do you agree with the Court's decision?
2. Why does the First Amendment's freedom of speech protection not extend to an employee who wishes to wear facial jewelry?
3. Do you think the rules regarding the right to wear jewelry and makeup as well as the right to wear skirts, dresses, and long hair should apply equally to men and women?

Homosexual Partners

Currently, gays and lesbians do not have the legal right to include their partners under their health coverage. However, some companies permit them to do so. Because homosexual marriages are not legally sanctioned except in Massachusetts and Vermont (the latter permits two people of the same sex to enter into a civil union) partners are considered mere friends who are not qualified for coverage. Family leave policies for sickness and death do not extend to gays and lesbians. A Hawaii Circuit Court was the first to legitimize same-sex marriages, but this was quickly overruled by the Hawaii state legislature and subsequently affirmed by the Hawaii Supreme Court. A few states have passed, and a number of states are attempting to pass, antigay marriage bills.

Employment Perspective

Bruce Wagner's gay partner, Paul, has passed away. Bruce asks for time off to attend Paul's wake and funeral. The firm is amenable as long as Bruce uses his personal days or takes a leave without pay. Bruce argues that if he were married, he would be entitled to leave with pay. The company asserts that neither it nor state law recognizes homosexual marriages. Does Bruce have any recourse? No! Sexual orientation is not included under the Family and Medical Leave Act.

The issue in the case that follows is whether persons of the same sex should be entitled to marry, thereby granting unto them all of the rights afforded to married couples.

Baker v. State of Vermont
Supreme Court of Vermont No. 98-032 (1999)

Amestoy, Chief Judge.

May the State of Vermont exclude same-sex couples from the benefits and protections that its laws provide to opposite-sex married couples? That is the fundamental question we address in this appeal, a question that the Court well knows arouses deeply-felt religious, moral, and political beliefs. Our constitutional responsibility to consider the legal merits of issues properly before us provides no exception for the controversial case. The issue before the Court, moreover, does not turn on the religious or moral debate over intimate same-sex relationships, but rather on the statutory and constitutional basis for the exclusion of same-sex couples from the secular benefits and protections offered married couples.

We conclude that under the Common Benefits Clause of the Vermont Constitution, which, in pertinent part, reads,

That government is, or ought to be, instituted for the common benefit, protection, and security of the people, nation, or community, and not for the particular emolument or advantage of any single person, family, or set of persons, who are a part only of that community, plaintiffs may not be deprived of the statutory benefits and protections afforded persons of the opposite sex who choose to marry. We hold that the State is constitutionally required to extend to same-sex couples the common benefits and protections that flow from marriage under Vermont law. Whether this ultimately takes the form of inclusion within the marriage laws themselves or a parallel "domestic partnership" system or some equivalent statutory alternative, rests with the Legislature. Whatever system is chosen, however, must conform with the constitutional imperative to afford all Vermonters the common benefit, protection, and security of the law.

Plaintiffs are three same-sex couples who have lived together in committed relationships for periods ranging from four to twenty-five years. Two of the couples have raised children together. Each couple applied for a marriage license from their respective town clerk, and each was refused a license as ineligible under the applicable state marriage laws. Plaintiffs thereupon filed this lawsuit against defendants—the State of Vermont, the Towns of Milton and Shelburne, and the City of South

Burlington—seeking a declaratory judgment that the refusal to issue them a license violated the marriage statutes and the Vermont Constitution.

The State, joined by Shelburne and South Burlington, moved to dismiss the action on the ground that plaintiffs had failed to state a claim for which relief could be granted. The trial court granted the State's and the Town of Milton's motions and dismissed the complaint. The court ruled that the marriage statutes could not be construed to permit the issuance of a license to same-sex couples. The court further ruled that the marriage statutes were constitutional because they rationally furthered the State's interest in promoting "the link between procreation and child rearing." This appeal followed.

Vermont's marriage statutes are set forth in Chapter 1 of Title 15, entitled "Marriage," which defines the requirements and eligibility for entering into a marriage, and Chapter 105 of Title 18, entitled "Marriage Records and Licenses," which prescribes the forms and procedures for obtaining a license and solemnizing a marriage. Although it is not necessarily the only possible definition, there is no doubt that the plain and ordinary meaning of "marriage" is the union of one man and one woman as husband and wife. This understanding of the term is well rooted in Vermont common law. The legislative understanding is also reflected in the enabling statute governing the issuance of marriage licenses, which provides, in part, that the license "shall be issued by the clerk of the town where either the bride or groom resides." "Bride" and "groom" are gender-specific terms.

These statutes, read as a whole, reflect the common understanding that marriage under Vermont law consists of a union between a man and a woman. Plaintiffs essentially concede this fact. They argue, nevertheless, that the underlying purpose of marriage is to protect and encourage the union of committed couples and that, absent an explicit legislative prohibition, the statutes should be interpreted broadly to include committed same-sex couples. Plaintiffs rely principally on our decision in In re B.L.V.B. There, we held that a woman who was co-parenting the two children of her same-sex partner could adopt the children without terminating the natural mother's parental rights. Although the statute provided generally that an adoption deprived the natural parents of their legal rights, it contained an exception where the adoption was by the "spouse" of the natural parent. Technically, therefore, the exception was inapplicable. We concluded, however, that the purpose of the law was not to restrict the exception to legally married couples, but to safeguard the child, and that to apply the literal language of the statute in these circumstances would defeat the statutory purpose and "reach an absurd result."

Contrary to plaintiffs' claim, B.L.V.B. does not control our conclusion here. We are not dealing in this case with a narrow statutory exception requiring a broader reading than its literal words would permit in order to avoid a result plainly at odds with the legislative purpose. Unlike B.L.V.B., it is far from clear that limiting marriage to opposite-sex couples violates the Legislature's "intent and spirit." Rather, the evidence demonstrates a clear legislative assumption that marriage under our statutory scheme consists of a union between a man and a woman. Accordingly, we reject plaintiffs' claim that they were entitled to a license under the statutory scheme governing marriage.

With these general precepts in mind, we turn to the question of whether the exclusion of same-sex couples from the benefits and protections incident to marriage under Vermont law contravenes Article 7. The first step in our analysis is to identify the nature of the statutory classification. As noted, the marriage statutes apply expressly to opposite-sex couples. Thus, the statutes exclude anyone who wishes to marry someone of the same sex.

Next, we must identify the governmental purpose or purposes to be served by the statutory classification. The principal purpose the State advances in support of the excluding same-sex couples from the legal benefits of marriage is the government's interest in "furthering the link between procreation and child rearing." The State has a strong interest, it argues, in promoting a permanent commitment between couples who have children to ensure that their offspring are considered legitimate and receive ongoing parental support. The State contends, further, that the Legislature could reasonably believe that sanctioning same-sex unions "would diminish society's perception of the link between procreation and child rearing . . . and advance the notion that fathers or mothers . . . are mere surplusage to the functions of procreation and child rearing." The State argues that since same-sex couples cannot conceive a child on their own, state-sanctioned same-sex unions "could be seen by the Legislature to separate further the connection between procreation and parental responsibilities for raising children." Hence, the Legislature is justified, the State concludes, "in using the marriage statutes to send a public message that procreation and child rearing are intertwined."

Do these concerns represent valid public interests that are reasonably furthered by the exclusion of same-sex couples from the benefits and protections that flow from the marital relation? It is beyond dispute that the State has a legitimate and long-standing interest in promoting a permanent commitment between couples for the security of their children. It is equally undeniable that the State's interest has been advanced by extending formal public sanction and protection to the union, or marriage, of those couples considered capable of having children, i.e., men and women. And there is no doubt that the overwhelming majority of births today continue to result from natural conception between one man and one woman.

It is equally undisputed that many opposite-sex couples marry for reasons unrelated to procreation, that some of these couples never intend to have children, and that others are incapable of having children. Therefore, if the purpose of the statutory exclusion of same-sex couples is to "further the link between procreation and child rearing," it is significantly under-inclusive. The law extends the benefits and protections of marriage to many persons with no logical connection to the stated governmental goal.

Furthermore, while accurate statistics are difficult to obtain, there is no dispute that a significant number of children today are actually being raised by same-sex parents, and that increasing numbers of children are being conceived by such parents through a variety of assisted-reproductive techniques (citing estimates that between 1.5 and 5 million lesbian mothers resided with their children in United States between 1989 and 1990, and that thousands of lesbian mothers have chosen motherhood through donor insemination or adoption); (estimating that numbers of children of either gay fathers or lesbian mothers range between six and fourteen million).

Thus, with or without the marriage sanction, the reality today is that increasing numbers of same-sex couples are employing increasingly efficient assisted-reproductive techniques to conceive and raise children. The Vermont Legislature has not only recognized this reality, but has acted affirmatively to remove legal barriers so that same-sex couples may legally adopt and rear the children conceived through such efforts. The State has also acted to expand the domestic relations laws to safeguard the interests of same-sex parents and their children when such couples terminate their domestic relationship. Therefore, to the extent that the State's purpose in licensing civil marriage was, and is, to legitimize children and provide for their security, the statutes plainly exclude many same-sex couples who are no different from opposite-sex couples with respect to these objectives. If anything, the exclusion of same-sex couples from the legal protections incident to marriage exposes their children to the precise risks that the State argues the marriage laws are designed to secure against. In short, the marital exclusion treats persons who are similarly situated for purposes of the law, differently.

The question thus becomes whether the exclusion of a relatively small but significant number of otherwise qualified same-sex couples from the same legal benefits and protections afforded their opposite-sex counterparts contravenes the mandates of Article 7. While the laws relating to marriage have undergone many changes during the last century, largely toward the goal of equalizing the status of husbands and wives, the benefits of marriage have not diminished in value. On the contrary, the benefits and protections incident to a marriage license under Vermont law have never been greater. They include, for example, the right to receive a portion of the estate of a spouse who dies intestate and protection against disinheritance through elective share provisions; preference in being appointed as the personal representative of a spouse who dies intestate; the right to bring a lawsuit for the wrongful death of a spouse; the right to bring an action for loss of consortium; the right to workers' compensation survivor benefits; the right to spousal benefits statutorily guaranteed to public employees, including health, life, disability, and accident insurance; the opportunity to be covered as a spouse under group life insurance policies issued to an employee; the opportunity to be covered as the insured's spouse under an individual health insurance policy; the right to claim an evidentiary privilege for marital communications; homestead rights and protections; the presumption of joint ownership of property and the concomitant right of survivorship; hospital visitation and other rights incident to the medical treatment of a family member; and the right to receive, and the obligation to provide, spousal support, maintenance, and property division in the event of separation or divorce.

While other statutes could be added to this list, the point is clear. The legal benefits and protections flowing from a marriage license are of such significance that any statutory exclusion must necessarily be grounded on public concerns of sufficient weight, cogency, and authority that the justice of the deprivation cannot seriously be questioned. Considered in light of the extreme logical disjunction between the classification and the stated purposes of the law—protecting children and "furthering the link between procreation and child rearing"—the exclusion falls substantially short of this standard. The laudable governmental goal of promoting a commitment between married couples to promote the security of their children and the community as a whole provides no reasonable basis for denying the legal benefits and protections of marriage to same-sex couples, who are no differently situated with respect to this goal than their opposite-sex counterparts.

We hold only that plaintiffs are entitled under Chapter I, Article 7, of the Vermont Constitution to obtain the same benefits and protections afforded by Vermont law to married opposite-sex couples.

Conclusion

The past provides many instances where the law refused to see a human being when it should have. The future may provide instances where the law will be asked to see a human when it should not (noting concerns that genetically engineering humans may threaten very nature of human individuality and identity). The challenge for future generations will be to define what is most essentially human. The extension of the Common Benefits Clause to acknowledge plaintiffs as Vermonters who seek nothing more, nor less, than legal protection and security for their avowed commitment to an intimate and lasting human relationship is simply, when all is said and done, a recognition of our common humanity.

The judgment of the superior court upholding the constitutionality of the Vermont marriage statutes under Chapter I, Article 7 of the Vermont Constitution is reversed. The effect of the Court's decision is suspended, and jurisdiction is retained in this Court, to permit the Legislature to consider and enact legislation consistent with the constitutional mandate described herein.

Case Commentary

Through this decision, the Vermont Supreme Court provided an impetus to the legislature to validate civil unions between persons of the same sex. Their reasoning was based upon the right of homosexuals who maintain permanent relationships to be afforded security through the legal protection granted to married couples. ■

CASE QUESTIONS

1. Do you believe this case was correctly decided?
2. How is it possible to marry someone of the same sex?
3. Are same-sex married couples no different than parents who adopt?

4. Should marriage be based on love and devotion, not the procreation of children?
5. Should all of the rights and privileges granted to married couples be afforded to couples of the same sex?

Federal Government's Policy

The federal government's treatment of homosexuals is inconsistent. Some agencies discriminate, while others do not. The Civil Service Commission was charged with actively implementing the Equal Employment Opportunity Act of 1972. On December 21, 1973, the commission issued a directive in its Civil Service Bulletin to supervisors in the employ of the federal government regarding the treatment of homosexuals. It provided that, with respect to employment, no action should be taken against a person because he or she is a homosexual.

The military has long had a policy of refusing to enlist homosexuals. Early in his tenure as president, Bill Clinton took an opposing viewpoint to the military's rigidness on the exclusion of gays. After being adjudicated in federal court, the ban on gays was lifted to the extent that the military will not inquire into the sexual preference of enlisted persons nor will it discharge someone who is gay on that basis alone. But if the homosexual engages in any overt acts ranging from hand holding to sexual conduct, the homosexual will be discharged from the military.

Professional license requirements often mandate good moral character as a criterion for acceptance. This often barred homosexuals from being admitted to a practice. Over time this obstacle has fallen into disuse because homosexual behavior is not evidence of a person's lack of morality. Furthermore, sexual orientation has nothing to do with the practice of a trade or profession.

Employment Perspective

Wilson Fredericks, who is gay, has just learned he has passed the bar exam. He is given an appointment before members of the character and fitness committee. During the interview, one member asks Wilson about his sexual orientation. Wilson refuses to answer on the grounds of his right to privacy. Has Wilson addressed this matter appropriately? Yes! Wilson's homosexuality is a private matter. The fact that he prefers men to women does not mean he is unethical and, therefore, any less qualified to practice law.

Teaching in Schools

Perhaps the most heated debate is over whether gays and lesbians should be allowed to teach in the public school system and work in day care centers. The fear persists among many that gays and lesbians will indoctrinate the children into the homosexual way of life and possibly persuade children into having homosexual acts with them. First, teachers must submit a plan book detailing their course content for each day. This must parallel the course curriculum. If a teacher substantially deviates from this requirement, appropriate disciplinary measures may be taken. The fact that a homosexual teacher may interject subtle references to the benefits of an alternative lifestyle is a given. However, there is no evidence that these remarks, if made, are enough to change a child's sexual orientation involuntarily. Second, homosexuality is not synonymous with pedophilia. Homosexuals usually engage in relationships with other adults, not little children. Being a homosexual is not indicative of being a pedophile. Within the pedophile constituency exist both homosexual and heterosexual adults. Allowing a homosexual to work in a day care center is no more dangerous for fear of pedophilia than allowing a heterosexual to work there. Pedophilia is a sickness unrelated to sexual orientation.

The important criterion for a teacher or a day care worker is job performance capability. A teacher or day care worker should be dismissed if the person is unfit to teach or unfit to exhibit care and concern, not on the basis of having chosen an alternative lifestyle.

The issue in the following case is whether a not-for-profit organization right of expressive association is compromised by New Jersey law.

Boy Scouts of America v. Dale
530 U.S. 640 (2000)

Chief Justice Rehnquist delivered the opinion of the Court.

Petitioners are the Boy Scouts of America and the Monmouth Council, a division of the Boy Scouts of America (collectively Boy Scouts). The Boy Scouts is a private, not-for-profit organization engaged in instilling its system of values in young people. The Boy Scouts asserts that homosexual conduct is inconsistent with the values it seeks to instill. Respondent is James Dale, a former Eagle Scout whose adult membership in the Boy Scouts was revoked when the Boy Scouts learned that he is an avowed homosexual and gay rights activist. The New Jersey Supreme Court held that New Jersey's public accommodations law requires that the Boy Scouts admit Dale. This case presents the question whether applying New Jersey's public accommodations law in this way violates the Boy Scouts' First Amendment right of expressive association. We hold that it does.

I

James Dale entered scouting in 1978 at the age of eight by joining Monmouth Council's Cub Scout Pack 142. Dale became a Boy Scout in 1981 and remained a Scout until he turned 18. By all accounts, Dale was an exemplary Scout. In 1988, he achieved the rank of Eagle Scout, one of Scouting's highest honors.

Dale applied for adult membership in the Boy Scouts in 1989. The Boy Scouts approved his application for the position of assistant scoutmaster of Troop 73. Around the same time, Dale left home to attend Rutgers University. After arriving at Rutgers, Dale first acknowledged to himself and others that he is gay. He quickly became involved with, and eventually became the copresident of, the Rutgers University Lesbian/Gay Alliance. In 1990, Dale attended a seminar addressing the psychological and health needs of lesbian and gay teenagers. A newspaper covering the event interviewed Dale about his advocacy of homosexual teenagers' need for gay role models. In early July 1990, the newspaper published the interview and Dale's photograph over a caption identifying him as the copresident of the Lesbian/Gay Alliance.

Later that month, Dale received a letter from Monmouth Council Executive James Kay revoking his adult membership. Dale wrote to Kay requesting the reason for Monmouth Council's decision. Kay responded by letter that the Boy Scouts "specifically forbid membership to homosexuals."

In 1992, Dale filed a complaint against the Boy Scouts in the New Jersey Superior Court. The complaint alleged that the Boy Scouts had violated New Jersey's public accommodations statute and its common law by revoking Dale's membership based solely on his sexual orientation. New Jersey's public accommodations statute prohibits, among other things, discrimination on the basis of sexual orientation in places of public accommodation.

The New Jersey Superior Court's Chancery Division granted summary judgment in favor of the Boy Scouts. The court held that New Jersey's public accommodations law was inapplicable because the Boy Scouts was not a place of public accommodation, and that, alternatively, the Boy Scouts is a distinctly private group exempted from coverage under New Jersey's law. The court rejected Dale's common-law claim holding that New Jersey's policy is embodied in the public accommodations law. The court also concluded that the Boy Scouts' position in respect of active homosexuality was clear and held that the First Amendment freedom of expressive association prevented the government from forcing the Boy Scouts to accept Dale as an adult leader.

The New Jersey Superior Court's Appellate Division affirmed the dismissal of Dale's common-law claim, but otherwise reversed and remanded for further proceedings. It held that New Jersey's public accommodations law applied to the Boy Scouts and that the Boy Scouts violated it. The Appellate Division rejected the Boy Scouts' federal constitutional claims.

The New Jersey Supreme Court affirmed the judgment of the Appellate Division. It held that the Boy Scouts was a place of public accommodation subject to the public accommodations law, that the organization was not exempt from the law under any of its express exceptions, and that the Boy Scouts violated the law by revoking Dale's membership based on his avowed homosexuality.

The forced inclusion of an unwanted person in a group infringes the group's freedom of expressive association if the presence of that person affects in a significant way the group's ability to advocate public or private viewpoints. But the freedom of expressive association, like many freedoms, is not absolute. We have held that the freedom could be overridden "by regulations adopted to serve compelling state interests, unrelated to the suppression of ideas, that cannot be achieved through means significantly less restrictive of associational freedoms."

To determine whether a group is protected by the First Amendment's expressive associational right, we must determine whether the group engages in "expressive association." The First Amendment's protection of expressive association is not reserved for advocacy groups. But to come within its ambit, a group must engage in some form of expression, whether it be public or private.

Because this is a First Amendment cas where the ultimate conclusions of law are virtually inseparable from findings of fact, we are obligated to independently review the factual record to ensure that the state court's judgment does not unlawfully intrude on free expression. The record reveals the following. The Boy Scouts is a private, nonprofit organization. According to its mission statement:

"It is the mission of the Boy Scouts of America to serve others by helping to instill values in young people and, in other ways, to prepare them to make ethical choices over their lifetime in achieving their full potential.
"The values we strive to instill are based on those found in the Scout Oath and Law":

Scout Oath
"On my honor I will do my best
To do my duty to God and my country
and to obey the Scout Law;
To help other people at all times;
To keep myself physically strong,
mentally awake, and morally straight."

Scout Law
"A Scout is:
Trustworthy Obedient
Loyal Cheerful
Helpful Thrifty
Friendly Brave
Courteous Clean
Kind Reverent."

Thus, the general mission of the Boy Scouts is clear: "To instill values in young people." *Ibid.* The Boy Scouts seeks to instill these values by having its adult leaders spend time with the youth members, instructing and engaging them in activities like camping, archery, and fishing. During the time spent with the youth members, the scoutmasters and assistant scoutmasters inculcate them with the Boy Scouts' values—both expressly and by example. It seems indisputable that an association that seeks to transmit such a system of values engages in expressive activity.

Given that the Boy Scouts engages in expressive activity, we must determine whether the forced inclusion of Dale as an assistant scoutmaster would significantly affect the Boy Scouts' ability to advocate public or private viewpoints. This inquiry necessarily requires us first to explore, to a limited extent, the nature of the Boy Scouts' view of homosexuality.

The values the Boy Scouts seeks to instill are "based on" those listed in the Scout Oath and Law. App. 184. The Boy Scouts explains that the Scout Oath and Law provide "a positive moral code for living; they are a list of 'do's' rather than 'don'ts.'" The Boy Scouts asserts that homosexual conduct is inconsistent with the values embodied in the Scout Oath and

Law, particularly with the values represented by the terms "morally straight" and "clean."

Obviously, the Scout Oath and Law do not expressly mention sexuality or sexual orientation. And the terms "morally straight" and "clean" are by no means self-defining. Different people would attribute to those terms very different meanings. For example, some people may believe that engaging in homosexual conduct is not at odds with being "morally straight" and "clean." And others may believe that engaging in homosexual conduct is contrary to being "morally straight" and "clean." The Boy Scouts says it falls within the latter category.

We must then determine whether Dale's presence as an assistant scoutmaster would significantly burden the Boy Scouts' desire to not "promote homosexual conduct as a legitimate form of behavior." As we give deference to an association's assertions regarding the nature of its expression, we must also give deference to an association's view of what would impair its expression. That is not to say that an expressive association can erect a shield against antidiscrimination laws simply by asserting that mere acceptance of a member from a particular group would impair its message. But here Dale, by his own admission, is one of a group of gay Scouts who have "become leaders in their community and are open and honest about their sexual orientation." Dale was the copresident of a gay and lesbian organization at college and remains a gay rights activist. Dale's presence in the Boy Scouts would, at the very least, force the organization to send a message, both to the youth members and the world, that the Boy Scouts accepts homosexual conduct as a legitimate form of behavior.

Here, we have found that the Boy Scouts believes that homosexual conduct is inconsistent with the values it seeks to instill in its youth members; it will not "promote homosexual conduct as a legitimate form of behavior." As the presence of GLIB in Boston's St. Patrick's Day parade would have interfered with the parade organizers' choice not to propound a particular point of view, the presence of Dale as an assistant scoutmaster would just as surely interfere with the Boy Scout's choice not to propound a point of view contrary to its beliefs.

The New Jersey Supreme Court determined that the Boy Scouts' ability to disseminate its message was not significantly affected by the forced inclusion of Dale as an assistant scoutmaster because of the following findings:

"Boy Scout members do not associate for the purpose of disseminating the belief that homosexuality is immoral; Boy Scouts discourages its leaders from disseminating *any* views on sexual issues; and Boy Scouts includes sponsors and members who subscribe to different views in respect of homosexuality."

We disagree with the New Jersey Supreme Court's conclusion drawn from these findings.

First, associations do not have to associate for the "purpose" of disseminating a certain message in order to be entitled to the protections of the First Amendment. An association must merely engage in expressive activity that could be impaired in order to be entitled to protection. For example, the purpose of the St. Patrick's Day parade in *Hurley* was not to espouse any views about sexual orientation, but we held that the parade organizers had a right to exclude certain participants nonetheless.

Second, even if the Boy Scouts discourages Scout leaders from disseminating views on sexual issues—a fact that the Boy Scouts disputes with contrary evidence—the First Amendment protects the Boy Scouts' method of expression. If the Boy Scouts wishes Scout leaders to avoid questions of sexuality and teach only by example, this fact does not negate the sincerity of its belief discussed above.

Third, the First Amendment simply does not require that every member of a group agree on every issue in order for the group's policy to be "expressive association." The Boy Scouts takes an official position with respect to homosexual conduct, and that is sufficient for First Amendment purposes. In this same vein, Dale makes much of the claim that the Boy Scouts does not revoke the membership of heterosexual Scout leaders that openly disagree with the Boy Scouts' policy on sexual orientation. But if this is true, it is irrelevant. The presence of an avowed homosexual and gay rights activist in an assistant scoutmaster's uniform sends a distinctly different message from the presence of a heterosexual assistant scoutmaster who is on record as disagreeing with Boy Scouts policy. The Boy Scouts has a First Amendment right to choose to send one message but not the other. The fact that the organization does not trumpet its views from the housetops, or that it tolerates dissent within its ranks, does not mean that its views receive no First Amendment protection.

Having determined that the Boy Scouts is an expressive association and that the forced inclusion of Dale would significantly affect its expression, we inquire whether the application of New Jersey's public accommodations law to require that the Boy Scouts accept Dale as an assistant scoutmaster runs afoul of the Scouts' freedom of expressive association. We conclude that it does.

We are not, as we must not be, guided by our views of whether the Boy Scouts' teachings with respect to homosexual conduct are right or wrong; public or judicial disapproval of a tenet of an organization's expression does not justify the State's effort to compel the organization to accept members where such acceptance would derogate from the organization's expressive message. "While the law is free to promote all sorts of conduct in place of harmful behavior, it is not free to interfere with speech for no better reason than promoting an approved message or discouraging a disfavored one, however enlightened either purpose may strike the government."

The judgment of the New Jersey Supreme Court is reversed, and the cause remanded for further proceedings not inconsistent with this opinion.

Dissent: Justice Stevens

In this case, Boy Scouts of America contends that it teaches the young boys who are Scouts that homosexuality is immoral. Consequently, it argues, it would violate its right to associate to force it to admit homosexuals as members, as doing so would be at odds with its own shared goals and values. This contention, quite plainly, requires us to look at what, exactly, are the values that BSA actually teaches.

BSA's mission statement reads as follows: "It is the mission of the Boy Scouts of America to serve others by helping to instill values in young people and, in other ways, to prepare them to make ethical choices over their lifetime in achieving their full potential." Its federal charter declares its purpose is "to promote, through organization, and cooperation with other agencies, the ability of boys to do things for themselves and others, to train them in scoutcraft, and to teach them patriotism, courage, self-reliance, and kindred values, using the methods which were in common use by Boy Scouts on June 15, 1916."

II

The Court seeks to fill the void by pointing to a statement of "policies and procedures relating to homosexuality and Scouting" signed by BSA's President and Chief Scout Executive in 1978 and addressed to the members of the Executive Committee of the national organization. The letter says that the BSA does "not believe that homosexuality and leadership in Scouting are appropriate." But when the *entire* 1978 letter is read, BSA's position is far more equivocal:

> "4. Q. May an individual who openly declares himself to be a homosexual be employed by the Boy Scouts of America as a professional or non-professional?"

> "A. Boy Scouts of America does not knowingly employ homosexuals as professionals or non-professionals. We are unaware of any present laws which would prohibit this policy".

> "5. Q. Should a professional or non-professional individual who openly declares himself to be a homosexual be terminated?"

> "A. Yes, *in the absence of any law to the contrary.* At the present time we are unaware of any statute or ordinance in the United States which prohibits discrimination against individual's employment upon the basis of homosexuality. *In the event that such a law was applicable, it would be necessary for the Boy*

Scouts of America to obey it, in this case as in Paragraph 4 above. It is our position, however, that homosexuality and professional or non-professional employment in Scouting are not appropriate."

BSA Position
"The Boy Scouts of America has always reflected the expectations that Scouting families have had for the organization.
"We do not believe that homosexuals provide a role model consistent with these expectations. "Accordingly, we do not allow for the registration of avowed homosexuals as members or as leaders of the BSA."

BSA's claim finds no support in our cases. We have recognized "a right to associate for the purpose of engaging in those activities protected by the First Amendment—speech, assembly, petition for the redress of grievances, and the exercise of religion." And we have acknowledged that "when the State interferes with individuals' selection of those with whom they wish to join in a common endeavor, freedom of association . . . may be implicated." But "the right to associate for expressive purposes is not . . . absolute"; rather, "the nature and degree of constitutional protection afforded freedom of association may vary depending on the extent to which . . . the constitutionally protected liberty is at stake in a given case." Indeed, the right to associate does not mean "that in every setting in which individuals exercise some discrimination in choosing associates, their selective process of inclusion and exclusion is protected by the Constitution." For example, we have routinely and easily rejected assertions of this right by expressive organizations with discriminatory membership policies, such as private schools, law firms, and labor organizations. In fact, until today, we have never once found a claimed right to associate in the selection of members to prevail in the face of a State's antidiscrimination law. To the contrary, we have squarely held that a State's antidiscrimination law does not violate a group's right to associate simply because the law conflicts with that group's exclusionary membership policy.

The only apparent explanation for the majority's holding, then, is that homosexuals are simply so different from the rest of society that their presence alone—unlike any other individual's—should be singled out for special First Amendment treatment. Under the majority's reasoning, an openly gay male is irreversibly affixed with the label "homosexual." That label, even though unseen, communicates a message that permits his exclusion wherever he goes. His openness is the sole and sufficient justification for his ostracism. Though unintended, reliance on such a justification is tantamount to a constitutionally prescribed symbol of inferiority. As counsel for the Boy Scouts remarked, Dale "put a banner around his neck when he . . . got himself into the newspaper . . . . He created a reputation. . . . He can't take that banner off. He put it on himself and, indeed, he has continued to put it on himself."

That such prejudices are still prevalent and that they have caused serious and tangible harm to countless members of the class New Jersey seeks to protect are established matters of fact that neither the Boy Scouts nor the Court disputes. That harm can only be aggravated by the creation of a constitutional shield for a policy that is itself the product of a habitual way of thinking about strangers. As Justice Brandeis so wisely advised, "we must be ever on our guard, lest we erect our prejudices into legal principles."

If we would guide by the light of reason, we must let our minds be bold. I respectfully dissent.

Case Commentary
The U.S. Supreme Court held that the right to freedom of expression entitles an association to exclude individuals based on sexual orientation. ∎

CASE QUESTIONS

1. Do you agree with the decision of the Court?
2. Do you believe the dissenting opinion has any validity?
3. Dale acknowledged his homosexuality; some do not. Do you think a screening process should be allowed to discover who is a homosexual?

Comparison to Other Discrimination Victims

Over time, significant inroads have been made by Jews, Catholics, and others with European ancestry. All of them are white males. It is difficult, at times, to determine religion or national origin by someone's demeanor. Intermarriage has also resulted in fewer homogeneous groups. The distinction for women and minorities remains because it cannot be disguised. Racial and gender differences are obvious. Although age, pregnancy, and disabilities are often obvious, sexual orientation may not be so. It can be evidenced through the display of overt acts such as exhibiting feminine mannerisms and speech, cross dressing, hand holding, and exhibiting other characteristics of the opposite sex. For the most part, homosexuality is not readily identifiable unless the individual chooses to speak about it. Many gays and lesbians want their lifestyles to be tolerated to the point where people will not be shocked to learn of their choice, snide remarks and jokes will not be made, and discrimination will not take place. Is this asking too much? No!

Prejudices of society should not have a deleterious effect on the rights of others, who for some particular reason are different because of their sex, race, religion, age, disability, pregnancy, sexual orientation, personality, hobbies, standard of living, social connections, or vices (drinking, smoking, gambling). Tolerance of differences should be preached. In diversity there is strength. Economic livelihood through the deprivation of employment opportunities should not be affected. Job qualifications and performance should rule. All other unrelated suspect classifications should not be considered. It is time for individuals to be judged on the merits of what they do rather than on the personal characteristics they cannot change.

A strong argument has been made to grant homosexuals Title VII protection under gender discrimination because they have the right to work. Equal employment opportunities should not be denied to them, as it is not denied to single and married heterosexuals who have many sex partners. Sexual orientation is a private matter that is not job related. As long as conduct such as hand holding, kissing, touching, and incessantly preaching the virtues of homosexuality is not displayed on the job, an employee's private affinity for members of his or her gender should be tolerated. A gay or lesbian should be held to the same standards as a so-called straight male or female, no more, no less.

Acceptance or Tolerance

Acceptance of gays and lesbians may never take place, but tolerance must. Acceptance means confirming a personal conviction in the person in question. Tolerance means keeping any personal hostility to oneself and refraining from causing harm to the individual because of his or her difference. This applies to race, religion, gender, national origin, age, pregnancy, and disability as well. We cannot delude ourselves into thinking someday everyone will accept everyone else. There have been a lot of "somedays" that have come and gone. Personal prejudices and traditions stand in the way. They have been instilled from generation to generation in family life, the community, the educational system, and the media. Personal prejudices exist on both sides. There are many minorities and people of foreign extraction who despise whites. Many women have hostile feelings toward men. Many claim justification because of past atrocities. Many white males feel resentful because of what they perceive to be favorable treatment given to others.

EMPLOYEE LESSONS

1. Check to see if your state or city affords protection on the basis of sexual orientation.
2. Realize that federal protection under the Civil Rights Act does not encompass sexual orientation.
3. Familiarize yourself with support groups and political organizations advocating employment rights on the basis of sexual orientation.
4. Understand the reasoning behind opponents of sexual orientation protection.
5. Inquire as to whether your employer covers or would consider covering homosexual partners under its health plan.
6. Appreciate that if you are a homosexual with AIDS or a sexually transmitted disease, you will be covered under the Americans with Disabilities Act.
7. Be aware that the military may not stop you from serving because of your sexual orientation.
8. Recognize that your ability to work in a school or day care center should not be compromised because of your sexual orientation.

Summary

The practical solution is to mandate tolerance. Society would like you to love everybody, but society cannot make you. However, society can require you to tolerate everyone. In your mind, if you choose to hate someone, that is up to you. It is subjective, and although society may try to alter your beliefs, society cannot enforce that because it is your state of mind. But any objective manifestation of your state of mind that results in harm to another can be disciplined. Society can judge people's objective actions, and it should where it results in unfair treatment of another. Political correctness is an example of this. People who are politically correct may hate their neighbor, but they do not show it. They keep their prejudices to themselves or amongst people who have the same feelings. Politically correct people do not offend anyone. They tolerate the behavior of others. Whether they accept it or not will never be known. Society may have a higher goal acceptance, but realistically, it should be looking to achieve removal of discrimination from the workplace and everyday life.

Review Questions

1. Is Title VII of the Civil Rights Act applicable to homosexuals?
2. Are there any laws prohibiting discrimination against gays and lesbians?
3. Why is sexual-orientation discrimination not covered under gender discrimination?
4. Is it ethical to discriminate against people having alternative lifestyles?
5. Can a homosexual wear a button saying "Support Gay Rights" at the workplace?
6. Are any homosexuals protected against discrimination?
7. Do family medical leave policies extend to homosexual partners?
8. What is the policy with regard to gays and lesbians in the military?
9. Should gays and lesbians be allowed to teach in the schools?
10. Can a homosexual be denied a professional license because he or she lacks good moral character?
11. Can homosexuals qualify as adoptive parents?
12. Could a homosexual person operate a day care center?
13. Ethically, should homosexuals be protected against discrimination under Title VII?
14. Should transsexuals be entitled to dress as they please?
15. Should a company be allowed to dictate what jewelry its male and female employees may wear?
16. Is it ethical for a school to refuse to hire a homosexual as a teacher?

Case Problems

1. The ERNSR-sponsored proposed charter amendment ultimately appeared on the November 2, 1993 ballot as:

    No special class status may be granted based upon sexual orientation conduct or relationships.

    The City of Cincinnati and its various boards and commissions may not enact, adopt, enforce or administer any ordinance, regulation, rule, or policy that provides that homosexual, lesbian, or bisexual orientation, status, conduct, or relationship constitutes, entitles, or otherwise provides a person with the basis to have any claim of minority or protected status, quota preference, or other preferential treatment. Issue 3 passed by a popular vote of approximately 62 percent in favor and 38 percent opposed.

On November 8, 1993, plaintiffs Equality Foundation, several individual homosexuals (Richard Buchanan, Chad Bush, Edwin Greene, Rita Mathis, and Roger Asterino), and Housing Opportunities Made Equal, Inc. ("H.O.M.E.") (a housing-rights organization) filed a complaint against the city under 42 U.S.C. 1983 that alleged that their constitutional rights had been, or would potentially be, violated by the adoption of Issue 3. The issue is whether homosexuals should be an identifiable class protected from discrimination.

Equality Foundation v. City of Cincinnati, 54 F.3d 261 (6th Cir. 1995)

2. The plaintiffs sought a declaration that ORS 659.165 is invalid. That statute provides that a political subdivision of the state may not enact or enforce any charter provision, ordinance, resolution, or policy granting special rights, privileges, or treatment to any citizen or group of citizens on account of sexual orientation, or enact or enforce any charter provision, ordinance, resolution, or policy that singles out citizens or groups of citizens on account of sexual orientation. A municipality granted special protection for sexual orientation. This action was in direct contravention of a state statute. The issue is whether both laws may coexist. *deParrie v. State*, 893 P.2d 541 (OR. App. 1995)

3. Barbara Renee James, an anatomically male transsexual, alleges sex discrimination under Title VII. From September 1, 1992, through August 19, 1993, James worked in the Ranch Mart hardware store "as a man," using the name "Glenn Wayne James." James did not wear women's clothing, a wig, or makeup.

   James told Bays that she wanted to start dressing and trying to appear as a woman and to use the name "Barbara Renee James." The question is whether a male transsexual may come to work dressed as a female. The employer argued that a transsexual is not a member of a protected class. Does James have any recourse? *James v. Ranch Mart Hardware, Inc.*, 881 F. Supp. 478 (D. Kan. 1995)

4. On April 29, 1997, both houses of the Hawaii legislature passed, upon final reading, House Bill No. 117, proposing an amendment to the Hawaii Constitution (the marriage amendment). "The legislature shall have the power to reserve marriage to opposite-sex couples." The plaintiffs seek a limited scope of relief in the present lawsuit, i.e., access to applications for marriage licenses and the consequent legally recognized marital status. The issue is whether individuals of the same sex should have the right to marry. *Baehr v. Lawrence Mike, Director of the Department of Health, State of Hawaii*, 910 P.2d 112 (Hi 1996)

5. Plaintiff Vernon Jantz has brought the present action under 42 U.S.C. 1983, alleging a violation of his right to equal protection. The plaintiff alleges that he was denied by the defendant, then school principal Cleofas Muci, employment as a public school teacher on the basis of Muci's perception that Jantz had "homosexual tendencies." According to Muci, he hired Silverthorne because he was the best candidate. Silverthorne had student-taught and coached at Wichita North. In Muci's opinion, Silverthorne had done a good job while coaching. Jantz cites the testimony of Sharon Fredin (Muci's secretary) and William Jenkins (the coordinator of social studies at Wichita North). Fredin has acknowledged in her deposition that during the 1987–88 school year she "made the off-hand comment" to Muci that Jantz reminded her of her husband, whom she believed to be a homosexual. Jenkins has testified that when he asked why Jantz was not hired for the new position, Muci told him it was because of Jantz's "homosexual tendencies."

   The issue is whether the denial of employment as a public school teacher to a man because of his sexual tendencies is justified. *Jantz v. Muci*, 759 F. Supp. 1543 (D.Kan. 1991)

HUMAN RESOURCE DILEMMAS

1. Bruce Fisher is a transvestite who works for Northern Bell Phone Company. One day when Bruce exits from the ladies room, he is warned by Red Jenson to use the men's room. Bruce refuses and he is fired. How would you advise Bruce to pursue this matter?

2. In Firefly Fashions, Inc., there is a corporate policy accommodating transvestites and their freedom of choice in restrooms. When Rita Hudson finds herself in the next stall

to Buck Wheaton, she files an invasion of privacy complaint with Firefly, alleging their allowance of anatomic males to use the women's restroom.

3. During an interview with Treetop Publishing, Simon Lefleur asks vice president Hadley Fairbanks if Treetop extends health care coverage to same-sex partners. Hadley replies, "I'm afraid not," while having a startled expression. Simon is not hired. Does Simon have any recourse?

WEB SITE ASSIGNMENT

As an associate, you have been asked to provide commentary regarding the pros and cons for protection against discrimination for homosexuals, transsexuals, and transvestites. Using the following Web sites, determine which states and municipalities afford protection based on affinity orientation. Then uncover the arguments for and against same-sex marriages. Discover the necessary procedure to put forth a constitutional amendment banning same-sex marriages.

www.findlaw.com
www.westbuslaw.com
www.law.cornell.edu/topics/employment_discrimination.html
www.aclu.org/issues/gay/hmgl.html
www.lager.dircon.co.uk
www.ibiblio.org/gaylaw/issue3/mison.html
www.findlaw.com/01topics/36civil/orient.html
www.ll.georgetown.edu/topics/sexual_orientation.cfm
www.eeoc.gov/facts/fs-orientation_parent_marital_political.html
www.lambdalegal.org/cgi-bin/iowa/documents/record?record=122

Chapter 14

Religious Discrimination

Employment Scenario

Arafa Habib is employed in the shipping and receiving department of The Long and the Short of It. He begins work before sunrise. At sunrise during a break and at noon during lunch he prays to Allah. One morning a huge shipment of suits arrives, and Arafa is told to work through his break. He refuses because of his prayer ritual. His supervisor informs Mark Short, copresident of L&S. Mark tells Arafa, in no uncertain terms, that his job comes before his religious practices. Furthermore, Mark stipulates that engaging in religious prayer at the workplace is disruptive. From now on, Arafa must discontinue it. Arafa explains that he is Muslim. Mark is unrelenting. Arafa resigns immediately and files a claim with the EEOC. Arafa stipulates that his accommodation request was reasonable and that L&S discriminated against him because of his religious beliefs. Mark consults with Susan North, L&S's attorney. Susan divides Arafa's request for accommodation into two parts: First, his religious belief requires him to pray at sunrise and noon and, second, he wishes to fulfill his religious practice by praying on the premises. What course of action should Susan recommend?

Chapter Checklist
➤ Become familiar with the religious implications of the First Amendment to the U.S. Constitution.
➤ Understand that employers must reasonably accommodate the religious beliefs of their employees.
➤ Appreciate that religious accommodation may not extend to situations creating an undue burden on the employer.
➤ Recognize that a bona fide occupational qualification exists for religious institutions wishing to hire members of their own faith.
➤ Realize that religious practices cannot compromise food safety, i.e., dreadlocks, long hair, and beards or seniority under collective bargaining agreements.

> *Know that employers generally cannot tell employees where to live.*

> *Learn that employers do not have to permit employees to promote their religious beliefs at the workplace.*

> *Be aware that employers do not have to allow religious services in the workplace.*

> *Be cognizant of the fact that employers do not have to accommodate an employee beyond what the religion itself requires.*

> *Recognize that religious discrimination is one of the suspect classifications under the Civil Rights Act.*

INTRODUCTION

The First Amendment to the U.S. Constitution provides for freedom of religion. It also states that Congress shall not establish a national religion, thus ensuring the right of individuals to engage in whatever religious practices they wish. These practices must not, however, violate other laws such as criminal laws prohibiting sacrificial offerings. The First Amendment applies directly to the federal government and to the states through the Fourteenth Amendment.

While the Constitution protects individuals from governmental infringement, Title VII protects them from employment discrimination. Religious affiliation is one of the classes protected under Title VII from invidious discrimination. Employers may not refuse to hire an individual because he or she is a member of a particular religion.

HUMAN RESOURCE ADVICE

- Decide what religious accommodations to provide for your employees.
- Realize that you cannot discriminate in making an employment decision because of the religion of an applicant or an employee.
- Recognize that food safety is paramount to religious practices involving facial hair or hair length.
- Learn the significance of the First Amendment of the U.S. Constitution for religion.
- Know that religion is a suspect class under Title VII of the Civil Rights Act.
- Understand that you do not have to permit religious services to be conducted at the workplace.
- Be aware that you do not have to allow employees to promote their religious or political beliefs at the workplace.
- Be cognizant of the fact that religious institutions may employ members of their own faith to promote their religion.
- Acknowledge the fact that a person's religion has no bearing on their ability to perform a job.

Employment Perspective

Herman Tuffle, an atheist, is the owner of a bookstore called "The Classics." Shamus O'Neill applies for a position in the bookstore. During the course of the interview, Shamus mentions that one of the priests of his parish saw The Classics' employment advertisement in the local paper. Herman, who never questioned Shamus about his religion, refused to hire him. Shamus, uncertain as to why he was not hired, relates the story to one of his friends. The friend tells him that Herman is a confirmed atheist. Shamus files a claim with the EEOC. Will he win? Yes! As long as Shamus was otherwise qualified for the position, Herman will have no valid defense for refusing to hire him. What if Herman had hired him and then, upon learning of Shamus's religious affiliation, terminated him? The result would be the same.

ACCOMMODATING RELIGIOUS BELIEFS

To require an employer to accommodate an employee's religious beliefs, the employee must first explain to the employer what his or her religious beliefs are and how they are being compromised by the employer because of the task at hand. The employer must acquiesce if such accommodation would not cause the employer undue hardship, compromise the rights of others, or not require more than minimal cost. If the employee resigns or is terminated for failing to perform the job because of religious beliefs, then the question of religious discrimination will be decided on the basis of the criteria of reasonable accommodation.

Many claims of religious discrimination relate to religious observance. Employers have a duty to make reasonable accommodations for the employee as long as it does not present an undue hardship for the employer.

Employment Perspective

John Edwards, a Catholic, is employed as an intern at Bay Ridge Hospital. At times, John must be physically present at the hospital for 36 hours. When this occurs mid-Saturday to Sunday evening, it conflicts with John's religious belief in attending Mass. When John informs the hospital, his plea is ignored. Is the hospital guilty of religious discrimination? Yes! Bay Ridge Hospital could make a reasonable accommodation for John to allow him 1 hour to attend Mass, either on Saturday evening or on Sunday. This provision does not present an undue hardship to the hospital, which could either rearrange his work hours or give him a 1-hour break.

Suppose that the hospital is able to rearrange John's work hours to allow him to have all Saturday evenings off. Some time ago, the Catholic Church permitted its members to attend a service after 4:00 P.M. on Saturdays to fulfill the Sunday obligation. John insists that he must attend Mass on Sunday because that is the way he was raised. He does not accept this Saturday night exception. Has Bay Ridge Hospital made a reasonable accommodation? Yes! After John advised Bay Ridge Hospital that he was a Catholic, it worked out a schedule to permit him to attend Mass on Saturday afternoon or evening, which is acceptable to the Catholic Church. John is being unreasonable in insisting that he be permitted to attend Mass on Sunday. He is asking for an exception on religious grounds that is not required by the religion itself.

The issue in the case that follows is whether a nurse should be terminated for refusing to participate in a life-threatening procedure that results in an abortion because of her religious belief.

Shelton v. University of Medicine & Dentistry of New Jersey

223 F.3d 220 (3rd Cir. 2000)

Scirica, Circuit Judge.

In this employment discrimination case, the issue on appeal is whether a state hospital reasonably accommodated the religious beliefs and practices of a staff nurse who refused to participate in what she believed to be abortions. The District Court held it had, and we agree. We will affirm.

BACKGROUND

Yvonne Shelton worked as a staff nurse in the Labor and Delivery section of the Hospital at the University of Medicine and Dentistry of New Jersey. The Hospital's Labor and Delivery section provides patients with routine vaginal and cesarean-section deliveries. The Labor and Delivery section does not perform elective abortions. On occasion, Labor and Delivery section patients require emergency procedures that terminate their pregnancies. Labor and Delivery section nurses are required to assist in emergency procedures as part of their job responsibilities.

Shelton is a member of the Pentecostal faith; her faith forbids her from participating "directly or indirectly in ending a life." The proscription includes abortions of live fetuses. Shelton claims she notified the Hospital in writing about her religious beliefs when she first joined the Hospital in 1989, and again in 1994. During this time, the Hospital accommodated Shelton's religious beliefs by allowing her to trade assignments with other nurses rather than participate in emergency procedures involving what Shelton considered to be abortions.

Two events precipitated Shelton's termination. In 1994, Shelton refused to treat a patient. According to the Hospital, the patient was pregnant and suffering from a ruptured membrane (which the Hospital describes as a life-threatening condition). Shelton learned the Hospital planned to induce labor by giving the patient oxytocin. Shelton refused to assist or participate.

Shelton maintains that she "refused to participate in a procedure that would end a life."

After the incident, Shelton's supervisor asked her to provide a note from her pastor about her religious beliefs. Instead, Shelton submitted her own note:

Before the foundations of the earth, God called me to be Holy. For this cause I must be obedient to the word of God. From his own mouth he said 'Thou shalt not kill.' Therefore, regardless of the situation, I will not participate directly or indirectly in ending a life. . . .

In November 1995, Shelton refused to treat another emergency patient. This patient—who was "standing in a pool of blood"—was diagnosed with placenta previa. The attending Labor and Delivery section physician determined the situation was life-threatening and ordered an emergency cesarean-section delivery. When Shelton arrived for her shift, she was told to "scrub in" on the procedure. Because the procedure would terminate the pregnancy, Shelton refused to assist or participate. Eventually, another nurse took her place. The Hospital claims Shelton's refusal to assist delayed the emergency procedure for thirty minutes.

Two months later, the Hospital informed Shelton she could no longer work in the Labor and Delivery section because of her refusal to assist in "medical procedures necessary to save the life of the mother and/or child." The Hospital claimed that staffing cuts prevented it from allowing Shelton to continue to trade assignments when situations arose she considered would lead to an abortion. The Hospital believed Shelton's refusals to assist risked patients' safety.

But the Hospital did not terminate Shelton. Instead, it offered her a lateral transfer to a staff nurse position in the Newborn Intensive Care Unit ("Newborn ICU"). The Hospital also invited Shelton to contact its Human Resources Department, which would help her identify other available nursing positions.

Shelton undertook her own investigation of the Newborn ICU position. She claims she spoke with a nurse (whose name she does not remember) in that unit, who said that "extremely compromised" infants who were not expected to survive would be "set aside" and allowed to die. Shelton did not attempt to confirm this information with the Hospital. Nor did she contact the Human Resources Department to investigate other available positions. Shelton claims she believed no other positions would be available.

The Hospital gave Shelton thirty days to accept the position in Newborn ICU, or to apply for another nursing position. Shelton did neither. Instead, on the thirtieth day, she wrote to her supervisor:

. . . The ultimatum given me however, doesn't align with the response I am unctioned to submit. The decision is not ours to make but the Lords'. The Living God is in control of that which concerns my life and job. "Many are the plans in a mans heart but it's Gods plan/purpose that will prevail."

On February 15, 1996, the Hospital terminated Shelton.

DISCUSSION

The Title VII Religious Discrimination Claim

Title VII of the 1964 Civil Rights Act requires employers to make reasonable accommodations for their employees' religious beliefs and practices, unless doing so would result in "undue hardship" to the employer. To establish a prima facie case, the employee must show:

1. she holds a sincere religious belief that conflicts with a job requirement;
2. she informed her employer of the conflict; and
3. she was disciplined for failing to comply with the conflicting requirement.

If the employee establishes a prima facie case, the burden shifts to the employer to show that it made good faith efforts to accommodate, or that the requested accommodation would work an undue hardship.

The District Court held Shelton established a prima facie case. We agree. There is no dispute that Shelton's religious beliefs are sincere, and that the Hospital ultimately terminated Shelton.

In sum, Shelton has not established she would face a religious conflict in the Newborn ICU. The Hospital's offer of a lateral transfer to that unit thus constituted a reasonable accommodation.

In another attempt to accommodate Shelton's religious conflict, the Hospital invited Shelton to meet with its Human Resources Department to discuss other available nursing positions. Once the Hospital initiated discussions with that proposal, Shelton had a duty to cooperate in determining whether the proposal was a reasonable one. By refusing to meet with Human Resources to investigate available positions, Shelton failed to satisfy her duty.

In sum, Shelton's refusal to cooperate in attempting to find an acceptable religious accommodation was unjustified. Her unwillingness to pursue an acceptable alternative nursing position undermines the cooperative approach to religious accommodation issues that Congress intended to foster.

It would seem unremarkable that public protectors such as police and firefighters must be neutral in providing their services. We would include public health care providers among such public protectors. Although we do not interpret Title VII to require a presumption of undue burden, we believe public trust and confidence requires that a public hospital's health care practitioners—with professional ethical obligations to care for the sick and injured—will provide treatment in time of emergency.

Shelton refused the Hospital's efforts to accommodate her religious beliefs and practices. Having done so, she cannot successfully challenge those efforts as legally inadequate.

In sum, Shelton has failed to establish that the Hospital was anything but neutral with respect to religion.

For the reasons stated, we will affirm the judgment of the District Court in favor of University of Medicine.

Case Commentary

The Third Circuit Court concluded that Shelton had refused a transfer that would have accommodated her beliefs. ■

CASE QUESTIONS

1. Do you agree with the reasoning of the Court?
2. Why would Shelton want to remain in a work environment where she would be confronted with an abortion procedure?
3. If those women she refused to treat had died or sustained severe injuries as a result, would she be liable for malpractice?

The issue in this case is whether an employer must make a good faith effort to try to accommodate an employee's Sabbath where the accommodation would place the employer in violation of the collective bargaining agreement.

In the Matter of New York Transit Auth. v. New York, Executive Dep't, Div. of Human Rights

89 N.Y.2d 79 (1996)

Titone, Judge.

Our State's Human Rights Law prohibits employers from discriminating against their employees because of their religiously-motivated Sabbath observance. Recognizing that there may be circumstances in which the mandate of the statute conflicts with the strictures of a collective bargaining agreement, we have previously held that an employer caught in such a conflict is obligated only to make a "good faith" effort to accommodate a Sabbath observing employee.

The present appeal requires us to apply that principle and to delineate some of the contours of what a "good faith" effort is.

Respondent Mary Myers is a practicing Seventh Day Adventist. The tenets of her religion forbid her from engaging in any form of work on the Sabbath, which extends from sundown on Friday to sundown on Saturday. In June of 1988, Myers was hired as a full-time bus operator trainee by the New York City Transit Authority, which operates its buses on a seven-day per week, twenty-four-hour per day basis. From the outset, Myers made it clear to her supervisors that her religious commitments would prevent her from working between sundown on Friday and sundown on Saturday. During her training period and the first week of her regular employment, Myers' Sabbath observance presented little conflict with the demands of her job. However, a problem arose shortly thereafter because she was assigned Wednesdays and Thursdays as her days off, a schedule requiring her regularly to work on her Sabbath. Under the terms of the collective bargaining agreement between the Authority and the Transport Workers Union, the privilege of selecting weekly days off was allocated in accordance with a strict seniority system. Ordinarily, employees were not able to choose weekend days as their days off under this system until they had accumulated as much as five years of seniority.

According to the testimony, Myers spoke with several of her employer's representatives in an effort to obtain some accommodation for her Sabbath observance. Her request for "split" days off was rebuffed on the ground that the practice was forbidden by the collective bargaining agreement. Her request to be permitted to work an early shift on Friday was initially granted, but the Authority denied her request to postpone her Saturday service until after sundown because there were no bus run shifts that began after 5:00 and because respondent had not been trained for other available work. After a few weeks, even her Friday afternoon accommodation was withdrawn. The only solution suggested to Myers was to find another worker in her depot who would be willing to trade shifts with her. However, the Authority did not offer to assist her in locating a willing co-worker. Instead, a supervisor told her that she would have to stand at the door as the bus drivers were leaving and ask each of them if they would consider an exchange of shifts. Having failed to obtain an accommodation or to locate a co-worker who was willing to "swap" shifts, Myers began taking unauthorized days off. Although she called in on several occasions to report her plans to absent herself, she did not think it necessary to call in each time, since her employers knew that she was unwilling to work on her Sabbath. Myers was ultimately discharged on October 10, 1988 because of her unexcused absences.

Following her discharge, Myers filed a complaint with the State Human Rights Division, alleging that the Transit Authority and the Transport Workers Union had violated Executive Law § 296(10)(a). The Division found probable cause to believe that a violation had occurred and directed that a hearing be held. At the hearing, a labor relations specialist for the Authority testified that the Authority had a policy to accommodate Sabbath observers only if it could be accomplished without additional cost, disruption of scheduled runs or risk of labor strife. He acknowledged that a Sabbath observers such as respondent were caught in a Catch-22 situation, since they would have difficulty securing accommodations unless they had seniority and they could not obtain seniority without working on weekends for several years.

On the basis of the evidence adduced at the hearing, the Human Rights Division concluded that both the Authority and the union had violated the statutory provisions prohibiting discrimination against Sabbath observers. The Division found that both parties had failed to make good faith efforts to accommodate respondent, despite a statutorily imposed duty to do so. The Division noted that there had been no efforts by either the Authority or the Union to make arrangements for a voluntary exchange of shifts, that the parties' collective bargaining agreement did not preclude such a voluntary exchange and that the Authority had not shown that accommodating Myers would result in economic hardship or serious labor difficulties. Accordingly, the Authority was directed to reimburse Myers, with interest, for her lost back pay. Additionally, the Authority and the union were each directed to compensate her for her mental anguish, and both were ordered to accommodate her Sabbath observance in the future.

On transfer from the Supreme Court, the Appellate Division annulled the agency's order, concluding that the seniority provisions of the Authority's collective bargaining agreement foreclosed any realistic possibility of accommodating Myers. Since the Division had erroneously ignored the effect of these provisions, the Appellate Division held, its ruling was not supported by substantial evidence. We now reverse the Appellate Division's order insofar as it exonerated the Transit Authority.

Before discussing the Transit Authority's duty, we turn briefly to the application of that statute to the collective bargaining agent, the Transport Workers Union. Executive Law § 296(10)(a), the sole predicate for this Human Rights Law proceeding, makes it unlawful "for any employer to prohibit, prevent or disqualify any person from, or otherwise to discriminate against any person in, obtaining or holding employment, because of his observance of any particular day or days * * * as a Sabbath * * * in accordance with the requirements of his religion." By its terms, the prohibition is aimed only at employers, a class that plainly does not include the Transport Workers Union in this situation.

Respondent Myers' contention that Executive Law § 296(10) should be construed to encompass union conduct is not convincing. "Labor organizations" and "employers" are defined separately in the Human Rights Law and their substantive obligations are also. Separately, this Court held that the State Human Rights Division had not erred in adjudging the employer guilty of violating Executive Law § 296(10)(a) under these circumstances, since the employer had made no efforts to accommodate the complainant's religious observance by at least trying to find an existing day-shift employee willing to exchange shifts for the critical Friday evening Sabbath. In so ruling, the Court was careful to note that an employer is not obligated to assist a Sabbath-observing worker to arrange a voluntary shift swap where "clearly prohibited from doing so by nondiscriminatory provisions of its collective bargaining agreement."

In this connection, we deem it significant that the disputed collectively bargained provision in this case involved a bona fide, nondiscriminatory system for distributing days off according to the public transportation employees' longevity of service. Where there is no prior history of invidious discrimination within the particular business or industry, such seniority systems often operate to promote anti-discriminatory values by providing a neutral and fair method for allocating scarce benefits and privileges among employees. Given the utility of these seniority systems, it would be unreasonable to construe and apply our State Human Rights Law in such a way as to compel employers to challenge a union's rational interpretation of the shop's existing seniority plan. There is no proof, for example, that the Authority's managers had approached the union in an effort either to negotiate an overall plan to accommodate Sabbath observers or to secure a specific waiver of seniority rules for Myers individually.

In the final analysis, what the "good faith" standard requires is that the employer show that it exerted reasonable efforts to accommodate its Sabbath observing employees. This standard does not require proof that an accommodation was actually found, but rather that a genuine search for reasonable alternatives was undertaken. Since there was no showing that such a search was conducted here and since it is undisputed that Myers was discharged only because of her inability to work a normal weekend shift, the finding of the Human Rights Division that the Authority violated § 296(10) was supported by substantial evidence and its determination should be upheld.

Judgment for Myers.

Case Commentary
The New York Court of Appeals held that although an employer does not have to violate a collective bargaining agreement to accommodate an employee's religious accommodation request, it must make a good faith effort to seek alternative means that do not place it in violation of the agreement. ∎

CASE QUESTIONS
1. Do you agree with the Court's decision?
2. Why should the onus be on the employer to seek out alternative ways to accommodate?
3. Are employees asking too much when they apply for a job in an organization that requires weekend work and then stipulate that they cannot work for what amounts to a day and a half on the weekend?

Employment Perspective
Sidney Green, who is Jewish, responds to an advertisement for a position as a manager in a Food King store. During the interview, Sidney is told that the position is for weekend work. Sidney tells Food King that his religion does not permit him to work on Saturdays. Food King says that that is the only position open and the hours cannot be altered with the weekday manager. Sidney argues that the advertisement did not specify weekend work and files a religious discrimination claim with the EEOC. Will he win? No! The advertisement does not have to specify every detail of the job. Sidney asked for an accommodation, and Food King recounted that the accommodation would impose an undue hardship on it because it would leave no managerial coverage for Saturdays. Sidney claims that once Food King learned he was Jewish, it told him that the position was for weekend work, knowing that he would have to decline because of his religious beliefs. If Sidney could prove this, he would win. But there is no evidence that Food King knew Sidney was Jewish when it told him that the opening was for a weekend job. Under the facts as stated, Sidney's claim would most likely fail.

BONA FIDE OCCUPATIONAL QUALIFICATION

Religious organizations are permitted to discriminate as long as the position relates to the promotion of the religion. Religious belief is considered a bona fide occupational qualification.

Employment Perspective

St. John's Lutheran Church has a position available as administrative assistant to the minister. MaryBeth Luciano, a Catholic, is refused the position because she is not Lutheran. Is this religious discrimination? No! St. John's Lutheran may discriminate in favor of its own parishioners because the position is involved with the operation of the Church.

Employment Perspective

Mount Franklin United Methodist Church runs a summer soccer camp for children age 6 through 12. It is open to children of all faiths. Al Kaplan, who is Jewish, applies for the position of soccer instructor. Al played 4 years as starting forward for the state university, and he is well qualified. Mount Franklin refuses to hire Al because he is not Methodist. Al claims that religious beliefs are not a bona fide occupational qualification of a soccer instructor. Who would win? Most likely Al! The determination would hinge upon whether Mount Franklin is trying to promote the Methodist religion to young children through their participation in the soccer camp. Because the camp is open to children of all faiths, this is not the case.

The term *religion* refers to religious practice as well as religious belief. There is often a conflict as to whether a group qualifies as a religion or is secular in nature. One test to apply would be to find whether its members belong to an organized religion in addition to the group.

Employment Perspective

During an interview for a supervisory position in the auto plant of Prestige Motors, Tom Westfield, the applicant, was asked whether he could start to work the evening shift every Tuesday night. Tom responded that on Tuesday nights, he was obligated to attend a Ku Klux Klan meeting but that he would be available every other evening. Tom was rejected because he was unavailable on Tuesday nights. Tom filed a claim with the EEOC under Title VII, claiming that Prestige would not make a reasonable accommodation for his religious practices. Prestige argued that the Ku Klux Klan is not a religious organization. Will Tom win? No! The Ku Klux Klan has been determined to be a political rather than a religious organization and that as such no accommodation has to be made.

Religious practices that require its members to wear certain clothing or to groom themselves in certain ways are protected unless they present an undue hardship to the employer.

Employment Perspective

Morris Gold was hired as a teller for Mid-Island Savings Bank. He wore his yarmulke for work the first day and was told to remove it because it was not proper attire. Because he refused, he was terminated. Morris filed a claim with the EEOC, stating that it was a recognized religious practice of the Jewish faith. Will he win? Yes! The practice of wearing a yarmulke is protected because it does not present an undue hardship to the employer.

The issue in the next case is whether an employer should accommodate an employee's request to wear a religious pin.

Daniels v. City of Arlington, Texas
246 F.3d 500 (5th Cir. 2001)

Wiener, Circuit Judge

FACTS AND PROCEEDINGS

Daniels was an Arlington police officer for thirteen years. While working in a plainclothes position, he began wearing on his shirt a small, gold cross pin ("the pin") as a symbol of his evangelical Christianity. He continued to wear the pin after he was reassigned to a uniformed position, which brought him into conflict with Arlington Police Department General Order No. 205.02(C)(2)(c) ("the no-pins policy"). The General Order, as revised in November 1997, states that: "No button, badge, medal, or similar symbol or item not listed in this General Order will be worn on the uniform shirt unless approved by the Police Chief in writing on an individual basis."

Daniels requested in writing that then-Police Chief David Kunkle make an exception to the policy and allow him to continue wearing the pin on his uniform. Kunkle declined, writing to Daniels that "I have not authorized any non-department related pins and I do not intend to do so." Daniels refused Kunkle's order to remove the pin from his uniform shirt and did not respond to the police chief's offer of accommodations, which included: (1) wearing a cross ring or bracelet instead of the pin; (2) wearing the pin under his uniform shirt or collar; or (3) transferring to a non-uniformed position, where he could continue to wear the pin on his shirt. Daniels declined these alternatives and ultimately was fired for insubordination.

Daniels sued, claiming that the no-pins policy is unconstitutional on its face, and that he had been the victim of intentional religious discrimination. The district court rejected Daniels's claims. It denied his motion for partial summary judgment on the facial challenge to the regulation and granted the city's summary judgment motion, dismissing the remainder of Daniel's claims.

ANALYSIS

Daniels asserts that Arlington Police Department General Order No. 205.02(C)(2)(c), one of many provisions regulating uniform standards for Arlington police, is an invalid prior restraint of speech protected by the First Amendment. He contends that the order is overbroad, impermissibly giving the police chief unfettered discretion to determine what expression may be displayed on an officer's uniform.

This argument is unavailing. As the district court correctly noted, "a police officer's uniform is not a forum for fostering public discourse or expressing one's personal beliefs." The Supreme Court has upheld appropriate restrictions on the First Amendment rights of government employees, specifically including both military and police uniform standards.

We have used two tests to determine whether speech relates to a "legitimate public concern." Daniels fails both. The first, the citizen-employee test, turns on whether a public employee "'speaks not as a citizen upon matters of public concern, but instead as an employee upon matters only of personal interest." The second evaluates the content, form, and context of a given statement. None of these three factors favors Daniels's argument. The content of his speech—symbolic conveyance of his religious beliefs—is intensely personal in nature. Its form melds with the authority symbolized by the police uniform, running the risk that the city may appear to endorse Daniels's religious message. The final factor, context, perhaps weighs most heavily against Daniels. Although the First Amendment protects an individual's right, for example, to shout, "Fire!" while riding a surfboard on the Pacific swells, it offers no such protection to the same speech uttered in a crowded theater. Visibly wearing a cross pin—religious speech that receives great protection in civilian life—takes on an entirely different cast when viewed in the context of a police uniform. Although personal religious conviction—even the honestly held belief that one must announce such conviction to others—obviously is a matter of great concern to many members of the public, in this case it simply is not a matter of "public concern" as that term of art has been used in the constitutional sense.

Because Daniels's communication of his personal religious views through the pin is not speech addressing a "legitimate public concern," the departmental policy does not offend the First Amendment. As recognized in FLRA, the city through its police chief has the right to promote a disciplined, identifiable, and impartial police force by maintaining its police uniform as a symbol of neutral government authority, free from expressions of personal bent or bias. The city's interest in conveying neutral authority through that uniform far outweighs an officer's interest in wearing any non-department–related symbol on it. Daniels's facial challenge to the no-pins policy fails.

Having reviewed de novo the legal claims Daniels asserts on appeal, we affirm the district court's decision to dismiss his case with prejudice on summary judgment.

Our conclusion that Daniels has not justified an exception to the police department's no-pins policy is analogous to the one we reached in rejecting a Muslim prison inmate's complaint after he was denied an exemption from the Texas prison policy requiring all inmates to be clean-shaven, even though wearing a beard was a tenet of his faith. After noting that the grooming policy of the prison has a legitimate penological justification, we found that the policy does not violate Muslim prisoners' free exercise of religion, but "merely removes or reduces one of many avenues by which they may manifest their faith." The same is equally true of Daniels's complaint: The no-pins policy serves a legitimate governmental purpose in the context of uniformed law enforcement personnel, and Daniels undoubtedly has myriad alternative ways to manifest this tenet of his religion.

CASE QUESTIONS

1. Do you agree with the Court's decision?
2. How can the freedoms of religion and speech be balanced against an employer's dress code?

Conclusion

A police department does not violate the First Amendment when it bars officers from adorning their uniforms with individually chosen adornments, even when those decorations include symbols with religious significance. Therefore, the decision of the district court is AFFIRMED for the City of Arlington.

Case Commentary

The Fifth Circuit Court held that in setting a dress code, an employer may prohibit visible religious pins. ∎

3. Why do some people insist on wearing religious paraphernalia, and why do some people find it intolerable?

In the following case, an employee selected the town in which he wished to relocate on the basis of its having an active religious community of his faith. His employer objected because it was too far from the place of employment. The first issue is whether an employee's residence may be determined by an employer. The second is, if so, then may an exception be carried out to accommodate this employee because of his religious beliefs.

Vetter v. Farmland Industries, Inc.
884 F. Supp. 1287 (N.D. Iowa 1995)

Bennett. District Judge.

Vetter and his wife are adherents of the Jewish faith. Although Mrs. Vetter had been born into the Jewish faith, Vetter had converted to Judaism in a ceremony only about four months prior to Vetter's employment with Farmland. Prior to his employment with Farmland, Vetter and his family were living in Muscatine, Iowa, a town without a significant Jewish community. While living in Muscatine, the Vetters travelled approximately thirty miles to attend regular religious services. Farmland is an agricultural products company that sells supplies to the farming community.

Vetter applied for a job with Farmland as a Livestock Production Specialist (LPS) in July of 1992. The principal job duties of an LPS are to work in conjunction with the management of the assigned cooperative to sell Farmland livestock feed and animal health products within the cooperative's trade territory. Vetter had an initial telephone interview with George Gleckler,

Gleckler offered Vetter the job in Webster City by telephone on August 21, 1992. In a follow-up telephone call on August 24, Vetter indicated that they had been looking for housing in Ames, approximately 35 miles from Webster City, because it had an active synagogue. Gleckler responded that Ames might be "a little far," but that he would check on it.

Later that evening, Gleckler called Vetter back to inform him that he had found out that there was a synagogue in Fort Dodge, Iowa. Vetter began working for Farmland on September 1, 1992, by attending a sales meeting in Des Moines, at which he again raised the issue of living in Ames with Gleckler. Gleckler reiterated that he thought that Ames would not be acceptable. Again during meetings in Kansas City on September 9th and 10th, 1992, Vetter discussed the possibility of living in Ames with Terry Allen, Farmland's regional Feed Manager. Allen also indicated that Ames would not be an acceptable place for Vetter to live. Gleckler and Allen suggested that Vetter look further in Webster city and Fort Dodge. The Vetters rejected Fort Dodge after learning that the synagogue there was essentially "inactive," providing services only every few months, and that there was no Jewish community of significant size or activity.

On September 21, 1992, Gleckler told Vetter that he had learned that Vetter was planning to rent housing in Ames. Vetter explained that he had put a small deposit on one residence in Ames. Vetter was therefore terminated effective September 21, 1992. Vetter asserts that he was not given any reason for his termination at the time he was discharged. The employee separation form filled out by Terry Allen has checked as the reason for discharge "other," and in the space provided for explanation "Relocation within trade territory was condition of employment. Employee refused to locate as required."

Juxtaposed to this dispute over the genuineness of Farmland's interest in where Vetter lives is the dispute of the parties over whether Vetter's desire to live in Ames was based on his religious beliefs or merely on personal preference. Vetter has provided the affidavit of Rabbi Stanley Herrnan, who affirms that "living in an active Jewish community with an active synagogue is essential to the sustenance of one's faith as a Jew, so much so it rises to the level of being a niitzvah (Jewish law)." However, Farmland points out that Vetter formerly lived in a community that had no such active Jewish community, and the court observes that a great many Jews in this area of the country do not live in such an "active Jewish community."

Vetter's complaint alleges discrimination on the basis of religion on two theories. First, Vetter alleges that he was subjected to disparate treatment, because other LPSs have been allowed to live either outside of their trade areas or at greater distances from cooperatives that they serve than he would have been if allowed to live in Ames, and further that other LPSs were not terminated, whereas he was, for desiring to live or living outside of their trade areas. Second, Vetter alleges that Farmland refused to make reasonable accommodations to his religious observances or practices by refusing to allow him to live in Ames, or to allow him to live in Webster City while his family lived in Ames. The court will consider whether Farmland is entitled to summary judgment on either of these claims.

Vetter argues that Farmland refused to make reasonable accommodations to his religious beliefs because Farmland refused to consider his suggestion that he maintain a residence for himself in Webster City while his family lived in Ames. Vetter has since argued that he also suggested as a reasonable accommodation that he bear any additional costs of his travel to his trade area that might result if he and his family were to live in Ames. Farmland argues that nothing about Vetter's religion required him to live in Ames, or outside of the trade area, therefore it was under no obligation to provide any accommodation. Farmland has also, at least implicitly, suggested that by pointing out that Fort Dodge had a synagogue and that Vetter could live there, they offered a reasonable accommodation.

Vetter must make the following prima facie showing in support of his claim of failure to accommodate his religion: (1) Vetter has a bona fide belief that compliance with an employment requirement is contrary to his religious faith; (2) Vetter informed Farmland about the conflict; and (3) Vetter asserts that a religious belief is incompatible with a requirement of employment. On this issue: Vetter was a recent convert to Judaism, and his children were endeavoring to pursue religious training in that faith. Thus, the growth of the family's faith during the period in question is uncontradicted. Because Vetter was a recent convert to Judaism, the court finds that his prior conduct in Muscatine

is of little relevance to the question of the sincerity of his belief in a need to live in a Jewish community. To the extent that is relevant, the court finds that Vetter's uncontradicted testimony is that even had Vetter not taken the job with Farmland, they would have attempted to move to the Quad Cities area, because of its active Jewish community. Their evidence, again uncontroverted, is that their plans to move to the Quad Cities for this reason before Vetter was offered the job with Farmland were thwarted by floods in the area. Furthermore, the sincerity of Vetter's belief is reinforced by his conduct of asserting the belief in the face of opposition from his employer, and in his offers to provide for that belief at some personal cost in his offers either to pay for extra travel costs or to live in Webster City while his family lives in Ames. Thus, the court finds as a matter of law that Vetter's religious beliefs in question here were indeed sincerely held. As to the third element, there is no dispute that Vetter was discharged because of noncompliance with the employment requirement that he live within his trade area. Vetter has established at least a genuine issue of material fact in each element of his prima facie case of disparate treatment because of religion and on the question of whether Farmland's proffered legitimate reason for his discharge is pretextual. The court concludes that the elements of a prima facie case of disparate treatment because of religion are as follows: (1) the plaintiff was a member of a protected class because of the plaintiff's religious affiliation or beliefs; (2) the employee informed the employer of his or her religious beliefs; (3) the plaintiff was qualified for the position; (4) despite plaintiff's qualifications, the plaintiff was fired or denied an employment benefit; and (5) similarly situated employees, outside of the plaintiff's protected class were treated differently or there is other evidence giving rise to an inference of discrimination.

Examining these elements in this light the court finds that there is no significant dispute that Vetter was a member of a protected class on the basis of his adherence to the Jewish faith, he informed his employer of his adherence to that faith, he was qualified for the position in which he was employed, and he was fired from that position. Vetter has generated a genuine issue of material fact to go with the final element of his prima facie case because, although he was hired and fired essentially by the same person, there is no presumption that the termination was not discriminatory, because it was only after he was hired that Farmland officials learned of his religious affiliation, and because of evidence of more favorable treatment of similarly situated LPSs who were not members of his faith.

Judgment for Vetter.

Case Commentary

The Northern District of Iowa decided that an employer has no right to determine where its employees live especially if the employees have chosen a community for religious reasons. ■

1. Are you in agreement with the court's decision?
2. Why do you think the employer cared where Vetter lived?

3. Under what circumstances should an employer be able to require a worker to live at or near the job?

Employment Perspective

Mustafa Darey, a Rastafarian, wore his hair in dreadlocks. When he was hired by Faster Food Service, he was told he would have to cut them. He refused. Mustafa filed a claim with the EEOC, citing the wearing of dreadlocks was part of his religion. Faster Food maintained it was unsanitary and in violation of health department regulations. Will Mustafa prevail? It may be possible to accommodate Mustafa by having him enclose his hair in a plastic cap. If Mustafa refuses, then his religious practice will be overridden for public health reasons.

FIRST AMENDMENT PROTECTION

The First Amendment to the U.S. Constitution addresses religion in two respects. First, it prohibits the government from establishing a national religion. Freedom from religious persecution is an important reason why many immigrants came to this country. Permitting people the freedom to choose how, when, and where to worship is an important consideration in this country. Allowing others to discriminate because of religion not only compromises this First Amendment right but also promotes the economic advantages of belonging to one religion. The latter factor violates the Establishment Clause.

The First Amendment also promotes the freedom to associate. If a person chooses to associate socially only with members of his or her own religion, that is a protected choice. Employment, however, is not social; it is economic. It is unfair for an employer to choose its employees on the basis of their religious preference. How is this characteristic job related? It is not. Employers should respect the right of employees to worship as they please on their own time and, if possible, should reasonably accommodate their employees to enable them to do so.

The issue in the following case is whether a religious institution can terminate a homosexual because that individual's lifestyle runs contrary to its core values.

Pedreira v. Kentucky Baptist Homes
186 F. Supp. 2d 757 (W.D. KY 2001)

Simpson III, J.

On October 23, 1998, after approximately seven months of employment, Alicia Pedreira ("Pedreira") was terminated from her position as a Family Specialist at Spring Meadows Children's Home, a facility owned and operated by Kentucky Baptist Homes for Children, Inc. ("KBHC").

The decision to terminate her was made after a photograph taken of her together with her acknowledged "life partner" was displayed at the Kentucky State Fair, and her lesbian lifestyle became known to KBHC. The termination statement she received stated "Alicia Pedreira is being terminated on October 23, 1998, from Kentucky Baptist Homes for Children because her admitted homosexual lifestyle is contrary to Kentucky Baptist Homes for Children core values."

KBHC then issued a public statement with respect to the termination to the effect that "it is important that we stay true to our Christian values. Homosexuality is a lifestyle that would prohibit employment."

KBHC has required that all its employees "exhibit values in their professional conduct and personal lifestyles that are consistent with the Christian mission and purpose of the institution." KBHC also adopted an employment policy which stated that homosexuality is a lifestyle that would prohibit employment with Kentucky Baptist Homes for Children. The Board does not encourage or intend for staff to seek out people within the organization who may live an alternative lifestyle, we will however, act according to Board policy if a situation is brought to our attention.

Pedreira filed this action challenging her termination and the policies adopted by KBHC on the ground that its actions constitute religious discrimination.

A second plaintiff in this action, Karen Vance ("Vance"), is a social worker living in California. She has alleged that she wishes to relocate to Louisville to be closer to her aging parents. She claims that there are employment positions open at KBHC for which she is qualified, but for which she has not applied because she is a lesbian. She has asserted that her application for a position with KBHC would be futile in light of its formal and well-publicized policy prohibiting gays and lesbians from employment. Vance claims that KBHC's hiring policy constitutes religion-based employment discrimination.

Seven individuals, identified in the complaint as Kentucky taxpayers, are also plaintiffs in this action. They claim that government funds provided to KBHC are used to finance staff positions which are filled according to religious tenets, and to provide services designed to instill Christian values and teachings in the children. These plaintiffs contend that state money is thus used for religious purposes, in violation of the United States Constitution.

The Commonwealth of Kentucky has been sued on the ground that it violated the Establishment Clause of the First Amendment by providing government funds to KBHC. There is no dispute that KBHC has contracted with Kentucky and received government funds for the operation of its facilities. KBHC provides services to youth placed in its care as wards of the state.

KBHC contends that its policy against the employment of homosexuals in general, and its treatment of Pedreira in particular, is openly discriminatory with regard to homosexual conduct, but does not constitute religious discrimination, and is therefore not prohibited under either Title VII or the Kentucky Civil Rights Act.

The plaintiffs concede that Title VII does not prohibit employment discrimination on the basis of homosexuality. Homosexuals have not been recognized as a class protected by Title VII. Thus, KBHC's intentional exclusion of homosexuals from employment does not run afoul of Title VII unless it constitutes discrimination on the basis of religion.

Title VII prohibits employers from using an individual's religion as a criterion for discharging or refusing to hire. The courts have found a corollary to this prohibition. Title VII

also precludes an employer from discriminating by utilizing an individual's failure to embrace the *employer's* faith. Pedreira and Vance contend that living a homosexual lifestyle constitutes a failure to embrace KBHC's religious faith or practice. Thus they contend that it is impermissible to base employment decisions upon this lifestyle choice.

The parties agree that KBHC does not require its employees to practice any religion. They are not required to attend religious services nor are they required to be members of or believers in any particular religion or religious group. The plaintiffs contend, however, that KBHC's behavioral requirement, although facially religion-neutral, requires conformity with KBHC's religious beliefs in actual practice. In order for an employee's professional and personal comportment to be acceptable in the eyes of KBHC, it must be "consistent with the Christian mission and purpose of the institution." Thus the plaintiffs argue that a requirement that employees behave in a manner which is consistent with KBHC's religious beliefs constitutes an unconstitutional imposition of KBHC's religion upon them as a condition of employment.

KBHC contends that it does not wish to be viewed as accepting homosexuality, and does not wish to employ homosexual individuals for that reason. KBHC's concern is with the projected persona of its employees which is said to reflect upon the public image of KBHC. KBHC urges that its policy on employee behavior is consistent with its religious values, but stands independent of any form of religious faith or practice.

This is an action brought under statutes that protect the religious freedom of individuals in the workplace. The complaint's second claim for relief contains the conclusory statement that Pedreira was discharged and Vance would not be hired because of their "failure to hold and adhere to KBHC's religious beliefs concerning homosexuality." However, there are no facts alleged which support this contention.

The plaintiffs do not allege that their individual lifestyle choices are premised upon their religious beliefs, or lack thereof. They do not state whether they accept or reject Baptist beliefs in particular, or whether they practice any religion. Rather, they focus on KBHC's so-called "impermissible religious motivation," in an attempt to turn this claim involving non-religious lifestyle choices into one based upon religious discrimination. However, Title VII does not prohibit an employer from having a religious motivation.

While KBHC seeks to employ only persons who adhere to a behavioral code consistent with KBHC's religious mission, the absence of religious requirements leaves their focus on behavior, not religion. KBHC imposes upon its employees a code of conduct which requires consistency with KBHC' s religious beliefs, but not the beliefs themselves.

Pedreira and Vance would place the focus on the underlying reasons for KBHC's policies regarding personal and professional comportment. The religious foundation for KBHC's policies is not relevant to the analysis however because KBHC does not condition employment on the acceptance or practice of its religious beliefs. Employees need not embrace the religion-based moral code which the KBHC espouses in order to comply with the conduct requirement. The code of conduct, although requiring behavior which is consistent with KBHC's values, leaves the religious freedoms of employees and potential employees unfettered. The civil rights statutes protect religious freedom, not personal lifestyle choices. There is no religious discrimination in an employment policy which does not require and does not inhibit the practice of or belief in any faith.

The religious freedoms of the plaintiffs have not been impaired by the conduct requirement of KBHC. Therefore, the claims of Pedreira and Vance for religious discrimination must be dismissed.

Judgment for the Kentucky Baptist Homes.

Case Commentary
The Western District Court of Kentucky ruled that a lesbian's religious beliefs are not infringed by a religious organization's right to discharge her for her affinity orientation. ■

CASE QUESTIONS

1. Do you believe this Court decided the case correctly?
2. Should religious groups be more accepting?

3. Why do homosexuals continue to argue for mainstream religious acceptance?

Religious Harassment

Every suspect classification has a subset for harassment. Religion is no different. Religious harassment has always existed against every religious minority. Jews, Catholics, Buddhists, Hindu, and Muslims, among others, have all experienced it. Since 9/11, religious harassment has been more pronounced against Muslims and other religions of Arab countries. Name-calling, jokes, and pictorials demeaning an employee's religion are all forms of racial harassment that employers have to guard against.

EMPLOYEE LESSONS

1. Familiarize yourself with the protections afforded your religious beliefs by the First Amendment.
2. Be aware that you cannot be discriminated against in employment because of your religion.
3. Be cognizant of the fact that if you choose to live in a certain area because of your religious affiliation, your employer cannot tell you otherwise.
4. Know that an employer must accommodate your religious belief if it is reasonable.
5. Learn that you may not promote your religious and political beliefs in the workplace.
6. Understand that religious institutions have the right to refuse employment to those not of the same faith in positions where knowledge or belief in that religion is necessary.
7. Realize that you cannot conduct a religious service at the workplace.
8. Appreciate that your seniority under a collective bargaining agreement will not be compromised by another employee's request for religious accommodation.
9. Be aware that religious practices can never take precedence over food safety.
10. Know that an employer may never have to grant a request for accommodation if that which is required exceeds what the religion itself requires of its members.

SUMMARY

Employers should not pry into the personal lives of their employees any more than they would like their employees seeking personal information about them or their top executives. If everyone converted to a particular religion, then job performance would not therefore improve. Thus, employers have no right to discriminate because of religion.

Employers need only consider global trade. It would be a foolish thought for an employer to trade only with countries having the same religion as the employer. More so, if an employer establishes a subsidiary overseas or otherwise employs foreign people to work on its behalf, it would be nearly impossible to discriminate on the basis of religion, race, or national origin. Religious discrimination is rendered impracticable in a global environment. The same philosophy should apply domestically. The practice of any form of discrimination weakens the employer by narrowing the pool of qualified candidates available for the job.

REVIEW QUESTIONS

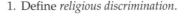

1. Define *religious discrimination*.
2. Explain the significance of the First Amendment with respect to religious discrimination.
3. Define *reasonable accommodation* for religious observances.
4. Can an employer refuse to accommodate an employee's religious belief because it imposes a hardship?
5. How can an employer discern whether a group to which an employee claims membership qualifies as a religion?
6. Can religious belief qualify as a bona fide occupational qualification?
7. May an employee dress in his or her religious garb at work?
8. Must an employer allow the wearing of a button saying "Stop Abortion Now"?
9. Is religious grooming an acceptable practice in the workplace?
10. Should religious beliefs be accorded reasonable accommodation in the workplace?
11. Should an employer be allowed to dictate where an employee lives in regard to his or her proximity to the workplace?
12. Should employees be allowed to express their religious beliefs through the wearing of buttons at the workplace?

CASE PROBLEMS

1. Ms. Bernstein began working at OPRF in 1982 as a school psychologist. On January 30, 1991, she received an anti–Semitic hate letter at her home that referenced administration and employees at OPRF, leading her to believe that it had been written by a fellow OPRF employee. Ms. Bernstein alleges in her complaint that OPRF, through its agent Mr. Offerman, conducted an "intentionally ineffective and/or negligently indifferent inquiry into the incident."

   Neither the letter, nor a copy thereof, was included in the record. However, Ms. Bernstein asserts that the letter contained "swastikas and threats along religious lines," characterizations OPRF does not refute.

   After complaining about the inadequate investigation, Ms. Bernstein asserts, OPRF began to treat her unfavorably. The issue is whether an employer is guilty of religious discrimination for adversely affecting a worker's employment by failing to investigate an anti–Semitic hate letter. *Bernstein v. Board of Ed*, 203 F.3d 1056 (7th Cir. 1999)

2. In late July 1990, Wilson, a Roman Catholic, made a religious vow that she would wear an antiabortion button "until there was an end to abortion or until she could no longer fight the fight." The button was 2 inches in diameter and showed a color photograph of an 18- to 20-week-old fetus. The button also contained the phrases "Stop Abortion" and "They're Forgetting Someone."

   Wilson began wearing the button to work in August 1990. Another information specialist asked Wilson not to wear the button to a class she was teaching. Wilson explained her religious vow and refused to stop wearing the button. The button caused disruptions at work. Employees gathered to talk about the button. U.S. West identified Wilson's wearing of the button as a "time robbing" problem. She cited religious discrimination, claiming that she was not reasonably accommodated. What result? *Wilson v. U.S. West Communications*, 58 F.3d 1337 (8th Cir. 1995)

3. The facts as found show that Mary E. Schumaker, a member of the United Pentecostal Church, was employed by the district as an interpreter and tutor for deaf students. Schumaker would neither take God's name in vain nor use everyday swear words. She interpreted the line in *Gone with the Wind*, "Frankly my dear, I don't give a damn," as "Frankly, I don't care."

The district board then adopted the committee's guidelines, including the requirement of literal word-for-word interpretation to the deaf students. Because she would not work at the district's high school under the new guidelines, she was terminated. What was the result? *Sedalia School Dist. v. Commission on Human Rights*, 843 S.W.2d 928 (Mo.App. W.D. 1992)

HUMAN RESOURCE DILEMMAS

1. In the law firm of Chris, Mike, Madden & Herman (MM&H), a request has been filed by two Sikhs to wear turbans. Although MM&H's dress code does not speak to this issue, MM7H decide to prohibit this attire. How would you advise the Sikhs to proceed?

2. At Prestige Motors, Muslim employees request to pray on their personal rugs on the factory floor during breaks. Prestige states this is disruptive to the work environment. Instead, Prestige assigns them space in the cafeteria. Coworkers complain that their annunciation of their prayers is disrupting their ability to converse during lunch. How would you advise Prestige to proceed?

3. In the Hillsdale Savings Bank, a Menorah and a Christmas tree are displayed. Maria McDougal, a teller, brings a small nativity scene for display. The bank manager refuses to display it for fear of offending non–Christians. After Maria writes to the bank headquarters, she is terminated. How would you advise her to proceed?

WEB SITE ASSIGNMENT

Using the Web, locate different situations where an individual has requested an accommodation because of religious beliefs.

www.eeoc.gov/facts/fs-relig.html
www.findlaw.com
www.chicagolegalnet.com/religion.htm
hydra.gsa.gov/eeo/newpage110.htm
www.multifaithnet.org/religdiscrim/reports.htm
www.westbuslaw.com
www.hrlawinfo.com/lawguide/Discrimination/religiousdiscriminaton.asp
www.usdoj.gov/crt/religdisc/religdisc.html
www.eeoc.gov/types/religion.html
www.business-humanrights.org/Categories/Issues/Discrimination/
Religiousdiscrimination

National Origin Discrimination

Employment Scenario

Faruq Salio and Mohammed Khad, both Pakistani immigrants, apply for a job as sales associates at The Long and the Short of It (L&S) men's clothing store. Both have 3 years' experience in the importation and sale of women's clothing. During an interview with Faruq and Mohammad, Tom Long discovers that their 3 years of experience is in women's clothing. Tom explains to the candidates that L&S is looking for experience in the sale of men's clothing. Faruq and Mohammed state that the skills are similar. Tom begs to differ. Tom explains that he has been in the business for 25 years, so he knows what is best for L&S. Faruq and Mohammed leave, feeling disgruntled. Tom brags to his partner, Mark, about how easily he got rid of those "towel heads." Mark agrees and tells Tom that that is why Tom is such a valuable partner. Meanwhile, Faruq asks his neighbor, Jim Byrnes, to visit L&S the next day and request an interview. As a favor, Jim does as Faruq requests. Jim is hired on the spot although he has no sales experience. Tom Long assures Jim that L&S will train him for the sales associate position. When they learn about this, Faruq and Mohammed file a claim with the EEOC. Upon being apprised of this Susan North, Esq., is livid. She is adamant about impressing upon Tom and Mark the fact that this is the twenty-first century—no ethnic discrimination is allowed. Tom and Mark argue that this is their business; why can't they choose to hire those individuals who fit the image L&S is seeking to project? Does their argument have any merit?

Chapter Checklist
➤ Define national origin.
➤ Know what rights to employment are afforded to resident aliens.
➤ Learn that discrimination against an applicant or employee because of his or her spouse's national origin is a violation of Title VII.
➤ Appreciate that discrimination against people because of the national origin of their surname is impermissible.
➤ Be aware of the documentation required to work in this country.

➤ *Understand that national origin is a suspect class covered under Title VII of the Civil Rights Act.*

➤ *Be apprised of the purpose of the Immigration Reform and Control Act.*

➤ *Be familiar with the number of employees required for the application of each act.*

➤ *Recognize that the Immigration Reform and Control Act applies to all workers employed in the United States, but it has no application to American workers employed abroad.*

➤ *Realize what is required to bring a disparate treatment case for national origin discrimination.*

INTRODUCTION

Individuals are protected from discrimination based on national origin under Title VII of the Civil Rights Act and the Immigration Reform and Control Act of 1986. National origin refers to a person's roots, that is, the country in which the person or the person's ancestors were born. The 4-step test for national origin discrimination is as follows:

1. The employee belongs to the protected class.
2. The employee wanted to retain or obtain the position.
3. The employee was terminated or the applicant was refused employment.
4. Termination or refusal to hire occurred because of the employee's or applicant's national origin.

HUMAN RESOURCE ADVICE

- Treat all applicants and employees the same regardless of their national origin.
- Know what employment rights are given to resident aliens.
- Guard against employing illegal aliens.
- Learn what documentation is required before hiring aliens.
- Do not advocate or tolerate ethnic harassment in the workplace.
- Understand that a person's surname, spouse's national origin, and affiliation with an ethnic school or association should not be considered in any employment decision.
- Develop an expertise in the Immigration Reform and Control Act.
- Appreciate why the Civil Rights Act includes national origin as a suspect class.
- Refrain from asking candidates for employment in which country they were born.
- Recognize that Title VII and the Immigration Reform and Control Act do not apply to Americans working outside the United States.

Employment Perspective

Manolo Fuentes is Spanish American; his ancestors came from Spain. When Manolo applies for a position as a stockbroker with Bull and Bear after graduating at the top of his university class, he is offered a job in the mailroom. When he questions this offer, a manager from Bull and Bear tells him that "this is where you

Puerto Ricans belong." Manolo corrects Bull and Bear about his heritage, but the manager retorts, "You are all the same." Manolo argues that it should not matter whether he is from Spain, Puerto Rico, Latin America, or Mexico and that he should be judged on the basis of his qualifications, not regional or ethnic stereotypes. Will Manolo win? Yes! Offering a person a low-level position solely because he or she is from Spain, Puerto Rico, Latin America, or Mexico is in violation of Title VII's prohibition against national origin discrimination.

Not only is discrimination against a person for his or her own national origin prohibited, but the issue can also be raised by a person who is discriminated against because of:

1. his or her spouse's national origin;
2. membership in an association of a particular national origin;
3. attendance at a school or religious institution identified with people of a specific national origin; or
4. the association of his or her name with persons of a particular national origin.

The Immigration Reform and Control Act (IRCA) requires that employers discern whether their employees are citizens or immigrants. If they are immigrants, the employer must verify the documentation of the employee to determine whether he or she has legal immigration status.

IRCA requires employers to examine genuine documentation of all employees hired for proof of identity and right to work. The employer must attest to this under penalty of perjury on Form I-9. The Illegal Immigration Reform and Immigrant Responsibility Act (IIRIRA) of 1996 lists the acceptable forms of identification and work authorization. The following are acceptable for identity and right to work: U.S. passport, foreign passport with I-551 stamp, permanent resident card (green card), temporary resident card, or employment authorization card. Documents that may be used for identification only include driver's license, school ID with photo, voter registration card, and a hospital record or school report card for minors. Documents that prove the authorization to work include Social Security card, birth certificate, and U.S. citizen ID card. These lists are representative, not all-inclusive.

English-Only Rule

Employers can stipulate an English-only rule, but if they are challenged, the employer must offer a reason for this requirement, such as communication with customers and coworkers.

The issue in the case that follows is whether an employee can be discharged for speaking Spanish in the workplace.

Rosario v. Cacace
767 A.2d 1023 (NJ 2001)

Kestin, J.

The gravamen of plaintiff's complaint was that she was discharged for speaking Spanish in the workplace and that the action taken on that basis was in contravention of protections afforded her under the Law Against Discrimination (LAD). She specifically posits the "national origin" feature of

N.J.S.A. 10:5–12 as the basis of her claim, but the pleading also implicates the protection against discrimination on account of "ancestry".

Defendant Cacace is a urologist, and defendant DeSantis is his office manager. Plaintiff, born in New Jersey of Puerto

Rican ancestry, was hired in late June 1997 as a secretary/medical assistant. She was discharged in early August of the same year. One qualification for the job was fluency in Spanish because most of Cacace's patients were Spanish-speaking. Plaintiff is bilingual in Spanish and English. Another bilingual medical assistant, Bertha Aranzazu, was also employed in the office. Cacace speaks English and Spanish as well, as does his wife who also worked in the office and is of Hispanic origin. DeSantis was the only employee who was not proficient in both languages; she spoke and understood English only.

Plaintiff's duties included translating for DeSantis in dealing with Hispanic patients and assisting Cacace in setting up the treatment rooms. On a job evaluation form prepared by DeSantis on July 21, 1997, for the school that had referred plaintiff, plaintiff was rated "good" in thirty-two areas and "fair" in three areas; all other areas on the form were marked "N/A". Additionally, DeSantis wrote that plaintiff was a "fast learner".

In her certification in opposition to the motion for summary judgment, plaintiff characterized DeSantis's treatment of her as follows:

During my employment at least once a week I was told on many occasions by Defendant Marge DeSantis not to speak Spanish on the job and on occasion not even speak Spanish to patients. One occasion, Defendant Marge DeSantis told me and another employee "I am going to let one of you go because there is too much chitchat in Spanish I don't understand." It is a common custom among people of Spanish national origin to speak Spanish to each other. Bilinguals even combine English with Spanish. It just happens. I have always habitually done this and to this day I still do it and no employer I have ever worked for to this day has ever complained except the above Defendant.

Plaintiff further certified that, on or about August 5, 1997, DeSantis fired plaintiff, telling her, "I'm sorry that I have to let you go like this because you are a nice girl and a quick learner but I cannot have you speaking Spanish in my office."

In her deposition, plaintiff recounted specific incidents of DeSantis's pique at her use of Spanish. All three of the staff worked in the same room. DeSantis would hear plaintiff and Aranzazu conversing in Spanish and "she would flip[,]" once saying "I am going to have to get rid of one of you. There's no reason for you, you know, to be talking Spanish." Plaintiff testified that DeSantis's objections were "constant." Plaintiff elaborated:

She would reprimand us. Sometimes we would do it unconsciously. You're talking to somebody and then they ask you something in Spanish so you answer in Spanish. It is just unconscious, and she would quickly pick up and we would go back to English. It's like a Spanish thing. Any little thing she would bark at you.

On one occasion DeSantis told plaintiff and Aranzazu, "This is America, you got to speak English, you don't have to be talking in Spanish. I am going to have to get rid of one of you. . . . "

Plaintiff's and Aranzazu's duties required that they share information with each other, which they often did in Spanish. Plaintiff conceded that it was possible that DeSantis thought they were talking about her, but DeSantis never said so. Plaintiff insisted that her occasional Spanish-speaking never affected her job duties and that she was always willing to let DeSantis know what she was saying.

DeSantis would often instruct plaintiff to talk to patients in Spanish, as was her regular job duty, and on those occasions DeSantis would not reprimand plaintiff for speaking Spanish. DeSantis seemed to object only when she did not know what was being talked about or when the exchange did not directly relate to instructions she had given.

During my employment at Dr. Cacace's office, Plaintiff, Gisela Rosario, and I were continually barred from speaking Spanish and continually harassed and threatened with the termination of our employment by our superior, Defendant Marge DeSantis, for speaking Spanish in the office in discrimination to my national origin. The office was filled with Spanish patients and other Spanish workers. On one occasion Defendant Marge DeSantis specifically told Plaintiff, Gisela Rosario, and me, "If you keep talking Spanish the first to initiate will have to go. I already had enough Spanish with the patients to be listening to both of you."

3. Plaintiff Gisela Rosario was terminated from her job and was replaced by a non Spanish speaking woman.

After Cacace was served with plaintiff's suit, Cacace's wife fired Aranzazu.

In his certification, Cacace discussed the reasons for plaintiff's termination:

Based on her lack of performance, Rosario was terminated by Marge on or about August 1, 1997.

Rosario was not terminated by my office because of her national origin. In fact, she was hired because she spoke Spanish.

This is a case that arises out of a dispute between an employer or the manager and the employee, and I do not see any basis . . . on which a jury could find, rationally, that there [was] discrimination in the firing. And since the doctor has a policy of hiring Spanish speaking people, there is no way a rational fact finder could find any discrimination in this case.

So, for that reason I have to grant the Motion for Summary Judgment. And the same thing is true with respect to Ms. DeSantis. She is not liable. She hasn't done anything legally wrong. Under the law an employee at will can be fired for no good reason. As long as it doesn't violate the law, the firing is proper.

A plaintiff who could prove that an English-only or English-mainly rule was used as a surrogate for discrimination on the basis of national origin, ancestry, or any other prohibited grounds, would qualify for relief under the LAD. But, evaluating the facts as a whole, this plaintiff has made no such showing, even only on the prima facie basis required to survive the motion for summary judgment.

Plaintiff's claims of unlawful discrimination implicate theories of disparate treatment and disparate impact, as well as hostile work environment. We do not regard the trial court's omission to analyze each theory separately to have been erroneous, for the LAD contains no per se rule that the use of one's own commonly spoken language is protected by the statute's national origin or ancestry provisions. We view the matter as simply involving a two-part employer's rule regarding the use of languages in the workplace, one element addressing the use of Spanish with patients who required such assistance and the other mandating the use of English in all other circumstances, including communications among co-workers.

On facts very similar to those at issue here, i.e., involving an essentially identical workplace rule and a native-born plaintiff for whom Spanish and English were both primary languages, the court in *Gloor* articulated what has become the majority judicial rule on the federal level that the protection contended for does not exist under federal law, i.e., Title VII, the Equal Employment Opportunity Act. With regard to considerations of discriminatory treatment, the court opined:

No authority cited to us gives a person a right to speak any particular language while at work; unless imposed by statute, the rules of the workplace are made by collective bargaining or, in its absence, by the employer. An employer's failure to forbid employees to speak English does not grant them a privilege. The refusal to hire applicants who cannot speak English might be discriminatory if the jobs they seek can be performed without knowledge of that language, but the obverse is not correct: if the employer engages a bilingual person, that person is granted neither right nor privilege by the statute to use the language of his personal preference. Mr. Garcia was bilingual. Off the job, when he spoke one language or another, he exercised a preference. He was hired by *Gloor* precisely because he was bilingual, and, apart from the contested rule, his preference in language was restricted to some extent by the nature of his employment. On the job, in addressing English-speaking customers, he was obliged to use English; in serving Spanish-speaking patrons, he was

required to speak Spanish. The English-only rule went a step further and restricted his preference while he was on the job and not serving a customer.

Given the uncontested facts, it is of no moment whether a rational fact finder could conclude that plaintiff was discharged simply because she spoke Spanish in the workplace in ways that contravened the employer's rule, for a discharge on that basis alone does not violate the LAD. Plaintiff's allegation ignores other patent facts: that the non-Spanish-speaking supervisory employee established a rule that, except where necessary to assist patients, only English be spoken so that all persons in the office, primarily she herself, could readily understand what was being said by any others; and that plaintiff may have been discharged for violating that rule. If we were managing such an operation, we might devise a different rule, but the one chosen by this supervisor cannot, by itself, be seen as a violation of law. There is no evidence in this record that the English-mainly requirement was a proxy for discrimination on the basis of national origin or ancestry or any other unlawful ground.

We note finally that plaintiff has also asserted a non-LAD claim, the independent tort of intentional infliction of emotional distress. That claim, however, is based on the very same allegations of conduct asserted to constitute disparate treatment under the LAD. As plaintiff is unable to make a prima facie case for unlawful discrimination, she is perforce unable to prevail on her claim for emotional distress damages based upon the same conduct.

We hold, accordingly, that plaintiff has not made a prima facie showing of the elements necessary to establish a potential for success in proving her case of discrimination based on national origin or ancestry sufficient to survive the motion for summary judgment. A discharge for speaking another language in the face of an employer's English-only or English-mainly rule is not by itself a violation of the Law Against Discrimination.

Affirmed for Cacace.

Case Commentary
The New Jersey Supreme Court decided that an employer who has an English-only speaking rule is not guilty of national origin discrimination for that fact alone. ∎

CASE QUESTIONS

1. Are you in agreement with the Court's decision?
2. Should English be declared the official language by constitutional amendment?

3. Why is it that you see conflicting decisions over this issue in different parts of the country?

Ethnic Harassment

Joke telling, disparaging remarks, and slang epithets about people's ethnic origins may create a hostile work environment if they are severe and pervasive.

The issue in the next case is whether the ethnic harassment suffered by the plaintiffs constituted infliction of emotional distress.

Perez v. Pavex Corporation

2002 U.S. Dist. LEXIS 21871 (Fla.)

Whittemore, United States District Judge.

INTRODUCTION

On January 11, 2001, Plaintiffs M. Perez and McKenna filed a Complaint against Defendant Pavex Corporation, alleging discrimination in violation of Title VII of the Civil Rights Act of 1964 and the Florida Civil Rights Act. Plaintiff M. Perez alleged that he was terminated and subjected to harassment because he is Hispanic. Plaintiff McKenna alleged that she was harassed and selected for lay-off because of her relationship with M. Perez.

On March 8, 2001, Plaintiffs Perez and McKenna amended the Complaint to add twenty-five additional Plaintiffs. (Three Plaintiffs are former employees asserting claims based on their Hispanic race. Twelve Plaintiffs are former employees asserting claims based on their race, African American. Five Plaintiffs are former white employees. Seven Hispanic non-employee Plaintiffs claim to work for trucking companies which delivered materials to Defendant's job sites).

Plaintiffs seek to add state tort claims of (1) intentional infliction of emotional distress; (2) negligent hiring, supervision and retention; (3) intentional interference with an advantageous business relationship; (4) battery; and (5) assault. Defendant opposes Plaintiffs' request for leave on the grounds that (1) Plaintiffs' state tort claims were brought after undue delay and will cause undue prejudice to Defendant and (2) Plaintiffs' state tort claims are futile.

Intentional Infliction of Emotional Distress

In order to state a cause of action for intentional infliction of emotional distress under Florida law, the plaintiff must plead the following elements: (1) deliberate or reckless infliction of mental suffering; (2) outrageous conduct; (3) the complained of conduct must have caused the suffering; and (4) the suffering must have been severe. Conduct is considered "outrageous", when it is "so outrageous in character, and so extreme in degree, as to go beyond all possible bounds of decency, and to be regarded as atrocious, and utterly intolerable in a civilized community."

"It is manifest that the subjective response of the person who is the target of the actor's conduct is not to control the question of whether the tort occurred. Rather, an evaluation of the claimed misconduct must be undertaken to determine as objectively as is possible, whether it is atrocious, and utterly intolerable in a civilized community." Whether conduct is sufficiently outrageous to support a cause of action for intentional infliction of emotional distress is a question of law.

Here, Plaintiffs allege that they were the subject of relentless verbal abuse, curses, ridicule, racial epithets and racial slurs, as well as threats of violence and physical abuse. In determining whether Plaintiffs' claims are futile, the Court cannot conclude that Plaintiffs' allegations of repeated verbal abuse, threats of violence, and physical injury are insufficient as a matter of law. Accordingly, Plaintiffs' request to add claims of intentional infliction of emotional distress are granted. (Nearly all of the Plaintiffs allege that they suffered verbal abuse and racial slurs, such as "s**c," "f***ing Cuban," "Cuban thief," "n***ers," "f***ing n****rs," and "stupid m****rf***ing Cuban.") Some Plaintiffs allege that they suffered abuse or hostility because of their relationships or associations with African American or Hispanic co-workers. Non-employee Plaintiffs contend that on several occasions they were not allowed to complete their assigned deliveries. Nearly all Plaintiffs allege that they suffered numerous acts of discrimination, such as work reassignments, demeaning tasks, restrictions on use of office restroom, reduction in work hours, refusal to report accidents, and mandatory drug tests which were allegedly fixed to result in a positive showing of drugs, as well as other discriminatory acts. Other Plaintiffs allege threats of violence, physical abuse and injury. Plaintiff N. Perez alleges that he was beaten by the foreman until he was unconscious, suffering permanent scarring and nerve damage. Plaintiff Abrams alleges that his supervisor "picked up the lute], swung it at him, a frail man of 62, and struck him in the back." Plaintiff Lluberes contends that during one of his deliveries the foreman picked up a shovel and threatened to hit him over the head. This altercation allegedly caused Lluberes to suffer a stroke, resulting in permanent damage to his right eye. Plaintiff Flournoy alleges supervisors threw their hats and tools at him to humiliate him.

Negligent Hiring, Supervision and Retention

All of the Plaintiffs seek leave to bring claims for negligent hiring, supervision and retention.

Here, Plaintiffs allege damages as a result of Defendant's failure to maintain a workplace free of "racial and ethnic discrimination, harassment and retaliation, assault, battery, intentional interference with advantageous relationships, and intentional infliction of emotional distress." As Plaintiffs N. Perez and Abrams meet Florida's impact rule and allege injuries resulting from a tort recognized under common law (battery), their claims are legally sufficient. Further, N. Perez and Abrams's negligent retention claims are not barred by Florida's Workers' Compensation law. Accordingly, these proposed claims are not futile and Plaintiffs N. Perez and

Abrams's request for leave to add negligent supervision and retention claims are granted.

Tortious Interference with an Advantageous Business Relationship

Non-employee Plaintiffs Abrahantes, Lluberes, Martinez, D. Perez, I. Perez, N. Perez, R. Perez and Vazquez-Falero seek leave to bring claims for tortious interference with an advantageous business relationship ("tortious interference claim"). Under Florida law, the elements of a claim of tortious interference with a business relationship are: (1) the existence of a business relationship that affords the plaintiff existing or prospective legal rights; (2) defendant's knowledge of the business relationship; (3) defendant's intentional and unjustified interference with the relationship; and (4) damage to the plaintiff.

In order to succeed on a tortious interference claim, the "alleged business relationship must afford the plaintiff existing or prospective legal or contractual rights." Here, all eight non-employee Plaintiffs allege that they were regularly assigned, via their contracts with certain trucking companies, to make deliveries to Defendant's work sites. Plaintiffs

Abrahantes, N. Perez, Vazquez-Falero, Martinez, and R. Perez allege that their deliveries were intentionally interfered with by Defendant. Plaintiffs Martinez, D. Perez, I. Perez, and R. Perez allege that they ceased working on Defendant's jobs, or were told that they would no longer be permitted to work on Defendant's work sites.

Accordingly, it is **ORDERED and ADJUDGED** that: Plaintiffs' Motion to add claims for intentional infliction of emotional distress is **GRANTED**.

Plaintiffs' N. Perez and Abrams's Motion to add claims for negligent hiring, supervision and retention is **GRANTED**.

Plaintiffs Abrahantes, Martinez, D. Perez, I. Perez, N. Perez, R. Perez and Vazquez-Falero's Motion to add claims for tortious interference with advantageous business relationships is **GRANTED**.

Case Commentary

The Florida District Court held that plaintiffs had made a prima facie case to show that Pavex Corporation was guilty of national origin discrimination, inflicting emotional distress, tortuously interfering with business relationships, and negligent supervision. ■

CASE QUESTIONS

1. Would Pavex have to have had notice of the harassment to hold it liable?
2. Do you believe the plaintiffs will succeed?

3. Are the language and actions severe and pervasive?

The questions presented in the following case are whether the plaintiff's claim of national origin harassment was severe and pervasive, and whether his claims for discrimination as well as harassment were time barred.

Filipovic v. K & R Express Systems, Inc.
176 F.3d 390 (7th Cir. 1999)

Coffey, Circuit Judge.

On July 19, 1993, the plaintiff-appellant, Momcilo Filipovic ("Filipovic"), filed charges with the Equal Employment Opportunity Commission ("EEOC"), alleging that his employer, the defendant-appellee K&R Express Systems, Inc., ("K&R") discriminated against him because of his Yugoslavian origin and in retaliation for prior complaints of discrimination. Specifically, Filipovic contended that he was denied a promotion, was "harassed and subjected to derogatory language," and was given written warnings for various rule infractions. On December 20, 1993, Filipovic filed additional charges with the EEOC, this time complaining of retaliation based on K&R's denial of overtime and vacation requests. Some seven months later, on July 19, 1994, Filipovic filed other charges with the EEOC, alleging that, on the basis of his age, he was "rejected for a promotion." The EEOC issued findings of no cause on all three filings, and Filipovic filed suit in the United States

District Court for the Northern District of Illinois, alleging discrimination based on national origin under Title VII of the Civil Rights Act of 1964. Filipovic did not pursue the age discrimination charge. K&R filed a motion for summary judgment which the trial court granted, ruling that certain allegedly discriminatory actions suffered by the plaintiff were time-barred under Illinois law and that the remaining actions did not create a hostile work environment. The plaintiff appeals, contending that he properly stated a claim of discrimination based on national origin under Title VII. We affirm.

I. BACKGROUND

Filipovic was born in Yugoslavia on July 10, 1939. In 1973, he emigrated to the United States, obtained citizenship, and took up residence in Illinois. On January 26, 1982, Filipovic was hired by K&R as a full-time dockman and joined the

International Brotherhood of Teamsters, Local Union No. 710 ("union"). Beginning in 1984 and throughout his employment with K&R, Filipovic contends that he was subjected to a "continuing violation" of discrimination based upon his national origin. The centerpiece of his charge of discrimination is Filipovic's allegation that he was repeatedly called names and subjected to vulgar language by his coworkers for the eleven years of his employment prior to his filing suit. For example, coworkers referred to him as "scumbag," "pyromaniac," "piece of a**," "piece of s***," "stupid a**h***," "sheep f***er," and "Russian d*** h***." According to Filipovic, K&R supervisory personnel also engaged in coarse language directed toward him at work. Sometime prior to 1990, Filipovic was called a "dirty Commie" by a former supervisor, and in 1993, another K&R supervisor called him a "f***ing foreigner," and commented, with respect to the civil war in Yugoslavia, that "it seems to me all Serbians are barbarians." The undisputed facts at trial establish that Filipovic engaged in similar behavior, often calling his coworkers names in response.

Filipovic also contends that he was singled out for unfair treatment by K&R's management as a result of his national origin. On April 17, 1984, Filipovic went to lunch with dockman Bill Bartuch ("Bartuch"). Bartuch was well known around the company as having a "big" drinking problem. Intoxication during working hours is a terminable offense at K&R. If management has probable cause to suspect an employee is intoxicated, that employee is sent to a clinic for a blood alcohol test. Furthermore, a blood alcohol test is required under union work rules. Filipovic's supervisor, Jeffery Epstein ("Epstein") was told that Bartuch and Filipovic were seen entering a bar during their lunch break. In accordance with K&R's policies and union rules, Epstein sent Bartuch and Filipovic to submit to a blood alcohol test upon their return from lunch. Filipovic refused because of religious reasons and was discharged. Bartuch, who was not Yugoslavian, took the blood test. The afternoon of his discharge, Filipovic went to a hospital and submitted to a urine alcohol test, which yielded a negative result for alcohol. After receiving the results, K&R reinstated Filipovic with no disciplinary action.

In 1985, Filipovic contends that he was discriminated against when he was investigated for possibly stealing company property. After freight is reported missing, K&R policy requires all persons who came in contact with the freight, as well as any persons who management believes might have information about the missing freight, to be interviewed by a private investigator. In this case, the investigator asked Filipovic whether he had stolen fifteen calculators from the company, and Filipovic responded that he had not. The investigator went on to interview all other dockworkers as well as Filipovic's supervisor, Epstein.

Filipovic also claims that he was discriminated against for being Yugoslavian when he was denied a promotion to the position of "spotter." Filipovic acknowledges that K&R is bound to follow union-imposed seniority rules in allocating spotter positions to workers. Filipovic admits that he is eleven places lower on the seniority list than the last worker in Filipovic's position who became a spotter. Furthermore, spotter positions are not available frequently; the last time a full-time dockman, such as Filipovic, was trained as a spotter occurred in 1993.

In response to all of these incidents of perceived discrimination against him, Filipovic filed three charges with the EEOC in 1993 and 1994. In each case, the EEOC concluded that Filipovic had not established violations of Title VII. On November 20, 1995, Filipovic filed suit in the U.S. District Court for the Northern District of Illinois, accusing K&R of discrimination based on national origin. The complaint provided that the objectionable conduct of his coworkers and supervisors had created a hostile work environment. K&R filed a motion for summary judgment, and the district court granted the same on December 16, 1997, and dismissed the case, finding that some of the discriminatory acts alleged by Filipovic were time barred under Illinois law and that the remaining acts did not constitute discrimination on the basis of national origin.

II.ISSUES

On appeal, we consider whether the district court erred in failing to find that: (1) allegedly discriminatory acts constituted a "continuing violation" which became cognizable as discrimination based on national origin only after the 300-day period of limitation imposed by 42 U.S.C. sec. 2000e-5(e) had elapsed; (2) a hostile work environment resulted from discrimination based on national origin directed at Filipovic; and (3) Filipovic had produced sufficient evidence of a prima facie case of retaliation by K&R beginning after he filed charges of discrimination with the EEOC.

III.DISCUSSION

According to the Federal Rules of Civil Procedure, a motion for summary judgment must be granted when "there is no genuine issue as to any material fact and . . . the moving party is entitled to a judgment as a matter of law." In determining whether a genuine issue of material fact exists, "a trial court must view the record and all reasonable inferences drawn therefrom in the light most favorable to the non-moving party." To defeat a motion for summary judgment, the non-moving party cannot rest on the mere allegations or denials contained in his pleadings, but "must present sufficient evidence to show the existence of each element of its case on which it will bear the burden at trial." An appellate court will review de novo the district court's grant of summary judgment.

A.Continuing Violation

Initially, we consider whether the district court erred in failing to find that Filipovic's allegedly discriminatory acts constituted a "continuing violation" which became cognizable as discrimination based on national origin only after the 300-day period of limitation had elapsed. In Illinois, a complainant must file a charge with the EEOC within 300 days of the alleged discriminatory act and failure to do so renders the charge untimely. Because Filipovic filed the first of his three charges of discrimination based on national origin with the EEOC on July 18, 1993, any discriminatory acts which occurred prior to September 21, 1992, would be time-barred, unless Filipovic can show that these acts were "related closely enough" to the acts occurring within the established time frame "to be considered one ongoing violation." The continuing violation doctrine allows a complainant to obtain relief for a time-barred act of discrimination by linking it with acts that fall within the statutory limitations period. Courts will then treat the series of acts as one continuous act ending within the limitations period. See id. Courts will consider three factors in making this determination: (1) whether the acts involve the same subject matter; (2) the frequency at which they occur; and (3) the degree of permanence of the alleged acts of discrimination, "which should trigger an employee's awareness of and duty to assert his or her rights." The continuing violation doctrine is applicable only if it would have been unreasonable to expect the plaintiff to sue before the statute ran on the conduct, as in a case in which the conduct could constitute, or be recognized, as actionable harassment only in the light of events that occurred later, within the period of the statute of limitations.

By contrast, many of the discriminatory acts which Filipovic has alleged occurred up to thirteen years prior to September 21, 1992, and of those incidents, many involve name-calling by eight fellow dockworkers. This Court has previously held that when "it is evident long before the plaintiff sues that he was the victim of actionable harassment, he cannot reach back and base his suit on conduct that occurred outside the statute of limitations. While a single comment may not be harassment, if the comment is repeated over a period of years, its cumulative effect likely precludes invocation" of the continuing violation doctrine.

With respect to the allegations of disparate treatment by K&R management, to establish a continuing violation, Filipovic must, as discussed earlier, demonstrate that the allegedly discriminatory acts which occurred outside the limitations period were "related closely enough to constitute a continuing violation" with those occurring within the limitations period and not "merely discrete, isolated, and completed acts" which must be regarded as individual violations. Furthermore, in making this determination, courts consider whether the acts involve the same subject matter, the frequency at which they occur, and the degree of permanence of the alleged acts of discrimination.

With respect to the third factor, Filipovic has not shown that these acts were either closely related or motivated by animus against Yugoslavians. Three incidents occurring over a nine year period "cannot reasonably be linked together into a single chain, a single course of conduct, to defeat the statute of limitations."

B. Hostile Work Environment

In determining the existence of a hostile work environment, the district court considered only those incidents that occurred within the statutory time frame, thus on or after September 21, 1992. This included some of the name-calling incidents by both coworkers and supervisors and one incident during which Filipovic was given the undesirable job of unloading a trailer full of rancid food. On this basis, the district court ruled that the conduct of Filipovic's supervisors and coworkers was insufficient to constitute a hostile work environment and that the comments were few in number, were not physically threatening, were spread out over more than a year, and were relatively mild compared to epithets that can be lodged against other racial, ethnic, and religious groups.

As a threshold matter, the district court ruled that Filipovic had shown that he had faced harassment "because of" his national origin, due to the ethnic content of the comments that had been made to him. However, "relatively isolated instances of nonsevere misconduct will not support a claim of a hostile environment." Furthermore, the ethnic slurs at issue were simply part of the normal dock environment and were too infrequent to constitute the "concentrated or insistent barrage" necessary to render Filipovic's claim actionable. Thus, the district court did not err in concluding that the harassment suffered by Filipovic was not severe or pervasive enough to create a hostile work environment.

IV. CONCLUSION

Filipovic has failed to establish that a genuine issue of material fact exists in his employment discrimination claim. In our opinion, the district court properly concluded that incidents of workplace harassment occurring prior to the statutory limitations period were time-barred and that the continuing violation doctrine is inapplicable to his claims of discrimination based on national origin. Further, we agree that Filipovic failed to demonstrate that the harassment he endured was sufficient to create a hostile work environment under Title VII. Finally, the district court correctly ruled that Filipovic fell short of establishing a prima facie case of retaliation by K&R since he offered no direct evidence of a causal connection between his filing charges of discrimination with the EEOC and his subsequent termination.

Affirmed.

Judgment for K&R Express Systems

Case Commentary

The Seventh Circuit Court ruled that Filipovic's claims of national origin discrimination and harassment were disconnected and time barred. ∎

CASE QUESTIONS

1. Do you think this case was decided correctly?
2. Why did the court believe Filipovic's claims were disconnected?
3. Was the language directed at Filipovic severe and pervasive?
4. Should the location where the harassing language was uttered make a difference?

The issues in the following case are whether the ethnic epithets the plaintiff was exposed to were severe and pervasive enough to constitute harassment and so intolerable as to warrant constructive discharge.

Amirmokri v. Baltimore Gas and Electric Company

60 F.3d 1126 (4th Cir. 1995)

Michael, Circuit Judge.

Homi Amirmokri appeals the district court's grant of summary judgment in favor of Baltimore Gas and Electric Co. (BG&E) on his Title VII claims stemming from alleged mistreatment due to his Iranian national origin. Amirmokri asserts three claims: discriminatory failure to promote, harassment, and constructive discharge. We affirm summary judgment for BG&E on the claim of failure to promote.

However, because genuine issues of material fact exist regarding Amirmokri's constructive discharge claim and because equitable relief may be available to him ultimately on his harassment claim, we reverse the district court's grant of summary judgment on these two claims and remand for further proceedings.

I.

Amirmokri, an Iranian immigrant, interviewed for an engineering position with BG&E in August 1989. During his interview he told BG&E that he was interested in a Senior Engineer position. In October 1989 Amirmokri accepted BG&E's offer for an Engineer position at the Calvert Cliffs nuclear power plant. He says he understood that he would be promoted to Senior Engineer within six months.

Amirmokri alleges the following sequence of events. At the end of March 1990 a Senior Engineer position opened up at Calvert Cliffs. Douglas Lenker, another BG&E employee, was chosen to fill the slot. Amirmokri believed that this was the position he had been promised at the time of his offer and sought an explanation from his supervisors. He first met with Al Thornton, the General Supervisor, in April 1990 to discuss the unrealized promotion. The following month he met with Larry Tucker, who had replaced Thornton as the General Supervisor, about the promotion issue and the way he was being treated by Michael Polak, his engineering work

group leader. Tucker, who was new, told Amirmokri that he didn't know anything about the situation but said he would talk to Polak.

Around the time of Amirmokri's meetings with Thornton and Tucker, Polak began to harass Amirmokri by making derogatory references to his Iranian national origin, calling him "the local terrorist," a "camel jockey," "the ayatollah," and "the Emir of Waldorf" (Amirmokri lived in Waldorf, Maryland). Polak encouraged others to do the same thing. He also intentionally embarrassed Amirmokri in front of other employees by saying Amirmokri did not know what he was talking about. Finally, Polak withheld company benefits, like meal money, from Amirmokri.

By late July 1990 the harassment had not ceased. Frustrated, Amirmokri complained to Charlie Cruse, the Department Manager, who arranged for Amirmokri to meet with Bill Dunson, the Employee Grievance Coordinator, in August. Dunson told Amirmokri that he would investigate and get back to him. Dunson claims that he spoke to Polak and several of Polak's superiors, none of whom provided support for Amirmokri's allegations. In September 1990 Amirmokri began to suffer from severe gastric pain. His doctor told him that he was developing an ulcer caused by work-related stress and that he should quit his job if the harassment and stress did not end. By October Amirmokri had not heard back from Dunson, and he went to George Creel, a Vice President of BG&E. Amirmokri requested a transfer to a different job so he would not have to report to Polak.

Creel told him he would investigate and get back to him. Creel also arranged for Amirmokri to see BG&E's clinical psychologist. By November 1990 Amirmokri felt his situation was hopeless, so he resigned. Shortly thereafter he filed complaints with the Equal Employment Opportunity Commission (EEOC) and the Maryland Commission on

Human Relations. In September 1992 the EEOC issued a determination that Title VII had not been violated. Amirmokri then sued BG&E in federal court, asserting three claims: (1) discriminatory failure to promote, (2) harassment based on national origin, and (3) constructive discharge. The court then granted BG&E's motion for summary judgment on all three claims.

II.

A. Failure to promote

The district court found that Amirmokri made out a prima facie case of discriminatory failure to promote, and we agree. Amirmokri is of Iranian national origin, placing him in a protected class. He produced evidence that he applied for, and was qualified for, the Senior Engineer position to which Lenker was ultimately promoted. Finally, the fact that the person selected (Lenker) was not of foreign origin gives rise to an inference of unlawful discrimination.

However, the district court also found that (1) BG&E produced evidence that Lenker was better qualified for the Senior Engineer position and (2) Amirmokri failed to rebut this with evidence showing BG&E's asserted reason for promoting Lenker was merely pretext.

Again, we agree with both of these determinations. BG&E claimed it promoted Lenker because he had hands-on experience as an engineer operating a nuclear submarine and had worked at Calvert Cliffs for two and one-half years with outstanding performance ratings. Amirmokri, on the other hand, had worked at Calvert Cliffs for only three months with mediocre performance ratings.

B. National origin harassment

To make out a claim of national origin harassment, Amirmokri must show (1) that the acts of BG&E employees were severe and pervasive enough to create a hostile working environment and (2) that some basis exists to impute liability to his employer. Liability may be imputed to the employer if the employer had actual or constructive knowledge of the existence of a hostile working environment and took no prompt and adequate remedial action.

Whether harassment is sufficiently severe or pervasive to create an abusive work environment is "quintessentially a question of fact." To show that harassment was severe or pervasive, a plaintiff must show that he perceived, and a reasonable person would perceive, the work environment to be abusive.

The district court found that Amirmokri produced sufficient evidence to show that harassment occurred and that it was severe and pervasive. He testified that for six months Polak and other co-workers abused him almost daily, calling him names like "the local terrorist," a "camel jockey" and "the Emir of Waldorf." He also asserted that Polak intentionally tried to embarrass him by giving him impossible tasks and by saying in front of co-workers that Amirmokri did not know what he was doing. He testified

that this abuse led to his ulcer and his ultimate resignation. A reasonable person could easily find this atmosphere to be hostile.

BG&E may be liable for Polak's harassment if it knew or should have known of the harassment and failed to take "prompt remedial action reasonably calculated to end the harassment." The adequacy of BG&E's response once it was aware of the harassment is a factual issue.

Here, BG&E's response was even less decisive than that in Paroline. To begin with, it is not clear whether anyone at BG&E ever investigated Amirmokri's complaint, even after Amirmokri complained to Dunson, the Employee Grievance Coordinator, in August 1990. Dunson claims that he spoke to Polak and several other members of the Calvert Cliffs supervisory staff, Richard Honaker (Employment Recruiter), Thornton, Creel (a company Vice President), and a Mr. Denton. However, Polak testified that he never heard about Amirmokri's allegations until after Amirmokri resigned and filed his EEOC complaint.

C. Constructive discharge

To prove constructive discharge, Amirmokri must show that BG&E deliberately made his working conditions "intolerable" in an effort to induce him to quit. He must prove two elements: (1) the "deliberateness of BG&E's actions" and (2) the "intolerability of the working conditions."

Amirmokri's testimony is sufficient to raise a factual issue about whether his working conditions were intolerable. He testified that Polak and other co-workers subjected him to epithets about his Iranian origin almost daily and tried to embarrass him in public. The constant stress created by this atmosphere caused him to get an ulcer and eventually to resign. A reasonable trier of fact could find these conditions intolerable.

The more difficult question is whether Amirmokri has shown that BG&E deliberately attempted to force his resignation. Intent may be shown by evidence that an employee's resignation was the reasonably foreseeable consequence of the employer's conduct. For example, intent may be inferred from a failure to act in the face of known intolerable conditions. A complete failure to act by the employer is not required; an employer may not insulate itself entirely from liability by taking some token action in response to intolerable conditions. The reasonably foreseeable consequence of token action by the employer would still be that the employee resign. In other words, the employer's response must be reasonably calculated to end the intolerable working environment.

As discussed above, when an employee suffers from discriminatory treatment, claims for workplace harassment and constructive discharge are both governed by two-part tests. The first prong of each test weighs the severity of the conditions the employee faces. For a harassment claim the conduct must be "severe and pervasive," whereas for a constructive discharge claim the environment must be "intolerable." The second prong examines the employer's response. For a harassment claim the employer must fail to take "prompt and adequate" remedial action, and for a constructive discharge claim the employer must intend for the employee to quit.

We hold that Amirmokri has produced evidence sufficient to allow a reasonable factfinder to conclude that BG&E's response was not reasonably calculated to end Amirmokri's intolerable working conditions and that Amirmokri's ultimate resignation was a reasonably foreseeable consequence of BG&E's insufficient response. Therefore, we reverse the district court's grant of summary judgment on Amirmokri's constructive discharge claim.

CASE QUESTIONS

1. Do you agree with the Court's decision?

III.

For the above reasons, we affirm the grant of summary judgment on Amirmokri's claim for failure to promote and reverse the summary judgment on Amirmokri's claims for national origin harassment and constructive discharge. We remand to the district court for further proceedings consistent with this opinion.

Judgment for Amirmokri

Case Commentary

The Fourth Circuit Court held that Amirmokri had presented evidence sufficient to prove that he had been subject to ethnic harassment and constructive discharge. ∎

2. Was the harassment Amirmokri complained of severe and pervasive?

IMMIGRATION REFORM AND CONTROL ACT

The Immigration Reform and Control Act of 1986, which applies to employers with four or more employees, prohibits discrimination for national origin or for citizenship when the latter is an alien lawfully admitted for permanent residence. Whereas Title VII affords no protection against discrimination for citizenship or against employers of four to 14 employees, the Immigration Reform and Control Act does. However, the Immigration Reform and Control Act makes no provision for the disparate impact that occurs unintentionally, as does Title VII. Intent to discriminate is mandated by the Immigration and Control Act. The Immigration Reform and Control Act has been amended by the Immigration Act of 1990.

The Immigration Reform and Control Act applies to foreign and domestic companies who employ people within the United States. It has no application to American workers who are employed by foreign or domestic companies abroad.

Employment Perspective

The law firm of Knapp and Schultz has 12 employees. Knapp and Schultz makes it their policy never to hire anyone who is not a U.S. citizen. Prasait Theesowatt, a permanent resident alien from Thailand, applies for a job with Knapp and Schultz, only to be informed of their policy. Prasait claims that Knapp and Schultz is in violation of the Immigration Reform and Control Act. Is he correct? Yes! The Immigration Reform and Control Act prohibits discrimination against permanent resident aliens and applies to employers with at least four employees.

Discriminating against people who are not citizens is permissible under the Civil Rights Act, but not under the Immigration Reform and Control Act if they have a certificate of naturalization or a resident alien card.

In the next case, an applicant was denied a position at a pizza franchise after an in-person interview. The applicant claimed that the denial was due to his national origin because others were hired after he had applied. The issue is whether the franchisor or the franchisee is ultimately responsible for the discriminatory acts.

Bahadirli v. Domino's Pizza
873 F. Supp. 1528 (M.D.Ala. 1995)

Albritton, District Judge.

On April 12, 1993, Mehrnet Bahadirli sought employment as a pizza delivery person at the Westgate Parkway store, a Domino's pizza franchise in Dothan, Alabama. According to the plaintiff, he visited the store and was told that he was well qualified for the position, but he never received word regarding the job. The plaintiff alleges that on his return to the store around April 25, 1993, he was told that he would not receive the position. According to the plaintiff, in the interim four other individuals were hired at the Westgate Parkway store.

Clarkfinn asserts that plaintiff returned to the store after approximately one month from his initial visit to inquire as to the status of his application. According to Clarkfinn, plaintiff was told that the application had been misfiled, that the Westgate Parkway store did not have any openings, but perhaps another location in Dothan did. Defendants allege that they contacted another store and that plaintiff said that he would pick up an application there.

Bahadirli contends that on learning he would not be hired, he went directly home and asked his wife to call the shop and inquire about employment. Plaintiff alleges his wife was offered a position over the phone.

As stated above, both Clark and Clarkfinn have filed Motions to Dismiss. Clarkfinn is the corporate entity that owns the Domino's Pizza franchise at issue here. Mr. Clark owns 75% of Clarkfinn's stock and serves as the corporation's president.

Until very recently, Eleventh Circuit law was very clear in holding that Title VII claims against a person in his individual capacity were "inappropriate." Accordingly, Clark may not be sued in his individual capacity. As stated above, in order to make out a case, plaintiff must show the plaintiff is of different nationality, plaintiff applied for a position, was qualified for that position; that the plaintiff was rejected for the position despite his qualifications; and that the defendant continued to accept applications for the position following the rejection of the plaintiff.

However, in addition to establishing a prima facie case, the plaintiff must show that the defendants named are properly before the court on these claims. Domino's argues that it is entitled to summary judgment on plaintiff's Title VII claims because it is not the employer in this case. The defendant Reams contends that he cannot be sued under Title VII in his individual capacity and that, because the employer is named in the suit, naming him in his official capacity is repetitive. The court agrees with the argument of both Domino's and Reams.

Reams is the individual who served as manager at the Domino's franchise that plaintiff is suing. According to plaintiff, Reams turned him down for a position at the Westgate Parkway store because of plaintiff's national origin. Reams no longer works for Clarkfinn.

Plaintiff admits that Reams cannot be sued in his individual capacity, but argues that the court should not grant summary judgment as to Reams in his official capacity. The Court disagrees. As stated above, a suit under Title VII brought against an employee as agent of the employer is properly regarded as a suit against the employer. Domino's contends that it did not have control over the day to day operations or over hiring and firing that would allow a finding of liability should Bahadirli prove his claim. In support of its argument, Domino's has submitted affidavits from Linda Popevich, a Divisional Vice President of Franchise Services for Domino's. According to these affidavits, the Westgate Parkway store was, and is, a franchise, operated by an independent contractor—Clarkfinn. Popevich also avers that "persons who work at a store operated by a franchisee, including the Westgate Parkway Store, are employees of the Franchisee Clarkfinn and not DPI Domino's." In her supplemental affidavit, Popevich stated that Domino's has no knowledge of individuals who apply for positions at Domino's franchises. In this case, the plaintiff has presented no evidence that the defendant Domino's had any control over the employees' day to day activities, or control over hiring and firing at the Westgate Parkway store. Accordingly, Domino's Motion for Summary Judgment is due to be granted.

Judgment for Domino's.

Case Commentary

The Middle District of Alabama decided that a franchisor is not liable for the discriminatory actions of its franchisee. Here, Bahadirli was refused employment by Clarkfinn, the Domino's franchisee, because of his national origin. ■

CASE QUESTIONS

1. Are you in accord with the Court's decision?
2. Do you believe Clarkfinn should be held liable?

3. Why do you think Clarkfinn refused Bahadirli employment?

EMPLOYEE LESSONS

1. Recognize that you are protected from national origin discrimination under Title VII of the Civil Rights Act.
2. Realize that this protection extends to your school, ethnic associations, surname, and spouse's national origin.
3. Be aware when an employer asks the country in which you were born.
4. Do not initiate or participate in ethnic harassment in the workplace.
5. Be familiar with the Immigration Reform and Control Act.
6. Inquire as to the applicability of this act as well as the Civil Rights Act to your employer.
7. Provide the necessary documentation for your employer if you are a resident alien.
8. Understand you may not be protected against national origin discrimination when working abroad.
9. Be aware of the reasons for national origin discrimination.
10. Apprise yourself of the requirements needed to file a disparate treatment case for national origin.

SUMMARY

The United States is a melting pot and is probably the most integrated country in the world. America derives its strength from the attributes of a population diverse in culture and tradition. Excluding individuals because of their national origin goes against the grain of American heritage; individuals should be judged only on the basis of their merit. Most immigrants have taken their lumps upon entering this country. One hundred years ago, the Irish and Germans were not well received. Seventy-five years ago, the Italians and Polish were resented. Twenty-five years ago, the Spanish and Latin Americans were not wanted. Today, Indians and Koreans are looked upon with contempt.

Many Americans want immigration laws tightened to the point of restricting most nonwhite immigrants. What these Americans are forgetting is the work ethic that their ancestors brought with them in building the infrastructure that exists today. Most immigrants are not freeloaders but rather are people seeking opportunities to put their talents to work to build a future for their families and themselves, a goal that everyone should encourage.

Immigrants are often used to performing the routine ministerial tasks that Americans refuse to do. Hard labor, landscaping, assembly-line factory work, janitorial maintenance, and gas pumping are a few occupations serviced by a significant number of immigrants. On the other side of the coin, as immigrants mesh themselves into our society and have children, those children will eventually compete with Americans for better-paying positions. Also, as the population grows, pollution and garbage increase proportionately. Development causes overuse of the land, natural resources, and water; erosion occurs; disease proliferates; and quality of life deteriorates. In areas of technology, communications, and product development, our innovation is unparalleled, but in purifying our air, water, and food supply, we are underachievers. Therefore, the number of people that can adequately be supported by America's vital resources is an issue to be seriously considered.

This problem pertains to the number of immigrants in the future. For those immigrants already here, America should embrace them into our society and encourage them to utilize their talents to their greatest potential for the benefit of all of us. Discrimination against immigrants serves no purpose, because they rarely leave involuntarily; it serves only to delay their inevitable amalgamation into American employment and society.

Thoughtful planning with regard to supporting future immigrants with the vital resources available to us is an intelligent policy, but purposeful discrimination against the ones among us is not. They should be treated as our own.

REVIEW QUESTIONS

1. Define *national origin discrimination*.
2. Explain the significance of the Immigration Reform and Control Act.
3. Can a person claim to be discriminated against because of his or her spouse's national origin?
4. Does discrimination because of membership in an association of a particular national origin qualify as national origin discrimination?
5. When a student is discriminated against because he or she is attending a school of a particular national origin, does Title VII apply?
6. Does the Civil Rights Act extend to a person's claiming discrimination because his or her surname is associated with a particular national origin?
7. Can an employer discriminate against someone on the basis of the person's lacking U.S. citizenship?
8. Does the Immigration Reform and Control Act apply to all employers?
9. Can national origin ever be considered a bona fide occupational qualification?
10. Must an employee be 100 percent of a particular national origin to qualify for protection under Title VII?
11. Should Title VII be extended to cover American citizens working abroad?
12. Should a franchisor be responsible for the unethical conduct of the franchisee?

CASE PROBLEMS

1. Dr. Muzquiz was born in Texas in 1932, is of Hispanic origin (Mexican–Indian), and graduated from a Mexican medical school in 1963. From 1985 to 1989, Dr. Muzquiz performed no cardiac catheterizations in Michigan, but did travel to Mexico for several weeks each year where he performed that procedure.

   In January 1989, Dr. Muzquiz became a member of the provisional staff of Defendant Hospital, which is a not-for-profit institution. A physician who seeks to independently perform invasive cardiology procedures must meet the following specific requirement:

   3b. A favorable review of medical charts and films of patients for whom the physician served as primary physician for diagnostic catheterizations in the past year selected at random.

   At the core of the instant dispute is the difficulty Dr. Muzquiz encountered in trying to meet requirement 3b. Dr. Muzquiz had performed all of his recent cardiac catheterizations during his trips to Mexico. Consequently, to comply with requirement 3b, it was necessary to obtain the films and charts of the catheterizations he had performed in the past year from the hospital in Mexico. Dr. Frank Morales, administrator and CEO of the hospital in Mexico, forwarded the English translation of 10 patient charts.

   On December 11, 1991, the Credentials Committee informed Dr. Muzquiz that they needed (1) a written explanation from Dr. Morales as to why the actual case logs and copies of the films corresponding to the 10 translated charts sent were not available, and (2) copies of the actual medical records that had been translated. Upon receipt and review of that documentation, the committee was prepared to recommend Dr. Muzquiz for provisional cardiac catheterization privileges conditioned on a favorable evaluation of his first 10 catheterization procedures. On January 15, 1992, however, the Medical Executive Committee voted to reject the recommendation of the Credentials Committee with respect to the 10 proctored cases and instead recommended proctoring Muzquiz' first 25 cases. Dr. Muzquiz registered his strong objection to the 25-proctored cases requirement and asked for reconsideration of the 10-proctored cases initially recommended by the Credentials Committee. On March 17, Dr. Muzquiz met with representatives of the hospital and refused to accept the terms of the provisional grant of catheterization privileges. The issue is whether the plaintiff was subject to national origin discrimination due to the employer's unfavorable treatment toward those physicians who had trained in Mexico. *Muzquiz, Jr., M.D. v. W.A. Foote Memorial Hospital, Inc.*, 70 F.3d 422 (6th Cir. 1995)

2. Plaintiff (who was 43 years old at the time he filed this appeal) is a native of Iran and has been a citizen of the United States since 1979. Because of his Iranian ethnicity, Plaintiff is dark complected and speaks with an accent. Plaintiff was admitted to the College of Dentistry ("College") at the University of Tennessee ("University") as a first-year dental student on August 12, 1994, after a 12-year career as a mechanical engineer in the aerospace industry.

   Dr. William F. Bowles, as well as Dr. Victor A. Fletcher, has a policy of barring first-year dental students from sitting in the last row of their classrooms. Dr. Bowles informed Plaintiff and his classmates on the first day of class of this policy. On January 31, 1995, Dr. Bowles and Dr. Lynch (Associate Dean of the College and a Professor in the Department of Orthodontics at the University) met with Plaintiff, at his request, regarding the "last row rule." Less than 1 week later, Plaintiff wrote a letter to Dr. Bowles reiterating the same concerns addressed at the meeting, including Plaintiff's displeasure with the "last row rule." The next day, February 7, 1995, Plaintiff sat in the last row of Dr. Bowles' class. Dr. Bowles warned Plaintiff that he would be instructed to leave the classroom if he violated the "last row rule" again.

   Plaintiff alleged that he desired to sit in the last row because he could see and hear better in that location, and that he found sitting elsewhere to be disruptive to his thinking process. It was decided that Plaintiff would be placed on disciplinary probation for the entirety of his matriculation at the College, and warned that he would be dismissed if found guilty of other academic infractions.

   Plaintiff filed suit against Defendants alleging ethnic discrimination. The issue is whether Plaintiff was subject to national origin discrimination by university professors who refused to allow him to sit in a particular row in their classrooms. *Salehpour v. University of Tennessee*, 159 F.3d 199 (6th Cir. 1998)

3. Rys once heard Lehman say that Adolf Hitler did not finish his job because he did not kill all the Polish and Jewish people. Lehman also said that he should shove those people into the ovens. Lehman once saw a woman having lunch and asked her what were "all those dumb Polacks" doing in the hallway. When Lehman fired the crew, Rys complained that Palka should be present. Lehman then said that he would fire "that dumb Polack, too." Are these events sufficient to constitute a claim for national origin discrimination? *ISS Intern. Service v. Human Rights Commission*, 651 N.E.2d 592 (Ill. App. 1 Dist. 1995)

HUMAN RESOURCE DILEMMAS

1. Josh Martinez applies for a job with American Heartland Corporation. Sparky Foster, personnel director, asks Josh if he is an American citizen. Josh replies in the negative, but then produces a green card signifying his status as a resident alien with working privileges. Sparky silences Josh and then tells Josh, "At American Heartland, we hire only American citizens." Josh is considering suing under Title VII. How would you advise him?

2. At Bayou Oil Drilling, the Mexican workers are often referred to as wetbacks, subjected to vulgar language about their mothers and wives, and taunted with ethnic

jokes and comic pictorials. Their complaints go unheeded. They are fearful of losing their jobs if they sue. How would you advise them?

3. Johnny Carlton attended the University of Lebanon while his father was stationed in the Armed Forces there. When Kurt Munson reviews Johnny's application for employment, he asks Johnny why he chose to attend college there. Johnny explains. When Johnny, who is qualified for the position, is subsequently denied, he reasons that Kurt's inquiry was a determining factor. Johnny initiates a Title VII claim for national origin discrimination. Kurt asserts that Johnny does not fall under that suspect classification. Is Johnny covered?

WEB SITE ASSIGNMENT

Check the Web to ascertain if any municipalities have adopted English as the official language. Then do the same for Spanish.

www.eeoc.gov/facts/fs-nator.html
www.ilo.org/public/english/protection/migrant/papers/usempir/ch6.htm
www.civiljustice.com/empnews2.htm#raceandethnic-baseddiscrimination
www.usdoj.gov/crt/legalinfo/natorigin.htm
www.discriminationattorney.com/nat_orig_des.html
www.elinfonet.com/fedarticles/15/1

Chapter 16

Age Discrimination

Employment Scenario

Beatrice McCormick has been a cashier for The Long and the Short of It since they opened 6 years ago. Beatrice is approaching 70. Tom Long and Mark Short have been urging her to retire, but so far they have had no luck. It seems Beatrice's life revolves around her work. Her children live far away and she has no hobbies. Tom and Mark ask Susan North, their attorney, if there is any way they can force Beatrice into retirement.

Susan asks them about Beatrice's job performance. Tom and Mark explain that Beatrice is extremely competent. However, Beatrice's age and appearance do not fit the youthful and up-to-date image that L&S wishes to project. They recently hired 19-year-old Tanya, whom they describe as being really "hot." Beatrice is training Tanya. Tom and Mark plan to make the switch in 2 weeks, on Beatrice's birthday. Are Tom and Mark justified?

Chapter Checklist

➤ Appreciate the ramifications of the Age Discrimination in Employment Act.

➤ Learn that age discrimination applies to employees 40 years old or older.

➤ Know that the mandatory retirement age has been eliminated.

➤ Consider that age discrimination usually occurs when an employer chooses to discharge an older employer because of his or her higher salary.

➤ Realize that older employees are often replaced by younger ones who earn far less.

➤ Be aware that executives can be forced to retire when they reach 65 years of age.

➤ Be concerned that forcing older employees to accept early retirement packages is age discrimination.

➤ Understand that an employer's justification for layoffs cannot be motivated by age discrimination.

➤ Appreciate that elderly people have the right to work.

INTRODUCTION

The Age Discrimination in Employment Act of 1967 (ADEA) was enacted to promote the employment of individuals over 40 years of age. Later, it was amended to discontinue mandatory retirement, thereby shifting the requirement for employment from age to ability. There are exceptions. Companies can force executives in high policy-making positions to retire at age 65.

HUMAN RESOURCE ADVICE

- Do not take age into account when making employment decisions.
- Understand the purpose of the Age Discrimination in Employment Act.
- Know that protection against age discrimination begins at 40.
- Consider that there is no longer mandatory retirement.
- Realize that employees may work as long as they are competent to do so.
- Refrain from coercing employees to accept early retirement packages.
- Be careful not to discharge an inordinate number of older workers when downsizing.
- Learn that the desire to project a more youthful and up-to-date image might have to give way to the rights of older workers.
- Be aware that company policy may dictate the mandatory retirement age of high-level executives.

Employment Perspective

Lawrence Wright is the chief financial officer (CFO) for Code Blue Medical Supplies, Inc. Miriam Hodges is a quality control analyst. Both will be 70 in March. Code Blue has a policy of compulsory retirement at age 70. Will Lawrence and Miriam both have to retire? Under the ADEA, Miriam can continue to work as long as she is able to do the job. Lawrence will be forced to retire as CFO because he is a high-ranking executive. However, he will not be prevented from doing consulting work for the company.

Employment Perspective

Professor Martin Ryan has been teaching mathematical statistics, differential equations, and complex variables at Moran University for 35 years. At the end of this academic year, he will turn 70. Martin is still highly competent, revered by his colleagues, and a favorite of the students. However, university policy mandates retirement of tenured professors at age 70. Martin implores Dean Margaret Stokes to make an exception, but Dean Stokes bellows that once Moran University makes one exception, it will set a precedent that will undermine university policy. Moran University may then be forced to permit scholars much less competent than Martin Ryan to continue working beyond age 70. The school may become stale, full of old codgers, and lose its stellar reputation. Does Professor Martin Ryan have any recourse? Unfortunately, No! The ADEA does not afford protection to tenured professors who reach age 70.

Discrimination Requirements

The initial test for determining age discrimination has four prongs:

1. Employee was qualified.
2. Employee was terminated.
3. Employee was a member of a protected class.
4. Employee was replaced by someone younger or was otherwise discharged because of age.

The employer must then provide a legitimate nondiscriminatory reason for the discharge. After satisfying this burden, the employee must prove that the employer's reasoning was false and that the real reason was to discriminate.

The issue in the following case is whether the Eleventh Amendment to the Constitution renders a state immune from liability under the ADEA.

Kimel v. Florida Board of Regents
528 U.S. 62 (2000)

Justice O'Connor delivered the opinion of the Court.

The Age Discrimination in Employment Act of 1967 (ADEA or Act) makes it unlawful for an employer, including a State, "to fail or refuse to hire or to discharge any individual or otherwise discriminate against any individual . . . because of such individual's age." In these cases, three sets of plaintiffs filed suit under the Act, seeking money damages for their state employers' alleged discrimination on the basis of age. In each case, the state employer moved to dismiss the suit on the basis of its Eleventh Amendment immunity. The District Court in one case granted the motion to dismiss, while in each of the remaining cases the District Court denied the motion. Appeals in the three cases were consolidated before the Court of Appeals for the Eleventh Circuit, which held that the ADEA does not validly abrogate the States' Eleventh Amendment immunity. In these cases, we are asked to consider whether the ADEA contains a clear statement of Congress' intent to abrogate the States' Eleventh Amendment immunity and, if so, whether the ADEA is a proper exercise of Congress' constitutional authority.

We conclude that the ADEA does contain a clear statement of Congress' intent to abrogate the States' immunity, but that the abrogation exceeded Congress' authority under § 5 of the Fourteenth Amendment.

I

A

Since its enactment, the ADEA's scope of coverage has been expanded by amendment. Of particular importance to these cases is the Act's treatment of state employers and employees. When first passed in 1967, the ADEA applied only to private employers. In 1974, in a statute consisting primarily of amendments to the FLSA, Congress extended application of the

ADEA's substantive requirements to the States. Fair Labor Standards Amendments of 1974 (1974 Act). Congress accomplished that expansion in scope by a simple amendment to the definition of "employer": "The term [employer] also means . . . a State or political subdivision of a State and any agency or instrumentality of a State or a political subdivision of a State . . . ." Congress also amended the ADEA's definition of "employee," still defining the term to mean "an individual employed by any employer," but excluding elected officials and appointed policymakers at the state and local levels. In the same 1974 Act, Congress amended 29 U.S.C. § 216(b), the FLSA enforcement provision incorporated by reference into the ADEA. Section 216(b) now permits an individual to bring a civil action "against any employer (including a public agency) in any Federal or State court of competent jurisdiction." Section 203(x) defines "public agency" to include "the Government of a State or political subdivision thereof," and "any agency of . . . a State, or a political subdivision of a State." Finally, in the 1974 Act, Congress added a provision prohibiting age discrimination generally in employment at the Federal Government. Under the current ADEA, mandatory age limits for law enforcement officers and firefighters—at federal, state, and local levels—are exempted from the statute's coverage.

B

In December 1994, Roderick MacPherson and Marvin Narz, ages 57 and 58 at the time, filed suit under the ADEA against their employer, the University of Montevallo, in the United States District Court for the Northern District of Alabama. In their complaint, they alleged that the university had discriminated against them on the basis of their age, that it had retaliated against them for filing discrimination charges with the

Equal Employment Opportunity Commission (EEOC), and that its College of Business, at which they were associate professors, employed an evaluation system that had a disparate impact on older faculty members. MacPherson and Narz sought declaratory and injunctive relief, backpay, promotions to full professor, and compensatory and punitive damages. The University of Montevallo moved to dismiss the suit for lack of subject matter jurisdiction, contending it was barred by the Eleventh Amendment. No party disputes the District Court's holding that the University is an instrumentality of the State of Alabama. On September 9, 1996, the District Court granted the University's motion. The court determined that, although the ADEA contains a clear statement of Congress' intent to abrogate the States' Eleventh Amendment immunity, Congress did not enact or extend the ADEA under its Fourteenth Amendment § 5 enforcement power. The District Court therefore held that the ADEA did not abrogate the States' Eleventh Amendment immunity.

In April 1995, a group of current and former faculty and librarians of Florida State University, including J. Daniel Kimel, Jr., the named petitioner in one of today's cases, filed suit against the Florida Board of Regents in the United States District Court for the Northern District of Florida. The complaint was subsequently amended to add as plaintiffs current and former faculty and librarians of Florida International University. The plaintiffs, all over age 40, alleged that the Florida Board of Regents refused to require the two state universities to allocate funds to provide previously agreed upon market adjustments to the salaries of eligible university employees. The plaintiffs contended that the failure to allocate the funds violated both the ADEA and the Florida Civil Rights Act of 1992 because it had a disparate impact on the base pay of employees with a longer record of service, most of whom were older employees. The plaintiffs sought backpay, liquidated damages, and permanent salary adjustments as relief. The Florida Board of Regents moved to dismiss the suit on the grounds of Eleventh Amendment immunity. On May 17, 1996, the District Court denied the motion, holding that Congress expressed its intent to abrogate the States' Eleventh Amendment immunity in the ADEA, and that the ADEA is a proper exercise of congressional authority under the Fourteenth Amendment.

In May 1996, Wellington Dickson filed suit against his employer, the Florida Department of Corrections, in the United States District Court for the Northern District of Florida. Dickson alleged that the state employer failed to promote him because of his age and because he had filed grievances with respect to the alleged acts of age discrimination. Dickson sought injunctive relief, backpay, and compensatory and punitive damages. The Florida Department of Corrections moved to dismiss the suit on the grounds that it was barred by the Eleventh Amendment. The District Court denied that motion on November 5, 1996, holding that Congress unequivocally expressed its intent to abrogate the States' Eleventh

Amendment immunity in the ADEA, and that Congress had authority to do so under § 5 of the Fourteenth Amendment.

The plaintiffs in the *MacPherson* case, and the state defendants in the *Kimel* and *Dickson* cases, appealed to the Court of Appeals for the Eleventh Circuit. The United States also intervened in all three cases to defend the ADEA's abrogation of the States' Eleventh Amendment immunity. The Court of Appeals consolidated the appeals and, in a divided panel opinion, held that the ADEA does not abrogate the States' Eleventh Amendment immunity.

We granted certiorari, 525 U.S. 1121 (1999), to resolve a conflict among the Federal Courts of Appeals on the question whether the ADEA validly abrogates the States' Eleventh Amendment immunity.

II

The Eleventh Amendment states:

"The Judicial power of the United States shall not be construed to extend to any suit in law or equity, commenced or prosecuted against one of the United States by Citizens of another State, or by Citizens or Subjects of any Foreign State."

Although today's cases concern suits brought by citizens against their own States, this Court has long "'understood the Eleventh Amendment to stand not so much for what it says, but for the presupposition . . . which it confirms.'" Accordingly, for over a century now, we have made clear that the Constitution does not provide for federal jurisdiction over suits against nonconsenting States. Petitioners nevertheless contend that the States of Alabama and Florida must defend the present suits on the merits because Congress abrogated their Eleventh Amendment immunity in the ADEA. To determine whether petitioners are correct, we must resolve two predicate questions: first, whether Congress unequivocally expressed its intent to abrogate that immunity; and second, if it did, whether Congress acted pursuant to a valid grant of constitutional authority.

A review of the ADEA's legislative record as a whole, then, reveals that Congress had virtually no reason to believe that state and local governments were unconstitutionally discriminating against their employees on the basis of age. Although that lack of support is not determinative of the § 5 inquiry Congress' failure to uncover any significant pattern of unconstitutional discrimination here confirms that Congress had no reason to believe that broad prophylactic legislation was necessary in this field. In light of the indiscriminate scope of the Act's substantive requirements, and the lack of evidence of widespread and unconstitutional age discrimination by the States, we hold that the ADEA is not a valid exercise of Congress' power under § 5 of the Fourteenth Amendment. The ADEA's purported abrogation of the States' sovereign immunity is accordingly invalid.

Our decision today does not signal the end of the line for employees who find themselves subject to age discrimination at the hands of their state employers. We hold only that, in the ADEA, Congress did not validly abrogate the States' sovereign immunity to suits by private individuals. State employees are protected by state age discrimination statutes, and may recover money damages from their state employers, in almost every State of the Union. Those avenues of relief remain available today, just as they were before this decision.

Because the ADEA does not validly abrogate the States' sovereign immunity, however, the present suits must be dismissed. Accordingly, the judgment of the Court of Appeals is affirmed in favor of the Florida Board of Regents.

Case Commentary
The U.S. Supreme Court held that states are immune from liability under the ADEA; however, an individual may proceed under state age discrimination laws. ■

CASE QUESTIONS

1. Are you in agreement with this decision?
2. Is the Eleventh Amendment immunity justifiable?

3. Can Congress extend ADEA coverage to state governments?

The issue in this case is whether an employee alleging age discrimination must be replaced by someone under 40 years of age.

O'Connor v. Consolidated Coin Caterers
517 U.S. 308 (1996)

Justice Scalia delivered the opinion of the Court.
This case presents the question whether a plaintiff alleging that he was discharged in violation of the Age Discrimination in Employment Act of 1967 (ADEA) must show that he was replaced by someone outside the age group protected by the ADEA to make out a prima facie case under the framework established by *McDonnell Douglas Corp. v. Green.*

Petitioner James O'Connor was employed by respondent Consolidated Coin Caterers Corporation from 1978 until August 10, 1990, when, at age 56, he was fired. Claiming that he had been dismissed because of his age in violation of the ADEA, petitioner brought suit in the United States District Court for the Western District of North Carolina. After discovery, the District Court granted respondent's motion for summary judgment and petitioner appealed. The Court of Appeals for the Fourth Circuit stated that petitioner could establish a prima facie case under *McDonnell Douglas* only if he could prove that (1) he was in the age group protected by the ADEA; (2) he was discharged or demoted; (3) at the time of his discharge or demotion, he was performing his job at a level that met his employer's legitimate expectations; and (4) following his discharge or demotion, he was replaced by someone of comparable qualifications outside the protected class. Since petitioner's replacement was 40 years old, the Court of Appeals concluded that the last element of the prima facie case had not been made out. Finding that petitioner's claim could not survive a motion for summary judgment without benefit of the *McDonnell Douglas* presumption, the Court of Appeals affirmed the judgment of dismissal. We granted O'Connor's petition for certiorari.

As the very name "prima facie case" suggests, there must be at least a logical connection between each element of the prima facie case and the illegal discrimination for which it establishes a "legally mandatory, rebuttable presumption." The element of replacement by someone under 40 fails this requirement. The discrimination prohibited by the ADEA is discrimination "because of an individual's age," though the prohibition is "limited to individuals who are at least 40 years of age." This language does not ban discrimination against employees because they are aged 40 or older; it bans discrimination against employees because of their age, but limits the protected class to those who are 40 or older. The fact that one person in the protected class has lost out to another person in the protected class is thus irrelevant, so long as he has lost out because of his age. Or to put the point more concretely, there can be no greater inference of age discrimination (as opposed to "40 or over" discrimination) when a 40 year-old is replaced by a 39 year-old than when a 56 year-old is replaced by a 40 year-old. Because it lacks probative value, the fact that an ADEA plaintiff was replaced by someone outside the protected class is not a proper element of the *McDonnell Douglas* prima facie case.

Perhaps some courts have been induced to adopt the principle urged by respondent in order to avoid creating a prima facie case on the basis of very thin evidence—for example, the replacement of a 68 year-old by a 65 year-old. While the respondent's principle theoretically permits such thin evidence (consider the example above of a 40 year-old replaced by a 39 year old), as a practical matter it will rarely do so, since the vast majority of age-discrimination claims come from older employees. In our view, however, the proper solution to the problem lies not in making an utterly irrelevant factor an element of the prima facie case, but rather in recognizing that the prima facie case requires "evidence adequate to create an inference that an employment decision was based on an illegal discriminatory criterion. . . ." In the age-discrimination context, such an inference can not be drawn from the replacement of one worker with another worker insignificantly younger. Because the ADEA prohibits discrimination on the basis of age and not class membership, the fact that a replacement is substantially younger than the plaintiff is a far more reliable indicator of age discrimination than is the fact that the plaintiff was replaced by someone outside the protected class. The judgment of the Fourth Circuit is reversed, and the case is remanded for proceedings consistent with this opinion.

It is so ordered.

Judgment for O'Connor.

Case Commentary

The U.S. Supreme Court decided that an older person who was discharged does not have to be replaced by someone under 40 years of age in order to allege age discrimination. The disparity in age is key. ■

CASE QUESTIONS

1. Are you in agreement with the decision of the U.S. Supreme Court?
2. If the age discrimination threshold is 40 years of age, why would the court allow an employee to sue when his or her replacement is over 40 years old?
3. Should the requirement for age discrimination be the age of the replacement, disparity in age, or both?

Mandatory Retirement

The mandatory retirement age was originally 65. In 1978, it was adjusted to 70, and more recently, it has been eliminated. Age discrimination can begin at 40.

Employment Perspective

Big Mac Kowalski is the quarterback for the Raleigh Rainbows. In the past year, he was ranked among the upper half of all quarterbacks in the league. Before the beginning of the season, Chubby Shelten, coach of the Rainbows, informs Kowalski that he is being discharged. Chubby explains that the team will be committing itself to younger players and that the younger players would prefer someone of similar age to be quarterback rather than an old man to whom they cannot relate. Kowalski is 38 years old. He sues the Rainbows for age discrimination. Will he score? No. Big Mac is under 40. The protection of the Age Discrimination in Employment Act does not apply to him. Big Mac will become an armchair quarterback.

Damages

Damages recoverable for age discrimination include reinstatement, back pay, differential in pay due to seniority, and pension-benefit contributions. Where the employer's motivation for discharge was intentional, double lost wages may be assessed as a form of liquidated damages. Interest and attorney's fees may also be awarded at the discretion of the court.

A victim of age discrimination must file a claim with the EEOC within 2 years of the incident. This statute of limitations is extended to 3 years if the employer acted with intent. After filing with the EEOC, the complainant himself or herself may proceed in state or federal court. It is possible for two corresponding suits, one brought by the EEOC and the other brought by the complainant, to take place at the same time.

Under Title VII, a separate suit may be commenced only when EEOC's determination is not to proceed. If the complaining party has not yet filed a separate suit and the EEOC has decided not to pursue the claim, the complainant has 90 days to bring a lawsuit from the receipt of the said notice.

The question presented in the case that follows is whether the employer's age discrimination toward an employee is mitigated by the fact that the employer later discovered the employee misappropriated company documents.

McKennon v. Nashville Banner Publishing Co.

513 U.S. 352 (1995)

Justice Kennedy delivered the opinion of the Court.

The question before us is whether an employee discharged in violation of the Age Discrimination in Employment Act of 1967 is barred from all relief when, after her discharge, the employer discovers evidence of wrongdoing that, in any event, would have led to the employee's termination on lawful and legitimate grounds.

I

For some 30 years, petitioner Christine McKennon worked for respondent Nashville Banner Publishing Company. She was discharged, the Banner claimed, as part of a work force reduction plan necessitated by cost considerations. McKennon, who was 62 years old when she lost her job, thought another reason explained her dismissal: her age. She filed suit in the United States District Court for the Middle District of Tennessee, alleging that her discharge violated the Age Discrimination in Employment Act of 1967 (ADEA). The ADEA makes it unlawful for any employer: "to discharge any individual or otherwise discriminate against any individual with respect to his compensation, terms, conditions, or privileges of employment, because of such individual's age." McKennon sought a variety of legal and equitable remedies available under the ADEA, including backpay. In preparation of the case, the Banner took McKennon's deposition. She testified that, during her final year of employment, she had copied several confidential documents bearing upon the company's financial condition. She had access to these records as secretary to the Banner's comptroller. McKennon took the copies home and showed them to her husband. Her motivation, she averred, was an apprehension she was about to be fired because of her age. When she became concerned about her job, she removed and copied the documents for "insurance" and "protection." A few days after these deposition disclosures, the Banner sent McKennon a letter declaring that removal and copying of the records was in violation of her job responsibilities and advising her again that she was terminated. The Banner's letter also recited that had it known of McKennon's misconduct it would have discharged her at once for that reason.

For purposes of summary judgment, the Banner conceded its discrimination against McKennon. The District Court granted summary judgment for the Banner, holding that McKennon's misconduct was grounds for her termination and that neither backpay nor any other remedy was available to her under the ADEA. We granted certiorari to resolve conflicting views among the Courts of Appeals on the question whether all relief must be denied when an employee has been discharged in violation of the ADEA and the employer later discovers some wrongful conduct that would have led to discharge if it had been discovered earlier. We now reverse.

II

We shall assume, as summary judgment procedures require us to assume, that the sole reason for McKennon's initial discharge was her age, a discharge violative of the ADEA. Our further premise is that the misconduct revealed by the deposition was so grave that McKennon's immediate discharge would have followed its disclosure in any event. The District Court and the Court of Appeals found no basis for contesting that proposition, and for purposes of our review we need not question it here. We do question the legal conclusion reached by those courts that after-acquired evidence of wrongdoing which would have resulted in discharge bars employees from any relief under the ADEA. That ruling is incorrect.

The Court of Appeals considered McKennon's misconduct, in effect, to be supervening grounds for termination. That may be so, but it does not follow, as the Court of Appeals said in citing one of its own earlier cases, that the misconduct renders it "'irrelevant whether or not McKennon was discriminated against.'" We conclude that a violation of the ADEA cannot be so altogether disregarded.

The ADEA, enacted in 1967 as part of an ongoing congressional effort to eradicate discrimination in the workplace, reflects a societal condemnation of invidious bias in employment decisions. The ADEA is but part of a wider statutory scheme to protect employees in the workplace nationwide. The ADEA incorporates some features of both Title VII and the Fair Labor Standards Act, which has led us to describe it as "something of a hybrid." The substantive, antidiscrimination provisions of the ADEA are modeled upon the prohibitions of Title VII. Its remedial provisions incorporate by reference the provisions of the Fair Labor Standards Act of 1938. When confronted with a violation of the ADEA, a district court is authorized to afford relief by means of reinstatement, backpay, injunctive relief, declaratory judgment, and attorney's fees. In the case of a willful violation of the Act, the ADEA authorizes an award of liquidated damages equal to the backpay award. The Act also gives federal courts the discretion to "grant such legal or equitable relief as may be appropriate to effectuate the purposes of the Act." The ADEA and Title VII share common substantive features and also a common purpose: "the elimination of discrimination in the workplace." Congress designed the remedial measures in these statutes to serve as a "spur or catalyst" to cause employers "to self-examine and to self-evaluate their employment practices and to endeavor to eliminate, so far as possible, the last vestiges" of discrimination. Deterrence is one object of these statutes. Compensation for injuries caused by the prohibited discrimination is another. The ADEA, in keeping with these purposes, contains a vital element found in both Title VII and the Fair Labor Standards Act: it grants an injured employee a right of action to obtain the authorized relief. The private litigant who seeks redress for his or her injuries vindicates both the deterrence and the compensation objectives of the ADEA. The private litigant in Title VII not only redresses his own injury but also vindicates the important congressional policy against discriminatory employment practices.

As we have said, the case comes to us on the express assumption that an unlawful motive was the sole basis for the firing. McKennon's misconduct was not discovered until after she had been fired. The employer could not have been motivated by knowledge it did not have and it cannot now claim that the employee was fired for the nondiscriminatory reason. Mixed motive cases are inapposite here, except to the important extent they underscore the necessity of determining the employer's motives in ordering the discharge, an essential element in determining whether the employer violated the federal antidiscrimination law.

The proper boundaries of remedial relief in the general class of cases where, after termination, it is discovered that the employee has engaged in wrongdoing must be addressed by the judicial system in the ordinary course of further decisions, for the factual permutations and the equitable considerations they raise will vary from case to case. We do conclude that here, and as a general rule in cases of this type, neither reinstatement nor front pay is an appropriate remedy. It would be both inequitable and pointless to order the reinstatement of someone the employer would have terminated, and will terminate, in any event and upon lawful grounds.

The proper measure of backpay presents a more difficult problem. Resolution of this question must give proper recognition to the fact that an ADEA violation has occurred which must be deterred and compensated without undue infringement upon the employer's rights and prerogatives. The object of compensation is to restore the employee to the position he or she would have been in absent the discrimination, but that principle is difficult to apply with precision where there is after-acquired evidence of wrongdoing that would have led to termination on legitimate grounds had the employer known about it. Once an employer learns about employee wrongdoing that would lead to a legitimate discharge, we cannot require the employer to ignore the information, even if it is acquired during the course of discovery in a suit against the employer and even if the information might have gone undiscovered absent the suit. The beginning point in the trial court's formulation of a remedy should be calculation of backpay from the date of the unlawful discharge to the date the new information was discovered. In determining the appropriate order for relief, the court can consider taking into further account extraordinary equitable circumstances that affect the legitimate interests of either party. An absolute rule barring any recovery of backpay, however, would undermine the ADEA's objective of forcing employers to consider and examine their motivations, and of penalizing them for employment decisions that spring from age discrimination.

Where an employer seeks to rely upon after-acquired evidence of wrongdoing, it must first establish that the wrongdoing was of such severity that the employee in fact would have been terminated on those grounds alone if the employer had known of it at the time of the discharge. The concern that employers might as a routine matter undertake extensive discovery into an employee's background or performance on the job to resist claims under the Act is not an insubstantial one, but we think the authority of the courts to award attorney's fees, mandated under the statute, will deter most abuses.

The judgment is reversed, and the case is remanded to the Court of Appeals for the Sixth Circuit for further proceedings consistent with this opinion.

It is so ordered.

Judgment for McKennon

Case Commentary

The U.S. Supreme Court ruled that the employer's subsequent discovery of the employee's theft of documents does not excuse its discharge of the employee due to age discrimination. ∎

CASE QUESTIONS

1. Are you in agreement with the Court?
2. Is the employer vindicated by the subsequent disclosure of the employee's document theft?
3. If the employer and the employee are both at fault, how can the case be resolved?

Employment Perspective

Myrtle Eldridge has been working for Marvin Wilson as his personal secretary for 35 years. Their employer is Seacrest Shipping. Marvin retired recently. His replacement is Buddy Johnson, who is 27 years old. After one look at Myrtle, he decides that he would prefer someone who is more youthful. Buddy replaces Myrtle with Rhonda, a 22-year-old whose office skills barely measure up to Myrtle's. Myrtle files a claim with EEOC. Before its determination, she sues Seacrest Shipping in state court. Seacrest argues that her suit cannot be brought until the EEOC determination has been made, as in Title VII cases. Are they correct? No! After the filing of the EEOC claim, Myrtle is free to pursue her own suit in state court, unlike under Title VII, which requires an EEOC dismissal before suing. With regard to the issue in her case, Seacrest claims that incompatibility was the reason why Buddy wanted her replaced. Is this a sufficient reason? No! Because Buddy had Myrtle dismissed immediately, there is no basis on which to draw a conclusion of incompatibility. Myrtle will win and will be reinstated in the secretarial position. Naturally, it would be ludicrous for Buddy and Myrtle to work together, given the EEOC investigation and the lawsuit. Myrtle will be entitled to double back pay. The doubling is a form of liquidated damages because Buddy's actions were intentional: He did not want her because of her age. In addition, she will receive compensation for lost benefits, loss of seniority, and possibly attorney fees and interest.

Employer's Justification for Layoffs

Many firms lay off older workers for financial reasons. They can save money by replacing older workers with young workers, who are willing to do the same work for an entry-level salary. For layoffs not to be in violation of the Age Discrimination in Employment Act, they must be made across the board.

The issue in the next case is whether the plaintiff's discharge was justified due to downsizing coupled with his lackluster performance.

Carlton v. Mystic Transportation
202 F.3d 129 (2nd Cir. 2000)

Cardamone, Circuit Judge.

Plaintiff Charles R. Carlton, formerly employed as director of marketing by defendants Mystic Transportation, Inc., Mystic Bulk Carriers, Inc. and Leonard Baldari, appeals from a grant of summary judgment in favor of defendants in the United States District Court for the Eastern District of New York. Carlton asserts he was fired on account of his age, but defendants declare plaintiff's discharge occurred as part of a company-wide reduction-in-force and because of his mediocre job performance.

One of the arguments the employer raises in this employment discrimination case is the "same actor inference." The premise underlying this inference is that if the person who fires an employee is the same person that hired him, one cannot logically impute to that person an invidious intent to discriminate against the employee.

Such an inference is strong where the time elapsed between the events of hiring and firing is brief. Here it is not. And, the enthusiasm with which the actor hired the employee years before may have waned with the passage of time because the relationship between an employer and an employee, characterized by reciprocal obligations and duties, is, like them, subject to time's "wrackful siege of battering days."

In reviewing a grant of summary judgment for an employer, we examine the record to see if any genuine issues of material fact exist regarding whether the non-discriminatory reasons the employer advanced for the employee's discharge were instead a pretext for intentional age discrimination. Because we find several unresolved issues of material fact in this record, we reverse and remand.

BACKGROUND

Mystic Transportation, Inc. is a trucking company that delivers heating oil within the New York metropolitan area, and Mystic Bulk Carriers, Inc. transports gasoline, asphalt, cement, and jet fuel in the same market. The two companies have consolidated financial statements and are inextricably intertwined. Leonard Baldari is Mystic's president and sole shareholder. The defendants will be collectively referred to as Mystic.

In August 1988, at age 49, plaintiff Carlton was hired as a salesman by Baldari, who shortly thereafter appointed him as director of marketing. The principal duties of that position included soliciting new accounts with the aim of increasing his employer's delivery income. Mystic's delivery income increased each year that Carlton was employed, and nearly doubled overall from $12,485,480 in 1989 to $23,622,567 in 1994. Carlton also brought in 65 new accounts.

Due to a mild winter in 1995, Mystic's profits dropped $1,400,000 in that year's first quarter from those the company had enjoyed in the first quarter of 1994. In April 1995 Carlton, then 56 years old, was terminated. He alleges that during a meeting regarding his discharge, Baldari suggested he should "retire." Ten other employees were also discharged in early 1995.

One year prior to plaintiff's dismissal, Mystic hired Lydia Gounalis (age 38) to assist with marketing. Immediately after plaintiff was fired, Gounalis assumed his position as director of marketing. Three months later, Mystic hired a former employee, John Oravets (age 31), to work in marketing. Oravets' previous employment with defendant had been terminated in 1993 for insubordination. After he was rehired, Oravets took over the director of marketing position in June 1996.

Carlton filed an age discrimination complaint with the EEOC on September 25, 1995. Mystic stated in response that it had a deficit of $1.5 million in the first quarter of 1995—it turned out Mystic actually had an operating profit of $584,108 during that quarter, but it was about $ 1.4 million less than the previous year's profits for the same period. Mystic also stated that Carlton's performance was not a factor in its decision to discharge him. After its investigation, the EEOC issued a determination in defendants' favor.

On August 19, 1996 Carlton commenced the instant action in the Eastern District alleging a violation of the Age Discrimination in Employment Act of 1967 (ADEA). In contrast to the EEOC proceeding, Mystic averred in the district court that it discharged Carlton not only as part of a reduction-in-force due to the economic downturn it experienced, but also because of his poor performance. The district court granted Mystic's motion for summary judgment finding that plaintiff had failed to establish a prima facie case of age discrimination. It further stated that even assuming arguendo that plaintiff had made out a prima facie case, he did not adequately demonstrate that his employer's purported reasons for discharging him were a pretext for age discrimination.

This appeal followed.

DISCUSSION
I. LEGAL PRINCIPLES
A. Summary Judgment

Because this is a discrimination case where intent and state of mind are in dispute, summary judgment is ordinarily inappropriate. Thus, a trial court should exercise caution when granting summary judgment to an employer where, as here, its intent is a genuine factual issue.

B. The ADEA and the Burden of Proof

Direct evidence of discrimination is not necessary, because proof is seldom available with respect to an employer's mental processes. Instead, plaintiffs in discrimination suits often must rely on the cumulative weight of circumstantial evidence, since an employer who discriminates against its employee is unlikely to leave a well-marked trail, such as making a notation to that effect in the employee's personnel file. Ordinarily, plaintiff's evidence establishing a prima facie case and defendant's production of a nondiscriminatory reason for the employment action raise a question of fact to be resolved by the factfinder after a trial. Summary judgment is appropriate at this point only if the employer's nondiscriminatory reason is dispositive and forecloses any issue of material fact.

II. ANALYSIS
A. Plaintiff's Prima Facie Case

Carlton has established the first three elements of his prima facie case. At age 57 when he was terminated, he was a member of the protected class and qualified for his position. The only remaining question is whether plaintiff showed that his discharge occurred under circumstances giving rise to an inference of age discrimination.

The proof on that issue reveals that upon Carlton's termination his duties were transferred in part to Gounalis, a co-worker, who was 18 years younger than Carlton, and his remaining duties were given to Oravets, an employee 25 years younger, who was hired three months after Carlton was discharged. Generally, a plaintiff's replacement by a significantly younger person is evidence of age discrimination. Indeed, we have previously held that a plaintiff has demonstrated an inference of age discrimination and thus established a prima facie case in nearly identical circumstances where the majority of plaintiff's responsibilities were transferred to a younger co-worker, and shortly thereafter some of plaintiff's other duties were transferred to a newly hired younger employee.

Carlton also alleges that Baldari suggested, during the meeting regarding his termination, that he should "retire," and that this constitutes additional evidence of age discrimination. Although evidence of one stray comment by itself is usually not sufficient proof to show age discrimination, that stray comment may "bear a more ominous significance" when considered within the totality of all the evidence. Hence, it furnishes support for Carlton's prima facie case.

In light of the foregoing, we think plaintiff demonstrated circumstances giving rise to an inference of discrimination, and conclude that Carlton established a prima facie case.

B. Mystic's Defense

After a plaintiff demonstrates a prima facie case of age discrimination, the defendant must produce evidence "which, taken as true, would permit the conclusion that there was a nondiscriminatory reason for the adverse action." This explanation "must be 'clear and specific.'" Mystic has established that it experienced a significant decline in delivery income and profits due to weather conditions, and that a reduction-in-force was necessary to redress the imbalance in its finances. Mystic also avers that it was dissatisfied with Carlton's job performance. These explanations are sufficient to rebut the presumption of age discrimination established by plaintiff's prima facie case.

C. Pretext for Age Discrimination

Even within the context of a legitimate reduction-in-force, however, an employer may not discharge an employee "because" of his age. But Carlton must demonstrate, at least in his individual case, that the reduction-in-force and the allegation of poor performance are actually a pretext and that the real reason for his discharge was his age.

Several questions arise regarding Mystic's assertion that Carlton was fired as part of a necessary reduction-in-force. In spite of the company's purported need to downsize, Oravets, who was 25 years younger than the plaintiff, was hired to fill Carlton's position as director of marketing only three months after plaintiff was discharged, tending to refute the reduction-in-force reason for plaintiff's discharge. Although Mystic asserts that a newly acquired account warranted the hiring of another employee, its contention does not explain why Mystic did not consider rehiring Carlton for the position. The inadequacy of Mystic's explanation is of some significance since Congress, as earlier noted, found

older workers especially disadvantaged in regaining employment after being displaced. Further, Mystic provided another employee with a recall option pending a financial turnaround, but did not extend this option to Carlton. And, defendant achieved relatively insignificant savings as a result of Carlton's termination. While Carlton had received $57,200 per year, Oravets was paid $46,800 per year. All of which suggests that perhaps some other motive—beyond the company's finances—motivated Carlton's dismissal.

Defendants' assertion that Carlton was terminated in part because of poor performance also appears questionable. In its response to the EEOC, Mystic cited its decline in profits as the only reason for Carlton's dismissal, and expressly stated that job performance was not a factor.

In light of the dispute in the proof on these issues, a rational jury could reject both of Mystic's non-discriminatory reasons. The conflict between plaintiff's evidence establishing a prima facie case and Mystic's proof in support of its non-discriminatory reasons creates genuine issues of material fact that can only be decided by a factfinder after trial.

Conclusion

In sum, we find that Carlton has established a prima facie case of age discrimination and that genuine issues of material fact exist regarding the non-discriminatory reasons Mystic has advanced for its decision to discharge him. As a result, summary judgment was wrongly granted. Accordingly, that judgment is reversed and the case remanded to the district court with instructions to reinstate plaintiff's complaint and to conduct further proceedings on the merits of Carlton's ADEA claim consistent with this opinion.

Judgment for Carlton.

Case Commentary

The Second Circuit Court found that Mystic's reasons for discharging Carlton were not justified. Therefore, Mystic's motion to dismiss was not granted. ■

CASE QUESTIONS

1. Are you in agreement with the Court's decision?
2. Do you believe employers should be granted more leeway in the termination of its employees?
3. Are you confident that Carlton will win when his case goes to trial?

Employment Perspective

Michael Ryan has worked as a driver for Yukon Bus Company for 35 years. He is 62 years old; his salary is $47,000. Ryan is laid off and then replaced by 22-year-old Jude West. West is paid $25,000. Ryan sues, citing age discrimination. Does he win? Yes! Unless Yukon can show cause, then it intentionally terminated Ryan because of his age and correspondingly higher salary. Ryan will be entitled to back pay, loss of pension benefits, and liquidated damages in the form of doubling the back pay that is owed.

Retirement Packages

Forcing older employees to accept retirement packages is another form of age discrimination. Retirement must not be mandatory; otherwise, the employer will be in violation of the ADEA. The retirement package must be accepted voluntarily, without coercion.

The Older Workers Benefit Protection Act

The Older Workers Benefit Protection Act (OWBPA) of 1990 amended the ADEA to protect older workers from discrimination in hiring by those employers who believe it would be a financial burden on their health and pension plans. Older workers can be forced to retire for safety reasons. Pilots and others involved in transportation often have mandatory retirement ages.

EEOC issued guidelines for layoffs. The individuals being laid off must fall into one of the following decisional units: category (engineers), facility (Boston Plant), division (minivans), department (software development), and those reporting to a particular superior (human resource VP). Then the individuals who are staying and who are leaving must be listed by age, job title, and whether they are accepting an early retirement package or being discharged involuntarily. After all this information has been disseminated to all departing employees, an employer can request they sign a waiver that the process has been fairly administered in line with the ADEA.

The issue in the following case is whether the release executed in return for severance pay was done so in accordance with the terms of the Older Workers Benefit Protection Act.

Oubre v. Entergy Operations, Inc.
522 U.S. 422(1998)

Justice Kennedy delivered the opinion of the Court.

An employee, as part of a termination agreement, signed a release of all claims against her employer. In consideration, she received severance pay in installments. The release, however, did not comply with specific federal statutory requirements for a release of claims under the Age Discrimination in Employment Act of 1967 (ADEA). After receiving the last payment, the employee brought suit under the ADEA. The employer claims the employee ratified and validated the nonconforming release by retaining the monies paid to secure it. The employer also insists the release bars the action unless, as a precondition to filing suit, the employee tenders back the monies received. We disagree and rule that, as the release did not comply with the statute, it cannot bar the ADEA claim.

I

Petitioner Dolores Oubre worked as a scheduler at a power plant in Killona, Louisiana, run by her employer, respondent Entergy Operations, Inc. In 1994, she received a poor performance rating. Oubre's supervisor met with her on January 17, 1995, and gave her the option of either improving her performance during the coming year or accepting a

voluntary arrangement for her severance. She received a packet of information about the severance agreement and had 14 days to consider her options, during which she consulted with attorneys. On January 31, Oubre decided to accept. She signed a release, in which she "agreed to waive, settle, release, and discharge any and all claims, demands, damages, actions, or causes of action . . . that I may have against Entergy. . . . " In exchange, she received six installment payments over the next four months, totaling $6,258.

The Older Workers Benefit Protection Act (OWBPA) imposes specific requirements for releases covering ADEA claims. In procuring the release, Entergy did not comply with the OWBPA in at least three respects: (1) Entergy did not give Oubre enough time to consider her options. (2) Entergy did not give Oubre seven days after she signed the release to change her mind. And (3) the release made no specific reference to claims under the ADEA.

Oubre filed a charge of age discrimination with the Equal Employment Opportunity Commission, which dismissed her charge on the merits but issued a right-to-sue letter. She filed this suit against Entergy in the United States

District Court for the Eastern District of Louisiana, alleging constructive discharge on the basis of her age in violation of the ADEA and state law. Oubre has not offered or tried to return the $6,258 to Entergy, nor is it clear she has the means to do so. Entergy moved for summary judgment, claiming Oubre had ratified the defective release by failing to return or offer to return the monies she had received. The District Court agreed and entered summary judgment for Entergy. The Court of Appeals affirmed, and we granted certiorari.

II

The employer rests its case upon general principles of state contract jurisprudence. As the employer recites the rule, contracts tainted by mistake, duress, or even fraud are voidable at the option of the innocent party. The employer maintains, however, that before the innocent party can elect avoidance, she must first tender back any benefits received under the contract. If she fails to do so within a reasonable time after learning of her rights, the employer contends, she ratifies the contract and so makes it binding. The employer also invokes the doctrine of equitable estoppel. As a rule, equitable estoppel bars a party from shirking the burdens of a voidable transaction for as long as she retains the benefits received under it. Applying these principles, the employer claims the employee ratified the ineffective release (or faces estoppel) by retaining all the sums paid in consideration of it. The employer, then, relies not upon the execution of the release but upon a later, distinct ratification of its terms. These general rules may not be as unified as the employer asserts. And in equity, a person suing to rescind a contract, as a rule, is not required to restore the consideration at the very outset of the litigation. Even if the employer's statement of the general rule requiring tender back before one files suit were correct, it would be unavailing. The rule cited is based simply on the course of negotiation of the parties and the alleged later ratification. The authorities cited do not consider the question raised by statutory standards for releases and a statutory declaration making nonconforming releases ineffective. It is the latter question we confront here. In 1990, Congress amended the ADEA by passing the OWBPA. The OWBPA provides: "An individual may not waive any right or claim under the ADEA unless the waiver is knowing and voluntary. . . . A waiver may not be considered knowing and voluntary unless at a minimum" it satisfies certain enumerated requirements, including the three listed above.

The statutory command is clear: An employee "may not waive" an ADEA claim unless the waiver or release satisfies the OWBPA's requirements. The policy of the Older Workers Benefit Protection Act is likewise clear from its title: It is designed to protect the rights and benefits of older workers. The OWBPA implements Congress' policy via a strict, unqualified statutory stricture on waivers, and we are bound to take Congress at its word. Congress imposed specific duties on employers who seek releases of certain claims created by statute. Congress delineated these duties with precision and without qualification: An employee "may not waive" an ADEA claim unless the employer complies with the statute. Courts cannot with ease presume ratification of that which Congress forbids. The OWBPA sets up its own regime for assessing the effect of ADEA waivers, separate and apart from contract law. The statute creates a series of prerequisites for knowing and voluntary waivers and imposes affirmative duties of disclosure and waiting periods. The OWBPA governs the effect under federal law of waivers or releases on ADEA claims and incorporates no exceptions or qualifications. The text of the OWBPA forecloses the employer's defense, notwithstanding how general contract principles would apply to non-ADEA claims.

Oubre's cause of action arises under the ADEA, and the release can have no effect on her ADEA claim unless it complies with the OWBPA. In this case, both sides concede the release the employee signed did not comply with the requirements of the OWBPA. Since Oubre's release did not comply with the OWBPA's stringent safeguards, it is unenforceable against her insofar as it purports to waive or release her ADEA claim. As a statutory matter, the release cannot bar her ADEA suit, irrespective of the validity of the contract as to other claims.

In further proceedings in this or other cases, courts may need to inquire whether the employer has claims for restitution, recoupment, or setoff against the employee, and these questions may be complex where a release is effective as to some claims but not as to ADEA claims. We need not decide those issues here, however. It suffices to hold that the release cannot bar the ADEA claim because it does not conform to the statute. Nor did the employee's mere retention of monies amount to a ratification equivalent to a valid release of her ADEA claims, since the retention did not comply with the OWBPA any more than the original release did. The statute governs the effect of the release on ADEA claims, and the employer cannot invoke the employee's failure to tender back as a way of excusing its own failure to comply.

We reverse the judgment of the Court of Appeals and remand for further proceedings consistent with this opinion.

It is so ordered.

Judgment for Oubre.

Case Commentary

The U.S. Supreme Court held that Oubre's signing of the release was not conducted according to the Older Workers Benefit Protection Act. The fact that Oubre did not return the severance pay does not preclude her ADEA claim. ∎

CASE QUESTIONS

1. Do you agree with the decision of the U.S. Supreme Court?
2. Why do you think Oubre did not make restitution?

3. What do you think Oubre is trying to achieve in trying to set aside her agreement to the severance package?

Employment Perspective

Mildred Greene is 58 years old. Her employer, Suds & Bubbles, a soap manufacturer, has offered her an attractive retirement package. Mildred, who has no family, would rather continue working in public relations, where she is able to meet new people. Suds & Bubbles tells Mildred that if she does not retire, she will be transferred to back-office bookkeeping work, where she will not be able to interact with anyone. Mildred files a claim with the EEOC and later brings an action in state court. Will she win? Of course! There is no reasonable basis for transferring her. The prospect of a transfer is being used as a threat to force her to retire.

Comparative Treatment of the Elderly

In many cultures, the elderly are looked upon as having much wisdom and are revered. In the United States, the elderly were often forced into retirement unless they were executives or politicians. Although mandatory retirement is gone because of the Age Discrimination in Employment Act, certain prejudices remain. Some prejudices are understandable in economic terms. For example, the performance of routine office work by a person with 24 years' seniority making a salary of $42,000 could easily be replaced by a young person for a salary of $28,000. With age often comes seniority, and with seniority often comes greater wages and benefits and sometimes greater knowledge. Although that may not be so in the telecommunications and software development fields, in many other cases it is. To automatically discount an older worker's skill, knowledge, and experience would not be prudent because it would not be utilizing the talents of all American workers.

EMPLOYEE LESSONS

1. Know what protections you are afforded under the Age Discrimination in Employment Act.
2. Consider whether age may have been a factor in your termination if you are 40 years of age or older.
3. Realize that you may work indefinitely as long as you are performing the essential functions of the job.
4. Appreciate that if you are in your 30s and are replaced by someone 10 to 15 years younger, you are not protected under the ADEA.
5. Be aware that you cannot be coerced into accepting an early retirement package.
6. Be careful when an employer downsizes that its motivation is not based on age.
7. Understand that age discrimination may occur when your position is terminated because of your high salary and age.
8. Be aware that age discrimination exists when an older employee is replaced by someone significantly younger, even when the younger person is over 40 years of age.
9. Be apprised that policy-making executives may be forced to retire at 65 years of age.
10. Be aware that tenured professors have no ADEA protection beyond age 70.

SUMMARY

In years gone by, most people worked either until they became disabled or until they died. Disabled workers were usually cared for by family members. There was no such thing as retirement unless a person was independently wealthy and could, therefore, live off the income from his or her investments. With the advent of Social

Security, when individuals retire they are entitled to a small amount of income. As pensions became more prevalent, workers were guaranteed a defined benefit. The income from Social Security and the pension enabled people to survive after mandatory retirement. How well they survived depended upon the size of their pension and of their investment income. Pensions remained fixed because they were not adjusted for inflation. Social Security recipients received cost-of-living adjustments. Investment income has a built-in guard against inflation.

Life expectancies have increased, and the majority of Americans now live beyond age 65. Surreptitiously prohibiting people from continuing to work because of their age when they are perfectly capable of doing so is discriminatory. The purpose of the Age Discrimination in Employment Act is to dispel this conduct and to give free access to the workplace to those people over the age of 65. Workers will be able to continue in their current jobs or to seek new employment elsewhere, thus broadening the pool of workers. As was stated, many older workers have special skills, knowledge, and experience. The freedom to employ these people is certainly a bonus for employers, especially those involved in the growing competitiveness of the global marketplace.

REVIEW QUESTIONS

1. What is the significance of the Age Discrimination in Employment Act?
2. At what age may an employee claim age discrimination?
3. Is there a mandatory retirement age?
4. Are there any exceptions?
5. Is an advertisement that specifies "recent college graduate" discriminatory?
6. Can age be considered a bona fide occupational qualification?
7. What must be the determining factor in the dismissal of an older worker?
8. Can a young person who is not hired because of his or her youth claim age discrimination?
9. Does the Civil Rights Act encompass those discriminated against because of age?
10. In many cultures, age is a sign of wisdom. Why is that not generally the case in the United States?
11. Is it possible to claim age discrimination even though the individual opted for early retirement?
12. Is it ethical for a supervisor to discharge an employee when he or she knows that the employer's motivation is age?
13. Are economic factors a justifiable defense to a suit based on age discrimination?

CASE PROBLEMS

1. The district court summarized the reasons for laying off plaintiffs: Unisys was losing billions of dollars, facing economic disaster, and had to implement drastic cost-cutting measures.

   However, as Unisys outlined in the 1991 layoffs, a slightly higher percentage of employees outside the protected age group were terminated compared with those in the protected group. Indeed, the percentage of employees in the age group before and after the reduction force was almost the same—about 69 percent. Statistics taken in isolation are generally not probative of age discrimination, and the statistics here do not support a finding of intent to discriminate.

   The only other purported case of age discrimination was a double heresay comment by a Unisys employee responsible for job posting, that "It's about time we unloaded some of this old driftwood." The issue is whether economic factors dictated the company's decision to downsize or whether they serve as a pretext for the company to discriminate. *Jones v. Unisys Corp.*, 54 F.3d 624 (10th Cir. 1995)

2. "Consistent with such decreasing sales, defendant began to reduce the number of Kollsman employees in order to save the business and save jobs. . . ." Between November 1989 and April 1993, when Kern was terminated, Kollsman reduced its workforce by approximately 1,100 employees on five separate occasions. It was understood by Kollsman employees, and Kern in particular, that the reason for such reductions was declining sales in the defense business.

   Kern claims that he was not dismissed pursuant to a reduction in force because many of his previous responsibilities were not eliminated with his position, but rather were allocated to younger employees. The case addresses the question of whether an older employee was terminated because of his age, with his work then reassigned to younger employees. *Kern v. Kollsman*, 885 F. Supp. 335 (D.N.H. 1995)

3. The Hazens hired respondent Walter F. Biggins as their technical director in 1977. They fired him in 1986, when he was 62 years old.

   Respondent brought suit against petitioners in the U.S. District Court for the District of Massachusetts, alleging a violation of the ADEA. He claimed that age had been a determinative factor in the petitioners' decision to fire him. The petitioners contested this claim, asserting instead that the respondent had been fired for doing business with competitors of Hazen Paper. What was the result? *Hazen Paper Company, et al. v. Walter F. Biggins*, 113 S. Ct. 1701 (1993)

HUMAN RESOURCE DILEMMAS

1. Crystal Advertising Agency is changing its sick policy from a specific number of days to occurrences. The number of occurrences will be reviewed in the year-end evaluation. Kevin Rogers is attempting to organize a class action claiming age discrimination because older workers get sick more often than younger workers. What advice would you give him?

2. Harvey Jameson was recently terminated as comptroller at the age of 66 from Better Beef, Inc. His replacement is Tammy Parker, age 45. Because both he and his replacement are covered under the ADEA, Harvey is wondering whether he is precluded from suing.

3. Multimatrix, Inc., has decided to phase out its production of cassette tapes and VHS tapes in favor of CDs and DVDs. Of the 224 workers, 95 percent are over the age of 40. Because it is fully staffed, Multimatrix cannot transfer these workers to other positions. Multimatrix is fearful of a class action lawsuit under the ADEA. What advice would you give Multimatrix?

WEB SITE ASSIGNMENT

Compare and contrast age discrimination laws of the United States and foreign countries. Make note of those countries that have no protection at all.

www.eeoc.gov/facts/age.html
www.aristotle.net/~hantley/hiedlegl/statutes/agedis67.htm
www.aarp.org
www.agerights.com
retireplan.about.com
www.dol.gov
benefitsattorney.com/links/ERISA
www.qdro.pair.com/erisa.htm

Chapter 17

Disability Discrimination

Employment Scenario

One day, Louise Fredricks enters the flagship store of The Long and the Short of It in a wheelchair. She encounters Tom Long and tells him that she is responding to L&S's advertisement for a sales associate. Tom responds in amazement, "You're kidding." Louise reiterates her intent to gain employment. Tom begins laughing uncontrollably and opens the exit door. Louise, visibly upset, departs in despair. After composing herself, Louise becomes infuriated over the treatment she endured. She contacts the EEOC, which notifies L&S that they will be investigating. What advice should their attorney, Susan North, give to L&S?

Chapter Checklist

➤ Be familiar with the intricacies of the Americans with Disabilities Act (ADA).

➤ Learn the four major categories of disabilities.

➤ Know that anyone perceived as having a disability will be covered under the ADA, even if they would not otherwise be covered.

➤ Realize that reasonable accommodations must be made if an employee is disabled.

➤ Consider that employees may seek ADA coverage for many ailments, injuries, and conditions, but not all of these qualify as disabilities.

➤ Understand that AIDS is covered under the ADA as a disease.

➤ Be aware that applicants should not be asked if they are disabled.

➤ Be apprised that disabled employees must be able to perform the essential functions of the job.

➤ Be concerned that if the accommodation requested amounts to an undue burden, the employer does not have to grant it.

➤ Appreciate that disabled individuals have the right to be gainfully employed.

INTRODUCTION

In 1990, Congress passed the Americans with Disabilities Act (ADA). The ADA has a profound effect on the many millions of Americans who live with some type of disability. The Americans with Disabilities Act requires employers having 15 or more employees to refrain from discriminating against any individual who has an impairment that limits major life activities, such as an impairment to sight, speech, hearing, walking, and learning. Also included are people with cancer, heart conditions, AIDS, and disfigurement, as well as people recovering from substance abuse.

The four largest categories of disabilities are physical (prosthetic, wheelchair, carpal tunnel), disease (heart, lung, cancer, AIDS), sensory (sight, speech, hearing), and mental (developmentally disabled, emotionally disabled, chemical dependency). The examples given are not all-inclusive. Physical and disease represent a much larger proportion than sensory or mental.

The forerunner of the ADA was the Rehabilitation Act of 1973. It prohibited disability discrimination in federal employment and with federal contractors.

HUMAN RESOURCE ADVICE

- Understand the provisions of the Americans with Disabilities Act.
- Treat disabled workers as you would treat other employees.
- Know what ailments, conditions, or sicknesses are covered under the ADA.
- Learn the four major categories of disabilities.
- Attempt to accommodate disabled workers if their requests are reasonable.
- Refrain from questioning applicants about whether they are disabled.
- Know that if the accommodation requested is an undue burden, then it does not have to be granted.
- Safeguard the confidentiality of the medical records of disabled employees.
- Do not speak to coworkers about an employee's disability.
- Be aware that the ADA does not mandate special treatment for the disabled; they must be able to perform the essential functions of the job.

REASONABLE ACCOMMODATIONS

The ADA requires employers to make reasonable accommodations to enable the disabled to work. This includes making the work site accessible, modifying equipment, and changing work schedules. Those businesses providing a service to the public must make their establishments accessible to the handicapped. This includes but is not limited to stores, restaurants, hotels, museums, theaters, historical landmarks, visitor centers, sports arenas, health and fitness facilities, and nightclubs. The disabled person must be qualified to do the job; that is, he or she must be able to perform the essential functions with reasonable accommodation. The ADA was not designed to force employers to hire disabled workers who are not qualified. The qualifications required, however, must be necessary to do the job. If someone is more qualified than the disabled individual, the employer is not required to give the disabled individual preferential treatment.

The issue in the following case is whether twin sisters with severe myopia, which has been corrected with eyewear, are covered under the ADA.

Sutton v. United Air Lines, Inc.

527 U.S. 471 (1999)

Justice O'Connor delivered the opinion of the Court.

The Americans with Disabilities Act of 1990 (ADA or Act), prohibits certain employers from discriminating against individuals on the basis of their disabilities. Petitioners challenge the dismissal of their ADA action for failure to state a claim upon which relief can be granted. We conclude that the complaint was properly dismissed. In reaching that result, we hold that the determination of whether an individual is disabled should be made with reference to measures that mitigate the individual's impairment, including, in this instance, eyeglasses and contact lenses. In addition, we hold that petitioners failed to allege properly that respondent "regarded" them as having a disability within the meaning of the ADA.

I

Petitioners are twin sisters, both of whom have severe myopia. Each petitioner's uncorrected visual acuity is 20/200 or worse in her right eye and 20/400 or worse in her left eye, but "with the use of corrective lenses, each . . . has vision that is 20/20 or better." Consequently, without corrective lenses, each "effectively cannot see to conduct numerous activities such as driving a vehicle, watching television or shopping in public stores," but with corrective measures, such as glasses or contact lenses, both "function identically to individuals without a similar impairment."

In 1992, petitioners applied to respondent for employment as commercial airline pilots. They met respondent's basic age, education, experience, and FAA certification qualifications. After submitting their applications for employment, both petitioners were invited by respondent to an interview and to flight simulator tests. Both were told during their interviews, however, that a mistake had been made in inviting them to interview because petitioners did not meet respondent's minimum vision requirement, which was uncorrected visual acuity of 20/100 or better. Due to their failure to meet this requirement, petitioners' interviews were terminated, and neither was offered a pilot position.

In light of respondent's proffered reason for rejecting them, petitioners filed a charge of disability discrimination under the ADA with the Equal Employment Opportunity Commission (EEOC). After receiving a right to sue letter, petitioners filed suit in the United States District Court for the District of Colorado, alleging that respondent had discriminated against them "on the basis of their disability, or because respondent regarded petitioners as having a disability" in violation of the ADA. Specifically, petitioners alleged that due to their severe myopia they actually have a substantially limiting impairment or are regarded as having such an impairment, and are thus disabled under the Act.

The District Court dismissed petitioners' complaint for failure to state a claim upon which relief could be granted. Because petitioners could fully correct their visual impairments, the court held that they were not actually substantially limited in any major life activity and thus had not stated a claim that they were disabled within the meaning of the ADA. The court also determined that petitioners had not made allegations sufficient to support their claim that they were "regarded" by the respondent as having an impairment that substantially limits a major life activity. The court observed that "the statutory reference to a substantial limitation indicates . . . that an employer regards an employee as handicapped in his or her ability to work by finding the employee's impairment to foreclose generally the type of employment involved."

But petitioners had alleged only that respondent regarded them as unable to satisfy the requirements of a particular job, global airline pilot. Consequently, the court held that petitioners had not stated a claim that they were regarded as substantially limited in the major life activity of working. Employing similar logic, the Court of Appeals for the Tenth Circuit affirmed the District Court's judgment.

The Tenth Circuit's decision is in tension with the decisions of other Courts of Appeals. We granted certiorari and now affirm.

II

The ADA prohibits discrimination by covered entities, including private employers, against qualified individuals with a disability. Specifically, it provides that no covered employer "shall discriminate against a qualified individual with a disability because of the disability of such individual in regard to job application procedures, the hiring, advancement, or discharge of employees, employee compensation, job training, and other terms, conditions, and privileges of employment." ("The term 'covered entity' means an employer, employment agency, labor organization, or joint labor-management committee.") A "qualified individual with a disability" is identified as "an individual with a disability who, with or without reasonable accommodation, can perform the essential functions of the employment position that such individual holds or desires." In turn, a "disability" is defined as:

"(A) a physical or mental impairment that substantially limits one or more of the major life activities of such individual;
"(B) a record of such an impairment; or
"(C) being regarded as having such an impairment."

Accordingly, to fall within this definition one must have an actual disability (subsection (A)), have a record of a disability (subsection (B)), or be regarded as having one (subsection (C)).

The parties agree that the authority to issue regulations to implement the Act is split primarily among three Government agencies. According to the parties, the EEOC has authority to issue regulations to carry out the employment provisions in Title I of the ADA. The Attorney General is granted authority to issue regulations with respect to Title II, which relates to public services. Finally, the Secretary of Transportation has authority to issue regulations pertaining to the transportation provisions of Titles II and III.

No agency, however, has been given authority to issue regulations implementing the generally applicable provisions of the ADA, which fall outside Titles I–V. Most notably, no agency has been delegated authority to interpret the term "disability." The EEOC has, nonetheless, issued regulations to provide additional guidance regarding the proper interpretation of this term. After restating the definition of disability given in the statute, the EEOC regulations define the three elements of disability: (1) "physical or mental impairment," (2) "substantially limits," and (3) "major life activities." Under the regulations, a "physical impairment" includes "any physiological disorder, or condition, cosmetic disfigurement, or anatomical loss affecting one or more of the following body systems: neurological, musculoskeletal, special sense organs, respiratory (including speech organs), cardiovascular, reproductive, digestive, genitourinary, hemic and lymphatic, skin, and endocrine." The term "substantially limits" means, among other things, "unable to perform a major life activity that the average person in the general population can perform;" or "significantly restricted as to the condition, manner or duration under which an individual can perform a particular major life activity as compared to the condition, manner, or duration under which the average person in the general population can perform that same major life activity." Finally, "major life activities means functions such as caring for oneself, performing manual tasks, walking, seeing, hearing, speaking, breathing, learning, and working." Because both parties accept these regulations as valid, and determining their validity is not necessary to decide this case, we have no occasion to consider what deference they are due, if any.

III

With this statutory and regulatory framework in mind, we turn first to the question whether petitioners have stated a claim under subsection (A) of the disability definition, that is, whether they have alleged that they possess a physical impairment that substantially limits them in one or more major life activities. Because petitioners allege that with corrective measures their vision "is 20/20 or better," they are not actually disabled within the meaning of the Act if the "disability" determination is made with reference to these measures. Consequently, with respect to subsection (A) of the disability definition, our decision turns on whether disability is to be determined with or without reference to corrective measures.

Looking at the Act as a whole, it is apparent that if a person is taking measures to correct for, or mitigate, a physical or mental impairment, the effects of those measures—both positive and negative—must be taken into account when judging whether that person is "substantially limited" in a major life activity and thus "disabled" under the Act.

Three separate provisions of the ADA, read in concert, lead us to this conclusion. The Act defines a "disability" as "a physical or mental impairment that *substantially limits* one or more of the major life activities" of an individual. Because the phrase "substantially limits" appears in the Act in the present indicative verb form, we think the language is properly read as requiring that a person be presently—not potentially or hypothetically—substantially limited in order to demonstrate a disability. A "disability" exists only where an impairment "substantially limits" a major life activity, not where it "might," "could," or "would" be substantially limiting if mitigating measures were not taken. A person whose physical or mental impairment is corrected by medication or other measures does not have an impairment that presently "substantially limits" a major life activity. To be sure, a person whose physical or mental impairment is corrected by mitigating measures still has an impairment, but if the impairment is corrected it does not "substantially limit" a major life activity.

The definition of disability also requires that disabilities be evaluated "with respect to an individual" and be determined based on whether an impairment substantially limits the "major life activities of such individual." Thus, whether a person has a disability under the ADA is an individualized inquiry.

The agency guidelines' directive that persons be judged in their uncorrected or unmitigated state runs directly counter to the individualized inquiry mandated by the ADA.

It explained that the estimates of the number of disabled Americans ranged from an overinclusive 160 million under a "health conditions approach," which looks at all conditions that impair the health or normal functional abilities of an individual, to an underinclusive 22.7 million under a "work disability approach," which focuses on individuals' reported ability to work.

Regardless of its exact source, however, the 43 million figure reflects an understanding that those whose impairments are largely corrected by medication or other devices are not "disabled" within the meaning of the ADA.

Because it is included in the ADA's text, the finding that 43 million individuals are disabled gives content to the ADA's terms, specifically the term "disability." Had Congress intended to include all persons with corrected physical limitations among those covered by the Act, it undoubtedly would have cited a much higher number of disabled persons in the findings. That it did not is evidence that the ADA's coverage is restricted to only those whose impairments are not mitigated by corrective measures. The use of a corrective device does not, by itself, relieve one's disability. Rather, one has a disability under subsection A if, notwithstanding the use of a corrective device, that individual is substantially limited in a major life activity. For example, individuals who use prosthetic limbs or wheelchairs may be mobile and capable of functioning in society but still be disabled because of a substantial limitation on their ability to walk or run. The same may be true of individuals who take medicine to lessen the symptoms of an impairment so that they can function but nevertheless remain substantially limited. Alternatively, one whose high blood pressure is "cured" by medication may be regarded as disabled by a covered entity, and thus disabled under subsection C of the definition. The use or nonuse of a corrective device does not determine whether an individual is disabled; that determination depends on whether the limitations an individual with an impairment *actually* faces are in fact substantially limiting.

Applying this reading of the Act to the case at hand, we conclude that the Court of Appeals correctly resolved the issue of disability in respondent's favor. As noted above, petitioners allege that with corrective measures, their visual acuity is 20/20, and that they "function identically to individuals without a similar impairment." In addition, petitioners concede that they "do not argue that the use of corrective lenses in itself demonstrates a substantially limiting impairment." Accordingly, because we decide that disability under the Act is to be determined with reference to corrective measures, we agree with the courts below that petitioners have not stated a claim that they are substantially limited in any major life activity.

IV

Under subsection (C), individuals who are "regarded as" having a disability are disabled within the meaning of the ADA. Subsection (C) provides that having a disability includes "being regarded as having," "a physical or mental impairment that substantially limits one or more of the major life activities of such individual." There are two apparent ways in which individuals may fall within this statutory definition: (1) a covered entity mistakenly believes that a person has a physical impairment that substantially limits one or more major life activities, or (2) a covered entity mistakenly believes that an actual, nonlimiting impairment substantially limits one or more major life activities. In both cases, it is necessary that a covered entity entertain misperceptions about the individual—it must believe either that one has a substantially limiting impairment that one does not have or that one has a substantially limiting impairment when, in fact, the impairment is not so limiting. These misperceptions often "result from stereotypic assumptions not truly indicative of . . . individual ability." ("By amending the definition of 'handicapped individual' to include not only those who are actually physically impaired, but also those who are regarded as impaired and who, as a result, are substantially limited in a major life activity, Congress acknowledged that society's accumulated myths and fears about disability and disease are as handicapping as are the physical limitations that flow from actual impairment.")

There is no dispute that petitioners are physically impaired. Petitioners do not make the obvious argument that they are regarded due to their impairments as substantially limited in the major life activity of seeing. They contend only that respondent mistakenly believes their physical impairments substantially limit them in the major life activity of working. To support this claim, petitioners allege that respondent has a vision requirement, which is allegedly based on myth and stereotype. Further, this requirement substantially limits their ability to engage in the major life activity of working by precluding them from obtaining the job of global airline pilot, which they argue is a "class of employment." In reply, respondent argues that the position of global airline pilot is not a class of jobs and therefore petitioners have not stated a claim that they are regarded as substantially limited in the major life activity of working.

Standing alone, the allegation that respondent has a vision requirement in place does not establish a claim that respondent regards petitioners as substantially limited in the major life activity of working. By its terms, the ADA allows employers to prefer some physical attributes over others and to establish physical criteria. An employer runs afoul of the ADA when it makes an employment decision based on a physical or mental impairment, real or imagined, that is regarded as substantially limiting a major life activity. Accordingly, an employer is free to decide that physical characteristics or medical conditions that do not rise to the level of an impairment—such as one's height, build, or singing voice—are preferable to others, just as it is free to decide that some limiting, but not *substantially* limiting, impairments make individuals less than ideally suited for a job.

Assuming without deciding that working is a major life activity and that the EEOC regulations interpreting the term "substantially limits" are reasonable, petitioners have failed to allege adequately that their poor eyesight is regarded as an impairment that substantially limits them in the major life activity of working. An otherwise valid job requirement, such as a height requirement, does not become invalid simply because it *would* limit a person's employment opportunities in a substantial way *if* it were adopted by a substantial number of employers. Because petitioners have not alleged, and cannot demonstrate, that respondent's vision requirement reflects a belief that petitioners' vision substantially limits them, we agree with the decision of the Court of Appeals affirming the dismissal of petitioners' claim that they are regarded as disabled.

CASE QUESTIONS

1. Do you agree with the U.S. Supreme Court's decision?
2. Should people with correctable disabilities still be covered under the ADA?

For these reasons, the decision of the Court of Appeals for the Tenth Circuit is affirmed.

Judgment for United Airlines.

Case Commentary

The U.S. Supreme Court resolved that the twins were not covered under the ADA because their vision problem was corrected with eyewear. Therefore, they no longer had a disability that limited a major life activity. ■

3. If the twins had argued that United Airlines regarded them as having a disability, do you believe they would have prevailed?

The question presented in the case that follows is whether an employer may incorporate a federal safety standard into a job qualification that, in effect, bars a disabled person from employment.

Albertsons, Inc. v. Kirkingburg

527 U.S. 555 (1999)

Justice Souter delivered the opinion of the Court.

The question posed is whether, under the Americans with Disabilities Act of 1990, an employer who requires as a job qualification that an employee meet an otherwise applicable federal safety regulation must justify enforcing the regulation solely because its standard may be waived in an individual case. We answer no.

I

In August 1990, petitioner, Albertsons, Inc., a grocery-store chain with supermarkets in several States, hired respondent, Hallie Kirkingburg, as a truckdriver based at its Portland, Oregon, warehouse. Kirkingburg had more than a decade's driving experience and performed well when Albertsons' transportation manager took him on a road test.

Before starting work, Kirkingburg was examined to see if he met federal vision standards for commercial truckdrivers. For many decades the Department of Transportation or its predecessors has been responsible for devising these standards for individuals who drive commercial vehicles in interstate commerce. Since 1971, the basic vision regulation has required corrected distant visual acuity of at least 20/40 in each eye and distant binocular acuity of at least 20/40. Kirkingburg, however, suffers from amblyopia, an uncorrectable condition that leaves him with 20/200 vision in his left eye and monocular vision in effect. Despite Kirkingburg's weak left eye, the doctor erroneously certified that he met the DOT's basic vision standard, and Albertsons hired him.

In December 1991, Kirkingburg injured himself on the job and took a leave of absence. Before returning to work in November 1992, Kirkingburg went for a further physical as required by the company. This time, the examining physician correctly assessed Kirkingburg's vision and explained that his eyesight did not meet the basic DOT standards. The physician, or his nurse, told Kirkingburg that in order to be legally qualified to drive, he would have to obtain a waiver of its basic vision standards from the DOT. The doctor was alluding to a scheme begun in July 1992 for giving DOT certification to applicants with deficient vision who had three years of recent experience driving a commercial vehicle without a license suspension or revocation, involvement in a reportable accident in which the applicant was cited for a moving violation, conviction for certain driving-related offenses, citation for certain serious traffic violations, or more than two convictions for any other moving violations. A waiver applicant had to agree to have his vision checked annually for deterioration, and to report certain information about his driving experience to the Federal Highway Administration, the agency within the DOT responsible for overseeing the motor carrier safety regulations. Kirkingburg applied for a waiver, but because he could not meet the basic DOT vision standard Albertsons fired him from his job as a truckdriver. In early 1993, after he had left Albertsons, Kirkingburg received a DOT waiver, but Albertsons refused to rehire him.

Kirkingburg sued Albertsons, claiming that firing him violated the ADA. Albertsons moved for summary judgment solely on the ground that Kirkingburg was "not 'otherwise qualified' to perform the job of truck driver with or without reasonable accommodation." The District Court granted the motion, ruling that Albertsons had reasonably concluded that Kirkingburg was not qualified without an accommodation because he could not, as admitted, meet the basic DOT vision standards. The court held that giving Kirkingburg time to get a DOT waiver was not a required reasonable accommodation because the waiver program was "a flawed experiment that has not altered the DOT vision requirements."

A divided panel of the Ninth Circuit reversed. In addition to pressing its claim that Kirkingburg was not otherwise qualified, Albertsons for the first time on appeal took the position that it was entitled to summary judgment because Kirkingburg did not have a disability within the meaning of the Act. The Court of Appeals considered but rejected the new argument, concluding that because Kirkingburg had presented "uncontroverted evidence" that his vision was effectively monocular, he had demonstrated that "the *manner* in which he sees differs significantly from the *manner* in which most people see." That difference in manner, the court held, was sufficient to establish disability.

II

Though we need not speak to the issue whether Kirkingburg was an individual with a disability in order to resolve this case, that issue falls within the first question on which we granted certiorari, and we think it worthwhile to address it briefly in order to correct three missteps the Ninth Circuit made in its discussion of the matter. Under the ADA:

"The term 'disability' means, with respect to an individual—

"(A) a physical or mental impairment that substantially limits one or more of the major life activities of such individual;
"(B) a record of such an impairment; or
"(C) being regarded as having such an impairment."

We are concerned only with the first definition. There is no dispute either that Kirkingburg's amblyopia is a physical impairment within the meaning of the Act, (defining "physical impairment" as "any physiological disorder, or condition . . . affecting one or more of the following body systems: . . . special sense organs"), or that seeing is one of his major life activities. The question is whether his monocular vision alone "substantially limits" Kirkingburg's seeing.

This is not to suggest that monocular individuals have an onerous burden in trying to show that they are disabled. On the contrary, our brief examination of some of the medical literature leaves us sharing the Government's judgment that people with monocular vision "ordinarily" will meet the Act's definition of disability, and we suppose that defendant

companies will often not contest the issue. We simply hold that the Act requires monocular individuals, like others claiming the Act's protection, to prove a disability by offering evidence that the extent of the limitation in terms of their own experience, as in loss of depth perception and visual field, is substantial.

III

Albertsons' primary contention is that even if Kirkingburg was disabled, he was not a "qualified" individual with a disability, because Albertsons merely insisted on the minimum level of visual acuity set forth in the DOT's Motor Carrier Safety Regulations. If Albertsons was entitled to enforce that standard as defining an "essential job function of the employment position," that is the end of the case, for Kirkingburg concededly could not satisfy it.

Under Title I of the ADA, employers may justify their use of "qualification standards . . . that screen out or tend to screen out or otherwise deny a job or benefit to an individual with a disability," so long as such standards are "job-related and consistent with business necessity, and . . . performance cannot be accomplished by reasonable accommodation. . . ."

In sum, the regulatory record made it plain that the waiver regulation did not rest on any final, factual conclusion that the waiver scheme would be conducive to public safety in the manner of the general acuity standards and did not purport to modify the substantive content of the general acuity regulation in any way. The waiver program was simply an experiment with safety, however well intended, resting on a hypothesis whose confirmation or refutation in practice would provide a factual basis for reconsidering the existing standards.

Nothing in the waiver regulation, of course, required an employer of commercial drivers to accept the hypothesis and participate in the Government's experiment. The only question, then, is whether the ADA should be read to require such an employer to defend a decision to decline the experiment. Is it reasonable, that is, to read the ADA as requiring an employer like Albertsons to shoulder the general statutory burden to justify a job qualification that would tend to exclude the disabled, whenever the employer chooses to abide by the otherwise clearly applicable, unamended substantive regulatory standard despite the Government's willingness to waive it experimentally and without any finding of its being inappropriate? If the answer were yes, an employer would in fact have an obligation of which we can think of no comparable example in our law. The employer would be required in effect to justify *de novo* an existing and otherwise applicable safety regulation issued by the Government itself. The employer would be required on a case-by-case basis to reinvent the Government's own wheel when the Government had merely begun an experiment to provide data to consider changing the underlying specifications. And what is even more, the employer would be required to do so when the Government had made an affirmative record indicating that contemporary empirical evidence was hard to come by. It is simply not credible that Congress enacted the ADA (before there was any waiver program) with the understanding that employers choosing to respect the Government's sole substantive visual acuity regulation in the face of an experimental waiver might be burdened with an obligation to defend the regulation's application according to its own terms.

CASE QUESTIONS

1. Are you in agreement with the Court's resolution?
2. Should all tests have to pass muster under the ADA before implementation?

The judgment of the Ninth Circuit is accordingly reversed.

Judgment for Albertsons, Inc.

Case Commentary

The U.S. Supreme Court decided that employers who use federal safety standards in determining whether an applicant is qualified for a position do not have to justify the validity of the standard under the ADA. ∎

3. Why are government standards immune from scrutiny?

The issue in the case that follows is whether an employee who controls his high blood pressure with medication is considered to be disabled under the ADA.

Murphy v. United Parcel Service, Inc.
527 U.S. 516 (1999)

Justice O'Connor delivered the opinion of the Court.

Respondent United Parcel Service, Inc. (UPS), dismissed petitioner Vaughn L. Murphy from his job as a UPS mechanic because of his high blood pressure. Petitioner filed suit under Title I of the Americans with Disabilities Act of 1990 (ADA or Act), in Federal District Court. The District Court granted summary judgment to respondent, and the Court of Appeals for the Tenth Circuit affirmed. We must decide whether the Court of Appeals correctly considered petitioner in his medicated state when it held that petitioner's impairment does not "substantially limit" one or more of his major life activities and whether it correctly determined that petitioner is not "regarded as disabled." In light of our decision in *Sutton v. United Air Lines, Inc.*, we conclude that the Court of Appeals' resolution of both issues was correct.

I

Petitioner was first diagnosed with hypertension (high blood pressure) when he was 10 years old. Unmedicated, his blood pressure is approximately 250/160. With medication, however, petitioner's "hypertension does not significantly restrict his activities and . . . in general he can function normally and can engage in activities that other persons normally do."

In August 1994, respondent hired petitioner as a mechanic, a position that required petitioner to drive commercial motor vehicles. Petitioner does not challenge the

District Court's conclusion that driving a commercial motor vehicle is an essential function of the mechanic's job at UPS. To drive such vehicles, however, petitioner had to satisfy certain health requirements imposed by the Department of Transportation (DOT). ("A person shall not drive a commercial motor vehicle unless he/she is physically qualified to do so and . . . has on his/her person . . . a medical examiner's certificate that he/she is physically qualified to drive a commercial motor vehicle.") One such requirement is that the driver of a commercial motor vehicle in interstate commerce have "no current clinical diagnosis of high blood pressure likely to interfere with his/her ability to operate a commercial vehicle safely." At the time respondent hired him, petitioner's blood pressure was so high, measuring at 186/124, that he was not qualified for DOT health certification. Nonetheless, petitioner was erroneously granted certification, and he commenced work. In September 1994, a UPS Medical Supervisor who was reviewing petitioner's medical files discovered the error and requested that petitioner have his blood pressure retested. Upon retesting, petitioner's blood pressure was measured at 160/102 and 164/104. On October 5, 1994, respondent fired petitioner on the belief that his blood pressure exceeded the DOT's requirements for drivers of commercial motor vehicles. Petitioner brought suit under Title I of the ADA in the United States District Court for the District of Kansas. The court granted respondent's motion for summary judgment. It held that, to determine whether petitioner is disabled under the ADA, his "impairment should be evaluated in its medicated state." Noting that when petitioner is medicated he is inhibited only in lifting heavy objects but otherwise functions normally, the court held that petitioner is not "disabled" under the ADA. The court also rejected petitioner's claim that he was "regarded as" disabled, holding that respondent "did not regard Murphy as disabled, only that he was not certifiable under DOT regulations."

The Court of Appeals affirmed the District Court's judgment. Citing its decision in *Sutton v. United Air Lines, Inc.,* that an individual claiming a disability under the ADA should be assessed with regard to any mitigating or corrective measures employed, the court held that petitioner's hypertension is not a disability because his doctor had testified that when petitioner is medicated, he "'functions normally doing everyday activity that an everyday person does.'" The court also affirmed the District Court's determination that petitioner is not "regarded as" disabled under the ADA. It explained that respondent did not terminate petitioner "on an unsubstantiated fear that he would suffer a heart attack or stroke," but "because his blood pressure exceeded the DOT's requirements for drivers of commercial vehicles." We granted certiorari, and we now affirm.

II

The first question presented in this case is whether the determination of petitioner's disability is made with reference to the mitigating measures he employs. We have answered that question in *Sutton* in the affirmative. Given that holding, the result in this case is clear. The Court of Appeals concluded that, when medicated, petitioner's high blood pressure does not substantially limit him in any major life activity. Petitioner did not seek, and we did not grant, certiorari on whether this conclusion was correct. Because the question whether petitioner is disabled when taking medication is not before us, we have no occasion here to consider whether petitioner is "disabled" due to limitations that persist despite his medication or the negative side effects of his medication. Instead, the question granted was limited to whether, under the ADA, the determination of whether an individual's impairment "substantially limits" one or more major life activities should be made without consideration of mitigating measures. Consequently, we conclude that the Court of Appeals correctly affirmed the grant of summary judgment in

respondent's favor on the claim that petitioner is substantially limited in one or more major life activities and thus disabled under the ADA.

III

The second issue presented is also largely resolved by our opinion in *Sutton*. Petitioner argues that the Court of Appeals erred in holding that he is not "regarded as" disabled because of his high blood pressure. As we held in Sutton, a person is "regarded as" disabled within the meaning of the ADA if a covered entity mistakenly believes that the person's actual, nonlimiting impairment substantially limits one or more major life activities. Here, petitioner alleges that his hypertension is regarded as substantially limiting him in the major life activity of working, when in fact it does not. To support this claim, he points to testimony from respondent's resource manager that respondent fired petitioner due to his hypertension, which he claims evidences respondent's belief that petitioner's hypertension—and consequent inability to obtain DOT certification—substantially limits his ability to work. In response, respondent argues that it does not regard petitioner as substantially limited in the major life activity of working but, rather, regards him as unqualified to work as a UPS mechanic because he is unable to obtain DOT health certification.

Consequently, in light of petitioner's skills and the array of jobs available to petitioner utilizing those skills, petitioner has failed to show that he is regarded as unable to perform a class of jobs. Rather, the undisputed record evidence demonstrates that petitioner is, at most, regarded as unable to perform only a particular job. This is insufficient, as a matter of law, to prove that petitioner is regarded as substantially limited in the major life activity of working. Accordingly, the Court of Appeals correctly granted summary judgment in favor of respondent on petitioner's claim that he is regarded as disabled. For the reasons stated, we affirm the decision of the Court of Appeals for the Tenth Circuit.

It is so ordered.

Judgment for UPS.

Case Commentary

The U.S. Supreme Court ruled that Murphy was not disabled under the ADA because he was under medication for his high blood pressure. Furthermore, the Court held that UPS did not regard Murphy as having a disability. ■

CASE QUESTIONS

1. Are you in agreement with the Court's decision?
2. Should a person with a disability lose ADA protection because the disability is being corrected by medication?

3. Do you believe UPS regarded Murphy as being disabled when it determined he was not certifiable under DOT regulations?

Employment Perspective

Lisa Conroy applied for a position as a paralegal with the law firm of Moran, Holochwost, and Mullins. Lisa is a paraplegic and is confined to a wheelchair. The firm is located on the second floor of an office building with no elevator. The firm employs 18 individuals. What must the law firm do? The law firm has to refuse to hire Lisa. Existing businesses are not required to install elevators. If the law firm occupied the first floor as well, it would be required to make a reasonable accommodation for Lisa on the first floor. If the law firm was going to construct its own office building, an elevator would be required if the building was three stories or more.

If the law firm was located on the first floor but had two steps inside and a bathroom entrance that was not wide enough for a wheelchair, what would the law firm have to do? It would have to install a ramp and make the bathroom entrance wider. These are modifications that are reasonable. To do otherwise would be to refuse to hire Lisa solely because her disability.

The issue in the case that follows is whether a professional golfer with a disability that restricts him from walking substantial distances is entitled to ride in a golf cart as a reasonable accommodation.

PGA Tour, Inc. v. Martin
532 U.S. 661 (2001)

Justice Stevens delivered the opinion of the Court.

This case raises two questions concerning the application of the Americans with Disabilities Act of 1990, to a gifted athlete: first, whether the Act protects access to professional golf tournaments by a qualified entrant with a disability; and second, whether a disabled contestant may be denied the use of a golf cart because it would "fundamentally alter the nature" of the tournaments, to allow him to ride when all other contestants must walk.

I

Petitioner PGA TOUR, Inc., a nonprofit entity formed in 1968, sponsors and cosponsors professional golf tournaments conducted on three annual tours. About 200 golfers participate in the PGA TOUR; about 170 in the NIKE TOUR; and about 100 in the SENIOR PGA TOUR. PGA TOUR and NIKE TOUR tournaments typically are 4-day events, played on courses leased and operated by petitioner. The entire field usually competes in two 18-hole rounds played on Thursday and Friday; those who survive the "cut" play on Saturday and Sunday and receive prize money in amounts determined by their aggregate scores for all four rounds. The revenues generated by television, admissions, concessions, and contributions from cosponsors amount to about $300 million a year, much of which is distributed in prize money.

There are various ways of gaining entry into particular tours. For example, a player who wins three NIKE TOUR events in the same year, or is among the top-15 money winners on that tour, earns the right to play in the PGA TOUR. Additionally, a golfer may obtain a spot in an official tournament through successfully competing in "open" qualifying rounds, which are conducted the week before each tournament. Most participants, however, earn playing privileges in the PGA TOUR or NIKE TOUR by way of a three-stage qualifying tournament known as the "Q-School."

Any member of the public may enter the Q-School by paying a $3,000 entry fee and submitting two letters of reference from, among others, PGA TOUR or NIKE TOUR members. The $3,000 entry fee covers the players' greens fees and the cost of golf carts, which are permitted during the first two stages, but which have been prohibited during the third stage since 1997. Each year, over a thousand contestants compete in the first stage, which consists of four 18-hole rounds at different locations. Approximately half of them make it to the second stage, which also includes 72 holes. Around 168 players survive the second stage and advance to the final one, where they compete over 108 holes. Of those finalists, about a fourth qualify for membership in the PGA TOUR, and the rest gain membership in the NIKE TOUR. The significance of making it into either tour is illuminated by the fact that there are about 25 million golfers in the country.

Three sets of rules govern competition in tour events. First, the "Rules of Golf," jointly written by the United States

Golf Association (USGA) and the Royal and Ancient Golf Club of Scotland, apply to the game as it is played, not only by millions of amateurs on public courses and in private country clubs throughout the United States and worldwide, but also by the professionals in the tournaments conducted by petitioner, the USGA, the Ladies' Professional Golf Association, and the Senior Women's Golf Association. Those rules do not prohibit the use of golf carts at any time.

Second, the "Conditions of Competition and Local Rules," often described as the "hard card," apply specifically to petitioner's professional tours. The hard cards for the PGA TOUR and NIKE TOUR require players to walk the golf course during tournaments, but not during open qualifying rounds. On the SENIOR PGA TOUR, which is limited to golfers age 50 and older, the contestants may use golf carts. Most seniors, however, prefer to walk.

Third, "Notices to Competitors" are issued for particular tournaments and cover conditions for that specific event. Such a notice may, for example, explain how the Rules of Golf should be applied to a particular water hazard or man-made obstruction. It might also authorize the use of carts to speed up play when there is an unusual distance between one green and the next tee.

Casey Martin is a talented golfer. As an amateur, he won 17 Oregon Golf Association junior events before he was 15 and won the state championship as a high school senior. He played on the Stanford University golf team that won the 1994 National Collegiate Athletic Association (NCAA) championship. As a professional, Martin qualified for the NIKE TOUR in 1998 and 1999, and based on his 1999 performance, qualified for the PGA TOUR in 2000. In the 1999 season, he entered 24 events, made the cut 13 times, and had 6 top-10 finishes, coming in second twice and third once.

Martin is also an individual with a disability as defined in the Americans with Disabilities Act of 1990 (ADA or Act). Since birth he has been afflicted with Klippel-Trenaunay-Weber Syndrome, a degenerative circulatory disorder that obstructs the flow of blood from his right leg back to his heart. The disease is progressive; it causes severe pain and has atrophied his right leg. During the latter part of his college career, because of the progress of the disease, Martin could no longer walk an 18-hole golf course. Walking not only caused him pain, fatigue, and anxiety, but also created a significant risk of hemorrhaging, developing blood clots, and fracturing his tibia so badly that an amputation might be required. For these reasons, Stanford made written requests to the Pacific 10 Conference and the NCAA to waive for Martin their rules requiring players to walk and carry their own clubs. The requests were granted.

When Martin turned pro and entered petitioner's Q-School, the hard card permitted him to use a cart during his successful progress through the first two stages. He made a request, supported by detailed medical records, for permission to use a golf cart during the third stage. Petitioner refused to review those records or to waive its walking rule

for the third stage. Martin therefore filed this action. A preliminary injunction entered by the District Court made it possible for him to use a cart in the final stage of the Q-School and as a competitor in the NIKE TOUR and PGA TOUR. Although not bound by the injunction, and despite its support for petitioner's position in this litigation, the USGA voluntarily granted Martin a similar waiver in events that it sponsors, including the U.S. Open.

Title III of the ADA prescribes, as a "general rule":

"No individual shall be discriminated against on the basis of disability in the full and equal enjoyment of the goods, services, facilities, privileges, advantages, or accommodations of any place of public accommodation by any person who owns, leases (or leases to), or operates a place of public accommodation."

The phrase "public accommodation" is defined in terms of 12 extensive categories, which the legislative history indicates "should be construed liberally" to afford people with disabilities "equal access" to the wide variety of establishments available to the nondisabled.

a. "(A) an inn, hotel, motel, or other place of lodging, except for an establishment located within a building that contains not more than five rooms for rent or hire and that is actually occupied by the proprietor of such establishment as the residence of such proprietor;

b. "(B) a restaurant, bar, or other establishment serving food or drink;

c. "(C) a motion picture house, theater, concert hall, stadium, or other place of exhibition or entertainment;

d. "(D) an auditorium, convention center, lecture hall, or other place of public gathering;

e. "(E) a bakery, grocery store, clothing store, hardware store, shopping center, or other sales or rental establishment;

f. "(F) a laundromat, dry-cleaner, bank, barber shop, beauty shop, travel service, shoe repair service, funeral parlor, gas station, office of an accountant or lawyer, pharmacy, insurance office, professional office of a health care provider, hospital, or other service establishment;

g. "(G) a terminal, depot, or other station used for specified public transportation;

h. "(H) a museum, library, gallery, or other place of display or collection;

i. "(I) a park, zoo, amusement park, or other place of recreation;

j. "(J) a nursery, elementary, secondary, undergraduate, or postgraduate private school, or other place of education;

k. "(K) a day care center, senior citizen center, homeless shelter, food bank, adoption agency, or other social service center establishment; and

l. "(L) a gymnasium, health spa, bowling alley, *golf course*, or other place of exercise or recreation."
§ 12181(7) (emphasis added).

It seems apparent, from both the general rule and the comprehensive definition of "public accommodation," that petitioner's golf tours and their qualifying rounds fit comfortably within the coverage of Title III, and Martin within its protection. The events occur on "golf courses," a type of place specifically identified by the Act as a public accommodation. In addition, at all relevant times, petitioner "leases" and "operates" golf courses to conduct its Q-School and tours. As a lessor and operator of golf courses, then, petitioner must not discriminate against any "individual" in the "full and equal enjoyment of the goods, services, facilities, privileges, advantages, or accommodations" of those courses. Certainly, among the "privileges" offered by petitioner on the courses are those of competing in the Q-School and playing in the tours; indeed, the former is a privilege for which thousands of individuals from the general public pay, and the latter is one for which they vie. Martin, of course, is one of those individuals. It would therefore appear that Title III of the ADA, by its plain terms, prohibits petitioner from denying Martin equal access to its tours on the basis of his disability.

Rather, petitioner reframes the coverage issue by arguing that the competing golfers are not members of the class protected by Title III of the ADA.

According to petitioner, Title III is concerned with discrimination against "clients and customers" seeking to obtain "goods and services" at places of public accommodation, whereas it is Title I that protects persons who work at such places. As the argument goes, petitioner operates not a "golf course" during its tournaments but a "place of exhibition or entertainment," and a professional golfer such as Martin, like an actor in a theater production, is a provider rather than a consumer of the entertainment that petitioner sells to the public. Martin therefore cannot bring a claim under Title III because he is not one of the "'clients or customers* of the covered public accommodation.'" Rather, Martin's claim of discrimination is "job-related" and could only be brought under Title I—but that Title does not apply because he is an independent contractor rather than an employee.

We need not decide whether petitioner's construction of the statute is correct, because petitioner's argument falters even on its own terms. If Title III's protected class were limited to "clients or customers," it would be entirely appropriate to classify the golfers who pay petitioner $3,000 for the chance to compete in the Q-School and, if successful, in the subsequent tour events, as petitioner's clients or customers. In our view, petitioner's tournaments (whether situated at a "golf course" or at a "place of exhibition or entertainment") simultaneously offer at least two "privileges" to the public— that of watching the golf competition and that of competing in it. Although the latter is more difficult and more expensive to obtain than the former, it is nonetheless a privilege that petitioner makes available to members of the general public. In consideration of the entry fee, any golfer with the requisite letters of recommendation acquires the opportunity to qualify

for and compete in petitioner's tours. Additionally, any golfer who succeeds in the open qualifying rounds for a tournament may play in the event. That petitioner identifies one set of clients or customers that it serves (spectators at tournaments) does not preclude it from having another set (players in tournaments) against whom it may not discriminate.

Our conclusion is consistent with case law in the analogous context of Title II of the Civil Rights Act of 1964. Title II of that Act prohibits public accommodations from discriminating on the basis of race, color, religion, or national origin.

Petitioner does not contest that a golf cart is a reasonable modification that is necessary if Martin is to play in its tournaments. Martin's claim thus differs from one that might be asserted by players with less serious afflictions that make walking the course uncomfortable or difficult, but not beyond their capacity. In such cases, an accommodation might be reasonable but not necessary. In this case, however, the narrow dispute is whether allowing Martin to use a golf cart, despite the walking requirement that applies to the PGA TOUR, the NIKE TOUR, and the third stage of the Q-School, is a modification that would "fundamentally alter the nature" of those events.

Indeed, the walking rule is not an indispensable feature of tournament golf either. As already mentioned, petitioner permits golf carts to be used in the SENIOR PGA TOUR, the open qualifying events for petitioner's tournaments, the first two stages of the Q-School, and, until 1997, the third stage of the Q-School as well.

Petitioner, however, distinguishes the game of golf as it is generally played from the game that it sponsors in the PGA TOUR, NIKE TOUR, and (at least recently) the last stage of the Q-School—golf at the "highest level." According to petitioner, "the goal of the highest-level competitive athletics is to assess and compare the performance of different competitors, a task that is meaningful only if the competitors are subject to identical substantive rules." The waiver of any possibly "outcome-affecting" rule for a contestant would violate this principle and therefore, in petitioner's view, fundamentally alter the nature of the highest level athletic event. The walking rule is one such rule, petitioner submits, because its purpose is "to inject the element of fatigue into the skill of shot-making," and thus its effect may be the critical loss of a stroke. As a consequence, the reasonable modification Martin seeks would fundamentally alter the nature of petitioner's highest level tournaments even if he were the only person in the world who has both the talent to compete in those elite events and a disability sufficiently serious that he cannot do so without using a cart.

Under the ADA's basic requirement that the need of a disabled person be evaluated on an individual basis, we have no doubt that allowing Martin to use a golf cart would not fundamentally alter the nature of petitioner's tournaments. As we have discussed, the purpose of the walking rule is to subject players to fatigue, which in turn may influence the outcome of tournaments. Even if the rule does serve that purpose, it is an uncontested finding of the District Court that Martin "easily endures greater fatigue even with a cart than his able-bodied competitors do by walking." The purpose of the walking rule is therefore not compromised in the slightest by allowing Martin to use a cart. A modification that provides an exception to a peripheral tournament rule without impairing its purpose cannot be said to "fundamentally alter" the tournament. What it can be said to do, on the other hand, is to allow Martin the chance to qualify for and compete in the athletic events petitioner offers to those members of the public who have the skill and desire to enter. That is exactly what the ADA requires. As a result, Martin's request for a waiver of the walking rule should have been granted.

The judgment of the Court of Appeals is affirmed for Martin.

Case Commentary

The United States Supreme Court ruled that Casey Martin is not afforded an unfair advantage through the use of the cart because he is still subject to fatigue by playing the game. ■

CASE QUESTIONS

1. Are you in favor of the Court's decision?
2. Could this ruling be applied to other professional sports?

3. Do you believe professional sports should be exempted from the ADA?

The issue in the following case is whether carpal tunnel syndrome qualifies as a disability under the ADA.

Toyota v. Williams
534 U.S. 184 (2002)

Justice O'Connor delivered the opinion of the Court.

Under the Americans with Disabilities Act of 1990 (ADA or Act), a physical impairment that "substantially limits one or more . . . major life activities" is a "disability." Respondent, claiming to be disabled because of her carpal tunnel syndrome and other related impairments, sued petitioner, her former employer, for failing to provide her with a reasonable accommodation as required by the ADA. The District Court granted summary judgment to petitioner, finding that respondent's impairments did not substantially limit any of her major life activities. The Court of Appeals for the Sixth Circuit reversed, finding that the impairments substantially limited respondent in the major life activity of performing manual tasks, and therefore granting partial summary judgment to respondent on the issue of whether she was disabled under the ADA. We conclude that the Court of Appeals did not apply the proper standard in making this determination because it analyzed only a limited class of manual tasks and failed to ask whether respondent's impairments prevented or restricted her from performing tasks that are of central importance to most people's daily lives.

I

Respondent began working at petitioner's automobile manufacturing plant in Georgetown, Kentucky, in August 1990. She was soon placed on an engine fabrication assembly line, where her duties included work with pneumatic tools. Use of these tools eventually caused pain in respondent's hands, wrists, and arms. She sought treatment at petitioner's in-house medical service, where she was diagnosed with bilateral carpal tunnel syndrome and bilateral tendinitis. Respondent consulted a personal physician who placed her on permanent work restrictions that precluded her from lifting more than 20 pounds or from "frequently lifting or carrying of objects weighing up to 10 pounds," engaging in "constant repetitive . . . flexion or extension of her wrists or elbows," performing "overhead work," or using "vibratory or pneumatic tools."

In light of these restrictions, for the next two years petitioner assigned respondent to various modified duty jobs. Nonetheless, respondent missed some work for medical leave, and eventually filed a claim under the Kentucky Workers' Compensation Act. The parties settled this claim, and respondent returned to work. She was unsatisfied by petitioner's efforts to accommodate her work restrictions, however, and responded by bringing an action in the United States District Court for the Eastern District of Kentucky alleging that petitioner had violated the ADA by refusing to accommodate her disability. That suit was also settled, and as part of the settlement, respondent returned to work in December 1993.

During the fall of 1996, petitioner announced that it wanted QCIO employees to be able to rotate through all four of the QCIO processes. Respondent therefore received training for the shell body audit job, in which team members apply a highlight oil to the hood, fender, doors, rear quarter panel, and trunk of passing cars at a rate of approximately one car per minute. The highlight oil has the viscosity of salad oil, and employees spread it on cars with a sponge attached to a block of wood. After they wipe each car with the oil, the employees visually inspect it for flaws. Wiping the cars required respondent to hold her hands and arms up around shoulder height for several hours at a time.

A short while after the shell body audit job was added to respondent's rotations, she began to experience pain in her neck and shoulders. Respondent again sought care at petitioner's in-house medical service, where she was diagnosed with myotendinitis bilateral periscapular, an inflammation of the muscles and tendons around both of her shoulder blades; myotendinitis and myositis bilateral forearms with nerve compression causing median nerve irritation; and thoracic outlet compression, a condition that causes pain in the nerves that lead to the upper extremities. Respondent requested that petitioner accommodate her medical conditions by allowing her to return to doing only her original two jobs in QCIO, which respondent claimed she could still perform without difficulty.

The parties disagree about what happened next. According to respondent, petitioner refused her request and forced her to continue working in the shell body audit job, which caused her even greater physical injury. According to petitioner, respondent simply began missing work on a regular basis. Regardless, it is clear that on December 6, 1996, the last day respondent worked at petitioner's plant, she was placed under a no-work-of-any-kind restriction by her treating physicians. On January 27, 1997, respondent received a letter from petitioner that terminated her employment, citing her poor attendance record.

Respondent filed a charge of disability discrimination with the Equal Employment Opportunity Commission (EEOC). Respondent based her claim that she was "disabled" under the ADA on the ground that her physical impairments substantially limited her in (1) manual tasks; (2) housework; (3) gardening; (4) playing with her children; (5) lifting; and (6) working, all of which, she argued, constituted major life activities under the Act. Respondent also argued, in the alternative, that she was disabled under the ADA because she had a record of a substantially limiting impairment and because she was regarded as having such an impairment.

The ADA requires covered entities, including private employers, to provide "reasonable accommodations to the known physical or mental limitations of an otherwise qualified individual with a disability who is an applicant or employee, unless such covered entity can demonstrate that the accommodation would impose an undue hardship." The Act defines a "qualified individual with a disability" as "an individual with a disability who, with or without reasonable accommodation, can perform the essential functions of the

employment position that such individual holds or desires." In turn, a "disability" is:

a. "(A) a physical or mental impairment that substantially limits one or more of the major life activities of such individual;
b. "(B) a record of such an impairment; or
c. "(C) being regarded as having such an impairment."

To qualify as disabled under subsection (A) of the ADA's definition of disability, a claimant must initially prove that he or she has a physical or mental impairment. The Rehabilitation Act regulations issued by the Department of Health, Education, and Welfare (HEW) in 1977, which appear without change in the current regulations issued by the Department of Health and Human Services, define "physical impairment," the type of impairment relevant to this case, to mean "any physiological disorder or condition, cosmetic disfigurement, or anatomical loss affecting one or more of the following body systems: neurological; musculoskeletal; special sense organs; respiratory, including speech organs; cardiovascular; reproductive, digestive, genitourinary; hemic and lymphatic; skin; and endocrine."

Merely having an impairment does not make one disabled for purposes of the ADA. Claimants also need to demonstrate that the impairment limits a major life activity. The HEW Rehabilitation Act regulations provide a list of examples of "major life activities," that includes "walking, seeing, hearing," and, as relevant here, "performing manual tasks."

To qualify as disabled, a claimant must further show that the limitation on the major life activity is "substantial." Unlike "physical impairment" and "major life activities," the HEW regulations do not define the term "substantially limits." The EEOC, therefore, has created its own definition for purposes of the ADA. According to the EEOC regulations, "substantially limited" means "unable to perform a major life activity that the average person in the general population can perform"; or "significantly restricted as to the condition, manner or duration under which an individual can perform a particular major life activity as compared to the condition, manner, or duration under which the average person in the general population can perform that same major life activity." In determining whether an individual is substantially limited in a major life activity, the regulations instruct that the following factors should be considered: "the nature and severity of the impairment; the duration or expected duration of the impairment; and the permanent or long-term impact, or the expected permanent or long-term impact of or resulting from the impairment."

We therefore hold that to be substantially limited in performing manual tasks, an individual must have an impairment that prevents or severely restricts the individual from doing activities that are of central importance to most people's daily lives. The impairment's impact must also be permanent or long-term.

It is insufficient for individuals attempting to prove disability status under this test to merely submit evidence of a medical diagnosis of an impairment. Instead, the ADA requires those "claiming the Act's protection . . . to prove a disability by offering evidence that the extent of the limitation [caused by their impairment] in terms of their own experience . . . is substantial." That the Act defines "disability" "with respect to an individual," makes clear that Congress intended the existence of a disability to be determined in such a case-by-case manner.

An individualized assessment of the effect of an impairment is particularly necessary when the impairment is one whose symptoms vary widely from person to person. Carpal tunnel syndrome, one of respondent's impairments, is just such a condition. While cases of severe carpal tunnel syndrome are characterized by muscle atrophy and extreme sensory deficits, mild cases generally do not have either of these effects and create only intermittent symptoms of numbness and tingling. Studies have further shown that, even without surgical treatment, one quarter of carpal tunnel cases resolve in one month, but that in 22 percent of cases, symptoms last for eight years or longer. Given these large potential differences in the severity and duration of the effects of carpal tunnel syndrome, an individual's carpal tunnel syndrome diagnosis, on its own, does not indicate whether the individual has a disability within the meaning of the ADA.

Even more critically, the manual tasks unique to any particular job are not necessarily important parts of most people's lives. As a result, occupation-specific tasks may have only limited relevance to the manual task inquiry. In this case, "repetitive work with hands and arms extended at or above shoulder levels for extended periods of time," the manual task on which the Court of Appeals relied, is not an important part of most people's daily lives. The court, therefore, should not have considered respondent's inability to do such manual work in her specialized assembly line job as sufficient proof that she was substantially limited in performing manual tasks.

At the same time, the Court of Appeals appears to have disregarded the very type of evidence that it should have focused upon. It treated as irrelevant "the fact that respondent can . . . tend to her personal hygiene and carry out personal or household chores." Yet household chores, bathing, and brushing one's teeth are among the types of manual tasks of central importance to people's daily lives, and should have been part of the assessment of whether respondent was substantially limited in performing manual tasks.

In addition, according to respondent's deposition testimony, even after her condition worsened, she could still brush her teeth, wash her face, bathe, tend her flower garden, fix breakfast, do laundry, and pick up around the house. The record also indicates that her medical conditions caused her to avoid sweeping, to quit dancing, to occasionally seek help dressing, and to reduce how often she plays with her children, gardens, and drives long distances. But these changes in her life did not amount to such severe restrictions in the activities that are of central importance to most people's daily lives that they establish a manual-task disability as a matter of law. On this record, it was therefore inappropriate for the Court of Appeals to grant partial summary judgment to respondent on the issue whether she was substantially limited in performing manual tasks, and its decision to do so must be reversed.

Case Commentary

The U.S. Supreme Court concluded that carpal tunnel syndrome would have to prevent the plaintiff from being able to perform major life necessities in order to qualify her as disabled under the ADA. ■

CASE QUESTIONS

1. Are you in favor of the Court's resolution?
2. Why is the determining factor whether she can perform hygiene and housework rather than tasks on the job?
3. Is it fair to terminate someone who can perform housework, but not the essential functions of their job without reasonable accommodation?

Employment Perspective

Patricia Krakowski is 52 years old. She applied for a position as a high school history teacher with the Monroe Township Academy. Although her credentials were superior, she was passed over for a younger applicant. Patricia had had a cancerous kidney removed. The academy feared that she might be a candidate for dialysis, which could cause its health costs to increase. Because the academy was operating within a tight budget, Patricia posed a potential financial risk that it did not want to take. Has Patricia been discriminated against? Yes! Were it not for her disability, Patricia would have been hired. The academy must give Patricia the position or reimburse her until she finds another suitable one.

The issue in the case that follows is whether the job would pose a direct threat to the employee's health.

Chevron v. Echazabal

536 U.S. 73 (2002)

Justice Souter delivered the opinion of the Court.

Beginning in 1972, respondent Mario Echazabal worked for independent contractors at an oil refinery owned by petitioner Chevron U.S.A. Inc. Twice he applied for a job directly with Chevron, which offered to hire him if he could pass the company's physical examination. Each time, the exam showed liver abnormality or damage, the cause eventually being identified as Hepatitis C, which Chevron's doctors said would be aggravated by continued exposure to toxins at Chevron's refinery. In each instance, the company withdrew the offer, and the second time it asked the contractor employing Echazabal either to reassign him to a job without exposure to harmful chemicals or to remove him from the refinery altogether. The contractor laid him off in early 1996.

Echazabal filed suit, ultimately removed to federal court, claiming, among other things, that Chevron violated the Americans With Disabilities Act in refusing to hire him, or even to let him continue working in the plant, because of a disability, his liver condition. Chevron defended under a regulation of the Equal Employment Opportunity Commission permitting the defense that a worker's disability on the job would pose a "direct threat" to his health. Although two medical witnesses disputed Chevron's judgment that Echazabal's liver function was impaired and subject to further damage under the job conditions in the refinery, the District Court granted summary judgment for Chevron. It held that Echazabal raised no genuine issue of material fact as to whether the company acted reasonably in relying on its own doctors' medical advice, regardless of its accuracy.

On appeal, the Ninth Circuit asked for briefs on a threshold question not raised before, whether the EEOC's regulation recognizing a threat-to-self defense exceeded the scope of permissible rulemaking under the ADA. The Circuit held that it did and reversed the summary judgment. The court rested its position on the text of the ADA itself in explicitly recognizing an employer's right to adopt an employment qualification barring anyone whose disability would place others in the workplace at risk, while saying nothing about threats to the disabled employee himself. The majority opinion reasoned that "by specifying only threats to 'other individuals in the workplace,' the statute makes it clear that threats to other persons—including the disabled individual himself—are not included within the scope of the direct threat defense," and it indicated that any such regulation would unreasonably conflict with congressional policy against paternalism in the workplace. The court went on to reject Chevron's further argument that Echazabal was not

"'otherwise qualified'" to perform the job, holding that the ability to perform a job without risk to one's health or safety is not an "'essential function'" of the job.

Section 102 of the Americans with Disabilities Act of 1990, prohibits "discrimination against a qualified individual with a disability because of the disability . . . in regard to" a number of actions by an employer, including "hiring." The statutory definition of "discrimination" covers a number of things an employer might do to block a disabled person from advancing in the workplace, such as "using qualification standards . . . that screen out or tend to screen out an individual with a disability." By that same definition, the Act creates an affirmative defense for action under a qualification standard "shown to be job-related for the position in question and . . . consistent with business necessity." Such a standard may include "a requirement that an individual shall not pose a direct threat to the health or safety of other individuals in the workplace," if the individual cannot perform the job safely with reasonable accommodation. By regulation, the EEOC carries the defense one step further, in allowing an employer to screen out a potential worker with a disability not only for risks that he would pose to others in the workplace but for risks on the job to his own health or safety as well: "The term 'qualification standard' may include a requirement that an individual shall not pose a direct threat to the health or safety of the individual or others in the workplace."

Chevron relies on the regulation here, since it says a job in the refinery would pose a "direct threat" to Echazabal's health. The first strike against the expression-exclusion rule here is right in the text that Echazabal quotes. Congress included the harm-to-others provision as an example of legitimate qualifications that are "job-related and consistent with business necessity."

Since Congress has not spoken exhaustively on threats to a worker's own health, the agency regulation can claim adherence under the rule in *Chevron*, so long as it makes sense of the statutory defense for qualification standards that are "job-related and consistent with business necessity." Chevron's reasons for calling the regulation reasonable are unsurprising: moral concerns aside, it wishes to avoid time lost to sickness, excessive turnover from medical retirement or death, litigation under state tort law, and the risk of violating the national Occupational Safety and Health Act of 1970. Although Echazabal claims that none of these reasons is legitimate, focusing on the concern with OSHA will be enough to show that the regulation is entitled to survive.

Echazabal points out that there is no known instance of OSHA enforcement, or even threatened enforcement, against an employer who relied on the ADA to hire a worker willing to accept a risk to himself from his disability on the job. In Echazabal's mind, this shows that invoking OSHA policy and possible OSHA liability is just a red herring to excuse covert discrimination. But there is another side to this. The text of OSHA itself says its point is "to assure so far as possible every working man and woman in the Nation safe and healthful working conditions," and Congress specifically obligated an employer to "furnish to each of his employees employment and a place of employment which are free from recognized hazards that are causing or are likely to cause death or serious physical harm to his employees." Although there may be an open question whether an employer would actually be liable under OSHA for hiring an individual who knowingly consented to the particular dangers the job would pose to him, there is no denying that the employer would be asking for trouble: his decision to hire would put Congress's policy in the ADA, a disabled individual's right to operate on equal terms within the workplace, at loggerheads with the competing policy of OSHA, to ensure the safety of "each" and "every" worker. Courts would, of course, resolve the tension if there were no agency action, but the EEOC's resolution exemplifies the substantive choices that agencies are expected to make.

Similarly, Echazabal points to several of our decisions expressing concern under Title VII, which like the ADA allows employers to defend otherwise discriminatory practices that are "consistent with business necessity," with employers adopting rules that exclude women from jobs that are seen as too risky. Those cases, however, are beside the point, as they, like Title VII generally, were concerned with paternalistic judgments based on the broad category of gender, while the EEOC has required that judgments based on the direct threat provision be made on the basis of individualized risk assessments.

Finally, our conclusions that some regulation is permissible and this one is reasonable are not open to Echazabal's objection that they reduce the direct threat provision to "surplusage." The mere fact that a threat-to-self defense reasonably falls within the general "job related" and "business necessity" standard does not mean that Congress accomplished nothing with its explicit provision for a defense based on threats to others. The provision made a conclusion clear that might otherwise have been fought over in litigation or administrative rulemaking. It did not lack a job to do merely because the EEOC might have adopted the same rule later in applying the general defense provisions, nor was its job any less responsible simply because the agency was left with the option to go a step further. A provision can be useful even without congressional attention being indispensable.

Accordingly, we reverse the judgment of the Court of Appeals and remand the case for proceedings consistent with this opinion.

Judgment for Chevron.

Case Commentary

The U.S. Supreme Court ruled that Chevron's reason for not hiring Echazabal was justifiable because his hepatitis would be exacerbated by exposure to the toxins in the work environment. ∎

CASE QUESTIONS

1. Are you in accord with the Court's decision?
2. Do you believe Echazabal could have been accommodated?
3. Is a person with hepatitis covered under the ADA?

AIDS Discrimination

AIDS is of great concern to employers. When an employee is questioned as to whether he or she has the disease or when that information is related to other employees, an invasion of privacy may occur. If the assertion that an employee has the AIDS virus turns out to be unfounded, defamation may occur. If an applicant is refused employment because he or she has the AIDS virus, employment discrimination may be asserted. When an existing employee who is capable of working is discharged because he or she has the AIDS virus, a violation of the Federal Rehabilitation Act, Americans with Disabilities Act, or state law protecting the handicapped may result. Under the circumstances, how can an employer maintain harmony in the workplace? Employers must develop policies regarding the treatment afforded existing employees who have AIDS regarding fringe benefits, including absences, dental care, and medical benefits; alternative work location; and reassurance of support by the company. Employees with AIDS who apply for positions within the company must be treated on an equal basis with those applicants not having the AIDS virus. As long as a person who has AIDS is capable of performing the work, he or she should be treated no differently from any other employee. Employers are encouraged to develop an educational program designed to ease the fears of coworkers who worry about catching the virus. The key is successful planning.

The issue in the case that follows is whether a person with HIV is a covered person under the ADA.

Bragdon v. Abbott
524 U.S. 624 (1998)

Justice Kennedy delivered the opinion of the Court.

We address in this case the application of the Americans with Disabilities Act of 1990 (ADA), to persons infected with the human immunodeficiency virus (HIV). We granted certiorari to review, first, whether HIV infection is a disability under the ADA when the infection has not yet progressed to the so-called symptomatic phase; and, second, whether the Court of Appeals, in affirming a grant of summary judgment, cited sufficient material in the record to determine, as a matter of law, that respondent's infection with HIV posed no direct threat to the health and safety of her treating dentist.

I

Respondent Sidney Abbott has been infected with HIV since 1986. When the incidents we recite occurred, her infection had not manifested its most serious symptoms. On September 16, 1994, she went to the office of petitioner Randon Bragdon in Bangor, Maine, for a dental appointment. She disclosed her HIV infection on the patient registration form. Petitioner completed a dental examination, discovered a cavity, and informed respondent of his policy against filling cavities of HIV-infected patients. He offered to perform the work at a hospital with no added fee for his services, though respondent would be responsible for the cost of using the hospital's facilities. Respondent declined.

Respondent sued petitioner under state law and §302 of the ADA, alleging discrimination on the basis of her disability. The state law claims are not before us. Section 302 of the ADA provides:

"No individual shall be discriminated against on the basis of disability in the full and equal enjoyment of the goods, services, facilities, privileges, advantages, or accommodations of any place of public accommodation by any person who . . . operates a place of public accommodation."

The term "public accommodation" is defined to include the "professional office of a health care provider." A later subsection qualifies the mandate not to discriminate. It provides:

"Nothing in this subchapter shall require an entity to permit an individual to participate in or benefit from the goods, services, facilities, privileges, advantages and accommodations of such entity where such individual poses a direct threat to the health or safety of others."

The United States and the Maine Human Rights Commission intervened as plaintiffs. After discovery, the parties filed cross-motions for summary judgment. The District Court ruled in favor of the plaintiffs, holding that respondent's HIV infection satisfied the ADA's definition of disability. The court held further that petitioner raised no genuine issue of material fact as to whether respondent's HIV infection would have posed a direct threat to the health or safety of others during the course of a dental treatment. The court relied on affidavits submitted by Dr. Donald Wayne Marianos, Director of the Division of Oral Health of the Centers for Disease Control and Prevention (CDC). The Marianos affidavits asserted it is safe for dentists to treat patients infected with HIV in dental offices if the dentist follows the so-called universal precautions described in the Recommended Infection-Control Practices for Dentistry issued by CDC in 1993.

The Court of Appeals affirmed. It held respondent's HIV infection was a disability under the ADA, even though her infection had not yet progressed to the symptomatic stage. The Court of Appeals also agreed that treating the respondent in petitioner's office would not have posed a direct threat to the health and safety of others. Unlike the District Court, however, the Court of Appeals declined to rely on the Marianos affidavits. Instead the court relied on the 1993 CDC Dentistry Guidelines, as well as the Policy on AIDS, HIV Infection and the Practice of Dentistry, promulgated by the American Dental Association in 1991.

II

We first review the ruling that respondent's HIV infection constituted a disability under the ADA. The statute defines disability as:

"(A) a physical or mental impairment that substantially limits one or more of the major life activities of such individual; "(B)a record of such an impairment; or "(C)being regarded as having such impairment."

We hold respondent's HIV infection was a disability under subsection (A) of the definitional section of the statute. In light of this conclusion, we need not consider the applicability of subsections (B) or (C).

Our consideration of subsection (A) of the definition proceeds in three steps. First, we consider whether respondent's HIV infection was a physical impairment. Second, we identify the life activity upon which respondent relies (reproduction and child bearing) and determine whether it constitutes a major life activity under the ADA. Third, tying the two statutory phrases together, we ask whether the impairment substantially limited the major life activity. In construing the statute, we are informed by interpretations of parallel definitions in previous statutes and the views of various administrative agencies which have faced this interpretive question.

A

The ADA's definition of disability is drawn almost verbatim from the definition of "handicapped individual" included in the Rehabilitation Act of 1973, and the definition of "handicap" contained in the Fair Housing Amendments Act of 1988. Congress' repetition of a well-established term carries the implication that Congress intended the term to be construed in accordance with pre-existing regulatory interpretations. In this case, Congress did more than suggest this construction; it adopted a specific statutory provision in the ADA directing as follows:

"Except as otherwise provided in this chapter, nothing in this chapter shall be construed to apply a lesser standard than the standards applied under title V of the Rehabilitation Act of 1973 or the regulations issued by Federal agencies pursuant to such title."

The directive requires us to construe the ADA to grant at least as much protection as provided by the regulations implementing the Rehabilitation Act.

1

The first step in the inquiry under subsection (A) requires us to determine whether respondent's condition constituted a physical impairment. The Department of Health, Education and Welfare (HEW) issued the first regulations interpreting the Rehabilitation Act in 1977. The regulations are of particular significance because, at the time, HEW was the agency responsible for coordinating the implementation and enforcement of §504. The HEW regulations, which appear without change in the current regulations issued by the Department of Health and Human Services, define "physical or mental impairment" to mean:

"(A) any physiological disorder or condition, cosmetic disfigurement, or anatomical loss affecting one or more of the following body systems: neurological; musculoskeletal;

special sense organs; respiratory, including speech organs; cardiovascular; reproductive, digestive, genito-urinary; hemic and lymphatic; skin; and endocrine;" or "(B) any mental or psychological disorder, such as mental retardation, organic brain syndrome, emotional or mental illness, and specific learning disabilities."

In issuing these regulations, HEW decided against including a list of disorders constituting physical or mental impairments, out of concern that any specific enumeration might not be comprehensive. The commentary accompanying the regulations, however, contains a representative list of disorders and conditions constituting physical impairments, including "such diseases and conditions as orthopedic, visual, speech, and hearing impairments, cerebral palsy, epilepsy, muscular dystrophy, multiple sclerosis, cancer, heart disease, diabetes, mental retardation, emotional illness, and . . . drug addiction and alcoholism." In 1980, the President transferred responsibility for the implementation and enforcement of §504 to the Attorney General. The regulations issued by the Justice Department, which remain in force to this day, adopted verbatim the HEW definition of physical impairment quoted above. In addition, the representative list of diseases and conditions originally relegated to the commentary accompanying the HEW regulations were incorporated into the text of the regulations.

HIV infection is not included in the list of specific disorders constituting physical impairments, in part because HIV was not identified as the cause of AIDS until 1983. HIV infection does fall well within the general definition set forth by the regulations, however. The disease follows a predictable and, as of today, an unalterable course. Once a person is infected with HIV, the virus invades different cells in the blood and in body tissues. Certain white blood cells, known as helper Tlymphocytes or CD41 cells, are particularly vulnerable to HIV. The virus attaches to the CD4 receptor site of the target cell and fuses its membrane to the cell's membrane. HIV is a retrovirus, which means it uses an enzyme to convert its own genetic material into a form indistinguishable from the genetic material of the target cell. The virus' genetic material migrates to the cell's nucleus and becomes integrated with the cell's chromosomes. Once integrated, the virus can use the cell's own genetic machinery to replicate itself. Additional copies of the virus are released into the body and infect other cells in turn. Although the body does produce antibodies to combat HIV infection, the antibodies are not effective in eliminating the virus.

The virus eventually kills the infected host cell. CD41 cells play a critical role in coordinating the body's immune response system, and the decline in their number causes corresponding deterioration of the body's ability to fight infections from many sources. Tracking the infected individual's CD41 cell count is one of the most accurate measures of the course of the disease.

The initial stage of HIV infection is known as acute or primary HIV infection. In a typical case, this stage lasts three months. The virus concentrates in the blood. The assault on the immune system is immediate. The victim suffers from a sudden and serious decline in the number of white blood cells. There is no latency period. Mononucleosis-like symptoms often emerge between six days and six weeks after infection, at times accompanied by fever, headache, enlargement of the lymph nodes (lymphadenopathy), muscle pain (myalgia), rash, lethargy, gastrointestinal disorders, and neurological disorders. Usually these symptoms abate within 14 to 21 days. HIV antibodies appear in the bloodstream within 3 weeks; circulating HIV can be detected within 10 weeks.

After the symptoms associated with the initial stage subside, the disease enters what is referred to sometimes as its asymptomatic phase. The term is a misnomer, in some respects, for clinical features persist throughout, including lymphadenopathy, dermatological disorders, oral lesions, and bacterial infections. Although it varies with each individual, in most instances this stage lasts from 7 to 11 years. The virus now tends to concentrate in the lymph nodes, though low levels of the virus continue to appear in the blood. It was once thought the virus became inactive during this period, but it is now known that the relative lack of symptoms is attributable to the virus' migration from the circulatory system into the lymph nodes. The migration reduces the viral presence in other parts of the body, with a corresponding diminution in physical manifestations of the disease. The virus, however, thrives in the lymph nodes, which, as a vital point of the body's immune response system, represents an ideal environment for the infection of other CD41 cells. Studies have shown that viral production continues at a high rate. CD41 cells continue to decline an average of 5% to 10% (40 to 80 cells/mm^3) per year throughout this phase.

A person is regarded as having AIDS when his or her CD41 count drops below 200 cells/mm^3 of blood or when CD41 cells comprise less than 14% of his or her total lymphocytes. During this stage, the clinical conditions most often associated with HIV, such as pneumocystis carninii pneumonia, Kaposi's sarcoma, and non-Hodgkins lymphoma, tend to appear. In addition, the general systemic disorders present during all stages of the disease, such as fever, weight loss, fatigue, lesions, nausea, and diarrhea, tend to worsen. In most cases, once the patient's CD41 count drops below 10 cells/mm^3, death soon follows.

In light of the immediacy with which the virus begins to damage the infected person's white blood cells and the severity of the disease, we hold it is an impairment from the moment of infection. As noted earlier, infection with HIV causes immediate abnormalities in a person's blood, and the infected person's white cell count continues to drop throughout the course of the disease, even when the attack is concentrated in the lymph nodes. In light of these facts, HIV infection must be regarded as a physiological disorder with a constant and detrimental effect on the infected person's hemic and lymphatic systems from the moment of infection. HIV infection satisfies the statutory and regulatory definition of a physical impairment during every stage of the disease.

2

The statute is not operative, and the definition not satisfied, unless the impairment affects a major life activity. Respondent's claim throughout this case has been that the HIV infection placed a substantial limitation on her ability to reproduce and to bear children.

From the outset, however, the case has been treated as one in which reproduction was the major life activity limited by the impairment. It is our practice to decide cases on the grounds raised and considered in the Court of Appeals and included in the question on which we granted certiorari. We ask, then, whether reproduction is a major life activity.

We have little difficulty concluding that it is. Reproduction falls well within the phrase "major life activity." Reproduction and the sexual dynamics surrounding it are central to the life process itself. While petitioner concedes the importance of reproduction, he claims that Congress intended the ADA only to cover those aspects of a person's life which have a public, economic, or daily character. Nothing in the definition suggests that activities without a public, economic, or daily dimension may somehow be regarded as so unimportant or insignificant as to fall outside the meaning of the word "major."

As we have noted, the ADA must be construed to be consistent with regulations issued to implement the Rehabilitation Act. The Rehabilitation Act regulations support the inclusion of reproduction as a major life activity, since reproduction could not be regarded as any less important than working and learning. We agree with the Court of Appeals' determination that reproduction is a major life activity for the purposes of the ADA.

3

The final element of the disability definition in subsection (A) is whether respondent's physical impairment was a substantial limit on the major life activity she asserts. The Rehabilitation Act regulations provide no additional guidance.

Our evaluation of the medical evidence leads us to conclude that respondent's infection substantially limited her ability to reproduce in two independent ways. First, a woman infected with HIV who tries to conceive a child imposes on the man a significant risk of becoming infected. The cumulative results of 13 studies collected in a 1994 textbook on AIDS indicates that 20% of male partners of women with HIV became HIV-positive themselves, with a majority of the studies finding a statistically significant risk of infection.

Second, an infected woman risks infecting her child during gestation and childbirth, i.e., perinatal transmission.

Petitioner concedes that women infected with HIV face about a 25% risk of transmitting the virus to their children. Published reports available in 1994 confirm the accuracy of this statistic.

The Act addresses substantial limitations on major life activities, not utter inabilities. Conception and childbirth are not impossible for an HIV victim but, without doubt, are dangerous to the public health. This meets the definition of a substantial limitation. The decision to reproduce carries economic and legal consequences as well. There are added costs for antiretroviral therapy, supplemental insurance, and long-term health care for the child who must be examined and, tragic to think, treated for the infection. The laws of some States, moreover, forbid persons infected with HIV from having sex with others, regardless of consent.

In the end, the disability definition does not turn on personal choice. When significant limitations result from the impairment, the definition is met even if the difficulties are not insurmountable. For the statistical and other reasons we have cited, of course, the limitations on reproduction may be insurmountable here. Testimony from the respondent that her HIV infection controlled her decision not to have a child is unchallenged. In the context of reviewing summary judgment, we must take it to be true. We agree with the District Court and the Court of Appeals that no triable issue of fact impedes a ruling on the question of statutory coverage. Respondent's HIV infection is a physical impairment which substantially limits a major life activity, as the ADA defines it. In view of our holding, we need not address the second question presented, i.e., whether HIV infection is a per se disability under the ADA.

"b. Did petitioner, Randon Bragdon, D. M. D., raise a genuine issue of fact for trial as to whether he was warranted in his judgment that the performance of certain invasive procedures on a patient in his office would have posed a direct threat to the health or safety of others?"

Notwithstanding the protection given respondent by the ADA's definition of disability, petitioner could have refused to treat her if her infectious condition "posed a direct threat to the health or safety of others." The ADA defines a direct threat to be "a significant risk to the health or safety of others that cannot be eliminated by a modification of policies, practices, or procedures or by the provision of auxiliary aids or services."

The ADA's direct threat provision stems from the recognition in *School Bd. of Nassau Cty. v. Arline*, of the importance of prohibiting discrimination against individuals with disabilities while protecting others from significant health and safety risks, resulting, for instance, from a contagious disease. In *Arline*, the Court reconciled these objectives by construing the Rehabilitation Act not to require the hiring of a person who posed "a significant risk of communicating an infectious disease to others." Congress amended the Rehabilitation Act and the Fair Housing Act to incorporate the language (excluding individuals who "would constitute a direct threat to the health or safety of other individuals"); it later relied on the same language in enacting the ADA. (ADA's direct threat provision codifies *Arline*.) Because few, if any, activities in life are risk free, *Arline* and the ADA do not ask whether a risk exists, but whether it is significant.

The existence, or nonexistence, of a significant risk must be determined from the standpoint of the person who refuses the treatment or accommodation, and the risk assessment must be based on medical or other objective evidence. As a health care professional, petitioner had the duty to assess the risk of infection based on the objective, scientific information available to him and others in his profession. His belief that a significant risk existed, even if maintained in good faith, would not relieve him from liability. To use the words of the question presented, petitioner receives no special deference simply because he is a health care professional. It is true that *Arline* reserved "the question whether courts should also defer to the reasonable medical judgments of private physicians on which an employer has relied." At most, this statement reserved the possibility that employers could consult with individual physicians as objective third-party experts. It did not suggest that an individual physician's state of mind could excuse discrimination without regard to the objective reasonableness of his actions.

Nor can we be certain, on this record, whether the 1991 American Dental Association Policy on HIV carries the weight the Court of Appeals attributed to it. The Policy does provide some evidence of the medical community's objective assessment of the risks posed by treating people infected with HIV in dental offices. It indicates:

"Current scientific and epidemiologic evidence indicates that there is little risk of transmission of infectious diseases through dental treatment if recommended infection control procedures are routinely followed. Patients with HIV infection may be safely treated in private dental offices when appropriate infection control procedures are employed. Such infection control procedures provide protection both for patients and dental personnel."

We note, however, that the Association is a professional organization, which, although a respected source of information on the dental profession, is not a public health authority. It is not clear the extent to which the Policy was based on the Association's assessment of dentists' ethical and professional duties in addition to its scientific assessment of the risk to which the ADA refers. Efforts to clarify dentists' ethical obligations and to encourage dentists to treat patients with HIV infection with compassion may be commendable, but the question under the statute is one of statistical likelihood, not professional responsibility. Without more information on the manner in which the American Dental Association formulated this Policy, we are unable to determine the Policy's value in evaluating whether petitioner's assessment of the risks was reasonable as a matter of law.

We conclude the proper course is to give the Court of Appeals the opportunity to determine whether our analysis of some of the studies cited by the parties would change its conclusion that petitioner presented neither objective evidence nor a triable issue of fact on the question of risk. In remanding the case, we do not foreclose the possibility that the Court of Appeals may reach the same conclusion it did earlier. A remand will permit a full exploration of the issue through the adversary process.

The determination of the Court of Appeals that respondent's HIV infection was a disability under the ADA is affirmed. The judgment is vacated, and the case is remanded for further proceedings consistent with this opinion. It is so ordered.

Case Commentary

The U.S. Supreme Court ruled that HIV substantially inhibits the right to procreate and that procreation qualifies as a major life activity. As such, an individual with HIV is covered under the ADA. The court sent the case back for reconsideration on the issue of whether a dentist who works on a patient with HIV is exposing himself to the risk of contracting the disease. ∎

CASE QUESTIONS

1. Are you in accord with the Court's determination?
2. Do you believe HIV and/or AIDS should be covered under the ADA?

3. Do you believe Bragdon's refusal to perform dental work on Abbott for fear of exposing himself to the HIV virus was reasonable?

WORKERS WITH CONTAGIOUS DISEASES

The Question of Disclosure

To disclose or not to disclose—that has been the question for employees who have AIDS. Disclosure may be necessary to excuse excessive absences and to explain poor performance on the job, which may result from a weakened physical condition. Although a person with AIDS has little choice, disclosure has generally compounded the problems. Once notified, many employers have fired or coaxed employees who have AIDS into leaving quietly, promising to retain confidentiality and not to tell the world. Many panic-stricken fellow employees react negatively upon learning the news. They refuse to share drinking fountains, pens, telephones, and toilets. Some employees who work in a confined area with a person who has AIDS refuse to breathe the same air. As a result, employees who have AIDS become isolated in much the same way as did lepers. However, unlike leprosy, AIDS cannot be transmitted through touching or any of the other unfounded ways that are responsible for the mass hysteria in the workplace. AIDS is communicable, but only through the exchange of body fluids, which allow for the AIDS virus to enter the bloodstream. AIDS cannot be transmitted by casual contact because the AIDS virus dies shortly after it is exposed to the air.

Preventative Planning

Preventative planning will diminish the worry over lawsuits involving discrimination, defamation, and invasion of privacy. It will also bolster the company's public image concerning the treatment of an employee with a life-threatening disease. Planning is the key. Developing a sound AIDS policy now will prepare companies for the AIDS cases that are sure to follow.

A company's first priority is to protect the privacy of an employee who has AIDS, thus shielding itself from an invasion of privacy or defamation suit. Employees should be encouraged, but not required, to inform their managers that they have AIDS. By advocating that employees who have AIDS discuss their illness with the human resource department, companies can assure employees that medical benefits and other accommodations, such as flexible work hours, may be arranged. The company may also place employees who have AIDS in contact with community groups that are concerned with the welfare of people who have AIDS and that provide counseling or medical assistance.

The implementation by companies of effective planning and educational programming will result in more humane treatment of employees who have AIDS.

A MODEL FOR A COMPANY POLICY ON AIDS

Employers should educate themselves concerning the legal and medical issues and then develop a company policy to deal with employees who have AIDS, incorporating an educational program such as the one set forth here.

1. Equal treatment will be accorded to employees who have AIDS with regard to their right to work, to seek promotion and raises, and to be protected from discrimination and harassment by managers and coworkers.

2. An employee suspected of having AIDS will not be approached, and no statement will be made regarding the suspected illness to coworkers. This guards against an invasion of privacy suit as well as a defamation action should the hunch turn out to be false.

3. A well-informed human resource staff will be provided, which will be trained in dealing with all aspects of the AIDS dilemma. Employees who have AIDS will be encouraged to confide in the human resource staff. The staff will help employees who have AIDS cope with unfriendly coworkers and protect the employees from harassment and/or discrimination through education and then disciplinary action, if necessary. The human resource staff will explore the possibility of flexible work hours or permitting the employee who has AIDS to work at home through a computer terminal and modem. The future course of the AIDS virus will be discussed with the employee by explaining the medical and disability benefits available. A counselor will be employed to help the AIDS patient cope with the psychological trauma he or she will be experiencing. The AIDS patient will be placed in contact with community service programs that are geared to helping the needs of the AIDS patient outside the workplace.

4. Confidentiality will be extended to information received by the company from the AIDS employee. This information will not be placed in the AIDS employee's personnel file, but may be documented in the employee's medical file with consent. This procedure guards against invasion of privacy.

5. An educational program will be implemented consisting of booklets and other printed information on the causes of AIDS, working with AIDS, or working with someone who has AIDS. Seminars may be set up where a physician and psychologist are invited to discuss the physical and emotional consequences of AIDS and how to deal with them. The theory behind the program will be to create a comfortable atmosphere in which both AIDS employees and their coworkers can function productively.

6. Coworkers will be educated and counseled to dispel their fear of catching the AIDS virus from casual contact. An employee's refusal to work with an AIDS patient will not be given preferential treatment beyond the normal request for a transfer.

7. Those employees who hold positions of leadership in the community will be encouraged to espouse their concern for the need for AIDS awareness.

8. An employer's right to dismiss an AIDS employee is restricted to evaluating the employee's caliber of work. If the quality of the AIDS patient's work has suffered due to excessive absences and/or a weakened physical condition, the employer may legally exclude the employee from the workplace by placing him or her on disability. Prior to this, the employer will sit down with the AIDS patient and discuss the health benefits the company will provide.

THE FUTURE FOR DISABLED WORKERS

With the increase in information-service positions, the computer and the telephone become great equalizers for the disabled. Couple this with the decline in the number of young people entering the job market, and the future for disabled workers looks promising. Disabled individuals represent the largest pool of potential workers. This is but another group of productive and dedicated workers whose abilities have remained untapped. They will prove to be useful resources to many companies in the future and will integrate themselves into the workforce similar to those other groups who have previously been unwanted. McDonald's McJobs program hires individuals with mental and physical disabilities. It began in the early 1980s and has proven to be a sound business solution to McDonald's need for dedicated and loyal employees with low turnover ratio.

EMPLOYEE LESSONS

1. Be familiar with the rights afforded to you under the Americans with Disabilities Act.
2. Know that you have the right to be accommodated as long as the accommodation is reasonable and does not create an undue burden on the employer.
3. Understand that you must be able to perform the essential functions of the job, albeit with accommodation.
4. Be aware that employers should not query you regarding whether you have any disabilities.
5. Be apprised that if an employer perceives you as having a disability, even though you do not, you are covered under the ADA.
6. Appreciate the fact that if an employer divulges information about your disability that is not readily apparent, it may be an invasion of your privacy.
7. Consider that AIDS is a protected disability.
8. Realize that if someone falsely accuses you of harboring a loathsome disease, it is defamation.
9. Learn what disabilities are protected under the ADA.
10. Recognize that disabled workers have as much right to employment as anyone else.

SUMMARY

The percentage of disabled workers who are unemployed is much greater than that of the general population. Public access and specific job accommodations have gone a long way to aid the gainful employment of many of the disabled. Encouraging a change in the mind-set of employers remains a formidable task. Many employers view disabled applicants as inferior to others. They represent an additional worry employers do not need. However, with reasonable accommodation, many disabled employees have proven to work as effectively as other workers because their disability has been alleviated. They are operating on a level playing surface with the rest of the work population.

REVIEW QUESTIONS

1. Explain the importance of the Americans with Disabilities Act of 1990.
2. What is the significance of the Rehabilitation Act of 1973?
3. Define *disability*.
4. Are disabled people covered under Title VII?
5. Explain the changes made to better accommodate the disabled in our society.
6. What types of reasonable accommodations have to be made for the disabled employee?

7. Can a disability ever preclude employment because it is considered a bona fide occupational qualification?
8. When can a request for disability accommodation be denied?
9. Are alcoholism and drug addiction disabilities?
10. How should the employer deal with alcoholism and drug addiction?
11. Define *AIDS*.
12. Is AIDS a contagious disease?
13. Can a person having a contagious disease be discriminated against?
14. Is AIDS considered to be a disability?
15. Can a coworker refuse to work with an employee who has AIDS?
16. Do coworkers have a right to know if an employee has AIDS?
17. If management discloses that an employee has AIDS, what recourse does the employee have?
18. Is harassing an employee who has AIDS actionable?
19. If false rumors are spread, stating that an employee has AIDS, on what principle of law could the employee sue?
20. Is it ethical to demote an employee who has become disabled?
21. What are the limits to which an employer must go in order to reasonably accommodate an employee?
22. Is the request for part-time work unreasonable when an employee becomes disabled?
23. How severe would a plaintiff's injury have to be to qualify as disabled?
24. Are the accommodations public establishments have been forced to make under the ADA reasonable or an undue burden?
25. Should people with AIDS be classified as victims deserving of accommodation or should they be treated as are alcoholics and drug addicts who are responsible for their actions?
26. Should the tort of invasion of privacy be extended to people with AIDS?
27. Is it ethical to spend so much money on research for one illness—AIDS—instead of spreading the money around?

CASE PROBLEMS

1. Plaintiff alleged that she was terminated from her assembly-line position with Toyota in violation of the Americans with Disabilities Act of 1990 (ADA) because of a physical disability caused by carpal tunnel syndrome. Plaintiff's impairment disqualified her from only a narrow range of repetitive-motion positions and not from working in the broader class of manufacturing jobs. The issue presented is whether a person who suffers with carpal tunnel syndrome is covered under the ADA. *McKay v. Toyota Motor Manufacturing, U.S.A., Inc.* 110 F.3d 369 (6th Cir. 1997)

2. Plaintiff Matthew T. Stone, a firefighter employed by defendant City of Mount Vernon (the "City"), appeals from a judgment dismissing his complaint alleging that defendants violated his rights by refusing to assign him to a light-duty position after an off-duty accident that left him a paraplegic. The district court granted summary judgment dismissing the complaint on the ground that no rational trier of fact could conclude that Stone was able to perform the essential functions of the job of firefighter. Stone contends principally that summary judgment was improper because there were genuine issues of fact to be tried as to whether fire suppression is an essential function of a position in certain of the department's specialized bureaus, and whether the department could reasonably accommodate his disability by assigning him to such a position. The issue is whether a firefighter is capable of performing the essential functions of the job in spite of being a paraplegic. *Stone v. City of Mount Vernon*, 118 F.3d 893 (2nd Cir. 1996)

3. Leckelt was a male hospital nurse. After he underwent an HIV test, the hospital insisted that he disclose the result. Leckelt refused. The hospital fired him because his

refusal prevented the hospital from having the information it felt necessary to ensure the safety of its patients and staff. Leckelt claimed that he was discriminated against because of the perception that he might be HIV positive. What was the result? *Leckelt v. Board of Commissioners*, 909 F.2d 820 (5th Cir. 1990)

HUMAN RESOURCE DILEMMAS

1. Stephanie Wilkens works in a typing pool for the law firm of Gunther, Wadkins, and Farmer. After 6 years, she has developed carpal tunnel syndrome. Stephanie's requests for wrist guards and armrests have been met, but to date they have not been effective in alleviating her dilemma. She has requested a transfer to a position with comparable pay, but none are available. Because Stephanie can no longer type, she was terminated. What advice would you give her?

2. George Wilson is national sales manager for Raytech. He travels extensively throughout the United States. George weighs 420 pounds. He has requested that Raytech accommodate his physical disability by purchasing a first-class ticket or two coach-class tickets for each of his flights. Raytech refused George's request for accommodation, claiming the request is not reasonable. George retorts that this operates as a constructive discharge. How would you advise Raytech?

3. Rita Hall has kidney failure and is forced to be on dialysis three times a week. She is a financial analyst for Bull and Bear. She is asking for three afternoons off. Rita is offering to work late two days and on Saturdays to make up the time. She does not believe this will adversely affect her duties. Bull and Bear refuses, claiming it is disruptive to the work environment. How would you advise Rita to proceed?

WEB SITE ASSIGNMENT

Using the following Web sites, research whether there are any employment situations in which carpal tunnel, lupus, or obesity are considered to be qualified disabilities under the ADA.

www.columbus.bcentral.com/columbus/stories/2001/02/19/daily11.html
www.mackinac.org/article.asp?ID = 1848
www.hmso.gov.uk/acts/acts1995/1995050.htm
www.hiredisability.com
www.lawguru.com
www.eeoc.gov/facts/fs-ada.html

Unions and Collective Bargaining Agreements

Employment Scenario

The Long and the Short of It is now in its seventh year of operation, with 8 stores and over 175 employees. A large number of employees have become disenchanted with the autocratic management style of Tom Long and Mark Short. These employees want to form a union. When Tom and Mark learn of this through their spies, they decide to nip this "subversive activity" in the bud by requiring all employees to sign off on an agreement not to participate in the formation of a union. Those employees who refuse to sign will be immediately terminated to set an example. Thirty-five employees refuse to sign L&S's yellow-dog contract requiring nonunion membership as a condition to continued employment. They are discharged.

Is this permissible?

Chapter Checklist

➤ *Understand that the right of workers to organize and participate in unions is viable.*

➤ *Appreciate that in certain parts of the country unions have flourished, whereas in other parts their existence has waned.*

➤ *Realize that the Norris–LaGuardia Act revoked the power of federal courts to end strikes through injunctive relief.*

➤ *Be aware that nonunion membership cannot be a condition of employment.*

➤ *Learn that the National Mediation Board encourages voluntary mediation between management and labor.*

➤ *Recognize the deleterious effect that GATT and NAFTA have had on unions.*

➤ *Know that a collective bargaining agreement is a binding contract between management and labor.*

> ➤ *Become familiar with the terms included in a collective bargaining agreement.*
>
> ➤ *Be apprised of the history and purpose of unions.*
>
> ➤ *Incorporate an arbitration clause in collective bargaining agreements to avoid protracted litigation.*

INTRODUCTION

The first unions were organized during the economic depression of the 1820s. The unions were against excessive taxation, prison labor as competition, and debtors' prisons. Unions stood for public schools and mechanics' liens, which tie up assets of those who refuse to pay their bills. Unions became politically active in their fight to limit the workday to 10 hours. They argued that the government, instead of protecting the poor and middle-class workers, protected the upper class, employers, and management by allowing them to maintain and at times increase their economic advantage.

In 1833, 20 to 30 percent of Manhattan's workforce formed a general trade union. Skilled and unskilled workers became members. By 1836, two-thirds of New York City workers and 15 percent of the entire American labor force were union members. Strikes were the unions' main weapon against employers. Strikes involved women as well as men—female bookbinders as well as male shoemakers. The general trade union admitted women to membership. Many other trade unions did not extend membership to women and blacks. Nonadmittance into unions impeded any rise in economic stature and public recognition of women and blacks.

HUMAN RESOURCE ADVICE

- Determine the propensity for workers to organize unions in your business field and in your region.
- Refrain from mandating that employees promise not to organize or participate in a union.
- Familiarize yourself with the various labor laws.
- Be cognizant of the movement of manufacturing outside the country.
- Realize the impact GATT and NAFTA have had on unions.
- Evaluate whether it is best to relocate to another region of the country or overseas if your employees are forming a union.
- Fulfill employees' demands when reasonable, rather than be forced to relocate or to confront a union.
- Hire a specialist to negotiate collective bargaining agreements.
- Appreciate the significance of the National Labor Relations Board.
- Know that the National Mediation Board is available to negotiate labor disputes.

SHERMAN ACT

Back in the early 1900s, monopolistic companies totally dominated labor. This trend was accepted more in Great Britain than in America, where it led to some unrest. Wage differences widened between skilled and unskilled workers.

Employers exhibited a weak sense of responsibility and began to hoard their wealth. Single women worked, while married women stayed home.

The Sherman Antitrust Act, enacted in 1890, was initially applied to any activity that interrupted the free flow of commerce. The term "every business combination" came into use to include the unions. Whereas citizens had hoped that the Sherman Act would be used to lessen the power of monopolies, instead it became a tool for big business to use against its employees.

CLAYTON ACT

The Clayton Act, enacted in 1914 with good intent toward labor, exacerbated the problem by strengthening the application of the Sherman Act against labor. Whereas before, applications for injunctive relief rested only with the federal courts, under the Clayton Act employers themselves could file applications against their employees.

The language of Sections 6 and 20 of the Clayton Act seemed to invalidate the use of injunctive relief under the Sherman Act with regard to labor. Section 6 provided that employees' work is not goods available in commerce and that labor unions and their members are not illegal combinations acting in restraint of free trade. Section 20 went on to provide that injunctive relief is not to be granted in a labor dispute unless damage to property was intended. The language could not be clearer that Congress's intent was that the Sherman Act and its remedy of injunctive relief should not apply to labor. However, the courts carved many exceptions by claiming that the Clayton Act does not apply to individuals who strike because they are no longer employees, to union organizers because they are not employees, and to employees who sign yellow-dog contracts.

Yellow-Dog Contract

A yellow-dog contract is a stipulation mandated by the employer that the employee will not join a union, as a condition of continued employment. Yellow-dog contracts were upheld by the courts in strict opposition to the legal principle of noninterference with contractual business relations. Interference with contracts is an actionable tort, which means that an individual can sue for money damages. In any event, this doctrine was overlooked and yellow-dog contracts were in effect until the passage of the Railway Labor Act of 1926 and the Federal Anti-Injunction Act of 1932.

RAILWAY LABOR ACT

The Railway Labor Act of 1926 outlawed yellow-dog contracts by prohibiting an agreement of nonunion membership as a condition to employment. It strengthened the right of unions to strike as long as the work stoppage and related protest were peaceful. The act instituted the National Mediation Board (NMB) to encourage voluntary mediation between management and labor. If no resolution could be reached, then the NMB would propose binding arbitration. If agreed, both sides would be bound by its decision.

NORRIS–LAGUARDIA ACT

This activity against labor continued until 1932, when the Federal Anti-Injunctive Act, more commonly known as the *Norris–LaGuardia Act*, was passed. Its first section relieved federal courts of the power to grant injunctions in labor disputes, with limited exceptions, thus marking the end of the use of the Sherman and Clayton Acts' injunctive relief against labor.

NATIONAL LABOR RELATIONS ACT

The National Labor Relations Act (NLRA) was enacted in 1935 to ensure the right of employees to organize and participate in unions without fear of reprisals from employers.

In 1935, with the passage of the NLRA, also known as the Wagner Act, unions organized with the power of enforcement. Certified bargaining agreements were forthcoming. Company attempts at domination were stymied with the creation of the National Labor Relations Board, with investigatory and enforcement power being placed at its discretion.

TAFT–HARTLEY ACT

The Taft–Hartley Act, also known as the *Labor Management Relations Act of 1947*, declared the closed shop illegal. Workers who did not want to join the union could not be discriminated against. This act delineated unfair labor practices by unions. One such practice prohibited was the use of coercion by unions to force workers to join.

THE FUTURE FOR UNIONS

The struggle waged by unions was certainly profitable for their members. From the 1940s until recently, skilled laborers have enjoyed a relatively high standard of living. However, many businesses have now taken advantage of lower living costs and cheaper office space outside the United States. With the emergence of the General Agreement on Tariffs and Trade (GATT) and the North American Free Trade Agreement (NAFTA), more jobs, especially those in manufacturing, are moving to Mexico and overseas. The power of the unions has been crippled. In the past, unions were a major political force in the Democratic Party. Now that is no longer true. Ironically, it was Democratic President Bill Clinton who signed off on the GATT, which signaled the death knell for unions.

In the global marketplace, comparative advantage will prevail. If goods can be manufactured somewhere cheaper with no loss in quality, then a company will move its operation there, and high-paying union jobs will be lost. The result will be the lowering of the standard of living for skilled, semiskilled, and unskilled laborers. The same phenomenon is happening even in the service sector with regard to certain data entry positions. Communications and computers are making this trend possible. Location is no longer a key factor. As a result, American office workers are working harder, lunch hours have been given up, longer hours are becoming the norm, and taking work home or coming into the office on weekends is commonplace. Workers had believed that using the computer to link their office with their home would cut their commuting time to 3 days a week. Instead, the office worker will still work a standard 5-day week at the office. The computer link will enable the worker to work at home in the evenings and on the weekends.

Office workers and laborers are also being continually forced to reeducate and retrain themselves. Developing skills that cannot be easily and efficiently replicated overseas is vital to keeping one's job and maintaining a comfortable standard of living.

The issue in the following case is whether, under the Coal Act, a company that purchases the assets of another company assumes responsibility for the retirees of the company purchased.

Barnhart, Comm. of Social Security v. Sigmon Coal Company

534 U.S. 438 (2002)

Justice Thomas delivered the opinion of the Court.

This case arises out of the Commissioner of Social Security's assignment, pursuant to the Coal Industry Retiree Health Benefit Act of 1992 (Coal Act or Act) of 86 retired coal miners to the Jericol Mining Company (Jericol). The question presented is whether the Coal Act permits the Commissioner to assign retired miners to the successors in interest of out-of-business signatory operators. The United States Court of Appeals for the Fourth Circuit held that it does not. We affirm.

I

The Coal Act reconfigured the system for providing private health care benefits to retirees in the coal industry. In restructuring this system, Congress had to contend with over half a century of collective-bargaining agreements between the coal industry and the United Mine Workers of America (UMWA), the coal miners' union. Tensions between coal operators and the UMWA had often led to lengthy strikes with serious economic consequences for both the industry and its employees. Confronted with an industry fraught with contention, Congress was faced with a difficult task.

This was not the first time that the Federal Government had been called on to intervene in negotiations within the industry. Such tensions motivated President Truman, in 1946, to issue an Executive Order directing the Secretary of the Interior to take possession of all bituminous coal mines and to negotiate with the UMWA over changes in the terms and conditions of miners' employment. These negotiations culminated in the first of many agreements that resulted in the creation of benefit funds compensating miners, their dependents, and their survivors.

Subsequently, the UMWA and several coal operators entered into a collectively bargained agreement, the National Bituminous Coal Wage Agreement of 1947 (NBCWA), which established a fund under which three trustees "were given authority to determine," among other things, the allocation of benefits to miners and their families. Further disagreement prompted the parties to negotiate another NBCWA in 1950. The following year, the Bituminous Coal Operators' Association (BCOA) was created as a multiemployer bargaining association and primary representative for the coal operators in their negotiations with the UMWA.

While the NBCWA was amended occasionally and new NBCWAs were adopted in 1968 and 1971, the terms and structure of the 1950 agreement remained largely unchanged between 1950 and 1974. In 1974, in order to comply with the Employee Retirement Income Security Act of 1974 (ERISA), the UMWA and the BCOA negotiated a new agreement to finance benefits. The 1974 NBCWA created four trusts that replaced the 1950 fund.

These benefit plans quickly developed financial problems. Thus, in 1978 the parties executed another NBCWA. This agreement assigned responsibility for the health care of active and retired employees to the respective coal mine operators who were signatories to the earlier NBCWAs, and left the 1974 Benefit Plan in effect only for those retirees whose former employers were no longer in business.

Nonetheless, financial problems continued to plague the plans "as costs increased and employers who had signed the 1978 NBCWA withdrew from the agreement, either to continue in business with nonunion employees or to exit the coal business altogether." "As more and more coal operators abandoned the Benefit Plans, the remaining signatories were forced to absorb the increasing cost of covering retirees left behind by exiting employers." Pursuant to yet another NBCWA, the UMWA and the BCOA in 1988 attempted to remedy the problem, this time by imposing withdrawal liability on NBCWA signatories that seceded from the benefit plans.

Despite these efforts, the plans remained in serious financial crisis and, by June 1991, the 120,000 individuals who received health benefits from the funds were in danger of losing their benefits. About 60% of these individuals were retired miners and their dependents whose former employers were no longer contributing to the benefit plans. Another 15% worked for employers that were no longer UMWA-represented or were never unionized. These troubles were further aggravated by rising health care costs.

The UMWA threatened to strike if a legislative solution was not reached. And BCOA members, which included those coal firms that were currently signatories to NBCWAs, threatened that they would not renew their commitments to cover retiree costs when their contracts expired. Following another strike and much unrest, Secretary of Labor Elizabeth Dole created the Advisory Commission on United Mine Workers of America Retiree Health Benefits (Coal Commission), which studied the problem and proposed several solutions. In particular, the Coal Commission focused on how to finance the health care benefits of orphaned retirees.

Congress considered these and other proposals and eventually reconfigured the allocation of health benefits for coal miner retirees by enacting the Coal Act in 1992. Crafting the legislative solution to the crisis, however, was no easy task. The Coal Act was passed amidst a maelstrom of contract negotiations, litigation, strike threats, a presidential veto of the first version of the bill and threats of a second veto, and high pressure lobbying, not to mention wide disagreements among Members of Congress. The Act "merged the 1950 and 1974 Benefit Plans into a new multiemployer plan called the United Mine Workers of America Combined Benefit Fund (Combined Fund)." The Combined Fund "is financed by annual premiums assessed against 'signatory coal operators,' i.e., coal operators that signed any NBCWA or any other agreement requiring contributions to the 1950 or 1974 Benefits Plans." Where the signatory is no longer in business, the statute assigns liability for beneficiaries to a defined group of "related persons." The Coal Act charged the Commissioner of Social Security with assigning each eligible beneficiary to a signatory operator or its related persons. The statute identifies specific categories of signatory operators (and their related persons) and requires the Commissioner to assign beneficiaries among these categories in a particular order. The Coal Act also ensures that if a beneficiary remains unassigned because no existing company falls within the aforementioned categories, then benefits will be financed by the Combined Fund, either with funds transferred from interest earned on the Department of the Interior's Abandoned Mine Reclamation Fund or from an additional premium imposed on all assigned signatory operators on a pro rata basis.

II

Respondent Jericol was formed in 1973 as Irdell Mining, Inc. (Irdell). Shortly thereafter, Irdell and another company purchased the coal mining operating assets of Shackleford Coal Company, Inc., a company that was a signatory to a coal wage agreement while it was in business. They acquired the right to use the Shackleford name and assumed responsibility for Shackleford's outstanding contracts, including its collective-bargaining agreement with the UMWA. "There was no common ownership between Irdell and Shackleford." Irdell subsequently changed its name, operating as the Shackleford Coal Company until 1977, when it again changed its name to Jericol. The new company was a signatory only to the 1974 NBCWA.

The Commissioner assigned premium responsibility for over 100 retired miners and dependents to Jericol.

Of these, 86 were assigned because they had worked for Shackleford and the Commissioner determined that as a "successor" or "successor in interest" to the original Shackleford, Jericol qualified as a "related person" to Shackleford. The others were assigned because they had actually worked for Jericol. Jericol appealed most of the Commissioner's determinations, arguing that the assignments were erroneous both because Jericol was not a successor in interest of Shackleford and because Jericol was not a related person to Shackleford.

Dissatisfied with the outcome of administrative proceedings, Jericol filed suit against the Commissioner, arguing that he wrongfully assigned retirees and dependents to Jericol. The District Court concluded that the classification regime of the Coal Act does not provide, directly or indirectly, "for liability to be laid at the door of successors of defunct signatory operators." The District Court ordered the Commissioner to withdraw the challenged assignments and enjoined the Commissioner from assigning additional retirees to Jericol on the basis that it is a related person to the original Shackleford.

The Commissioner appealed, arguing that a "straight reading" of the statute shows that a successor in interest to a signatory operator qualifies as a related person, thereby permitting the assignment of the retirees and dependents to Jericol. Alternatively, the Commissioner argued that the District Court's "reading . . . produces inexplicable, anomalous results that are clearly at odds with congressional intent."

"Declining the Commissioner's invitation to rewrite the Coal Act," the United States Court of Appeals for the Fourth Circuit affirmed. The Court of Appeals concluded that the "statute is clear and unambiguous," and that the court was "bound to read it exactly as it is written." Accordingly, the court held that Jericol was not a "related person" to Shackleford and thus could not be held responsible for Shackleford's miners.

We granted certiorari, 532 U.S. 993 (2001), and now affirm.

III

With respect to the question presented in this case, this statute is unambiguous. The statutory text instructs that the Coal Act does not permit the Commissioner to assign beneficiaries to the successor in interest of a signatory operator. The statute provides:

"For purposes of this chapter, the Commissioner of Social Security shall, before October 1, 1993, assign each coal industry retiree who is an eligible beneficiary to a signatory operator which (or any related person with respect to which) remains in business in the following order:
"(1) First, to the signatory operator which—
"(A) was a signatory to the 1978 coal wage agreement or any subsequent coal wage agreement, and
"(B) was the most recent signatory operator to employ the coal industry retiree in the coal industry for at least 2 years.
"(2) Second, if the retiree is not assigned under paragraph (1), to the signatory operator which—
"(A) was a signatory to the 1978 coal wage agreement or any subsequent coal wage agreement, and
"(B) was the most recent signatory operator to employ the coal industry retiree in the coal industry.
"(3) Third, if the retiree is not assigned under paragraph (1) or (2), to the signatory operator which employed the coal industry retiree in the coal industry for a longer

period of time than any other signatory operator prior to the effective date of the 1978 coal wage agreement."

In this case, the Commissioner determined that because Shackleford is a pre-1978 signatory and employed the disputed miners for over 24 months, assignment must be made under category 3. It then assigned the miners to Jericol after determining that Jericol was a successor in interest to Shackleford and was therefore a "related person" to Shackleford.

We disagree with the Commissioner's reasoning. Because the disputed retirees were employees of Shackleford, the "signatory operator" that sold its assets to Jericol (then-Irdell) in 1973, the Commissioner can only assign them to Jericol if it is a "related person" to Shackleford. The statute provides that "a person shall be considered to be a related person to a signatory operator if that person" falls within one of three categories:

"(i) a member of the controlled group of corporations (within the meaning of section 52(a)) which includes such signatory operator;

"(ii) a trade or business which is under common control (as determined under section 52(b)) with such signatory operator; or

"(iii) any other person who is identified as having a partnership interest or joint venture with a signatory operator in a business within the coal industry, but only if such business employed eligible beneficiaries, except

that this clause shall not apply to a person whose only interest is as a limited partner."

In addition, the last sentence of §9701(c)(2)(A) states that "[a] related person shall also include a successor in interest of any person described in clause (i), (ii), or (iii)."

Although the Commissioner maintains that Jericol is a "related person" to Shackleford, Jericol does not fall within any of the three specified categories defining a "related person." There is no contention that it was ever a member of a controlled group of corporations including Shackleford, that it was ever a business under common control with Shackleford, or that it ever had a partnership interest or engaged in a joint venture with Shackleford. Therefore, liability for these beneficiaries may attach to Jericol only if it is a successor in interest to an entity described in §§9701(c)(2)(A)(i)–(iii). Because Jericol is a successor in interest only to Shackleford, Jericol will be liable only if a signatory operator itself, here Shackleford, falls within one of these categories. None of the three categories, however, includes the signatory operator itself.

Accordingly, the judgment of the Court of Appeals is affirmed for Sigmon Coal Co.

Case Commentary

The U.S. Supreme Court ruled that Jericol was an independent entity that purchased the assets of Shackleford; as such, Jericol is not responsible for the retired miners of Shackleford. ∎

CASE QUESTIONS

1. Are you in favor of the Court's ruling?
2. Do you think the coal miners got the shaft?

3. If Jericol bought Shackleford's assets, should it not be responsible for Shackleford's liabilities as well?

COLLECTIVE BARGAINING

Collective bargaining is the negotiation process undertaken by a union on behalf of its members with the management of an organization with the intent of entering into a contract after the resolution of labor issues. The contract, known as the *collective bargaining agreement*, is binding on all union members. The advantage of collective bargaining is that the union has greater bargaining strength than an individual employee would have in attempting to negotiate the best possible deal.

Key Terms

The key terms to be negotiated in a collective bargaining agreement include full-time wages, minimum number of hours required for full-time status, overtime pay, vacation time, personal days, pension benefits, health care coverage for the employees and their dependents, description and classification of jobs, work schedules, rules regarding employee behavior, cost of living adjustments in pay, determination of promotion, policy termination committee to handle grievances, and procedure for arbitration to handle contract disputes.

The issue in the following case is whether a collective bargaining agreement precludes an employee from bringing an invasion of privacy claim under state law.

Cramer v. Consolidated Freightways
255 F.3d 683 (9th Cir. 2001)

Fisher, Circuit Judge.

This appeal requires us to decide whether a plaintiff's state law privacy claim, based on California's penal code, is preempted under § 301 of the Labor Management Relations Act ("LMRA"). Resolution of this issue, in turn, leads us to clarify our Circuit's approach to § 301 preemption. We hold that because plaintiffs' privacy claims are not even arguably covered by the collective bargaining agreement ("CBA"), the claims are independent of the CBA and thus are not subject to § 301 preemption. Moreover, we hold that when an employer's surreptitious surveillance constitutes a per se violation of established state privacy laws, the employees affected thereby may bring an action for invasion of privacy regardless of the terms of the collective bargaining agreement governing their employment.

I.

Consolidated Freightways ("Consolidated"), the defendant in this action, is a large trucking company. It concealed video cameras and audio listening devices behind two-way mirrors in the restrooms at its terminal in Mira Loma, California, ostensibly to detect and prevent drug use by its drivers. Employees at the terminal discovered the surveillance equipment when a mirror fell off the men's restroom wall, exposing a camera with a wire leading out through a hole in the wall behind it. Subsequent investigation revealed a similar hole in the wall behind the mirror in the adjoining women's restroom.

Under California Penal Code § 653n, "any person who installs or who maintains . . . any two-way mirror permitting observation of any restroom, toilet, bathroom, washroom, shower, locker room, fitting room, motel room, or hotel room, is guilty of a misdemeanor." Thus, Consolidated's installation of the two-way mirror was a direct violation of California criminal law.

Soon after discovery of the camera, truck driver Lloyd Cramer, an employee at the Mira Loma terminal, brought a class action suit in state court alleging invasion of privacy on behalf of all "individuals lawfully on the premises . . . who had a reasonable expectation of privacy while using Consolidated's restrooms." Guillermo Alfaro, another Consolidated employee, and 281 others brought a separate suit seeking damages for invasion of privacy and infliction of emotional distress. They also sought injunctive relief to end the use of the surveillance devices.

Consolidated removed both cases to federal court, contending that plaintiffs' state claims were preempted under § 301 of the LMRA because the claims required interpretation of the CBA between Consolidated and its employees'

union to determine the employees' reasonable expectations of privacy.

The history of § 301 preemption doctrine is well known, but worth summarizing again to explain how we have arrived at the current state of the law and to provide context for our discussion. As this court has noted, "familiarity with the subject matter has not bred facility."

Section 301 is on its face a jurisdictional statute, under which "suits for violation of contracts between an employer and a labor organization representing employees in an industry affecting commerce as defined in this chapter, or between any such labor organizations, may be brought in any district court of the United States having jurisdiction of the parties." Finally, *Livadas v. Bradshaw* summarized and advanced the state of preemption doctrine. Livadas explained:

> Finally, we were clear that when the meaning of contract terms is not the subject of dispute, the bare fact that a collective-bargaining agreement will be consulted in the course of state-law litigation plainly does not require the claim to be extinguished.

Based on these principles, Livadas held that because the plaintiff's claim required the court only to "look to" the CBA to determine her rate of pay, there was not even a "colorable argument" for preemption, because her claim was "entirely independent of any understanding embodied in the collective-bargaining agreement between the union and the employer." Even though the Court looked to the CBA to determine the absence of a waiver of state law protections, it concluded that preemption was not required.

If the claim is plainly based on state law, § 301 preemption is not mandated simply because the defendant refers to the CBA in mounting a defense.

We turn now to the specifics of the case before us. In arguing in favor of dismissal, Consolidated cites provisions of the CBA it negotiated with the International Brotherhood of Teamsters, Local No. 63, claiming these provisions brought its covert surveillance within the purview of the CBA. Article 26, Section 2 of the agreement forbids the use of camera surveillance for disciplinary reasons except to prove a charge of property theft or dishonesty. The section also specifies the procedure to be employed for the use of videotapes in the context of theft or dishonesty allegations. Article 35, Section 3 discusses alcohol and drug use and the procedures to be employed for drug testing. Consolidated contends that any employee claim based on its covert restroom surveillance requires recourse to these provisions of the CBA to determine the employees' reasonable expectations of privacy. Without such an analysis,

Consolidated argues, the court would be unable to determine whether these expectations were violated.

The relevant section reads as follows:

> The Employer may not use video cameras to discipline or discharge an employee for reasons other than theft of property or dishonesty. If the information on the video tape is to be used to discipline or discharge an employee, the Employer must provide the Local Union, prior to the hearing, an opportunity to review the video tape used by the Employer to support the discipline or discharge. Where a Supplement imposes more restrictive conditions upon use of video cameras for discipline or discharge, such restrictions shall prevail.

As discussed above, we may look to a CBA to determine whether a plaintiff's claim necessarily implicates its terms without "interpreting" the agreement, as that word is used in the context of § 301 preemption. Doing so here, we find Consolidated's argument unpersuasive. The plaintiffs based their claims on the protections afforded them by California state law, without any reference to expectations or duties created by the CBA. Their claims are neither founded directly upon rights conferred in the CBA nor "substantially dependent upon" interpretation of the CBA terms. Rather, those claims are based on California's constitutional and statutory rights of privacy guaranteed to all persons, whether or not they may happen to work subject to a CBA. Although some such rights of privacy might well be subject to negotiation and be conditioned by the terms of a CBA, that is not the case here. The claims are independent of the CBA and not subject to § 301 preemption.

Consolidated's insistence that we must refer to the CBA because one provision mentions drug use and another contemplates the use of surveillance videotapes in certain specified circumstances does not change our analysis. Neither of these provisions purports to have any bearing on secret spying on Consolidated's employees in company restrooms—no matter how well-intentioned Consolidated's alleged purpose may have been in doing so. Indeed, the surreptitious nature of the violation of plaintiffs' privacy belies any notion of bargaining or consent to hidden cameras behind two-way mirrors. Consolidated cannot create a dispute as to the meaning of the terms of the CBA by picking out terms that refer to videotapes and drug use, particularly when a cursory examination of those provisions makes clear they apply to a completely different context and set of circumstances. In short, this is a classic example of a defendant's attempt to "inject a federal question into an action that asserts what is plainly a state-law claim [in order to] transform the action into one arising under federal law, thereby selecting the forum in which the claim shall be litigated."

Even if the CBA did expressly contemplate the use of two-way mirrors to facilitate detection of drug users, such a provision would be illegal under California law. Section 653n of the California Penal Code makes the installation and maintenance of two-way mirrors permitting the observation of restrooms illegal without reference to the reasonable expectations of those so viewed. Determination of guilt under the statute is not dependent on context or subjective factors; use of the mirrors is a per se violation of the penal code, and an assumption that the mirrors will not be used is per se reasonable.

When companies employ drug testing, the parameters of the tests are often outlined in CBAs so that employees know exactly what to expect. Moreover, drug testing, unlike covert restroom surveillance, is not performed surreptitiously and—most importantly—is not illegal under state law. Issues of privacy implicated by drug testing programs may well be context-dependent. Issues of privacy implicated by the use of two-way mirrors for surreptitious surveillance are not.

Because a CBA cannot validly sanction illegal action, we hold the terms of the CBA were irrelevant to plaintiffs' claim of privacy violation. The district court's finding of pre-emption was therefore improper.

Because the state law privacy claims in these cases were not preempted by § 301, the district court lacked removal jurisdiction over these actions. They must therefore be remanded to state court.

REVERSED and REMANDED with judgment for Cramer.

Case Commentary

The Ninth Circuit Court decided that a CBA cannot preclude the filing of an invasion of privacy claim that occurred due to a violation of the criminal law. ∎

CASE QUESTIONS

1. Is the Court's decision justifiable?
2. Was there any justification for the cameras or two-way mirrors?
3. Ethically, how could the employer hide behind the CBA to cover up a criminal act?

Purpose

Collective bargaining serves a useful purpose in allowing management to negotiate with one union rather than the hundreds or thousands of individual employees that the union represents. In most cases, it is an expeditious and inexpensive method of resolving labor issues.

Unlawful Practices

Where there is a valid collective bargaining agreement, it would be an unlawful practice to compromise employees' contracted rights, such as seniority and shift preference, in order to accommodate the religious beliefs of a particular employee. This would present an undue hardship for the employer.

Employment Perspective

Mitchell Feldstein, an Orthodox Jew, has been employed at the Giant Motors Lexington, Kentucky, plant, where he has seniority. Mitchell is granted a transfer to the Flint, Michigan, plant. According to the collective bargaining agreement, seniority is determined by years at the plant, not at the company. At Flint, Mitchell, having no seniority, is required to work Saturdays. Mitchell asserts that this requirement is against his religious beliefs. Giant Motors refuses to accommodate him, claiming undue hardship in that the accommodation will compromise the seniority rights of other employees as determined by the collective bargaining agreement. Mitchell is subsequently discharged for excessive absenteeism on Saturdays. Mitchell files an EEOC claim for religious discrimination. Will he be successful? No! To accommodate Mitchell would be a breach of the collective bargaining agreement and an unlawful employment practice. It is an undue hardship for Giant Motors.

The issue in the next case is whether the arbitrator's decision to reinstate a driver who twice tested positive for drugs is arbitrary and capricious.

Eastern Associated Coal Corporation v. United Mine Workers of America
531 U.S. 57 (2000)

Justice Breyer delivered the opinion of the Court.

A labor arbitrator ordered an employer to reinstate an employee truck driver who had twice tested positive for marijuana. The question before us is whether considerations of public policy require courts to refuse to enforce that arbitration award. We conclude that they do not. The courts may enforce the award. And the employer must reinstate, rather than discharge, the employee.

I

Petitioner, Eastern Associated Coal Corp., and respondent, United Mine Workers of America, are parties to a collective-bargaining agreement with arbitration provisions. The agreement specifies that, in arbitration, in order to discharge an employee, Eastern must prove it has "just cause." Otherwise the arbitrator will order the employee reinstated. The arbitrator's decision is final.

James Smith worked for Eastern as a member of a road crew, a job that required him to drive heavy trucklike vehicles on public highways. As a truck driver, Smith was subject to Department of Transportation (DOT) regulations requiring random drug testing of workers engaged in "safety-sensitive" tasks.

In March 1996, Smith tested positive for marijuana. Eastern sought to discharge Smith. The union went to arbitration, and the arbitrator concluded that Smith's positive drug test did not amount to "just cause" for discharge. Instead the arbitrator ordered Smith's reinstatement, provided that Smith (1) accept a suspension of 30 days without pay, (2) participate in a substance-abuse program, and (3) undergo drug tests at the discretion of Eastern (or an approved substance-abuse professional) for the next five years.

Between April 1996 and January 1997, Smith passed four random drug tests. But in July 1997 he again tested positive for marijuana. Eastern again sought to discharge Smith. The union again went to arbitration, and the arbitrator again concluded that Smith's use of marijuana did not amount to "just cause" for discharge, in light of two mitigating circumstances. First, Smith had been a good employee for 17 years.

And, second, Smith had made a credible and "very personal appeal under oath . . . concerning a personal/family problem which caused this one time lapse in drug usage."

The arbitrator ordered Smith's reinstatement provided that Smith (1) accept a new suspension without pay, this time for slightly more than three months; (2) reimburse Eastern and the union for the costs of both arbitration proceedings; (3) continue to participate in a substance-abuse program; (4) continue to undergo random drug testing; and (5) provide Eastern with a signed, undated letter of resignation, to take effect if Smith again tested positive within the next five years.

Eastern brought suit in federal court seeking to have the arbitrator's award vacated, arguing that the award contravened a public policy against the operation of dangerous machinery by workers who test positive for drugs. The District Court, while recognizing a strong regulation-based public policy against drug use by workers who perform safety-sensitive functions, held that Smith's conditional reinstatement did not violate that policy. And it ordered the award's enforcement.

The Court of Appeals for the Fourth Circuit affirmed on the reasoning of the District Court. We granted certiorari in light of disagreement among the Circuits. We now affirm the Fourth Circuit's determination.

II

Eastern claims that considerations of public policy make the arbitration award unenforceable. In considering this claim, we must assume that the collective-bargaining agreement itself calls for Smith's reinstatement. That is because both employer and union have granted to the arbitrator the authority to interpret the meaning of their contract's language, including such words as "just cause." They have "bargained for" the "arbitrator's construction" of their agreement. And courts will set aside the arbitrator's interpretation of what their agreement means only in rare instances. Of course, an arbitrator's award "must draw its essence from the contract and cannot simply reflect the arbitrator's own notions of industrial justice." "But as long as an honest arbitrator is even arguably construing or applying the contract and acting within the scope of his authority," the fact that "a court is convinced he committed serious error does not suffice to overturn his decision." Eastern does not claim here that the arbitrator acted outside the scope of his contractually delegated authority. Hence we must treat the arbitrator's award as if it represented an agreement between Eastern and the union as to the proper meaning of the contract's words "just cause."

We must then decide whether a contractual reinstatement requirement would fall within the legal exception that makes unenforceable "a collective bargaining agreement that is contrary to public policy." The Court has made clear that any such public policy must be "explicit," "well defined," and "dominant." And, of course, the question to be answered is not whether Smith's drug use itself violates public policy, but whether the agreement to reinstate him does so.

III

In Eastern's view, these provisions embody a strong public policy against drug use by transportation workers in safety-sensitive positions and in favor of random drug testing in order to detect that use. Eastern argues that reinstatement of a driver who has twice failed random drug tests would undermine that policy—to the point where a judge must set aside an employer–union agreement requiring reinstatement.

Eastern's argument, however, loses much of its force when one considers further provisions of the Act that make clear that the Act's remedial aims are complex. The Act says that "rehabilitation is a critical component of any testing program," that rehabilitation "should be made available to individuals, as appropriate," and that DOT must promulgate regulations for "rehabilitation programs." The DOT regulations specifically state that a driver who has tested positive for drugs cannot return to a safety-sensitive position until (1) the driver has been evaluated by a "substance-abuse professional" to determine if treatment is needed; (2) the substance-abuse professional has certified that the driver has followed any rehabilitation program prescribed; and (3) the driver has passed a return-to-duty drug test. In addition, (4) the driver must be subject to at least six random drug tests during the first year after returning to the job. Neither the Act nor the regulations forbid an employer to reinstate in a safety-sensitive position an employee who fails a random drug test once or twice. The congressional and regulatory directives require only that the above-stated prerequisites to reinstatement be met.

Moreover, when promulgating these regulations, DOT decided not to require employers either to provide rehabilitation or to "hold a job open for a driver" who has tested positive, on the basis that such decisions "should be left to management/driver negotiation." That determination reflects basic background labor law principles, which caution against interference with labor–management agreements about appropriate employee discipline.

The award before us is not contrary to these several policies, taken together. The award does not condone Smith's conduct or ignore the risk to public safety that drug use by truck drivers may pose. Rather, the award punishes Smith by suspending him for three months, thereby depriving him of nearly $ 9,000 in lost wages, it requires him to pay the arbitration costs of both sides; it insists upon further substance-abuse treatment and testing; and it makes clear (by requiring Smith to provide a signed letter of resignation) that one more failed test means discharge.

The award violates no specific provision of any law or regulation. It is consistent with DOT rules requiring completion of substance-abuse treatment before returning to work, for it does not preclude Eastern from assigning Smith to a non-safety-sensitive position until Smith completes the pre-scribed treatment program. It is consistent with the Testing Act's 1-year and 10-year driving license suspension requirements, for those requirements apply only to drivers who, unlike Smith, actually operated vehicles under the influence of drugs. The award is also consistent with the Act's rehabilitative concerns, for it requires substance-abuse treatment and testing before Smith can return to work.

The fact that Smith is a recidivist—that he has failed drug tests twice—is not sufficient to tip the balance in Eastern's favor. The award punishes Smith more severely for his second lapse. And that more severe punishment, which included a 90-day suspension, would have satisfied even a "recidivist" rule that DOT once proposed but did not adopt—a rule that would have punished two failed drug tests, not with discharge, but with a driving suspension of 60 days.

We recognize that reasonable people can differ as to whether reinstatement or discharge is the more appropriate remedy here. But both employer and union have agreed to entrust this remedial decision to an arbitrator. We cannot find in the Act, the regulations, or any other law or legal precedent an "explicit," "well defined," "dominant" public policy to which the arbitrator's decision "runs contrary." We conclude that the lower courts correctly rejected Eastern's public policy claim.

The judgment of the Court of Appeals is Affirmed for the United Mine Workers.

Case Commentary
The U.S. Supreme Court concluded that the arbitrator's award is binding because the parties contracted for this type of resolution of disputes. ■

CASE QUESTIONS

1. Are you in agreement with the Court's reasoning?
2. Should an exception to arbitration be carved out in cases involving drug use?
3. How could the arbitrator send this employee back to work after the second time he failed the drug test?

EMPLOYEE LESSONS

1. Be aware of the history and purpose of unions.
2. Develop an understanding of the various labor laws.
3. Determine the likelihood that your employer will remain at its current location before purchasing a home or becoming entrenched in the community.
4. Evaluate whether you will search for other employment or remain with your employer if it decides to relocate.
5. Recognize that mediation is available to settle disputes.
6. Become knowledgeable concerning the terms and conditions in a collective bargaining agreement.
7. Appreciate that unions have, on occasion, secured higher wages and benefits for their members, only to have employers as a result relocate.
8. Acknowledge the impact of GATT and NAFTA on employment.
9. Realize that many manufacturing jobs have been replaced by lower paying nonunion service jobs.
10. Understand that arbitration clauses are incorporated into many employment contracts, thereby eliminating the opportunity to have your case heard before a jury.

REVIEW QUESTIONS

1. Why did workers have so much difficulty organizing?
2. How was the Sherman Antitrust Act used against workers?
3. When was the first union formed? – *K20*
4. What is beneficial about unions?
5. How have the GATT and NAFTA affected unions?
6. Why did unions switch their political support from the Labor Party to the Democratic Party?
7. Why was the American Federation of Labor successful?
8. Define *yellow-dog contract*.

9. Explain the function of the National Labor Relations Board.
10. A union shop mandates that the employer hire only union members. Is a union shop legal?
11. Can an individual be paid as a union representative without forgoing his rights under the NLRA?
12. Define *collective bargaining*.
13. What is a collective bargaining agreement?
14. Is a collective bargaining agreement binding on all union members?
15. Explain the terms in the agreement.
16. What is the method for dispute resolution?
17. Explain the purpose served by collective bargaining.
18. Give an example of when contract rights secured through collective bargaining conflict with civil rights.
19. How is this conflict resolved?
20. Explain the advantage of collective bargaining from an employer's perspective.
21. What law secured the right of workers to bargain collectively?
22. Can provisions of a collective bargaining agreement survive its termination?
23. Is it ethical to compel a nonunion member to pay union dues as a condition of his or her employment?

CASE PROBLEMS

1. Congress enacted the Federal Service Labor-Management Relations Statute (FSLMRS), which provides certain protections, including union representation, to a variety of federal employees. The question is whether an investigator employed in NASA's Office of Inspector General (NASA–OIG) can be considered a "representative" of NASA when examining a NASA employee, such that the right to union representation in the FSLMRS may be invoked.

    In January 1993, in response to information supplied by the Federal Bureau of Investigation (FBI), OIG conducted an investigation of certain threatening activities of an employee at the Space Flight Center in Huntsville, Alabama, a component of NASA. A NASA–OIG investigator contacted the employee to arrange for an interview and, in response to the employee's request, agreed that both the employee's lawyer and union representative could attend. The conduct of the interview gave rise to a complaint by the union representative that the investigator had improperly limited his participation. The union filed a charge with the Federal Labor Relations Authority (Authority) alleging that NASA and its OIG had committed an unfair labor practice. The issue is whether an investigator employed in NASA's Office of Inspector General is considered to be a representative of NASA.

    The FSLMRS provides, in relevant part,

    "(2) An exclusive representative of an appropriate unit in an agency shall be given the opportunity to be represented at—...
    "(B) any examination of an employee in the unit by a representative of the agency in connection with an investigation if—
    "(i) the employee reasonably believes that the examination may result in disciplinary action against the employee; and
    "(ii) the employee requests representation."

    In this case, it is undisputed that the employee reasonably believed the investigation could result in discipline against him, that he requested union representation, that NASA is the relevant "agency," and that, if the provision applies, a violation of §7114(a)(2)(B) occurred. *National Aeronautics and Space Administration v. Federal Labor Relations Authority*, 527 U.S. 229 (1999)

2. Clause 15(F) of the CBA provides as follows:

"The Union agrees that this Agreement is intended to cover all matters affecting wages, hours, and other terms and conditions of employment and that during the term of this Agreement the Employers will not be required to negotiate on any further matters affecting these or other subjects not specifically set forth in this Agreement. Anything not contained in this Agreement shall not be construed as being part of this Agreement. All past port practices being observed may be reduced to writing in each port." When the stevedoring companies realized that Wright had previously settled a claim for permanent disability, they informed the union that they would not accept Wright for employment, because a person certified as permanently disabled (which they regarded Wright to be) is not qualified to perform longshore work under the CBA. The union responded that the employers had misconstrued the CBA, suggested that the ADA entitled Wright to return to work if he could perform his duties, and asserted that refusing Wright employment would constitute a "lock-out" in violation of the CBA.

A magistrate judge recommended that the district court dismiss the case without prejudice because Wright had failed to pursue the grievance procedure provided by the CBA. The district court adopted the report and recommendation and subsequently rejected Wright's motion for reconsideration. The question is whether an employee who is asserting a violation of the Americans with Disabilities Act (ADA) must arbitrate this dispute in accordance with the arbitration provision of the collective bargaining agreement. *Wright v. Universal Maritime Service Corp.*, 525 U.S. 70 (1998)

3. The question here is whether an employer may disavow a collective bargaining agreement because of a good-faith doubt about a union's majority status at the time the contract was made, when the doubt arises from facts known to the employer before its contract offer is accepted by the union. On November 18, 1988, the picketing stopped, and 9 days later, on a Sunday evening, the union telegraphed its acceptance of the outstanding offer. The very next day, however, Auciello told the union that it doubted that a majority of the bargaining unit's employees supported the union and, for that reason, disavowed the collective bargaining agreement and denied it had any duty to continue negotiating. Auciello traced its doubt to knowledge acquired before the union accepted the contract offer, including the facts that 9 employees had crossed the picket line, that 13 employees had given it signed forms indicating their resignation from the Union, and that 16 had expressed dissatisfaction with the union.

The issue is whether an employer with a good-faith doubt that the union has majority status prior to approval of the collective bargaining agreement may wait until after the collective bargaining agreement has been accepted before raising the issue of lack of majority status.

Auciello Iron Works, Inc. v. National Labor Relations Board, 517 U.S. 781 (1996)

HUMAN RESOURCE DILEMMAS

1. Steven Goldberg, who is Jewish, is a factory worker at Uranus Umbrella Company. His work shift has been changed on weekdays to 11 A.M. to 7 P.M. He asks for an accommodation to have his shift adjusted on Fridays to allow him to return home before sunset. Uranus claims this accommodation would place it in violation of the seniority provision of the collective bargaining agreement it has with Steven's union. How would you advise Uranus?

2. Jimmy Ryan is a nonunion employee. As a condition of his employment with Sun Aerospace, he is required to pay union dues. Jimmy claims his constitutional rights are violated by the collective bargaining unit's service fee. Do you believe Jimmy's assessment is correct?

3. Tanya Gilbert and 12 of her coworkers were terminated by Asteroid Enterprises after signing union authorization forms. They claim that Asteroid's action was antiunion and thus constituted an unfair labor practice. How would you advise Tanya to proceed?

WEB SITE ASSIGNMENT

Using the following Web sites, determine the public policy exceptions to collective bargaining agreements.

www.findlaw.com
www.unionmuscle.com
kids.infoplease.lycos.com/spot/laborl.html
www.nrtw.org/legal.htm
stats.bls.gov/news.release/wkstp.toc.htm
www.bls.gov/cba/home.htm
www.thelaborers.net/collective_bargaining_agreements/DEFAULT.HTM
www.ers.dol.govt.nz/bargaining
www.bls.gov/opub/mlr/1999/01/art4exc.htm

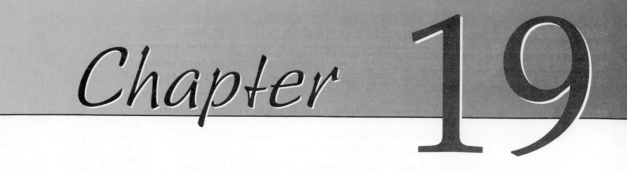

Chapter 19

Wage and Hour Regulation

Employment Scenario

The Long and the Short of It employs several newly arrived legal immigrants. L&S pays them a flat $4 per hour off-the-books for stocking inventory, cleaning the store and its bathrooms, and performing general maintenance work. Hours tallied by these workers usually exceed 60 hours per week. Regina Matthews, the new bookkeeper at L&S, discovers the scam. She relays this information to Susan North, L&S's attorney. Susan calls Tom Long and Mark Short, copresidents of L&S, to her office. What position should Susan take with regard to L&S's violation?

Chapter Checklist

➤ *Learn the significance of the Fair Labor Standards Act.*

➤ *Know what the minimum wage is.*

➤ *Appreciate why wage and hour laws exist.*

➤ *Be aware when overtime pay is required.*

➤ *Be apprised of the minimum wage and maximum hours exemptions.*

➤ *Realize that children may not be employed during school hours or in certain hazardous jobs.*

➤ *Understand that the number of hours worked cannot be averaged over several weeks to avoid overtime pay.*

➤ *Evaluate the argument that eliminating the minimum wage would keep more companies from relocating abroad.*

➤ *Recognize that children under the age of 14 may work for their parents.*

➤ *Be apprised that court approval of entertainment and athletic contracts is required for children under 14 years of age.*

INTRODUCTION

Wage and hour regulation has a two-fold purpose: first, to set an hourly subsistence wage for workers; and second, to regulate the number of hours individuals have to work before becoming entitled to overtime compensation of $1\frac{1}{2}$ times their regular wage. In reality, minimum wage workers must work overtime to support themselves, unless their spouse is also working or they are being subsidized in part by another family member. Arguments are often made that eliminating the minimum wage would stop manufacturers from relocating to Mexico or overseas. Realistically, it is difficult to imagine anyone, except possibly newly arrived immigrants or illegal aliens, working for less than the minimum wage.

HUMAN RESOURCE ADVICE

- Understand the provisions of the Fair Labor Standards Act (FLSA).
- Pay at least the minimum wage.
- Compensate employees with overtime pay after a 40-hour workweek.
- Recognize that averaging hours worked over several weeks to avoid time-and-a-half pay for overtime is illegal.
- Know the occupations exempted from minimum wage and maximum hours laws.
- Avoid hiring illegal aliens who will work for less than the minimum wage.
- Refrain from paying workers off-the-books.
- Appreciate that children may not be employed during school hours or in certain jobs deemed hazardous.
- Learn that children under the age of 14 may work for their parents.
- Be aware that children under the age of 14 who engage in athletics and entertainment must have their contracts approved by the court.

FAIR LABOR STANDARDS ACT

In 1938, Congress enacted the Fair Labor Standards Act to regulate both the minimum compensation that could be given to a worker on an hourly basis and the maximum number of hours an employee could be required to work before being compensated at an overtime rate of $1\frac{1}{2}$ times the normal rate of pay. The minimum wage has risen through the years, but it is not indexed to the cost of living. Since October 1, 1996, the minimum wage rate was $4.75. On September 1, 1997, the minimum wage was increased to $5.15. The maximum number of hours before the overtime is required is 40 hours per workweek. The regular rate of pay, which is used to determine the maximum wage, may include the reasonable cost of room, board, and other facilities; gifts; bonuses; days compensated for vacation, illness, or personal reasons; reimbursed expenses for meals, lodging, and travel expenses; contributions toward pensions; premiums for life, disability, and health insurance; and extra compensation for work performed on a Saturday or Sunday.

Federal law does not require overtime pay for work in excess of 8 hours in a day or work on weekends or holidays, but some states do. Record keeping is required under the FLSA relating to straight and overtime pay, hourly rate of pay, hours worked each day and each week, sex, and occupation.

Students may be paid 85 percent of minimum wage. Employees who receive tips have a minimum wage of $2.13 per hour.

Employment Perspective

Brittany Robinson works at the Baked Cake Shop in Vernon. She is a full-time employee who works Wednesday through Sunday, 8 hours a day. Brittany's gross pay per week is $190. The Bake Cake Shop pays $6.50 per hour on Saturdays and Sundays. Is the Baked Cake Shop in violation of the minimum wage law established in the FLSA? Yes! The extra compensation Brittany received for Saturday and Sunday work cannot be used in determining the regular rate of hourly pay. Subtracting her Saturday and Sunday wages of $104 ($6.50 per hour times 16 hours), Brittany is paid $86 for the 24 hours of work. This amounts to $3.58 per hour, which is below the minimum wage.

Employment Perspective

Hector Jiminez is a Mexican farm worker in Southern California. Pine Valley Farm pays Hector $3.50 per hour throughout the year and then makes up the difference between that rate and the minimum wage rate at the end of the year. Is Pine Valley in violation of the minimum wage standard? Yes! The minimum wage is determined on the basis of each workweek. The year-end payment must be looked on as extra compensation or a bonus and may not be factored in. Pine Valley is in violation of the minimum wage requirement. The first week it paid Hector at the rate of $3.50 per hour. Pine Valley is not given a grace period of an entire year to make up the difference.

The issue in the case that follows is whether the delivery workers were employees entitled to minimum wage or independent contractors.

Ansoumana v. Gristede's
255 F. Supp. 2d 184 (S.D. NY 2003)

Alvin K. Hellerstein, U.S.D.J.

Plaintiffs Faty Ansoumana et al., and the class they represent, were delivery workers for supermarkets and drugstore chains, including stores owned and operated by Duane Reade, Inc., a defendant. The delivery workers were hired by the Hudson/Chelsea group of defendants and assigned to Duane Reade stores to make deliveries to customers and to provide general in-store services, as directed by the store supervisors. I am asked to decide, on these cross-motions for summary judgment, whether, as to the Hudson/Chelsea defendants, the plaintiffs were independent contractors or employees entitled to be paid a minimum wage and time-and-a-half for overtime and, if plaintiffs were employees, whether Duane Reade was a "joint employer," jointly obligated with the Hudson/Chelsea defendants to pay minimum wages and overtime. I will be applying, in determining the issues put to me, the Fair Labor Standards Act ("FLSA"), and the New York Minimum Wage Act.

The defendant, Duane Reade, Inc. is a large retail drugstore chain in the New York metropolitan area. Duane Reade outsourced its requirements for delivery workers by engaging the Hudson/Chelsea defendants to provide delivery workers to the Duane Reade stores, at the rate of $250 to $300 per week, per worker. The Hudson/Chelsea defendants, in turn, paid the delivery workers whom they assigned $20–$30 per day, characterizing them as independent contractors in order to avoid the minimum wage and overtime provisions of federal and New York law.

I hold in this decision that those delivery workers who were assigned to work in Duane Reade stores and made deliveries on foot were not independent contractors, that the

Hudson/Chelsea defendants are liable to them for violations of the FLSA and the New York Labor law, and that Duane Reade and the Hudson/Chelsea defendants were joint employers within the meaning of those laws and were jointly and severally obligated to pay minimum wages and overtime to the delivery workers.

I. BACKGROUND

Plaintiffs filed this action on January 13, 2000 against three large chains of New York supermarkets and drugstores, and several companies and individuals who hired employees to work as deliverymen in such chains. Plaintiffs alleged that the defendants were operating in violation of the FLSA and the New York Minimum Wage Law. They claimed that the defendants, who had hired the delivery workers, and the chains to which they were assigned and in which they worked were jointly and severally liable to them. In May 2001, I certified a class of delivery workers and dispatchers who had worked for defendants between January 13, 1994 and May 24, 2001 and who had not been paid the minimum wage or overtime required under New York law. More than 500 delivery workers have filed consents and are participating in this lawsuit pursuant to the collective action provisions of the FLSA.

The delivery workers involved in the motion before me were hired by the Hudson/Chelsea defendants and were assigned to and worked for Duane Reade stores in Manhattan. The workers are mainly unskilled immigrants, mostly from West Africa. They provided services in the stores and made deliveries from the stores, and, despite working eight to eleven hours a day, six days a week, were paid a flat rate of between $20–$30 per day, well below minimum wage requirements.

The record developed in discovery shows that the Hudson/Chelsea defendants hired the delivery workers for 45 to 60 of the 200 Duane Reade stores located in Manhattan and the boroughs. By oral agreement between Duane Reade and the Hudson/Chelsea defendants, Duane Reade has depended on the Hudson/Chelsea defendants exclusively, since 1994, to supply its stores with delivery workers and has been paying the Hudson/Chelsea defendants a flat weekly rate of $250–$300 per worker. The Hudson/Chelsea defendants hired their workers essentially without advertising, from recommendations by one worker to another, and provided them with uniforms and delivery carts. Since 1989, the Hudson/Chelsea defendants have regarded their delivery workers as independent contractors, not employees, and have required some of the workers to sign statements so acknowledging. The Hudson/Chelsea defendants have not withheld federal, state, or local taxes, nor made FICA or other statutory required withholdings from the payments to the workers, and have given them IRS Forms 1099 rather than W-2s to reflect their compensation. The Hudson/Chelsea defendants did not maintain a system for tracking the delivery workers' hours or pay and did not keep records of any tips the delivery workers received.

In March 2000, the Hudson/Chelsea defendants entered into a collective bargaining agreement with those of its delivery workers who had joined Local 338, Retail, Wholesale and Department Store Workers Union, AFL-CIO. That agreement required that all employees hired by the Hudson/Chelsea defendants earn at least $5.15 an hour and time and a half for overtime. Employees assigned to drug stores are allowed $1.65 of the wage to be credited as tip allowance. Since the agreement was signed, the Hudson/Chelsea defendants have been issuing IRS Forms W-2 to their delivery workers.

The delivery workers assigned to Duane Reade stores reported to the Duane Reade store to which they had been assigned and received directions from Duane Reade personnel in that store. Generally, they were assigned to the pharmacy departments and made deliveries of pharmaceutical items to customers. Duane Reade personnel provided the pharmaceutical stickers, issued the delivery instructions and, if payment was to be collected, instructed the delivery workers how much money to bring back from the customer. The Duane Reade stores maintained logs at the stores, and the delivery workers signed in and out of the logs upon each delivery, recording deliveries and receipts. In their spare time, the delivery workers were often asked to help customers with heavy items, provided bagging services at check-out registers, helped with security, stocked shelves, and moved products from one Duane Reade store to another. If a delivery worker was unsatisfactory, the Duane Reade manager asked Hudson/Chelsea to reassign the worker and provide another to replace him. Thus, the delivery worker, although not hired or paid by Duane Reade, was directed by Duane Reade managers and supervisors and provided services essentially similar to other Duane Reade employees.

II. LEGAL FRAMEWORK
The Fair Labor Standards Act

The Fair Labor Standards Act mandates that "employees" receive a minimum wage and overtime pay of time and a half of the workers' regular hourly rate for each hour worked in excess of forty hours per workweek. The FLSA defines an "employee," with certain exceptions not relevant here, as "any individual employed by an employer." The statute in turn defines "employ" as "to suffer or permit to work," and "employer" to include "any person acting directly or indirectly in the interest of an employer."

The regulations implementing the FLSA contemplate that an employee may have more than one employer. Such "joint employment" arises when the employee "performs work which simultaneously benefits two or more employers" and "one employer is acting directly or indirectly in the interest of the other employer (or employers) in relation to the employee." This question of joint employment of plaintiffs, by Duane Reade and by the Hudson/Chelsea defendants, is a central issue in these cross motions.

New York Law

The New York Minimum Wage Act, like the FLSA, requires employers to pay a minimum wage—$4.25 before March 31, 2000, and $5.15 thereafter, and time and a half for overtime. Like the FLSA, the New York Labor law defines "employee" broadly, as "including any individual employed or permitted to work by an employer in any occupation." Because New York Labor Law and the FLSA embody similar standards with respect to the legal issues before me, I will consider the federal law in deciding whether defendants were joint employers.

An employer's characterization of an employee is not controlling, however, for otherwise there could be no enforcement of any minimum wage or overtime law. There would be nothing to prevent old-fashioned labor contractors from rounding up workers willing to sell their labor cheaply, and assigning them to perform outsourced work, without complying with minimum wage requirements. Thus, not the characterization of a hiring hall, but the test of "economic reality," governs how a relationship of employment is to be characterized in relation to the FLSA.

In *Brock v. Superior Care, Inc.*, the Court set out an "economic reality" test to distinguish between employees and independent contractors. The test considers five factors: (1) the degree of control exercised by the employer over the workers; (2) the workers' opportunity for profit or loss and their investment in the business; (3) the degree of skill and independent initiative required to perform the work; (4) the permanence or duration of the working relationship; and (5) the extent to which the work is an integral part of the employer's business. No one factor is dispositive; the "ultimate concern" is "whether, as a matter of economic reality, the workers depend upon someone else's business for the opportunity to render service or are in business for themselves."

The Hudson/Chelsea defendants' relationship with plaintiffs satisfies the first of the Brock considerations, showing a substantial degree of control over the workers. The fact that the Hudson/Chelsea defendants hired, fired, transferred and paid the delivery workers weighs substantially in favor of finding an employment relationship between the Hudson/Chelsea defendants and plaintiffs.

The second consideration of Brock—opportunity for investment, and profit or loss—also weighs heavily in favor of an employment relationship. As defendants conceded, plaintiffs' investment in the business was negligible. Plaintiffs are not asked to invest in Duane Reade, Hudson/Chelsea, or their own jobs. Hudson/Chelsea provided the delivery workers with delivery carts that they could rent and uniforms that they could purchase; the workers did not have to make an up-front investment in such things in order to be hired or assigned to a Duane Reade store.

Hudson/Chelsea argues that delivery services require plaintiffs to exercise "skill and independent initiative," the third consideration of Brock, but clearly this is not so in any objective sense. The Duane Reade stores are located throughout Manhattan and the boroughs, and customers typically reside within a neighborhood of a few blocks. Little "skill" or "initiative" is needed to find one's way from a Duane Reade store to a customer's residence. The third consideration, then, also argues for finding plaintiffs to be employees, not independent contractors.

The fourth consideration, the permanence and duration of the plaintiffs' working relationship with the Hudson/Chelsea defendants, is disputed. Many delivery workers do not endure for long periods of time in this line of work due to the long hours, the low pay, the dangers of the streets, and the vagaries of the weather inherent in delivery work. Any transience of the work force therefore reflects "the nature of the profession and not the workers' success in marketing their skills independently."

The fifth consideration looks at the extent to which the work is integral to the business, and it also weighs heavily in favor of an employment relationship. The Hudson/Chelsea defendants concede that they are engaged primarily in the business of providing delivery services to retail establishments and that plaintiffs perform the actual delivery work. Thus, plaintiffs' services constitute an integral part of the Hudson/Chelsea defendants' business.

It is clear, from the "economic reality" and the totality of circumstances, that the delivery workers depend upon the Hudson/Chelsea defendants for the opportunity to sell their labor and are not in any real sense in business for themselves. The delivery workers, as a matter of law, are employees, not independent contractors, and are entitled to summary judgment against the Hudson/Chelsea defendants.

Duane Reade is a Joint Employer

The FLSA contemplates that more than one employer may be responsible for underpayments of minimum wages and overtime. Duane Reade may be liable to plaintiffs for such underpayments, jointly and severally with the Hudson/Chelsea defendants, if Duane Reade was also their "employer" under the FLSA. The issue is determined by an "economic reality" test, which takes into account the real economic relationship between the employer who uses and benefits from the services of workers and the party that hires or assigns the workers to that employer.

Duane Reade offers an analogy to Federal Express, United Parcel, and other delivery services, but the analogy is misplaced. Duane Reade's delivery workers worked out of the Duane Reade stores, and not from a central depot; deliveries were made directly from the pharmacy counters to customers' homes, and not via a central facility; and control was exercised throughout by Duane Reade, and not by some independent service. Duane Reade used the delivery workers to extend its shelves and counters to the homes of customers, allowing them the convenience of shopping from home instead of having to come physically into a store.

Duane Reade managers and supervisors directed the delivery workers in their tasks, instructing them what to pick up, where to make deliveries, how to log their deliveries, and how much to receive in payment. The delivery workers worked as individuals, and not as a group shifting from store to store according to seasonal and hourly needs. Indeed, it was not until they were organized by Local 338, in March 2000, that they even had a bargaining representative to negotiate for them as a collective. Clearly, the economic reality of the relationship between Duane Reade and the delivery workers reveals that Duane Reade was an employer of the delivery workers, responsible for assuring that they were paid the wages required by the FLSA and the New York Minimum Wage Act as a condition of their employment.

Additionally, the relationship between Duane Reade and the Hudson/Chelsea defendants establishes joint employment. That relationship was "so extensive and regular as to approach exclusive agency." The Hudson/Chelsea defendants acted directly in the interest of Duane Reade in relation to the delivery workers, and Duane Reade used the Hudson/Chelsea defendants' services almost exclusively, for a lengthy period of years, since 1994, showing consistent dependence on them for delivery services.

I therefore hold, looking at the "circumstances of the whole activity," that plaintiffs were economically dependent on both the Hudson/Chelsea defendants and Duane Reade,

and that both were their "employers" under the FLSA and the New York Minimum Wage Act.

Conclusion

Duane Reade had the right to "outsource" its requirement for delivery services to an independent contractor, here the Hudson/Chelsea defendants, and seek, by such outsourcing, an extra measure of efficiency and economy in providing an important and competitive service. But it did not have the right to use the practice as a way to evade its obligations under the FLSA and the New York Minimum Wage Act. Both Duane Reade and the Hudson/Chelsea defendants were the "employers" of the plaintiffs under these laws, jointly and severally obligated for underpayments of minimum wage and overtime during the period between January 13, 1994 and March 26, 2000.

All plaintiffs who were hired by or worked for the Hudson/Chelsea defendants, were assigned to a Duane Reade store, and made deliveries mainly on foot are entitled to summary judgment against the Hudson/Chelsea defendants and Duane Reade, jointly and severally.

Judgment for Ansoumana.

Case Commentary

The Southern District Court of New York held that the delivery workers were employees who were entitled to be paid minimum wage. ■

CASE QUESTIONS

1. Do you agree with the court's ruling?
2. Why would a large company like Duane Reade begrudge its workers minimum wage?
3. Why would the company spend thousands to litigate this case when it could have given that money to the workers in the beginning?

Employment Perspective

Angela Montalbano is a floral arranger for Violets and Roses Flower Shop. She is a full-time employee. During Valentine's Day week, Angela worked 50 hours, and the following week Angela worked 30 hours. Angela is paid every 2 weeks. In her paycheck, she was compensated at her regular rate of pay for 80 hours. Is Violets and Roses in violation of the overtime pay provision of the maximum hours requirement of the FLSA? Yes! Each workweek must be looked at unto itself. One cannot offset against the other. The fact that Violets and Roses does not have enough work for Angela the week following Valentine's Day is immaterial. Angela is entitled to the hours of overtime pay for Valentine's week at the rate of $1\frac{1}{2}$ times the regular rate of pay. In the second week, Angela will receive her regular rate of pay for 30 hours unless she was hired with the proviso that she would be guaranteed a 40-hour workweek. Then she must be paid for the additional hours even if there is no work to do.

Overtime pay is not required when the employee is receiving up to 10 hours per week of remedial education that is not specific job training. Overtime would be required in excess of the 10 hours if this remediation was mandated by the company. If it were a voluntary after-work program, no pay at all would be required.

Employment Perspective

Rufus Buttonwod is an employee at Maple Woods Convention Center. At times, Rufus is asked to fill in as a customer service representative. Rufus's grammar is poor. Maple Woods provides him with remedial tutoring 1 hour per day, in addition to his normal 8-hour day. Rufus's attendance is mandatory. He is paid at his regular rate for 45 hours. Is Maple Woods adhering to the provisions of the maximum-hour laws? Yes! The 5 hours' remediation is compensable at the regular rate of pay.

The issue in the case that follows is whether on-call time should be compensated as working time.

Andrews v. Town of Skiatook, Oklahoma
123 F.3d 1327 (10th Cir. 1997)

Ebel, Circuit Judge.

The parties consented to trial before a United States Magistrate Judge.

The magistrate judge expressed his decision in well-reasoned Findings of Fact and Conclusions of Law with which we substantially agree. We thus attach the Findings of Fact and Conclusions of Law as an Appendix and AFFIRM for substantially the reasons stated therein.

FINDINGS OF FACT

1. Plaintiff, Michael Andrews, is a resident of the town of Skiatook, State of Oklahoma, and was employed by the Town of Skiatook as an Emergency Medical Technician (EMT) from February 28, 1993 to January 6, 1995.
2. Defendant, Town of Skiatook, is a political subdivision of the State of Oklahoma, existing under the laws of the State of Oklahoma, and was engaged in the business of managing, maintaining and operating an emergency ambulance service at all times relevant to this litigation.
3. During his employment as an EMT with the Town of Skiatook, Plaintiff was required to work four regular twelve-hour shifts per week and four twelve-hour on-call shifts per week which immediately followed his regular twelve-hour shift. Every third week Plaintiff was required to work one additional twelve-hour on-call shift. EMTs were permitted to trade their on-call shifts with another EMT and would then be expected to pay back the other EMT by covering an on-call shift for him/her.
4. The Town of Skiatook operated two emergency ambulances. One ambulance was staffed by two EMTs who remained at the ambulance station. The second ambulance was staffed by two "on-call EMTs" who were required to respond to calls in the second ambulance when an emergency call was received while the first ambulance was on another run. A call serviced by the second ambulance staffed by on-call EMTs is called a "second run."
5. While on-call, Plaintiff was required to monitor a pager which could be utilized to summon him for a second run. In addition to summoning the on-call personnel, the pager would advise the on-call personnel when the first ambulance had gone on a run. On-call EMTs could also monitor a police radio, which would advise them when the first ambulance had completed its run and returned to the ambulance station. Thus, the on-call EMTs would be aware when the first ambulance was on a run and there was an increased likelihood they could be summoned to make a second run.
6. While on-call, the EMTs were required to remain clean and appropriately attired, although not required to report in uniform, to refrain from drinking alcohol, and to respond to an on-call page within a reasonable period of time.
7–8. Omitted
9. Plaintiff was not compensated for the time spent on-call unless he was called back to make a second run, in which case, Plaintiff was compensated for a minimum of two hours at time and one/half pay. Of the 76 second runs Plaintiff made, none lasted more than two hours.
10. In 1993, the Town of Skiatook ambulance service made a total of 1,071 runs, 115 of which were second runs. Plaintiff made 28 second runs.
11. In 1994, the Town of Skiatook ambulance service made a total of 1,171 runs of which 140 were second runs. Plaintiff made 48 second runs.
12. Plaintiff worked ten months in 1993. At four on-call shifts per week and one extra on-call shift every three weeks, Plaintiff would have worked a total of 173 on-call shifts in 1993. Considering that Plaintiff went on 28 second runs in 1993, the Court calculates

that Plaintiff was actually called back to service during 16.18% of his on-call shifts in 1993.

13. Plaintiff worked a full twelve months in 1994. At four on-call shifts per week and one extra on-call shift every three weeks, Plaintiff would have worked a total of 209 on-call shifts. Considering that Plaintiff went on 48 second runs in 1994, the Court calculates that Plaintiff was called back to service during 22.96% of his on-call shifts in 1994.

CONCLUSIONS OF LAW

This Court has jurisdiction of this matter pursuant to the Fair Labor Standards Act. Defendant Town of Skiatook is a public agency and employer within the meaning of the Fair Labor Standards Act, is located within the jurisdiction of this Court, and is subject to the provisions of the Fair Labor Standards Act.

The test to determine whether an employee's on-call time constitutes working time is whether the time is spent predominantly for the employer's benefit or for the employee's. That test requires consideration of the agreement between the parties, the nature and extent of the restrictions, the relationship between the services rendered and the on-call time and all surrounding circumstances. The sole 10th Circuit authority finding on-call time compensable is *Renfro*. Plaintiff argues that his case is controlled by the decision in *Renfro*. This Court disagrees.

In *Renfro* the firefighters, although not required to remain on the premises while on-call, were required to report to the station within twenty minutes of being called back, were called back as many as 13 times in one shift, and averaged 3 to 5 callbacks per on-call shift. In *Renfro*, the 10th Circuit affirmed the district court which found:

The frequency with which Emporia firefighters are subject to call-backs readily distinguishes this case from cases which have held that on-call time is non-compensable. In many of those cases, the probability of an employee being called in, and thus, the probability of disruption of the employee's personal activities, was minimal.

CASE QUESTIONS

1. Are you in agreement with the court's determination?
2. How did the court determine whether Andrews spent the on-call time for his employer's benefit or for his own personal benefit?

The infrequency of callbacks in this case distinguishes it from *Renfro*.

Instead of being called back to work on average between 3 to 5 times per on-call shift, Plaintiff was only called back 16.18% of the time during his on-call shifts in 1993 and 22.96% of the time for his on-call shifts in 1994. On the facts before this Court, it is clear that Plaintiff's on-call time was predominantly for his personal benefit. While on-call, Plaintiff was free to engage in any activity of his choosing as long as he remained clean, did not drink alcohol and could respond to the ambulance station within five to ten minutes. The five to ten minute requirement gave Plaintiff access to all of the small town of Skiatook. Further, the fact that Plaintiff was notified when the first ambulance had gone on a run enabled Plaintiff to prepare for the possibility of a second run and to structure his activities so his on-call time would be as least restrictive as possible. In this regard it is fair to conclude that Plaintiff felt only slight restrictions on his personal activities while the first ambulance was not out on a call. It was only when the first ambulance was out on a call that Plaintiff had any significant chance of having to respond to a second run call and, based upon actual experience, Plaintiff knew that the percentage of time when a second run call would be required was small. Thus, Plaintiff was predominantly free to pursue his personal activities during his on-call time.

Based upon the above FINDINGS OF FACT AND CONCLUSIONS OF LAW, the Court finds that Plaintiff has failed to prove by a preponderance of the evidence that his on-call time was spent predominantly on behalf of Defendant employer. THE COURT, THEREFORE, FINDS IN FAVOR OF DEFENDANT.

Judgment will be entered accordingly.

Case Commentary

The Tenth Circuit Court ruled that Andrews did not spend his on-call time predominantly for his employer; therefore, he was not entitled to compensation for his time. ∎

3. Should on-call employees be entitled to some remuneration?

Exemptions

Certain employees are exempted from the minimum wage and the maximum hour requirements. These include executives, administrators, professionals, salespeople, elementary and secondary schoolteachers, domestic helpers who reside in the household, baby-sitters, and people who provide companionship and care to the elderly. Camp counselors are also exempted if the camp is not in operation for more than 7 months in the calendar year.

Employment Perspective

Tiffany O'Toole works as a camp counselor for 3 months each summer at Camp Fooey. The camp operates 13 weeks each year. She often works 8 hours a day, 7 days a week. Tiffany is paid a flat rate of $3,000 plus room and board, which has a reasonable value of $1,000. Is Camp Fooey in violation of the minimum wage and maximum hour requirement? No! Camp counselors are exempt even though Tiffany's cumulative compensation of $4,000 is less than the $4,284.80 minimum wage including overtime required by the FLSA. The $4,284.80 figure is arrived at as follows: 13 weeks times 40 hours times $5.15 equals $2,678.00 plus 13 weeks times 16 hours (Saturday and Sunday) times $7.725 equals $1,606.80 for a total of $4,284.80.

The issue in the following case is whether the plaintiffs are salaried employees and thus exempt from overtime pay.

Carpenter v. City & County of Denver, Colorado

115 F.3d 765 (10th Cir. 1996)

Porfilio, Circuit Judge.

In this appeal, we are asked to decide whether plaintiffs, lieutenants, captains, and division chiefs in the Denver Police Department, are salaried employees exempt from the overtime requirement of the Fair Labor Standards Act (FLSA). This resolution pivots on our reading of 29 C.F.R. 541.118(a), which states an employee whose salary is "subject to reduction because of variations in the quality or quantity of the work performed," is not exempt from payment of overtime. Because we read the language of the regulation to mean what it says, that the possibility of reduction defeats salaried status, we conclude plaintiffs are not exempt from the FLSA's overtime requirement. We reverse.

I.

Generally, the FLSA requires all employers, including state and local governments, to pay their employees a minimum wage for a 40-hour work week. Hours worked over the 40-hour week must be compensated at an overtime rate of time and a half. However, payment of overtime does not apply to "any employee employed in a bona fide executive, administrative, or professional capacity. . . . " Congress delegated fleshing out this status to the Department of Labor (DOL), which devised a "short test," providing:

The term "employee employed in a bona fide executive * * * capacity . . . shall mean any employee:

(a) Whose primary duty consists of the management of the enterprise in which he is employed. . . .

(b) Who customarily and regularly directs the work of two or more other employees therein; and

(c) Who has the authority to hire or fire other employees or whose suggestions and recommendations as to the hiring or firing and as to the advancement and promotion or any other change of status of other employees will be given particular weight; and

(d) Who customarily and regularly exercises discretionary powers; and

(e) Who does not devote more than 20 percent . . . of his hours of work in the workweek to activities which are not directly or closely related to the performance of the work described in paragraphs (a) through (d) . . . ; and

(f) Who is compensated for his services on a salary basis at a rate of not less than . . . $250 per week . . . and whose primary duty consists of the management of the enterprise in which the employee is employed or of a customarily recognized department or subdivision thereof, and includes the customary and regular direction of the work of two or more other employees therein, shall be deemed to meet all the requirements of this section."

The employer bears the burden of showing "the employee fits 'plainly and unmistakenly within the exemption's terms'—under both the 'salary' test and the 'duties' test."

Exempt employees receive straight-time overtime compensation. The City classifies plaintiffs as falling within the executive exemption.

Challenging this status, plaintiffs sued the City for declaratory relief, contending they are not exempt from coverage of the FLSA overtime requirements and seeking back pay for each hour of overtime worked at time and a half for approximately three years from 1990 through 1993, in addition to liquidated damages authorized by the FLSA. Their complaint attacked their exempt status solely on the basis of the salary test, alleging the City's practice of fining certain plaintiffs for violations of minor safety rules and docking pay for military leave after 15 days defeated its claim to the exemption. The City responded the executive, administrative, and professional exemptions barred plaintiffs' claims.

Finding no factual issues in dispute, the district court concluded plaintiffs are exempt employees, rejecting the Second, Seventh, and District of Columbia Circuits' interpretation and aligning itself with the Eighth, Eleventh, and Fifth Circuits which hold that absent an actual deduction from salary, the practice of offsetting leave with leave will not defeat an employee's exempt status.

The only material issue presented in this case is whether plaintiffs are paid on a salary basis as defined by DOL's regulations.

DOL's definition of salaried status, 29 C.F.R. 541.118(a), which states:

An employee will be considered to be paid "on a salary basis" within the meaning of the regulations if under his employment agreement he regularly receives each pay period on a weekly, or less frequent basis, a predetermined amount constituting all or part of his compensation, which amount is not subject to reduction because of variations in the quality or quantity of the work performed. Subject to the exceptions provided below, the employee must receive his full salary for any week in which he performs any work without regard to the number of days or hours worked. This policy is also subject to the general rule that an employee need not be paid for any workweek in which he performs no work.

It is the phrase, "subject to reduction" which the parties challenge, each citing those factual allegations which serve its partisan interpretation.

Plaintiffs maintain salaried employees are paid a fixed amount for doing a job. That is, they "are paid on a job function basis," in contrast to non-salaried employees "whose compensation depends on the number of hours they put in." The opposite of payment on a salary basis, then, is payment on an hourly basis. Consequently, plaintiffs contend the City's express policies on disciplinary infractions, military leave, and leave for jury duty, which require "fining" the employee by deducting leave days from their "leave banks" or other leave offsets, render their fixed salaries "subject to reduction" because ultimately these contingent deductions reflect the "quality or quantity" of the work performed.

The City counters no plaintiff has had a reduction in salary as a consequence of any City policy or practice. Further, only a plaintiff's leave bank, the repository of all accumulated leave inuring to each plaintiff's position, is tapped, the City maintains; and, even then, only leave is offset against leave.

We believe if we are to construe exceptions to the FLSA narrowly, giving substantial deference to DOL's interpretation of its own rules, we must conclude the City's express policy on discipline does not conform to DOL's parameters. Its "safety rules," in fact, are more often rules of behavior involving an officer's daily conduct on the force. Because the rules fall short, the City's punishing an errant officer by removing leave time from the officer's leave repository creates the potential for reducing pay. When leave is exhausted, the record makes clear a plaintiff's salary is "subject to reduction." That is, then, the quality of the officer's work may ultimately reduce the predetermined amount of salary the officer receives. Reading the regulations narrowly, we cannot say that employee is salaried.

Reversed.

Judgment for Carpenter

Case Commentary
The Tenth Circuit Court resolved that lieutenants, captains, and chiefs of the Denver police force are not salaried employees exempt from overtime, because they are subject to salary deduction. ■

CASE QUESTIONS

1. Are you in accord with the court's resolution in this case?
2. Do you believe the plaintiffs are paid on a wage basis rather than on a salary basis?

3. Did not the court use the term *salary* in discussing the plaintiff's compensation?
4. Can the plaintiffs be compared to managers in business who are not paid overtime?

There are many exceptions to the maximum hours requirement, a few of which include domestic helpers, taxi drivers, and movie theater employees.

Employment Perspective
Myrtle Dover is a domestic helper who resides with the Remingtons. At times, she works more than 8 hours per day and always works on Saturdays and Sundays unless the family is vacationing. Myrtle is paid a set fee each week in

accordance with the minimum wage law, but she is not paid overtime. Are the Remingtons in violation of the maximum hour laws? No! There is an exception for domestic helpers.

CHILD LABOR

Children who are at least 16 years of age may work in any occupation as long as it has not been deemed hazardous by the Secretary of Labor. Children who are 14 or 15 years of age are not permitted to work in manufacturing, mining, and other occupations that interfere with their schooling and/or their health and well-being. Children under 14 are not permitted to work unless it is for their parents or approved by the court for entertainment or athletic contracts.

Employment Perspective

Robby Landry, who is 17, was hired by Major Waste Materials Corp. to load hazardous and radioactive containers for shipment. Is this permissible? No! The transport of hazardous and radioactive waste is a dangerous activity. Therefore, children may not work in this occupation.

Employment Perspective

Lawrence Connery is an attorney with his own practice. He employs his 12-year-old daughter, Tiffany, to work for him 2 hours after school each day. Her responsibilities include photocopying, stapling, dusting, and making coffee. Is this permissible? Yes! Parents may employ the services of their children as long as it is not in a hazardous occupation.

Employment Perspective

Michele Goldsmith is a 14-year-old freshman at Richmond Hill High. She works from 2 P.M. until 10 P.M. at Foodway 3 days a week. In order to get to work on time, she has to cut her last class, which, because of a rotating schedule, changes each day and is not particularly noticeable. Is this permissible? No! The FLSA would prohibit Michele's current employment because it interferes with her schooling in that it forces her to leave school early and leaves her no time to do her homework.

Employment Perspective

Cindy Masterson is a 4-year-old model of children's clothes. She also performs in a television commercial occasionally and is employed by various manufacturers and retail clothing stores. Is this employment permissible? Yes! Cindy's contracts must be court-approved. If the court determines this action is in Cindy's best interest, she will be allowed to perform.

The issue in the case that follows is whether Vidtape violated the FLSA, particularly its child labor provisions.

Chao, Secretary of Labor v. Vidtape, Inc.
196 F. Supp. 2d 281 (E.D. NY 2002)

Boyle, J.

The Secretary of Labor (hereinafter "Plaintiff" or "Secretary)") commenced this action on May 1, 1998, pursuant to Fair Labor Standards Act, after an investigation of the labor practices of the defendants.

On April 9, 2002, the Secretary moved, pursuant to Rule 59(e) to amend this court's judgment dated March 29, 2002. In particular, the Secretary moved: (1) to remove the award of pre-judgment interest; (2) to include violations of 29 U.S.C. § 215(a)(1) in the judgment; and (3) to rescind the award of $11,000 in civil money penalties for child labor violations. Defendants do not oppose the Secretary's motion. The Secretary's motion is granted.

The complaint, which was amended on July 20, 2000, alleges that from the period of May 1, 1995 to approximately June 10, 1997, the corporate defendants Vidtape, Inc. ("Vidtape") and Inventive and the individual defendants Mohinder Singh Anand ("Mohinder"), Satinder Singh Anand ("Satinder") and Arjan Singh Anand ("Arjan") willfully violated various provisions of the Act. These violations include: (1) failing to pay employees proper minimum wage; (2) failing to pay employees adequate overtime wages; (3) employing a child in violation of the child labor provision; (4) violating the "hot goods" provision of the Act by putting in the stream of commerce goods manufactured in violation of these laws; and (5) violating the Act's record-keeping provisions. The Secretary seeks an injunction to prevent defendants from future violations of the Act, and a judgment ordering defendants to pay: (1) minimum wage compensation in the amount of $50,649.25; (2) overtime wages in the amount of $70,716.30; (3) liquidated damages in the amount of $121,365.55; and (4) costs.

FINDINGS OF FACT

A. Introduction

Defendant Vidtape is a New York corporation incorporated in January, 1988. Defendant Inventive is a Delaware corporation incorporated on June 18, 1997. Prior to April, 1998, Vidtape manufactured and duplicated videocassette tapes. On February 26, 1998, Vidtape sold its manufacturing operation to Inventive. Currently, Inventive manufactures and duplicates videocassettes, while Vidtape markets and sells Inventive's product. Vidtape and Inventive were located at the same property in West Babylon, New York and are currently located at the same property in Farmingdale New York.

Defendant Mohinder Singh Anand is the president, sole officer, and sole shareholder of Vidtape. Satinder Singh Anand, Mohinder's brother, was formerly employed at

Vidtape, and is currently the president of Inventive. Arjan Singh Anand, the father of Mohinder and Satinder, was never employed by Vidtape, but currently works as Inventive's general manager. The Nihang Nivas trust is the sole shareholder of Inventive's stock. Arjan is the trustee of the Nihang Nivas trust, and the beneficiaries of the trust are Mohinder's wife, children, and mother. Satinder is also a beneficiary of the trust.

B. Employer Status of the Individual Defendants

1. Mohinder Singh Anand

   Mohinder, the president of Vidtape, controls and manages the operations at his company. He hired employees, terminated employees, set wage rates, set Vidtape's pay system, and signed Vidtape pay checks. He also supervised employees.

2. Satinder Singh Anand

   Employees testified that Satinder gave them work assignments and supervisory directions. Satinder hired some of the Vidtape employees. Employees reported to Satinder in the absence of Mohinder. Satinder directed some employees to report to work on Sundays and he directed employees not to report to work after the Department of Labor commenced its investigation. Satinder also had the authority to sign checks for Vidtape and did so when Mohinder was unavailable.

   Satinder testified that he was not an employer of Vidtape and that he only worked there on commission as its salesman. He stated he never fired employees, never set work hours or work schedules, never directed or supervised employees, and never dealt with payroll issues. The court does not credit this testimony by Satinder. It is undisputed that Satinder is the current president and employer of Inventive, the portion of the enterprise that manufactures the videotapes and employs the majority of the minimum wage employees.

3. Arjan Singh Anand

   Arjan, the father of Mohinder and Satinder, has never been a shareholder, corporate officer, or employee of Vidtape. He testified that he never gave orders, hired, fired, or set policies for employees. Arjan did visit his sons at work during the midday and discussed financial matters with them at lunch. Hardeep Anand testified that Arjan brought lunch for his sons a few days a week and that during the time he was at the office, he read a religious book. Vidtape employees testified that they viewed Arjan as a "boss." This testimony is credited. Arjan is currently employed part-time as Inventive's general manager, where he maintains Inventive's inventory and procures spare parts.

B. Enterprise

Vidtape manufactured videotapes at its factory in West Babylon. Inventive was formed on June 18, 1997, days after the Department of Labor commenced its formal investigation of Vidtape. Inventive began manufacturing videotapes on April 30, 1998, one day before the Department of Labor filed its complaint in this action.

Vidtape sold its manufacturing operations to Inventive for $175,000. The book value of the assets was $120,000. To pay for this, Inventive assumed Vidtape's $175,000 Keybank corporate bank loan. Mohinder and Vidtape are guarantors of this loan. The asset sale agreement did not include warranties of merchantability or fitness.

Vidtape is Inventive's primary customer, with approximately 90% of Inventive's product marketed by Vidtape under Vidtape's label. Vidtape sales are over $500,000 annually and Vidtape and Inventive ship their product in interstate commerce.

When Inventive began its manufacturing operations, Vidtape employees resigned and were hired as Inventive employees. They signed a waiver stating:

I [name], of [address] hereby acknowledge that I am resigning as an employee of Vidtape, Inc. as of April 30, 1998. I further acknowledge that during the course of my employment with Vidtape, Inc. I have had no claims for past due wages, or anything else. My period of employment with Vidtape, Inc. has been satisfactory.
This acknowledgment is being signed by me voluntarily and of my own free will. There has been no pressure exerted upon me by anyone to sign this document. The contents of this document have been translated for me in [language], which is my native language.

Employees observed no change between employment at Vidtape and employment at Inventive, other than a different corporate name on their pay check. The court credits this testimony.

D. Knowledge of Fair Labor Standards Act

Since the early 1990s, Mohinder had knowledge of minimum wage and overtime laws. Specifically, he knew that employers must pay employees one and a half times their hourly rate when they worked over forty hours per week, that the minimum wage was $5.15 at the time of his deposition, and that the law required employers to keep time cards. Vidtape posted a Department of Labor poster in the lunchroom. The court credits this testimony.

Employees testified that after the Department of Labor commenced its investigation, Mohinder held a meeting where he instructed Vidtape employees to tell investigators that their work schedule was 8:30 A.M–5:00 P.M., Monday–Friday. He also instructed employees to tell investigators that they were paid the proper minimum wage of $4.25 per hour and that they received overtime wages at a rate of one and one-half their regular rate. The court credits this testimony of employees and does not credit the conflicting testimony of Mohinder.

E. Vidtape's Record-Keeping Practices

Prior to June 10, 1997, Vidtape did not maintain proper records as required by the F.L.S.A. Employees recorded their hours using time cards when they arrived in the morning and when they left at the end of the day. Hardeep Anand, Vidtape's bookkeeper, testified that Vidtape maintained these time cards for approximately two weeks after it issued employee paychecks. If no corrections to employee wages were necessary, she discarded the time cards. The latter testimony is not credited. Mohinder directed her to discard the time cards. After June 10, 1997, the date the Department of Labor began its formal investigation, Vidtape began preserving its time cards.

Vidtape's payroll records for 1995, 1996, and part of 1997 show that Vidtape employees received two pay checks per month. Vidtape's two pay periods during this time were the first to fifteenth day of the month, and the sixteenth to last day of the month. Vidtape's payroll records for this period did not contain the employees' hourly rates, number of hours worked per day, the number of hours worked per week, or the number of hours worked for each bi-monthly pay period. No other records containing this information were maintained or preserved by Vidtape.

Vidtape paid most employees by check. On pay day, employees received a pay check, but no pay stub or other information that indicated the hourly rate, hours worked, gross pay, or amount of deductions taken.

TESTIMONY OF PLAINTIFF'S WITNESSES

At trial, twenty-one former Vidtape employees testified for the Secretary as to the hours they worked and the pay they received. These employees testified in English, Spanish, and Punjabi.

1. Work Schedule
   The employees testified that they typically worked from 8:30 A.M. to 7:00 P.M., Monday through Saturday. They took thirty minute lunch breaks and had one or two short breaks as well. Some employees also worked on Sundays. This consistent testimony indicates that employees worked an average of sixty hours per week and the court credits this testimony offered by the Secretary.
2. Hourly Wage and Overtime
   The employees testified that their wage was $4.00 per hour, and $3.50 per hour after taxes. Some employees testified that Vidtape never told them what wage the company paid its employees. Beginning about June 10, 1997, immediately following the commencement of the Department of Labor investigation by a visit to the

defendants' premises, employees received wages of $4.75 per hour, which was the statutory minimum wage at that time. The employees also testified that they did not receive overtime pay prior to June 10, 1997. The court credits this testimony.

RECONSTRUCTION OF THE EMPLOYEES' BACK WAGES

Child Labor

Wilber Amaya testified that he was fourteen years old when Vidtape hired him to pack videos and move boxes using a "hand truck." At his interview, he presented his INS work permit to Mohinder and Hardeep Anand, which indicated that Amaya was born on September 2, 1982. Amaya worked ten hour days, six days a week, during the months when school was in session. Vidtape terminated Amaya after the Department of Labor began its investigation. The court credits this testimony.

G. Testimony of Defense Witnesses

1. Hardeep Anand
   Hardeep Anand, the aunt of Mohinder and Satinder, testified that she worked as Vidtape's bookkeeper and secretary. She calculated the payroll every two weeks. She stated that she used the minimum wage figures of $4.25, $4.75 and $5.15 to calculate the payroll. She also testified that she calculated overtime wages for the employees. The court does not credit this testimony.

   On cross-examination, Hardeep was not able to calculate the gross wage that she had written in the payroll records. She stated that she needed the time cards to perform this function.

2. Delia Alvarado
   Delia Alvarado who is presently employed by Inventive, testified that when she was hired in June, 1995 she earned $4.25 per hour. She stated her hours were Monday–Friday, 8:30 A.M. to 7:00 P.M. She also testified that when she received her pay check, she reviewed the amount to be sure she was paid the proper wage and overtime. The court does not credit this testimony.

3. Mohinder Singh Anand
   Mohinder stated employees were always informed of their wage rates, they worked Monday to Friday, 8:30 A.M. to 7:00 P.M., and they received overtime pay. He testified that the policies he set were in compliance with the F.L.S.A. He also testified that he directed Hardeep Anand to dispose of the time cards. The court does not credit this testimony.

CONCLUSIONS OF LAW

Defendants Mohinder and Satinder, but not Arjan, were employers under the Act. "Employer" is defined as "any person acting directly or indirectly in the interest of an employer in relation to an employee." Factors examined under the Second Circuit's economic reality test in determining whether an individual is an employer include: (1) whether the alleged employer had the power to hire and fire employees; (2) whether he or she supervised and controlled employee work schedules or conditions of employment; (3) whether he or she determined the rate and method of payment; and (4) whether he or she maintained employment records. Since this is a "totality of the circumstances test," any relevant evidence can be examined, and not all factors are required to be present.

Vidtape and Inventive were a unified operation. After the sale of Vidtape's assets to Inventive, the two remained integrally related to each other and their business activities were intertwined. The sale of Vidtape's assets was not an arms length transaction. The purchase price was exactly equal to the outstanding loans on the assets of the corporation.

Record-Keeping Violations

Defendants violated the Act's record-keeping provisions. Under § 211(c), "every employer subject to . . . this Act . . . shall make, keep, and preserve such records of the persons employed by him and of the wages, hours, and other conditions and practices of employment maintained by him, and shall preserve such records for such periods of time."

Additionally, employees testified that they never received a pay stub or a calculation of their wages or hourly rates when they received their pay checks. Vidtape did not establish a 7-day, 168-hour established "work week". Payroll records indicate that instead of establishing a work week, the employees were paid twice a month, on approximately a fifteen day pay period.

Minimum Wage Violations

Under § 206, the rate of pay per hour must be at least $4.25 (ending September 30, 1996), $4.75 (ending August 31, 1997), and $5.15 (currently). Minimum wage should be calculated on a work week basis, defined as a 7-day, 168 hour period.

Overtime Violations

Under § 207, no employees engaged in commerce shall work longer than forty hours per week unless the employee "receives compensation for his employment in excess of the hours above specified at a rate not less than one and one-half the regular rate at which he is employed." Plaintiff's witnesses consistently testified that they did not receive overtime pay for the extra hours they worked. Since their average work week was between sixty to seventy hours, overtime compensation is owed to them.

Child Labor Violation

In employing Wilbur Amaya, defendants violated the Act's child labor provision. Section 212(c) of the Act provides that "no employer shall employ any oppressive child labor in commerce or in the production of goods for commerce or in any enterprise engaged in commerce or in the production of goods for commerce." "Oppressive child labor" is defined as a "condition of employment under which . . . any employee under the age of sixteen years is employed by an employer . . . in any occupation." Children between the age of 14 and 16 cannot be employed for more than three hours a day, 18 hours per week when school is in session, and 8 hours a day, 40 hours a week when school is not in session. Children may only work between 7 A.M. and 7 P.M. during school, and until 9 P.M. in the summer. The regulations also state that minors are not permitted to work in occupations that involve manufacturing of goods.

Wilber Amaya testified that he was hired by Mohinder. At his interview, Amaya presented Mohinder with his work card, which stated his date of birth was 1982. Amaya worked at Vidtape in 1997 for approximately one year. He was fourteen years old when he began working. He worked six days a week between the hours of 8:30 A.M. and 7:00 P.M. He packed videos, used a lift, a hand cart, and machinery such as the video cassette machine. Vidtape terminated Amaya when the Department of Labor's investigation began. Although Mohinder testified and defendants asserted as an affirmative defense that the minor child was hired at the request of a relative and that defendants were not aware they violated child labor law intent or willfulness is not an element of this offense.

Hot Goods

The defendants violated the "hot goods" provision by manufacturing products in violation of the Act. The "hot goods" provision provides that it is unlawful for any person to "transport . . . ship . . . deliver or sell in commerce, or to ship, deliver, or sell with knowledge that shipment or delivery or sale thereof in commerce is intended, any goods in the production of which any employee was employed" in violation of minimum wage, overtime or child labor restrictions. The remedy for violation of this provision is an injunction. Vidtape violated the "hot goods" provision by manufacturing videotapes in violation of the Act and then shipping them in interstate commerce. An injunction is warranted.

J. Willful

The court finds that defendants acted willfully. More than one witness indicated that before the Department of Labor interviewed employees, Mohinder had a meeting and told his employees to lie about their wages and hours worked. Further, a poster in the break room notified the employees of their rights under the Act. For these reasons, a three year period for compensation of back wages beginning on May 1, 1995 is applicable.

The Secretary seeks compensation for sixty-seven employees. The Secretary seeks the following amount of damages: $50,649.25 in minimum wage violations for the period of May 1, 1995–June 10, 1997 and $70,716.30 in unpaid overtime wages for the period of May 1, 1995–October 5, 1997. The Secretary also seeks liquidated damages in the amount of $121,365.55, for a total award of $242,731.10.

JUDGMENT
A. INJUNCTION

I. ORDERED, ADJUDGED AND DECREED, that defendants Vidtape, Inc., Inventive Technology Systems, Inc, Mohinder Singh Anand, Satinder Singh Anand and Arjan Singh Anand, their officers, agents, servants, employees, and those persons in active concert or participation with them who receive actual notice of this Order by personal service, or otherwise, be, and they hereby are, permanently enjoined and restrained from violating the provisions of the Fair Labor Standards Act of 1938, as amended.

"Hereinafter" called the Act, in the following manners:

1. Defendants Vidtape, Inc., Inventive Technology Systems, Inc, Mohinder Singh Anand, Satinder Singh Anand and Arjan Singh Anand shall not, contrary to § 6 of the Act, pay to any of their employees who in any work week are engaged in commerce or in the production of goods for commerce, or employed in an enterprise engaged in commerce or in the production of goods for commerce, within the meaning of the Act, wages at rates less than those which are now, or which in the future may become, applicable under § 6 of the Act.

2. Defendants Vidtape, Inc., Inventive Technology Systems, Inc, Mohinder Singh Anand, Satinder Singh Anand and Arjan Singh Anand shall not, contrary to § 7 of the Act, employ any of their employees in any work week who are engaged in commerce or in the production of goods for commerce, or employed in an enterprise engaged in commerce or in the production of goods for commerce, within the meaning of the Act, for work weeks longer than the hours now, or which in the future become, applicable under §§ 7 and 15(a)(2) of the Act, unless the said employees receive compensation for their employment in excess of the prescribed hours at rates not less than one and one-half times the employees' regular rates.

3. Defendants Vidtape, Inc., Inventive Technology Systems, Inc, Mohinder Singh Anand, Satinder Singh Anand and Arjan Singh Anand shall not, contrary to §§ 12(c) and 15(a)(4) of the Act, employ minors under the age of eighteen years in commerce or in the production of goods for commerce, or in an enterprise engaged in commerce or in the production of goods for commerce, within the meaning of the Act, on jobs or during hours which constitute oppressive child labor as defined in § 3(l) of the Act.

4. Defendants Vidtape, Inc., Inventive Technology Systems, Inc, Mohinder Singh Anand, Satinder Singh Anand and Arjan Singh Anand shall not fail to make, keep, and preserve adequate records of their employees and of the wages, hours, and other conditions and practices of employment maintained by them, as prescribed by the Regulations issued pursuant to §§ 11(c) and 12 of the Act.

B. BACK PAY AND LIQUIDATED DAMAGES

ORDERED, ADJUDGED AND DECREED that Defendants Vidtape, Inc., Inventive Technology Systems, Inc., Mohinder Singh Anand and Satinder Singh Anand shall not withhold the back wages due the employees and former employees listed on Exhibit A. Defendants Vidtape, Inc., Inventive Technology Systems, Inc., Mohinder Singh Anand and Satinder Singh Anand shall pay to plaintiff's representatives $119,853.58 in unpaid minimum wage and overtime compensation, and $ 119,853.50 in liquidated damages, for a total amount of $ 239,707.58; and it is further

ORDERED that any monies due persons named in Exhibit A, annexed hereto and not so distributed by plaintiff within one (1) year, because of plaintiff's inability to locate the proper person or said persons' refusal to accept such money, shall be deposited with the Clerk of the Court who shall forthwith deposit such money with the Treasurer of the United States and it is further

ORDERED, that if payment is not tendered within such time, additional interest shall be due defendants' employees and former employees at the applicable adjusted prime rate, and it is further

ORDERED, ADJUDGED AND DECREED that the costs of this action shall be taxed by the Clerk against defendants Vidtape, Inc., Inventive Technology Systems, Inc., Mohinder Singh Anand and Satinder Singh Anand.

Judgment for Chao, Secretary of Labor.

Case Commentary

The Eastern District Court of New York ruled that Vidtape violated the minimum wage, overtime, and child labor provisions of the FLSA. ■

CASE QUESTIONS

1. Are you in accord with the court's actions?
2. Do you believe the owners of Vidtape should have been subject to criminal prosecution?
3. Does it seem unfair that those who make the least are often the ones exploited most?

EMPLOYEE LESSONS

1. Become familiar with the Fair Labor Standards Act.
2. Be apprised of what the minimum wage is currently.
3. Learn that overtime pay begins after 40 hours, not 35 hours, which is the usual workweek.
4. Understand that payroll deductions are necessary.
5. Ascertain if the amount withheld from your check is accurate.
6. Do not accept payments that are off-the-books.
7. Know which occupations are exempted from the minimum wage and maximum hours laws.
8. Be aware that your children may not work during school hours or in certain jobs deemed to be hazardous.
9. Recognize that your children under the age of 14 may work for you.
10. Be cognizant that children under the age of 14 who participate for compensation in entertainment or athletics must have court approval.

REVIEW QUESTIONS

1. Explain the significance of the Fair Labor Standards Act.
2. Is the current minimum wage adequate?
3. Explain the purpose of the minimum wage law.
4. What is the rule regarding maximum hours and overtime?
5. Why is there a need to cap the number of hours worked?
6. Explain the child labor laws.
7. What are the exceptions to the child labor laws?
8. Explain what would happen if there was no Fair Labor Standards Act.
9. Is it ethical to employ illegal immigrants at a wage below the minimum?
10. What effect will the General Agreement on Tariffs and Trade (GATT) and North American Free Trade Agreement (NAFTA) have on wage and hour regulation?

CASE PROBLEMS

1. This dispute centers around Harris County's policy of not permitting accrued comp time for nonexempt employees to rise above a predetermined level by directing employees to reduce the number of hours of accrued comp time. More precisely put, we must decide whether Harris County violates the FLSA when it involuntarily shortens an employee's workweek with pay. The issue is whether an employer may designate limits on the accrual of comp time. *Moreau v. Harris County*, Texas 158 F.3rd 241 (5th Cir. 1998)

2. Skidmore was required by his employer, Swift Co., to be "on call." His hours exceeded the 40-hour workweek. Skidmore was not paid overtime. Swift argued that Skidmore was not entitled to compensation. Whether "waiting time" is "working time" depends on the particular case and is a question of fact to be resolved by the trial court. The FLSA requires the payment of time and one-half of an employee's regular rate of pay for each hour worked in excess of 40 hours in any workweek. What was the result? *Skidmore v. Swift Co.*, 323 U.S. 134 (1994)

3. Police officers' overtime pay was calculated on the basis of a different number of hours from other city workers. The city argued that as long as all police officers were treated equally, the formula was acceptable. The officers complained that it violated the Fair Labor Standards Act in that one class of employees was treated differently from the others. What was the result? *Marie v. City of New Orleans*, 612 So.2d 244 (La. App. 4 Cir. 1992)

HUMAN RESOURCE DILEMMAS

1. In Kona, on the Big Island of Hawaii, Mexican workers with green cards are brought in for the harvesting of coffee beans. The workers are paid a commission per pound of beans picked. Can this be in violation of the FLSA?

2. Veronica is a waitress at Didi's Diner. She is paid $2.13 per hour, and she is entitled to keep all of her tips, which average $8.50 per hour. Is Didi's in compliance with the FLSA?

3. Neptune Fish Market hires a group of 15 Mexican workers who have green cards to cleanse, sanitize, and overhaul the marketplace. They are paid a flat fee of $10,000. It takes them 15 days working 10 hours a day. The average pay works out to $4.44 per hour. Is Neptune in violation of the FLSA?

WEB SITE ASSIGNMENT

Use the following Web sites to compare the minimum wage in the United States with that of foreign countries. Determine why there are no universal child labor laws. Then find an article on a company that has a sweatshop and uses child labor overseas.

www.findlaw.com
www.hrnext.com/content/view.cfm?subs_articles_id = 1876
www.opm.gov/flsa/overview.htm
www.dol.gov/elaws/flsa.htm
www.2mediate.com/articles/federal_fair_labor_standards_act.html
www.expertlaw.com/experts/Employment/Wage_and_Hour_Regulation.html
www.credencia.net/products/detail.asp?ProductID = 501
www.dol.state.nc.us/wh/wh.htm
www.legal-term.com/fairlaborstandardsact-definition.htm
www.awb.org/calendar/Seminars/wageandhourdetails.htm

Chapter 20

Occupational Safety and Health Introduction

Employment Scenario

In The Long and the Short of It's Woodmere store, the plaster in the bathroom ceiling is loose and cracking. It also leaks, which makes the floor extremely slippery. Sylvia Norton contacted OSHA, telling them of the unsafe working conditions. She also told OSHA that there was no heat in the stockroom and employee lounge. An OSHA inspector arrived at the L&S store 2 weeks later. The inspector found the conditions to be as Sylvia had reported. L&S's attorney, Susan North, was notified of the fine and was served with a 10-day notice to cure the defect before reinspection. She asked Tom Long and Mark Short why they had neglected the repairs. Mark responded that they believed no one would complain, but now they stand ready to correct the violations. How should she counsel them to avoid future violations?

Chapter Checklist

➤ *Recognize the significance of the Occupational Safety and Health Act.*

➤ *Understand the purpose of the Occupational Safety and Health Administration (OSHA).*

➤ *Appreciate the function of the Occupational Safety and Health Review Commission.*

➤ *Know that the National Institute of Occupational Safety and Health (NIOSH) recommends health and safety measures. Learn that the Secretary of Labor establishes safety and health standards.*

➤ *Be cognizant of when emergency standards can be implemented.*

➤ *Define permanent disability.*

➤ *Acknowledge the extent of work-related injuries that occur each year.*

➤ *Discover the major causes of work-related injuries.*

➤ *Realize the meaning of the greater hazard defense.*

INTRODUCTION

The Occupational Safety and Health Act of 1970 (OSHAct) was designed to set forth a standard that would provide for the safety and health of employees while on the job. Employers are required to provide a place of employment free from occupational hazards. Employees are required to follow rules and regulations established to promote their safety and to use equipment designed to ensure their safety.

HUMAN RESOURCE ADVICE

- Understand that NIOSH makes recommendations regarding health and safety measures.
- Know that the Secretary of Labor takes into account those recommendations in promulgating safety standards.
- Appreciate that the OSHA inspects the plants and offices of employers to assure compliance.
- Be aware that the Occupational Safety and Health Review Commission (OSHRC) holds hearings and imposes fines and penalties on derelict employers.
- Maintain a clean, safe, and healthy work environment.
- Look for possible OSHA violations and correct them immediately.
- Differentiate between the various gradations of disabilities.
- Be apprised of the annual figure regarding work-related injuries.
- Be cognizant that on occasion a repair may lead to a greater hazard.
- Educate your employees regarding executing their work in a safe and responsible manner.

ADMINISTRATIVE AGENCIES

The OSHAct created three administrative agencies. The first is the Occupational Safety and Health Administration, also known as *OSHA*. Its purpose is to set health and safety standards and see to it that these standards are implemented by employers through plant and office inspections. If an employer is in violation, OSHA seeks corrective action voluntarily by the employer through a hearing conducted by the OSHRC. If OSHRC rules against an employer, it may impose fines or other penalties against the employer. The employer has the right of appeal to the circuit court. OSHRC is the enforcement arm created by the OSHAct. Finally, the NIOSH was created to conduct research and make health and safety recommendations to OSHA for consideration.

OSHAct was enacted to reduce safety and health hazards, thereby preventing injuries, loss of wages, lost production, and incurrence of medical and disability expenses. Employees must be provided with a safe environment free of toxic substances, asbestos dust, and cotton dust. Precautions must be taken for first aid, eye and face protection, and safety at excavation sites to prevent cave-ins. Employees must be accorded a work environment with adequate lighting, ventilation, and heat, as well as tools and equipment that are in proper working order. The Department of Labor has the right to inspect the work environment to ensure adherence to the OSHA requirements. The OSHRC is the initial review body for violations of the act.

SECRETARY OF LABOR

The addition or deletion of occupational health and safety standards is promulgated by the Secretary of Labor. Interested parties may submit written comments regarding a proposal. If the Secretary reiterates a proposal, an objection can be entered and a hearing held, after which the Secretary will submit the final document.

In establishing standards, the Secretary of Labor must set forth standards to prevent employees from suffering substantial harm to their health even if the employee worked at this job for most of his or her adult life. The Secretary of Labor must rely on research and experiments to establish reliable standards, which will be set forth objectively. The specific actions and the desired results must be set forth.

Employees may request a temporary variance from the Secretary of Labor if they do not have the technical know-how or materials and/or equipment needed to comply or the plant or equipment cannot be altered by the required date. Employers must make every effort to comply as soon as possible. The time limit is 1 year, which can be renewed twice.

Although it was thought that employers would have enough incentive to ensure a safe working environment because of the absolute liability imposed upon them under Workers' Compensation, Congress did not feel employers were doing all that they could do, so they created OSHAct.

Before OSHAct was enacted, most employees who were injured on the job were not successful in suing their employers if they were injured by a coworker, were negligent themselves, or were held to have assumed the risk. This situation was not a sufficient impetus for employers to improve the workplace, knowing that they would not have to compensate most employees for their injuries. The purpose of OSHAct was to ensure that employees would not sustain the injuries in the first place.

Employers are required to comply with certain mandates of the Department of Labor regarding safety and health. Furthermore, the employment environment must be a safe and healthy place in which to work without hazards.

PERMANENT STANDARDS

Permanent standards are the standards originally introduced when OSHA was created as well as standards promulgated thereafter. The latter are referred to as *National Consensus Standards*. When OSHA develops a new standard, it is published in the *Federal Register*. The public, especially employees, has 30 days to request a hearing. If requested, notice of a public hearing will be made. After the hearing, OSHA must publish the standard incorporating the changes, if any, and the date of its commencement, within 60 days. The Secretary of Labor must explain the need for the new standard, else it will be null and void. He or she may delay the date of its commencement. In one case, a delay of 4 years was imposed. An employer may file an appeal in the circuit court of appeals within 60 days from OSHA's final announcement. If there is an appeal, the Secretary of Labor must demonstrate for the court that the standard mitigates a significant health risk. If the circuit court is convinced that the Secretary of Labor has provided sufficient evidence, the standard will become permanent.

The issue in the case that follows is whether OSHA has the power to regulate the safety characteristics of the tools and materials used at a work site.

Steel Joist Institute v. Occupational Safety & Health Administration

287 F.3d 1165 (D.C. Cir. 2002)

Henderson, Circuit Judge.

On August 13, 1998 the Occupational Safety and Health Administration (OSHA) proposed revised "Safety Standards for Steel Erection" based on a consensus document submitted by a rulemaking advisory committee in a negotiated rulemaking. After a public hearing, two comment periods and a public consultation meeting, OSHA issued its final rule on January 18, 2001. The Steel Joist Institute (Institute) asks the court to invalidate three provisions of the final rule's safety standard for open web steel joists. As explained below, we reject the Institute's objections, which require "field bolting" of steel joists, because they are authorized by the Occupational Safety and Health Act of 1970 (Act) and they are supported by substantial evidence.

Each of the two challenged provisions requires that joists be field bolted temporarily during steel erection to protect employees working on and around the joists until the joists are welded permanently in place. Specifically, they provide:

(1) Except as provided in paragraph (a)(2) of this section, where steel joists are used and columns are not framed in at least two directions with solid web structural steel members, a steel joist shall be field-bolted at the column to provide lateral stability to the column during erection. For the installation of this joist:

. . .

(iii) Hoisting cables shall not be released until the seat at each end of the steel joist is field-bolted, and each end of the bottom chord is restrained by the column stabilizer plate.

. . .

(8) Field-bolted joists.

  (i) Except for steel joists that have been pre-assembled into panels, connections of individual steel joists to steel structures in bays of 40 feet (12.2 m) or more shall be fabricated to allow for field bolting during erection.

  (ii) These connections shall be field-bolted unless constructibility does not allow.

First, the Institute contends that the provisions constitute an *ultra vires* attempt to regulate joist design and consequently the off-site joist manufacturers. We disagree. It is true that the Act authorizes OSHA to regulate only the employer's conduct at the worksite; but the challenged provisions do not exceed OSHA's statutory authority. OSHA has made it clear that the challenged provisions are not enforceable, or intended to be enforced, against joist manufacturers. Regulation 1926.750 expressly declares that "this subpart sets forth requirements to protect employees from the hazards *associated with steel erection activities*," and includes several examples of what constitutes such activities. ("Steel erection activities include hoisting, laying out, placing, connecting, welding, burning, guying, bracing, bolting, plumbing and rigging structural steel, steel joists and metal buildings; installing metal decking, curtain walls, window walls, siding systems, miscellaneous metals, ornamental iron and similar materials; and moving point-to point while performing these activities.") Insofar as the challenged provisions regulate the design of the joists used by the steel joist erector, OSHA's authority to regulate the safety characteristics of tools and materials used at a worksite is well established. We therefore reject the Institute's *ultra vires* argument.

OSHA acknowledges, as the Institute asserts, that there is no record evidence of injury or death attributable to joist instability. OSHA responds, however, that the "data in many cases do not provide enough detail as to the role of welding in the reported accidents involving joists," and further notes, correctly, that the Act does not require specific evidence of past injury to justify standards to prevent future injury from a likely hazard. The Act does not wait for an employee to die or become injured. It authorizes the promulgation of health and safety standards and the issuance of citations in the hope that these will act to prevent deaths or injuries from ever occurring. As OSHA points out, unattached joists constitute such a hazard because they can be displaced "by wind or construction activity, by the movement of employees, by trailing welding leads, by accidental impact against the supporting structure by a crane or other equipment, or by harmonic motion, or vibration."

The objection here is surprising because below the Institute expressly approved subsection (a)(1) generally as a required safety measure: "The requirement for joist and girders at columns to be field-bolted is a carryover from the previous standard and has long been an effective method for preventing adjacent parallel beams from opening up. Providing a bolted connection for joists at columns is a very necessary safety issue and has been supported by the joist industry for years." The Institute's comments did not single out subsection (a)(1)(iii) for objection or revision.

Ultimately the Institute does not deny that unsecured joists pose a hazard and has in fact proposed, in order to obviate it, that joists be temporarily "tack welded" in place until a permanent weld is applied. The Institute maintains that tack welding is safer than bolting because bolting subjects a worker to the hazard of an unstable joist twice, once when he bolts it initially and again when he permanently welds it. As OSHA pointed out below, however, tack welding likewise requires two separate trips, one for the temporary tack weld and a second for the permanent weld. Further, OSHA offers two persuasive reasons why bolting is preferable to tack welding, namely that (1) "joists can roll and pop welds due to the movement of a worker on the joist or the stresses caused by removing the sweep, which could cause a collapse" and (2) welding has "unique hazards," including "impairment of the vision and balance of an employee working at elevation while wearing a welding hood." The likelihood of these hazards supports the fieldbolting requirements imposed in section 1926.757(a)(1)(iii) and section 1926.757(a)(8).

For the preceding reasons, the petition for review is *Denied.*

Case Commentary

The D.C. Circuit Court ruled that OSHA has the authority to promulgate safety standards for tools and materials used on the job site. ■

CASE QUESTIONS

1. Do you agree with the court's determination?
2. Are you of the opinion that OSHA is interfering in a situation where the company has the expertise?

3. Why is the company adamantly opposed to OSHA's requirements if the standards are for the safety of the workers?

Employment Perspective

Veggie King has just begun irradiating fruits and vegetables for a longer shelf life. OSHA has promulgated a standard that all workers who are subjected to the low levels of radiation used on the fruits and vegetables must wear radiation-proof jumpsuits and headwear. These suits are very expensive. Veggie King asks for a hearing, but OSHA's final determination is unchanged. On appeal before the circuit court, Veggie King proclaims that low levels of radiation have no impact on humans. The Secretary of Labor counters that studies have shown that subjecting a human to low levels of radiation for 20 years or longer will cause cancer. What is the likely result? If the circuit court believes that the studies introduced by the Secretary of Labor have merit, then the standard of requiring radiation-protective garments will become permanent.

The occupational safety and health standard requires the employer to adopt appropriate practices necessary to ensure that the place of employment is a safe and healthy environment.

The national consensus standard is an occupational safety and health standard designated by the Secretary of Labor after its formulation by a nationally recognized safety and/or health organization that has conducted hearings.

The issue in the following case is whether the new standard for respiratory protection in the workplace is legal.

American Iron v. OSHA
182 F.3d 1261 (11th Cir. 1999)

Anderson, Chief Judge.

These consolidated cases seek judicial review of the Occupational Safety and Health Administration's ("OSHA") new standard for respiratory protection in the workplace. The separate challenges are brought by the American Iron and Steel Institute ("Industry") and the American College of Occupational and Environmental Medicine ("Doctors") and relate to different aspects of the new standard. For the reasons that follow, we conclude that OSHA correctly applied the law and that its factual determinations were supported by substantial evidence, and therefore the petitions for review are DENIED.

I. BACKGROUND

The Occupational Safety and Health Act of 1970 was enacted to ensure safe and healthy working conditions for employees. The OSH Act empowers OSHA to promulgate standards "dealing with toxic materials or harmful physical agents . . . which most adequately assure, to the extent feasible, on the basis of the best available evidence, that no employee will suffer material impairment of health or functional capacity even if such employee has regular exposure to the hazard dealt with by such standard for the period of his working life." One such hazard is caused by harmful dusts, fumes, gases, and the like that contaminate the atmospheres in many workplaces. OSHA began to regulate employee exposure to such contaminants as early as 1971. In January 1998, OSHA issued a new regulatory standard representing a comprehensive revision of those portions of the old standard which addressed the manner and conditions of respirator use ("Standard"). It is the Standard that is at issue in this case.

Highlights of the Standard

The Standard retains the Hierarchy-of-Controls Policy, which as a general matter prefers engineering controls over respirators worn by individual employees. However, the employer is required to provide respirators for its employees when respirators are necessary to protect their health. The Standard requires certain employers to develop and implement a written respiratory protection program that includes several mandatory items. Employers are required to select particular types of respirators based on certain criteria, such as the nature of harmful contaminants and workplace and user factors. In this regard, atmospheres in workplaces are classified into two categories: "immediately dangerous to life and health" ("IDLH"), and non-IDLH. Only certain highly effective types of respirators may be used in IDLH atmospheres. With respect to non-IDLH atmospheres, the Standard permits an employer to choose between atmosphere-supplying respirators (i.e., those with a self-equipped oxygen tank) and the less burdensome air-purifying respirators (i.e., those which merely filter the incoming air). However, air-purifying respirators are usable only if certain specified steps are taken to ensure that the filtering device is working and maintained properly. The medical evaluation provisions of the Standard require the employer "to provide a medical evaluation to determine the employee's ability to use a respirator, before the employee is fit tested or required to use the respirator in the workplace." The medical evaluation provisions spell out the procedures in this regard much more specifically than the prior standard. In addition, whereas licensed physicians were responsible for such medical evaluations under the prior standard, the Standard allows non-physician "licensed health care professionals" to perform such evaluations to the extent allowed under state law. The new Standard also contains detailed provisions relating to initial and periodic fit-testing to ensure respirators fit an employee-user's face properly, proper day-to-day use of respirators, maintenance and care of respirators, the required quality of the breathing gases used in conjunction with an air-supplying respirator, proper identification and labeling of filters, cartridges, and canisters,

provision of training and information to employees, periodic self-evaluations of an employer's written respiratory protection program to ensure that it continues to work properly, and appropriate record-keeping regarding medical evaluations and fit-testing.

Provisions Under Attack and Alignment of the Parties

The instant petitions for review are brought by the Industry and the Doctors. The Industry challenges three particular aspects of the Standard. First, it challenges the retention of the Hierarchy-of-Controls Policy, and OSHA's failure even to consider revising or abrogating that policy in light of its revision of the rest of the regulation. Second, it challenges the conditions placed upon the use of air-purifying respirators, as opposed to air-supplying respirators. Third, it challenges the requirements regarding, respectively, annual fit-testing and annual retraining, contending that less frequent fit-testing and retraining would have sufficed.

The Doctors, on the other hand, challenge only one aspect of the Standard: the provision enabling non-physician licensed health care professionals (e.g., nurses, physician's assistants, etc.) to perform the medical evaluation services that were previously conducted only by physicians ("Non-Physician Involvement Provision"). They contend that the Non-Physician Involvement Provision is defective because OSHA failed to notify interested parties that it was considering the elimination of mandatory physician involvement, that it is void for vagueness, and that it is not amply supported by the factual evidence.

II. DISCUSSION
A. Standard of Review

We must uphold OSHA's factual determinations underlying its regulations if they are supported by substantial evidence in the record considered as a whole. Substantial evidence is "such relevant evidence as a reasonable mind might accept as adequate to support a conclusion." "All that need be shown is that OSHA's determination is supported by substantial evidence presented to or produced by it and does not rest on faulty assumptions or factual foundations." OSHA's policy decisions are entitled to the same deference.

B. The Industry's Challenge
1. Retention of the Hierarchy-of-Controls Policy

The Industry's first challenge to the Standard is addressed to the retention of the Hierarchy-of-Controls Policy from the prior standard. The Hierarchy-of-Controls Policy reflects a general preference for engineering controls, which eliminate or arrest pollution at the source, over respirators in reducing employee exposure to airborne contaminants. Although it comprehensively revised those aspects of the prior standard relating to the manner and conditions of respirator use, OSHA altogether excluded the Hierarchy-of-Controls Policy from the rulemaking proceeding. Consequently, the

Hierarchy-of-Controls Policy was not open to comment or scrutiny. In the issuing release for the Standard, OSHA explained its position in the following way:

By leaving paragraphs (a)(1) and (a)(2) of the final rule unchanged from the corresponding paragraphs of the respiratory protection standard that has been in effect since 1971, OSHA . . . . continues the protection that employees have relied on, ... retains the language that employers are familiar with, ... [and] allows OSHA and the affected public to continue to rely on OSHA interpretations. . . .

. . . .

The unchanged language of paragraph (a)(1) was included in the language of the proposed rule only to enable interested parties to view the rule as it would ultimately appear in the Code of Federal Regulations in its entirety. Since OSHA neither proposed nor adopted modifications to proposed paragraph (a)(1), the Agency believes that it is not legally required to reconsider this issue at this time. OSHA has the authority to identify which regulatory requirements it is proposing to revise and which issues are to receive regulatory priority. Limiting this rulemaking to issues concerning respirator programs is appropriate because such programs are the exclusive focus of this rulemaking and to collect comments and data on additional issues would divert resources from the task at hand. We do not find a requirement that OSHA include all possible substances in one rulemaking. OSHA has never claimed that the Air Contaminants Standard constituted the entire universe of substances needing regulation, and it seems reasonable that some limit needed to be set as to what substances could be considered in this rulemaking. The list of [the standard-setting organization's] recommendations is a rational choice as the source for that limitation. [Those] recommendations are well known to industry and the safety and health community. Therefore, we find that the agency's choice to so limit this rulemaking is a valid exercise of OSHA's authority to set priorities for rulemaking.

The Industry also implies that the Hierarchy-of-Controls Policy has outlived its validity under § 6(a) because it no longer represents a national consensus standard. This argument is without merit because the Industry has proffered no evidence that the Hierarchy-of-Controls Policy no longer represents the national consensus standard. To the contrary, the most recent national consensus standard, ANSI Standard Z88.2–1992, § 4.2, retains the Hierarchy-of-Controls Policy. Thus, the Industry has failed to demonstrate that OSHA's decision to limit the instant rulemaking to issues relating to the manner and conditions of respirator use was unreasonable. For the foregoing reasons, we reject the Industry's challenge to the retention of the Hierarchy-of-Controls Policy.

2. Change Schedule Requirement for Air-Purifying Respirators

Because the Industry's challenge to the Change Schedule Condition is exclusively factual in nature, our review is limited to whether OSHA's determinations are "supported by substantial evidence in the record considered as a whole." After reviewing the record, we conclude that OSHA's decision to replace the subjective adequate-warning-properties approach with the Change Schedule Condition is supported by substantial evidence. There was a consensus among commentors that inherent unreliability problems exist with odor and irritation thresholds. Change schedules based on "objective information or data" better promote worker safety by ensuring on a consistent basis that APRs are properly serviced and maintained. Moreover, the record belies the Industry's argument that OSHA entirely failed to consider the fact that ASRs tend to be bulky and cumbersome. The record reflects that OSHA did consider the uncomfortableness and mobility restrictions caused by APRs and weighed those factors in the balance. Thus, the factual determinations and policy choices underlying the Change Schedule Condition are consistent with the OSH Act and supported by substantial evidence.

3. Annual Fit-Test and Retraining Requirements

We turn next to the Industry's challenge to the provisions in the Standard requiring annual fit-testing and retraining of respirator-using employees. With respect to the annual fit-testing requirement, a respirator cannot function properly unless it is properly fitted to the wearer's face. Accordingly, the Standard requires that an employee be fit tested with a respirator of the same make, model, style, and size as is proposed to be used, before he actually begins to use one in the course of employment. The Industry does not object to this initial-test requirement, but does object to a requirement that wearers be tested at least annually following the initial test.

We find that the annual retraining requirement is also supported by substantial evidence. "OSHA's compliance experience had demonstrated that inadequate respirator training is a common problem, and is often associated with respirator program deficiencies that could lead to employee exposures to workplace contaminants." OSHA stated that annual retraining is necessary so that "employees know about the respiratory protection program and . . . cooperate and actively participate in the program," "so that employees will be confident when using respirators," and to "eliminate complacency on the part of both the employer and employees." OSHA noted that commenters requesting less frequent or no retraining submitted no data indicating that less frequent training "would be sufficient for respirator users to retain information critical to the successful use of respirators on an individual basis." Additionally, OSHA explained that annual retraining is the norm with respect to a number of other, substance-specific OSHA standards that involve respirators.

While retraining at some other periodic interval might also be defensible, OSHA was entitled to require annual retraining as a precautionary measure to assure "that no employee will suffer material impairment of health or functional capacity even if such employee has regular exposure to the hazard." Moreover, OSHA could conclude based on the record that annual retraining is reasonably necessary to ensure that employee knowledge about respirators does not fall into obsolescence. Given that conscientiousness among employees is such a critical element in the formula for success of a respirator program, OSHA could reasonably find that the Industry's suggested alternative of screening employees to determine who needed retesting would not serve its goal of preventing misuse and "ensuring a reasonable amount of recall and performance on the part of the respirator user." We see no basis for disturbing OSHA's factual conclusions and policy decisions in this regard.

C. The Doctors' Challenge

In their petition for review, the Doctors challenge the Non-Physician Involvement Provision in paragraph (e) of the Standard, which for the first time allows non-physician licensed health care professionals, as opposed to only physicians, to perform the required medical evaluations to the extent permitted under state law. The Doctors contend that OSHA gave insufficient notice to interested parties of its intent to adopt this new policy, that the Non-Physician Involvement Provision is void for vagueness, and that the Non-Physician Involvement Provision is not supported by substantial evidence.

The Standard does not distinguish between physicians and other licensed health care professionals. Rather, it allows all of the tasks associated with medical evaluations to be performed by any licensed health care professional to the same extent as they may be performed by a physician, to the extent permitted under state law. The Standard uses the term "physician or other licensed health care provider," which is defined as "an individual whose legally permitted scope of practice (i.e., license, registration, or certification) allows him or her to independently provide, or be delegated the responsibility to provide, some or all of the health care services required by paragraph (e) of this section." Because licensure, registration, and certification of health care professionals is

basically a matter of state law, the Standard essentially defers to state law on the question of who may provide the medical evaluation services. In contrast, the prior standard provided that "persons should not be assigned to tasks requiring use of respirators unless it has been determined that they are physically able to perform the work and use the equipment. The local physician shall determine what health and physical conditions are pertinent."

We have reviewed the record and find OSHA's decision to be supported by substantial evidence. While the comments were extremely varied, a common thread running through many of the comments was that registered nurses, physician's assistants, and other such health care providers are well-equipped to perform basic medical functions, such as assessing responses to medical questionnaires, provided that appropriate measures are in place for referring non-routine cases to a physician. There also was evidence from several commenters to the effect that they had safely and efficaciously used non-physician licensed health care professionals in the past for medical evaluations involving respirators. Moreover, the Non-Physician Involvement Provision does not automatically allow non-physician individuals to perform medical evaluation services; rather, it merely defers to state law on the extent of permissible involvement. State licensure laws can be trusted, as they are relied upon in similar contexts, to ensure that individuals performing medical evaluations under the Standard have the requisite competence, and such laws in fact typically provide for physician oversight over other health care professionals.

III. CONCLUSION

For the foregoing reasons, the petitions for review are Denied.

Judgment for OSHA.

Case Commentary

The Eleventh Circuit Court determined that the standards adhered to by OSHA in enacting a new regulation regarding respiratory protection in the workplace were lawful. ■

CASE QUESTIONS

1. Are you in accord with the court's decision?
2. Why does the industry not want to accept the new OSHA standard?

3. Why do the physicians refuse to support the OSHA respiratory standard?

Inspections

Inspections of business premises and records may be made during working hours and at other times deemed reasonable by OSHA compliance officers. The employees and the employer may be questioned privately. Record keeping relating to occupational accidents and illnesses is required and must be produced upon demand. Exposure of employees to toxic chemicals must be documented. Employees have the right of free access to the documents relating to their exposure. If the level exceeds the occupational safety and health standard, the employer must immediately notify the employee and take corrective action. If the employees believe a standard is being violated, they may notify the Secretary of Labor in writing. If the Secretary determines that there is a viable issue, he or she will authorize an investigation.

Employment Perspective

Dolores Wright, an employee of Green Bay Rental Apartments, is in charge of tenant complaints regarding lack of heat and hot water. She is a part-time employee who works only during the winter months. Wright's office is in a 3-story building located in the downtown section. In February, the building's oil burner malfunctioned. Dolores Wright made numerous calls to her superiors, but no action was taken. When Dolores called the oil company people, they said the burner needed to be replaced. It was not replaced. Of her own volition, she bought and paid for a heater, insulated her office, and continued to work through the month of February. At that time, she became ill with pneumonia and was hospitalized. Because she was a part-time employee, her employer did not pay for her medical plan. She thereupon sued Green Bay Rental for her medical bills, loss of compensation while she was hospitalized, and the expenses she incurred in attempting to make the office habitable during the month of February. Is she entitled to be reimbursed? Yes! Green Bay Rental is liable for her medical expenses because it failed to provide her with a safe and healthy working environment. She is entitled to compensation for the time she lost from work because the lost time was directly caused by the employer's negligence. Also she is entitled to reimbursement for the expenses she incurred in attempting to create a healthy environment in the office.

Citations and Penalties

If an employer has committed a violation, an OSHA director will issue a citation, which will describe the particulars as well as reference to the occupational safety and health standard that the Secretary believes has been violated. The employer, upon receipt, has 15 business days to contest the citation or it will become a final order not subject to judicial review.

If the employer fails to correct the violation of a safety and health standard, a penalty will be assessed against the employer. The employer has 15 days to object to the penalty. Otherwise, it will become a final order not subject to judicial review.

Penalties may be assessed between $5,000 and $70,000 for each violation of an occupational safety and health standard. These penalties may be made in increments of up to $7,000 per day per violation. Payment for these penalties is made to the Secretary of Labor and deposited in the U.S. Treasury.

With regard to any issues of occupational safety and health not addressed by the Secretary of Labor, the individual states are free to develop their own standards.

If an employer contests the citation or penalty in a timely manner, the matter is referred to the OSHRC which is an administrative agency composed of three commissioners, each of whom has been appointed by the President. The Secretary of Labor has the burden of proving that the employer violated an OSHA standard, in a hearing held before an administrative law judge. The judge's decision is then given to the commission, which has the option of reviewing it.

The commission may render its own decision or allow the administrative law judge's decision to be final. An appeal may be made in either case within 60 days from the commission's decision to the Federal Circuit Court of Appeals.

There are no specific standards set forth in the OSHAct itself. OSHA was empowered to adopt existing standards and to develop new ones as conditions warrant.

Employment Perspective

Stan Meyers was installing aluminum siding on a house, working on a platform 22 feet high. The platform was flat and had no guardrails. An OSHA standard requires guardrails to be installed on all platforms that are 10 feet or higher above the ground. Stan has asked his employer to install guardrails, without success. Finally, Stan notifies OSHA, which sends a compliance officer to the work site. The compliance officer investigates and makes a determination that there is a violation of the OSHA standard regarding guardrails. The OSHA director then issues a citation. Must the employer install the guardrails? Yes!

The issue in the case that follows is whether the company filed a lawsuit objecting to OSHA's survey requirement with the proper court.

Eastern Bridge v. Chao, Secretary of Labor
320 F.3d 84 (1st Cir. 2003)

Torruella, Circuit Judge.

Four New Hampshire companies ("plaintiffs")—Eastern Bridge, LLC, Isaacson Structural Steel, Inc., Vanguard Manufacturing, Inc., and Monadnock Forest Products, Inc. ("Monadnock")—claim that the Occupational Safety and Health Administration ("OSHA") acted ultra vires when it mandated that plaintiffs complete a Data Collection Initiative Survey ("DCI Survey" or "Survey"). They argue that OSHA did not have a final regulation requiring employers to maintain the information sought in the DCI Surveys. The United States District Court for the District of New Hampshire granted defendants' motion to dismiss, holding that it lacked subject matter jurisdiction over plaintiffs' claims. We affirm.

I. BACKGROUND
A. The History of the DCI Survey

In 1970, Congress enacted the Occupational Safety and Health Act ("OSH Act"), giving the Secretary of Labor ("Secretary") the responsibility to protect the health and safety of American workers. The OSH Act gives the Secretary authority to promulgate implementing regulations and requires that employers comply with OSHA's standards and regulations.

To enforce the OSH Act, Congress provides the following administrative mechanism. If the Secretary believes, after a workplace inspection, that an employer has violated a standard or regulation, the Secretary can issue the employer a citation, classify the citation, and set a penalty. If the employer contests the citation or the proposed assignment of penalty, the Occupational Safety and Health Review Commission ("Commission") will provide the employer with a hearing before an administrative law judge ("ALJ"). Following the hearing, the ALJ makes a report of the hearing, which becomes a final order of the Commission unless the Commission decides to conduct

further review. The employer can appeal the Commission's final order to a United States court of appeals.

The Secretary first sent the challenged DCI Surveys to various employers in February 1996. In March of that year, a consortium of employers filed suit against the Secretary of Labor under the Administrative Procedures Act ("APA"), claiming that the Secretary did not have the regulatory authority to distribute the DCI Surveys. A district court in the District of Columbia Circuit held that OSHA's DCI Survey, as it then existed, violated the APA because OSHA attempted to accomplish its data collection without a final regulation in place requiring employers to complete and return the Survey.

Following American Trucking, the Secretary promulgated a final regulation explicitly requiring employers to complete the DCI Survey:

Each employer shall, upon receipt of OSHA's Annual Survey Form, report to OSHA or OSHA's designee the number of workers it employed and number of hours worked by its employees for periods designated in the Survey form, and such information as OSHA may request from records required to be created and maintained.

OSHA uses the DCI Survey to gather injury and illness data about specific establishments. The Survey asks for information about the number of employees at the company, the number of hours the employees worked over a specified period, and the number of injuries and illnesses the employees suffered during that period. Based on this information, OSHA calculates the workplace's injury/illness incidence rate and decides whether to target the establishment for inspection.

B. Plaintiffs were Sent DCI Surveys

In 2000, OSHA sent a DCI Survey to three of the four plaintiffs seeking information based upon 1999 data.

Plaintiffs completed the 2000 DCI Survey, leading to the placement of Monadnock and Eastern Bridge on OSHA's primary inspection list. Although OSHA never initiated an inspection of Monadnock, it attempted to inspect Eastern Bridge. When Eastern Bridge withdrew its consent to inspection, OSHA obtained an administrative search warrant from the district court. Eastern Bridge moved to quash the warrant, but the motion was denied. Subsequently, OSHA carried out the inspection and issued Eastern Bridge a citation.

In 2001, OSHA sent all four plaintiffs a DCI Survey requesting data from 2000. All of the plaintiffs completed the Survey. OSHA placed Eastern Bridge on the primary inspection list and placed the other three plaintiffs on the supplemental inspection list. Because OSHA had already inspected Eastern Bridge that year, it deleted Eastern Bridge from its inspection list. On the record before us, OSHA has not subjected any of the plaintiffs on the supplemental list to an inspection, and there is no indication that any inspection is pending.

C. District Court Proceeding

In April of 2002, before they received their 2002 DCI Surveys requesting data from 2001, plaintiffs brought suit seeking to have the district court declare the DCI Survey ultra vires and the use of information gathered in the DCI Survey illegal. Plaintiffs sought declaratory and injunctive relief, arguing that the DCI Survey violated the OSH Act and the APA because it required plaintiffs to report information that they were not required by regulation to maintain, and that the Survey violated their Fourth Amendment privacy right. Plaintiffs argue that 29 C.F.R. § 1904.17(b) simply required employers to "report" the information, but did not require them to record and maintain the requested information. In response, OSHA argues that the plaintiffs are required to channel and exhaust their claims administratively pursuant to the OSH Act's statutorily provided review scheme. The district court dismissed plaintiffs' action due to lack of subject matter jurisdiction.

Effective January 1, 2002, OSHA issued a final rule revising its employer injury and illness record keeping and reporting requirements. This rule explicitly requires employers to record, maintain, and report the information requested in the DCI Survey. The January 1, 2002 effective date means that employers must maintain the requested information starting with that date. Plaintiffs concede that the 2003 DCI Survey (requesting 2002 information) will be valid even under the theory on which they challenge the prior Surveys, and they do not seek to enjoin it.

II. ANALYSIS

To determine whether Congress intended to preclude district court review of plaintiffs' claims, we first examine the OSH Act for explicit language of preclusion. Because no such language exists, we look next for other indicia of congressional intent.

Committing initial review to the agency is often sensible policy. Because the administrative agency may possess greater expertise with respect to the organic statute, agency review can be more informed and thus more expeditious, and scarce judicial resources can be conserved for other areas of pressing concern. Moreover, streamlined agency adjudication and deferential appellate review can induce greater compliance by ensuring that penalties are paid reasonably close in time to violations and by deterring frivolous and dilatory challenges.

Plaintiffs have not alleged any facts demonstrating that the potential penalty for refusing to complete the DCI Survey is such that no rational actor would test the law. Similarly, plaintiffs have not made any factual showing that the cost of completing the DCI Survey is so high that it would cause irreparable harm. The DCI Survey asks for information about the number of employees at the company, the number of hours worked by the employees, and the number of injuries and illnesses the employees suffered during that period. But employers were already required by regulation to "maintain . . . a log and summary of all recordable occupational injuries and illnesses." The marginal cost of maintaining the incremental data (number of employees the company employs and the number of hours worked) does not appear to create a burden that causes irreparable harm. Instead, plaintiffs have successfully completed the 2000 and 2001 DCI Surveys. If the cost of compliance created an imperiling burden, we would expect the plaintiffs to have alleged such facts in this challenge. Plaintiffs have made no such argument.

We think it clear—and OSHA concedes—that the district court would have jurisdiction if OSHA sought an administrative warrant for an inspection, and plaintiffs moved to quash the warrant on the theory that the warrant was based on illegally collected Survey data. But in this case, the only plaintiff (Eastern Bridge) to have challenged an administrative warrant below has chosen not to appeal that issue to this court. As matters now stand, Eastern Bridge has already been cited for violations following a completed inspection, and ordinary principles of exhaustion require us to defer to an administrative process that is already in motion.

Affirmed for Secretary of Labor, Chao.

Case Commentary

The First Circuit Court concluded that after an ALJ makes a decision with respect to an OSHA requirement, an appeal is made by a company wishing to litigate with the appropriate circuit court of appeals, not a district court. ■

CASE QUESTIONS

1. Are you in accord with the court's reasoning?
2. How could the company file suit with a court having no jurisdiction to hear and decide the matter?

3. Do you believe it was bad legal advice or could there have been an ulterior motive for filing with the district court?

EMERGENCY STANDARDS

The Secretary of Labor has the power to institute health and safety standards for OSHA. These standards may be emergency or permanent.

Emergency standards are imposed where an immediate concern for the health and safety of workers has just arisen and needs to be addressed in an expeditious manner. Emergency standards are effective for only 6 months. The Secretary of Labor must explain what the emergency is and then follow regular procedures to have the standard become permanent, if it is believed that the problem will continue to exist.

Employment Perspective

Pesto, Inc., created a new cleanser for industrial ovens. When workers began to use the cleanser, they felt a burning sensation on the hands and face. It was discovered that the product contained a caustic acid that would burn areas of the skin that were exposed to its fumes. What recourse is available? Through the Secretary of Labor, an emergency standard can be imposed, requiring breathing ventilators and appropriate gloves, uniforms, and masks to guard against the caustic effects of the acid in the oven cleanser.

PARTIAL AND PERMANENT DISABILITY

Over 10,000 workers die on the job each year. Approximately 100,000 workers are permanently disabled. Permanent disability means that the worker is unable to work again and has suffered a serious physical impairment. Over 2 million workers are partially disabled, meaning that they have missed one or more days from work as a result of the work-related injury. All together, approximately $2\frac{1}{2}$ million workers suffer some form of disabling injury each year. In addition, in excess of 6 million more suffer minor injuries for which no time is taken off from work.

In about half of the cases, manually handling an object or falling is the cause. Other major types of injuries include being struck by falling or moving objects; machinery-related injuries; motor-vehicle and other types of vehicle-induced injuries; stepping on or striking against objects; the use of hand tools, elevators, hoists, or conveyors; and being in the proximity of electric heat and explosives. Motor-vehicle accidents and falling account for a significant portion of fatalities.

Ancillary Expenses

There are numerous ancillary expenses that must be absorbed by an employer when a worker is injured on the job. At the time of the injury, other employees and their supervisors may have to stop working to assist their injured coworker or to view and discuss the event. This constitutes a loss of working time. If the injured worker suffered a temporary disability and remained away from work for a short duration, the injured employee would still be entitled to wages, and the employer would have to bear the corresponding loss of productivity. When the injury is permanent or death results, the costs for these losses are substantial. A replacement will have to be hired, and the cost of his or her training must be recognized. The time devoted to investigatory questioning about the accident is time lost for supervisors and coworkers. There is the cost to repair or replace the equipment and/or premises involved in the incident. Another consideration is the time taken for the repair or replacement that may have resulted in a partial work stoppage for those dependent on that equipment or access to the premises in question. The loss of productivity caused by the accident could result in overtime needed to facilitate a return to status quo. These ancillary costs may on occasion exceed the payments made on behalf of the insured worker.

Two criteria must be satisfied before an employer is held to be in violation of OSHAct. The first criterion is that the employer did not provide a workplace free from recognized hazards. A hazard is considered recognized when the employer either knew of it or should have known of it because the hazard is of the type that is understood throughout the industry. The second is that the hazard is likely to cause serious harm or death to the employees. When the Secretary of Labor brings an action against an employer, he or she must set forth the OSHA standard held to be violated. Standards vary among the four designated industries: general, maritime, construction, and agriculture. The Secretary must describe how, when, and where the violation took place and whether the employer knew or should have known of it, as well as the proximity of the employees to the hazard. The proximity requirement does not suggest that an employee must have been injured by the hazard—only that the potential for injury exists because the employee was in the vicinity of the hazard.

Employment Perspective

The Boxer is a company that manufactures and recycles cardboard boxes. A mechanical forklift is used to carry and stack the flattened boxes. OSHA requires that all motorized vehicles emit a beeping sound when they are in reverse. Forklift 17's beeper is not functional, but the forklift is being used until Friday, when the repair is scheduled. On Wednesday morning, Ryan Madison has just turned a corner and is now walking in the aisle when forklift 17, operating in reverse, just misses hitting him. Is The Boxer in violation? Yes! The Boxer knew of the violation, because forklift 17 was scheduled for repair; an employee, Ryan Madison, was in proximity of the recognized hazard; and the potential for an injury to occur existed.

Employer Defenses

The greater hazard defense is applicable where the imposition of a safety standard while remedying one hazard actually has caused a greater hazard in its place. The employer should request a variance for noncompliance; otherwise, the employer's excuse for not adhering to the safety standard may be denied.

Employment Perspective

Assume that during roadway construction, orange cones must be laid for $\frac{1}{4}$ mile before the construction work commences, and, furthermore, a flag-waver must stand by the first cone to wave off oncoming traffic. On days when there is fog, snow, or heavy rain, poor visibility makes it difficult for drivers to see the flag-waver. Does this situation pose a greater hazard? Yes! The imposition of this safety standard on clear days makes sense, but on days of poor visibility it exposes the flag-waver to a greater hazard than those workers $\frac{1}{4}$ mile down the road. A variance should be requested for days when there is inclement weather.

Another defense exists where compliance with the safety standard requires a device that is not available on the market. Finally, an employee's negligence or refusal to comply with an OSHA safety standard does not justify the employer's inaction. The employer will still be held in violation.

The following case addresses the question of whether a State Hazardous Waste Laborers Licensing Act must yield to the OSHAct when they are in conflict.

Mary Gade, Director, Illinois EPA v. Nat'l Solid Wastes Management Assoc.

509 U.S. 88 (1992)

Justice O'Connor delivered the opinion of the Court.

In 1988, the Illinois General Assembly enacted the Hazardous Waste Crane and Hoisting Equipment Operators Licensing Act, and the Hazardous Waste Laborers Licensing Act, (together, licensing acts). The stated purpose of the acts is both "to promote job safety" and "to protect life, limb and property." In this case, we consider whether these "dual impact" statutes, which protect both workers and the general public, are preempted by the federal Occupational Safety and Health Act of 1970, (OSH Act), and the standards promulgated thereunder by the Occupational Safety and Health Administration (OSHA).

The OSH Act authorizes the Secretary of Labor to promulgate federal occupational safety and health standards. In the Superfund Amendments and Reauthorization Act of 1986 (SARA), Congress directed the Secretary of Labor to "promulgate standards for the health and safety protection of employees engaged in hazardous waste operations" pursuant to her authority under the OSH Act. In relevant part, SARA requires the Secretary to establish standards for the initial and routine training of workers who handle hazardous wastes.

In response to this congressional directive, OSHA, to which the Secretary has delegated certain of her statutory responsibilities, promulgated regulations on "Hazardous Waste Operations and Emergency Response," including detailed regulations on worker training requirements. The OSHA regulations require, among other things, that workers engaged in an activity that may expose them to hazardous wastes receive a minimum of 40 hours of instruction off the site, and a minimum of three days actual field experience under the supervision of a trained supervisor. Workers who are on the site only occasionally or who are working in areas that have been determined to be under the permissible exposure limits must complete at least 24 hours of off-site instruction and one day of actual field experience. On-site managers and supervisors directly responsible for hazardous waste operations must receive the same initial training as general employees, plus at least eight additional hours of specialized training on various health and safety programs. Employees and supervisors are required to receive eight hours of refresher training annually. Those who have satis-

fied the training and field experience requirement receive a written certification; uncertified workers are prohibited from engaging in hazardous waste operations.

In 1988, while OSHA's interim hazardous waste regulations were in effect, the State of Illinois enacted the licensing acts at issue here. The laws are designated as acts "in relation to environmental protection," and their stated aim is to protect both employees and the general public by licensing hazardous waste equipment operators and laborers working at certain facilities. Both acts require a license applicant to provide a certified record of at least 40 hours of training under an approved program conducted within Illinois, to pass a written examination, and to complete an annual refresher course of at least eight hours of instruction. In addition, applicants for a hazardous waste crane operator's license must submit "a certified record showing operation of equipment used in hazardous waste handling for a minimum of 4,000 hours." Employees who work without the proper license, and employers who knowingly permit an unlicensed employee to work, are subject to escalating fines for each offense.

The respondent in this case, National Solid Waste Management Association (the Association), is a national trade association of businesses that remove, transport, dispose, and handle waste material, including hazardous waste. The Association's members are subject to the OSH Act and OSHA regulations, and are therefore required to train, qualify, and certify their hazardous waste remediation workers. For hazardous waste operations conducted in Illinois, certain of the workers employed by the Association's members are also required to obtain licenses pursuant to the Illinois licensing acts. Thus, for example, some of the Association's members must ensure that their employees receive not only the three days of field experience required for certification under the OSHA regulations, but also the 500 days of experience (4,000 hours) required for licensing under the state statutes. The Association sought to enjoin Illinois Environmental Protection Agency (IEPA) from enforcing the Illinois licensing acts, claiming that the acts were pre-empted by the OSH Act and OSHA regulations and that they violated the Commerce Clause of the United States Constitution.

"The question whether a certain state action is pre-empted by federal law is one of congressional intent. The purpose of Congress is the ultimate touchstone."

In the OSH Act, Congress endeavored "to assure so far as possible every working man and woman in the Nation safe and healthful working conditions." To that end, Congress authorized the Secretary of Labor to set mandatory occupational safety and health standards applicable to all businesses affecting interstate commerce, and thereby brought the Federal Government into a field that traditionally had been occupied by the States. Federal regulation of the workplace was not intended to be all-encompassing, however. First, Congress expressly saved two areas from federal pre-emption. Section 4(b) (4) of the OSH Act states that the Act does not "supersede or in any manner affect any workmen's compensation law or . . . enlarge or diminish or affect in any other manner the common law or statutory rights, duties, or liabilities of employers and employees under any law with respect to injuries, diseases, or death of employees arising out of, or in the course of, employment." Section 18(a) provides that the Act does not "prevent any State agency or court from asserting jurisdiction under State law over any occupational safety or health issue with respect to which no federal standard is in effect."

Congress not only reserved certain areas to state regulation, but it also, in 18(b) of the Act, gave the States the option of pre-empting federal regulation entirely. That section provides:

"Submission of State plan for development and enforcement of State standards to preempt applicable Federal standards."
"Any State which, at any time, desires to assume responsibility for development and enforcement therein of occupational safety and health standards relating to any occupational safety or health issue with respect to which a Federal standard has been promulgated by the Secretary under the OSH Act shall submit a State plan for the development of such standards and their enforcement."

About half the States have received the Secretary's approval for their own state plans as described in this provision. Illinois is not among them.

Looking at the provisions of 18 as a whole, we conclude that the OSH Act precludes any state regulation of an occupational safety or health issue with respect to which a federal standard has been established, unless a state plan has been submitted and approved pursuant to 18(b). Our review of the Act persuades us that Congress sought to promote occupational safety and health while at the same time avoiding duplicative, and possibly counterproductive, regulation.

It thus established a system of uniform federal occupational health and safety standards, but gave States the option of pre-empting federal regulations by developing their own occupational safety and health programs. In addition, Congress offered the States substantial federal grant monies to assist them in developing their own programs. To allow a State selectively to "supplement," certain federal regulations with ostensibly nonconflicting standards would be inconsistent with this federal scheme of establishing uniform federal standards, on the one hand, and encouraging States to assume full responsibility for development and enforcement of their own OSH programs, on the other.

The OSH Act defines an "occupational safety and health standard" as "a standard which requires conditions, or the adoption or use of one or more practices, means, methods, operations, or processes, reasonably necessary or appropriate to provide safe or healthful employment and places of employment." Any state law requirement designed to promote health and safety in the workplace falls neatly within the Act's definition of an "occupational safety and health standard." Clearly, under this definition, a state law that expressly declares a legislative purpose of regulating occupational health and safety would, in the absence of an approved state plan, be pre-empted by an OSHA standard regulating the same subject matter.

We recognize that "the States have a compelling interest in the practice of professions within their boundaries, and that as part of their power to protect the public health, safety, and other valid interests they have broad power to establish standards for licensing practitioners and regulating the practice of professions." But under the Supremacy Clause, from which our pre-emption doctrine is derived, "any state law, however clearly within a State's acknowledged power, which interferes with or is contrary to federal law, must yield" ("even state regulation designed to protect vital state interests must give way to paramount federal legislation"). We therefore reject petitioner's argument that the State's interest in licensing various occupations can save from OSH Act pre-emption those provisions that directly and substantially affect workplace safety.

The judgment of the Court of Appeals is hereby Affirmed.

Judgment for National Solid Wastes Management Association.

Case Commentary

The U.S. Supreme Court concluded that an Illinois state law regulating occupational safety and health must yield because it is in conflict with the OSH Act. ∎

CASE QUESTIONS

1. Are you in agreement with the court's decision?
2. Why cannot Illinois enact measures stricter than OSHA requirements in certifying individuals who deal with hazardous waste?

3. Would National Solid Wastes Management Association's argument that requiring its members to comply with individual state standards more stringent than OSHA standards be an undue burden?

An employer is required to provide its employees with a safe working environment. Inherent in this requirement is the employer's duty to inspect and maintain the working environment. An employer breaches its duty when it knows or should have known of a workplace hazard and failed either to correct the defect or notify its employees of it.

An employer is not an ensurer of the employee's safety. Liability attaches when the employer had a better understanding of the hazards to be anticipated. However, the employer's liability ceases when the employee's knowledge of the hazard is at least the equivalent of the employer's.

EMPLOYEE LESSONS

1. Be apprised of the significance of the OSHAct.
2. Learn what safety measures are required in your place of employment.
3. Determine whether your employer is adhering to the required standards.
4. Consider whether to report your employer for OSHA violations.
5. Know who to contact for reporting unsafe conditions.
6. Be aware of the numerous injuries that occur each year during the scope of employment.
7. Guard against injuring yourself on the job by wearing safety equipment and following safety procedures.
8. Appreciate the distinctions among the various types of disabilities.
9. Make sure you have adequate disability insurance.

REVIEW QUESTIONS

1. Explain the significance of the OSHAct.
2. Who is responsible for establishing OSHA standards?
3. If an employer is unable to comply with an OSHA standard, what alternative is available to it?
4. Absent OSHAct, what should provide employers with enough incentive to ensure a safe working environment?
5. Explain the purpose of OSHA.
6. May OSHA representatives inspect an employer's place of business?
7. Explain the purpose of the NIOSH.
8. What kind of record keeping is mandated by OSHA?
9. Explain National Consensus Standards.
10. What is the procedure once a determination has been made that an employer is in violation of OSHA standards?
11. Is the burden and cost of compliance with OSHA standards justified by the injuries and lives saved?
12. How should a decision ethically be made when compliance with OSHA standards perpetuates discrimination against women?
13. Should OSHA take precedence in all conflicts with state law?

CASE PROBLEMS

1. We consider the question of to whom should a reviewing court defer when the Secretary of Labor and the OSHRC furnish reasonable but conflicting interpretations of an ambiguous regulation promulgated by the Secretary under the OSHAct of 1970.

The act charges the Secretary with responsibility for setting and enforcing workplace health and safety standards. The Secretary establishes these standards through the exercise of rule-making powers. If the Secretary (or the Secretary's designate) determines upon investigation that an employer is failing to comply with such a standard, the Secretary is authorized to issue a citation and to assess the employer a monetary penalty.

The commission is assigned to "carry out adjudicatory functions" under the act. If an employer wishes to contest a citation, the commission must afford the employer an evidentiary hearing and "thereafter issue an order, based on findings of fact, affirming, modifying, or vacating the Secretary's citation or proposed penalty." Who should have the power to interpret the OSHA? *Lynn Martin, Secretary of Labor v. Occupational Safety and Health Review Commission*, 499 U.S. 144 (1991)

2. Albert Dayton, a respondent in No. 90–114, applied for black lung benefits in 1979, after having worked as a coal miner for 17 years. The ALJ found that Dayton invoked the presumption of eligibility based on ventilatory test scores showing a chronic pulmonary condition. The judge then determined that petitioner Consolidated Coal Company had successfully rebutted the presumption under 15 727.203 (b) (2) and (4) by demonstrating that Dayton did not have pneumoconiosis and, in any event, that Dayton's pulmonary impairment was not totally disabling. The Benefits Review Board affirmed, concluding that the medical evidence demonstrated that Dayton's pulmonary condition was unrelated to coal and dust exposure, but was instead secondary to his smoking and "other ailments," and that the ALJ had correctly concluded that Consolidation had rebutted the presumption. *Consolidation Coal Co. v. Director, Office of Workers' Compensation Programs, U.S. Dept. of Labor*, 501 U.S. 680 (1991)

3. In 1986, while walking in a dark train tunnel, Sinclair fell over a depression in a bent trap door covering a manhole. Sinclair immediately experienced "sharp low back pains" and could not stand straight or walk normally. He was out of work for almost 3 weeks, during which time he was treated and examined twice by a private physician and three times by Long Island Rail Road (LIRR) physicians.

Sinclair commenced this FELA (Fair Employment Labor Authority) action in September 1989, alleging a single theory of liability: The LIRR breached its duty to exercise reasonable care in providing a safe workplace. The claim was limited to the September 1986 incident with the manhole cover. What was the result? *Sinclair v. Long Island R.R.*, 985 F.2d 74 (2nd Cir. 1993)

HUMAN RESOURCE DILEMMAS

1. At Paradise Elementary School, the cleaning staff uses a strong chemical containing bleach to clean the rest rooms. Breathing masks are provided, but the workers refuse to wear them because the children laugh. The principal is concerned that this may constitute an OSHA violation. How would you advise her?

2. In constructing the Omega Tower, an 85-story structure, the use of asbestos came into question. Asbestos is an excellent fire retardant, especially for use in the upper stories where fire may prevent escape. However, asbestos poses respiratory risks for installers and possibly office workers. Which is the greater hazard?

3. In the 1,200-attorney law firm of Moran, Mullins, and Hall, 300 individuals are employed in the typing pool. These workers clock more than 8 hours a day, and their keystrokes are counted. The typists constantly complain about back pains, eyestrain, carpal tunnel, and poor leg circulation. They want the following accommodations to ease their pain: chairs with built-in massages for neck and back, footstools, armrests, and liquid crystal display monitors. The law firm does not want to make the office environment more ergonomically sound due to the cost. How would you advise the firm?

WEB SITE ASSIGNMENT

Using the following Web sites, research an industry to ascertain the particular OSHA regulations with which it must comply.

www.osh.net
www.findlaw.com
www.westbuslaw.com
www.worksafe.org
www.eng.auburn.edu/ie/ose/laborsafety.about.com/?once = true&
www.osha.gov
www.epa.gov/region5/defs/html/osha.htm
www4.law.cornell.edu/uscode/29/ch15.html
www.dol.gov/dol/compliance/comp-osha.htm
www.usda.gov/oce/oce/labor-affairs/oshapage.htm

Chapter 21

Workers' Compensation

Employment Scenario

Mary Fields, an inventory control analyst for The Long and the Short of It, was injured when a shelf containing heavy boxes collapsed, knocking her to the floor. The injury occurred in the stockroom while Mary was taking inventory. She suffered a severe concussion, broken collarbone, and injuries to her ribs. Tom Long and Mark Short were very sympathetic to Mary until they learned she intended to file a workers' compensation claim.

They attempted to dissuade Mary, telling her that they would cover all of her medical expenses. Mary replied that she wanted compensation for her pain and suffering. Tom empathized with Mary, saying that he felt Mary's pain, but then rebuked her, telling Mary that she would feel his wrath if she filed with the Workers' Compensation Board. Tom admonished Mary that she could take her time convalescing, because her days at L&S were over.

Tom and Mark were afraid of an increase in L&S's workers' compensation insurance premiums. Susan North, L&S's attorney, was notified by Mary's attorney of Tom Long's outburst and threats. What course of action should Susan recommend?

Chapter Checklist

➤ Appreciate the purpose of workers' compensation.

➤ Know the function of the Workers' Compensation Board.

➤ Learn that eligibility hinges upon the injury occurring within the scope of employment.

➤ Be aware that an employee must notify the employer of the injury sustained.

➤ Be apprised that employees may not sue their employer in court.

➤ Be cognizant that employers will pay for medical expenses, lost wages, retraining, and death benefits.

➤ Realize that workers' compensation is governed by each state.

> *Recognize that some employees submit fraudulent claims, hoping to collect benefits.*

> *Understand that workers' compensation is absolute regardless of fault.*

> *Appreciate that workers' compensation is a form of no-fault insurance.*

INTRODUCTION

Workers' compensation originated under the Master/Servant Doctrine, where a master was liable for the death or injury of his servant. Master/Servant evolved into Employer/Employee. Originally the liability of the employer was not absolute. If the employee was contributorily negligent, assumed the risk, or was injured by another employee, he or she would be barred from recovery. As employee issues gained importance, those roadblocks to recovery were removed, and the employer's negligence became absolute.

HUMAN RESOURCE ADVICE

- Understand that workers' compensation applies only to work-related injuries.
- Learn that employees must give notice that a work-related injury was sustained.
- Know that employers are immune from lawsuits for employee work-related injuries.
- Be aware that, as an employer, you are absolutely liable for all injuries to employees occurring within the scope of employment.
- Be cognizant that workers' compensation is governed by a state board.
- Realize that employees may fraudulently claim that their injuries occurred on the job.
- Appreciate that you can contest an employee's claim if it is fraudulent.
- Be apprised that employees may collect workers' compensation even if they were negligent.
- Recognize that employers pay into the state funded workers' compensation program.
- Attempt to minimize work-related injuries to avoid having to pay workers' compensation.

PURPOSE

In return for absolute liability for injury or death, employers are immune from lawsuits for unintentional torts. When an injury occurs on the job, the employer is liable without regard to fault. It makes no difference whether the negligent act was committed on the part of the employee, employer, or coworker. The term *injury* also includes diseases that occur in the workplace, such as lung-related diseases from asbestos.

Workers' compensation affords employers and employees the following benefits. Employers save the time and expense of defending a lawsuit. Employees, in turn, receive immediate medical benefits, continued wage earnings, retraining, and death or disfigurement benefits, if applicable.

Employment Perspective

P's and Q's Grammar School has discovered that its building is laced with asbestos. An asbestos removal firm has estimated the cost of removal at $175,000. School administrators decide to have Oscar Clark, their maintenance man, do the work over the summer. Oscar is not particularly knowledgeable about what asbestos is and how to remove it properly. Oscar works all summer on the job, without proper clothing or equipment. Seventeen years later, he is diagnosed with lung cancer. He sues P's and Q's Grammar School in court, claiming that the school administrators intentionally exposed him to asbestos, knowing its harmful effects. Will Oscar win? Yes!

The question presented in the case that follows is whether the employee's disability was completely caused by asbestosis.

In The Matter of Blair v. Bendix Corporation

85 N.Y.2d 834 (1995)

Memorandum:

The order of the Appellate Division should be affirmed, with costs.

Until July 1, 1974, an employee disabled by a dust disease, such as asbestosis, was entitled to workers' compensation only in the event of total disability. Workers' Compensation Law § 39 was amended, effective July 1, 1974, to afford a remedy to any employee disabled, whether partially or completely, as a result of exposure to noxious dust in the course of employment, provided such exposure occurred on or after July 1, 1974.

Claimant-appellant was exposed to asbestos from August 1956 through September 1970 in the course of her employment as a stenciler and packer of brake linings for Respondent.

Claimant became totally disabled and stopped working in 1978 as a result of asthma and emphysema, diseases that were unrelated to her employment. She was awarded Social Security disability benefits accordingly. On March 15, 1988, claimant was diagnosed with asbestosis and, subsequently, instituted this workers' compensation proceeding against respondent alleging injurious exposure to asbestos as a result of her employment.

The Workers' Compensation Board found that claimant's asbestosis was causally related to her employment at respondent's plant. However, it also found that claimant was previously partially disabled, as a result of a "pre-existing lung disability from unrelated pulmonary emphysema and asthma" and that the combination of the two unrelated conditions—asbestosis and pulmonary disease—caused her total disablement.

This Court agrees with that part of the Appellate Division's reasoning that concluded claimant's pre-existing lung disability and her asbestosis were not inseparable causative agents of her total disability. The Workers' Compensation Board, therefore, erroneously found that claimant sustained a compensable injury and was entitled to benefits. Since claimant's period of exposure to asbestos predated the 1974 amendment to section 39, the recovery of workers' compensation was contingent on her complete disablement as a result of asbestosis, a fact not evidenced by this record. The fact that claimant's asbestosis contributed to her pre-existing lung disability could not create an entitlement to compensation, prior to the 1974 amendment to section 39, absent proof that the disabling causative agents were inseparable or that the asbestosis completely disabled her.

Judgment for Bendix Corp.

Case Commentary

The New York Court of Appeals concluded that Blair's lung deficiency was not completely due to asbestosis. Therefore, she was not entitled to benefits under workers' compensation. ■

CASE QUESTIONS

1. Are you in accord with the court's decision?
2. Do you think it was unfair that Blair received no compensation?
3. Do you believe the 1974 amendment, which granted benefits where asbestosis was only partially responsible, should have been retroactive?

An employee must report an injury to his or her employer and then file a claim with the Workers' Compensation Board.

The issue in the next case is whether an employer is entitled to workers' compensation immunity where it is guilty of an intentional tort.

Sierra v. Associated Marine Institutes
850 So. 2d 582 (Fla. 2003)

Northcutt, Judge.

For these purposes we must treat the material factual allegations of Mrs. Sierra's pleadings as true. They reflect that Big Cypress Wilderness Institute was a "level 8" high-risk residential juvenile detention facility commonly known as a "boot camp," housing felons aged fourteen to eighteen. It was located on federal land in the Big Cypress National Preserve by virtue of an agreement between the National Park Service and the Florida Department of Juvenile Justice. The boot camp was operated by Big Cypress Wilderness Institute, Inc., pursuant to a contract between DJJ and BCWI's parent, Associated Marine Institutes, Inc.

That contract acknowledged that a high-risk residential placement required "close supervision in a standard residential setting that provides 24-hour secure custody, care, and supervision." Juveniles with a history of "serious felony offenses" were placed in such facilities out of "concern for public safety that outweighs placement in lower risk programs."

Commensurate with this risk level, AMI's contract and an amalgam of DJJ rules and procedural manuals imposed stringent security requirements. Thus, for example, high risk facilities such as Big Cypress were to have twelve-foot fences topped by razor wire. Staff members were required to undergo a rigorous orientation that included training in verbal and physical use of force, familiarization with policies and procedures, and "job shadowing" of experienced staffers. Until this training was completed, a new staff member was not to have direct contact with youths except under the direct supervision of a certified drill instructor or camp commander.

The DJJ Residential Commitment Service Manual, applicable to Big Cypress pursuant to the DJJ/AMI contract, called for continual assessment of each youth in the program to monitor his level of risk. The program was to devise and maintain an "alert system," whereby all members of the staff would be apprised of specific developments affecting an individual youth's level of risk. These included, for example, such things as an escape attempt or an assault or threat against another resident within the previous 30 days. The manual warned that youths assessed as risks should not be allowed off-campus or to participate in work projects

in which they had access to work tools that could be used as weapons or means of escape. Moreover, all off-site work projects were to be supervised by at least two trained staff members.

The two youths who murdered Michael Sierra had been assessed as risks for escape. Jermaine Jones had a record of offenses including aggravated assault, cocaine possession, battery, resisting arrest, and a prior escape. He had attacked a staff member in the past and had made threatening remarks on three separate occasions. Mazer Jean's record included burglary and possession of a short-barreled rifle, and he had made threatening remarks twice.

On the Sunday before Sierra's death, Jones and Jean had a verbal confrontation, culminating in Jones's threat to "split Jean's head to the white meat." On learning of the altercation, supervisor Erroll Denson placed them both on "contract," a form of punishment requiring the offender to "pay off" the contract with heavy manual labor. Jones in particular expressed anger about this, prompting one staffer to warn that he feared Jones would try to escape and that he should be closely watched.

At 7:19 P.M. on the second day after the altercation between Jones and Jean, Denson instructed Sierra to accompany them and a third youth named Sal Beatty to a work site next to a pond roughly 100 yards outside the Big Cypress compound, where the youths were to fell trees as part of their "contract" punishments. Denson ordered Sierra to oversee the work project until 9:00 P.M., when the group was to return to the compound.

Sierra had been employed as a youth counselor at Big Cypress only eight days. According to Mrs. Sierra's second amended complaint, BCWI had failed to provide Sierra with the required new staff orientation or a copy of the employee handbook. It had never given him the DJJ-required written test on the policies and procedures governing Florida juvenile boot camps, nor had it given him the mandated video training about the boot camp's policies and procedures. Further, Sierra was never warned of the violent threats by Jones or that his fellow staff member thought Jones might try to escape.

Sierra retrieved his car keys from a locked box located in the administrative office, and took his jacket from the trunk of his car. But he did not return the keys to the office as required by policy. Instead, he placed them in his pocket. Sierra next took the three youths to select tools for the work project. Jean and Beatty chose machetes, and Jones took a pickaxe. The four then walked out to the work site.

During a water break at approximately 8:25 P.M., Jones and Jean killed Sierra by repeatedly striking him about the head with their work tools. They took Sierra's car keys, rolled him into the pond, returned to the Big Cypress compound, and escaped in Sierra's car.

WORKERS' COMPENSATION IMMUNITY

Workers' compensation immunity, like other affirmative defenses, may justify dismissing a suit at the pleadings stage only if the plaintiff's complaint affirmatively and clearly demonstrates the conclusive applicability of the defense. We conclude that Mrs. Sierra's second amended complaint did not conclusively demonstrate that Florida's Workers' Compensation Law immunized AMI and BCWI from liability.

Section 440.11, Florida Statutes protects employers from tort liability for injuries to their employees except in limited situations identified in the statute. In addition, Florida courts recognize an exception for intentional torts where an employer has either exhibited a deliberate intent to injure or engaged in conduct that is substantially certain to result in injury or death.

Here, in waning daylight the employer allegedly sent a new, inexperienced, and incompletely trained employee into the woods 100 yards from the relative safety of the workplace to supervise, on his own, three teenaged felony offenders. Two of the employee's charges had violent histories, and the employer knew, but the employee did not, that these two were specifically assessed as escape risks. The youths were armed with machetes and a pickaxe. The employee wielded only a walkie-talkie.

CASE QUESTIONS

1. Are you in accord with the court's reasoning?
2. What prompted the supervisor to give axes to juveniles who were determined to be dangerous?

If proved, the facts alleged could convince a jury that when Sierra was sent into those woods his employer should have known there was a substantial certainty that doing so would result in his injury or death. Therefore, the circuit court should not have dismissed the action based on workers' compensation immunity.

Even assuming AMI's and BCWI's status as agents of the state, the circuit court should not have dismissed the suit on the ground that these defendants enjoyed sovereign immunity from liability for intentional torts. This holding was predicated on the defendants' argument that if Mrs. Sierra could avoid their workers' compensation immunity by proving her husband's supervisor knew or should have known there was a substantial certainty that he would be injured or killed, they necessarily would be immunized from liability under the wanton and willful acts exception to state liability contained in section 768.28(9)(a).

As a preliminary matter, we note that the defendants do not dispute that they owed Sierra a duty of care. Indeed, it is easy to see that the defendants' actions foreseeably placed their employee, Sierra, in a zone of increased risk, giving rise to a common law duty on their part either to lessen the risk or to protect him against it.

Conclusion

Mrs. Sierra's second amended complaint did not affirmatively and clearly demonstrate the conclusive applicability of the defendants' affirmative defenses based on workers' compensation immunity and sovereign immunity. Accordingly, we reverse the order dismissing her suit with prejudice and remand for further proceedings.

Judgment for Sierra.

Case Commentary

The Florida Supreme Court decided that where an employer is guilty of an intentional tort against an employee, workers compensation will not render it immune from a lawsuit. ■

3. How could the employer justify immunity under these circumstances?

Employment Perspective

Peter Hallmark worked at Freedom Printing Press. One day, Sam Houseman, a coworker, caught his hand in a press. When Peter attempted to extricate Sam from his peril, Peter banged his head on the press and suffered a bad head injury that resulted in his death. Peter's widow filed a claim with the Workers' Compensation Board for Peter's wrongful death. Sam filed a claim for the injury to his hand. Will they be successful? Yes! Fault is not at issue here. Peter may have been contributorily negligent. Sam may have been contributorily negligent in jamming his hand. Freedom may have been negligent if the machine was not functioning properly. All that matters is that the injuries occurred on the job. Freedom is liable for the medical expenses, loss of wages, death benefits, and a possible benefit for disfigurement depending on the severity of the injury to Sam's hand.

Employment Perspective

Tom Woodstock was working on the third floor of a new office building. While walking along a beam, his attention was distracted when two waitresses came out of the Masters Restaurant across the street. Tom slipped off the beam and fell 30 feet. As a result, he became quadriplegic. Tom filed a claim with the Workers' Compensation Board for permanent disability. His employer, Build-Rite, claimed that Tom should have watched where he was walking. Will Tom recover? Yes! Although Tom was clearly negligent, he will recover because his injury occurred on the job.

Employment Perspective

Sidney Wood was cleaning debris off the railroad tracks that are owned and operated by Northwest Railway System. Billy Thomas, a teenager, threw a rock that hit Sidney on the head. Sidney suffered a concussion and blurred vision and was out of work for 1 month. He filed a workers' compensation claim. Northwest Railway claimed that only the perpetrator of this intentional tort can be held liable. Is Northwest correct? No! Sidney was injured on the job. Northwest Railway is liable for medical expenses and lost wages. This situation does not preclude Sidney from suing Billy for pain and suffering for the intentional tort of battery or from pressing criminal charges against him for assault.

Employment Perspective

Herman Munsun worked for the West Virginia Coal Mining Company for 30 years. At 51 years of age, while still employed, Herman was diagnosed with black lung disease. He filed a claim under workers' compensation for a work-related disease. West Virginia Coal disputed the claim, asserting it was not conclusive that Herman contracted the disease while on the job. Will Herman be successful? Yes! Expert opinion is on the side of Herman because of the multitude of case histories. West Virginia Coal Mining Company will probably be liable.

The issue in the following case is whether an employee who sustained injuries when she fell in a parking lot designated for use by the general public is covered under workers' compensation.

Wal-Mart v. The Industrial Commission
761 N.E.2d 768 (Ill. 2001)

Justice O'Malley delivered the opinion of the court:

On November 11, 1995, Parry was employed by Wal-Mart and was scheduled to work a 4:30 P.M. to 11 P.M. shift. Parry left the store at 8:30 P.M. for her meal break. She did not return that night; instead, she called the store from her home and told the assistant manager that she had slipped on ice in the parking lot on the way to her car and injured her back. After seeking medical care, Parry was released to work on December 26, 1995.

Parry filed an application for adjustment of claim on February 15, 1996. Following an evidentiary hearing, the arbitrator found that Parry's injury arose out of and in the course of her employment and that her current condition of ill-being was causally related to her injury. Therefore, the arbitrator awarded Parry temporary total disability benefits, permanency benefits, and payment of medical bills. The Commission, with one dissenting opinion, affirmed and adopted the arbitrator's decision.

In its appeal, Wal-Mart contends that the Commission erred as a matter of law in finding that Parry sustained a compensable injury. The evidence showed that the Wal-Mart parking lot was covered with ice as the result of an ice storm on November 10 or 11, 1995. There was only one parking lot at Wal-Mart, used by both employees and patrons. Employees were requested, but not required, to park on the south side of the lot so that customers would have better access to the front door. However, the south side of the lot was not restricted from patron use.

Parry testified that, as she walked to her car at about 8:30 P.M. on Saturday, November 11, her feet came out from underneath her. She twisted around to catch herself but her back hit the ground. She then testified that her back did not actually hit the ground but that she felt something pull as she was falling. She drove to her home approximately one block away and called Wal-Mart, speaking to Sharon. She did not return to work that night or the next day. She sought medical attention on Monday.

On cross-examination, Parry admitted that she had not driven herself to work on November 11. Instead, her roommate, Amber Samples, had borrowed her car and was waiting to pick up Parry when Parry fell in the parking lot. According to Parry, Samples, who was not a Wal-Mart employee, was waiting with the car in the section of the lot in which the employees were encouraged to park.

Sharon Lynn Nielsen testified that she was a support manager for Wal-Mart in November 1995 and received the call from Parry on the night of November 11. Parry told her that she had gone home for lunch and had fallen in the parking lot of her apartment building. Nielsen could not remember what time the call came in, but estimated that it was between 6:30 and 7:30 P.M. She made no written report of the incident that day.

Wilda Mae Land testified that she was an assistant manager at Wal-Mart and received a call from Parry on November 12, 1995. Parry told her that she would not be coming in to work because she had slipped and fallen. When Land asked where she had fallen, Parry said that she had fallen at home. Land could not remember what time the call came in, who else was present, or how long the call lasted. She made no written record of the conversation.

The burden lies with the claimant to establish the elements of her right to compensation. For accidental injuries to be compensable, a claimant must show that the injuries arose out of and in the course of employment. To arise out of one's employment, an injury must (1) have an origin in some risk connected with or incidental to the employment; or (2) be caused by some risk to which the employee is exposed to a greater degree than the general public by virtue of his employment.

The mere fact that duties take the employee to the place of injury and that, but for the employment, the employee would not have been there is not sufficient to give rise to the right to compensation. The evidence is clear that the entire Wal-Mart parking lot was available for use by both patrons and employees alike. Parry did not park her own car in the lot that night. Although Samples was waiting for Parry in the section of the lot in which employees were asked to park, Samples was not an employee, and there was no evidence that anyone, including Parry, asked her to park there. Parry's fall resulted from a hazard to which she and the general public were equally exposed; thus, her injury did not arise out of her employment.

The court noted that the object of comparing the exposures to risk of an employee and the general public "is to isolate and identify the distinctive characteristics of the employment." Here, there are no such distinctive characteristics. Both Parry and every member of the general public were free to park anywhere in the lot. Parry's employment at Wal-Mart did not place her in any special position vis-à-vis the general public in that lot.

We conclude that Parry's injuries did not did not arise out of her employment. Therefore, the Commission's decision was against the manifest weight of the evidence.

Judgment for Wal-Mart.

Case Commentary

The Illinois Supreme Court held that Parry was not on the job when she exited the store. ∎

CASE QUESTIONS

1. Does the decision of the court make sense?
2. After an employee clocks out and leaves the store, is she still within the scope of employment until she exits the parking lot?

3. If the employees had had a designated parking lot, would that have resulted in a different decision?

WORKERS' COMPENSATION BOARD

The social purposes of workers' compensation are to provide injured workers with support and medical treatment expeditiously and to provide an incentive to employers to create and maintain a safe working environment for their employees.

The Workers' Compensation Board is administered by the state. Each employer must carry its own workers' compensation insurance unless it is a self-insurer.

Insurance companies assess premiums on the basis of the number of claims that are made. There has been an abuse of the system by some lawyers and physicians. Certain lawyers steer individuals with skeptical claims to physicians who will always diagnose a work-related injury. In deciding whether to pay, insurance companies have to weigh the investigation and litigation expenses against the cost of the settlement. Employers should consult with their insurers before a settlement to assess whether the claim is bogus and what the potential pubic relations ramifications are. Employers are concerned with keeping premiums low. Litigating bogus claims may result in fewer doubtful claims in the future.

Employers often do not want to hire people who have a condition that could be aggravated on the job, for they fear an almost certain workers' compensation claim in the future. If an individual is not hired because of his or her physical condition and he or she could perform the job at the present time, the person may file a claim with the EEOC for violation of the Americans with Disabilities Act (ADA).

Employment Perspective

Susan Hampton is a registered nurse. She applies for a position with the Midway Hospital. While Susan is undergoing a physical exam, it is discovered that she suffered a lower back strain. Midway refuses to hire Susan, although she can do the job required. Susan files a claim with the EEOC, alleging a violation of the ADA. Midway claims that eventually Susan will reinjure her back and file a workers' compensation claim. Will Susan win? Yes! Midway is discriminating against Susan for a past disability. Although the odds may favor a reinjury, this is discrimination. There is no way for Midway to guard against a future workers' compensation claim by Susan if she reinjures her back.

Employment Perspective

Ken Warren delivers groceries for Foodway. His main hobby is playing racquetball. One night, Ken is late for a match and forgoes his usual preplay routine. During the intensive match, Ken injures his groin muscle. Ken will be out of work for at least 6 weeks. The next day, he files a workers' compensation claim, alleging that the injury resulted from carrying two heavy packages up the flights of stairs to Thelma Johnson's apartment, one of the previous day's deliveries. Foodway does not believe Ken. North Star Insurance wants to settle the claim. What should Foodway do? It should insist that North Star investigate by speaking to Ken's racquetball partners and by questioning how he could play at night if he suffered such a painful injury earlier during the day. This investigation will keep costs down and discourage other employees from submitting fraudulent claims.

FALSE REPRESENTATIONS

A worker who makes a false representation with regard to his or her physical or mental state of health will be prevented from recouping compensation if the following are true: The representation was made intentionally; reliance was justifiably placed on the representation; the representation influenced the employer in the hiring of the employee; and the resulting injury is of the same condition as the one falsely represented. The burden of proving this is on the employer.

During the Industrial Age, many workers labored under the most deplorable conditions, such as the lack of heat, lighting, and ventilation, and having to use unsafe equipment and machinery. Workers for the most part assumed the risk of injury. Recovering damages for loss of earnings, medical expenses, and pain and suffering was rare. The employee suffered not only an injury but also the possible loss of his or her job for nonperformance. Coworkers were afraid to testify for fear of employer retaliation. Even worse than that was the courts' allowance of the legal defenses of fellow servant negligence and assumption of risk. The fellow servant rule prohibited an employee from suing the employer when the injury occurred because of the negligence of a coworker. The employer's deep pocket was immune from liability. The injured employee's only recourse was to sue the coworker.

When a worker is injured, the employer sustains an economic loss due to the nonproductivity of the worker. The employer must absorb this loss. The employee's entitlement to compensation depends on whether the injury was in the scope of employment. If the employer provides health and disability benefits, this will compensate the employee for medical expenses and loss of earnings while temporarily or partially disabled because of an injury or illness that occurred outside the scope of employment. The employee must make up the difference.

When the injury occurs on the job and is within the scope of employment, the employee may seek retribution from the employer's workers' compensation plan.

The issue in the case that follows is whether the employee's involvement in a customer-sponsored bowling league was in some way work related.

In the Matter of Dorosz v. Green & Seifter and Workers' Compensation Board
92 N.Y.2d 672 (1999)

Rosenblatt, Judge.

Decedent, an accountant who worked for a private accounting firm, suffered a fatal heart attack while bowling for a team sponsored by one of the firm's clients. We must decide whether the Workers' Compensation Board properly denied his widow's claim for Workers' Compensation benefits. Reversing the Workers' Compensation Law Judge, the Board ruled that decedent's death did not arise out of an injury sustained in the course of his employment. In disallowing the claim, the Board concluded that decedent's participation in bowling was an after-hours, voluntary athletic activity for which benefits are barred by section 10 of the Workers' Compensation Law. The Appellate Division, by a divided court, upheld the Board's decision. We affirm.

The Workers' Compensation Law requires every employer to carry workers' compensation insurance, so that employees, or those claiming through them, may recover for "accidental injuries arising out of and in the course of employment." Pursuant to Workers' Compensation Law § 10, this entitlement exists without regard to fault as a cause of the injury, but the section contains a number of restrictions, including the one at issue in this case. The pertinent restriction reads:

"There shall be no liability for compensation under this chapter where the injury was sustained in or caused by voluntary participation in an off-duty athletic activity not constituting part of the employee's work related duties unless the employer (a) requires the employee to participate in such activity, (b) compensates the employee for participating in such activity or (c) otherwise sponsors the activity."

The Board found that decedent bowled in a Monday night league, on a team sponsored by Tom Cardinal, a client of decedent's firm. The two were friends, and, as was their custom, would discuss business before and after bowling on these Monday nights. No other employees of Cardinal's or decedent's firm were involved in the activity. On the night in question, Cardinal picked decedent up and the two went to the bowling alley, where they discussed business and then bowled three games. Minutes later, decedent had a cardiovascular collapse and died. The Board noted that there was conflicting evidence as to whether the act of bowling caused the decedent's heart attack, or whether, owing to his pre-existing severe obstructive coronary artery disease, it would have happened at that time, no matter what he was doing. The Board, however, made no determination as to that issue, and it is not before us.

By enacting section 10, the Legislature narrowed the standards for what constitutes a compensable work-related sports injury, so that an award would not be based upon insufficient employer involvement. In the record before us it is obvious that the decedent, who was an accountant, was not engaging in work-related duties when he was bowling. To conclude otherwise would be inconsistent with the Board's findings, which are supported by substantial evidence.

Under section 10, an award is thus foreclosed here unless one of three conditions permitting compensation for off-duty athletic-related injuries exists: that the employer (1) required the employee to participate in the activity, (2) paid the worker to do so, or (3) sponsored the activity. In the case before us, none of these conditions is met. The employer did not require the decedent to bowl in the Monday league, nor did it pay him to do so.

As to the third condition, that the employer "otherwise sponsors the activity," we note that the legislative

memorandum to the 1983 amendment of section 10 states that the amendment "will not change the liability of the employer when participation in an activity is overtly encouraged by the employer." In the case before us, there is no evidence of overt encouragement by the employer. That the employer may have known of the activity, and even acquiesced in it, does not constitute overt encouragement, let alone formal sponsorship of the activity. An employee's activity may be beneficial to his or her health or morale or may confer a benefit on the employer, but that alone is not enough to justify an award, given the restrictions set forth in section 10.

Based on the testimony adduced, we conclude that the Board's determination was supported by substantial evidence.

Accordingly, the order of the Appellate Division should be affirmed, with costs.

Judgment for Green & Seifter.

Case Commentary

The New York Court of Appeals decided that Dorosz's death did not occur within the scope of employment. The bowling league was not company sponsored, and Dorosz was not otherwise obligated to be at the bowling alley. ∎

CASE QUESTIONS

1. Are you in agreement with the court's decision?
2. Was it not enough that Dorosz and Cardinal were discussing business at the bowling alley?

3. Why should the employer be responsible if it sponsored the bowling league?

The next case deals with an injury to a teacher arising out of a faculty/student basketball game. Being present on the court or in the stands was required of each teacher. The teacher claimed that the game was work-related and filed for workers' compensation for the injury sustained during that game.

Highlands Cty. School v. Savage
609 So.2d 133 (Fla. App. 1 Dist. 1992)

Wolf, Judge.

Highlands County School Board and McCreary Corporation (E/C), appeal from a final order of the judge of compensation claims (JCC) determining that the injury sustained by claimant, Rosalie Savage, was compensable. The E/C asserted that the JCC erred in finding that claimant's injury while participating in a basketball game was a result of an incident of her employment, and therefore, compensable. We find that the basketball game during which claimant was injured constituted part of her employment rather than social or recreational activity and is, therefore, compensable.

The facts are undisputed. The claimant, a teacher at Sebring Middle School, was injured in December 1990 during a basketball game between the teachers and students. The game

was an annual charity event. The game occurred during regular school hours, and the teachers received their regular salary. The teachers were required to participate in the game, either as a spectator or a player. No benefit or detriment resulted from a teacher's decision to play or to act as a spectator.

The claimant's claim for benefits to cover the injury sustained in the faculty basketball game was denied by the E/C, on the grounds that the recreational or social activity was not an expressly required incident of employment nor did it produce a benefit to the employer beyond improvement in employee health and morale. The JCC found, following a June 7, 1991, hearing, that the claimant's participation was an incident of her employment and, therefore, compensable.

The E/C's main argument on appeal is that the JCC erred in finding the accident to be compensable in light of section 440.092(1), Florida Statutes (1991), where there was no proof that playing in the basketball games was expressly required as an incident of employment. Section 440.092(1) was created in 1990 and was in effect on December 21, 1990, the date of the claimant's injury. The statute provides as follows:

Recreational or social activities are not compensable unless such recreational or social activities are an expressly required incident of employment and produce a substantial direct benefit to the employer beyond improvement in employee health and morale that is common to all kinds of recreation and social life.

Prior to the adoption of the statute, the law concerning compensability of recreational and social activities was as follows:

Social activities . . . are deemed to be in the course and scope of employment when *any one* of the following criteria are met: (1) They occur on the premises during a lunch or recreation period as a regular incident of the employment; or (2) the employer, by expressly or impliedly requiring participation, or by making the activity part of the services of an employee, brings the activity within the orbit of the employment; or (3) the employer derives substantial direct benefits from the activity beyond the intangible value of improvement in employee health and morale that is common to all kinds of recreation and social life.

It appears that the statutory change was enacted to avoid compensability in situations where the activity in question was neither part of the job duties of an individual or expressly required by the employer. There is nothing in the statute as adopted which would indicate a desire to preclude compensation where a person was injured in conducting actual job duties. Thus, the JCC did not ignore the requirement for a finding of an "express incident of employment" as argued by the E/C. As a matter of fact, the JCC specifically found that the activity in which the claimant was injured was *not* social and recreational but was a regular incident of her employment. This finding is supported by competent substantial evidence; therefore, the E/C's reliance on the statute to deny benefits was inappropriate.

Even if the JCC had found that the facts of this case are controlled by section 440.092 (1), there would be record support for finding of both "an expressly required incident of employment" *and* "a substantial direct benefit to the employer beyond improvement in employee health and morale" as required by the statute. It was uncontradicted that the basketball game was a school activity which required attendance of both students and faculty. Teachers were expressly required to participate in the basketball game in some manner. The event was a part of developing community awareness by requiring students to participate in a community service project. The order of the JCC is affirmed.

Judgment for Savage.

Case Commentary

The Florida Appellate District Court decided that the teacher's participation in the playing of a faculty/student basketball game, which resulted in an injury to her, occurred within the scope of employment. ■

CASE QUESTIONS

1. Are you in agreement with the court's decision?
2. Why should the school be liable when Savage could have watched the game, instead of playing?
3. Did Savage not assume the risk of injury when she stepped onto the court?

Temporarily debilitating injuries are paid according to a schedule of benefits that determines the amount of compensation given during each pay period and its duration. Once the time limit has been reached, payments cease. The benefit to both the employer and the employee is the time and expense saved by not engaging in litigation. Also, employees do not have to lay out money for medical expenses and wonder how they will support themselves until the case is tried or a settlement is reached.

Workers' compensation is a form of no-fault insurance. Under most workers' compensation plans, medical expenses for on-the-job injuries resulting in permanent disability or death will be fully covered, and disability payments for loss of earnings will be payable for life at a fixed rate, i.e., two-thirds of the wage earned at the time the employee was disabled. In cases of death, benefits will be paid to the surviving spouse until remarriage or death and to any children until they reach the age of majority.

Injured workers may also seek compensation for pain and suffering. An employee must file an accident report at the time of the injury, and if the injury results in a disability, then a workers' compensation claim must also be filed with the insurance company administering the plan. Some states administer the plan themselves. In other jurisdictions, the employer may choose a private carrier or may self-insure. After an award is made, the employee will be notified. If the employee is not satisfied with the amount given, he or she may appeal to the state workers' compensation board. If the board affirms the award, the employee may appeal the decision in court. This will result in legal fees, court costs, and the loss of time. However, it may be a necessary evil when an award is unjustifiably deficient.

EMPLOYEE LESSONS

1. Learn the history of the Master/Servant relationship.
2. Know that employers are not liable for work-related injuries if employees are partially negligent.
3. Understand that the purpose of workers' compensation is to hold the employer absolutely liable for work-related injuries.
4. Appreciate that employees give up their right to sue in return for workers' compensation coverage.
5. Be aware that you must report an injury to your employer.
6. Be cognizant that you must then file a claim with the Workers' Compensation Board.
7. Recognize that workers' compensation is governed by each state.
8. Realize that the injury must occur on the job.
9. Do not submit a claim for an injury that is not work related and/or do not fake an injury.
10. Understand that discharge in retaliation for filing a workers' compensation claim is an exception to at-will termination.

REVIEW QUESTIONS

1. Define *workers' compensation*.
2. Before workers' compensation, what procedure was followed when an employee was injured?
3. What defenses were available before workers' compensation that are no longer applicable?
4. Are there any instances in which an employer is not liable for an injured employee?
5. Explain the advantages of workers' compensation.
6. Define the *fellow servant rule*.
7. Who administers workers' compensation claims?
8. Prior to workers' compensation, why were employees afraid to testify?
9. Explain the benefits that an employee who suffers a temporary disability is entitled to receive.
10. What factor will determine an employer's liability?
11. Is an employer absolutely liable for an employee's injuries when the employee has voluntarily exposed himself or herself to danger?
12. How does one arrive at a decision regarding permanent disability?

CASE PROBLEMS

1. Duncan Stone was injured at work. He received workers' compensation payments from Fluid Air Components, his employer, through Liberty Northwest, the employer's insurance carrier, (collectively, "the employer") in the amount of approximately $74,408. He subsequently recovered a $600,000 judgment in a suit against a third-party tortfeasor. The employer filed a petition for reimbursement of the payments already made to Stone. Stone filed an answer to the petition, contending that he owed the employer no money, because the amount of its right to reimbursement was exceeded by the employer's prorated share of the attorney's fees and costs based on

the total of past and future benefits. The employer conceded that its reimbursement should be reduced by a prorated share of fees and costs, but contended that the apportionment should be based on past compensation payments alone. The issue is whether the awarding of attorney's fees should be based solely on past workers' compensation benefits or should also include the amount of future benefits that would have been paid had the worker not recovered from a third-party tortfeasor. *Stone v. Fluid Air Components of Alaska*, 990 P.2d 621 (Alaska 1999)

2. The question before us is whether the director of the Office of Workers' Compensation Programs in the U.S. Department of Labor has standing under the Longshore and Harbor Workers' Compensation Act (LHWCA) to seek judicial review of decisions by the Benefits Review Board that in the director's view deny claimants compensation to which they are entitled. The question is whether it is within the power of the director of the Office of Workers' Compensation to seek compensation for an employee who has been denied by the Benefits Review Board. *Director, OWCP v. Newport News Shipbuilding*, 514 U.S. 122 (1995)

3. Cory Grote, 16 years old, was a high school rodeo champion. After receiving permission from Bruce Bushnell, foreman, he was allowed to visit his brother Brad at Joy Ranch, a division of Meyers. During his visit, Cory helped Brad release 12 colts into a corral. One of the colts, known to the ranchers to be uncontrollable, kicked Cory, causing him to have a skull fracture. Cory sued the ranch, claiming that the ranch was negligent in not informing him of the colt's dangerous propensities. Does Cory qualify for workers' compensation? *Grote v. Meyers Land and Cattle Co.*, 485 N.W.2d 748 (Neb. 1992)

HUMAN RESOURCE DILEMMAS

1. Marissa Campbell injured her lower back while working in the shipping department for her employer, Venus Cosmetics. Marissa is out on workers' compensation. Venus is also requiring FMLA leave to run concurrently. After 6 years, Marissa's physician has authorized Marissa to return to light duty. Under FMLA, Venus is entitled to the job she previously held. How would you advise her?

2. On Saturn Salvage Company's application for employment, candidates are asked whether they have previously filed for worker's compensation. Saturn employs 42 workers. Saturn wants to know if this question is permissible because it is trying to reduce the number of its employees filing for workers' compensation. How would you advise Saturn?

3. The Health Insurance Portability and Accountability Act (HIPAA) prohibits the communication of an employee's medical reports unless consent is given. Pluto Publishing asserts that when an employee files for workers' compensation, it must send the employee's medical report to the state workers' compensation board. Does the federal law supersede the state requirement?

WEB SITE ASSIGNMENT

Using the following Web sites, compare and contrast the workers' compensation laws of your home state with another.

www.findlaw.com
www.westbuslaw.com
www.benefitsnext.com/content/cats.cfm?cats_id-10&source=MiQ&effort=50
www.workcompsite.com
www.business.com/directory/human_resources/compensation_and_benefits
www.encyclopedia.com/searchpool.asp?target=@DOCTITLE%20workers'%20 compensation

Chapter 22

Employee Benefits

Employment Scenario

The Long and the Short of It, which is now in its 10th year of operation, set up a pension plan during its second year of operation. L&S's pension plan provides for a generous 12 percent contribution based on current salary for employees who contribute 5 percent to the plan. L&S's motivation for creating this plan was to entice superior salespeople to work for L&S. To date, their plan is severely underfunded due to L&S's failure to make any contributions to the pension plan after its third year of existence. Fourteen of L&S's employees have reached retirement age. L&S began funding payouts to the retirees from current operations, but now with layoffs and the closing of four stores, operating losses are mounting. Paying retirees is no longer possible. Susan North is notified of the ERISA violations. What course of action should she recommend?

Chapter Checklist
➤ *Define ERISA.*

➤ *Understand why ERISA was enacted.*

➤ *Learn what motivates employers to underfund their companies' pension plans.*

➤ *Know what a defined benefit plan is.*

➤ *Be aware that a defined benefit pension is fixed.*

➤ *Be cognizant of what a defined contribution plan is.*

➤ *Appreciate the concept of vesting.*

➤ *Recognize the concept of graduated vesting.*

➤ *Realize the significance of pension income to retirees.*

➤ *Be apprised of the age for eligibility to participate in pension plans.*

INTRODUCTION

The Employee Retirement Income Security Act of 1974 (ERISA) divides employee benefit plans into pension plans and welfare plans. Pension plans provide income for retirement. Welfare plans include, but are not limited to, medical and insurance benefits.

HUMAN RESOURCE ADVICE

- Understand the ramifications of ERISA.
- Keep your pension plan fully funded.
- Learn what constitutes a defined benefit plan.
- Know how to construct a defined contribution plan.
- Realize that a defined contribution plan invites employees to allocate income to the plan.
- Recognize that a defined contribution plan may guard against inflation.
- Be cognizant that defined benefit plans are fully funded by employers.
- Be aware that an employer can determine the amount, if any, that it wants to allocate to a defined contribution plan.
- Determine when an employee becomes vested.
- Be apprised that the age for pension eligibility is 21.

DEFINED BENEFIT PLAN

Originally, pension plans provided a defined benefit based on the employee's salary and the number of years of service. The determination of the "employee's salary" may be based on an average over more than 1 year. The amount determined to be paid will be fixed for the remainder of the retiree's life. This amount, which may be generous on the date of retirement, may become seriously eroded after many years. Though providing a larger percentage of a retiree's income initially, this will gradually decrease in comparison with social security and investment income, which will move to some extent with inflation.

DEFINED CONTRIBUTION PLAN

A more popular type of pension is the defined contribution plan. The income generated at retirement is not guaranteed as in the defined benefit plan. Rather, it depends on the contributions made by the employee. The employer may also contribute to this plan. The amount of the employer's contribution may be conditioned on the employee's contribution or it may be independent. A positive element of this plan is that the payment upon retirement may either be fixed or vary with the investments in the employee's retirement plan.

Profit-sharing plans provide for employer contributions based on a formula or at the discretion of the employer.

Eligibility

An employee must be 21 years of age and have worked 1 year with the employer before becoming eligible to participate in that employer's pension plan.

The issue in the case that follows is whether the workers were employees entitled to benefits under ERISA.

Vizcaino v. Microsoft
120 F.3d 1006 (9th Cir. 1997)

Fernandez, Circuit Judge.

Donna Vizcaino, Jon R. Waite, Mark Stout, Geoffrey Culbert, Lesley Stuart, Thomas Morgan, Elizabeth Spokoiny, and Larry Spokoiny brought this action on behalf of themselves and a court-certified class (all are hereafter collectively referred to as "the Workers"). They sued Microsoft Corporation and its various pension and welfare plans, including its Savings Plus Plan (SPP), and sought a determination that they were entitled to participate in the plan benefits because those benefits were available to Microsoft's common law employees. The district court granted summary judgment against the Workers, and they appealed the determinations that they were not entitled to participate in the SPP or in the Employee Stock Purchase Plan (ESPP). We reversed the district court because we decided that the Workers were common law employees who were not properly excluded from participation in those plans.

BACKGROUND

At various times before 1990, Microsoft hired the Workers to perform services for it. They did perform those services over a continuous period, often exceeding two years. They were hired to work on specific projects and performed a number of different functions, such as production editing, proofreading, formatting, indexing, and testing. "Microsoft fully integrated [the Workers] into its workforce: they often worked on teams along with regular employees, sharing the same supervisors, performing identical functions, and working the same core hours. Because Microsoft required that they work on site, they received admittance card keys, office equipment and supplies from the company." However, they were not paid for their services through the payroll department, but rather submitted invoices to and were paid through the accounts payable department.

Microsoft did not withhold income or Federal Insurance Contribution Act taxes from the Workers' wages, and did not pay the employer's share of the FICA taxes. Moreover, Microsoft did not allow the Workers to participate in the SPP or the ESPP. The Workers did not complain about those arrangements at that time.

However, in 1989 and 1990 the Internal Revenue Service examined Microsoft's records and decided that it should have been withholding and paying over taxes because, as a matter of law, the Workers were employees rather than independent contractors. It made that determination by applying common law principles. Microsoft agreed with the IRS and

made the necessary corrections for the past by issuing W–2 forms to the Workers and by paying the employer's share of FICA taxes to the government.

Microsoft also realized that, because the Workers were employees, at least for tax purposes, it had to change its system. It made no sense to have employees paid through the accounts payable department, so those who remained in essentially the same relationship as before were tendered offers to become acknowledged employees. Others had to discontinue working for Microsoft, but did have the opportunity to go to work for a temporary employment agency, which could then supply temporary Workers to Microsoft on an as-needed basis. Some took advantage of that opportunity, some—like Vizcaino—did not.

The Workers then asserted that they were employees of Microsoft and should have had the opportunity of participating in the SPP and the ESPP because those plans were available to all employees who met certain other participation qualifications, which are not relevant to the issues before us. Microsoft disagreed, and the Workers asked the SPP plan administrator to exercise his authority to declare that they were eligible for the benefits. A panel was convened; it ruled that the Workers were not entitled to any benefits from ERISA plans—for example, the SPP—or, for that matter, from non-ERISA plans—for example, the ESPP. That, the administrative panel seemed to say, was because the Workers had agreed that they were independent contractors and because they had waived the right to participate in benefit plans. This action followed.

DISCUSSION

Although the Workers challenge both their exclusion from the SPP and their exclusion from the ESPP, the two plans are subject to rather different legal regimes. The former is a 26 U.S.C. § 401(k) plan, which is governed by ERISA; the latter is a 26 U.S.C. § 423 plan, which is not governed by ERISA. It, instead, is governed, at least in large part, by principles arising out of the law of the State of Washington. Nevertheless, certain issues, perhaps the most critical ones, cut across both regimes, and we will address them first.

I. GENERAL CONSIDERATIONS.
A. The Workers' Status.

It is important to recognize that there is no longer any question that the Workers were employees of Microsoft, and not independent contractors. The IRS clearly determined that they were. In theory one could argue that what the IRS said was fine for withholding and FICA purposes, but that is as far as it goes.

However, the IRS made its determination based upon the list of factors which is generally used to decide whether a person is an independent contractor or an employee. That question is obviated here for, perhaps more to the purpose, both Microsoft and the SPP have conceded for purposes of this appeal that the Workers were common law employees. In fact, they have asserted that the Workers' status is a "nonissue" because they concede that the Workers were common law employees. That is to say, they were employees of Microsoft.

B. The Employment Agreements.

The concession that the Workers were employees would, at first blush, appear to dispose of this case. It means that for legal purposes they, along with the other employees of Microsoft, were subject to Microsoft's control as to both "the manner and means" of accomplishing their job, that they worked for a substantial period, that they were furnished a workplace and equipment, that they were subject to discharge, and the like.

Microsoft also entered into special agreements with the Workers, and it is those which complicate matters to some extent. Each of the Workers and Microsoft signed agreements which stated, among other things not relevant here, that the worker was "an Independent Contractor for Microsoft," and nothing in the agreement should be construed as creating an "employer-employee relationship." As a result, the worker agreed "to be responsible for all of his federal and state taxes, withholding, social security, insurance, and other benefits." At the same time, Microsoft had the Workers sign an information form, which explained: "As an Independent Contractor to Microsoft, you are self employed and are responsible to pay all your own insurance and benefits. . . . Microsoft . . . will not subject your payments to any withholding. . . . You are not either an employee of Microsoft, or a temporary employee of Microsoft." We now know beyond peradventure that most of this was not, in fact, true because the Workers actually were employees rather than independent contractors. What are we to make of that?

We now know that as a matter of law Microsoft hired the Workers to perform their services as employees and that the Workers performed those services. Yet we are also obligated to construe the agreements. In doing so, we could take either a negative or a positive view of Microsoft's intent and motives. We could decide that Microsoft knew that the Workers were employees, but chose to paste the independent contractor label upon them after making a rather amazing series of decisions to violate the law. Or we could decide that Microsoft mistakenly thought that the Workers were independent contractors and that all else simply seemed to flow from that status.

Were we to take the former approach, we would have to determine that Microsoft, with the knowledge that the

Workers were simply a group of employees, decided to engage in the following maneuvers:

(1) Despite the requirements of federal law that amounts be withheld from employee wages, Microsoft decided it would not withhold.
(2) Despite the fact that the SPP states that "employee" means "any common law employee . . . who is on the United States payroll of the employer," Microsoft decided to manipulate the availability of that benefit by routing the wages of these employees through the accounts payable department, so that it could argue that they were not on the United States payroll. Beyond that, it also determined that it would tell the IRS in its "Application for Determination for Defined Contribution Plan," that Microsoft did, indeed, basically include all employees, a category that it knew included the Workers, even though it had contrived to exclude them. Beyond even that, Microsoft excluded these employees when it filed its tax returns for the SPP, even though it knew better.
(3) Despite the fact that the ESPP must, essentially, be made available to all employees, Microsoft excluded these employees and thereby intentionally risked the possibility that the plan would not qualify for favorable tax treatment. It did that, even though the plan itself stated that it covered all regular employees and that it was to be construed to comply with 26 U.S.C. § 423, a law which basically requires that all employees be covered. The officers of Microsoft also decided to eliminate one group of common law employees from the benefits, even though the board of directors and the shareholders had already made the benefits of the ESPP available to those employees. In doing that, the officers intentionally violated the corporate law of Delaware, to which Microsoft was subject, because the terms of coverage of stock option plans are not in the hands of corporate officers; they are in the hands of the board itself.

On the other hand, in construing the agreements we can view the label as a simple mistake. That is, Microsoft honestly thought that the Workers were independent contractors and took its various actions and inactions based upon that misapprehension. Its actions and the conclusions conveyed to the Workers in the agreements and in the explanation in the information form, which accompanied the agreements, were simply an explication of what the effect of independent contractor status would be and had no separate purpose or effect aside from that explanatory function. That is to say, of course there could neither be withholding from wages nor participation in the benefit plans because those keyed on common law employment status. If the Workers were independent contractors, those would be the inevitable results, even if nothing were said about them in the agreement or the information form. Explaining the meaning of independent contractor status was simply a helpful disclosure.

Absent evidence that the officers of Microsoft used their daedalian talents to follow the first route we have just outlined, we must decide that the second route is a more accurate portrayal of what occurred here. In other words, we should, and we do, consider what the parties did in the best light. In so doing, we do not believe that we are being panglossian; we are merely acting in accordance with the ancient maxim which assumes that "the law has been obeyed."

The evidence does not undercut our approach; it supports it. As soon as Microsoft realized that the IRS, at least, thought that the Workers were employees, it took steps to correct its error. It put some of them on its United States payroll forthwith. It also gave the Workers retroactive pay for overtime hours. If Microsoft had been withholding taxes while failing to provide benefits, that would have suggested that it knew that the Workers were a species of employee. However, its failure to withhold indicates that it did not think that the Workers were a special breed of employee; it simply thought that they were not employees at all. That was underscored when Microsoft told its managers about the status of the Workers. It distinguished the Workers from other employees, both regular full-time and temporary. It did not say that the Workers were employees in some special category; rather, it said that they were not employees at all.

But they were employees, which returns us to the contracts themselves. Viewed in the proper light, it can be seen that the Workers were indeed hired by Microsoft to perform services for it. We know that their services were rendered in their capacities as employees. The contracts indicate, however, that they are independent contractors, which they were not. The other terms of the contracts do not add or subtract from their status or, indeed, impose separate agreements upon them. In effect, the other terms merely warn the Workers about what happens to them if they are independent contractors. Again, those are simply results which hinge on the status determination itself; they are not separate freestanding agreements. Therefore, the Workers were employees, who did not give up or waive their rights to be treated like all other employees under the plans. The Workers performed services for Microsoft under conditions which made them employees. They did sign agreements, which declared that they were independent contractors, but at best that declaration was due to a mutual mistake, and we know that even Microsoft does not now seek to assert that the label made them independent contractors.

In short, Microsoft has already recognized that the Workers were employees and that the "no withholding" consequence of the independent contractor label has fallen; we now hold that the "benefit" consequence has fallen also. Having thus burned off the brumes which threatened to obscure our view, we will now turn to the plans themselves.

II. THE PLANS.
A. The SPP.
The SPP is an ERISA plan. The Workers seek enforcement of the terms of that plan. That is, they seek to have us review the determination of the plan administrator and to require that the plan make its benefits available to them. As we have

already pointed out, the administrative panel of the SPP determined that the Workers are not entitled to benefits. The reasons appear to have been that the Workers were independent contractors and that they waived the benefits. We must review those determinations to see if they were arbitrary or capricious. Based upon what we have already said, it is pellucid that they were. To the extent that the decision was based upon the supposed independent contractor status of the Workers, the plan conceded that the decision was wrong when it conceded that the Workers were, in fact, employees. To the extent that the decision was based upon a supposed waiver of benefits, the plan administrator purported to construe the agreements rather than the plan itself. But, as we have pointed out, our construction is the opposite. We, therefore, determine that the reasons given for denying benefits were arbitrary and capricious because they were based upon legal errors which "misconstrued the Plan and applied a wrong standard to a benefits determination."

B. The ESPP.
The ESPP was a plan adopted for the purpose of taking advantage of the benefits conferred under 26 U.S.C. § 423. It was approved by the board of directors and by the shareholders of Microsoft. Their action was an offer to employees, as that term is defined in § 423. As we have already suggested, we doubt that the corporate officers set out to withdraw the offer from some employees, even if they could have done that. The Workers knew about the fact of that offer, even if they were not aware of its precise terms. Under the law of the State of Washington, which all agree applies here, a contract can be accepted, even when the employee does not know its precise terms. In *Dorward* the court pointed out that a pension is not a gratuity, but "rather is deferred compensation for services rendered." We think that that same form of reasoning applies to all employee benefits. Few of them are mere gratuities or a result of unadulterated altruism. Most are for services rendered or for the purpose of inducing the further rendering of services. They help to guarantee a competent and happy labor force. The Washington Supreme Court went on to say:

> The consideration rendered for the promise in the pension contract of the employer to pay a pension is established when the employee is shown to have knowledge of the pension plan and continues his employment. An enforceable contract will arise in such instances even though the pensioner does not know the precise terms of the pension agreement.

Again, we are confident that the court would apply the same reasoning to this employee benefit. The ESPP was created and offered to all employees, the Workers knew of it, even if they were not aware of its precise terms, and their labor gave them a right to participate in it. Of course, Microsoft's officers would not allow that participation because they were under the misapprehension that the board and the shareholders had not extended the offer to the Workers. That error on the officers' part does not change the fact that there was an offer, which was accepted by the Workers' labor. Of course, the ESPP provides for a somewhat unusual benefit. An employee, who chooses to participate, must pay for any purchase of stock, and the Workers never did that.

Conclusion

Microsoft, like other advanced employers, makes certain benefits available to all of its employees, who meet minimum conditions of eligibility. For some time, it did not believe that the Workers could partake of certain of those benefits because it thought that they were independent contractors. In that it was mistaken, as it now knows and concedes.

CASE QUESTIONS

1. Does the decision of the court make sense?
2. Was Microsoft really mistaken or was the independent contractor label done intentionally?

The mistake brought Microsoft difficulties with the IRS, but it has resolved those difficulties by making certain payments and by taking other actions. The mistake has also brought it difficulties with the Workers, and the time has come to resolve those. Therefore, we now determine that the reasons for rejecting the Workers' participation in the SPP and the ESPP were invalid.

Judgment for Vizcaino.

Case Commentary

The Ninth Circuit Court ruled that Microsoft's attempt to exclude workers from receiving benefits by labeling them as independent contractors was invalid. ■

3. What motivates a company the size of Microsoft to exclude its low-level workers from receiving benefits?

Vesting

Vesting occurs when the employee acquires the right to the contribution made on his or her behalf by the employer. An employee may be partially or fully vested. An employee becomes partially vested if, beginning in the third year, the plan provides for 20 percent vesting for each of the next 5 years. In that way, by the end of the seventh year, the employee will be completely vested. This means that all contributions made by the employer belong to the employee. Vesting applies only to the employer's contribution. When the employee contributes his or her own money in a defined contribution plan, it always belongs to the employee.

The question presented in the following case is whether the employer's demand for a release of employment-related claims by an employee before payments are made according to an early retirement program is in violation of ERISA.

Lockheed Corp. v. Spink
517 U.S. 882 (1996)

Justice Thomas delivered the opinion of the Court.
In this case, we decide whether the payment of benefits pursuant to an early retirement program conditioned on the participants' release of employment-related claims constitutes a prohibited transaction under the Employee Retirement Income Security Act of 1974 (ERISA). We also determine whether the 1986 amendments to ERISA and the Age Discrimination in Employment Act of 1967 (ADEA), forbidding age-based discrimination in pension plans apply retroactively.

I.

Respondent Paul Spink was employed by petitioner Lockheed Corporation from 1939 until 1950, when he left to work for one of Lockheed's competitors. In 1979, Lockheed persuaded

Spink to return. Spink was 61 years old when he resumed employment with Lockheed. At that time, the terms of the Lockheed Retirement Plan for Certain Salaried Individuals (Plan), a defined benefit plan, excluded from participation employees who were over the age of 60 when hired. This was expressly permitted by ERISA.

Congress subsequently passed the Omnibus Budget Reconciliation Act of 1986 (OBRA). Section 9203(a)(1) of OBRA repealed the age-based exclusion provision of ERISA, and the statute now flatly mandates that "no pension plan may exclude from participation (on the basis of age) employees who have attained a specified age." In an effort to comply with these new laws, Lockheed ceased its prior practice of age-based exclusion from the Plan, effective December 25, 1988. As of that date, all employees, including Spink, who had previously been ineligible to participate in the Plan due to their age at the time of hiring became members of the Plan. Lockheed made clear, however, that it would not credit those employees for years of service rendered before they became members.

Spink brought this suit, in his individual capacity and on behalf of others similarly situated, against Lockheed and several of its directors and officers. Among other things, the complaint alleged that Lockheed and the members of the board of directors violated ERISA's duty of care and prohibited transaction provisions by amending the Plan to create the retirement programs. The complaint also asserted that the OBRA amendments to ERISA and the ADEA required Lockheed to count Spink's pre–1988 service years toward his accrued pension benefits. Lockheed moved to dismiss the complaint for failure to state a claim, and the District Court granted the motion.

The Court of Appeals for the Ninth Circuit reversed in relevant part. The Plan was unlawful under ERISA, which prohibits a fiduciary from causing a plan to engage in a transaction that transfers plan assets to a party in interest or involves the use of plan assets for the benefit of a party in interest. The court reasoned that because the amendments offered increased benefits in exchange for a release of employment claims, they constituted a use of Plan assets to "purchase" a significant benefit for Lockheed. In addition, the Court of Appeals agreed with Spink that Lockheed had violated the OBRA amendments by refusing to include Spink's service years prior to 1988 in determining his benefits. In so holding, the court found that the OBRA amendments apply retroactively. We issued a writ of certiorari and now reverse.

II.

Nothing in ERISA requires employers to establish employee benefits plans. Nor does ERISA mandate what kind of benefits employers must provide if they choose to have such a plan. ERISA does, however, seek to ensure that employees will not be left empty-handed once employers have guaranteed them certain benefits. Accordingly, ERISA tries to "make as certain as possible that pension fund assets will be adequate" to meet expected benefits payments.

To increase the chances that employers will be able to honor their benefits commitments—that is, to guard against the possibility of bankrupt pension funds—Congress incorporated several key measures into the Act. Section 302 of ERISA sets minimum annual funding levels for all covered plans and creates tax liens in favor of such plans when those funding levels are not met. Sections 404 and 409 of ERISA impose respectively a duty of care with respect to the management of existing trust funds, along with liability for breach of that duty, upon plan fiduciaries. Finally, Section 406 of ERISA prohibits fiduciaries from involving the plan

and its assets in certain kinds of business deals. It is this last feature of ERISA that is at issue today.

Congress enacted Section 406 "to bar categorically a transaction that is likely to injure the pension plan." That section mandates, in relevant part, that "a fiduciary with respect to a plan shall not cause the plan to engage in a transaction, if he knows or should know that such transaction constitutes a direct or indirect . . . transfer to, or use by or for the benefit of a party in interest, of any assets of the plan." The question here is whether this provision of ERISA prevents an employer from conditioning the receipt of early retirement benefits upon the participants' waiver of employment claims. For the following reasons, we hold that it does not.

III.

Section 406(a)(1) regulates the conduct of plan fiduciaries, placing certain transactions outside the scope of their lawful authority. When a fiduciary violates the rules set forth in Section 406(a)(1), Section 409 of ERISA renders him personally liable for any losses incurred by the plan, any ill-gotten profits, and other equitable and remedial relief deemed appropriate by the court. But in order to sustain an alleged transgression of Section(s) 406(a), a plaintiff must show that a fiduciary caused the plan to engage in the allegedly unlawful transaction. Unless a plaintiff can make that showing, there can be no violation of Section(s) 406(a)(1) to warrant relief under the enforcement provisions.

A.

We first address the allegation in Spink's complaint that Lockheed and the board of directors breached their fiduciary duties when they adopted the amendments establishing the early retirement programs. Plan sponsors who alter the terms of a plan do not fall into the category of fiduciaries. "Employers or other plan sponsors are generally free under ERISA, for any reason at any time, to adopt, modify, or terminate welfare plans."

Lockheed acted not as a fiduciary but as a settlor when it amended the terms of the Plan to include the retirement programs.

According to Spink and the Court of Appeals, however, Lockheed's early retirement programs were prohibited transactions within the meaning of Section(s) 406(a)(1)(D) because the required release of employment-related claims by participants created a "significant benefit" for Lockheed. Spink concedes, however, that among the "incidental" and thus legitimate benefits that a plan sponsor may receive from the operation of a pension plan are attracting and retaining employees, paying deferred compensation, settling or avoiding strikes, providing increased compensation without increasing wages, increasing employee turnover, and reducing the likelihood of lawsuits by encouraging employees who would otherwise have been laid off to depart voluntarily.

We do not see how obtaining waivers of employment-related claims can meaningfully be distinguished from these admittedly permissible objectives. Each involves, at bottom, a quid pro quo between the plan sponsor and the participant: that is, the employer promises to pay increased benefits in exchange for the performance of some condition by the employee. By Spink's admission, the employer can ask the employee to continue to work for the employer, to cross a picket line, or to retire early. The execution of a release of claims against the employer is functionally no different; like these other conditions, it is an act that the employee performs for the employer in return for benefits. Certainly, there is no basis in Section(s) 406(a)(1)(D) for distinguishing a valid from an invalid quid pro quo. Section 406(a)(1)(D) simply does not address what an employer can and cannot ask an employee to do in return for benefits. "The private parties, not the Government, control the level of benefits." Furthermore, if an employer can avoid litigation that might result from laying off an employee by enticing him to retire early, as Spink concedes, it stands to reason that the employer can also protect itself from suits arising out of that retirement by asking the employee to release any employment-related claims he may have.

The judgment of the Court of Appeals is reversed, and the case is remanded for further proceedings consistent with this opinion.

Judgment for Lockheed Corp.

Case Commentary

The U.S. Supreme Court concluded that requesting a release of employment-related claims before the payment of employee benefits is a justifiable *quid pro quo* between the employer and the employee. ■

CASE QUESTIONS

1. Are you in accord with the court's reasoning?
2. Why should an employee forfeit valid claims against the employer in order to receive proceeds under an established employee benefit plan?
3. Do you think this release encompasses discrimination and harassment claims as well?

Employment Perspective

Tanya Redding worked as a customer service representative for the Fifth Avenue Fund. After 4 years, she left for another company. During that period, Fifth Avenue contributed $5,000 to Tanya's pension fund. The plan called for a graduated method of vesting. Tanya is 40 percent vested after the fourth year. After the fifth year, she will be entitled to 60 percent of the employer's contributions, and after the seventh year, 100 percent. If the pension is a defined contribution plan, the contributions she makes herself will always belong to her. How much will Tanya be entitled to when she leaves? The amount is $2,000.

An alternative to the graduated method of vesting is complete vesting after 5 years. Before the fifth year, if the employer terminates the employee or if the employee resigns, the employee is not entitled to any of the contributions made on the employee's behalf by the employer.

Employment Perspective

Mary Lou Shelby is an editor for Book World Publishing. Book World subscribes to complete vesting after 5 years. Two months prior to her fifth anniversary on the job, Mary Lou is terminated. Is she entitled to any part of her employer's contributions? No! Those contributions will revert back to the employer. Had she survived the fifth year, all of the contributions would have been hers.

When an employee becomes vested, he or she has the right to the employer's contributions but does not have access until he or she retires.

The issue in the following case is whether an employer terminated an employee to avoid the high cost of making contributions to his pension plan.

Lehman v. Prudential Insurance Co.

74 F.3d 323 (1st Cir. 1996)

Campbell, Senior Circuit Judge.

William R. Lehman, a former employee of the Prudential Insurance Company of America ("Prudential"), sued in the district court for age discrimination in violation of the Massachusetts Fair Employment Practices Act and for pension discrimination in violation of the Employment Retirement Income Security Act ("ERISA"). The district court granted Prudential's motion for summary judgment on both counts and denied plaintiff's motion for reconsideration. Lehman appealed. We affirm.

I.

We summarize the facts in the light most favorable to Lehman, the party opposing summary judgment. Prudential hired Lehman in late 1974 to work as a brokerage manager for the Greater New York Brokerage Agency. In 1978, Lehman was relocated and promoted to agency manager of the brokerage agency in Boston, Massachusetts. In 1986, Prudential expanded the territory of the agency run by Lehman, making him director of its New England Brokerage Agency which included all of New England except Fairfield County in Connecticut. Even after the expansion, the New England agency was relatively small; nevertheless, it performed very well under Lehman's direction. In 1988, Prudential created Pru Select, a separate sales division of Prudential's life insurance business, to supervise the twelve regional brokerage agencies. Ira Kleinman was appointed President of Pru Select, and he hired Roger Dunker as Pru Select's Senior Vice President. Dunker, along with Lehman's prior supervisors, gave Lehman glowing performance reviews.

Effective January 1, 1990, Pru Select revised its pension plan by changing the commencement year for calculating average eligible earnings from 1979 to 1983, benefitting more senior employees, and by providing a 50% annuity to widows without charge to the employee, benefitting Lehman whose wife is fifteen years younger than he. Lehman projected the additional cost to Prudential of his pension, in light of the above modifications, to be $500,000.

Also at that time, Pru Select overhauled and streamlined its brokerage agencies. It consolidated its twelve regions and directors into five regions and seven directors. In December of 1990, Dunker told Lehman that as of April 1, 1991, his New England office was going to be consolidated with the entire New York territory and part of the New Jersey territory. Lehman was to assume the duties and compensation scheme of a brokerage manager and report to the co-managing directors in the newly created Northeast region: Robert Kiley, the pre-consolidation director of the New York office, and the newly hired David Dietz. According to Lehman, his income potential as brokerage manager could be less than 25% of what it had been as a director. Lehman was instructed to formulate his own unit of brokers in New England from whom he could solicit business. However, he did not feel that this was possible, and after several meetings in which he attempted to define his new unit, he wrote to Dunker stating that the reassignment of his responsibilities constituted involuntary termination motivated by age discrimination. Lehman then accepted an early retirement package.

Before the merger, Lehman, aged 61, directed the New England office, and Kiley, aged 57, directed the New York office. After consolidation of the two offices into the new Northeast region, the latter was headed jointly by Kiley and the 42-year-old Dietz.

II. THIS COURT REVIEWS THE DISTRICT COURT'S GRANT OF SUMMARY JUDGMENT

Pension Discrimination Claim (ERISA) Lehman's second claim against Prudential was for unlawful pension discrimination in violation of section 510 of ERISA: any person to discharge, fine, suspend, expel, discipline, or discriminate against a participant or beneficiary for exercising any right to which he is entitled under the provisions of an employee benefit plan . . . for the purpose of interfering with the attainment of any right to which such participant may become entitled under the plan.

Lehman alleged that Prudential hired a younger person for the co-managing director position to avoid the high cost of funding his pension. This circuit, along with most others, analyzes ERISA discrimination claims under the same three stage burden-shifting paradigm described above. In the first stage, Lehman must set forth a prima facie case by demonstrating that: (1) he had the opportunity to attain rights under an ERISA benefit plan; (2) he was qualified for the position at issue; and (3) he was subjected to adverse action under circumstances that give rise to an inference of discrimination. We again assume *arguendo*, without deciding, that Lehman set forth a prima facie case.

To dispel the inference of discrimination arising from a prima facie case, Prudential must only articulate, it need not prove, a non-discriminatory reason for its hiring decision. Lehman conceded that Prudential "articulated a legitimate, non-discriminatory reason for its action . . . namely that it selected Dietz instead of Lehman for the position of co-Managing Director because of Dietz' supposedly superior qualifications for the position."

At the third stage, Lehman must show that Prudential was motivated by "the specific intent of interfering with the employee's ERISA benefits." ERISA provides no relief if the loss of an employee's benefits was incidental to, and not the reason for, the adverse employment action. Were this not so, every discharged employee who had been a member of a benefit plan would have a potential cause of action against his or her former employer under ERISA. To demonstrate that Prudential acted with the specific intention of interfering with Lehman's ERISA benefits, Lehman must show "(1) that Prudential's articulated reason for its employment actions was a pretext; *and* (2) that the true reason was to interfere with Lehman's receipt of benefits." On this record, we find no genuine issue of fact either that Prudential was motivated by a discriminatory purpose or that Prudential's reason for not hiring Lehman co-managing director was not credible.

Effective January 1, 1990, Prudential made adjustments to its company-wide pension plan which Lehman estimates increased Prudential's cost of funding his pension by about $500,000 over time. Lehman contends that Prudential was aware of the high cost of his benefits and refused to offer him the co-managing director position in an effort to reduce this cost (pension benefit obligations being lesser for younger people). Lehman again points to Kleinman's statement that benefits actually cost more than they had been estimating because of "the age of some of the Directors."

Viewing the evidence in the light most favorable to Lehman, we find nothing that would cause a reasonable fact-finder to doubt Prudential's explanation for its hiring decision. Prudential's mere awareness of the high cost of pension obligations combined with the single isolated ambiguous remark by Kleinman were insufficient, by themselves, to establish Prudential's discriminatory intent. Lehman did not contradict deposition testimony that Prudential's benefit costs were calculated on a company-wide basis, and that Pru Select's top management, who made the hiring decision, received no individual employee calculation of pension costs. Nor did Lehman contradict deposition testimony that Prudential did not have knowledge of his wife's age, knowledge that would be necessary to compute his pension obligation. No material connection appears between the cost of funding Lehman's pension and Prudential's decision to hire Dietz rather than Lehman. We are satisfied that the record would not support a finding that Prudential did not hire Lehman as co-managing director because of the cost of funding his pension.

Affirmed.

Judgment for Prudential Ins. Co.

Case Commentary

The First Circuit Court of Appeals resolved that Prudential was not guilty of pension discrimination when it terminated Lehman and replaced him with a younger worker who was more experienced. ■

CASE QUESTIONS

1. Are you in agreement with the court's decision?
2. Do you believe the cost of funding Lehman's pension had nothing to do with his termination?

3. Is there any protection afforded to Lehman in this situation?

PURPOSE

ERISA was introduced in response to unfair practices by employers. Numerous pension funds were underfunded. Therefore, when an employee retired, there was no guarantee that the money would be there for his or her pension. This situation occurred often in companies that went out of business. ERISA imposed minimum funding standards in response to this problem. Companies also had peculiar rules regarding age and years of service, as the following examples will illustrate.

Employment Perspective

Joan Thompson worked for 41 years for Bullseye Distillery in Memphis, Tennessee. When the plant closed down, Joan was offered a position in the Lexington, Kentucky, plant. She refused because she was $63\frac{1}{2}$ years old. When she reached age 65, she applied to Bullseye for pension benefits but was turned down because she had left the company before retirement. How would ERISA have addressed this problem? Joan would have been completely vested after either 5 years or 7 years if the graduated method had been used. The retirement benefits lost by leaving the job $1\frac{1}{2}$ years before her retirement would have been negligible.

Employment Perspective

Dennis Lynch worked as a blackjack dealer for Shore Road Casino for 17 years. He left for a job in Crazy Horse Casino when he was 55 years old. At age 65, he applied to Shore Road for pension benefits. Dennis was denied because he had worked for Shore Road only 10 out of the last 20 years, whereas 15 years out of 20 years immediately prior to retirement is required. How would this situation work out under ERISA? Dennis would have been completely vested for the contributions made by Shore Road Casino for his 17 years of service and would have been entitled to collect these upon his retirement.

Employment Perspective

Marjorie Quinn worked as a legal stenographer for Westfield, Morgan, and Kane (WMK) for 15 years before resigning at age 35 after the birth of her son. At age 50, after her son had entered high school, she resumed stenographic work with WMK until retirement. When she applied for pension benefits, the law firm denied her because she had not served 20 years consecutively. Under ERISA, what would happen today? Marjorie would have become fully vested during her first service with the firm. Her 15-year absence would have had no effect on the situation. On her return, she would have continued to be fully vested in all the contributions made both before and after her absence. Marjorie would have been entitled to all these benefits upon retirement.

Employment Perspective

Matthew Price had worked as a foreman for the Stingray Automobile Company for 35 years when he was forced to resign because of kidney failure. He was 53 years old at the time. When he reached age 65, he applied for pension benefits. Matthew was turned down because only those who worked with the company until age 55 were entitled to a pension. How would he be treated under ERISA? Matthew would have been fully vested and entitled to all the employer contributions made during his 35 years of service. Under ERISA, mistreatment of an individual who had contributed lengthy service to one employer would have been prevented.

The issue in the case that follows is whether employees are entitled to severance pay even though they were immediately rehired by the purchaser of the business.

Anstett v. Eagle-Picher
203 F.3d 501 (7th Cir. 2000)

Rovner, Circuit Judge.

Eagle-Picher sold its Plastics Division to Cambridge Industries, Inc., which immediately re-employed nearly all of the Plastics Division personnel. Eagle-Picher's Divisional Separation Policy provided severance benefits to its employees under certain circumstances, and the Plastics Division employees believed that the sale triggered application of the policy to them. Eagle-Picher declined to grant the benefits and the employees sued. The district court granted summary judgment in favor of Eagle-Picher. We reverse and remand.

I.

The plaintiffs were all salaried, at-will employees of Eagle-Picher's Plastics Division. Eagle-Picher entered into an asset purchase agreement with Cambridge on July 9, 1997, and on July 10, 1997, all of the plaintiffs began working for Cambridge without any interruption in employment. One of the benefits offered by Eagle-Picher was a severance policy that provided in relevant part:

> Salaried employees terminated other than for cause or voluntary separation, due to the exigencies of the business situation, will be entitled to the following benefits:
> One week's pay, for each year of service to the Plastics Division (final year to be prorated), with a minimum of two months pay (eight weeks) granted to the employee.
> Payment for both unused and accrued vacation.
> Group Medical and Life Insurance coverage of one week's coverage for each year of service, or until covered by another employer's program (minimum of eight weeks).

The Plastics Division employee handbook also contained a statement regarding the purpose of the plan benefits:

> It has always been the policy of Eagle-Picher Plastics Division to improve working conditions and promote the welfare of all employees. In line with this policy, the Company has established and maintains a number of benefit plans to meet the needs of its employees. The primary purpose of these plans is to afford a measure of security for all of us. Some allow us to lead fuller lives, through time off without loss of pay. Others provide for a reasonable amount of protection against unforeseen circumstances.

Cambridge had no such separation policy, but did provide other comparable benefits to the Plastics Division employees affected by the sale.

After the sale, Eagle-Picher refused to pay out separation benefits, maintaining that the employees had not been terminated as required by the plan. The affected employees sued Eagle-Picher under ERISA seeking approximately $1 million in separation benefits. Eagle-Picher contended that the policy was intended only to cover employees who suffered a loss of income, and was never intended to cover a corporate asset sale in which the employees were immediately re-hired by the purchaser.

Eagle-Picher disputes whether the employees were terminated because they were immediately re-employed and suffered no real interruption in employment. Eagle-Picher treated the plaintiffs as terminated for every purpose other than the determination of eligibility for separation benefits. For example, Eagle-Picher sent the employees the required COBRA notification, explaining how to continue their health insurance coverage after the qualifying event of "termination of service." In the case of persons eligible for certain pension benefits, Eagle-Picher sent notices to those employees describing the deferred vested benefits to which the employees were entitled as a result of their termination from service on the date of the sale of the division. In internal and external correspondence, Eagle-Picher referred to the employees as terminated or "termed" as of the date of the sale. Only in determining eligibility for separation benefits was Eagle-Picher unwilling to consider the employees terminated.

Eagle-Picher could have limited the salary benefit in the same manner, but did not. Indeed, the company conceded that it would have paid the separation benefit if the terminated employees had obtained jobs on their own and suffered no period of unemployment as a result of their own efforts. The key employee severance policy provides:

> If you are terminated by the Company other than for cause, you will receive benefits under the Plan. However, if the operation you work for is sold and you continue to work for the buyer, you will not be entitled to benefits under the Plan.

The inclusion of this provision in the key employees' policy allows us to draw the following inferences in favor of the plaintiffs. First, Eagle-Picher was aware that a sale of a division could trigger severance benefits unless other language in the policy limited eligibility. Second, Eagle-Picher knew how to draft that limiting language, and did so for its key employees. The absence of similar limiting language in the Plastics Division Employee Handbook can thus be construed as an intent on Eagle-Picher's part not to limit severance benefits for those non-key employees terminated by a sale and re-hired by a buyer. We therefore hold that the plan at issue is clear and unambiguous. The effect of the plan is to grant separation benefits to the employees when they are terminated from their employment. Termination includes a sale of the Plastics Division to another company, which then re-employs the workers. Entitlement to separation benefits is not predicated on a period of unemployment, but is triggered solely by termination. There is no dispute that these employees were terminated from Eagle-Picher and subsequently re-hired by Cambridge. The plaintiffs are therefore entitled to their separation benefits, and we reverse and remand so that the district court may resolve any remaining factual issues, such as the amount of the damages.

Reversed and Remanded.

Judgment for Anstett.

Case Commentary

The Seventh Circuit Court held that the employees were entitled to severance pay when the employees were terminated at the time of the sale of the business. The fact that the new owners rehired most of the workers immediately was inconsequential. ■

1. Do you agree with the court's decision?
2. Is not the purpose of severance pay to compensate someone who will not be working for the same pay at the same job?

3. If the company had foreseen this dilemma, what could have been done to alleviate this?

Minimum Funding Requirements

ERISA requires minimum funding requirements. The fiduciaries that administer the plan are required to act prudently when making investments. In addition, ERISA established the Pension Benefit Guarantee Corporation (PBGC), a not-for-profit enterprise administered by the Secretary of Labor to guard against loss of benefits when pension plans are terminated by companies. Employers are required to purchase pension termination insurance. There are maximum limits; retirees are insured up to the full value of their pensions, as long as the value does not exceed the maximum limit. Employees currently working who are vested are insured up to the value of the pension upon termination.

Employment Perspective

Nancy Woodward worked for Z Mart Department Stores for 40 years. Two years after her retirement at age 65, Nancy began to collect her pension. When Z Mart went out of business, her benefits were reduced by 70 percent because the pension plan was underfunded. How would she be treated under ERISA? The likelihood is that Z Mart's pension would be better funded and more prudently invested under ERISA to guard against loss of benefits. But if the plan was still inadequate, PBGC would step in and provide proceeds from its termination insurance fund. The amount that Z Mart was underfunded would be covered up to a maximum amount.

FIDUCIARY DUTIES

A fiduciary's duty is one of trust and confidence. A pension plan trustee is required to exercise prudence in the management of a pension's investments. In a defined contribution plan, the employee usually has discretion to allocate risk by selecting among a number of mutual funds. The range of funds will usually be from conservative to aggressive.

In a defined benefit plan, the employee has no say over the risk level of the pension plan's investments. Because of this, the duty of care owed by the fiduciary is greater in that the total responsibility falls upon him or her to act in a prudent manner. The defined benefit is paid according to a formula such as an average of the 3 final years of salary times the number of years of service times 2 percent.

Employment Perspective

Ronald Fishburn was employed by Marvelous Muffins, a gourmet bakery chain, where he worked for 30 years until retirement. Ronald's salaries for his final 3 years were $38,000, $40,000, and $42,000. How much will Ronald's pension be? His average salary was $40,000; $40,000 × 30 years of service = $1,200,000 × 2% = $24,000 per year pension.

The issue in the following case is whether a group of beneficiaries who transferred out of the company's welfare benefit plan base because of false information provided by the company can seek reinstatement into the company's plan.

Varity Corp. v. Howe
516 U.S. 489 (1996)

Justice Breyer delivered the opinion of the Court.

A group of beneficiaries of a firm's employee welfare benefit plan, protected by the Employee Retirement Income Security Act of 1974 (ERISA) have sued their plan's administrator, who was also their employer. They claim that the administrator, through trickery, led them to withdraw from the plan and to forfeit their benefits. They seek, among other things, an order that, in essence, would reinstate each of them as a participant in the employer's ERISA plan. The lower courts entered judgment in the employees' favor, and we agreed to review that judgment. In conducting our review, we do not question the lower courts' findings of serious deception by the employer, but instead consider three legal questions. First, in the factual circumstances (as determined by the lower courts), was the employer acting in its capacity as an ERISA "fiduciary" when it significantly and deliberately misled the beneficiaries? Second, in misleading the beneficiaries, did the employer violate the fiduciary obligations that ERISA 404 imposes upon plan administrators? Third, does ERISA 502(a)(3) authorize ERISA plan beneficiaries to bring a lawsuit, such as this one, that seeks relief for individual beneficiaries harmed by an administrator's breach of fiduciary obligations?

We answer each of these questions in the beneficiaries' favor, and we therefore affirm the judgment of the Court of Appeals.

The key facts, as found by the District Court after trial, include the following: Charles Howe, and the other respondents, used to work for Massey-Ferguson, Inc., a farm equipment manufacturer, and a wholly-owned subsidiary of the petitioner, Varity Corporation. (Since the lower courts found that Varity and Massey-Ferguson were "alter egos," we shall refer to them interchangeably.) These employees all were participants in, and beneficiaries of, Massey-Ferguson's self-funded employee welfare benefit plan—an ERISA-protected plan that Massey-Ferguson itself administered. In the mid-1980's, Varity became concerned that some of Massey-Ferguson's divisions were losing too much money and developed a business plan to deal with the problem. The business plan—which Varity called "Project Sunshine"—amounted to placing many of Varity's money-losing eggs in one financially rickety basket. It called for a transfer of Massey-Ferguson's money-losing divisions, along with various other debts, to a newly created, separately incorporated subsidiary called Massey Combines.

The plan foresaw the possibility that Massey Combines would fail. But it viewed such a failure, from Varity's business perspective, as closer to a victory than to a defeat. That is because Massey Combine's failure would not only eliminate several of Varity's poorly performing divisions, but it would also eradicate various debts that Varity would transfer to Massey Combines, and which, in the absence of the reorganization, Varity's more profitable subsidiaries or divisions might have to pay.

Among the obligations that Varity hoped the reorganization would eliminate were those arising from the Massey-Ferguson benefit plan's promises to pay medical and other nonpension benefits to employees of Massey-Ferguson's money-losing divisions. Rather than terminate those benefits directly (as it had retained the right to do), Varity attempted to avoid the undesirable fallout that could have accompanied cancellation by inducing the failing divisions' employees to switch employers and thereby voluntarily release Massey-Ferguson from its obligation to provide them benefits (effectively substituting the new, self-funded Massey Combines benefit plan for the former Massey-Ferguson plan). Insofar as Massey-Ferguson's employees did so, a subsequent Massey Combines failure would eliminate—simply and automatically, without distressing the remaining Massey-Ferguson employees—what would otherwise have been Massey-Ferguson's obligation to pay those employees their benefits.

To persuade the employees of the failing divisions to accept the change of employer and benefit plan, Varity called them together at a special meeting and talked to them about Massey Combines' future business outlook, its likely financial viability, and the security of their employee benefits. The thrust of Varity's remarks was that the employees' benefits would remain secure if they voluntarily transferred to Massey Combines. As Varity knew, however, the reality was very different. Indeed, the District Court found that Massey Combines was insolvent from the day of its creation and that it hid a $46 million negative net worth by overvaluing its assets and underestimating its liabilities.

After the presentation, about 1,500 Massey-Ferguson employees accepted Varity's assurances and voluntarily agreed to the transfer. (Varity also unilaterally assigned to Massey Combines the benefit obligations it owed to some 4,000 workers who had retired from Massey-Ferguson prior to this reorganization, without requesting permission or informing them of the assignment.) Unfortunately for these employees, Massey Combines ended its first year with a loss of $88 million, and ended its second year in a receivership, under which its employees lost their nonpension benefits. Many of those employees (along with several retirees whose benefit obligations Varity had assigned to Massey Combines and others whose claims we do not now consider) brought this lawsuit, seeking the benefits they would have been owed under their old, Massey-Ferguson plan, had they not transferred to Massey Combines.

After trial, the District Court found, among other things, that Varity and Massey-Ferguson, acting as ERISA fiduciaries, had harmed the plan's beneficiaries through deliberate deception. The court held that Varity and Massey-Ferguson thereby violated an ERISA-imposed fiduciary obligation to administer Massey-Ferguson's benefit plan "solely in the interest of the participants and beneficiaries" of the plan. ERISA 404(a). The Court added that ERISA 502(a)(3) gave the former Massey-Ferguson employees a right to "appropriate equitable relief . . . to redress" the harm that this deception had caused them individually. Among other remedies the Court considered "appropriate equitable relief," was an order that Massey-Ferguson reinstate its former employees into its own plan (which had continued to provide benefits to employees of Massey-Ferguson's profitable divisions). The court also ordered certain monetary relief which is not at issue here. The Court of Appeals later affirmed the District Court's determinations, in relevant part.

We granted certiorari in this case primarily because the Courts of Appeals have disagreed about the proper interpretation of ERISA 502(a)(3), the provision the District Court held authorized the lawsuit and relief in this case. ERISA protects employee pensions and other benefits by providing insurance for vested pension rights, specifying certain plan characteristics in detail (such as when and how pensions vest), and by setting forth certain general fiduciary duties applicable to the management of both pension and nonpension benefit plans.

We begin with the question of Varity's fiduciary status. In relevant part, the statute says that a "person is a fiduciary with respect to a plan," and therefore subject to ERISA fiduciary duties, "to the extent" that he or she "exercises any discretionary authority or discretionary control respecting management" of the plan, or "has any discretionary authority or discretionary responsibility in the administration" of the ERISA plan.

Varity was both an employer and the benefit plan's administrator, as ERISA permits. But, obviously, not all of Varity's business activities involved plan management or administration. Varity argues that when it communicated with its Massey-Ferguson workers about transferring to Massey Combines, it was not administering or managing the plan; rather, it was acting only in its capacity as an employer and not as a plan administrator.

The eight questions and answers on the question-and-answer sheet include three that relate to welfare benefits or to the ERISA pension plan Varity also administered:

"Q. 3. What happens to my benefits, pension, etc.?
"A. 3. When you transfer to MCC [Massey Combines], pay levels and benefit programmes will remain unchanged.
There will be no loss of seniority or pensionable service.
"Q. 4. Do you expect the terms and conditions of employment to change?
"A. 4. Employment conditions in the future will depend on our ability to make Massey Combines Corporation a success and if changes are considered necessary or appropriate, they will be made.

. . .

"Q. 8. Are the pensions protected under MCC?
"A. 8. Responsibility for pension benefits earned by employees transferring to Massey Combines Corporation is being assumed by the Massey Combines Corporation Pension Plan.

"The assets which are held in the Massey Ferguson Pension Plan to fund such benefits as determined by actuarial calculations, are being transferred to the Massey Combines Corporation Plan. Such benefits and assets will be protected by the same legislation that protect the Massey Ferguson Pension Plan.

"There will be no change in pension benefits as a result of your transfer to Massey Combines Corporation."

The transcript of the 90-second videotape message repeated much of the information in the question-and-answer sheet, adding assurances about Massey Combines' viability.

The cover letter, in five short paragraphs, repeated verbatim these benefit-related assurances.

Given this record material, the District Court determined, as a factual matter, that the key meeting, to a considerable extent, was about benefits, for the documents described them in detail, explained the similarity between past and future plans in principle, and assured the employees that they would continue to receive similar benefits in practice. The District Court concluded that the basic message conveyed to the employees was that transferring from Massey-Ferguson to Massey Combines would not significantly undermine the security of their benefits. And, given this view of the facts, we believe that the District Court reached the correct legal conclusion, namely, that Varity spoke, in significant part, in its capacity as plan administrator.

The second question—whether Varity's deception violated ERISA-imposed fiduciary obligations—calls for a brief, affirmative answer. ERISA requires a "fiduciary" to "discharge his duties with respect to a plan solely in the interest of the participants and beneficiaries." To participate knowingly and significantly in deceiving a plan's beneficiaries in order to save the employer money at the beneficiaries' expense, is not to act "solely in the interest of the participants and beneficiaries."

The remaining question before us is whether or not the remedial provision of ERISA that the beneficiaries invoked, ERISA 502(a)(3), authorizes this lawsuit for individual relief. That subsection is the third of six subsections contained within ERISA's "Civil Enforcement" provision (as it stood at the times relevant to this lawsuit):

"Sec. 502. (a) A civil action may be brought—

"(1) by a participant or beneficiary—

"(A) for the relief provided for in subsection (c) of this section [providing for liquidated damages for failure to provide certain information on request], or

"(B) to recover benefits due to him under the terms of his plan, to enforce his rights under the terms of the plan, or to clarify his rights to future benefits under the terms of the plan;

"(2) by the Secretary, or by a participant, beneficiary or fiduciary for appropriate relief;

"(3) by a participant, beneficiary, or fiduciary (A) to enjoin any act or practice which violates any provision of this title or the terms of the plan, or (B) to obtain other appropriate equitable relief (i) to redress such violations or (ii) to enforce any provisions of this title or the terms of the plan;

"(4) by the Secretary, or by a participant, or beneficiary for appropriate relief in the case of a violation of 105(c) [requiring disclosure of certain tax registration statements];

"(5) except as otherwise provided in subsection (b), by the Secretary (A) to enjoin any act or practice which violates any provision of this title, or (B) to obtain other appropriate equitable relief (i) to redress such violation or (ii) to enforce any provision of this title; or

"(6) by the Secretary to collect any civil penalty under subsection (i)

The District Court held that the third subsection, which we have italicized, authorized this suit and the relief awarded. Varity concedes that the plaintiffs satisfy most of this provision's requirements, namely that the plaintiffs are plan "participants" or "beneficiaries," and that they are suing for "equitable" relief to "redress" a violation of 404(a), which is a "provision of this title."

CASE QUESTIONS

1. Are you in accord with the court's resolution?
2. What motivated the company to provide false information to the beneficiaries?
3. How did the company think it was going to get away with this deception?

Section 409(a), in turn, reads:

"Liability for Breach of Fiduciary Duty
Sec. 409. (a) Any person who is a fiduciary with respect to a plan who breaches any of the responsibilities, obligations, or duties imposed upon fiduciaries by this title shall be personally liable to make good to such plan any losses to the plan resulting from each such breach, and to restore to such plan any profits of such fiduciary which have been made through use of assets of the plan by the fiduciary, and shall be subject to such other equitable or remedial relief as the court may deem appropriate, including removal of such fiduciary. . . ."

ERISA makes clear that a fiduciary has obligations other than, and in addition to, managing plan assets. The plaintiffs in this case could not proceed under the first subsection because they were no longer members of the Massey-Ferguson plan and, therefore, had no "benefits due them under the terms of the plan."

They could not proceed under the second subsection because that provision, tied to 409, does not provide a remedy for individual beneficiaries. They must rely on the third subsection or they have no remedy at all. We are not aware of any ERISA-related purpose that denial of a remedy would serve. Rather, we believe that granting a remedy is consistent with the literal language of the statute, the Act's purposes, and pre-existing trust law.

For these reasons, the judgment of the Court of Appeals is Affirmed.

Judgment for Howe.

Case Commentary

The U.S. Supreme Court ruled that the company must reinstate those beneficiaries who opted out of the welfare benefit program because of false information provided by the company. The company was a fiduciary and was guilty of deception. The beneficiaries have the right to maintain an action for reinstatement under ERISA. ∎

4. Do you believe that the officers who devised this scheme should be held personally accountable?

INFLATION

In a defined benefit pension, the amount per year is fixed. What may seem to be a generous amount initially will erode over time because of inflation. Defined contribution plans usually offer a choice of graduated payments that will increase as time goes by. If a fixed amount is taken, the retiree must be disciplined enough to save a portion to offset the loss of purchasing power down the road.

Employment Perspective

John Jacobs retired from Bull and Bear Investment Company after 40 years of service at age 65. The defined benefit pension plan paid him $7,000, which was a generous amount at the time. He is now 92 years old. The pension, which by itself provided for him and his wife at retirement, today provides about one-quarter of their needs.

A multifunded pension plan is one into which several companies contribute. It is usually formed in response to provisions in collective bargaining agreements, which stipulate that employees be given credit for length of service toward a pension when they work for more than one member of the plan.

TAX INCENTIVES

Although employers are not obligated to offer any benefits, a tax incentive exists for an employer that makes contributions to a qualified plan. A qualified plan is one that meets the requirements of the Internal Revenue Code. The tax incentive is a deduction for all employer contributions to the pension trust fund from which benefits will ultimately be paid to the employees. The monies paid into the trust fund do not have to be reported by the employees until they receive the benefits. This deferral helps the income grow faster because it is tax free. Thus, pension benefits can be paid out with smaller initial investments by the employer. This tax-free deferral plan can be withdrawn if the plan no longer qualifies under the Internal Revenue Code because of violations surrounding vesting or other fiduciary responsibilities. Enforcement of ERISA is spread out among various federal departments. The Department of Labor receives ERISA plan reports and initiates civil suits for violations of reporting and disclosure. The employee plans and exempt organizations component of the Internal Revenue Service deal with tax law violations of the Internal Revenue Code and can authorize removal of qualified plan status for tax deferral of pension contributions. The Pension Benefit Guaranty Corporation actively pursues employers that have underfunded plans, particularly those employers that are in bankruptcy. Finally, the Department of Justice pursues criminal violations of ERISA, such as embezzlement of funds.

COBRA

The Consolidated Omnibus Budget Reconciliation Act (COBRA) of 1985 requires employers with 20 or more employees to provide group health care coverage for the departing employee and qualified beneficiaries for at least 18 months after an employee departs. Former employees can be charged no more than the rate for regular employees plus a 2 percent administrative fee. A covered employee must select the family plan to have qualifying beneficiaries. A qualifying beneficiary includes a spouse and dependent children up to age 19 or age 23, if the children are in school. Children whose dependency ceases as well as divorced, separated, and widowed spouses are entitled up to 36 months of extended coverage. Qualifying beneficiaries who are or who become disabled are entitled to 29 months of coverage. Some employers extend coverage to domestic partners, but this is not required by COBRA,

COBRA is administered by the Department of Labor in conjunction with the IRS, who will assess violations with excise tax penalties.

Employers must notify employees on their departure of their eligibility for COBRA. Separate notice must be sent for the qualifying beneficiaries. Election of COBRA coverage must be made within 60 days of the date the employee loses coverage or the date he or she was notified of his or her right to elect coverage under COBRA, whichever is later.

HIPAA

The Health Insurance Portability and Accountability Act (HIPAA) of 1996 stipulates that employers must certify health care coverage of departing employees. The certificate must state the name of the plan; the covered employee and qualifying beneficiaries, if any; the plan administrator; and the date issued. This certificate is used if and when the individual participates in another group health care plan. It is used to determine if there are any limitations on the length of existing conditions such as mental health, vision impairments, dental problems, use of prescription drugs, and use of narcotics. HIPAA mandates against discrimination by health care plans based on health, genetics, medical conditions, disabilities, or number of claims submitted. Health care plans cannot exclude activities with a high degree of serious injuries; however, they may exclude injuries that occur due to the participation in illegal activities. HIPAA also has strict rules of privacy relating to the oral and written transfer and disclosure of medical documents. Patient notification and consent are required.

EMPLOYEE LESSONS

1. Know the impact that ERISA has on your pension plan.
2. Determine whether your employer is fully funding your pension plan.
3. Know whether your employer offers a defined benefit plan or a defined contribution plan.
4. Understand each plan.
5. Learn whether your employer will match your pension contribution up to a predetermined amount.
6. Realize the importance pension income has on your retirement income.
7. Appreciate the concept of vesting.
8. Be apprised of the amount of time required before you become vested.
9. Be cognizant of the fact that pension eligibility begins at 21 years of age.
10. Recognize that the PBGC aids retirees who are victimized by underfunded pension plans.

REVIEW QUESTIONS

1. Define *ERISA*.
2. Explain the difference between a defined benefit plan and a defined contribution plan.
3. Define *profit-sharing plans*.
4. When does an employee become eligible to participate in a company's pension plan?
5. Define *vesting*.
6. Explain the graduated method of vesting.
7. If an employee is discharged prior to vesting, what happens to his or her contributions?
8. When can employees access their contributions?
9. Are many pension plans underfunded?

10. Who administers pension plans?
11. Can a company's contributions to its employees' pension fund be something other than cash?
12. Why would a company want to be part of a multifunded pension plan?

CASE PROBLEMS

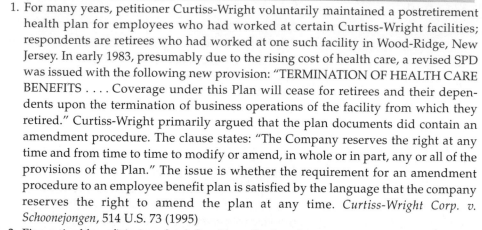

1. For many years, petitioner Curtiss-Wright voluntarily maintained a postretirement health plan for employees who had worked at certain Curtiss-Wright facilities; respondents are retirees who had worked at one such facility in Wood-Ridge, New Jersey. In early 1983, presumably due to the rising cost of health care, a revised SPD was issued with the following new provision: "TERMINATION OF HEALTH CARE BENEFITS . . . . Coverage under this Plan will cease for retirees and their dependents upon the termination of business operations of the facility from which they retired." Curtiss-Wright primarily argued that the plan documents did contain an amendment procedure. The clause states: "The Company reserves the right at any time and from time to time to modify or amend, in whole or in part, any or all of the provisions of the Plan." The issue is whether the requirement for an amendment procedure to an employee benefit plan is satisfied by the language that the company reserves the right to amend the plan at any time. *Curtiss-Wright Corp. v. Schoonejongen*, 514 U.S. 73 (1995)

2. Five retired beneficiaries of a defined benefit plan claim that Hughes violated ERISA by amending the plan to provide for an early retirement program and a noncontributory benefit structure.

    Section 3.2 provides that Hughes' contributions will not fall below the "amount necessary to maintain the qualified status of the Plan . . . and to comply with all applicable legal requirements." But §6.2 of the plan gives Hughes "the right to suspend its contributions to the Plan at any time," as long as doing so does not "create an 'accumulated funding deficiency'" under ERISA.

    By 1986, as a result of employer and employee contributions and investment growth, the plan's assets exceeded the actuarial or present value of accrued benefits by almost $1 billion. In light of this plan surplus, Hughes suspended its contributions in 1987, which it has not resumed. The issue is whether employees who participate in a defined benefit pension plan have a right to the surplus that has accrued in the plan. *Hughes Aircraft Company v. Jacobson*, 525 U.S. 432 (1999)

3. The issue is whether federal courts possess ancillary jurisdiction over new actions in which a federal judgment creditor seeks to impose liability for a money judgment on a person not otherwise liable for the judgment. We hold that they do not. Thomas unsuccessfully attempted to collect the judgment from Tru-Tech. Thomas then sued Peacock in federal court, claiming that Peacock had entered into a civil conspiracy to siphon assets from Tru-Tech to prevent satisfaction of the ERISA judgment. Thomas also claimed that Peacock fraudulently conveyed Tru-Tech's assets in violation of South Carolina and Pennsylvania law. Thomas later amended his complaint to assert a claim for "Piercing the Corporate Veil Under ERISA and Applicable Federal Law." The district court ultimately agreed to pierce the corporate veil and entered judgment against Peacock in the amount of $187,628.93—the precise amount of the judgment against Tru-Tech—plus interest and fees, notwithstanding the fact that Peacock's alleged fraudulent transfers totaled no more than $80,000.

    The issue is whether an officer of the corporation was a fiduciary under ERISA and thus personally liable for fraudulent transfers of corporate assets that were going to be used to fund an ERISA judgment against the corporation. *Peacock v. Thomas*, 516 U.S. 349 (1996)

HUMAN RESOURCE DILEMMAS

1. Mercury Manufacturing is considering closing its employee aerobic, yoga, and fitness facility. Employees are adamantly opposed to this and threaten a lawsuit claiming violation of ERISA. How would you advise?

2. Jupiter Jars is located in a small mid-western town. Its factory workers have come to rely on overtime pay for subsistence. Due to a projection for slower growth in glass jar sales, Jupiter has eliminated overtime pay. Its employees are contemplating a lawsuit under ERISA. How would you advise them?

3. Cindy Johnson graduated from Podink University at the age of 18. Cindy immediately began working in the office of Mars Maintenance Company. After meeting the 1-year requirement, she wanted to participate in the pension plan. Mars rebuffed her due to her age. Cindy wishes to sue under ERISA. How would you advise her?

WEB SITE ASSIGNMENT

Using the following Web sites, determine the protection afforded by ERISA in the case of bankruptcy.

www.law.cornell.edu/topics/pensions.html
www.findlaw.com
www.westbuslaw.com
www.eric.org
www.freeerisa.com
retireplan.about.com
www.dol.gov
benefitsattorney.com/links/ERISA
www.erisalitigation.net/erisalit/newslett/newshome.htm
www.qdro.pair.com/erisa.htm

Case Index

All entries that appear in italic are major cases within the text. Cases in regular type appear in the review questions.

SUBJECT INDEX